Data Science and Simulation in Transportation Research

Davy Janssens
Hasselt University, Belgium

Ansar-Ul-Haque Yasar
Hasselt University, Belgium

Luk Knapen
Hasselt University, Belgium

A volume in the Advances in Data Mining
and Database Management (ADMDM)
Book Series

Information Science
REFERENCE
An Imprint of IGI Global

Managing Director:	Lindsay Johnston
Editorial Director:	Myla Merkel
Production Manager:	Jennifer Yoder
Publishing Systems Analyst:	Adrienne Freeland
Development Editor:	Austin DeMarco
Acquisitions Editor:	Kayla Wolfe
Typesetter:	Christina Barkanic
Cover Design:	Jason Mull

Published in the United States of America by
Information Science Reference (an imprint of IGI Global)
701 E. Chocolate Avenue
Hershey PA 17033
Tel: 717-533-8845
Fax: 717-533-8661
E-mail: cust@igi-global.com
Web site: http://www.igi-global.com

Library of Congress Cataloging-in-Publication Data

Data science and simulation in transportation research / Davy Janssens, Ansar-Ul-Haque Yasar, and Luk Knapen, editors.
    pages cm
 Includes bibliographical references and index.
   ISBN 978-1-4666-4920-0 (hardcover) -- ISBN 978-1-4666-4921-7 (ebook) -- ISBN 978-1-4666-4922-4 (print & perpetual access) 1. Transportation--Planning--Data processing. 2. Transportation--Research--Data processing. 3. Traffic estimation--Mathematical models. 4. Traffic engineering--Data processing. 5. Transportation demand management--Data processing. I. Janssens, Davy, 1978- II. Yasar, Ansar-Ul-Haque, 1983- III. Knapen, Luk, 1954-
   HE147.6.D37 2014
   388.072--dc23
                                            2013035206

This book is published in the IGI Global book series Advances in Data Mining and Database Management (ADMDM) (ISSN: 2327-1981; eISSN: 2327-199X)

British Cataloguing in Publication Data
A Cataloguing in Publication record for this book is available from the British Library.

All work contributed to this book is new, previously-unpublished material. The views expressed in this book are those of the authors, but not necessarily of the publisher.

For electronic access to this publication, please contact: eresources@igi-global.com.

Advances in Data Mining and Database Management (ADMDM) Book Series

ISSN: 2327-1981
EISSN: 2327-199X

MISSION

With the large amounts of information available to businesses in today's digital world, there is a need for methods and research on managing and analyzing the information that is collected and stored. IT professionals, software engineers, and business administrators, along with many other researchers and academics, have made the fields of data mining and database management into ones of increasing importance as the digital world expands. The **Advances in Data Mining & Database Management (ADMDM) Book Series** aims to bring together research in both fields in order to become a resource for those involved in either field.

COVERAGE

- Cluster Analysis
- Customer Analytics
- Data Mining
- Data Quality
- Data Warehousing
- Database Security
- Database Testing
- Decision Support Systems
- Enterprise Systems
- Text Mining

IGI Global is currently accepting manuscripts for publication within this series. To submit a proposal for a volume in this series, please contact our Acquisition Editors at Acquisitions@igi-global.com or visit: http://www.igi-global.com/publish/.

Titles in this Series

For a list of additional titles in this series, please visit: www.igi-global.com

Data Science and Simulation in Transportation Research
Davy Janssens (Hasselt University, Belgium) Ansar-Ul-Haque Yasar (Hasselt University, Belgium) and Luk Knapen (Hasselt University, Belgium)
Information Science Reference • copyright 2014 • 350pp • H/C (ISBN: 9781466649200) • US $175.00 (our price)

Big Data Management, Technologies, and Applications
Wen-Chen Hu (University of North Dakota, USA) and Naima Kaabouch (University of North Dakota, USA)
Information Science Reference • copyright 2014 • 342pp • H/C (ISBN: 9781466646995) • US $175.00 (our price)

Innovative Approaches of Data Visualization and Visual Analytics
Mao Lin Huang (University of Technology, Sydney, Australia) and Weidong Huang (CSIRO, Australia)
Information Science Reference • copyright 2014 • 373pp • H/C (ISBN: 9781466643093) • US $200.00 (our price)

Data Mining in Dynamic Social Networks and Fuzzy Systems
Vishal Bhatnagar (Ambedkar Institute of Advanced Communication Technologies and Research, India)
Information Science Reference • copyright 2013 • 412pp • H/C (ISBN: 9781466642133) • US $195.00 (our price)

Ethical Data Mining Applications for Socio-Economic Development
Hakikur Rahman (University of Minho, Portugal) and Isabel Ramos (University of Minho, Portugal)
Information Science Reference • copyright 2013 • 359pp • H/C (ISBN: 9781466640788) • US $195.00 (our price)

Design, Performance, and Analysis of Innovative Information Retrieval
Zhongyu (Joan) Lu (University of Huddersfield, UK)
Information Science Reference • copyright 2013 • 508pp • H/C (ISBN: 9781466619753) • US $195.00 (our price)

XML Data Mining Models, Methods, and Applications
Andrea Tagarelli (University of Calabria, Italy)
Information Science Reference • copyright 2012 • 538pp • H/C (ISBN: 9781613503560) • US $195.00 (our price)

Graph Data Management Techniques and Applications
Sherif Sakr (University of New South Wales, Australia) and Eric Pardede (LaTrobe University, Australia)
Information Science Reference • copyright 2012 • 502pp • H/C (ISBN: 9781613500538) • US $195.00 (our price)

Advanced Database Query Systems Techniques, Applications and Technologies
Li Yan (Northeastern University, China) and Zongmin Ma (Northeastern University, China)
Information Science Reference • copyright 2011 • 410pp • H/C (ISBN: 9781609604752) • US $180.00 (our price)

www.igi-global.com

701 E. Chocolate Ave., Hershey, PA 17033
Order online at www.igi-global.com or call 717-533-8845 x100
To place a standing order for titles released in this series, contact: cust@igi-global.com
Mon-Fri 8:00 am - 5:00 pm (est) or fax 24 hours a day 717-533-8661

Table of Contents

Detailed Table of Contents

    Mirco Nanni, ISTI-CNR, Italy
    Roberto Trasarti, ISTI-CNR, Italy
    Paolo Cintia, ISTI-CNR, Italy
    Barbara Furletti, ISTI-CNR, Italy
    Chiara Renso, ISTI-CNR, Italy
    Lorenzo Gabrielli, ISTI-CNR, Italy
    Salvatore Rinzivillo, ISTI-CNR, Italy
    Fosca Giannotti, ISTI-CNR, Italy

The ability to understand the dynamics of human mobility is crucial for tasks like urban planning and transportation management. The recent rapidly growing availability of large spatio-temporal datasets gives us the possibility to develop sophisticated and accurate analysis methods and algorithms that can enable us to explore several relevant mobility phenomena: the distinct access paths to a territory, the groups of persons that move together in space and time, the regions of a territory that contains a high density of traffic demand, etc. All these paradigmatic perspectives focus on a collective view of the mobility where the interesting phenomenon is the result of the contribution of several moving objects. In this chapter, the authors explore a different approach to the topic and focus on the analysis and understanding of relevant individual mobility habits in order to assign a profile to an individual on the basis of his/her mobility. This process adds a semantic level to the raw mobility data, enabling further analyses that require a deeper understanding of the data itself. The studies described in this chapter are based on two large datasets of spatio-temporal data, originated, respectively, from GPS-equipped devices and from a mobile phone network.

Nicola Corona, University of Pisa, Italy & ISTI-CNR, Italy

Fosca Giannotti, ISTI-CNR, Italy

Anna Monreale, University of Pisa, Italy & ISTI-CNR, Italy

Roberto Trasarti, ISTI-CNR, Italy

The pervasiveness of mobile devices and location-based services produces as side effects an increasing volume of mobility data, which in turn creates the opportunity for a novel generation of analysis methods of movement behaviors. In this chapter, the authors focus on the problem of predicting future locations aimed at predicting with a certain accuracy the next location of a moving object. In particular, they provide a classification of the proposals in the literature addressing that problem. Then the authors preset the data mining method WhereNext and finally discuss possible improvements of that method.

Sungjin Cho, Hasselt University, Belgium

Tom Bellemans, Hasselt University, Belgium

Lieve Creemers, Hasselt University, Belgium

Luk Knapen, Hasselt University, Belgium

Davy Janssens, Hasselt University, Belgium

Geert Wets, Hasselt University, Belgium

Activity-based approach, which aims to estimate an individual induced traffic demand derived from activities, has been applied for traffic demand forecast research. The activity-based approach normally uses two types of input data: daily activity-trip schedule and population data, as well as environment information. In general, it seems hard to use those data because of privacy protection and expense. Therefore, it is indispensable to find an alternative source to population data. A synthetic population technique provides a solution to this problem. Previous research has already developed a few techniques for generating a synthetic population (e.g. IPF [Iterative Proportional Fitting] and CO [Combinatorial Optimization]), and the synthetic population techniques have been applied for the activity-based research in transportation. However, using those techniques is not easy for non-expert researchers not only due to the fact that there are no explicit terminologies and concrete solutions to existing issues, but also every synthetic population technique uses different types of data. In this sense, this chapter provides a potential reader with a guideline for using the synthetic population techniques by introducing terminologies, related research, and giving an account for the working process to create a synthetic population for Flanders in Belgium, problematic issues, and solutions.

Won Do Lee, Kyung Hee University, Korea

Chang-Hyeon Joh, Kyung Hee University, Korea

Sungjin Cho, Hasselt University, Belgium

Bruno Kochan, Hasselt University, Belgium

Over the last decades, the trip-based approach, also known as the four-step model, has been playing an unrivaled role in transportation demand research in Korea. It has been used to predict changes in traffic volume resulting from new transportation policy measures, and also has allowed conducting benefit-cost analyses for new infrastructure provisions. It has been increasingly difficult for the trip-based model to anticipate individual responses to new transportation policy inputs and infrastructure provision as the society becomes personalized and diversified. Activity-Based Modeling (ABM) approaches, predicting travel demand derived from individual activity participations, were introduced to complement the trip-based approach in this regard. The chapter introduces the Seoul ABM project that aims to first apply FEATHERS as an ABM to the data collected in Seoul Metropolitan Area (SMA) and then develop a prototype of the ABM framework for Korea. More specifically, the chapter first briefly describes SMA in comparison with Flanders in Belgium and other countries. It then introduces related research works in Korea and the background of the Seoul ABM project. After these, a FEATHERS framework applied for the Seoul ABM project is described with its data requirements. Major issues of and solutions to the Seoul ABM project are then discussed with regard to the data preprocessing. The chapter ends with a summary and future work.

Chapter 5

    Karthik C. Konduri, University of Connecticut, USA

    Ram M. Pendyala, Arizona State University, USA

    Daehyun You, Arizona State University, USA

    Yi-Chang Chiu, The University of Arizona, USA

    Mark Hickman, University of Queensland, Australia

    Hyunsoo Noh, University of Arizona, USA

    Paul Waddell, University of California – Berkeley, USA

    Liming Wang, Portland State University, USA

    Brian Gardner, U.S. Department of Transportation, USA

This chapter demonstrates the feasibility of applying an integrated microsimulation model of activity-travel demand and dynamic traffic assignment for analyzing the impact of pricing policies on traveler activity-travel choices. The model system is based on a dynamic integration framework wherein the activity-travel simulator and the dynamic traffic assignment model communicate with one another along the continuous time axis so that trips are routed and simulated on the network as and when they are generated. This framework is applied to the analysis of a system-wide pricing policy for a small case study site to demonstrate how the model responds to various levels of pricing. Case study results show that trip lengths, travel time expenditures, and vehicle miles of travel are affected to a greater degree than activity-trip rates and activity durations as a result of pricing policies. Measures of change output by the model are found to be consistent with elasticity estimates reported in the literature.

Chapter 6

    Muhammad Adnan, NED University of Engineering and Technology, Pakistan

    Mir Shabbar Ali, NED University of Engineering and Technology, Pakistan

Underreporting of road accidents has been widely accepted as a common phenomenon. In many developing countries this remains a critical problem as inappropriate information regarding road accidents does not provide a base to analyse its root causes. Therefore, effectiveness of implemented interventions are always questionable. In Pakistan, responsibility of collecting initial information regarding road accidents lies with the Police Department; however, reported figures are reflecting underestimation of the situation. This chapter reports the effectiveness of prevailing approaches for recording accident information in developing countries like Pakistan, India and Bangladesh, etc. Furthermore, it presents a unique methodology that has been adopted in Karachi for recording road accident information through an institute established on the notions of public-private partnership. Various features of that unique data collection mechanism are presented along with the discussion of some success stories, where the collected data has contributed significantly in improving road safety conditions.

Chapter 7

Ali Pirdavani, Hasselt University, Belgium

Tom Bellemans, Hasselt University, Belgium

Tom Brijs, Hasselt University, Belgium

Bruno Kochan, Hasselt University, Belgium

Geert Wets, Hasselt University, Belgium

Travel Demand Management (TDM) consists of a variety of policy measures that affect the transportation system's effectiveness by changing travel behavior. Although the primary objective to implement such TDM strategies is not to improve traffic safety, their impact on traffic safety should not be neglected. The main purpose of this study is to investigate differences in the traffic safety consequences of two TDM scenarios: a fuel-cost increase scenario (i.e. increasing the fuel price by 20%) and a teleworking scenario (i.e. 5% of the working population engages in teleworking). Since TDM strategies are usually conducted at a geographically aggregated level, crash prediction models that are used to evaluate such strategies should also be developed at an aggregate level. Moreover, given that crash occurrences are often spatially heterogeneous and are affected by many spatial variables, the existence of spatial correlation in the data is also examined. The results indicate the necessity of accounting for the spatial correlation when developing crash prediction models. Therefore, Zonal Crash Prediction Models (ZCPMs) within the geographically weighted generalized linear modeling framework are developed to incorporate the spatial variations in association between the Number Of Crashes (NOCs) (including fatal, severe, and slight injury crashes recorded between 2004 and 2007) and a set of explanatory variables. Different exposure, network, and socio-demographic variables of 2200 traffic analysis zones in Flanders, Belgium, are considered as predictors of crashes. An activity-based transportation model is adopted to produce exposure metrics. This enables a more detailed and reliable assessment while TDM strategies are inherently modeled in the activity-based models. In this chapter, several ZCPMs with different severity levels and crash types are developed to predict the NOCs. The results show considerable traffic safety benefits of conducting both TDM scenarios at an average level. However, there are certain differences when considering changes in NOCs by different crash types.

Chapter 8

Christine Kopp, Fraunhofer Institute for Intelligent Analysis and Information Systems (IAIS), Germany

Bruno Kochan, University of Hasselt, Belgium

Michael May, Fraunhofer Institute for Intelligent Analysis and Information Systems (IAIS), Germany

Luca Pappalardo, ISTI-CNR, Italy & University of Pisa, Italy

Salvatore Rinzivillo, ISTI-CNR, Italy

Daniel Schulz, Fraunhofer Institute for Intelligent Analysis and Information Systems (IAIS), Germany

Filippo Simini, University of Bristol, UK

The increasing expressiveness of spatio-temporal microsimulation systems makes them attractive for a wide range of real world applications. However, the broad field of applications puts new challenges to the quality of microsimulation systems. They are no longer expected to reflect a few selected mobility characteristics but to be a realistic representation of the real world. In consequence, the validation of spatio-temporal microsimulations has to be deepened and to be especially moved towards a holistic view on movement validation. One advantage hereby is the easier availability of mobility data sets at present, which enables the validation of many different aspects of movement behavior. However, these data sets bring their own challenges as the data may cover only a part of the observation space, differ in its temporal resolution, or not be representative in all aspects. In addition, the definition of appropriate similarity measures, which capture the various mobility characteristics, is challenging. The goal of this chapter is to pave the way for a novel, better, and more detailed evaluation standard for spatio-temporal microsimulation systems. The chapter collects and structure's various aspects that have to be considered for the validation and comparison of movement data. In addition, it assembles the state-of-the-art of existing validation techniques. It concludes with examples of using big data sources for the extraction and validation of movement characteristics outlining the research challenges that have yet to be conquered.

Chapter 9

Qiong Bao, Hasselt University, Belgium

Bruno Kochan, Hasselt University, Belgium

Tom Bellemans, Hasselt University, Belgium

Davy Janssens, Hasselt University, Belgium

Geert Wets, Hasselt University, Belgium

Activity-based models of travel demand employ in most cases a micro-simulation approach, thereby inevitably including a stochastic error that is caused by the statistical distributions of random components. As a result, running a transport micro-simulation model several times with the same input will generate different outputs. In order to take the variation of outputs in each model run into account, a common approach is to run the model multiple times and to use the average value of the results. The question then becomes: What is the minimum number of model runs required to reach a stable result? In this chapter, systematic experiments are carried out by using the FEATHERS, an activity-based micro-simulation modeling framework currently implemented for Flanders (Belgium). Six levels of geographic detail are taken into account, which are building block level, subzone level, zone level, superzone level, province level, and the whole Flanders. Three travel indices (i.e., the average daily number of activities per person, the average daily number of trips per person, and the average daily distance travelled per person), as well as their corresponding segmentations with respect to socio-demographic variables, transport mode alternatives, and activity types are calculated by running the model 100 times. The results show that application of the FEATHERS at a highly aggregated level only requires limited model runs. However, when a more disaggregated level is considered (the degree of the aggregation here not only refers to the size of the geographical scale, but also to the detailed extent of the index), a larger number of model runs is needed to ensure confidence of a certain percentile of zones at this level to be stable. The values listed in this chapter can be consulted as a reference for those who plan to use the FEATHERS framework, while for the other activity-based models the methodology proposed in this chapter can be repeated.

Chapter 10

Marco Lützenberger, Technische Universität Berlin, Germany

Over the last decade, traffic simulation frameworks have advanced into an indispensible tool for traffic planning and infrastructure management. For these simulations, sophisticated models are used to "mimic" traffic systems in a lifelike fashion. In most cases, these models focus on a rather technical scope. Human factors, such as drivers' behaviours are either neglected or "estimated" without any proven connection to reality. This chapter presents an analysis of psychological driver models in order to establish such a connection. In order to do so, human driver behaviour is introduced from a psychological point of view, and state-of-the-art conceptualisations are analysed to identify factors that determine human traffic behaviour. These factors are explained in more detail, and their appliances in human behaviour models for traffic simulations are discussed. This chapter does not provide a comprehensive mapping from simulation requirements to particular characteristics of human driver behaviour but clarifies the assembly of human traffic behaviour, identifies relevant factors of influence, and thus, serves as a guideline for the development of human behaviour models for traffic simulations.

The focus of this chapter is on issues surrounding the development and applications of large-scale agent-based traffic models. Following a brief overview of Agent-Based Modeling and Simulation (ABMS) applications in transportation modeling, the chapter proceeds to describe the authors' continued efforts and experiences with the development, calibration, validation, and application of a regional agent-based traffic model of the Buffalo-Niagara metropolitan area. The model is developed using the TRansportation ANalysis SIMulation System (TRANSIMS), an open-source, agent-based suite of transportation models. A unique feature of the chapter is its focus on unplanned or extreme events, such as severe snowstorms and major incidents on the freeways, and how the models may be calibrated and applied under such situations. The chapter concludes by summarizing the main lessons learned from the Buffalo case study and providing suggestions for future research.

Modeling activities and travel for individuals in order to estimate traffic demand leads to large scale simulations. Most current models simulate individuals acting in a mutually independent way except for the use of the shared transportation infrastructure. As soon as cooperation between autonomous individuals is accounted for, the individuals are linked to each other in a network structure and interact with their neighbours in the network while trying to achieve their own goals. In concrete traffic-related problems, those networks can grow very large. Optimization over such networks typically leads to combinatorially explosive problems. In this chapter, the case of providing optimal advice to combine carpooling candidates is considered. First, the advisor software structure is explained; then, the characteristics for the carpooling candidates network derived for Flanders (Belgium) are calculated in order to estimate the problem size.

In this chapter, an overview of electric power systems is presented. The purpose is to describe the structure and operation of the power system and its evolution to the new smart grids. The first section gives an introduction about the electric grid and its evolution. Then, there is a section with a brief description of the different components of the electric power system: generation, transmission, distribution, and consumption. The third section is related to power system control, explaining why control actions are necessary in the power system to maintain the balance between supply and consumption and to keep constant the system frequency (at 50 or 60 Hz). In order to understand future applications of electric vehicles, it is important to present a fourth section related to fundamentals of the electricity markets. The chapter finishes with a description of the future power systems with high penetration of intermittent renewable energies, energy storage capacity, active demand management, and integration with telecommunication infrastructure.

Chapter 14

Rashid A. Waraich, ETH Zurich, Switzerland

Gil Georges, ETH Zurich, Switzerland

Matthias D. Galus, ETH Zurich, Switzerland

Kay W. Axhausen, ETH Zurich, Switzerland

Battery-electric and plug-in hybrid-electric vehicles are envisioned by many as a way to reduce CO_2 traffic emissions, support the integration of renewable electricity generation, and increase energy security. Electric vehicle modeling is an active field of research, especially with regards to assessing the impact of electric vehicles on the electricity network. However, as highlighted in this chapter, there is a lack of capability for detailed electricity demand and supply modeling. One reason for this, as pointed out in this chapter, is that such modeling requires an interdisciplinary approach and a possibility to reuse and integrate existing models. In order to solve this problem, a framework for electric vehicle modeling is presented, which provides strong capabilities for detailed electricity demand modeling. It is built on an agent-based travel demand and traffic simulation. A case study for the city of Zurich is presented, which highlights the capabilities of the framework to uncover possible bottlenecks in the electricity network and detailed fleet simulation for CO_2 emission calculations, and thus its power to support policy makers in taking decisions.

Chapter 15

Jesus Fraile-Ardanuy, Universidad Politecnica de Madrid, Spain

Dionisio Ramirez, Universidad Politecnica de Madrid, Spain

Sergio Martinez, Universidad Politecnica de Madrid, Spain

Roberto Alvaro, Universidad Politecnica de Madrid, Spain

Jairo Gonzalez, Universidad Politecnica de Madrid, Spain

Luk Knapen, University of Hasselt, Belgium

Davy Janssens, University of Hasselt, Belgium

Electric mobility is becoming an option for reducing greenhouse gas emissions of road transport and decreasing the external dependence on fossil fuels. However, this new kind of mobility will introduce additional loads to the power system, and it is important to determine its effects on it. As a direct scenario from DATA SIM FP7 EU project, an application related to electric mobility and its impact on the electric grid from Flanders region is presented in this chapter. The chapter begins with a brief description of the electric transmission network for Flanders region and the electric vehicles energy requirements for different mobility zones in this region, obtained from FEATHERS, an activity-based model. In the following section, the main assumptions that allow estimating the total electricity consumption for each mobility area is presented. Once this total consumption per zone has been estimated, an algorithm to link the mobility areas with the nearest substation is developed. Finally, the impact of charging electric vehicles on the transmission substations is examined.

Chapter 16

Fjo De Ridder, EnergyVille, Belgium

Reinhilde D'hulst, EnergyVille, Belgium

Luk Knapen, Hasselt University, Belgium

Davy Janssens, Hasselt University, Belgium

This chapter presents a coordination algorithm for charging electric vehicles that can be used for avoiding capacity problems in the power distribution grid and for decreasing imbalance costs for retailers. Since it is expected that the fraction of electric vehicles will exceed 50% in the next decades, charging these vehicles will roughly double the domestic power consumption. Not all parts of the grid are expected to be able to provide the required power. Good estimates of the vehicles' use (routes driven, trip duration and length, when and where cars are parked) is crucial information to test the grid. The authors have chosen to use FEATHERS, an agent-based behavioral model, to provide this information. In a first case study, charging is coordinated to prevent grid capacity problems. In a second case study, charging and discharging of electric vehicles is employed by retailers to lower imbalance costs and by vehicle owners to lower charging costs. The coordination scheme can halve the imbalance cost if only charging is considered. If, on the other hand, electric vehicles can both charge and discharge, imbalance costs can completely be avoided and some revenues can be generated. The proposed coordination algorithm is a distributed algorithm, where all sensitive information that is privately owned, such as parking times, trip information, battery management, etc. is only used by the EVs. The functioning of the proposed algorithm is illustrated by simulations. It is shown that the charging can be rescheduled so that grid capacity violations are avoided. The novelty of this work is that both spatial and temporal information is used.

Chapter 17

Niels Leemput, KU Leuven, Belgium

Juan Van Roy, KU Leuven, Belgium

Frederik Geth, KU Leuven, Belgium

Johan Driesen, KU Leuven, Belgium

Sven De Breucker, VITO, Belgium

This chapter assesses the impact of different technical solutions and their impact on the ability of a fleet of plug-in hybrid electric vehicles to drive in electric mode as much as possible. The technical solutions covered in this chapter to attain this objective include: charging at low and medium power; charging at home, at work, and at other locations; and using fleets with small, medium, and large battery sizes. The driving behavior of the fleet is modeled using an availability analysis based on statistical data from Flanders and The Netherlands. The fleet itself is based on data of the Flemish vehicle segmentation, while the electric consumption of each segment is determined based on realistic vehicle data and driving cycles. This data is combined into different scenarios for which the utility factor, the energy consumption, the grid impact, and the battery utilization is investigated. Based on these scenario guidelines concerning the appropriate charge power at different locations and the distribution of charge locations, the expected grid impact and utility factor of different fleets are formulated.

Foreword

New technology and changing social and economic environments have a potentially substantial impact on the travel behavior of individuals and households. Current thinking about transport policy is heavily influenced by the discussion on sustainable transport. A wide variety of policies, ranging from new urbanism and land use planning to transport demand management initiatives and pricing mechanisms have been suggested and implemented to trigger individuals to switch from cars to alternative transport modes. Whether such spatial, transportation, and economic policies are sufficient is doubtful: it is likely that sustainable transport also requires a dramatic shift to alternative transport modes such as electric cars.

To provide adequate academic answers to emerging policy questions, novel methodologies need to be developed and enhanced. It has become increasingly clear that individuals differ widely in terms of their preferences, behavior, acceptance of new technology, and reaction to these new policies. Classic modeling approaches and underlying theories of human choice and decision making only partially address the relevant issues. Moreover, they are often too stringent to sufficiently represent this behavioral heterogeneity.

Agent-based models that are increasingly explored in travel behavior research have the potential to establish the required breakthrough. Only a few such models that go beyond toy problems are available. This book should be applauded by bringing together some state of the art agent-based models applied to current policy issues and new technological developments. It is complemented by underexplored issues in the application of these models such as uncertainty analysis and the creation of synthetic populations.

The chapters witness the creative ideas, academic rigor, and professionalism of the authors. They can serve as benchmarks for other researchers to improve.

The book is important reading for new researchers entering this field of travel behavior research. It offers new perspectives and documents important progress in modeling travel behavior.

Harry Timmermans
Technical University of Eindhoven, The Netherlands

Harry Timmermans (1952) holds a PH D degree in Geography/Urban and Regional Planning. He studied at the Catholic University of Nijmegen, The Netherlands. His dissertation concerned a theory of the functional and spatial structure and the dynamics of central place systems. Since 1976, he is affiliated with the Faculty of Architecture, Building and Planning of the Eindhoven University of Technology, The Netherlands. First as an assistant professor of Quantitative and Urban Geography, later as an associate professor of Urban Planning Research. In 1986, he was appointed chaired professor of Urban Planning at the same institute. In 1992, he founded the European Institute of Retailing and Services Studies (EIRASS) in Eindhoven, The Netherlands (a sister institute of the Canadian Institute of Retailing and Services Studies). His main research interests concern the study of human judgment and choice processes, mathematical modeling of urban systems, and spatial interaction and choice patterns and the development of decision support and expert systems for application in urban planning. He has published several books and many articles in journals in the fields of marketing, urban planning, architecture and urban design, geography, environmental psychology, transportation research, urban and regional economics, urban sociology, leisure sciences, and computer science.

Preface

This provides an overview of latest state-of-the-art research about spatial-temporal micro-simulation methodologies for human mobility, grounded on massive amounts of big data of various types and from various sources (e.g. GPS, mobile phones, and social networking sites). One of the applications explored in this book is the forecasting of nationwide consequences of a massive switch to electric vehicles, given the intertwined nature of mobility and power distribution networks. Many scientists have already pointed out that the goal of the social sciences is not simply to understand how people behave in large groups but to understand what motivates individuals to behave the way they do. If this fundamental insight can be gained, it certainly is a large step forward towards the solution of this important challenge; it can help us to better understand the dynamics of our society and, in the longer run, have an impact on overall societal well-being. In a nutshell, this book will help achieve some very novel objectives in the field of data-mining, transportation sciences, and its applications. Some of these objectives include:

1. **Big data challenges:** Big data coming from mobile call records, GPS trackers, and social networking sites (e.g. Facebook), along with microscopic energy consumption, land-use, road network, and public transport level-of-service data pose an enormous challenge in terms of data storage, integration, management, and privacy.

2. **Big data joined with behavioral motivation leading to truly novel social science laws:** Big data needs to be merged with behaviorally rich activity-travel diaries, generating a novel data-driven theory that enables us to analyze mobility demand from the individual point-of-view, not neglecting the behavioral and contextual situation of the individual.

3. **The behavioral sensitivity of the individual as the core entity in the novel simulation standard:** Agent-based reality mining of big data is combined with behavioral sensitivity of the agent, accounting for changes in human behavior when circumstances change, either due to control (e.g. policy actions to prevent peak loads in the power network) or due to general trends (e.g. the use of electric vehicles).

4. **A novel standard for evaluation and benchmarking:** The massive amounts of big data can be used to estimate origin-destination matrices, setting a novel, better, and more detailed standard for evaluating, validating, and benchmarking agent-based micro-simulation models.

5. **An issue of scalability:** Computational power needs to be enhanced by orders of magnitude using state-of-the-art advances in high-performance fine-grain parallel computing systems, addressing scalability problems resulting from the behavioral theory extraction from big data and from the adoption of this theory in a nationwide simulation environment of electrification of road transport.

The ability to understand dynamics of human mobility is crucial for tasks like urban planning and transportation management. The rapid growth of large spatio-temporal datasets gives us the possibility to develop more sophisticated and accurate methods and algorithms going towards a complete view on mobility. Private and public institutions have recognized mobility data as a source of information to assess the lifestyle, habits, and demands of citizens in terms of mobility. Chapter 1 provides an overview of a few approaches to extract mobility profiles of individuals from two important examples of big data sources: the GPS traces of vehicles and the GSM traces of mobile phones. The key of all the methods presented is that from the analysis of the individual histories it is possible to derive better information about the collectivity. Similarly, the pervasiveness of mobile devices and location-based services produces as side effects an increasing volume of mobility data, which in turn creates the opportunity for a novel generation of analysis methods of movement behaviors. Chapter 2 relies upon the same amount of big data but focuses on the specific problem of predicting future locations, which is aimed at predicting with a certain accuracy the next location of a moving object.

An activity-based approach, which estimates an individual induced traffic demand derived from activities, has been applied for traffic demand forecast research. The activity-based approach normally uses different types of input data: daily activity-trip schedule and population data, as well as environment information. In general, for privacy reasons, population data is made available only as aggregated frequency distributions; furthermore, that data is snapshots that apply to a specific moment in time. Therefore, it is indispensable to develop disaggregation and evolution simulation methods to population data. A synthetic population technique that provides a solution to this problem is presented in chapter 3.

Over the last decades, the trip-based approach, also known as the four-step model, has been playing an unrivalled role in transportation demand research in Korea. It has been used to predict changes in traffic volume resulting from new transportation policy measures and has allowed benefit-cost analyses for new infrastructure provisions. It has been increasingly difficult for the trip-based model to anticipate individual responses to new transportation policy inputs and infrastructure provision as the society becomes personalized and diversified. Activity-Based Modeling (ABM) approaches, predicting travel demand derived from individual activity participations, were introduced to complement the trip-based approach in this regard. Chapter 4 provides some deep insights on using an activity-based approach for a real world scenario (i.e. Seoul city). Similarly, chapter 5 demonstrates the feasibility of applying an integrated micro-simulation model of activity-travel demand and dynamic traffic assignment for analyzing the impact of pricing policies on traveler activity-travel choices. From a market's point of view, the realistic example presented in both of these chapters show strong valorisation potential of the approaches used.

Proper, accurate, and on time data collection is an important challenge for transportation scientists. For example, the underreporting of road accidents has been widely accepted as a common phenomenon. In many developing countries this remains a critical problem as inappropriate information regarding road accidents does not provide a base to analyse its root causes. Chapter 6 shows various features of a unique data collection mechanism along with the discussion of some success stories where the collected data has contributed significantly to improving road safety conditions.

Travel Demand Management (TDM) consists of a variety of policy measures that affect the transportation system's effectiveness by changing travel behavior. Although the primary objective to implement such TDM strategies is not to improve traffic safety, their impact on traffic safety should not be neglected.

Chapter 7 explains that activity-based transportation models provide an adequate range of in-depth information about individuals' travel behavior to realistically simulate and evaluate TDM strategies. The main advantage of these models is that the impact of applying a TDM strategy will be accounted for, for each individual, throughout a decision making process instead of applying the scenario to a general population level.

The increasing expressiveness of spatio-temporal micro-simulation systems makes them attractive for a wide range of real world applications. However, the broad field of applications puts new challenges to the quality of micro-simulation systems. They are no longer expected to reflect a few selected mobility characteristics but to be a realistic representation of the real world. In consequence, the validation of spatio-temporal micro-simulations has to be deepened and to be especially moved towards a holistic view on movement validation. Chapter 8 paves the way for a novel, better, and more detailed evaluation standard for spatio-temporal micro-simulation systems. The chapter collects and structures' various aspects that have to be considered for the validation and comparison of movement data.

In the next chapter, the issue of validation is explained further because in the specific case of activity-based models of travel demand, a micro-simulation approach is adopted, thereby inevitably including a stochastic error that is caused by the statistical distributions of random components. As a result, running a transport micro-simulation model several times with the same input will generate different outputs. In order to take the variation of outputs in each model run into account, a common approach is to run the model multiple times and to use the average value of the results. The question then becomes: What is the minimum number of model runs required to reach a stable result? Chapter 9 provides details on systematic experiments that are carried out by using FEATHERS, an activity-based micro-simulation modeling framework currently implemented for Flanders (Belgium). Six levels of geographic detail are taken into account, which are building block level, subzone level, zone level, superzone level, province level, and the whole Flanders. Three travel indices (i.e. the average daily number of activities per person, the average daily number of trips per person, and the average daily distance travelled per person) as well as their corresponding segmentations with respect to socio-demographic variables, transport mode alternatives, and activity types are calculated by running the model 100 times. The results show that application of FEATHERS at a highly aggregated level only requires limited model runs. However, when a more disaggregated level is considered (the degree of the aggregation here not only refers to the size of the geographical scale but also to the detailed extent of the index), a larger number of model runs is needed to ensure confidence of a certain percentile of zones at this level to be stable.

Over the last decade, traffic simulation frameworks advanced into an indispensable tool for traffic planning and infrastructure management. For these simulations, sophisticated models are used to "mimic" traffic systems in a lifelike fashion. In most cases, these models focus on a rather technical scope. Human factors, such as the drivers' behaviour, are either neglected or estimated without any proven connection to reality. Chapter 10 presents an analysis of psychological driver models in order to establish such connection.

Chapter 11 describes the authors' continued efforts and experiences with the development, calibration, validation, and application of a regional agent-based traffic model of a medium-sized metropolitan area with the goal of shedding light on the challenges, lessons learned, and the opportunities of regional agent-based transportation models. Specifically, the chapter highlights efficient procedures for identifying network coding errors and describes how one might go about validating and calibrating such complex models so as to achieve a good match between the model's simulated results and the field counts.

Modeling activities and travel for individuals in order to estimate traffic demand leads to large-scale simulations. Most current models simulate individuals acting in a mutually independent way except for the use of the shared transportation infrastructure. As soon as cooperation between autonomous individuals is accounted for, the need for agent-based simulation emerges. Chapter 12 presents a novel agent-based model for the carpooling application.

The last series of chapters in this book relate to the rise in both development and usage of electric vehicles all around the world. This rise has influenced not only the transportation infrastructure but also has an impact on the electricity grid. Chapter 13 provides an overview of electric power systems. The purpose is to describe the structure and operation of the power system and its evolution to the new smart grids.

Battery-electric and plug-in hybrid-electric vehicles are envisioned by many as a way to reduce CO_2 traffic emissions, support the integration of renewable electricity generation, and increase energy security. Electric vehicle modeling is an active field of research, especially with regards to assessing the impact of electric vehicles on the electricity network. Chapter 14 presents a framework for electric vehicle modeling that provides strong capabilities for detailed electricity demand modeling. This model is built on an agent-based travel demand and traffic simulation.

As mentioned earlier, electric mobility is becoming an option for reducing greenhouse gas emissions of road transport and decreasing the external dependence on fossil fuels. However, this new kind of mobility will introduce additional loads to the power system, and it is important to determine its effects on it. An application related to electric mobility and its impact on the electric grid from Flanders region is presented in chapter 15.

Similarly, chapter 16 presents a coordination algorithm for charging electric vehicles that can be used for avoiding capacity problems in the power distribution grid and for decreasing imbalance costs for retailers. Since it is expected that the fraction of electric vehicles will exceed 50% in the next decades, charging these vehicles will roughly double the domestic power consumption, and not all parts of the grid are expected to be able to provide the required power. Therefore, this chapter is quite interesting for the stakeholders from the power industry to be able to manage the future needs.

Last, but not the least, chapter 17 assesses the impact of different technical solutions and their impact on the ability of a fleet of plug-in hybrid-electric vehicles to drive in electric mode as much as possible. The technical solutions covered in this chapter to attain this objective include: charging at low and medium power; charging at home, at work, and at other locations; and using fleets with small, medium, and large battery sizes. The driving behavior of the fleet is modeled using an availability analysis based on statistical data from Flanders and The Netherlands.

This book is mostly based on the work performed within the European FP7 project called Data Science for Simulating the Era of Electric Vehicles (DATASIM) (www.datasim-fp7.eu). Many researchers are working on the problems defined above in the framework of this project. However, it would be difficult for any small group of people to cover such a broad topic with the appropriate depth and expertise. In order to tackle this challenge for this book, we, the editors, looked to our colleagues from within and outside the DATASIM project consortium to find experts from the domain in question. You can see that the list of authors has grown quite large and contains a good mixture of academics, consultants, and people from the industry. We are very fortunate to have received contributions from the knowledgeable authors in this book, and we are extremely grateful for this. We applaud the efforts of our contributors, partners, advisory board, reviewers, and all the others who helped us make this book a success. We all hope to see the important research work presented in this book used in our everyday lives soon!

Davy Janssens
Hasselt University, Belgium

Ansar-Ul-Haque Yasar
Hasselt University, Belgium

Luk Knapen
Hasselt University, Belgium

Acknowledgment

We are thankful to the EU FP7 programme for their support throughout the project's life cycle. The work presented in this book is mostly based on the work performed within the Data Science for Simulating the Era of Electric Vehicles (DATASIM) (www.datasim-fp7.eu) project funded by the European Union Seventh Framework Programme (FP7/2007-2013) under grant agreement number 270833. We would like to show our gratitude for the contributions from the authors in this book. We also applaud the efforts of our project partners, editorial advisory board, reviewers, and all others who helped us make this book a success.

Davy Janssens
Hasselt University, Belgium

Ansar-Ul-Haque Yasar
Hasselt University, Belgium

Luk Knapen
Hasselt University, Belgium

Chapter 1
Mobility Profiling

Mirco Nanni
ISTI-CNR, Italy

Chiara Renso
ISTI-CNR, Italy

Roberto Trasarti
ISTI-CNR, Italy

Lorenzo Gabrielli
ISTI-CNR, Italy

Paolo Cintia
ISTI-CNR, Italy

Salvatore Rinzivillo
ISTI-CNR, Italy

Barbara Furletti
ISTI-CNR, Italy

Fosca Giannotti
ISTI-CNR, Italy

ABSTRACT

The ability to understand the dynamics of human mobility is crucial for tasks like urban planning and transportation management. The recent rapidly growing availability of large spatio-temporal datasets gives us the possibility to develop sophisticated and accurate analysis methods and algorithms that can enable us to explore several relevant mobility phenomena: the distinct access paths to a territory, the groups of persons that move together in space and time, the regions of a territory that contains a high density of traffic demand, etc. All these paradigmatic perspectives focus on a collective view of the mobility where the interesting phenomenon is the result of the contribution of several moving objects. In this chapter, the authors explore a different approach to the topic and focus on the analysis and understanding of relevant individual mobility habits in order to assign a profile to an individual on the basis of his/her mobility. This process adds a semantic level to the raw mobility data, enabling further analyses that require a deeper understanding of the data itself. The studies described in this chapter are based on two large datasets of spatio-temporal data, originated, respectively, from GPS-equipped devices and from a mobile phone network.

INTRODUCTION

The ability to understand dynamics of human mobility is crucial for tasks like urban planning and transportation management. The rapidly growing of large spatio-temporal datasets gives us the possibility to develop always more sophisticated and accurate methods and algorithms, going towards a complete view on mobility. Private and public institutions have been recognized mobility data

DOI: 10.4018/978-1-4666-4920-0.ch001

as a source of information to assess the lifestyle, habits and demands of citizens in terms of mobility.

The traditional approaches in this field mainly focuses on inferring simple measurements and aggregations, such as density of traffic and car flows in road segments: mobility profiles are an evolution, in terms of richness of information, of those results. Profiles lie in between single trajectories and a whole population, i.e. the individual person, with his regularities and habits. Analysing individuals, rather than large groups, provides the basis for an understanding of systematic mobility, which is fundamental in some mobility planning applications.

Related Work

In the literature there are different views on mobility data mining, depending on the granularity of the results obtained. Studying and inferring the properties of some big indicators, such as radius of gyration, is the goal of (Song et al., 2010): using trajectory data from GSM phones, they made an exploration of the statistical properties of the population's mobility patterns, measuring the distance between user's positions at consecutive calls. The distribution of displacements over all users is well approximated by a truncated power law. With this result, they show how the human trajectories have an high degree of temporal and spatial regularity, in contrast with random trajectories predicted by the prevailing Lévy flight and random walk models (Brockmann et al., 2006). The concept of mobility pattern is, indeed, the basis of a really active research field. Since the time-dimension is considered an important factor for most social activities, understanding the dynamics of the daily mobility patterns is essential for the management and planning of urban facilities and services. An early approach on mobility pattern mining is given in (Gaffney and Smyth, 1999), where the problem tackled is to *find groups of objects that follow a common trajectory, allowing a limited amount of random noise*: they proposed a mixture

model-based clustering method for continuous trajectories, which groups together objects that are likely to be generated from a common core trajectory by adding Gaussian noise.

T-Pattern (defined in (Giannotti et al., 2007) as a sequence of points with a temporal annotation) is a spatio-temporal model used to represent similar mobility behaviors of different users, mined from a dataset of GPS trajectories. A step further from identifying aggregated mobility pattern has been made by (Yuan and Raubal, 2012), using hourly time series to extract and represent dynamic mobility patterns in different urban areas, then applying a dynamic time warping (DTW) algorithm to measure similarity between this time series. Dynamic time warp find an optimal matching between two given time-dependent sequences, since it has better performance on distinguishing different time series than other well-known methods like Euclidean or Frechét distance. Mobility pattern can be derived also with a visual analytic approach: the work of (Sagl et al., 2012) relies entirely on visualization and mapping techniques, purposefully avoiding statistical or probabilistic modeling. With a dataset of 88 million of handovers, coming from a GSM network operator and regarding an entire geographical region, they uncover the typical spatio-temporal patterns of the collective human mobility per day of the week. Solely relying on the intrinsic power of different visualization techniques, an effective and intuitive way to derive both characteristic and exceptional mobility patterns has been provided.

A methodology for extracting mobility profiles of individuals has been introduced in (Trasarti et al., 2011). Starting from defining the concept of mobility profile of a user as the set of his/her routine trips, they define a general method based on trajectory clustering to extract such profiles. In that context, mobility profiles was used to develop a car pooling service: with a further profiles matching task, a sort of recommendation system was given, in order to help users to find a possible host for their trips. In (Furletti et al., 2012) has been proposed a methodology to partition a population of users tracked by GSM mobile phones into four predefined user profiles: residents, commuters, in transit and tourists/visitors. This has been performed with two steps: a first top-down step, to identify classes of users based on a predefined call behavior that may approximate a given typology of users, then a second bottom-up step to compute sets of users with similar calling behavior, integrating the results of the top-down step. A more meaningful definition of mobility profile has been defined in (Phithakkitnukoon et al. 2010), where user's habits are represented by the sequence of the activities he performed. Activities are inferred using the activity-aware map, which provides information about the most probable activity associated with a specific area in the map. The activity-aware map is defined dividing the reference area in cells with the same dimension, then associating a most probable activity for each of them. This activity is derived from the distribution of the types of Point of Interest contained in the cell. Once obtained the activity-aware map, it is possible to calculate the daily activity pattern for every user, inferring which of the five activities (Working, Eating, Shopping, Entertainment, Recreational) the user has performed at every time-slot of the day. In the next sections, will be better introduced the work done in (Nanni et al., 2012): mobility profiles are there used to compute the state of traffic, avoiding a too big increase of communication costs and being ready to be an optimal input for real-time monitoring systems.

In this chapter we focus on the analysis and understanding of relevant individual habits in order to assign a profile to an individual on the basis of his/her mobility. To sense the movement of a user we adopt two large dataset of spatio-temporal data. The trajectories of a moving object are a powerful proxy to explore the mobility of a territory. They enable us to explore relevant mobility phenomena like, for example, the distinct access paths to a territory, the groups of persons that move together

in space and time, the regions of a territory that contains an high density of traffic demand. All these paradigmatic perspectives focus on a collective view of the mobility, where the interesting phenomenon is the result of the contribution of several moving objects.

A relevant aspect to consider when analyzing trajectory data is the fact that, in general, multiple trajectories can be produced by the same moving object. In such a case, the analytical methods applied on the history of a single moving object can provide a very precise and personal characterization of each movement. For example, we can select the trips of a user that are repeated several times during a time interval, meaning that such a particular movement has an important meaning for that user, whereas the trips that are performed rarely have minor importance.

Clearly, the movement of an individual is the reflection of his/her life style. For example, a full-time employee presents a strong regularity in the trip from home to work, whereas an unemployed person would miss such regularity. Thus, since the mobility reflects what people do, it is advisable to understand individual characteristics to better model the corresponding mobility habits. The relevant mobility characteristics are exploited to derive a *mobility profile*. Such profiling approach is meant to provide an abstraction of mobility features at different levels of granularity. For instance, we can assign specific profiles to a particular trip that a user frequently follows, or we can provide a characterization of the mobility of a user as a whole, like for example the distinction between commuters and unemployed.

Chapter Organization

The chapter is organized as follows. In Section *"The Big Data Challenge in mobility: GPS and GSM data"* we describe in details the two datasets used in this chapter, namely a set of GPS traces of private vehicles circulating in Tuscany, Italy, and a set of call records provided by a main mobile telecommunication company, again located in Italy. In Section *"Individual mobility profiling"* we tackle the problem of profiling individual mobility by means of GPS data analysis, while Sections *"Case of Study I: Distributed computation application"* and *"Case of Study II: Car pooling application"* report two applications where mobility profiles play a major role: a car traffic monitor application, where the traffic density is estimated by collecting the position sensed by each vehicle (Section *"Case of Study I: Distributed computation application"*); and a proactive car pooling application, where profiles are used to suggest to the users possibilities of sharing the car for common movements. In Section *"Discovery Call Behaviors"* we analyze the individual behavior of users observed by means of GSM logs. Then, the methods presented are used in Section *"Real Case of Study III: Discovering Call Behaviors in Pisa"* to automatically group users with similar behavior and provide a series of profile prototypes that can be used to classify new individuals. Finally, Section *"Conclusion"* draws some conclusions and discusses some open lines of research in this domain.

THE BIG DATA CHALLENGE IN MOBILITY: GPS AND GSM DATA

This section is devoted to the description of two large datasets that capture the mobility of individuals through two different technologies available today: GPS and GSM data. These two datasets will be used later in the chapter as basis for defining profiling methods as well as experimentation ground for a few representative applications.

GPS Dataset

A first dataset consists of a set of GPS traces (seen in Figure 1) of private vehicles circulating in central Italy, in the region of Tuscany. The owners of these cars are subscribers of a *pay-as-you-drive*

car insurance contract, under which the tracked trajectories of each vehicle are periodically sent (through the GSM network) to a central server for anti-fraud and anti-theft purposes. This dataset has been donated for research purposes by *Octo Telematics Italia S.r.l* (oct), the leader for this sector in Europe. The whole dataset describes about 40,000 cars tracked during 5 weeks (from June 14th through July 18th, 2011) in coastal Tuscany, a 100 km x 100 km square centered on the city of Pisa. The average sampling rate of the GPS receivers is 30 seconds. Globally, the dataset consists of about 20 Million observations, each consisting of a quadruple *(id, lat, long, t)*, where *id* is the car identifier, *(lat, long)* are the spatial coordinates, and *t* the time of the observation. The car identifiers are pseudonymized, in order to achieve a basic level of anonymity. The error of the positioning system is estimated at 10-20 m in normal conditions, while the temporal resolution is in seconds. All the observations of the same car *id* over the entire observation period are chained together in increasing temporal order into a global *trajectory* of car *id*. The global trajectory is then split into several sub-trajectories, corresponding to *trips* or *travels*, by using various criteria. For instance, if a cut-off temporal threshold of 30 minutes is applied (i.e., when the time interval between two subsequent observations of the car is larger than 30 minutes, the first observation is considered as the end of a travel, and the second observation is considered as the start of another travel) we obtained about 1,500,000 different travels. An alternative splitting approach is discussed in Section *"Individual mobility profiling."*

GSM Dataset

The GSM dataset consists of a large set of call records provided by Wind S.p.A., one of the main mobile telecommunication company in Italy.

GSM (Global System for Mobile Communications) Network is a mobile network that enables the communications between mobile devices.

Figure 1. Sample of the GPS dataset used in the chapter

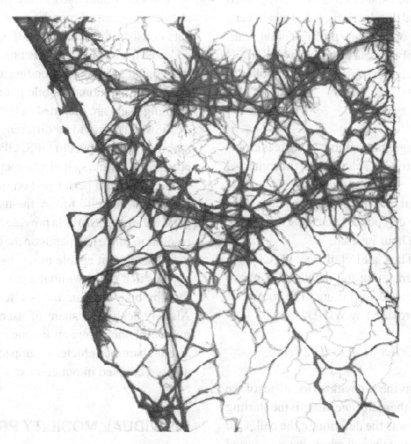

The GSM protocol is based on a so called *cellular network architecture*, where a geographical area is covered by a number of antennas (or Base Transceiver Stations, BTS) emitting a signal to be received by mobile devices. Each antenna covers an area called cell. In this way, the covered area is partitioned into a number of, possibly overlapping, cells, uniquely identified by the antenna. Cell horizontal radius varies depending on antenna height, antenna gain, population density and propagation conditions from a couple of hundred meters to several tens of kilometers. In urban areas cells are close to each other and small in area whose diameter can be down to one hundred meters and up to a kilometer. In rural areas the radius of a cell can reach a maximum of 30 kilometers. The presence of a mobile device in a cell is periodically detected by the system to maintain correctness and validity of the location information subsystem. Position data is maintained in GSM location databases (called VLR/HLR - Visitor/Home Location Register). These registers maintain location information within substructure of the network such as Location Areas, a group of antennas covering a quite extended area (100 - 300 km²). The actual location of a device in GSM network is registered at this level. Each BTS contains a radio transceiver and a controller and provides radio communication to the mobile units located in its cell.

Handover data: In cellular telecommunication domain, the term handover (or handoff) refers to the process of transferring an ongoing call or data session from one channel connected to the network to another. The most basic form of handover is when a phone connection is redirected from its current cell (called source) to a new cell (called target). In general this data is recorded whenever a mobile phone is on, not only during a phone call.

The format of the data provided by WIND as handover can be represented (Figure 2a) as follows:

<Cell 1, Cell 2, t, N>

where N is the aggregate number of devices crossing from *Cell 1* to *Cell 2* during the time interval t.

This temporal interval is set to one hour, thus N represents the cell phones that passed from the two cells in one hour interval.

CDR data: The Call Detail Record (CDR) is a log data documenting the details of a phone communication used for billing. The format of the CDR data provided by WIND is:

< Timestamp, Caller id, d, Cell 1, Cell 2 >

where *Caller id* is the anonymous identifier of the user originating the call, *Timestamp* is the starting time of the call, *d* is the duration of the call, *Cell 1* is the identifier of the cell where the call started and *Cell 2* is the identifier of the cell where the call ended. This is illustrated by Figure 2b.

The GSM data used in the examples of this chapter cover a full month of call activities. The data consist of around 7.8 million CDR records collected from January 9th to February 8th 2012. The data contains calls corresponding to about 232,200 users with a national mobile phone contract (no roaming users are included in the dataset).

GSM data provide a different perspective on mobility with respect to GPS. GPS data are very precise in time and spatial accuracy but are limited to the movement performed on private vehicles: it is not possible to follow the user once he has parked the car. GSM data provide a coarser spatial resolution, since it depends on the cell coverage of the network, but enable us to observe also those persons that move without a car, for example by foot, by bike or using the public transportation. Also, typically the share of users covered by a mobile phone company is much larger than the actual share of vehicles equipped with the GPS devised adopted in our context.

INDIVIDUAL MOBILITY PROFILING

In this section we tackle the problem of profiling individual mobility by means of GPS data analysis,

Figure 2. Schema of the Handover data (left) and Call Detail Records (right)

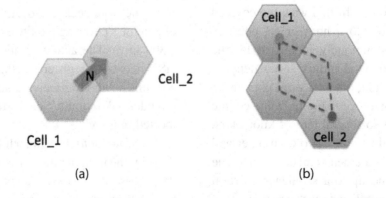

(a)　　　　　　　　　　(b)

taking as a pivot of our analytical approach the *mobility profile* concept introduced in (Trasarti et al., 2011).

Despite the great attention that mobility data and corresponding analysis methods have attracted, current work on mobility analysis largely neglects a key element that lies in between single trajectories and a whole population, i.e. the individual person, with his/her regularities and habits, that can be differed from the population. In fact, analysing individuals (rather than just large groups) provides the basis for an understanding of systematic mobility, as opposed to occasional movements, which is fundamental in some mobility planning applications, e.g. public transport. In this section we summarize the main approach presented in (Trasarti et al., 2011), where a framework was proposed, providing a two-phase process: first an individual-centered mobility model extraction; then a population-wide analysis based on the individual models. Our framework can be seen as a new approach in the learning paradigm since it provides a local-to-global analysis.

The daily mobility of each user can be essentially summarized by a set of single trips that the user performs during the day. When trying to extract a mobility profile of users, our interest is in the trips that are part of their habits, therefore neglecting occasional variations that divert from their typical behavior. Therefore in order to identify the individual *mobility profiles* of users from their GPS traces, the following steps will be performed - see Figure 3:

1. divide the whole history of the user into trips (Figure 3(a));
2. group trips that are similar, discarding the outliers (Figure 3(b));
3. from each group, extract a set of representative trips, to be used as mobility profiles (Figure 3(c)).

Trips Extraction

The history of a user is represented by the set of points in space and time recorded by their mobility device:

Definition 1 (User history): *The user history is defined as an ordered sequence of spatio-temporal points $H = <p_1, ..., p_n>$ where $p_i = (x, y, t)$ and x, y are spatial coordinates and t is an absolute timestamp.*

This continuous stream of information contains different trips made by the user, therefore in order to distinguish between them we need to detect when a user stops for a while in a place. This point in the stream will correspond to the end of a trip and the beginning of the next one. In the literature there are two main approaches: clustering-based (Bogorny et al., 2010) and heuristic-based (Xiao et al., 2010). In this paper we adopt the latter for computational efficiency reasons. Thus we look for points that change only in time; i.e. they keep the same spatial position for a certain amount of time quantified by the temporal threshold $th_{temporal}^{stop}$. Specularly, a spatial threshold $th_{spatial}^{stop}$ is used to remove both the noise introduced by the imprecision of the device and the small movements that are of no interest for a particular analysis.

Definition 2 (Potential stops): *Given the history H of a user and the thresholds $th_{spatial}^{stop}$ and $th_{temporal}^{stop}$, a potential stop is defined as a maximal subsequence S of the user's history H where the points remain within a spatial area for a certain period of time:*

$$S = <p_m, ..., p_k> | 0 < m \leq k \leq n \, \forall \, m \leq i \leq k \, Dist(p_m, p_i) \leq th_{spatial}^{stop} \wedge Dur(p_m, p_k) \, th_{temporal}^{stop}.$$

where *Dist* is the Euclidean distance function defined between the spatial coordinates of the

Figure 3. Mobility profile extraction process: (a) trip identification; (b) group detection/outlier removal; (c)selection of representative mobility profiles.

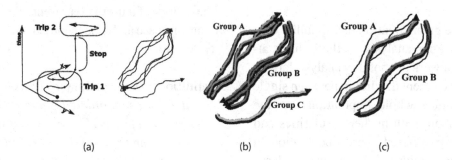

| | | |
| (a) | (b) | (c) |

points, and *Dur* is the difference in the temporal coordinates of the points. Potential stops can overlap with each other (yet, none of them can completely contain the other, for the maximality condition), making it difficult to use them as a basis for further analysis. In order to avoid this, a criterion of early selection is adopted to remove any overlaps.

Definition 3 (Actual stops): *Given a sequence of potential stops S_{set} = $<S_1, ..., S_N>$, sorted by starting time (i.e., $S \leq S' \Leftrightarrow S =<(x, y, t), ...> \wedge S' = <(x', y', t'), ...> \wedge t \leq t')$, the corresponding sequence of actual stops ActS is defined as the minimal sequence of potential stops such that:*
1. $S_1 \in$ ActS
2. *if* $S_i \in$ ActS $\wedge k = \min\{j \mid j > i \wedge S_j \cap S_i = \varnothing\} < \infty \Rightarrow S_k \in$ ActS

We indicate with $\bar{S}$ = $<S_1, ..., S_t>$ the set of all actual stops over *H*. Once we have found the stops in the users history we can identify the trips.

Definition 4 (Trip): *A trip is defined as a subsequence T of the user's history H between two consecutive actual stops in the ordered se $\bar{S}$ t or between an actual stop and the first/last point of H (i.e., p_1 or p_n):*
- $T = <p_m, ..., p_k> \mid 0 < m \leq k \leq n \wedge \exists i (S_i = <..., p_m> \wedge S_{i+1} = <p_k, ...>)$,

or
- $T = <p_1, ..., p_m> \mid 0 < m \leq n \wedge \exists i (S_i = <p_m, ...>)$, *or*
- $T = <p_k, ..., p_n> \mid 0 < k \leq n \wedge \exists i (S_i = <..., p_k>)$.

The set of extracted trip $\bar{T}$ = $<T_1, ..., T_c>$ in Figure 3(a), are the basic steps to create the user mobility profile. Notice that the thresholds $th_{spatial}^{stop}$ and $th_{temporal}^{stop}$ are the knobs for expressing specific analytical requirements.

Mobility Profiles Extraction

Our objective is to use the set of trips of an individual user to find his/her routine behaviors. We do this by grouping together similar trips based on concepts of spatial distance and temporal alignment, with corresponding thresholds for both the spatial and temporal components of the trips. In order to be defined as routine, a behavior needs to be supported by a significant number of similar trips. The above ideas are formalized as follows:

Definition 5 (Trip Group): *Given a set of trips $\bar{T}$, spatial and temporal thresholds $th_{spatial}^{group}$ and $th_{temporal}^{group}$, a spatial distance function $\delta : \bar{T}^2 \to \mathcal{R}$ and a temporal alignment constraint $\alpha : \bar{T}^2 x \mathcal{R} \to \mathcal{B}$ between pairs of trips, and a minimum support threshold*

$th_{support}^{group}$, *a trip group for* $\bar{T}$ *is defined as a subset of trips* $g \subseteq \bar{T}$ *such that:*

1. $\forall t_1, t_2 \in g . \delta(t_1, t_2) \leq th_{spatial}^{group} \wedge \alpha(t_1, t_2, th_{temporal}^{group})$;

2. $|g| \geq th_{support}^{group}$

Condition 1 requires that the trips in a group are approximately co-located, both in space and time, while condition 2 requires that the group is sufficiently large. Again, the thresholds are the knobs that the analyst will progressively tune the extraction process with.

Each group obtained in the previous step represents the typical mobility habit of a user, i.e., one of his/her routine movements. Here we summarize the whole group by choosing the central element of such a group.

Definition 6 (Routine): *Given a trip group g and the distance function used to compute it, its routine is defined as the medoid of the set, i.e.:*

$$routine(g, \delta) = argmin_{t \in g} \sum_{t' \in g \setminus \{t\}} \delta(t, t')$$

Notice that the temporal alignment is always satisfied over each pair of trips in a group, therefore the alignment relation does not appear in the definition.

Now we are ready to define the users mobility profile.

Definition 7 (Mobility Profile): *Given a set of trip groups G of a user and the distance function used to compute them, the user's mobility profile is defined as his/her corresponding set of routines:*

$$profile(G, \delta) = \{routine(g, \delta) \mid g \in G\}$$

Implementation of the Method

The whole mobility profile extraction - from the initial user history to the final mobility profiles - can be summarized in the following four steps, which are applied separately for each user: (1) the user's observations are sorted chronologically, in order to form his/her mobility history; (2) from such history the corresponding trips are built, based on spatial $(th_{spatial}^{stop})$ and temporal $(th_{temporal}^{stop})$ thresholds; (3) some heuristics is applied to define a set of suitable trip groups, satisfying all the requirements described in Definition 5; (4) each trip group of sufficient size w.r.t. threshold $th_{support}^{group}$ becomes a routine, for which a representative trip is selected.

The definitions provided in the previous section were kept generic w.r.t. the distance function δ. Different choices can satisfy different needs, possibly both conceptually (which criteria define a good group/routine assignment) and pragmatically (for instance, simpler criteria might be preferred for the sake of scalability). Obviously, the results obtained by different instantiations can vary greatly.

A crucial point left to define is the heuristics to select trip groups. Our proposal is to use a clustering method to carry out this task. We choose the clustering algorithm for trajectories proposed in (Andrienko et al., 2009), consisting of two steps. First, a density-based clustering is performed, thus removing noisy elements and producing dense - yet, possibly extensive - clusters. Secondly, each cluster is split through a bisection k-medoid procedure. Such method splits the dataset into two parts through k-medoid (a variant of k-means) with $k = 2$, then the same splitting process is recursively applied to each sub-group. Recursion stops when each resulting sub-cluster is compact enough to fit within a distance threshold of its medoid, by removing sub-clusters that are too small. The bisection k-medoid procedure guarantees that requirements 1 and 2 of Definition

5 are satisfied. The adopted clustering method is parametric w.r.t. a repertoire of similarity functions, that includes: *Ends* and *Starts* functions, comparing trajectories by considering only their last (respectively, first) points; *Route similarity*, comparing the paths followed by trajectories from a purely spatial viewpoint (time is not considered); *Synchronized route similarity*, similar to *Route similarity* but considering also time.

Experimental Validation

In this section we present the results of our method applied to a subset of the GPS dataset introduced in Section *"The Big Data Challenge in mobility: GPS and GSM data."* In particular, 2107 users were considered, in a time period of 12 days, covering different kind of territories such as urban and suburban areas. The analysis process was implemented using the Data Mining Query Language provided by the M-Atlas system [Giannotti et al., 2011]. The objective of these experiments is to generally evaluate the impact of different choices of the parameters, as well as to assess the persistence of the mobility profiles extracted, i.e. how well our definitions capture the notion of systematic mobility behavior.

We processed the dataset of observations using the *mobility profile construction* method, with the following parameters:

δ and α: we adopt the *route similarity* function described in (Andrienko et al., 2009) as spatial distance function (δ). The route similarity function performs an alignment between points of the trajectories (trips) that are going to be compared, and then computes the sum of distances between corresponding points. In addition, we adopt a temporal alignment constraint (α) which simply computes the temporal distance between the starting points of the two trips, and compares it against the temporal threshold.

$th_{spatial}^{stop}$ and $th_{temporal}^{stop}$: 50 meters and 1 hour, this means that we consider a stop when a user stays with his/her car in an area of 50 m^2 for at least one hour. Single trips of a user are thus the movements between these stops.

$th_{spatial}^{group}$ and $th_{temporal}^{group}$: 250 meters and 1 hour, we want to group trips which are similar considering a maximum of 250 meters and a temporal alignment of 1 hour.

$th_{support}^{group}$: 4 trips, only the groups with at least 4 trips survive the pruning process, the others are not considered interesting enough for the mobility profiles.

An example of how the *mobility profile construction* works is shown in Figure 5. As can be seen, two main routes are frequently repeated, each time with small variations. In addition, they appear to represent symmetric trips, such as home-to-work and work-to-home routine movements. The corresponding mobility profiles are depicted at the bottom of the figure. Notice that seven user trips were occasional trips that did not fit any consistent habit, and therefore were (correctly) filtered out by our algorithm.

Globally during the execution of the algorithm, a set of 46,163 trips is generated (Figure 4 (left)) and the result of the mobility profile construction is a set of 1,504 routines that form 919 mobility profiles (i.e., for 43.6% of the 2,107 users a profile was extracted). Figure 4 (right) shows the distribution of the number of routines per user, with almost every user having one or two routines, which usually correspond to the commute to (and from) work (not always at the same time).

To understand how the process is affected by the parameters, using different configurations we analyzed the percentage of users with a mobility profile. The results are shown in Figure 6.

They confirm that by using loose constraints, a profile can be built for almost 77% of users. Such percentage decreases to 12% when a strict set of constraints is applied. When looking at the

Figure 4. The set of trips extracted from the user observations (top) and the distribution of routines by the users (bottom).

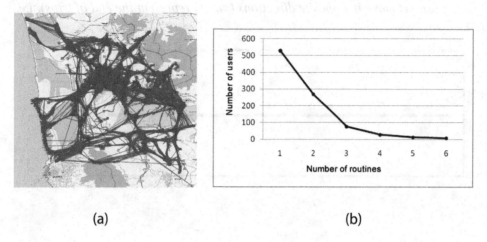

(a)   (b)

results obtained with a low spatial constraint, we must consider that the clustering method groups together fewer trips and thus pruning using the support threshold becomes more effective. Finally, the temporal threshold for the mobility profile construction does not seem to have much influence, most likely because we mixed together trips in different periods of the day. For the sake of claritywe will only show the case of the threshold set to one hour.

The purpose of the following analysis is to show to what degree the mobility profiles remain persistent and stable considering two time windows: days 1-6 and days 7-12. Figure 7 (left) presents the number of profiles extracted in the two time windows and the number of common profiles. It is important to note that the percentage of users profiled in both periods is around 50%, which means that their behavior is persistent in time. However although they are profiled in both periods, we want to understand if their routines are similar considering the same spatial threshold used for the grouping phase. In other words, if a routine extracted in the first period remains in the same hypothetical group.

The results in Figure 7 (right) show that for the same experiment we have a percentage of 74% of routines remaining stable.

The thresholds used in the rest of the paper correspond to the ones presented at the beginning of this section. There are two reasons why we chose this configuration: (i) from Figure 6 it seems that the process reaches a critical point before the decay in performance, and (ii) we want to maintain a critical point of view in order to discover the real capability of the process.

CASE OF STUDY I: DISTRIBUTED COMPUTATION APPLICATION

Mobility profiles describe to some extent the expected behaviour of an individual. In this sense, from an information theoretical viewpoint, the systematic movements of an individual are scarcely informative, since they follow faithfully known paths, while erratic movements are highly informative, since they deviate from expected ways. The scenario described in this section adopts this viewpoint, with the objective of reducing at the minimum the amount of data that a real-time

Figure 5. Trajectories of a user and the corresponding groups and routines extracted (A and B). Of the 30 trips, 11 are part of group A, and 12 of group B, while the remaining 7 are noise. The two routines are spatially similar, yet move in opposite directions (points represent the end of trips), i.e., south (A) vs. north (B).

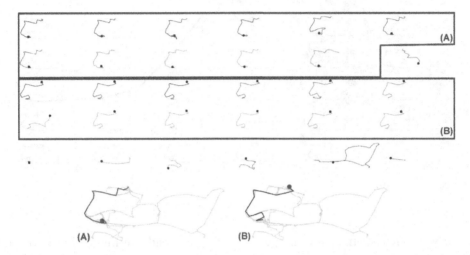

monitoring application needs to receive from mobility sensors.

In this scenario, we define a car traffic monitor application where the traffic density is estimated by collecting the position sensed by each vehicle. A single vehicle should send its position every time it moves. To reduce the impact of the communication, each vehicle computes a predictive model of its movements (based, as we will see, on its mobility profiles), and communicate to a central coordinator such model. The model provides the predictive base for the coordinator to estimate the position of each vehicle at a specific time instant. Each vehicle checks the current position against the predictive model it has computed: if the position is coherent with the model no communication to the coordinator is necessary; otherwise, the current position is sent to the coordinator.

Figure 6. Different settings of parameters lead to a different mobility profile extraction

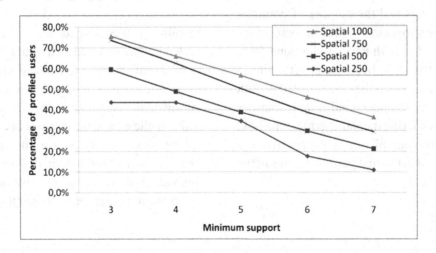

Figure 7. The process is performed on two different time windows and then compared to show how many mobility profiles are persistent (left) and stable (right)

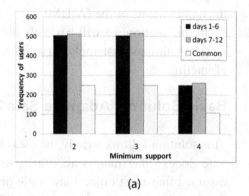

(a)

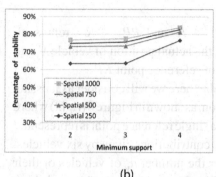

(b)

Our reference application consists in evaluating the density of vehicles in correspondence of a given set RP of n_{RP} points in space, called *reference points*. In particular, density is estimated through a kernel-based approach, i.e., the density in a point is computed by counting all vehicles in space, yet weighted according to their distance from the point (see Figure 8 (left) for a visual example).

The application involves a central controller that computes (or estimates) the vehicle densities, and a set of nodes, each representing a vehicle. Each node receives a stream of location updates (coming from the on-board GPS device) and

communicates the new location to the controller whenever needed to keep the global density estimates correct.

Definition 8 (DMP: Density Monitoring Problem): *Given a set $RP = \{RP_1, ..., RP_{nRP}\}$ of n_{RP} reference points, a set $V = \{V_1, ..., V_{nV}\}$ of vehicles and a kernel function $K(.)$, the* density monitoring problem *consists in computing, at each time instant, the function $f_{DMP}(V)$, defined as $f_{DMP}(V) = [K_1, ..., K_{nRP}]^T$, where:*

Figure 8. Examples of vehicle density estimation: for two reference points RP_1 and RP_2 (left), and, on a single dimension and with a Gaussian kernel, for a single reference point RP_1 (right).

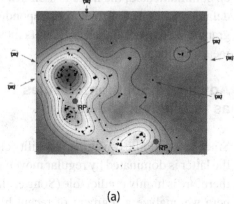

(a)

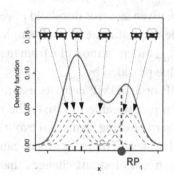

(b)

$$\forall 1 \le i \le n_{RP}.K_i = \sum_{j=1}^{n_V}K(V_j^{xy} - RP_i^{xy})$$

Here, $V_j^{xy} \in \mathcal{R}^2$ and $RP_i^{xy} \in \mathcal{R}^2$ represent, respectively, the actual position of vehicle V_j and the position of reference point RP_i.

In particular, here we will consider a Gaussian kernel function, as shown in Figure 8 (right) where the DMP for a single reference point is represented as sum of the contributions given by six vehicles.

Whenever the number n_V of vehicles or their location update frequency (or both) reach high values, it is necessary to trade the exactness of the estimation defined above with a reduction of information exchange and processing. The loss of precision, in our context, is bounded by a parameter ε, that represents the deviation from the exact output for the DMP.

Definition 9 (ADMP: Approximate DMP):
Given a DMP with reference points RP = {RP_1, ..., RP_{nRP}}, vehicle set V = {V_1, ..., V_{nV}} and kernel function K(.), and given an error tolerance parameter ε, the approximate density monitoring problem consists in computing, at each time instant, a function $f_{ADMP}(V)$ that approximates f_{DMP}. In particular, given the following error function:

error(K^A, K) = $max_{i=1}^{n_{RP}}$ |K_i^A-K_1|

where $K = f_{DMP}(V)$ and $K^A = f_{ADMP}(V)$, it always holds that error $(f_{ADMP}(V), f_{DMP}(V)) \le \varepsilon$.

In other words, given an error threshold ε we require that the density estimate of each single RP provided by f_{ADMP} differs at most of ε from the corresponding value provided by f_{DMP}.

Solving a DMP or a ADMP consists essentially in defining a process able to satisfy their requirements in every possible status and evolution of the overall system. The latter aspect can be modeled by a stream of status changes that each node senses during the monitoring period; the "process", then, basically defines a protocol used by nodes and controller to communicate only the essential information needed to satisfy the requirements of the (A)DMP.

In this section we will basically discuss two ADMP solutions, that apply very different levels of intelligence.

Basic Solution: Adaptive Safe Zones

This solution follows strictly the ideas based on Safe Zones (Sharfman et al., 2007), where it is assumed that most objects are static or most of the time they move around some specific points in space, such as the home or work location. The basic idea, then, is to define a *default location* for each object v, and when no update arrives to the controller, it assumes that v is inside its default location.

However, since the context of mobility is characterized by massive and rapid changes in the data and locations are highly dynamic, we adopted a variant that better fits our scenario.

The basic assumption behind this approach is that the objects are not necessarily static, yet their movements are relatively slow. As an effect, when an object visits a given location, its associated region will most likely contain several of the next locations of the object, yet no single location is able to capture a large part of the mobility of the object.

Operationally, the protocol works as for the case discussed above, but when an update must be communicated, the node is assigned to a new default location and to its corresponding geographical area, computed around its most recent measured location.

Advanced Solution: Profiles as Predictive Models

Since recent studies on human mobility claim that the latter is dominated by regular movements and therefore is highly predictable (Song et al., 2010), here we analyze a segment of recent history of each node, in order to identify its regularities and use them as models to predict their locations in the next future.

The basic idea is to use a predictive model based on Mobility Profiles. Here we make a strong assumption, i.e. that the user tends to repeat the same trips everyday (home-to-work, and vice versa, for instance), thus involving an higher level concept of *frequent trip*, that requires a coherent sequence of spatiotemporal locations.

Having extracted the user's mobility profile, we want to use it to predict the user's position at a certain time. It is important to notice that a mobility profile does not necessarily cover the whole daily schedule of a user. Let consider the two possible cases shown in Figure 9: (i) the prediction is made for the time instant t_1, corresponding to a period of the day where the profile is *defined*, and (ii) the prediction is made for the time instant t_2 corresponding to a period of the day where the profile is *not defined*.

In the first case the prediction will be the spatial interpolation between the two temporally closest points which surround t_1, namely p_1 and p_2. In the other case the prediction will be the last known point of the routine preceding temporally t_2, namely p_3.

Experimental Validation

A crucial aspect of the application is the position of the RPs in space. In order to test the effectiveness of the methods on a real scenario, we use the positions of a set actual sensors used by the Mobility Agency in Tuscany, placed on the main gates of the city of Pisa plus one over the main bridge of the city center and two on two important neighboring towns. In Figure 10 the complete set of sensors is shown, and in Figure 11 a detail of Pisa is shown where each entrance of the city is monitored. The physical devices placed on the territory are permanent sensors based on laser technology, which count the number and estimate the speed of cars passing nearby.

In this section we present the performances obtained using the Profiles approach. During the initial phase each node builds a profile and sends it to the controller. Then, when the system starts, the nodes check if their actual positions are coherent with their profiles. If not, they communicate to the controller, otherwise nothing is communicated, since the controller can predict the position using the profiles. In Figure 12 (left) we show how the Profile spatial radius value (essentially corresponding to the spatial threshold $th_{spatial}^{group}$ introduced in the previous section) changes the number of profiles extracted during the initialization phase: increasing the radius, the number of profiles increases, i.e. the number of nodes who have a profile. Indeed, higher radii make the similarity between the user's trips less strict, thus making the formation of groups and profiles easier. It is interesting to notice how the number have a big increasing when the radius passes from 0.3 to 0.5 detecting a crucial point for the profile construction.

Having more profiles does not mean to have better performances. Indeed, loose profiles lead

Figure 9. A profile composed by three routines. Only part of the day is covered, while holes are filled by the default model.

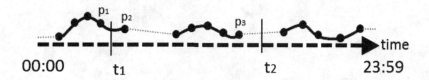

15

Figure 10. Location of RPs adopted in the experiments, and buffers representing kernel widths for the density computation.

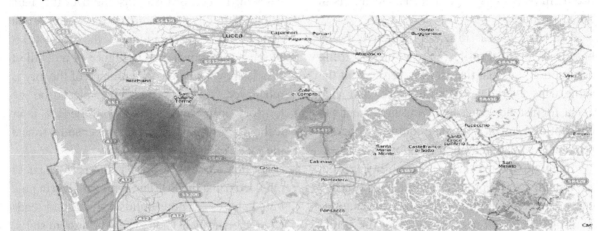

to loose predictions. This can be seen in the Figure12 (right), which shows the percentage of communications that the system had to perform during the monitoring: the baseline is the communication of every update received by each vehicle, which corresponds to 100%; the basic solution based on adaptive safe zones is depicted as a dashed blue line, while the profile-based solution is shown in green. We can see that the performances of the profile-based solution -

Figure 11. A detailed view of the sensors and the focal area in the city of Pisa

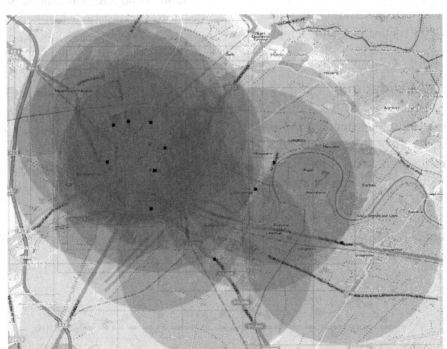

Figure 12. Number of profiles created by the nodes using different tolerance values (left) and corresponding performances obtained, expressed as fraction of the total amount of updates received by the nodes that were also sent to the controller (right).

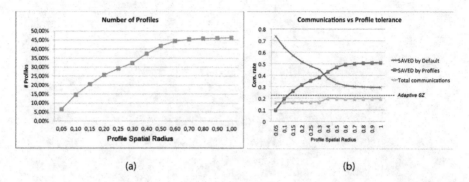

(a)   (b)

though consistently better than the basic solution - remain almost the same for increasing values of the Profile radius (and thus for increasing numbers of nodes with a profile). Moreover, with radius equal to 0.3 the performances decrease, meaning that a critical point is reached and the profiles become too loose and the errors in profile prediction becomes higher. Analyzing the communications saved by the profiles (red line) and the basic solution (violet line, used when there is no profile to apply) we can see that profiles tend to replace the default model, improving the overall performances.

As a last evaluation, we provide an exploration of the performance results on the map. Figure 13 shows where the relative errors occur during the execution of the system. The color scale goes from red, representing a big percentage of errors, to blue which represents a small percentage of errors. Clearly, the error percentage is affected by the proximity to the RPs, in fact the error threshold is more likely exceeded in proximity of each focal point where the kernel function reaches the maximum. In other words, in those areas a small error in the location prediction leads to a big error on the density computation, therefore causing more likely a communication from the node to the controller.

CASE OF STUDY II: CAR POOLING APPLICATION

A direct exploitation of mobility profiles is provided by the second application scenario we discuss in this chapter: a proactive car pooling application. Each vehicle computes and provides to a central server a summary of its relevant *routines*. The central server collects such routines by several registered user and elaborates the systematic behavior of each participant to find possible matches among two or more users. If such a match exists, the system suggests to the users the possibility of sharing the car for a common movement. Clearly, the matching procedure is rather complex, and requires to account different factors. For example, when evaluating when a person can pick up another one we should check if their mutual position is consistent with the trips of the user providing the car and that the passenger could be able to walk to the pick up checkpoint. From the initial simulations we found out that the potential reduction of circulating vehicles is significant, since 30% of the systematic trips have a corresponding match with another user.

Figure 13. Distribution of relative errors occurred during the system execution

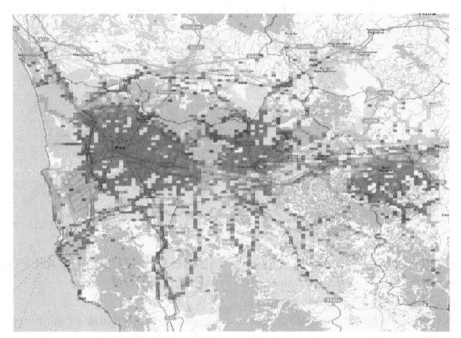

Definitions and Methodology

The basic building block of this application scenario is the concept of share-ability of trips between users, focusing in particular on the systematic ones, i.e. their sets of routines:

Definition 10 (Mobility profile share-ability):
Given two mobility profiles $\tilde{T}_1$ and $\tilde{T}_2$, and thresholds $th_{dis\tan ce}^{walking}$ and $th_{time}^{wasting}$, the Mobility profile share-ability measure between $\tilde{T}_1$ and $\tilde{T}_2$ is defined as the fraction of routines in profiles $\tilde{T}_1$ which are contained in at least one routine in $\tilde{T}_2$:

$$profileShare(\tilde{T}_1,\tilde{T}_2,th_{distance}^{walking},th_{time}^{wasting}) = \frac{\left| \left\{ p \in \tilde{T}_1 \mid \exists q \in \tilde{T}_2 . Share(p,q,th_{distance}^{walking},th_{time}^{wasting}) \right\} \right|}{\left| \tilde{T}_1 \right|}$$

By applying this definition to all possible pairs of users (i.e., to their corresponding profiles) we can build a matrix of share-ability, thus expressing how good the match of each pair is. The process includes a first phase where a *routine containment matrix* is built by comparing each pair of single mobility routines; then, in a second phase, the results corresponding to each pair of users are collapsed to form a mobility *profile share-ability matrix*, by applying the Definition 10. A visual example of the result is shown in Figure14.

Experimental Results

Here we apply the methodology sketched in the previous section to perform the matching on our data (the same dataset presented in Section *"Individual mobility profiling"*) with different parameter settings. The results in Figure 16 show how the performances are affected, in terms of percentage routines and mobility profiles that have at least one match. Note that by allowing a *walking distance* of 5 km and a *wasting time* of 1 hour, 89% of profiled users have (at least) one match, which decreases to 66% if the wasting time becomes half an hour. Figure 15 shows two

Figure 14. Example of the mobility profile matching process: the routines of the same color belong to the same mobility profile. On the right the matrix of containment between routines (top) and the matrix of the profile share-ability (bottom) with instantiated values.

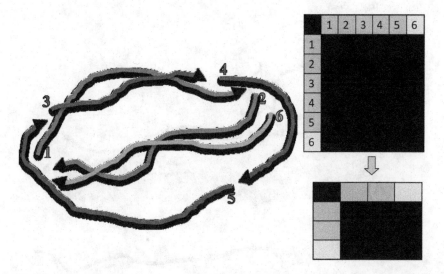

examples of matching between two users. The red user can be served by the violet user on the basis of the routines shown. In the two examples it is interesting to see that in the first case (A), the starts and ends of the routines are quite close, therefore these users can both serve or be served by each other; in the second case (B) the relation is unidirectional, since the red routine ends much earlier than the other, and therefore the *contain* relation does not hold in the opposite direction.

Considering a hypothetical car pooling service built on top of the proposed method, using a *walking distance* of 2.5 km and a *wasting time* of 1 hour, we can calculate some statistics regarding the potential impact of the service. In fact 684 users, corresponding to 32.4% of participants, receive at least one indication of a possible host for one of their routines. This means that if everybody takes the opportunity of sharing a/their car using this system, traffic could be decreased significantly. As previously mentioned, one advantage of the system is that users do not need to manually declare their common trips (indeed, routines are automatically detected), which is a major flaw of current car pooling systems, and

probably contributes substantially to their failure. As already discussed in section *"Experimental Validation"* devoted to generally validate profiles, the system can keep reasonably up-to-date routines and profiles by executing the profiling process once every two weeks (or more), using a temporal sliding window on the data.

DISCOVERY CALL BEHAVIORS

In this section we explore a form of user profiling alternative to that discussed in the previous section, based on mobility data coming from the mobile phone infrastructures. In particular, we will introduce a method to infer a possible segmentation of a population of GSM users into different behavior categories.

This is an essential step for better understanding and studying people mobility from unsupervised mobility data. Indeed, being able to differentiate population into a set of clear and well defined semantic categories enables a large number of new applications. However, when the mobility data is not directly annotated with the user profile, the

Figure 15. Examples of routine containment: red routines are contained in the violet ones

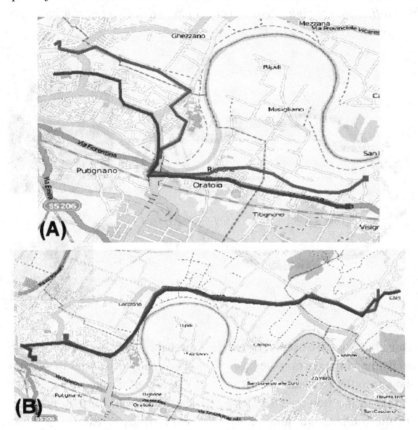

association of an anonymous trajectory to a given segment is far to be trivial.

We remark that, at the present, the individuals described by mobile phone data and GPS data are typically different and very difficult to link. Therefore, the profiling methods presented here and in previous sections are expected to be applicable only in independent analysis processes, though possibly describing the same territory and the same mobility-related phenomena. In the near future, however, with the larger diffusion of location-aware smart phones and related data collection infrastructures, the two worlds might converge and make it possible to join the different profiling techniques described in this chapter.

The strategy we present here is based on the identification of four categories of users, based on the analysis of GSM call records: *residents*, *commuters*, *people in transit* and *visitors/tourists*.

Mobile Users Profiles

Our concrete objective is to infer the profile of users moving in a city. To this purpose, given the spatial area A under analysis, the four categories we are interested in will be characterized as follows:

- **Resident**: A person is resident in an area A when his/her home is inside. Therefore, the mobility tends to be focused on movements from and towards his/her home.
- **Commuter:** A person is a commuter between an area B and an area A if his/her home is in B while the workplace is in A. Therefore the daily mobility of this person is mainly between B and A.
- **In Transit**: An individual is "in transit" over an area A if his/her home and work places are outside A, and his/her pres-

Figure 16. Matching percentages of users (upper curves) and routines (lower curves) for different settings of the spatial and temporal thresholds.

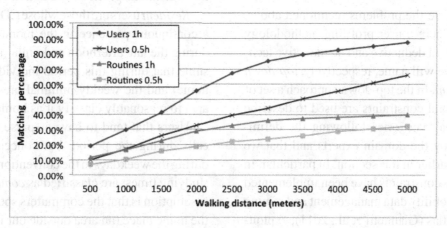

ence inside area *A* is limited by a temporal threshold T_{tr} representing the time necessary to transit through *A*. In other words, the user does not perform any main activity inside *A*. Depending on the application this temporal threshold T_{tr} may vary from few minutes to few hours.

- **Tourist or Visitor**: The definition given by The World Tourism Organization defines tourists as people "traveling to and staying in places outside their usual environment for not more than one consecutive year for leisure, business and other purposes" (Wikipedia). We can rephrase and formalize this definition as: a person is a tourist in an area *A* if his/her home and work places are outside *A*, and the presence inside the area is limited to a certain period of time T_{to} that can allow him/her to spend some activities in *A*. In particular, here the presence has to be concentrated in a finite temporal interval inside the time window. Should also be "occasional" therefore, he/she does not appear anymore during the observation period. It is also important to point out that this definition includes not only the classical "tourism" as visiting cultural and natural attractions, but also the

activities related to work, visiting relatives, health reasons, etc.

The proposed analytical process is based on a step-wise approach: first, domain knowledge is used to label each user according to a set of rules that define each profile; second, the profiles that do not fit in any of the hypothesis templates are analyzed by means of a machine learning approach to determine relevant groups of users according to their calling behavior. When an individual makes (at least) a phone call inside a network cell we say this individual is *present* into the cell area. The presence pattern is then defined by temporal constraints on the detected presence.

However, these definitions combined with the characteristics of the GSM call data may give misleading classifications. For example, a resident user who rarely calls may be misclassified as a tourist or a person in transit, while a resident that only use phone at work may be classified as a commuter. Again, defining a good threshold to identify tourists may be difficult and certainly depends on the application. Although the "in transit" profile is well defined once a temporal threshold is fixed, the other profiles, especially the "tourist" population, is characterized by a "fuzzy" and unclear characterization.

Top-Down vs. Bottom-Up Approach

In order to face the problems mentioned above, we describe here a user profiling methodology that combines a deductive and an inductive technique, that we will name, respectively, *top-down* and *bottom-up*. In the top-down approach a set of spatio-temporal constraints are used to describe the individual categories following the definitions given by the domain experts and that we introduced earlier in this section. In particular, in this work the constraints have been implemented within the mobility data management and mining system M-Atlas (Giannotti et al., 2011), exploiting its query language. In the bottom-up step, the assignment of users to categories is refined using a clustering algorithm based on Self Organizing Maps (SOM) (Kohonen, 2001).

Clearly, since the top-down step is based on a set of rules provided by the domain experts, they may fail at classifying behaviors that lie on the borders of the category definitions adopted. Therefore, all those individuals that have few phone calls or whose phone calls behavior does not clearly fall into the well-defined categories remain unassigned. The bottom-up approach aims at integrating the results of the first step by using a data-driven approach to identify relevant groups of users that present similar behaviors, and that can be classified as one of the available profiles.

The advantages of the described technique lie on the fact that GSM data - due to the widespread use of mobile phones and the heterogeneous classes of their users - allow to analyze the mobility behavior of a huge amount of people and a broad range of user categories. Furthermore, the use of an inductive step allows a refinement of the preliminary results obtained with the top-down approach.

Top-down Approach: During this phase the residents, commuters and in transit categories are retrieved from the CDR dataset with a proposed set of spatio-temporal constraints that depend on

the time window of the data collection and reflect the indications given by the domain experts.

Resident users are those whose CDR data show a continuous presence in the monitored period during the late afternoon and night (since we assume that during this period individuals stay at home) and the weekly minimal presence in the area to reasonably classify it as home.

Users that tend to have a sparse presence of calls during the period, but concentrated only during the weekdays in the conventional working/ studying times, are classified as *commuters*. The assumption is that the commuters spend nights at the home place (an area outside our interest) and weekdays at the work/study place in the area of interest, and never appear during the weekends.

People in transit are directly identified by a simple constraint that limits the presence to a fixed time range depending on the dimension of the area under analysis. The constraint tries to encode the average time needed to cross the area without stops for activities. The idea is to capture people passing on motorways and freeways near a city or crossing the city by using urban roads. This gap can vary from less than 1 hour, for small towns, up to several hours, for big cities.

Of course a number of users whose call behavior does not precisely fall in these three definitions remain unclassified after this first step. The bottom-up step is thus necessary to analyse the unclassified set of users trying to assign a category based on a temporal profiling.

Bottom-Up Approach: The bottom-up approach has the twofold purpose of both identifying tourists and refining the results obtained by the top-down phase for residents and commuters.

The behavior of each user is modeled by means of the concepts of space (where a call is started and where it is terminated) and time. We exploit these two dimensions to define a temporal profile for each user.

Given a user u, a *Temporal Profile* TP_u is a vector of call statistics according to a given temporal discretization. For example, each entry of

TP_u might contain the number of calls performed by the user on each day of the week. Since we are interested in a specific area, we define a *Space constrained Temporal Profile $TP_A{}^u$* as a Temporal Profile where only the calls performed in the cells contained within the area A are considered. This spatial projection is crucial when studying commuters in order to distinguish the call behavior at work and at home.

To explore different time patterns, we define also two time transformations of a (Space constrained) Temporal Profile: (i) *time projection* by a cycle period, where the time intervals of the vector are referred to relative position in a time cycle like week, month, and so on; (ii) *time shifting*, where the time intervals of the vector are shifted in order to have the first entry corresponding to the first activity of the user. Clearly, the available statistics can be chosen according to the specific analytical scenario. For example, it can be considered the number of calls, the total duration of the calls, or a boolean operator that yields true if at least a call has been performed in a specific time period. Figure 17 shows two examples of extraction of temporal profiles from the call behaviors of two users, using call frequency as measure for each cell.

The temporal profiles defined above are analyzed according to their relative similarities by means of a Self Organizing Map (Kohonen, 2001). A SOM is a type of neural network based on unsupervised learning. It produces a one/two dimensional representation of the input space using a neighborhood function to preserve the topological properties of the input space. As most neural nets, a SOM constructs a map in a training phases using input examples and uses the map for classifying a new input vector. SOMs form a sort of semantic map where similar samples are mapped close together and dissimilar ones are far apart. With respect to other clustering techniques, the SOM allows an easier and clearer visualization of the results.

In our case the weighted vectors used for the analysis are the TP_u extracted for each user. For example, using a discretization of one hour, a daily temporal profile for a user consists of a vector with 24 entries. The dimensions of the vector may change accordingly with different aspects of the analysis like, for example, the temporal profile in a week, in a single day, or in the whole period by hour (see Figure 17).

The SOM algorithm produces a set of nodes, where each node represents a group of users with similar temporal profile. By analyzing the profile that describes each group, it is possible to assign it to the class (resident, commuter and tourist) that best fits, based on the definitions given above. In particular, as stated before, the temporal profile of a tourist cannot be defined a priori because it has a wide variability depending on the season, the location and other unpredictable events. This method can thus help to discover the touristic degree of an area without using particular apriori knowledge. This phase is useful also to re-calibrate the top-down results. In fact, the analysis of the profiles emerging from the groups may give information about local habits and may suggests how to set the temporal constraints to adapt the model to the local habits of the area of study.

The analysis described above has been performed from two distinct perspectives, dependent on the chosen temporal profile: (i) applying a left shifting operator (see Figure 17 (g) and (h)), which leads to lose an absolute temporal reference (thus it is not directly possible to associate each entry to a specific

time period) yet allows to identify the typical duration of presence of the users and, hence, assign the tourist/visitor class to the nodes with compatible temporal profiles; (ii) extract the original temporal profile according to the absolute time alignment, in which case the resulting SOM tends to highlight similar and compatible presence profile of longer stay people, better allowing to separate commuters and residents.

Figure 17. Example of the extraction of temporal profiles from the call activities of two users. Each square represents a day and the number within a cell is the number of calls of the corresponding user in that day.

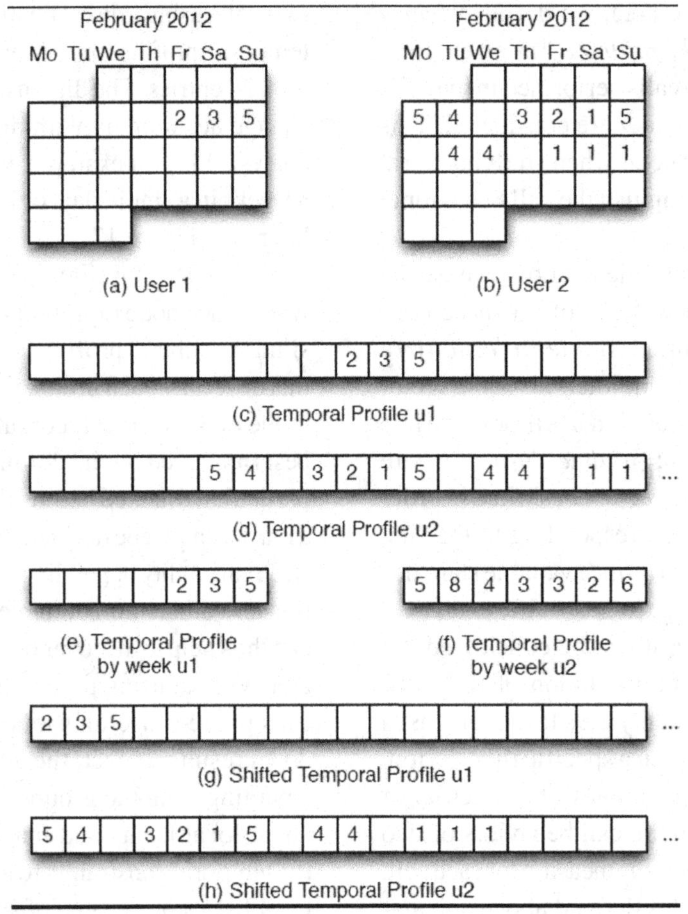

REAL CASE OF STUDY III: DISCOVERING CALL BEHAVIORS IN PISA

The approach described in Section *"Discovery Call Behaviors"* has been applied to a case study in the city of Pisa. In particular, we used a large GSM dataset collected in the province of Pisa by one of the Italian mobile operators, also described in Sub Section *"GSM dataset"*.

Our approach is based on a set of temporal constraints over the users' temporal profiles. As a preliminary validation analysis of the method, we analyze the temporal presence of users in the province of Pisa. Figure 18 shows the cumulative (decreasing) distribution of the duration of stay of users in the province: a point *(x, y)* on the chart represents the number of distinct users *y* that were observed in the area at least for *x* days. From the chart we can roughly partition the population on the basis of the domain knowledge: people staying less than four days are candidate visitors or in transit, while the others can be considered as residents/commuters. This very naive segmentation allows us to estimate how effective this approach is, and the candidate resident commuters that result are around 107k. This number is compatible with the customer statistics provided by the telecom operator in the area, thus providing a first indirect validation of the approach.

Since our aim is to study the mobility of residents and visitors in the area of Pisa, from the whole network we first selected the cells overlapping the urban area of the city, obtain through a simple geometric intersection of the base station positions (the antennas) with the urban census surface. Then, we filtered the calls by considering only those performed in the selected cells.

Top-Down Analysis

While the spatial constraints described above remain the same along the whole process, the temporal constraints adopted for the top-down approach are different for all the categories of users we want to identify, as detailed in the following:

Resident

C1: Temporal range: at least 1 call in [19:00 - 6:59] during the weekdays.
C2.1: Daily presence: at least 2 distinct weekdays per week, that satisfy C1.
C2.2: Daily presence: at least 1 day in the weekend without temporal range.
C3: Weekly presence: at least 3 weeks, in which C1, C2.1 and C2.2 are satisfied.

Commuter

C1.1: Temporal range: at least 1 call in [9:00 - 18:59] during the weekdays.
C1.2: Temporal range: no calls in [19:00 - 8:59] during the weekdays.
C2.1: Daily presence: at least 2 distinct weekdays per week, that satisfy C1.1 and C1.2.
C2.2: Daily presence: never during the weekends.
C3: Weekly presence: at least 3 weeks, in which C1.1, C1.2, C2.1, C2.2 and C3 are satisfied.

People in Transit

C1: Temporal range: calls during at most 1 hour.
C2: Daily presence: at most 1 day in which C1 is satisfied.
C3: Weekly presence: at most 1 week, in which C1 and C2 are satisfied.

A first statistics on the result of the top-down approach is shown in Figure 19.

This method is able to capture only a low number of commuters and residents because the temporal constraints are very strict and selective. On the contrary, people in transit are well identified. The high percentage of this kind of users is

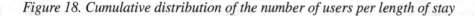

Figure 18. Cumulative distribution of the number of users per length of stay

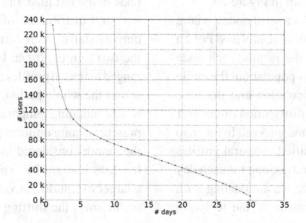

Figure 19. People profiles after the top-down phase

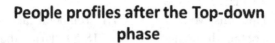

People profiles after the Top-down phase

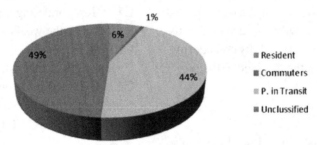

justified by the presence of a highway and a freeway close to the town, which are (partially) covered by some of the selected GSM cells.

Bottom-Up Analysis

Starting from the unclassified users left by the previous steps, we can apply the SOM method to identify temporal profiles with similar characteristics, i.e. we can group together people who have the same calling patterns. In particular, we are interested in two aspects of the temporal profile: the duration of the stay in the city and the typical temporal location of a user call. To address the first problem, we perform a transformation of the temporal profiles by applying a temporal shift. The objective it to align all the user activities at the beginning of the time window. The results provided by SOM are shown in Figure 20.

The resulting map shows a set of nodes, where each node contains a set of user profiles. For an immediate readability of the results, each node shows the cardinality of its population, the circle is proportional to the population and the time chart shows the temporal distribution of the user activities in the specific time interval. In the map of Figure 20 (left), the shifted temporal profiles consist of vectors of 31 entries, one for each day of the time window. Since we are dealing with shifted profiles, the extension of the temporal

distribution in each node provides an immediate estimation of the duration of the stay of the corresponding users. From the map it is evident how the temporal profiles are grouped: on the bottom left corner of the figure there are the temporal profiles corresponding to short visits of the city; the upper right side of the figure shows the profiles that span for the whole period and it is possible to identify even nodes that present a clear commuter-like pattern with high frequency during the workdays and a smaller activity during weekends. It is important to point out the presence of three larger nodes corresponding to short visits ranging from one day (node with 5750 profiles) to three days (nodes in the upper left corner).

The shifts can be inverted to observe the actual temporal distribution of the activities during the period of study. Figure 20 (right) shows, for each node in the left map, the corresponding absolute temporal distribution of the activities. The cardinality statistics are left as a reference between the two figures. It can be noted how the short-ranged temporal profiles are uniformly distributed across the whole period. For instance, the larger node containing temporal profiles of a single day presents a quite uniform presence of users across the month considered in the study. On the other hand, as it could be expected, the profiles with a larger extent do not vary too much, since their width limits the shifting transformation.

Figure 20. SOM clusters with shifted Temporal Profiles. (a) Each node shows the distribution for shifted temporal profiles. (b) Each node shows the actual temporal distribution for the corresponding set of users.

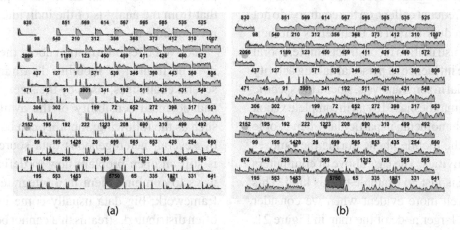

(a)   (b)

To better understand the temporal distribution of user activities in the period, we apply the SOM method to the un-shifted temporal profiles. The resulting SOM map is showed in Figure 21. In this map, we can notice how the commuter-like

patterns are even more evident in the bottom left corner. The population corresponding to these nodes is even larger than the nodes present in the shifted version. Actually, these nodes are contributed by users with different habits: the

Figure 21. SOM clusters with (un-shifted) Temporal Profiles

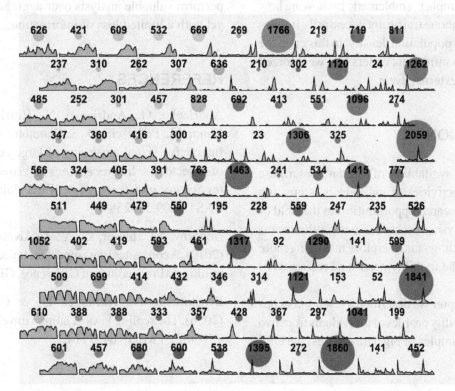

frequent callers have a regular temporal profile that remains unchanged even after the temporal shift; the infrequent callers, on the contrary, do not present such distribution by themselves but their aggregated distribution reconstructs this temporal pattern. The influence of personal calling activity may be crucial in some analysis, since a too specific distribution may be biased by an incomplete vision of the real phenomena, in particular when people do not use the mobile phone during their movements or activities. The case above of commuters distribution is just an example of this kind. This aspect is even more evident when we consider some of the larger node of the map in Figure 21. According to the node with 2059 entries (on the center right side of the figure), a lot of people were present in Pisa for a single day, specifically on January 26. Actually, that day, around 4:00 in the afternoon, an earthquake happened in northern Italy and it was perceived by the population in Pisa. That event triggered the need for a lot of users to communicate and call their relatives producing the peak we observed in the node. This particular example is emblematic in showing how a peak in the phone traffic not necessarily implies an increase in population density. In this case, the peak is due to infrequent callers that were forced to call by an external event.

CONCLUSION

The growing availability of big data describing the life and activities of individuals is creating several big research opportunities. In the field of mobility analysis, that means having the means for understanding - and therefore managing more efficiently - the mobility needs and resources of a territory.

In this chapter we described a few approaches to extract mobility profiles of individuals from two important examples of big data sources: the GPS traces of vehicles and the GSM traces of mobile phones. The key of all the methods presented is that from the analysis of the individual histories it is possible to

derive better information about the collectivity. The frontier of mobility data mining poses several challenges, risen by the size, complexity and potential sensibility of the available data, such as the following: mobility can be described by several, heterogeneous data sources, and it is still an open problem how to define optimal ways to combine them in a integrated analysis framework; big data usually come in fast, and often distributed, streams that cannot be analyzed with standard, off-line and centralized methods, thus requiring clever way to handle them; finally, individual data clearly poses risks of privacy leaks, calling for methods and framework to protect the individual data from the source to the publishing/exploitation of the analysis results. On this direction, the idea of creating temporal profiles from raw GSM calls data records provides a first way to overcome the privacy issues, since it allows to perform valuable analysis over aggregated data, yet with a limited loss of information.

REFERENCES

Andrienko, G., Andrienko, N., Rinzivillo, S., Nanni, M., Pedreschi, D., & Giannotti, F. (2009). Interactive visual clustering of large collections of trajectories. In *Proceedings of Visual Analytics Science and Technology*. IEEE. doi:10.1109/VAST.2009.5332584.

Bogorny, V., Heuser, C. A., & Alvares, L. O. (2010). A conceptual data model for trajectory data mining. In Proceedings of GIScience. GIScience..

Brockmann, D., Hufnagel, L., & Geisel, T. (2006). The scaling laws of human travel. *Nature*, *439*(462). PMID:16437114.

Furletti, B., Gabrielli, L., Rinzivillo, S., & Renso, C. (2012). Identifying users profiles from mobile calls habits. In *Proceedings of UrbComp12*. Urb-Comp. doi:10.1145/2346496.2346500.

Gaffney, S., & Smyth, P. (1999). Trajectory clustering with mixture of regression models. In *Proceedings of the 5th International Conference on Knowledge Discovery and Data Mining (KDD'99)*, (pp. 63-72). ACM.

Giannotti, F., Nanni, M., Pedreschi, D., Pinelli, F., Renso, C., Rinzivillo, S., & Trasarti, R. (2011). Unveiling the complexity of human mobility by querying and mining massive trajectory data. *The VLDB Journal, 20*(5), 695–719. doi:10.1007/s00778-011-0244-8.

Giannotti, F., Nanni, M., Pinelli, F., & Pedreschi, D. (2007). Trajectory pattern mining. In *Proceedings of KDD*, (pp. 330-339). KDD.

Kohonen, T. (2001). *Self-organizing maps*. Berlin: Springer. doi:10.1007/978-3-642-56927-2.

Nanni, T. Rossetti, & Pedreschi. (2012). Efficient distributed computation of human mobility aggregates through user mobility profiles. In Proceedings of UrbComp12. UrbComp..

Octotelematics. (n.d.). Retrieved from http://www.octotelematics.it/

Phithakkitnukoon, S. Horamont, Lorenzo, G. D., Shibasaki, R., & Ratti, C. (2010). Activity-aware map: Identifying human daily activity pattern using mobile phone data. In *Proceedings of HBU2010*, (pp. 14-25). HBU.

Sagl, G., Loidl, M., & Beinat, E. (2012). A visual analytics approach for extracting spatio-temporal urban mobility information from mobile network traffic. *ISPRS International Journal of Geo-Information*, 256-271.

Sharfman, I., Schuster, A., & Keren, D. (2007). A geometric approach to monitoring threshold functions over distributed data streams. *ACM Transactions on Database Systems, 32*(4). doi:10.1145/1292609.1292613.

Song, C., Koren, T., Wang, P., & Baràbsi, A.-L. (2010). Modelling the scaling properties of human mobility. *Nature Physics, 7*, 713.

Tourism. (n.d.). *Wikipedia*. Retrieved from http://en.wikipedia.org/wiki/Tourism

Trasarti, R., Pinelli, F., Nanni, M., & Giannotti, F. (2011). Mining mobility user profiles for car pooling. In *Proceedings of the 17th ACM SIGKDD International Conference on Knowledge Discovery and Data Mining*, (pp. 1190-1198). ACM.

Xiao, X., Zheng, Y., Luo, Q., & Xie, X. (2010). Finding similar users using category-based location history. In *Proceedings of the 18th SIGSPATIAL International Conference on Advances in Geographic Information Systems*. ACM.

Yuan, Y., & Raubal. (2012). Extracting dynamic urban mobility patterns from mobile phone data. In *Proceedings of GIScience*, (pp. 354-367). GIScience.

Chapter 2
On Predicting the Future Locations of Moving Objects:
The State of the Art

Nicola Corona
University of Pisa, Italy & ISTI-CNR, Italy

Fosca Giannotti
ISTI-CNR, Italy

Anna Monreale
University of Pisa, Italy & ISTI-CNR, Italy

Roberto Trasarti
ISTI-CNR, Italy

ABSTRACT

The pervasiveness of mobile devices and location-based services produces as side effects an increasing volume of mobility data, which in turn creates the opportunity for a novel generation of analysis methods of movement behaviors. In this chapter, the authors focus on the problem of predicting future locations aimed at predicting with a certain accuracy the next location of a moving object. In particular, they provide a classification of the proposals in the literature addressing that problem. Then the authors preset the data mining method WhereNext and finally discuss possible improvements of that method.

INTRODUCTION

In the last years, we have witnessed a considerable increase of the number of mobile devices used by the people and an extensive use of wireless communication, such as Bluetooth, Wi-Fi and GPRS. The mobile devices often, are equipped with positioning sensors that utilize Global Positioning System (GPS) to accurately provide the location of a device. Therefore, nowadays, the movement of people or vehicles within a given area can be observed from the digital traces left behind by the personal or vehicular mobile devices, and collected by the wireless network infrastructures. For instance, mobile phones leave positioning logs, which specify their localization at each

DOI: 10.4018/978-1-4666-4920-0.ch002

moment they are connected to the GSM network; analogously, GPS-equipped portable devices can record their latitude-longitude position at each moment they are exposed to a GPS satellite, and transmit their trajectories to a collecting server. The pervasiveness of ubiquitous technologies guarantees that there will be an increasing availability of large amount of data pertaining to individual trajectories, with increasing localization precision.

Knowledge about the positions of mobile objects has led to location-based services and applications, which need to know the approximate position of a mobile user in order to operate. Examples of such services are navigational services, traffic management and location-based advertising. In a typical scenario, a moving object periodically informs the positioning framework of its current location. Due to the unreliable nature of mobile devices and the limitations of the positioning systems, the location of a mobile object is often unknown for a long period of time. In such cases, a method to predict the possible next location of a moving object is required in order to anticipate or pre-fetch possible services in the next location. A hot topic in mobility management research field is *location prediction*. Location prediction can be defined as the prediction of the next locations where the mobile user is traveling between the cells of a personal communications services (PCS) network or a GSM network. The predicted movement can then be used to increase the efficiency of PCSs. By using the predicted movement, the system can effectively allocate resources to the most probable-to-move cells instead of blindly allocating excessive resources in the cell-neighborhood of a mobile user. Effective allocation of resources to mobile users would improve resource utilization and reduce the latency in accessing the resources.

Problem Statement

The Location Prediction task is composed of two main steps: a) learning a prediction model by observing historical movement data; and b) applying the prediction model for forecasting the next location visited by a specific user. More formally we can define the location prediction problem as follows:

Definition 1 (Location Prediction Problem): *Given a set of mobility data describing the user movements, first we want to learn a model called predictor P. Then, for any new trajectory t of a moving object o we want to apply the predictor P for forecasting the next location that the moving object o probably will visit.*

Several proposals in the literature have addressed this interesting problem. The strong interest is due to the fact that this task enables novel applications in a wide range of scenarios.

APPLICATIONS

The ability to predict future locations, which will be visited by people, enables a rich set of novel pervasive applications and systems. In general the knowledge about the mobile objects positions fosters location-based services and applications, which need to know the approximate position of a mobile user in order to provide their functionality.

In the following we discuss examples of applications where the location prediction could help to improve a service:

- **Location-based Advertising**: Embedding a location prediction system in a service such as Groupon, Foursquare and Facebook Places may provide location-aware sponsored advertisements together with search results that are relevant to the predicted user movement patterns. As an example, it is possible to offer discounts at shops or restaurants near to user or his followed path.

- **Navigational Services and Traffic Management:** In a "proactive" in-car navigator the prediction of the next location can be used to understand where the user is going and this may enable the suggestion of different paths looking at the traffic in future roads; moreover, knowing where a user will be can help to understand which cells or access-points in a city will be used.

- **LBS Mobile Applications:** LBS mobile applications need to know the current position of a user to satisfy the user's request; due to limited battery lifetime typically these applications guess the current location of a user by using some recent sampled positions. Clearly, these services can be improved by using a system of location prediction.

Plan of the Chapter

In this chapter we focus on the problem of predicting future locations. In Section 2 we provide an overview of the proposals in the literature addressing that problem. In particular, we discuss the different approaches proposed to solve this challenging problem: approaches based on frequent patterns and association rules that define a trajectory as an ordered sequence of locations, where the time is used as a time-stamp; approaches that try to predict the next location of a moving object by using the movements of all the moving objects in a database; approaches that base the prediction only on the movement history of the object itself; and approaches that use probabilistic models. In Section 3 we focus on the data mining method *WhereNext*, proposed in (Monreale et al., 2009) aimed at predicting with a certain level of accuracy the next location of a moving object. The prediction uses previously extracted movement patterns named *Trajectory Patterns*, which are a concise representation of behaviors of moving objects as sequences of regions frequently visited

with a typical travel time. The basic assumption is that people often follow the crowd: individuals tend to follow common paths. In Section 4 we present a discussion on the possible improvements of the *WhereNext* method. Finally, Section 5 concludes the chapter.

Overview of the Current Proposals

The prediction approaches proposed in the literature can be classified on the basis of different criteria. As an example, we could classify the approaches on the basis of: (a) the type of data that they use (GSM data, GPS data, wireless data); (b) the ability to predict the next route followed by the user or the next visited location; (c) the mobility models describing the typical mobility behavior of users and that represent the base of a predictor (sequential frequent patterns, association rules, time-series, Markovian models); (d) the prediction strategy.

We propose a classification based on the criterion (d). In particular, we discuss prediction methods that use the movements of all objects in a certain area to learn a predictor (*global prediction strategy*); methods that use the movements of the individual object whose future location is to be guessed for learning the predictor (*individual prediction strategy*), and methods that for the prediction use both global knowledge and mobility information extracted from the individual mobility history (*combined prediction strategy*).

Predictors Learnt on Global Movements

The prediction approaches we discuss in this section use a prediction strategy that we call *global strategy*. Specifically, these approaches extract movement behaviors from the movement history of all the moving objects in the database and use this global knowledge for forecasting the next location visited by a specific moving object. The basic assumption in this case is that people often follow the crowd, i.e., individuals tend to follow common paths; for example, people go to work every day by similar routes and public transportations crossing similar routes in different time periods.

This strategy was followed in many papers addressing the location prediction problem (Morzy, 2006, 2007; Yavas et al., 2005; Jeung et al., 2008; Monreale et al., 2009; Lu et al., 2011; Chen et al., 2010; Burbey, 2011; Liu et al., 2011; Lei et al., 2011; Juyoung Kang, 2010; Li et al., 2010; Gidofalvi & Dong, 2012; Baraglia et al., 2012; Xue et al., 2012). Most of them extract frequent patterns and association rules from data (Morzy, 2006, 2007; Yavas et al., 2005; Jeung et al., 2008; Monreale et al., 2009; Lu et al., 2011; Chen et al., 2010; Liu et al., 2011; Lei et al., 2011; Juyoung Kang, 2010; Li et al., 2010) using methods based on *Apriori*, *PrefixSpan* and *FP-Growth* techniques. Some recent works instead use probabilistic models and in particular Markovian models (Burbey, 2011; Gidofalvi & Dong, 2012; Baraglia et al., 2012; Xue et al., 2012).

Some of the above approaches are suitable for predicting the next location by using GSM data that are composed by sequence of cells ID (Yavas et al., 2005; Lu et al., 2011; Juyoung Kang, 2010; Li et al., 2010). However, most of the approaches work well with GPS data (Morzy, 2006, 2007; Jeung et al., 2008; Monreale et al., 2009; Chen et al., 2010; Liu et al., 2011; Lei et al., 2011; Gidofalvi & Dong, 2012; Xue et al., 2012). Only in (Burbey, 2011) Wi-Fi data logs have been used, reporting the access points which a Wi-Fi device has been associated to.

The solutions that are based on GPS data typically apply a spatial discretization to make easier finding frequent or interesting locations. Two main types of discretization are applied: the first one allows to extract interesting places frequented by many users applying density based clustering techniques on spatial points (Jeung et al., 2008; Liu et al., 2011; Lei et al., 2011; Li et al., 2010); while the second one simply uses a grid

on the space, determining for each trajectory the sequence of intersected cells (Morzy, 2006, 2007; Monreale et al., 2009; Chen et al., 2010; Lei et al., 2011; Gidofalvi & Dong, 2012). The discretization step allows of reducing the complexity of spatio-temporal data, of removing spatial differences on sampled positions due to signal imprecision and of considering only potential useful information for prediction. Approaches based on GSM and Wi-Fi data do not need to apply a discretization step because the space is already implicitly discretized due to the nature of this kind of data.

Most of the above approaches use the temporal information only as a time-stamp of an ordered sequence of visited locations without exploit it during the mobility behavior extraction and so during the prediction. Some exceptions are the approaches presented in (Jeung et al., 2008; Lei et al., 2011) which allow to choose when predicting by specifying the temporal information for the prediction. Other works such as (Monreale et al., 2009) base their location prediction approach on trajectory patterns which are intrinsically equipped with temporal information.

The main advantage of the approaches that use the *global strategy* is that only one predictor must be constructed and it is a compact representation of all users' mobility information. Moreover, this kind of predictors are capable to predict the next location of a moving object also when it is following a path that is not typical in its movement history. Clearly, the prediction can be provided if that path is globally frequent, i.e., it is a typical path of many objects. Unfortunately, there are some drawbacks for this strategy. For example, it has some problems due to the presence of some very frequent places, which are not necessarily relevant for the mobility analysis. Suppose one bridge that connects two cities, all users have to use that bridge if they want go from one side to the other side. This leads to fact that the area covered by that bridge will be detected as frequent (and so interesting). The same effect happens in case of main roads. In these cases, it becomes even problematic to set a threshold value for establishing when a movement is frequent or not, because it could remove less frequent information that could be very relevant for predicting a user's movement.

Predictors Learnt on Individual Movements

In the literature, a lot of works addressing the location prediction problem propose methods that for forecasting the next location visited by a specific moving object base the prediction only on the movement history of the object itself (Scellato et al., 2011; Ceci et al., 2010; Nishino et al., 2010; Anagnostopoulos et al., 2011; Tran et al., 2012; Zhu et al., 2012). We say that these approaches use the *individual strategy* for the location prediction. Clearly, this leads to the construction of a predictor for each moving object in the database. Typically, solutions adopting this strategy are capable to obtain predictors with good performance in terms of accuracy because it has been shown in many works (e.g., in (Trasarti et al., 2011)) that each user has some regularity in his daily movements.

Some approaches of this category adopt time series analyses (Scellato et al., 2011; Ceci et al., 2010) for forecasting user behavior in different locations from a spatio-temporal point of view. Time series analyses enable estimations as the time of the future visits and expected residence time in those locations (Scellato et al., 2011). In this kind of works it is necessary defining the set of interesting locations to be considered in the analysis. In (Ceci et al., 2010) these locations are areas defined statically while (Scellato et al., 2011) provides a method for extracting significant locations among which users move more frequently.

Others prediction approaches are based on Markovian processes (Nishino et al., 2010) and on machine learning techniques such as classification techniques (Anagnostopoulos et al., 2011; Tran et al., 2012). In particular, in these two works the location prediction problem is treated as a *classification problem*: in (Anagnostopoulos et

al., 2011) the location information considered for classification refers to the history of user movements that is represented by a vector of k time-ordered locations crossed by a user (i.e., we have a location for each vector dimension); while in (Tran et al., 2012) the classification tree is built based on simple, intuitive features extracted from the user visit sequence data with associate a semantic meaning.

Most of the above discussed works use GPS data and exploit the specific properties of this kind of data; only (Anagnostopoulos et al., 2011) is based on GSM data.

The main problem of approaches implementing the individual strategy is that when the analysis is related to a very short time period could happen that we do not have enough information to extract individual mobility behaviors. That is due to the fact that a location or a route is defined frequent with respect to a predefined threshold value; therefore, if there is not enough information it becomes hard distinguishing noise data from useful information and understanding if a location visited by a user is a new location or a typical one.

There is another policy which takes advantages from both strategies, individual one and global one, that we call *collective strategy* (Ying et al., 2011; Domenico et al., 2012; Krumm & Horvitz, 2006). Prediction approaches belonging to this category first extract mobility behavior for each user considering only the user's movement history, like in the individual strategy, and then they merge the entire individual models for the construction of the predictor. Clearly, by following this strategy, it could happen that when a prediction is requested the location provided could be computed using mobility information of other users.

The main difference between the global strategy and the collective one is that the last one is based on the assumption that different users can share some common routes and/or mobility characteristics. Note that, if many users follow some route only once, in this case it will not be detected as a frequent movement, and so the predictor will not exploit any knowledge about it.

Predictor Learnt with Combined Strategy

Another interesting way to exploit user mobility information for predicting the next user location is based on the idea to combine the previous *global* and individual *strategies* in order to obtain more accurate predictions. In particular, the idea is to have a global predictor constructed using all users' mobility data and for each user also producing a predictive model based only on his individual movements. Therefore, during the prediction the idea is to use one of these two predictors: when using the individual predictor is not possible to provide a valid and accurate prediction then the global predictor could be used.

This strategy has been applied only recently in few papers in the literature (Zhao et al., 2011; Ashbrook & Starner, 2003; Barth et al., 2012). Among them only (Ashbrook & Starner, 2003) is based on GPS data and for this reason applies a discretization based on clustering; while the others are based on GSM data. These works use Markovian models for the prediction; in particular, (Zhao et al., 2011) uses a Markovian process for the global model and mobility patterns for individual models. The authors measure people's predictability on discrete trajectory by *discrete entropy*. People's movements are regular if their discrete entropies are low and vice versa.

WHERENEXT

As already stated, *WhereNext* (Monreale et al., 2009) is a method for location prediction based on global strategy that uses trajectory patterns as mobility information's for the prediction model construction. Specifically, the goal of this method is the following: given a database of trajectories D construct a predictive model WN_D using the set of T-patterns extracted by D; given a new trajectory T use WN_D to predict the next location of T.

The basic assumption behind *WhereNext* is that people often follow the crowd: individuals tend to follow common paths; for example, people go to work every day by similar routes and public transportations cross similar routes in different time period. Hence, if we have enough data to model typical behaviors, we may use such knowledge to predict the future movements of most individuals: at least those whose past movements are similar to the typical ones.

This method uses the movement patterns extracted by using the *Trajectory Pattern* algorithm developed in (Giannotti et al., 2006) that mines movement patterns as sequences of regions with typical travel times frequently followed. Before explaining the details of *WhereNext* we introduce the trajectory patterns.

Trajectory Pattern Mining

During the past half decade, attempts have been made to extend many techniques for knowledge discovery in classical relational or transactional data to knowledge discovery in the context of movement data (Nanni et al., 2008). Typical techniques adapted to the spatio-temporal context are association rule mining, frequent pattern discovery, clustering, classification, prediction and time-series analysis. Most approaches tend to define clustering algorithms, which group together moving object trajectories using some notion of trajectory similarity, typically distance-based. When searching for concise representations of interesting behaviors of moving objects, we define local patterns, which are patterns that aim at characterize small portions of the data space. T-pattern is an example introduced in (Giannotti et al., 2007). The authors develop an extension of the sequential pattern mining paradigm, introduced in (Giannotti et al., 2006), which analyzes the trajectories of moving objects. A trajectory of a moving object is a sequence of time-stamped locations, representing the traces collected by some wireless/mobility infrastructure (GSM, GPS, etc). The location is abstracted by using ordinary Cartesian coordinates, as formally stated by the following definition:

Definition 2: *A Trajectory or spatio-temporal sequence is a sequence of triples* $T = <x_0, y_0, t_0>$, ..., $<x_n, y_n, t_n>$ *where* t_i *(i = 0 ... n) denotes a timestamp such that* $\forall\ 0 < i < n\ t_i < t_{i+1}$ *and* $(x_i,\ y_i)$ *are points in* $\mathbf{R}^2$.

Intuitively, each triple $<x_i, y_i, t_i>$ indicates that the object is in the position $(x_i,\ y_i)$ at time t_i. Trajectory Pattern is an efficient algorithm to extract a set of frequent temporally-annotated sequences of dense spatial regions extracted from trajectories with respect to two thresholds σ and τ: the former represents the minimum support and the latter a temporal tolerance. The threshold σ denotes the minimum support as well as in the standard frequent sequential pattern algorithms. In the case of *Trajectory Pattern*, it is also used as spatial density threshold. Indeed, the algorithm discretizes the working space through a regular grid with cells of user-set size. Then the density of each cell is computed by considering each single trajectory and incrementing the density of all the cells that contain any of its points. Finally a set of most frequent regions is extracted by means of a simple heuristics considering only the cells with a density greater than σ. Each T-pattern extracted is a concise description of frequent behaviors, in terms of both space (i.e., the regions of space visited during movements) and time (i.e., the duration of movements). As an example, consider the following T-pattern over regions of interest in the center of a town:

$$\text{Railway Station} \xrightarrow{15\,\text{min}} \text{Castle Square} \xrightarrow{50\,\text{min}} \text{Museum}$$

Intuitively, people typically move between railway station to Castle Square in 15 minutes and then to Museum in 50 minutes. Now we recall the T-patterns definition introduced in (Giannotti et al., 2007):

Definition 3: *A T-pattern is a pair (S, A), where* $S = <R_0, ..., R_n>$ *is a sequence of regions, and* $A = \alpha_1, ..., \alpha_n \in R_+^k$ *is the (temporal) annotation of the sequence. A T-pattern is also represented as* $(S, A) = R_0 \xrightarrow{\alpha_1} R_1 \xrightarrow{\alpha_2} \cdots \xrightarrow{\alpha_n} R_n$.

As explained in (Giannotti et al., 2006), the extraction of a representative transition time as annotation is formalized as density estimation problem. Therefore the resulting set of temporal annotations of a sequence is a set of temporal intervals, whose width depends on the temporal tolerance τ, and everyone represents a side of a dense (hyper)cube. A visual example of T-pattern is shown in Figure 1, where between regions (red areas) we have the transition times.

The Prediction Method

WhereNext is composed of different steps that can be summarized in four main phases:

1. **Data Selection**: by using spatio-temporal primitives, a spatial area and a time period are selected, in order to take only the portion of trajectories crossing that area in that time period.
2. **Local Models Extraction**: the *Trajectory Pattern* mining algorithm is executed to extract from the selected trajectories the frequent movement patterns called *Trajectory Patterns* with respect to a temporal threshold τ and a minimum support σ. Different settings of the two parameters τ and σ return different collection of T-patterns. In order to choose the best T-pattern collection among

Figure 1. An Example of T-pattern

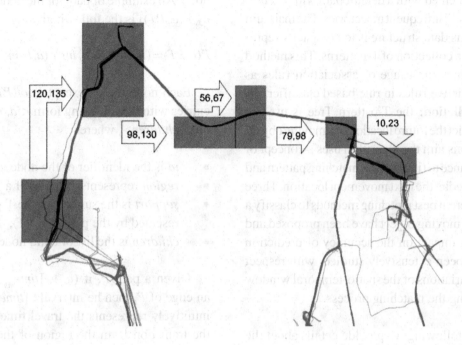

the extracted ones their predictive power is measured against different evaluation functions considering spatial coverage, dataset coverage, and region separation.

3. **T-pattern Tree Building**: the extracted local models, T-patterns, are combined in a prefix tree called *T-pattern Tree* (Figure

2). The nodes of the tree are regions frequently visited and the edges represent travel among regions and are annotated with the typical travel time. Each common prefix of T-patterns becomes a common path on the tree. This tree may be viewed as a global model of the underlying mobility data, once

Figure 2. T-pattern Tree construction

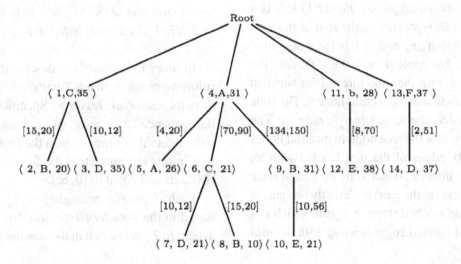

augmented with a default path which represents all infrequent trajectories. The main aim of this data structure is to compactly represent a collection of T-patterns. This method reminds the usage of association rules as predictive rules in rule based classifier.

4. **Prediction:** the T-pattern Tree is used to predict the future location of a moving object. To this aim the algorithm uses a concept of distance to find the best matching pattern and to predict the next movement location. Three different best matching methods to classify a new moving object have been proposed and their impact on the accuracy of prediction has been extensively studied, with respect to variations of the spatio-temporal window during the matching process.

In the following we provide details about the last two phases that represent the core of the method.

T-Pattern Tree

In order to compactly represent a collection of T-patterns *WhereNext* adopts a prefix tree, named *T-pattern Tree*.

T-pattern Tree Definition: The *T-pattern Tree* is a prefix tree and is defined as a triple $PT = (N, E, Root(PT))$, where N is a finite set of nodes, E is a set of labeled edges and $Root(PT) \in N$ is a fictitious node, representing the root of the tree. Each edge belonging to E is labeled with a time interval *int*. The triple $(u, v, int) \in E$ denotes the edge labeled with the time interval *int* between the parent node u and the child node v. The time interval *int* has the form $[time_{min}, time_{max}]$. The edges which link the root node to its child nodes are the only edges of the tree labeled with an empty time interval, denoted by int_e. Each node of the tree (except the root) has exactly one parent and it can be reached through a path, which is a sequence of labeled edges starting with the root

node. An example of path for the node c (denoted by $P(c, PT)$) is the following:

$$P(c, PT) = (Root(PT), a, int_e), (a, b, int_1), (b, c, int_2).$$

Each node $v \in N$, except $Root(PT)$, contains entries with the following form *<id, region, support, children>*, where:

- *id* is the identifier of the node v;
- *region* represents a region of a T-pattern;
- *support* is the support of the T-pattern represented by the path $P(v, PT)$;
- *children* is the list of child nodes of v.

Given a path P, if $(u, v, [time_{min}, time_{max}])$ is an edge of P, then he interval , $[time_{min}, time_{max}]$ intuitively represents the travel time interval of the transition from the region of the node u to the region of v.

T-pattern Tree Construction: In the following we describe how to build the *T-pattern Tree* given a set of T-patterns T_p_Set. Before that we introduce the notion of prefix of a T-pattern that will be used in the description.

Definition 4: *Let (S, A) and (S', A') be two T-patterns such that $(S, A) = R_0 \xrightarrow{\alpha_1} R_1 \xrightarrow{\alpha_2} \dots \xrightarrow{\alpha_n} R_n$ and $(S', A') = R_0 \xrightarrow{\beta_1} R_1 \xrightarrow{\beta_2} \dots \xrightarrow{\beta_k} R_k$. (S', A') is a prefix of (S, A) if and only if $k \leq n$ and $\forall i=1 \dots k\ \alpha_i$ is included in β_i.*

In order to simplify the description of algorithm we consider that a T-pattern is a sequence of pairs *<interval, region>*. Specifically, given the sequence $<i_1, r_1> \dots <i_n, r_n>$ we denote by i_k the interval of time to reach the region r_k from r_{k-1}. In this representation the first interval i1 is fictitious and equal to $[0, \infty]$.

Each T-pattern belonging to T_p_Set, is inserted in the *T-pattern Tree*. Intuitively, given a T-pattern T_p, we search in the tree the path which corresponds to the longest prefix of T_p. Next, we append a branch which represents the rest of the elements of T_p to this path. A T_p is appended to a path in the tree if this last is prefix of T_p.

Prediction Strategy

How to predict the next location for a given moving object in space and time using the *T-pattern Tree*? The main idea behind *WhereNext* is to find the best path on the tree, namely the best T-pattern, which matches the given trajectory. Hence, for a given trajectory we compute the best matching score among all admissible paths of the *T-pattern Tree*. The children of the best node that produces a prediction are selected as next possible locations. A preliminary step for computing the score of a whole path is to compute a local score for each node of this path called *punctual score*.

Punctual Score: The punctual score $pScore_r$ indicates the goodness of a node with respect to a trajectory. It aims at measuring the grade of reachability of a node r by a trajectory T that has already reached the parent node $r - 1$. Considering the moving object that follows the trajectory T, we introduce the notation of $WhereNext_{r-1}$ to identify a spatio-temporal window where the moving object *will be* after the time interval specified in the edge towards r. For example, in the Figure 3 the segment [begin,end] is the $WhereNext_{r-1}$ while [nextBegin, nextEnd] identifies the *Wher-*

eNext$_r$. Therefore, the punctual score of r can be defined in terms of spatio-temporal distance between $WhereNext_{r-1}$ and the spatial region of the node r. It is possible to identify three different cases that require a specific computation of the punctual score:

- **Case A**: the $WhereNext_{r-1}$ intersects the region of the node r. This is the optimal case and the punctual score is equal to the support value of the node. This case is reported in Figure 3(a).
- **Case B**: the $WhereNext_{r-1}$ enlarged by temporal tolerance th_t intersects the region of the node r. In this case, the punctual score is the support value of the node divided by the minimum time distance between the intersection point and the region. This case is reported in Figure 3(b).
- **Case C**: the $WhereNext_{r-1}$ enlarged by temporal tolerance th_t does not intersect the region of the node r. In this case the punctual score is the support value of the node divided by the weighted sum of the spatial and temporal distances between the region and the nearest neighbor point of the enlarged window. This case is reported in Figure 3(c).

Here th_t is a parameter which defines the tolerance for the time window during the process. If

Figure 3. The three possible cases during the punctual score computation

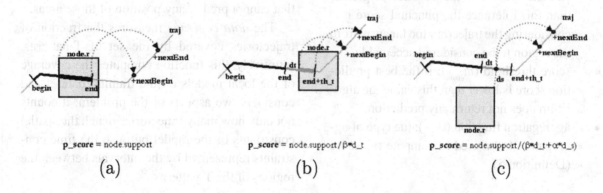

p_score = node.support   p_score = node.support/β*d_t   p_score = node.support/(β*d_t+α*d_s)

(a)   (b)   (c)

WhereNext$_r$ does not exist as the trajectory ended, the punctual score is not defined.

Path Score: The overall score of a path is based on the value of the punctual score for each node of the path. (Monreale et al., 2009) studied three different functions:

Definition 5 (Score Functions): *Given a trajectory tr, a path P = [p$_1$, ..., p$_n$] and a punctual score pScore$_k$ defined on each p$_k$ $\in$ P, we define:*

○ $avgScore_{(tr,P)} = \dfrac{\sum_n^1 pScore_k}{n}$

○ $sumScore_{(tr,P)} = \sum_n^1 pScore_k$

○ $\max Score_{(tr,P)} = Max\{pScore_1, ..., pSCore_n\}$

Each method produces a different behavior in terms of prediction. The *avgScore* tries to generalize the concept of *similarity* as average distance between the trajectory and each node. The *sumScore* is based on the concept of depth, i.e. privileges the longest path that matches the trajectory. The *maxScore* is a greedy measure: if a trajectory has a good match with a node, this has priority on the other ones.

Prediction: The prediction step uses a set of parameters described below:

- time tolerance (*th$_t$*): represents the tolerance to enlarge the *WhereNext* window in Figure 3(b) and Figure 3(c).
- space tolerance (*th$_s$*): represents the admissible spatial distance between trajectory and the region. If the distance is greater than this tolerance the punctual score is 0 considering the trajectory too far away from the region to be considered acceptable.
- score threshold (*th$_{score}$*): if the best prediction score is lower than this value the algorithm does not return any prediction.
- aggregation function (*th$_{agg}$*): the type of aggregation to be used to compute the score (Definition 5).

Given a trajectory *T* and a *T-pattern Tree PT*, the location prediction algorithm computes the path score for each path of the *PT* relatively to *T*, according to the selected aggregation function. When for a node is not available a punctual score this node is a candidate for the prediction with score equal to the path score from the root to its parent node. When the visit of the tree is finished to each possible path a score is computed. The algorithm thus selects the best path matching the trajectory *T*; in other words the path of the tree with the higher score is selected as best path and the next region associated to associated to the candidate path is returned as prediction. Notice that there might exist several predictions with the same score corresponding to all children of the last node of the path with the best score. In those cases all children are returned as a prediction.

A Priori Prediction Power Evaluation

The performance of the predictor (prediction rate and accuracy rate) depends on the quality of the T-pattern collection selected to build the predictor. Therefore, to evaluate a priori the predictive power of a T-pattern set it could be used an evaluation function taking into consideration three aspects: the spatial coverage, the dataset coverage and the region separation.

The *spatial coverage* measures the fraction of space covered by the set of T-patterns. A low value of this function means that there are many areas of the considered space that are not covered by the T-patterns and this leads to have a predictor that cannot predict any position of those areas.

The *data coverage* measures the fraction of trajectories covered by the set of T-patterns. Intuitively, this function computes the coverage of the local models on the training dataset and considers two aspects of the problem: it counts not only how many trajectories match the spatial constraints of the model but also the time constraints represented by the intervals between the regions of the T-patterns.

The *region separation* measures the fraction of regions crossed by the analyzed T-patterns. This function represents two important aspects: the precision during the prediction (smaller regions lead to a more specialized local patterns) and the granularity of our prediction (larger regions lead to less accurate predictions).

The combination of the above three measures provides the overall evaluation of the quality of a pattern collection; in particular they are combined in a unique measure called *Rate*:

$$Rate = spatialCoverage \times dataCoverage \times regionSeparation.$$

Note that, all above functions are defined in the interval [0, 1].

Prediction Performance Analysis

Data: The prediction performance of *WhereNext* was deeply analyzed on real-world data, provided by the GeoPKDD project: a set of trajectories of cars equipped with a GPS receivers moving in the city of Milan in a week. Given the whole dataset we select the trajectories on Wednesday and Thursday in the city center between 7AM and 10AM. Then, the data of Wednesday (4000 trajectories) was used as training set and a part of the data of Thursday was used as test set (a sampling of 500 trajectories).

Evaluation Measures: In order to assess the quality of the prediction of *WhereNext* three performance measures were used:

- **Prediction Rate:** the number of predicted trajectories over the total number of trajectories we want to predict.
- **Accuracy Rate:** the rate of the correctly predicted locations divided by the predicted ones.
- **Average Error:** the average spatial distance between the predicted location and the real position of the moving object at the predicted time.

In order to appreciate the quality of the results a *spatial tolerance* is used as an acceptable distance between the predicted location and the real position of the trajectory. The *spatial tolerance* is expressed in units, where a unit is the minimum granularity in the considered space.

Results: After the data preparation, different of collection of T-patterns were extracted by running the *Trajectory Pattern* algorithm changing the support value, the temporal threshold and the resolution. The prediction power of the T-pattern collections was evaluated and Figure 4 shows the behavior of the different measures for the apriori evaluation of discriminative power. This evaluation leaded to the selection of a set of 7039 T-patterns extracted with a temporal threshold equal to 200 seconds, a resolution of the regions of 100 meters and a support threshold of 1.85%. Then, this set of patterns allowed of building the *T-pattern Tree*. The results of a first set of experiments are shown in Figure 5. These summarize the model accuracy w.r.t. the prediction rate. We observe how the prediction accuracy changes while the number of predicted trajectories is growing without a selection of particular setting of the thresholds, summarizing the general trend of the model. The three groups of curves represent the three values of tolerance used: 0, 2, 4. The three curves of each group represent the use of a different aggregation function. The best result is obtained with the tolerance threshold set up to 4 and using the sum as aggregation function. This result justifies the quality of our approach showing the desirable behavior for a predictor, i.e., if we want to predict more cases we clearly lose accuracy. *WhereNext* obtains very good results in terms of accuracy when the algorithm predicts 45,7% trajectories; up to this value the prediction accuracy is greater than 40% without any tolerance; when some tolerance is set the results are greater than 54%.

Other experiments, Figures 6 (a,b,c,d), show the impact of the thresholds th_{space} and th_{score} (used in the prediction phase) on the quality of the results, i.e., accuracy, and the number of predicted

Figure 4. Apriori prediction evaluation of T-patterns

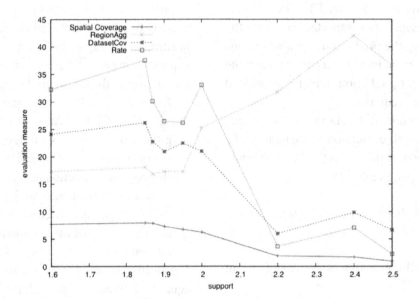

trajectories, i.e., Prediction Rate. In Figure 6 (c) prediction rate increases when we adopt a greater spatial threshold while in Figure 6 (d) there is a decrement of the accuracy when setting a higher value of th_{space}. Both represent an understandable behavior of the model. The enlargement of the spatial threshold allows the punctual score computation in different situations; so that the prediction is possible for more trajectories but, at same time, the prediction results are affected by more noise. The opposite behavior can be detected analyzing Figures 6 (a)&(b) where the impact of th_{score} on accuracy and prediction rate is shown. Indeed, while the th_{score} is increasing the prediction rate decreases (Figure 6 (a)) and the accuracy increases (Figure 6 (b)). The th_{score} impact is easy to explain considering that we select few paths on the Prediction Tree but very accurate when this threshold has a high value. In general, the prediction rate is never below 20%; this is probably due to the dataset coverage of the used set of T-patterns with respect to the test set adopted, i.e. at least 20% of the trajectories in the test set are completely covered by the selected set of T-patterns.

IMPROVING WHERENEXT

In this section we discuss possible extensions of *WhereNext* to improve the quality of the prediction. As stated in Section 3.2.3 the performance of *WhereNext* depends on the quality of the T-pattern set used for building the T-pattern tree. Some experiments highlighted that in some conditions the use of T-patterns could generate some problem. As an example, a territory characterized by a deep difference of trajectory density in different areas could bring to the extraction of a set of T-patterns unsuitable for the prediction. Suppose the case where we have a highway with higher density with respect to smaller streets around it. The *trajectory pattern mining* algorithm tends to not capture all the mobility behaviors in the secondary streets because of the too big difference of density between the areas. Other problems could depend on the sparsity of the trajectory data on the territory, which could make it hard finding global common behavior.

How can we address the problems deriving from the use of T-patterns for the construction of a predictor? Here, we discuss possible solu-

Figure 5. Accuracy versus Prediction rate

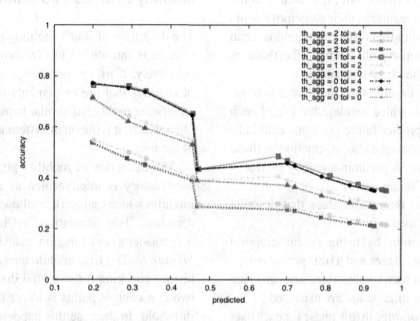

Figure 6. Accuracy and Prediction rate w.r.t th$_{space}$ and th$_{score}$

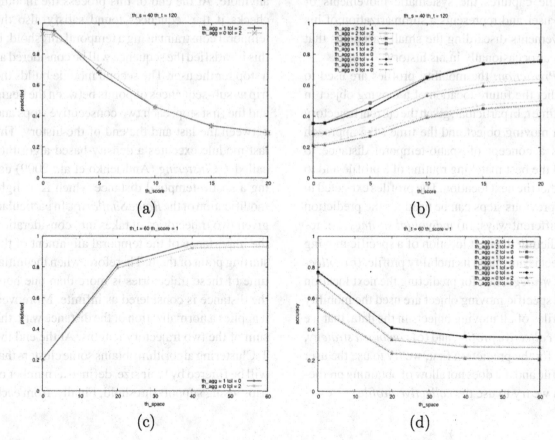

tions capable to exploit both the tendency of the individual to be regular in their daily movements and the possibility that different individuals can share some common paths due to the fact that they have to reach the same destination.

A predictor capable to exploit these two important aspects, which regulate the life of each individual, to predict future positions could obtain good performance also in situation as those described above. A preliminary study on that is presented in (Corona, 2013).

We consider three main steps that describe this prediction method:

Data Selection: by using spatio-temporal primitives a spatial area and a time period are selected. Then, for each user his trajectories crossing that area in that time period are extracted.

Mobility Profiling: in this phase for each user we extract the *Mobility Profile* from the historical movements of that user. Intuitively, the user profile captures the systematic movements of that user and represents a summarization of his movements discarding the small variations that appear occasionally in his history.

Prediction: the mobility profiles are used to predict the future location of a moving object in the time t. In particular, given the current trajectory of a moving object and the time t the approach uses a concept of spatio-temporal distance to find the best matching routine of a profile and to predict the next location. The profiles extracted in the previous steps can be used for the prediction in different ways: (a) *individual strategy*, i.e, for predicting the next location of a specific moving object is only used its mobility profile; (b) *collective strategy*, i.e., for predicting the next location of a specific moving object are used the mobility profiles of all moving objects in the data, that we call *collective profile*; and (c) *combined strategy*, i.e., for the prediction first, we try to use the user profile and if it does not allow of obtaining prediction we try to use the *collective profile*.

Mobility Profiles Extraction

The definition of user's mobility profile that we refer to is introduced in (Trasarti et al., 2011). Intuitively, a *user's mobility profile* is the set of routines that are movements supported by a significant number of similar trips of the user. In other words, it is the set of systematic movements of the user.

The extraction of mobility profiles from the user history is implemented as a sequence of modules which realizes the following steps: Stop detection, Trip generation, T-Clustering using a spatio-temporal function called *Synch Route Similarity*. The first module analyzes the user's history checking if the spatial distance between two consecutive points is lower than a specific threshold. In the case this happens the modules incrementally checks, and eventually stores, the following points until the constraint is not satisfied anymore. At the end of this process the module checks if the sequences found satisfy also the temporal constraint using a temporal threshold; if this is satisfied the sequence will be considered as a stop for the user. The second module builds the trip as sub-sequences of points between the begin and the first stop, each two consecutive stops and between the last and the end of the history. The last module executes a density-based algorithm called *T-Clustering* (Andrienko et al., 2009) using a spatio-temporal distance which is a slight modification of the *Route Similarity*. In particular, given two trajectories, it takes into consideration the importance of the temporal alignment of the starting point of them. Therefore, when the initial time of these trajectories is more than one hour the distance is considered as infinite. Moreover, it applies a normalization of the distance w.r.t. the sum of the two trajectory lengths. At the end the T-Clustering algorithm obtains some clusters that will be filtered by their size, defined as number of trips, using support threshold. Finally, from each survived cluster a medoid is extracted and grouped obtaining the mobility profile of the user. Note that the medoid represents the routine.

Prediction Strategies

As stated above the extracted user's profile can be used in different ways for the location prediction. The *individual strategy* uses the routine of the user profile for predicting the next movements of that user. This means that it exploits the systematic behavior of that user for the prediction. Clearly, a user could not have a mobility profile or could follow in a given instant a different path. In those cases this strategy does not provide any good prediction. This problem can be solved by means the *collective strategy*. In this case the idea is to use the routines of all user profiles for the prediction. In other words, with the union of all routines of users in the data we generate a *collective profile*. Therefore, in that case the strategy exploits the possibility that a user in a specific instant could follow a not standard path that is a typical routine of another user. Finally, the *combined strategy* tries to obtain advantages from both previous strategies. In other words, in this strategy it uses the individual strategy when this is possible and the collective strategy when the first is not applicable. In other words, this strategy exploits the possibility to use two levels of knowledge.

CONCLUSION

In this chapter, we presented an overview of the main techniques for the prediction of the next location visited by a user. In particular, we proposed a classification of the techniques on the basis of the prediction strategy. We identified the following strategies: the *global strategy*, the *individual strategy* and *combined strategy* and the *collective strategy*. Then, we presented the details of the data mining method *WhereNext*, proposed in (Monreale et al., 2009), that for the prediction of the next location of a moving object uses the global strategy.

Finally, we concluded our chapter with a discussion on the limitations of *WhereNext* and with the proposal of possible extensions and solutions that could improve the quality and accuracy of the prediction and that could eliminate the limitations of *WhereNext*.

REFERENCES

Anagnostopoulos, T., Anagnostopoulos, C., & Hadjiefthymiades, S. (2011). Mobility prediction based on machine learning. *Mobility Data Management*, (2), 27-30.

Andrienko, G., Andrienko, N., Rinzivillo, S., Nanni, M., Pedreschi, D., & Giannotti, F. (2009). Interactive visual clustering of large collections of trajectories. In *Proceedings of IEEE VAST*. IEEE.

Ashbrook, D., & Starner, T. (2003). Using gps to learn significant locations and predict movement across multiple users. *Personal and Ubiquitous Computing*, 7(5), 275–286. doi:10.1007/s00779-003-0240-0.

Baraglia, R., Frattari, C., Muntean, C. I., Nardini, F. M., & Silvestri, F. (2012). A trajectory-based recommender system for tourism. In *Proceedings of AMT*, (pp. 196-205). AMT.

Barth, D., Bellahsene, S., & Kloul, L. (2012). Combining local and global profiles for mobility prediction in lte femtocells. [MSWiM.]. *Proceedings of MSWiM*, *12*, 333–342.

Burbey, I. (2011). *Predicting future locations and arrival times of individuals*. (PhD thesis). Virginia Polytechnic Institute and State University, Blacksburg, VA.

Ceci, M., Appice, A., & Malerba, D. (2010). Time-slice density estimation for semantic-based tourist destination suggestion. In *Proceedings of ECAI* (pp. 1107-1108). ECAI.

Chen, L., Lv, M., & Chen, G. (2010). A system for destination and future route prediction based on trajectory mining. *Pervasive and Mobile Computing, 6*(6), 657–676. doi:10.1016/j.pmcj.2010.08.004.

Corona, N. (2013). *Un metodo per la predizione della locazione futura mediante la profilazione degli utenti.* (Master thesis). University of Pisa, Pisa, Italy.

Domenico, D. Lima, & Musolesi. (2012). Interdependence and predictability of human mobility and social interactions. In *Proceedings of the Mobile Data Challenge 2012*. IEEE.

Giannotti, F., Nanni, M., & Pedreschi, D. (2006). Efficient mining of temporally annotated sequences. In *Proceedings of SDM*. SDM.

Giannotti, F., Nanni, M., Pinelli, F., & Pedreschi, D. (2007). Trajectory pattern mining. In *Proceedings of KDD '07* (pp. 330-339). KDD.

Gidofalvi, G., & Dong, F. (2012). When and where next: Individual mobility prediction. [MobiGIS.]. *Proceedings of MobiGIS, 12,* 57–64. doi:10.1145/2442810.2442821.

Jeung, H., Liu, Q., Shen, H. T., & Zhou, X. (2008). A hybrid prediction model for moving objects. [ICDE.]. *Proceedings of ICDE, 08,* 70–79.

Juyoung Kang, H.-S. Y. (2010). A frequent pattern based prediction model for moving objects. *IJCSNS, 10*(3), 200–205.

Krumm, J., & Horvitz, E. (2006). Predestination: inferring destinations from partial trajectories. [UbiComp.]. *Proceedings of UbiComp, 06,* 243–260.

Lei, P.-R., Shen, T.-J., Peng, W.-C., & Su, I.-J. (2011). Exploring spatial-temporal trajectory model for location prediction. *Mobile Data Management, (1),* 58-67.

Li, H., Tang, C., Qiao, S., Wang, Y., Yang, N., & Li, C. (2010). Hotspot district trajectory prediction. [WAIM.]. *Proceedings of WAIM, 10,* 74–84.

Liu, K., Deng, K., Ding, Z., Zhou, X., & Li, M. (2011). Pattern-based moving object tracking. [TDMA.]. *Proceedings of TDMA, 11,* 5–14. doi:10.1145/2030080.2030083.

Lu, E. H.-C., Tseng, V. S., & Yu, P. S. (2011). Mining cluster-based temporal mobile sequential patterns in location-based service environments. *IEEE Transactions on Knowledge and Data Engineering, 23*(6), 914–927. doi:10.1109/TKDE.2010.155.

Monreale, A., Pinelli, F., Trasarti, R., & Giannotti, F. (2009). WhereNext: A location predictor on trajectory pattern mining. In *Proceedings of KDD '09* (pp. 637-646). KDD.

Morzy, M. (2006). Prediction of moving object location based on frequent trajectories. [ISCIS.]. *Proceedings of ISCIS, 06,* 583–592.

Morzy, M. (2007). Mining frequent trajectories of moving objects for location prediction. [MLDM.]. *Proceedings of MLDM, 07,* 667–680.

Nanni, M., Kuijpers, B., Korner, C., May, M., & Pedreschi, D. (2008). Spatiotemporal data mining. In F. Giannotti, & D. Pedreschi (Eds.), *Mobility, data mining, and privacy: Geographic knowledge discovery.* Berlin: Springer-Verlag. doi:10.1007/978-3-540-75177-9_11.

Nishino, M., Nakamura, Y., Yagi, T., Muto, S., & Abe, M. (2010). A location predictor based on dependencies between multiple lifelog data. In *Proceedings of GIS-LBSN,* (pp. 11-17). GIS-LBSN.

Scellato, S., Musolesi, M., Mascolo, C., Latora, V., & Campbell, A. T. (2011). Nextplace: A spatio-temporal prediction framework for pervasive systems. [Pervasive.]. *Proceedings of Pervasive, 2011*, 152–169.

Tran, L.-H., Catasta, M., McDowell, L. K., & Aberer, K. (2012). Next place prediction using mobile data. In *Proceedings of Nokia Mobile Data Challenge*. Nokia..

Trasarti, R., Pinelli, F., Nanni, M., & Giannotti, F. (2011). Mining mobility user profiles for car pooling. In *Proceedings of KDD '11* (pp. 1190-1198). KDD.

Xue, G., Luo, Y., Yu, J., & Li, M. (2012). *A novel vehicular location prediction based on mobility patterns for routing in urban vanet.* EURASIP J. Wireless Comm., & Networking. doi:10.1186/1687-1499-2012-222.

Yavas, G., Katsaros, D., Ulusoy, O., & Manolo-poulos, Y. (2005). A data mining approach for location prediction in mobile environments. *DKE, 54*(2), 121–146. doi:10.1016/j.datak.2004.09.004.

Ying, J. J.-C., Lee, W.-C., Weng, T.-C., & Tseng, V. S. (2011). Semantic trajectory mining for location prediction. [GIS.]. *Proceedings of GIS, 11*, 34–43.

Zhao, N., Huang, W., Song, G., & Xie, K. (2011). Discrete trajectory prediction on mobile data. *APWeb*, 77-88.

Zhu, Y., Sun, Y., & Wang, Y. (2012). Predicting semantic place and next place via mobile data. In *Proceedings of Nokia Mobile Data Challenge*. Nokia..

Chapter 3
Synthetic Population Techniques in Activity–Based Research

Sungjin Cho
Hasselt University, Belgium

Luk Knapen
Hasselt University, Belgium

Tom Bellemans
Hasselt University, Belgium

Davy Janssens
Hasselt University, Belgium

Lieve Creemers
Hasselt University, Belgium

Geert Wets
Hasselt University, Belgium

ABSTRACT

Activity-based approach, which aims to estimate an individual induced traffic demand derived from activities, has been applied for traffic demand forecast research. The activity-based approach normally uses two types of input data: daily activity-trip schedule and population data, as well as environment information. In general, it seems hard to use those data because of privacy protection and expense. Therefore, it is indispensable to find an alternative source to population data. A synthetic population technique provides a solution to this problem. Previous research has already developed a few techniques for generating a synthetic population (e.g. IPF [Iterative Proportional Fitting] and CO [Combinatorial Optimization]), and the synthetic population techniques have been applied for the activity-based research in transportation. However, using those techniques is not easy for non-expert researchers not only due to the fact that there are no explicit terminologies and concrete solutions to existing issues, but also every synthetic population technique uses different types of data. In this sense, this chapter provides a potential reader with a guideline for using the synthetic population techniques by introducing terminologies, related research, and giving an account for the working process to create a synthetic population for Flanders in Belgium, problematic issues, and solutions.

DOI: 10.4018/978-1-4666-4920-0.ch003

INTRODUCTION

Since its introduction in transportation, ABM (activity-based model), which purpose is to estimate an individual induced traffic demand derived from activities, have been applied for traffic demand forecasts. The ABM typically uses different types of input data including daily activity-trip survey data and population data. The individual daily activity-trip schedule data describes the different trips, its purpose, locations, transport modes, as well as its temporal dimension. The population data, including socio-demographic features, are used to estimate population characteristics such as gender, household composition, income, home location, etc. In general, it seems to be hard to use those datasets because they are rather expensive and normally protected by a privacy law. Thus, it is indispensable to find a solution to substitute population data in a synthetic manner.

Several synthetic population generators have been used in the literature to generate synthetic population data in transportation. Examples are techniques like Iterative Proportional Fitting and Combinatorial Optimization. Despite these advancements in research, using those techniques is not easy for non-expert researchers not only due to the fact that there are no explicit terminologies and concrete solutions to some existing issues and problems so far, but also every synthetic population technique handles different types or structures of input and output data.

In this sense, the chapter is supporting a potential reader with a guideline for using synthetic population techniques by introducing terminologies and related research, and giving an account of the working process to create a synthetic population, along with problematic issues and solutions. In detail, the following sections provide common terminologies and related research in this field. Then, section 3 introduces related research. The next section describes the whole process of generating a synthetic population, which consists of three steps: data preprocessing, fitting and drawing

(sampling). The section of issues and proposed solutions deals with some issues and solutions addressed by previous research. Finally, the chapter ends with a summary and by suggesting future work in this field.

RELATED RESEARCH

Synthetic population techniques can be largely divided into two groups: IPF and CO. Most techniques in these two groups have a similar concept of fitting seed data to a target marginal distribution, but they generate the required synthetic population in totally different way. This section covers the different ways by introducing related research in each group.

IPF

Deming and Stephan (1940) developed a basic algorithm in *IPF* (Iterative Proportional Fitting), which has been widely applied for synthetic population research in several fields, including transportation. The basic algorithm, which is called 'a least squares adjustment', is based on the assumption that the source and target have the same correlation structure. The correlation structure is defined by odds ratios, for example the odds ratio in a 2 x 2 cross-table is calculated as follows:

$$\emptyset = \frac{p_{1,1}p_{2,2}}{p_{1,2}p_{2,1}}$$

where $p_{i,j}$ is a cell proportion of the cell (i, j). Based on that assumption, the IPF adjusts seed data to target marginal distribution to keep the correlation between source and target. We do not explain further details of the IPF algorithm in this chapter, but we are dealing with how it can be applied within the synthetic population process in the next section.

In general, Beckman *et al.* (1996) are cited as the first scholar who generated synthetic populations using the IPF. They applied the IPF to predict synthetic populations of households and persons in a census tract using 1990 census data (summary tables and PUMS). The summary tables provide target marginals, and the PUMS (public use microdata sample) are a representative 5% sample of households and persons, used as seed data. There are two steps in building synthetic populations: a fitting step and a drawing step (also referred to this chapter). At first, a cross-table in the source is made of seed data. A cross-table in the target area is also formed, which is not a complete table because the cell values are not known for the target area. The IPF is used to complete the target cross-table by iteratively revising the cell values in the source area based on the target marginal distribution. Once the cross-table in the target area is completed, the synthetic population of households is generated by sampling the desired number of households from the seed data in the source by means of a household selection probability. The household selection probability is calculated using the complete cross-table in the target area. After Beckman *et al.* (1996), several researches have been conducted for the synthetic population using the IPF algorithm.

Guo and Bhat (2007) generated synthetic population for the Dallas/Fort-Worth area in Texas based on the conventional IPF, proposed by Beckman *et al.* (1996). They also advanced the conventional IPF by dealing with two issues: zero-cell value and multi-level fitting. We will discuss these issues in the following sections.

Arentze *et al.*, (2007) proposed a relation matrix as a new solution to multi-level fitting in synthetic population research. The relation matrix is constructed by converting *individual* marginal distributions to *household* distributions by assigning individuals to household positions, e.g. '2-adult households', '1-male households', 'males living in' and so on. In addition, they introduced data segmentation algorithms (CART and CHAID) for analyzing spatial heterogeneity in population.

Ye *et al.*, (2009) developed synthetic population software (named 'PopGen') with a new algorithm, IPU. The IPU (Iterative Proportional Updating) algorithm is for matching both household and person marginals by updating sample household weights. In the fitting step, household and person type constraints are estimated using the IPF procedure, followed by the calculation of sample household weights by the IPU algorithm. Then, the synthetic population is predicted by a household sampling process that expands sample households according to household selection probabilities. The household selection probabilities are computed by sample household weights calculated in the fitting step. This drawing step is repeated until a best-fit synthetic population is obtained. Note that the next section will cover details of these processes using the IPU algorithm.

Pritchard and Miller (2009) implemented the IPF with a sparse list-based structure, which is composed of a large number of records with household and person attributes, in the fitting step. Then, a conditional Monte-Carlo simulation is used for the drawing step to fit both household and person marginal distribution simultaneously. Moreover, their study insisted a rounding issue on target marginal and seed cross-table. The rounding issue will be discussed later in this chapter.

Auld and Mohammadian (2010) proposed a new methodology for synthesizing population on multiple levels of household and person using household selection probabilities. On the one hand, the existing household selection probability is calculated by a certain type of households' weight that is divided by the sum of the weights of all other households having the same type in the seed. On the other hand, a new household probability they proposed considers both household marginal distributions and person marginal distributions by combining the person probabilities with the existing household selection probabilities. The details of the selection probability will be handled in the following section.

CO

For the second group of the synthetic population techniques, *CO* (combinatorial optimization) is an iterative algorithm, which is also known as '*entropy maximization*' and '*hill climbing*'. The CO algorithm begins with a random assignment of sample households, and then iteratively replaces an assigned household with another one until reaching a given termination criterion to find a best-fit synthetic population. Compared to IPF, the number of related research using the CO algorithm is limited. Voas and Williamson (2000) proposed a 'sequential fitting procedure' as a new solution to the improvement in the estimation accuracy of synthetic population. In addition, they discussed error measurements for evaluating the quality of the synthetic population. Huang and Williamson (2001) compared the CO with the IPF algorithm by comparing the result of the synthetic population in a small area. At the end, they concluded that both techniques generated a well-fitted synthetic population, but the CO shows a better result in the variability of synthetic population. Melhuish *et al.*, (2002) generated synthetic households using the CO to build the socio-demographic profiles of each CDs (census collection district)[1] in Australia. Then, they evaluated the accuracy of the socio-demographic profiles by comparing with data from the census BCP (basic community profile)[2].

Ryan *et al.*, (2009) applied the CO to predict synthetic population of firms for the City of Hamilton, Ontario, in 1990, in order to compare the performance of the two algorithms. As a result, they concluded that the performance of the CO is better than the IPF. Through the comparison test, they found that the quality of synthetic population depends more on a tabular detail, rather than sample size.

Discussion

The heuristic methods used in IPF and CO techniques show some similarities, but there are also some differences in processing and application perspective. First, the IPF sequentially adjusts a seed marginal to a target marginal distribution, but, on the other hand, the CO first assigns individual sample and then iteratively changes the individual sample with another to find a best solution of synthetic population (Kurban et al., 2011). Second, the IPF has been generally applied in transportation, but the CO has been used for research in geography.

According to related research, there does not seem to exist one single best technique in synthetic population research, because every technique has pros and cons depending on its theoretical feature and purpose. For example, the IPF approach strongly depends on representativeness of the seed data and consistency of the target marginals (Barthelemy and Cornelis, 2012). The CO has also some weaknesses: inability of preserving consistency between attributes and an expensive computation. Therefore, it is important to figure out what data we have (input data) and what shape of output we want (output data) in selecting and applying synthetic population techniques. Note that this chapter only treats the IPF, not the CO algorithm. Table 1 in the appendix lists some of the synthetic population techniques using the IPF with information about using data and features.

WORKING PROCEDURE AND EMPIRICAL CASE

There are two main steps in the process of generating synthetic population using the IPF: a fitting step and a drawing step. The fitting step is to adjust seed data to target marginal distribution by iteratively re-scaling the value of a cell in the seed cross-table. The drawing step is to draw synthetic population by adding individuals/households to the population up to the desired size of the population. In addition to those two steps, there are also other steps before and after the above process: data-processing step and validation step.

This section explains the whole procedure from the data preprocessing to the validation test in the synthetic population research with some examples. Figure 4 in the appendix depicts the whole procedure considering both cases using the IPF and the IPU algorithm, because those algorithms do not require significantly different data structures of input. It also illustrates two different drawing methods, MC sampling and random sampling.

For our empirical case, we generated a synthetic population for Flanders (Belgium) using the IPU algorithm to provide examples in each step of the working procedure. Marginals corresponding to entities at the lowest spatial level (e.g. Building Block or SUBZONE) are assumed to be mutually independent. Furthermore each household belongs to exactly one such spatial area and each person belongs to exactly one household. As a consequence each spatial entity for which marginals need to be approximated constitutes an independent case. Remember that such area either is a basic area (Building Block, SUBZONE and so on) or an aggregate of basic entities used to resolve the zero

marginal problems. The computational structure of the problem is embarrassingly parallel due to the spatial independency. Hence we partitioned the input data and were able to run cases in parallel on the VSC (Vlaams Supercomputer Centrum) cluster machines.

In our study area, there is a spatial hierarchy that is composed of three levels; SUPERZONE (a highest level and compatible with a municipality), ZONE (a higher resolution), and SUBZONE (a lowest level with highest resolution) (see Figure 1). We used seed data from a travel survey (OVG) and target marginals from a population in 2010. For the synthetic population technique, we considered both household attributes (income and size) and person attributes (age, job, gender and driver license) (see Table 2 in the appendix).

Data Preprocessing

Obviously the first step in the process is a data preprocessing step in order to prepare input data for the synthetic population technique. To do this,

Figure 1. Study area with zoning system

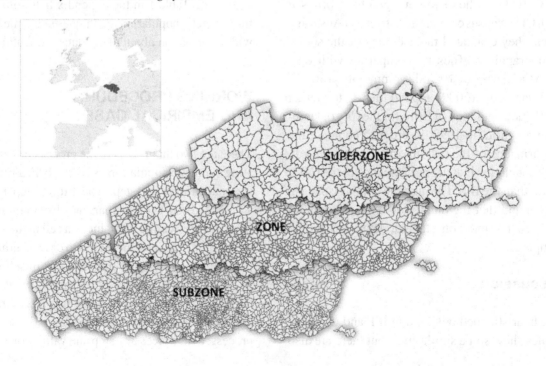

Figure 2. Example of zero-cell problem

| Subzone 25 | Gender | | Sum | Target margin |
Income	Male	Female		
1	706	359	1065	1278
2	878	793	1671	1838
3	564	677	1241	1737
4	481	0	481	673
Sum	2629	1829	4458	
Target margin	3418	2561	5350	

we first have to check the data requirement of the synthetic population technique we use, because the data requirement is slightly different depending on the synthetic population techniques. For example, the typical IPF technique needs a cross-table as input, but on the other hand, the IPU uses a list-based data for generating a synthetic population. However, two types of data are typically required for the synthetic population techniques: seed data and target marginal information. The seed data

contain disaggregate population which normally describes enough details of the population, but there are only a small number of individual elements in the seed data. On the other hand, the target marginal only has information about the sum of one dimension in an attribute, and not multi-dimensional distribution of several attributes. In general, the seed data can be acquired from a census institute and the target marginals can be easily collected from any institute. The most

Figure 3. Example of zero-marginal problem

| Subzone 47 | Gender | | Sum | Target margin |
Income	Male	Female		
1	643	525	1168	2518
2	787	802	1589	2225
3	950	886	1836	4751
4	0	0	0	629
Sum	2380	2213	4593	
Target margin	3094	2877	5052	

important thing in data collection is that attributes in the seed data must be the same as the ones in the target marginals because the basic algorithm in the IPF is to match the marginal distributions of attributes in the seed with the target marginals. Thus, when some attributes in the target marginal are not included in the seed data (or the opposite case), the process does not work due to the mismatching of the attribute dimensions in the marginals. Table 3, Table 4 , and Table 5 in the appendix show an example of source data, which normally includes a small number of household and person data, and target data, which is zone-based and contains a joint set of attributes of the household and person, respectively.

Once input data are available, we have to clean the data if necessary. This is because in the following steps an error may result from such erroneous values, e.g. typo and incorrect value types. After that, the data structure needs to be changed in order to make it feasible for using synthetic population techniques. There are two types of data structures commonly used for synthetic population techniques: a cross-table and a list-based data structure. The cross-table, also called a contingency-table, consists of rows and columns that represent one dimension with cells and marginal totals in each attribute. The ordinary IPF uses a cross-table as input. When the numbers of attributes increase, the size of a cross-table grows exponentially (Muller and Axhausen, 2011). To solve this problem, Williamson et al. (1998) first recommended the sparse list-based data structure as a solution. In addition, it can be applied without any additional processing due to its similarity to a list of attributes in raw data. For these reasons, we used the list-based data structure in our empirical case. Figure 5 and Table 6 in the appendix illustrate an example of the cross-table and the list-based data structure, respectively.

Fitting Step

The fitting process between the IPF and the IPU algorithm is different. First, an IPF fitting process is applied to the household data to make them comply with household marginals. Then, a person distribution is determined in the same way as the household distribution. Lastly, the two distributions are combined using a person-per-household ratio at the end of the fitting step or using conditioned MC sampling in the drawing step (or in the preprocessing step; Arentze *et al.*, 2007). On the other hand, the IPU first initializes household weights as '1'. Next, a (household) adjustment is calculated by computing the proportion to a target marginal. Finally, the household weights are updated by the adjustment. During the updating process, person marginals automatically match with household marginals (also see Figure 4 in the appendix).

The fitting step can be differently operated according to the synthetic population we generate. For example, depending on the levels in the synthetic population, one can chose a single-level or multi-level fitting. However, one cannot apply a multi-level fitting without multi-level data (e.g. household and person data).

Another classification of the fitting process distinguishes between zone-by-zone and multi-zones fitting. In the zone-by-zone fitting, one zone is adjusted to the marginal of that zone alone at a time. On the contrary, the multi-zone fitting matches all zones by aggregating all marginals. While the multi-zone fitting typically shows a better performance than the zone-by-zone fitting, it requires more data storage than the other (Muller and Axhausen, 2011). Therefore, the fitting approach selected depends on the zoning system and data status (both target and source). For example, when the study area has a few small zones, then the multi-zones fitting is a feasible solution. However, in the opposite case, when the study area consists of a few big zones, then the other approach, multi-zones fitting probably is a better solution. This approach is also related to the zero-cell and zero-marginal problems. If the sample size for some of the zones is too small to apply the IPF, then one has to use the multi-zones fitting by aggregating data in those small zones to avoid the zero-cell or zero-marginal problem. Algorithms 1 and 2 indicate the algorithms of zone-by-zone fitting and multi-zone fitting (In the algorithm, a sentence after '#' in each line is a comment on the function or the parameter used in the algorithm. Figures 6 and 7 in the appendix describe an example of zone-by-zone and multi-zones fitting, respectively.

1. Reading seed data in a study area of interest, on a SUBZONE level.
2. Reading target marginal in a corresponding area.
3. Fitting the seed data to the target marginal.
4. Drawing a synthetic population for the study area.

Algorithm 1. Zone-by-zone fitting algorithm

```
### Zone-by-Zone fitting algorithm ###

SUBZONE = '1234'  # SUBZONE is a study area of interest
SUBZON.seed = Read_Seed(SUBZONE)   # loading seed data
SUBZONE.target.marginal = Read_Marginal(SUBZONE)    # loading marginal
fitted.SUBZONE.seed = Fitting(SUBZONE.seed, SUBZONE.target.marginal)    # fitting step
SUBZONE.population = Drawing(fitted.SUBZONE.seed)    # drawing step
                                                     # synthetic population in the study area
```

Algorithm 2. Multi-zone fitting algorithm

```
### Multi-Zone fitting algorithm ###

SUBZONES = [ '1111', '1112', '1113', ...]    # SUBZONES are a group of a study area of interest
For subzone in [SUBZONES]
{
    subzone.seed = Read_Seed(subzone)
    zone.seed + = subzone.seed    # aggregating subzone seed into zone seed
}
zone.target.marginal = Read_Marginal(subzone)
fitted.zone.seed = Fitting(zone.seed, zone.target.marginal)   # fitting step
zone.population = Drawing(fitted.zone.seed)   # drawing step
For subzone.population in [zone.population]   # disaggregating zone population
{
    SUBZONE.population = subzone.population    # synthetic population in the study area
}
```

Algorithm 3. Spatial fitting algorithm

```
### Spatial fitting algorithm ###

SUBZONE = '1234'  # SUBZONE is a study area
For subzone in [SUBZONES]   # SUBZONES contains the study area
{
    subzone.seed = Read_Seed(subzone)
    zone.seed += subzone.seed   # aggregating subzone seed into zone seed
}
zone.target.marginal = Read_Marginal(subzone)
fitted.zone.seed = Fitting(zone.seed, zone.target.marginal)   # fitting step
zone.population = Drawing(fitted.zone.seed)   # drawing step
For subzone.population in [zone.population]   # disaggregating zone population
{
    if subzone == SUBZONE   # if subzone is the study area
    {
        SUBZONE.population = subzone.population   # synthetic population in the study area
    }
}
```

1. Reading seed data in all areas, where are belonged to the study area on a SUBZONE level.
2. Merging the see data to a corresponding ZONE, where is an upper-level area of the SUBZONE.
3. Reading target marginal in the ZONE area.
4. Fitting the aggregative seed data to the target marginal.
5. Drawing a synthetic population on a ZONE level.
6. Disaggregating the synthetic population to a SUBZONE level.

Depending on target population, there are two types of fitting process: temporal fitting and spatial fitting. In detail, if the target is a synthetic population at a different time (either past or future), the temporal fitting process needs to be applied. Namely, the base year of the seed data is different from the target year. If the target is a synthetic population in a different spatial level (or other region), a spatial fitting process is feasible. In other words, the spatial level (or location) of the seed data is different from that of the target marginal. Algorithms 3 and 4 describe the algorithm of the spatial fitting and the temporal fitting, respectively. Figures 8 and 9 in the appendix show an example of spatial fitting process and temporal fitting process, respectively.

1. Reading all target marginal in all SUBZONE areas, where belong to the same ZONE area.
2. Merging the target marginal to the ZONE area.
3. Reading seed data in the ZONE area.
4. Fitting the see data to the aggregative target marginal.
5. Drawing a synthetic population in the ZONE area.
6. Disaggregating the synthetic population on a SUBZONE level.

Algorithm 4. Temporal fitting algorithm

```
### Temporal fitting algorithm ###

SUBZONE = '1234'  # SUBZONE is a study area
T0 = 2010  # Base year
T1 = 2020  # Target year
SUBZON.T0.seed = Read_Seed(SUBZONE.T0)  # loading seed data in the base year
SUBZONE.T1.target.marginal = Read_Marginal(SUBZONE.T1)  # loading marginal in the target year
fitted.SUBZONE.T1.seed = Fitting(SUBZONE.T0.seed, SUBZONE.T1.target.marginal)  # fitting step
SUBZONE.T1.population = Drawing(fitted.SUBZONE.T1.seed)  # drawing step
                                    # synthetic population in the target year
```

7. Reading the seed data on a SUBZONE level, from the synthetic population.
8. (Again) reading the target marginal in the SUBZONE area.
9. Fitting the seed data to the target marginal.
10. Drawing a synthetic population for the SUBZONE area.

1. Reading seed data in a base year.
2. Reading target marginal in a target year.
3. Fitting the seed data to the target marginal.
4. Drawing a synthetic population for the target year.

Once the fitting step is terminated, you will get either a complete target cross-table in using the normal IPF or a household weight list in using the IPU algorithm. Those are the result of adjusting the seed data to the target marginal distributions so that both the seed and the target marginal totals (almost) match each other in all dimensions of attributes. This means that seed data have been successfully expanded to target marginal. Otherwise, the fitting step has failed. Therefore, a consistency between seed and target marginal needs to be checked before the next step.

Drawing Step

The next step is a drawing process which is to generate synthetic population by drawing population. There are two kinds of drawing methods: household selection probability and MC sampling. The household selection probabilities are calculated by the following formula (Auld and Mohammadian, 2010) using the result of either the complete cross-table or household weights list from the fitting step.

$$P_{i,c} = \frac{W_i}{\sum_{k=1}^{N_c} W_k}$$

where $P_{i,c}$ is a probability of selecting household i with household type c, W_i is a household weight for household i, and N_c is remaining households in sample with household type c. This formula accounts that the probability of selecting household with type c is equal to the current household weight divided by the sum of the other households' weights in the sample. It indicates that as the household weight is higher, the household is more often chosen in the synthetic population. The drawback of this method is that it does not conserve compliance with person-marginals. For this reason, Auld and Mohammadian (2010) suggested a solution of an additional person selection probability with the existing formula. However, it is a quite expensive computation because the selection probability should be calculated after each selection processing.

The other method in the drawing step is a MC sampling which is a random sampling method to obtain numerical results. The MC sampling method selects household with the household weights in a random way. The MC sampling allows selecting an almost infinite number of different set of population so that the probability of generating a best-fit synthetic population becomes higher. Like the previous one, the MC sampling also has a drawback. It could happen that there are only few persons to be sampled left with a few desired numbers of person marginals. In this case, it is not possible to add the rest of the desired persons by sampling from few persons left. When you use the MC sampling in generating synthetic population, you need to be careful of the processing time because the MC sampling is quite sensitive to the number of iterations for the sampling. Although more iterations in the MC sampling can produce a better result, they result in a longer processing time. Hence, finding the optimal number of iterations is important in using Monte-Carlo sampling. Therefore, if you have a lot of combination sets of attribute, then the MC sampling is a better solution in terms of an efficient processing. Otherwise, the household selection probability is a better solution to keep a higher chance to produce complete synthetic population without marginals left (also see Figure 4 in the appendix).

Validation Step

After the drawing step, you will acquire synthetic population in your study area of interest. To check the accuracy of estimation, the synthetic population needs to be validated against real population using a goodness-of-fit measure. In statistics, there are three types of error measurements: *traditional* statistics, *information-based* statistics and general *distance-based* statistics.

In the traditional statistics, R^2 and chi-square are the two most commonly-applied goodness-of-fit measurements. However, the R^2 statistics has been argued by several researchers due to its insensitivity to variations in model specification and missing concept to evaluate model performance across different data sets (Black and Salter, 1975; Wilson, 1976). The information-based statistics originated from "information gain statistics" in Kullback and Leibler (1951) includes the phi statistics, the psi statistics, and the measure of absolute entropy difference. The information-based statistics have a limitation in that the information gain is sensitive to the distribution of over and under estimations (Smith and Hutchinson, 1981). The general distance statistics are defined by functions of an element of the observed matrix and estimated matrix. Among the general distance statistics, a standardized root mean square error (SRMSE) has been commonly used for the validation test for synthetic population in transportation because of its theoretical relevance in statistical modeling (Hyndman and Koehler, 2006). The SRMSE is calculated as follows (Pitfield, 1978):

$$SRMSE \sqrt{\sum \sum \frac{(t_{ij} - \hat{t}_{ij})^2}{m \times n} / (\sum_i \sum_j \frac{t_{ij}}{m \times n})}$$

where $\hat{t}_{ij}$ is the estimated number of population elements with attributes i and j, and t_{ij} is an observed number of population. m and n are the number of attribute values for attributes i and j, respectively. A value of zero in the SRMSE means a perfect match, and '1' means no matching between estimated and observed data. Even its popularity in error measurements, the SRMSE cannot always serve as a best measurement with some problems. For example, the SRMSE is only feasible in a specific condition that the sum of observed frequencies is exactly the same as the sum of the estimated frequencies (Knudsen and Fotheringham, 1986). In practice, this condition is not always met, especially in evaluating synthetic population data. This is because the only case that perfectly matches between seed and target marginals can satisfy this condition.

$$\sum_i \sum_j t_{ij} = \sum_i \sum_j \hat{t}_{ij}$$

Now, what is the best measurement for a validation test? According to related research, there seems to be no concrete answer to this question because every measurement has merits and drawbacks depending on data and validation purpose. Table 7 in the appendix lists error measurements for testing the performance of synthetic population techniques. Voas and Williamson (2001) proposed some criteria on the decision of error measurements.

We seek a goodness-of-fit statistic that:

- *Can be used for comparisons across tables;*
- *Produces results corresponding to our intuitive sense of fit;*
- *Will measure both tabular fit and (via its components) internal fit;*
- *Will compare counts or totals and not just relative frequencies;*
- *Is not burdensome to calculate or (where appropriate) to test;*
- *Has a known, tractable sampling distribution;*
- *Will be familiar or at least acceptable to the user community. (pp. 196 in Voas and Williamson (2001)*

Summary

In this section, we described every processing step with examples: preprocessing step, fitting step, drawing step and validation step. The preprocessing step is to collect and clean input, and change the data structure if necessary. The fitting step is to adjust seed data to target marginal distribution using different fitting approach (single- and multi-level, zone-by-zone and multi-level, temporal and spatial fitting) feasible for the target synthetic population. Then, the drawing step is to draw synthetic population by expanding the seed to the desired number of population using a sampling tool (household selection probability and MC sampling). At the end, the validation step is to evaluate the performance of the synthetic population technique by computing an estimation error using an error measurement.

ISSUES AND PROPOSED SOLUTIONS

This section deals with some problems that we could experience during the working procedure of generating a synthetic population using whatever techniques. This is because even using a very good technique may have to deal with data problems. We also propose a solution to each problem with an example.

Zero-Cell and Zero-Marginal

A zero-cell problem, also referred to as missing values in the literature, is first addressed by Beckman *et al.* (1996). The zero-cell problem occurs when a target marginal is not zero in an attribute dimension without a corresponding sample in the source. This normally happens when generating synthetic population in rather small regions, because there is a high probability of no representative sample in a certain combination of attributes. In this case, the IPF process cannot converge to a solution because the corresponding cell in the cross-table always takes a zero value during the process due to a zero division error. Figure 2 shows an example of the zero-cell in a two-dimension cross-table.

There are few solutions to the zero-cell problem. The simplest solution is to assign an arbitrarily small value (e.g. 0.01) to the zero cells, which is called as 'tweaking approach' in Beckman *et al.* (1996). However, Beckman et al. (1996) and Guo and Bhat (2006) addressed that the solution may introduce an arbitrary bias. Another solution is to substitute for a zero-cell value by a derived value from overall distribution in the whole sample. Although this solution is quit suitable for the zero-cell problem in the small area, it is possible to over-represent and ignore the local characteristic in that area, for example no population with high income in a rural area (Ye et al., 2009). Another two solutions, using a maximum-iteration value and a category reduction, are indirect solutions to preventing from the zero-cell problem during the IPF process (Guo and Bhat, 2006). The former solution is to avoid non-convergence occurred by the zero-cell problem by terminating the IPF process when reaching the pre-specified maximum-iteration value. The latter one is to lower the chances to get the zero-cells in a cross-table by reducing the sparse categories. For instance, a cross-table with 5 categories has lower chance to get the zero-cell value than a cross-table with 10 categories (the section of category reduction deals with this category reduction in detail). However, those two solutions can affect on other factors, for example computing resource and model performance, and also trigger another problem in the IPF process.

A zero-marginal problem occurs with the same reason as the zero-cell problem, but it is limited to the case of using the IPU algorithm. As for the theoretical features of the IPU algorithm, all households corresponding to the zero-marginal category in the source will get a zero weight. Then, the household with zero weights never get positive weights even if some of the households have to be assigned with non-zero weights. This is because the IPU algorithm can normally update the household weights after each iteration, but it is not possible to update the zero weights due to fact that the denominator for adjusting marginal totals will always take a zero value. Ye *et al.* (2009) suggested a solution to this problem that assigns an arbitrary small number, e.g. 0.001, to the zero-marginal categories. The effect of the arbitrary small margins can be alleviated after little iteration, and the process of updating weights can avoid the zero-marginal problem. Figure 3 shows an example of the zero-marginal problem in the IPU algorithm.

Rounding

The IPF process estimates the value of a cell in a target cross-table by adjusting seed marginal to the target marginal by means of linearly rescaling the value of a cell in the seed cross-table. As a result, the IPF process outputs the value of a cell with a real number, which indicates the number of households (or persons) with certain socio-demographic attributes (e.g. age, gender, income and so on) in the population. Thus, the number should be an integer in the drawing step, otherwise, the number needs to be converted to an integer number by rounding up or down. In rounding a number, an expected problem is that after rounding those numbers, the marginal totals in the source cannot keep consistent with the target marginals. This means that rounding the numbers, also referred to as *"integerization"*, in a cross-table can lead to an unexpected biased distribution in the synthetic population process (Bowman, 2004). In addition to simple rounding methods (e.g. rounding up/down and rounding ceiling/floor), there are a number of rounding methods, such as an arithmetic rounding, a bucket rounding and stochastic rounding (introduced by Ye *et al.*, 2009). Note that after rounding, the marginal totals in the seed cross-table should be at least consistent with the marginal totals in the target cross-table, as far as possible.

Category Reduction

As mentioned in the section of zero-cell and zero-marginal, the category reduction serves as a solution to two problems, a zero-cell (or zero-marginal) and memory, in using synthetic population techniques. Compared to the IPU algorithm with a sparse list-based data structure, the ordinary IPF with a cross-table requires exponentially bigger memory as the number of categories in attributes increase. For example, consider a two-dimension cross-table that consists of two attributes each with three categories. In this case, there are nine cells (3 by 3) in the cross-table. Next, consider a two-dimension cross table consisting of two attributes with 3+1 categories, and then the cross-table has sixteen cells (4 by 4). As you can see in this example, an increase in the number of cells, which consumes more memory, is exponentially proportional to an increase in the number of categories. In addition, the more cells, the more often zero-valued cells will occur in a cross-table.

As always, the category reduction has not only those advantages but also some disadvantages. First, this solution cannot guarantee a better performance because using less categories means that less control variables are used for the synthetic population process (Auld *et al.*, 2008). Furthermore, this solution may ignore a local characteristic, for example reducing an income category would overlook the significant difference between urban area and rural area. Hence, it is important to find the optimal number of categories in the synthetic population research. Auld *et al.* (2008) proposed a user-specified percentage threshold as a category reduction method. At first, a user specifies the percentage threshold. Then, a category which does not exceed the percentage

threshold is combined with a neighboring category. For instance, for a given percentage threshold of 20%, there is no attribute with more than five categories. In addition, this solution should be applied to resolve the zero-cell issue together with adapting an input and model itself to fit the local characteristics lost by the category reduction.

CONCLUSION

As the ABM becomes more popular in transportation, the demand of micro-data increases. Generally, it is difficult to collect such micro-data due to privacy protection and high cost. Thus, more researchers are trying to produce synthetic population as an alternative resource using synthetic population techniques. However, generating a synthetic population is relatively complicated for non-experts or beginners because there is no explicit terminology and there are no concrete solutions to some issues and problems in the field. In this sense, this chapter aims at providing a beginner with a guideline on how to generate synthetic population using some techniques.

The chapter accounts for why we need synthetic population techniques and the chapter goal and structure in the introduction section. For a beginner, some terminologies which are commonly referred to in related research are described in the section of related research. Then, two groups of related research, IPF and CO, are separately introduced in the following two sections. The next section describes the whole process from data collection to the validation test in building a synthetic population (using the IPU algorithm). In the section of issues and proposed solutions, we introduce some issues (e.g. zero-cell and zero-marginal, rounding, and category reduction) in the synthetic population research, and also provide a solution to each issue.

Due to a limited space, this chapter cannot cover everything about the synthetic population techniques, but instead we made effort to give an answer to some practical questions of why, what and how generating synthetic population can be done. The research was supported by means of an empirical case where a synthetic population was generated for Flanders (Belgium). In our future work, we will provide more details of the working process and further issues and challenges in this field, and also introduce new research developing a new synthetic population technique without sample data.

ACKNOWLEDGMENT

For the empirical case we used the infrastructure of the VSC - Flemish Supercomputer Center, funded by the Hercules foundation and the Flemish Government - department EWI.

REFERENCES

Arentze, T. A., Timmermans, & Hofman. (2007). Population synthesis for microsimulating travel behavior. *Transportation Research Record*, (11): 85–91. doi:10.3141/2014-11.

Auld, J. Mohammadian, & Wies. (2008). *Population synthesis with control category optimization*. Paper presented at the 10th International Conference on Application of Advanced Technologies in Transportation. Athens, Greece.

Auld, J. Mohammadian, & Wies. (2010). *An efficient methodology for generating synthetic populations with multiple control levels*. Paper presented at the the 89th Annual Meeting of the Transportation Research Board. Washington, DC.

Barthelemy, J., & Cornelis, E. (2012). *Synthetic populations: review of the different approaches*. CEPS/INSTEAD..

Beckman, R. J., Baggerly, & McKay. (1996). Creating synthetic baseline populations. *Transportation Research Part A, Policy and Practice*, *30*(6), 415–429. doi:10.1016/0965-8564(96)00004-3.

Black, J. A., & Salter, R. T. (1975). A statistical evaluation of the accuracy of a family of gravity models. *Proceedings - Institution of Civil Engineers*, *2*(59), 1–20. doi:10.1680/iicep.1975.3839.

Deming, W. E., & Stephan. (1940). On the least squares adjustment of a sampled frequency table when the expected marginal totals are known. *Annals of Mathematical Statistics*, *11*(4), 427–444. doi:10.1214/aoms/1177731829.

Guo, J. Y., & Bhat. (2007). Population synthesis for microsimulating travel behavior. *Transportation Research Record*, (12): 92–101. doi:10.3141/2014-12.

Huang, Z., & Williamson, P. (2001). *Comparison of synthetic reconstruction and combinatorial optimisation approaches to the creation of small-area microdata* (Working Paper, 2001/2). Liverpool, UK: Department of Geography, University of Liverpool.

Hyndman, R. J., & Koehler, A. B. (2006). Another look at measures of forecast accuracy. *International Journal of Forecasting*, *22*(4), 679–688. doi:10.1016/j.ijforecast.2006.03.001.

Knudsen, D. C., & Fotheringham. (1986). Matrix comparison, goodness-of-fit, and spatial interaction modeling. *International Regional Science Review*, *10*(2), 127–147. doi:10.1177/016001768601000203.

Kullback, S., & Leibler, R. A. (1951). On information and sufficiency. *Annals of Mathematical Statistics*, *22*(1), 79–86. doi:10.1214/aoms/1177729694.

Kurban, H., Gallagher, R., Kurban, G. A., & Persky, J. (2011). A beginner's guide to creating small-area cross-tabulations. *Cityscape (Washington, D.C.)*, *13*(3), 225–235.

Melhuish, T., Blake, M., & Day, S. (2002). An evaluation of synthetic household populations for census collection districts created using optimisation techniques. *Australasian Journal of Regional Studies*, *8*(3), 269–387.

Muller, K., & Axhausen. (2011). *Population synthesis for microsimulation: State of the art.* Paper presented at the 90th Annual Meeting of the Transportation Research Board. Washington, DC.

Pitfield, D. E. (1978). Sub-optimality in freight distribution. *Transportation Research*, *12*(6), 403–409. doi:10.1016/0041-1647(78)90028-X.

Pritchard, D. R., & Miller. (2009). *Advances in agent population synthesis and application in an integrated land use and transportation model.* Paper presented at the 88th Annual Meeting of the Transportation Research Board. Washington, DC.

Ryan, J., Maoh, & Kanaroglou. (2009). Population synthesis: Comparing the major techniques using a small, complete population of firms. *Geographical Analysis*, *41*(2), 181–203. doi:10.1111/j.1538-4632.2009.00750.x.

Smith, D. P., & Hutchinson, B. G. (1981). Goodness-of-fit statistics for trip distribution models. *Transportation Research*, *15*(4), 295–303. doi:10.1016/0191-2607(81)90011-X.

Voas, D., & Williamson, P. (2000). An evaluation of the combinatorial optimisation approach to the creation of synthetic microdata. *International Journal of Population Geography*, *6*(5), 349–366. doi:10.1002/1099-1220(200009/10)6:5<349::AID-IJPG196>3.0.CO;2-5.

Voas, D., & Williamson, P. (2001). Evaluating goodness-of-fit measures for synthetic microdata. *Geographical and Environmental Modelling*, *5*(2), 177–200. doi:10.1080/13615930120086078.

Williamson, P., Birkin, M., & Rees, P. H. (1998). The estimation of population microdata by using data from small area statistics and samples of anonymised records. *Environment & Planning A*, *30*(5), 785–816. doi:10.1068/a300785 PMID:12293871.

Wilson, S. R. (1976). Statistical notes on the evaluation of calibrated gravity models. *Transportation Research*, *0*(5), 343–345. doi:10.1016/0041-1647(76)90114-3.

Ye, X. Konduri, Pendyala, Sana, & Waddell. (2009). *A methodology to match distributions of both household and person attributes in the generation of synthetic populations.* Paper presented at the 88th Annual Meeting of the Transportation Research Board. Washington, DC.

KEY TERMS AND DEFNITIONS

CO (Combinatorial Optimization): A synthetic population technique that adjusts seed data to target marginals by swapping the household randomly selected from the seed data to another until getting a best-fit output.

Drawing: Sampling procedure in synthetic population research that synthesizes population by adding a household up to the desired number of households in the target marginal.

Fitting: Matching procedure in synthetic population research that adjusts seed data to target marginal distribution.

IPF (Iterative Proportional Fitting): A synthetic population technique that iteratively estimates cell values of a cross-table in the source in order to match given target marginal distributions.

IPU (Iterative Proportional Updating): A synthetic population technique that iteratively updates household weights of each sample record to match seed data to target marginals.

Marginal: A row or column total in a cross-table, normally calculated along each of the row or column dimension.

Source (or Seed Data): Initial value for the matrix cells that has been derived from domain knowledge, e.g. census survey.

Sparse List-Based Data Structure: A data structure consisting of the microdata (sample) entries and weights attached to each entry. List based data structures are used in cases where only a small part of the possible attribute combinations occur in reality (sparseness).

Target: Aggregate data for which the marginal distribution is given in a study area of interest.

APPENDIX

Table 1. List of synthetic population techniques

Researcher	Model	Goal	Input	Fitting	Drawing	Validation
Beckman *et al.* (1996)	Original IPF	Tarrant County, Texas, 1990	Census STF-3A (margin) PUMS (seed)	Single-level (only house-hold)	Household selection probability	
Arentze *et al.* (2007)	Relation matrix	Dutch population, 1995	1995 OVG (seed)	Multi-level (dealt in a preprocessing step)		CHAID
Guo & Bhat (2007)	Original IPF	Dalla/Fort-Worth Metropolitan Area, Texas, 2000	2000 US census SF1 (margin) 2000 PUMS (seed)	Multi-level	Advanced household selection probability	PD (percentage difference) APD (absolute PD) AAPD (average APD)
Ye *et al.* (2009)	IPU algorithm	Maricopa County Region, Arizona, 2000	2000 Census summary file (margin) 2000 PUMS (seed)	Multi-level (by updating house-hold weights)	MC (Monte-Carlo) sampling	Chi-square statistic
Auld *et al.* (2010)	Advanced IPF	Chicago-land six-country region		Multi-level Zone-by-zone	MC sampling New household selection prob-ability	WAAPD (weighted average absolute percent-age difference) FT (Freeman-Tukey) statistic
Muller & Ax-hausen (2011)	Hierarchical IPF	Switzerland, 2000	2000 Swiss census	Multi-level (us-ing an entropy-optimizing method)		G^2 SRMSE (stan-dardized root mean square error)
Ptrichard & Miller (2012)	Advanced IPF	Toronto Census Metropolitan Area	1986 Toronto census	Multi-level Multi-zone	Conditioned MC sampling	SRMSE

Figure 4. Working process of synthetic population technique

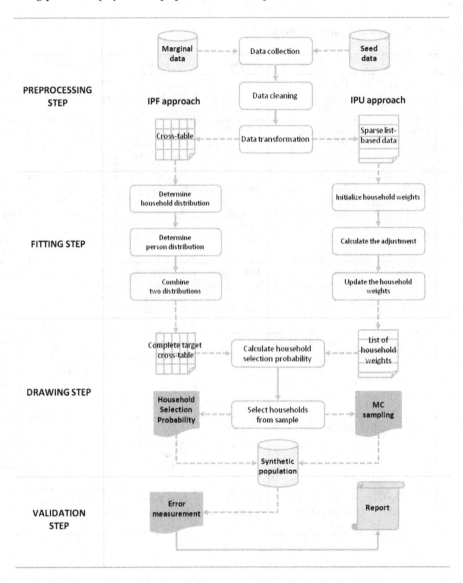

Table 2. List of household and person attributes

Attribute	Category
Residence	**Subzone ID**
Income	'1' = 0 – 1249 '2' = 1250 – 2249 '3' = 2250 – 2249 '4' = 3250+ Unit: euro
Number of members	'1' = 1 '2' = 2
Age	'1' = 18 – 34 '2' = 35 –54 '3' = 55 – 64 '4' = 65 – 74 '5' = 75+
Job	'0' = No work '2' = Work
Gender	'1' = Male '2' = Female
Driver license	'0' = No '1' = Yes

Table 3. Example of source data: household data

Household ID	Residence	Income	Size
1	3	1	1
2	15	1	1
3	20	4	2
4	12	1	1
5	19	5	2
6	25	4	2

Table 4. Example of source data: person data

Person ID	Household ID	Age	Job	Gender	Driver License
1	1	2	2	2	1
2	2	3	0	2	0
3	3	4	0	2	0
4	3	4	0	1	1
5	4	1	2	1	1
6	5	2	2	2	1
7	5	2	2	1	1
8	6	3	0	1	1
9	6	3	0	2	1

Table 5. Example of target data

Subzone	Households	Persons	Income 1	Income 2	Size 1	Size 2	Age1
0	4138	7207	734	711	1451	2686	782
1	767	1442	136	132	269	498	141
2	1496	2709	265	257	525	972	314
3	8073	9169	1896	1905	3591	4483	1367
Age2	**No Work**	**Work**	**Male**	**Female**	**No Driving License**	**Driving License**	
1117	3031	4177	4052	3155	1688	5519	
202	679	763	751	691	416	1026	
448	1043	1666	1578	1131	566	2144	
1952	4267	4902	5074	4094	2533	6635	

Figure 5. Example of (multi-zone) cross-table

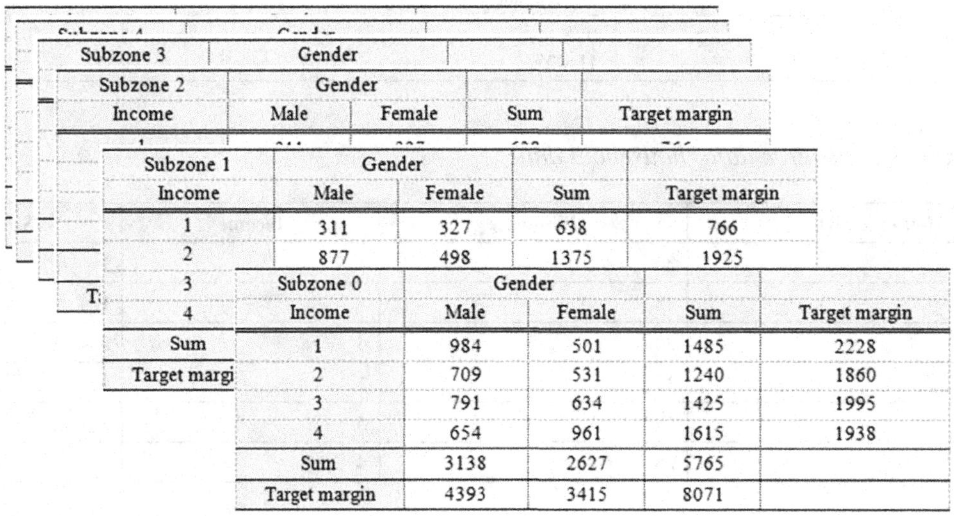

Subzone 1	Gender			
Income	Male	Female	Sum	Target margin
1	311	327	638	766
2	877	498	1375	1925

Subzone 0	Gender			
Income	Male	Female	Sum	Target margin
1	984	501	1485	2228
2	709	531	1240	1860
3	791	634	1425	1995
4	654	961	1615	1938
Sum	3138	2627	5765	
Target margin	4393	3415	8071	

Table 6. Example of sparse list-based data structure

Index	Residence	Income	Size	Age	Job	Gender	Driver License	Weight
1	3	1	1	2	2	2	1	39.3
2	15	1	1	3	0	2	0	41.2
3	20	4	2	4	0	2	0	33.10
4	20	4	2	4	0	1	1	50.10
5	12	1	1	1	2	1	1	47.8
6	19	5	2	2	2	2	1	47.3
7	19	5	2	2	2	1	1	17.6
8	25	4	2	3	0	1	1	35.1
9	25	4	2	3	0	2	1	11.10

Figure 6. Example of zone-by-zone fitting process

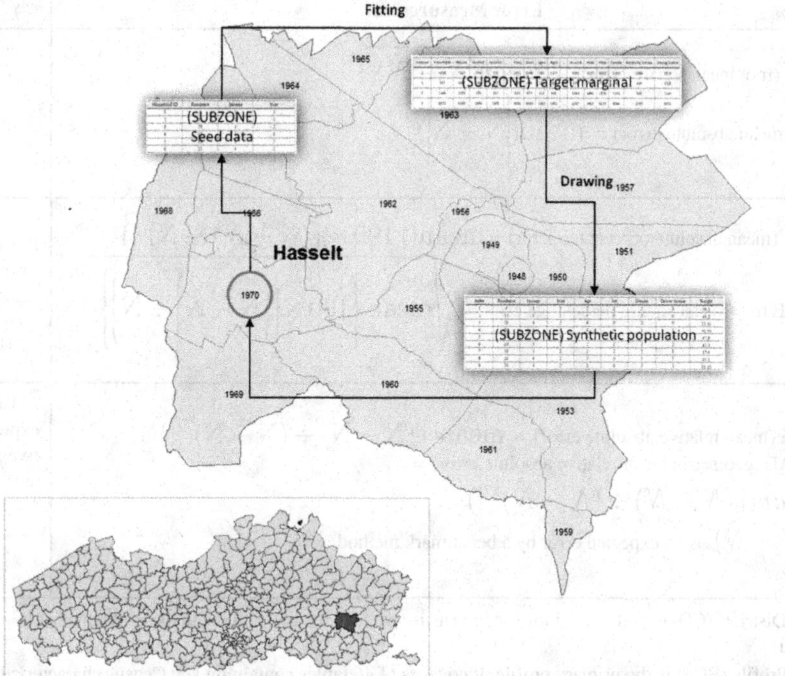

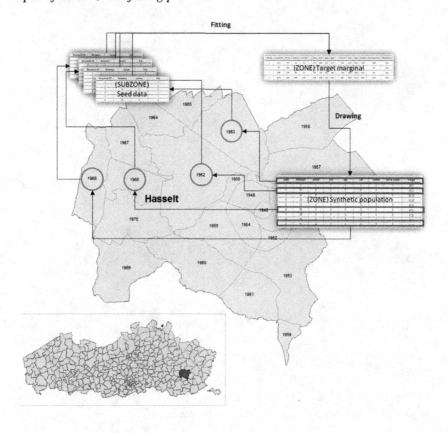

Figure 7. Example of multi-zones fitting process

Table 7. List of error measurements (Hyndman and Koehler, 2006)

Category	Error Measurement	Limit
Scale-dependent error	RMSE (root mean square error)= $\sqrt{mean(N - \hat{N})^2}$ MAE (mean absolute error) = $mean(\lvert N - \hat{N} \rvert)$	- sensitive to outliers
Percentage error	MAPE (mean absolute percentage error) = $mean(\lvert 100 \times \{(N - \hat{N}) \div N\} \rvert)$ RMSPE (root mean square percentage error = $\sqrt{mean\left\{100 \times \left(\left(N - \hat{N}\right) \div N\right)\right\}^2}$	- infinite or undefined if $N=0$ - skewed distribution if N is close to zero
Relative error	MRAE (mean relative absolute error) = $mean(\lvert (N - \hat{N}) \div (N - \hat{N})^* \rvert)$ GMRAE (geometric mean relative absolute error) = $gmean(\lvert (N - \hat{N}) \div (N - \hat{N})^* \rvert)$ $\#(N - \hat{N})^*$ is an expected error by a benchmark method	- infinite variance if an expected error has positive probability density at 0

[1]Census Collection Districts (CDs) are designed for use in census years for the collection and dissemination of Population Census data (http://www.abs.gov.au)

[2]Basic Community Profile (BCP) is the primary profile. It consists of 46 tables containing key Census characteristics on persons, families and dwellings (http://www.abs.gov.au).

Chapter 4
Issues in Feathers Application in the Seoul Metropolitan Area

Won Do Lee
Kyung Hee University, Korea

Chang-Hyeon Joh
Kyung Hee University, Korea

Sungjin Cho
Hasselt University, Belgium

Bruno Kochan
Hasselt University, Belgium

ABSTRACT

Over the last decades, the trip-based approach, also known as the four-step model, has been playing an unrivaled role in transportation demand research in Korea. It has been used to predict changes in traffic volume resulting from new transportation policy measures, and also has allowed conducting benefit-cost analyses for new infrastructure provisions. It has been increasingly difficult for the trip-based model to anticipate individual responses to new transportation policy inputs and infrastructure provision as the society becomes personalized and diversified. Activity-Based Modeling (ABM) approaches, predicting travel demand derived from individual activity participations, were introduced to complement the trip-based approach in this regard. The chapter introduces the Seoul ABM project that aims to first apply FEATHERS as an ABM to the data collected in Seoul Metropolitan Area (SMA) and then develop a prototype of the ABM framework for Korea. More specifically, the chapter first briefly describes SMA in comparison with Flanders in Belgium and other countries. It then introduces related research works in Korea and the background of the Seoul ABM project. After these, a FEATHERS framework applied for the Seoul ABM project is described with its data requirements. Major issues of and solutions to the Seoul ABM project are then discussed with regard to the data preprocessing. The chapter ends with a summary and future work.

DOI: 10.4018/978-1-4666-4920-0.ch004

INTRODUCTION

The trip-based approach, also known as the four-step model (FSM), has been used for transportation demand researches to develop policy measures, such as transportation infrastructure provision, in Korea. It has however been increasingly difficult for the FSM to anticipate individual responses to new transportation policy inputs and infrastructure provision as the society becomes personalized and diversified. The FSM is hard to capture the secondary consequences of social phenomena, such as aging and CO_2 emissions, which need to concern the efficiency of transportation system both at the macro and micros (Park et al., 2012). Moreover, the FSM does not take the temporal trip distribution into account and ignores spatio-temporal information about the trip segment.

This chapter introduces an activity-based model (ABM), developed by the Seoul ABM project, to complement the FSM and to better predict travel demand derived from individual activity participations. The Seoul ABM project (Lee et al., 2012) in Korea aims to first analyze individual travel demand in the Seoul Metropolitan Area (SMA) using FEATHERS and to develop a prototype of the ABM framework for Korean context. The chapter therefore focuses on introducing the Seoul ABM project with discussions on issues of and solutions to the data processing. To this end, Section 2 provides an overview of the study area and a comparison between the SMA in Korea and other countries including Flanders in Belgium. Section 3 then reviews related research on transportation demand forecast in Korea. Section 4 details the FEATHERS framework and data requirements. Section 5 addresses major issues of and solutions to the data processing of the Seoul ABM project using FEATHERS. Section 6 concludes the chapter with a summary and the future work.

STUDY AREA

The SMA consists of three local governments, including Seoul, Inchon and Gyeonggi with 23,836,272 inhabitants (49% of the population in Korea). Metropolitan Transportation Authority (MTA) organizes the metropolitan transportation planning, and Korea Transportation Institute (KOTI) collects for MTA the network data from local governments and their institutions. The recent household travel survey was conducted in 2010 in the SMA, to collect household activity-travel data involving 665,801 respondents (2.79% of the population in SMA). Table 1 shows descriptive statistics of the survey data.

Table 1 shows trip frequencies 2.51, time 84.04 in min and distance 13.73 in km on daily average. 31.6% and 31.3% of the trips account for walk and car drivers/passengers, respectively. Public transportation (e.g. bus and metro) use amounts to approximately 30% of the trips, which is higher than most large cities in western countries, likely resulting from the transportation infrastructure and policy measures in the area. Regarding the trip purpose, commuting, except for a private education, is of the highest proportion as 31.3% of the trips. Leisure and shopping take only 3.7% and 2.8%, respectively. This result is concerned likely with the lack of diversity in activities, dominated by work-related activities in the area. Time-use of each activity type therefore confirms its importance in the travel behavior research.

Figure 1 illustrates the temporal distributions of commuters' trip participation in Korea and other countries. The distributions in Korea and Japan are similar in the morning peak from 6 to 8, while the off-morning peak differs; 6 to 8 in Korea (6 to 8) and 4 to 6 in Japan. U.S. shows peak hours earlier by almost one hour than other countries. Netherlands have an exceptionally high proportion of trip participations at noon. Korea presents higher proportions of the trips in the evening hours, unlike other countries.

Table 1. Activity-travel behavior in household travel survey in SMA (Lee, et al., 2012)

Overall Indicator	
trip frequency	2.51
transfer frequency	0.06
travel time (min)	84.04
transfer time (min)	0.51
travel distance (km)	13.73
inner-trip chain frequency	1.91
outer-trip chain frequency	0.54
Travel Mode (%)	
walk	31.6
car	23.5
passenger	7.8
local-line bus	3.8
main-line bus	10.7
inter-city bus	3.1
metro/train	12.5
taxi	0.9
motorbike	0.7
bike	2.1
etc.	3.4
Trip Purpose	
pickup	1.0
back home	45.7
go to work	19.5
go to school	11.8
go to private education	5.3
business	4.1
shopping	2.8
leisure	3.7
etc.	6.1

Figure 2 illustrates an average annual work time per workers in OECD countries. Korea is almost 8.7 hours per day, which is 1.7 hours longer than the average of OECD countries. Overall, the Dutch workers work for 5.5 hours per day, which means that they work 3.2 hours shorter than Korean workers.

Figure 3 shows an average commuting time in Korea and other countries. Commuters in Korea spend 33 minutes, shorter than in China and India. Those in U.S. and Canada spend less time than in Korea. In other words, Korea is quite different in individual travel pattern from other countries. Moreover, commuters in the SMA spend 8 minutes longer than the average of Korea. Spatial attributes, personal characteristics and household properties contribute to this difference (Kim et al., 2012), which reflect unique characteristics of activity time-use and culture of Korea and in particular of the SMA.

TRAVEL DEMAND RESEARCH IN KOREA

Four-Step Model

The FSM has been a primary method for estimating future travel demands and evaluating the performance of a transportation system typically at regional and sub-regional scales. The model systems were developed for evaluating large-scale infrastructure projects (McNally, et al., 2000). The FSM has been heavily used in Korea for the travel demand research, partly due to the fact that these models easily collect and simplify data averaged from TAZ, which is equivalent to the census block in Korea. The FSM processes contain sequential four steps: trip generation, trip distribution, mode choice and route choice. Trip generation step in the FSM generates trip productions from and attractions to each TAZ, which are in turn input into trip distribution step. Trip distribution step generates trip frequencies between origin and destination of TAZs, which results in an origin-destination (OD) matrix. Mode choice step generates modal splits across transportation modes for each OD pair. Route choice step finally assigns trips across routes of the network connecting origin and destination for each transportation mode. Outputs from the

Figure 1. Commuter's temporal distribution
Data: Korea (Kim, et al., 2012), Japan (Tokyo Metropolitan Household Survey, 2008), U.S.A (Bureau of Labor Statistics, 2005), U.K (Department for Transport Statistics, 2012), Netherlands (Statistics Netherlands, 2008).

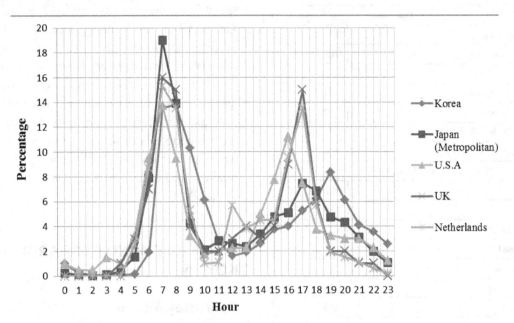

Figure 2. Average annual hours actually worked per worker based in 2010 year (OECD, 2012)
Data: OECD Stat Extracts (http://stats.oecd.org/Index.aspx?DataSetCode=ANHRS)

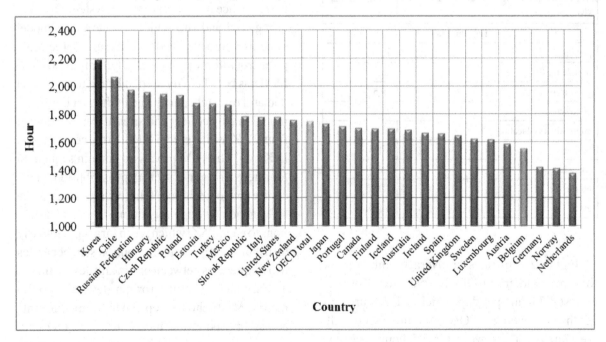

Figure 3. Average commute to work; commuting time (sorted by commuting time ascending)
Data: Korea (Kim, et al., 2012), other countries (The Economist, 2009)

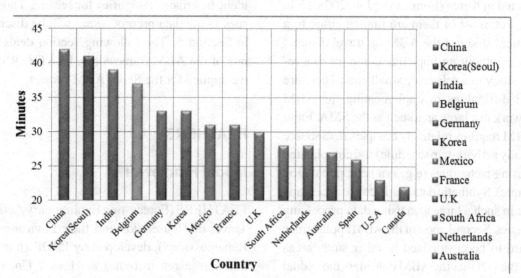

FSM are OD matrices with modal splits and trip purpose distribution for each TAZ.

KDI (Korea Development Institute) conducts preliminary feasibility study for large infrastructure investments in the country. The study consists of economic and policy feasibility investigations. Transportation section within these studies is to examine the benefits, such as decrease in travel time, gas usage and traffic accident, from particular investment plan. Economic feasibility computes benefit-cost ratio, NPV (Not Present Value), IRR (Internal Rate of Return) and sensitiveness of each input variable. The results are then used to determine the feasibility of the concerned future plan. Transportation infrastructure buffer is however narrow and includes only a few TAZs. TAZs are often arbitrarily sub-divided by the researchers because of this problem. Lim et al. (2008) analyzed the correlation in the computed feasibility between network-level and zone-scale, and suggested checking the balance with OD matrix and network-level when TAZs are sub-divided. However, the sub-division process is not included yet in Korea.

Activity-Based Model

In response to change in transport planning goals from supplying global infrastructure to satisfying individual travel demands, the ABM was first introduced by transportation researchers to complement the conventional models (the FSM in this chapter) at the third international conference on travel behavior in Australia in 1977 (Jovicic, 2001). The ABM was firmly based on the theories of two researchers, Hägerstrand and Chapin. Hägerstrand (1970) explained individual activity demand by personal and social constraints in his 'time-geography theory'. On the other hand, Chapin (1974) focuses more on natural human needs that derive activities. Based on their pioneering works, the ABM emerged to forecast disaggregate travel demands derived from activity participation, whereas the FSM predicts aggregate travel demands by typically using averaged mobility factors, such as population and land use of zones. The ABM becomes popular in transportation research as it has potential to provide the evaluation of complex policy measures and reflecting the effect of individual decision making process on transportation environment.

Only a few studies on the ABM have been conducted in Korea (Eom, 2007; Joh, 2008; Noh, 2011). Yet, most of them are limited either to a theoretical study of the ABM on travel demand research without an implementation, or to a regional study in a relatively small area. There are several difficulties in implementing the ABM framework in a large area such as the SMA. First, the ABM requires relatively complex data source (e.g. daily activity-trip schedule) and complicated computing techniques (e.g. synthetic population technique). Synthetic data is difficult to access and handle in such a large area using data processing techniques. Second, most of the ABM applications are hard to be customized in other study areas due to the fact that the ABM considers individual activities conducted in the particular context of socio-economic and spatial characteristics in the given study area. A relatively big difference in socio-economic and spatial attributes may attract a caution when adjusting the ABM framework to a large.

The Seoul ABM project presented in the chapter is the first in travel demand implementation research in Korea using an ABM framework. As mentioned earlier, it is difficult to develop an ABM in Korean context because of several reasons, including difficulties in data collection, synthesizing data, and so on. First, the ABM requires micro-data as input, e.g. individual schedule diary, which consists of trip sequences including transportation mode, travel party, travel time and cost. It requires much time to collect and handle such individual level data. Second, when the data at hand does not provide an ABM with the full details required, the missing details should be synthesized properly. Third, when applying an existing ABM framework to a new study area, one has to examine two important considerations; transportation environment and cultural difference. Activity-travel behavior in the model is likely affected by activity and travel specifications. For instance, household travel survey data in the SMA of Korea recognizes only one activity category for

leisure while travel survey in Flanders of Belgium identifies many categories for leisure. Those issues in the data preprocessing will be discussed in Section 5. The following section deals with one of the ABM frameworks, FEATHERS, that we applied for the Seoul ABM project.

FEATHERS

Model Framework

FEATHERS (Forecasting Evolutionary Activity-Travel of Households and their Environmental RepercussionS), developed by IMOB (transportation research institute) at Hasselt University in Belgium, is an activity-based transportation demand forecast model framework sponsored by the Flemish government. FEATHERS is a modular-based framework, where users can easily insert his/her own functions or modules, exchange functions or modules with other ones, and remove existing functions or modules from the framework. Hence, in principle, users can apply FEATHERS even to a different study area by modifying the components of the framework.

Figure 4 shows the FEATHERS framework with the main modules; configuration, data, population, schedule, schedule execution, learning, statistics and visualization, and training modules (Kochan, 2012). More specifically, the configuration module (ConfMod) is to obtain a specific setting required for other modules in the framework. It makes the FEATHERS framework extensible and flexible for users' study interests. Second, the data module (DatMod) as one of the core modules is to supply access to the data, e.g. supply and demand data, used for other modules and to provide a standardization tool. Next, the population module (PopMod) manages the different agents that are used in synthetic population, consisting of agents with a number of attributes. The schedule module (SchedMod) is to generate individual daily schedule for population based on

Figure 4. A schematic overview of the FEATHERS modules (Kochan, 2012)

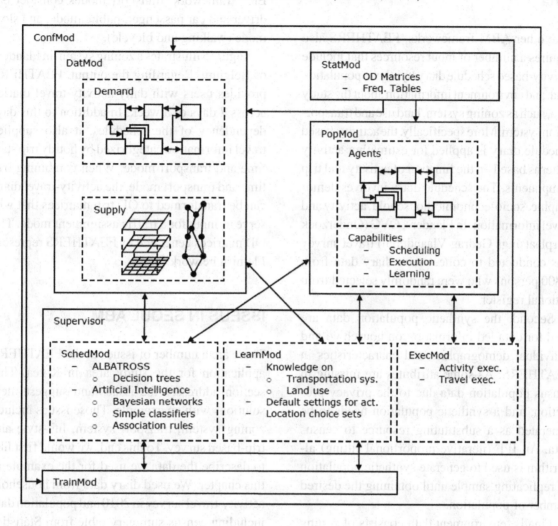

the training data (which is an activity-trip survey data) using a rule-based algorithm (a decision tree algorithm in FEATHERS). Currently the schedule module in the FEATHERs framework incorporates with the activity-based scheduler in ALBATROSS (A Learning-Based Transportation Oriented Simulation System). The schedule execution module (ExecMod) is to simulate synthetic activities and journeys simultaneously and synchronously. During the execution process, uncertainty on scheduled activities is also simulated by means of changing activity components by

unexpected events. The learning module (LearnMod) is to simulate an agent's learning process by re-scheduling the mismatching activity or trip with executed one. The statistics (StatMod) and visualization (VisMod) module are to provide reports regarding the synthetic population and the activity-travel schedules to users and to create graphical reports, respectively. The reports include information about household, person, activity, journey and lags. Finally, the training module (TrainMod) supplies the function for calibrating a user's model for real-life data.

Data

Like other ABM frameworks, FEATHERS also requires a number of input resources that include activity-based schedule diary, synthetic population data, and environment information about the study area, such as zoning system, land use and transportation system. More specifically, the activity-based schedule diary is applied for estimating activity patterns based on the function of activity and trip components. The schedule diary involves demographic, socio-economic, household, activity and travel information. In Flanders, OVG (Onderzoek Verplaatsings Gedrag Vlaanderen) travel survey was conducted to collect such diary data from 8,800 persons who were randomly selected from national register.

Second, the synthetic population data are used for detailed information on household and individual demographics and characteristics in FEATHERS. As some attributes are missing in census population data due to the privacy protection, and a synthetic population needs to be generated as a substituting resource to census data. An IPF (iterative proportional fitting) algorithm is used to generate synthetic population by replicating sample until obtaining the desired number of population.

Finally, environment data consists of zoning system and transportation system. Regarding location data, there is a spatial hierarchy in a zoning system; SUPERZONE, ZONE and SUBZONE. SUPERZONE is the highest spatial level that is compatible with the Municipality. ZONE is the second highest level with a higher resolution and compatible with administrative units. SUBZONE consists of virtual areas that were constructed based on homogeneous characteristics with a highest resolution. There are 327 SUPERZONEs, 1145 ZONEs and 2386 SUBZONEs in Flanders of Belgium. Transportation system is represented by a level of service (LOS) matrices by a transport mode containing information about travel distance, travel time, egress and access time. In the FEATH-

ERS framework, transport modes consider car driver and car passenger, public mode, and slow mode (walking and bicycle).

Figure 5 illustrates a zoning system in Flanders of Belgium. Regarding the output, FEATHERS provides users with daily activity-travel diaries across 7 days of a week. In addition to this day-dependency of the schedules, it also supplies travel information categorized by hourly trip start time and transport mode. When combining trip time and transport mode, the activity-travel diary can be transformed to OD trip matrices that will serve as input for a traffic assignment mode. The OD matrices generated by FEATHERS represent Flemish network links.

ISSEUS IN SEOUL ABM

There are a number of issues in the FEATHERS application for the study area in Korea. This section addresses the issues and suggests new solutions with an example. Those issues include zoning system, transport system, life-style and trip-based survey. To this end, we would first like to describe the data we used for the example in this chapter. We used diary data from household activity-travel survey in 2010 and population data including census summary table from Statistics Korea, for training the schedule module and generating synthetic population, respectively. In addition, environment information about transport network (from Korea Transport Institute), land-use (from the local government) and zoning system were also used for the FEATHERS application. Figure 6 shows the SMA with its zoning system.

Zoning System

We first discuss a zoning system in the FEATHERS implementation. The Flemish zoning system consists of three levels of spatial hierarchy: SUPERZONE, ZONE and SUBZONE. The Korean zoning system consists of three groups of admin-

Figure 5. Zoning system in Flanders, Belgium

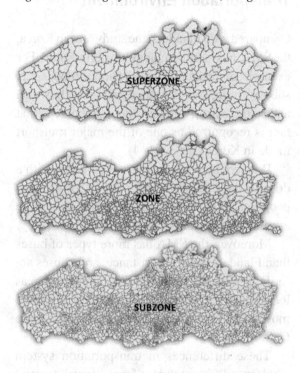

Figure 6. Study area with zoning system

istrative units; i) megalopolis and Province (Do), ii) Si, Gun and Gu, and iii) Eup, Myeon and Dong. The first group (megalopolis and Do) is the biggest administrative unit with a lowest resolution in Korea. The second group (Si, Gun and Gu) is the administrative unit of local governments. The last group (Eup, Myeon and Dong) is the smallest administrative unit with the highest resolution. The original zoning system of Korea is not feasible for the FEATHERS implementation because there are only three regions (Seoul, Incheon and Gyeonggi-Do) in the SUPERZONE level, which is too few to be considered as the SUPERZONE level given the FEATHERS framework. To solve this problem, we decided to assign the second group to the SUPERZONE level, TAZ as the ZONE level and the last group to the SUBZONE. TAZ that contains several homogeneous areas in terms of transportation is normally used in the conventional transportation model. Figure 6 shows the zoning

system of Korea. Table 2 accounts for the zoning systems of Korea and Flanders.

Second, there are other issues on the zoning system: temporal inconsistency and two co-existing different spatial units in Korea. Since 1990s, administrative units in Korea have changed several times. For example, they were raised to the upper level by combining other regions, or merged into another big region. Hence, it is difficult to keep the consistency of the zoning system between base year when data were generated and target year when travel demand is to be predicted. The temporal consistency should be maintained in the zoning system for the FEATHERS framework. If it is not possible to do so for some reasons, the zoning system should be manually matched by combining or separating the mismatching units. Table 3 illustrates an example of the temporal inconsistency in the administrative units of Korea.

Third, Korea has two administrative unit systems, namely legal and administrative districts. Legal district is in most cases the same with administrative district. But in some cases, two legal districts are merged to one administrative district to save the cost for maintaining the offices. In some other cases, one legal district is divided into several administrative districts to properly support large population. These changes cause inconsistency and complicate the data pre-processing. Indeed, respondents often confused administrative districts with legal districts. The legal district not only has a different location ID but also different spatial boundary from administrative districts in many cases. We had to translate the location ID of a legal district into that of the administrative district to solve this problem.

Table 2. Zoning system in SMA and Flanders

Level	Superzone	Zone	Subzone
SMA (Total)	Gu (79)	TAZ (350)	Dong (1,107)
Flanders (Total)	Municipality (327)	Administrative units (1,145)	Homogeneous area (2,386)

Transportation Environment

Compared with Flanders, the study area in Korea, the SMA, has more complex transport systems. For example, more than six types of public modes, e.g. subway, train, (regular, areal and local) bus, taxi and so on, exist. An interesting point here is that taxi is recognized as one of the major transport mode in Korea (see Table 4).

Due to a fact that taxi serves 24 hours with a door-to-door service and privacy protection, people use taxi for a back-home trip late in the evening and business (see Table 5).

Moreover, the SMA has more types of buses than Flanders have. For instance, areal buses are for long-trips with relatively high fares, whereas local buses are for short-trips with low fares and mostly link between subway stations (see Table 6)

These differences in transportation system result in a different output from a travel demand research because some constraints are dependent on available transport modes at a certain moment. The FEATHERS framework assumes one type of public transport mode because there is no big difference in trip components, e.g. travel time and cost. This is however not the case in Korea because travel time and distance (even fare) are different between types of bus, for example. Configuration of particular transport system therefore needs caution when FEATHERS framework is implemented for a different transport system.

The last and biggest issue is a single-mode concept in the FETHERS framework that does not handle more than one trip chains, for example a bus-to-subway trip. Since the current model framework takes a transport mode for the longest journey, rest of the transport modes with short travel time are ignored in the model. There is a preliminary solution to this problem when one journey consists of one big trip and several small trips. We assume in such cases that there is an additional journey based on information about a

Table 3. Inconsistency in administrative units in SMA

Region	2005 yr		Type	2006 yr		Solution
	Name	Code		Name	Code	
Seoul	Ahyeon-3 dong	1114053	merge	Ahyeon-2 dong	1114052	remove
	Dohwa-2 dong	1114058	merge	Dohwa-dong	1114057	remove
	Nogosan-dong	1114062	merge	Daeheung-dong	1114060	remove
	Changjeon-dong	1114064	merge	Seogang-*dong*	1114076	revise
	Sangsu-dong	1114065	merge	Seogang-*dong*	1114076	remove
Incheon	Dongchun -2 dong	2304058	split	songdo-dong	2304061	add
	Samsan- dong	2306065	split	Samsan-1 dong	2306072	revise
			split	Samsan-2 dong	2306073	add
	Geomdan-1 dong	2308068	split	Geomdan-4 dong	2308071	add
Gyeonggi-do	Taean-eup	3124011	split	Jinan-dong	3124052	revise
			split	Byeongjeom-1 dong	3124053	add
			split	Byeongjeom-2 dong	3124054	add
			split	Banwol-dong	3124055	add
			split	Gibae-*dong*	3124056	add
			split	Hwasan-dong	3124057	add

Table 4. Taxi usage in SMA

Region	Average Trip Number (Number/Day)	Average Passenger (Person/Trip)	Average Trip Duration (Duration/Trip)
Seoul	24.4	1.3	14.1
Incheon	36.9	1.3	9.7
Gyeonggi-do	27.5	1.5	9.4

Table 5. Percentage of trip purpose using taxi in each region

Region	Back Home	Work	School	Private Institute	Business	Back to Work	Shopping	Leisure	Others
Seoul	37.4%	13.2%	1.8%	1.0%	21.5%	2.5%	3.9%	8.8%	9.9%
Incheon	37.3%	13.0%	2.4%	0.7%	15.9%	1.7%	5.0%	10.0%	14.0%
Gyeonggi	36.9%	11.3%	2.2%	1.0%	18.2%	2.4%	4.7%	8.4%	14.9%

Table 6. Percentage of trip mode in each time period

Hour	Private	Bus					Subway/ Train	Taxi	Others
		Regular	Areal	Local	Others	Total			
0:00-4:00	64.6%	2.1%	0.3%	0.5%	2.3%	5.2%	0.9%	21.6%	7.7%
4:00-7:00	47.0%	15.0%	1.7%	2.3%	3.2%	22.2%	8.9%	8.1%	13.8%
7:00-9:00	37.4%	22.1%	2.5%	4.5%	5.4%	34.5%	17.8%	3.8%	6.5%
9:00-11:00	37.9%	20.0%	2.7%	4.5%	2.9%	30.1%	15.6%	7.0%	9.4%
11:00-13:00	38.8%	19.6%	2.4%	4.4%	2.1%	28.5%	13.0%	9.2%	10.5%
13:00-18:00	36.8%	20.9%	2.4%	4.5%	7.1%	34.9%	13.1%	8.0%	7.2%
18:00-20:00	38.6%	19.7%	2.8%	3.6%	5.7%	31.8%	19.7%	4.4%	5.5%
20:00-22:00	40.7%	19.5%	2.9%	3.4%	5.5%	31.3%	16.2%	6.6%	5.2%
22:00-24:00	39.5%	18.2%	2.0%	3.3%	6.1%	29.6%	12.0%	14.6%	4.3%
Total	39.1%	19.8%	2.5%	4.0%	5.1%	31.4%	15.0%	7.2%	7.3%

trip location, e.g. departure and destination. Table 7 shows percentages of single mode and multi mode for communing per day.

Cultural Difference

As we can easily expect, Korean culture is much different with Flemish one. The dissimilarity in culture accounts for the difference in activity and travel patterns in individual daily schedule because the details of activity and travel are strongly dependent on the life-style. For example, a lot of employees in Korea work until evening time, so that the work activity occupies a big proportion of daily activities, and only few activities are executed after working, comparing with Flanders. Hence, trip participation shows higher frequency in the evening hours, from 18:00 to 20:00 (see Table 8).

There are therefore often more than two work episodes a day in Korea. Since only two work episodes are considered in the schedule module of FEATHERS, more than two work episodes are not feasible to handle. We had either to adapt a new schedule module that can handle the third work episodes, or to assume the third work episode as another flexible activity. Following the second solution, the FEATHERS framework becomes able to handle the third work episode, which is normally flexible in a time constraint, without any effort for developing a new module.

There is no clear difference in a daily shopping and non-daily shopping in Korea. The household travel survey form does not have such activity. On the contrary, those are differently defined in the schedule data for the FEATHERS framework. A daily shopping activity is rather more regular activity in terms of activity time and location,

Table 7. Single-mode and multi-mode (only for commute trips)

Region	Frequency (per day)			Percentage (per day)		
	Single-Mode	Multi-Mode	Total	Single-Mode	Multi-Mode	Total
Seoul	3,088,295	678,355	3,766,650	82%	18%	100%
Incheon	870,456	110,811	981,267	89%	11%	100%
Gyeonngi-do	3,810,343	445,315	4,255,658	90%	10%	100%

Table 8. Percentage of trips in each time period

Hour	0:00-4:00	4:00-7:00	7:00-9:00	9:00-11:00	11:00-13:00	13:00-18:00	18:00-20:00	20:00-22:00	22:00-24:00
(%)	2.0%	2.7%	21.8%	11.4%	8.2%	27.7%	14.1%	7.5%	4.5%

whereas a non-daily shopping is rather irregular and flexible in time and location. As for the issue on the shopping activity, we can manually divide the shopping activity in half. This manipulation can provide the model framework with both daily shopping and non-daily shopping activities, and it is also not harmful because two shopping activities are dissolved by the little difference in the schedule module that defines activity-travel patterns.

In addition to the above two cases concerned with the life-style, there also exist differences in socio-demographic characteristics, e.g. income level and age class. Korean household travel survey recognizes 10 income categories and continuous scale of age. Flanders has 4 income categories and 5 age categories. This difference in the categories reflects difference in social settings. More categories of income in Korea may represent more diversity in socio-economic class, and more specifying age class in Flanders likely indicates clear difference between age classes in their activity-travel patterns.

Trip-Based Survey

This is the last and most important issue in not only the FEATHERS framework, but also any other activity-based transport demand models. It is the activity-travel diary data that is used for training the decision tree in the schedule module. MTA of the SMA has conducted household travel survey every four years, which is not activity-based. More specifically, the main information of the survey includes when, what transport mode and how long people travel, but does not include activity details in the sense that activity information is only involved as the trip purpose. Some activi-

ties cannot be recorded by the survey because no activity without a trip can be identified. There is no record of activity after a back-home trip, and also of flexible activities during lunch time between the first and the second work episodes, involving no trips in-between. The prediction of trips derived from activity participations is likely affected by this.

CONCLUSION

The FSM has been typically used for traffic demand research in Korea because most data are based on zoning system, which is administrative district in Korea. Nevertheless, the FSM is not an appropriate approach to the evaluation of the current transport policy focusing on traffic demand control, optimal operation and micro transport strategy, because of its inability of analysis of disaggregate and micro transport demand. This chapter aims at introducing the Seoul ABM project as an alternative approach, which has a goal of the FEATHERS implementation for the study area, with a focus on issues of and solutions to the data processing for the FEATHERS framework. According to the related research in Korea, there has no experience of implementation of the ABM framework until Park, et al. (2012) due to several difficulties in the input data processing, for example zoning system, different transportation system, cultural difference and trip-based survey. As a future research, we will develop a new schedule module for considering activity-travel behavior in Korea different from that in Flanders. We will also assess transport demands forecasted by the FEATHERS framework by comparing with the observed data in the SMA. We would then identify whether the FEATHERS framework is applicable for evaluation of the sensitivity to the transport policy and socio-demographic trend in Korea.

ACKNOWLEDGMENT

This paper was supported by the National Research Foundation of Korea (NRF) grant funded by the Korea government (MSIP) (NRF-2010-0029444).

REFERENCES

Bowman, J. L., & Ben-Akiva, M. E. (1996). *Activity based travel forecasting*. Paper presented at Activity-Based Travel Forecasting Conference. New Orleans, LA.

Chapin, F. S. (1974). *Human activity patterns in the city: Things people do in time and in space*. New York, NY: Wiley..

Eom, J. K. (2007). Introducing a spatial-temporal activity-based approach for estimating travel demand at KTX stations. In *Proceedings of the 2007 Autumn Conference of Korean Society for Railway*, (pp. 730-739). IEEE.

Hägerstraand, T. (1970). What about people in regional science? *Papers in Regional Science, 24*, 7–24. doi:10.1111/j.1435-5597.1970.tb01464.x.

Joh, C. H., Kim, C. S., & Song, H. M. (2008). An activity-based analysis of heavy-vehicle trip chains. *Journal of the Economic Geographical Society of Korea, 11*(2), 192–202.

Jovicic, G. (2001). *Activity-based travel demand modeling-A literature study*. Copenhagen: Denmark's Transport Forskning & The Danish Transport Research Institute..

Kim, C. S., Cheon, S. H., & Hwang, S. Y. (2012). *A decade of change in Korean travel patterns and policy implications*. Seoul, Korea: The Korea Transport Institute..

Kim, T. J. (2012). *Application of activity-based transport simulation model to the gangnam-gu area*. (Unpublished Master thesis). University of Seoul, Seoul, Korea.

Kochan, B. (2012). *Application of an activity-based transportation model for Flanders: Activity-based models and transportation demand management policies. LAP LAMBERT*. Academic Publishing..

Korea Development Institute. (2008). *A study on general guidelines for pre-feasibility study* (5th ed.). Seoul: Author..

Lee, W. D., Cho, S. J., Bellemans, T., Janssens, D., Wets, G., Choi, K. C., & Joh, C. H. (2012). Seoul activity-based model: An application of feathers solutions to Seoul metropolitan area. *Procedia Computer Science, 10*, 840–845. doi:10.1016/j.procs.2012.06.109.

Lee, W. D., Kim, C. S., Choi, K. C., Choi, J. M., Joh, C. H., Rasouli, S., & Timmermans, H. J. P. (2012). *Analyzing changes in activity-travel behavior in time and space using household travel surveys in Seoul metropolitan area over 10 years*. Paper presented at the Workshop on Transportgraphy: Advances in Spatial-Temporal Transport Analysis. Hong Kong, China.

Lim, Y. T., Kang, M. G., & Lee, C. H. (2008). Impacts of number of O/D zone and network aggregation level in transportation demand forecast. *Journal of Korean Society of Transportation, 26*(2), 147–156.

McNally, M. G. (2000). The four step model. In *Handbook of Transport Modeling* (pp. 35–52). London: Elsevier Science Ltd.

Metropolitan Transport Association. (2007). *Seoul metropolitan area household travel survey (2006)*. Seoul: Author..

Metropolitan Transport Association. (2012). *National household travel survey (2010)*. Seoul: Author..

Noh, S. H., & Joh, C. H. (2011). Change in travel behavior of the elderly: An analysis of household travel survey data sets in Seoul metropolitan area. *Journal of the Korean Geographical Society*, *46*(6), 781–796.

OECD. (2012). *OECD fact book 2011-2012: Economic, environmental and social statistics*. Paris: OECD Publishing..

Park, J. Y., Lee, J. S., Kim, Y. H., & Yu, J. B. (2012). *Forecasting individual travel behavior based on activity-based approach*. Seoul: The Korea Transport Institute..

Seo, S. U., Jung, J. H., & Kim, S. K. (2006). Analysis of the elderly travel characteristics and travel behavior with daily activity schedules: The case of Seoul, Korea. *Journal of Korean Society of Transportation*, *24*(5), 89–108.

ADDITIONAL READING

Arentze, T. A., Hofman, F., & Timmermans, H. J. P. (2001). Deriving rules from activity diary data: A learning algorithm and results of computer experiments. *Journal of Geographical Systems*, *3*(4), 325–346. doi:10.1007/s101090100069.

Arentze, T. A., & Timmermans, H. J. P. (2000). *ALBATROSS: A Learning-Based Transportation Oriented Simulation System*. The Hague: European Institute of Retailing and Services Studies..

Janssens, D., Wets, G., Brijs, T., Vanhoof, K., Arentze, T. A., & Timmermans, H. J. P. (2006). Integrating Bayesian networks and decision trees in a sequential rule-based transportation model. *European Journal of Operational Research*, *175*(1), 16–34. doi:10.1016/j.ejor.2005.03.022.

Joh, C. H., Arentze, T. A., & Timmermans, H. J. P. (2004). Activity-travel scheduling and rescheduling decision processes: empirical estimation of Aurora model. *Transportation Research Record*, *1898*, 10–18. doi:10.3141/1898-02.

Ortuzar, J. D., & Willumsen, L. G. (2011). *Modeling Transport* (4th ed.). John Wiley & Sons Ltd. doi:10.1002/9781119993308.

Timmermans, H. J. P., Arentze, T. A., & Joh, C. H. (2002). Analysing space-time behaviour: New approaches to old problems. *Progress in Human Geography*, *26*, 175–190. doi:10.1191/0309132502ph363ra.

Chapter 5
The Application of an Integrated Behavioral Activity–Travel Simulation Model for Pricing Policy Analysis

Karthik C. Konduri
University of Connecticut, USA

Ram M. Pendyala
Arizona State University, USA

Daehyun You
Arizona State University, USA

Yi-Chang Chiu
The University of Arizona, USA

Mark Hickman
University of Queensland, Australia

Hyunsoo Noh
University of Arizona, USA

Paul Waddell
University of California – Berkeley, USA

Liming Wang
Portland State University, USA

Brian Gardner
U.S. Department of Transportation, USA

ABSTRACT

This chapter demonstrates the feasibility of applying an integrated microsimulation model of activity-travel demand and dynamic traffic assignment for analyzing the impact of pricing policies on traveler activity-travel choices. The model system is based on a dynamic integration framework wherein the activity-travel simulator and the dynamic traffic assignment model communicate with one another along the continuous time axis so that trips are routed and simulated on the network as and when they are generated. This framework is applied to the analysis of a system-wide pricing policy for a small case study site to demonstrate how the model responds to various levels of pricing. Case study results show that trip lengths, travel time expenditures, and vehicle miles of travel are affected to a greater degree than activity-trip rates and activity durations as a result of pricing policies. Measures of change output by the model are found to be consistent with elasticity estimates reported in the literature.

DOI: 10.4018/978-1-4666-4920-0.ch005

INTRODUCTION

In an era of rising concerns about traffic congestion, energy sustainability, greenhouse gas emissions that potentially contribute to global climate change, and limited financial resources, many jurisdictions around the world are contemplating the implementation of pricing policies and strategies to address the growing demands for transport infrastructure. Some of the pricing policies that are being considered include system-wide mileage based fees that may vary by time of day and location, gas taxes, auto ownership/registration fees, parking pricing, corridor-based tolls that may vary by time of day and vehicle occupancy, high-occupancy toll (HOT) lanes, variable pricing that is demand responsive and ensures free flow conditions at all times, and area- or cordon-based pricing limited to certain subareas such as a central business district. There is considerable interest in the implementation of pricing policies for two reasons; first, pricing policies are viewed as a mechanism to manage travel demand and better distribute the demand for travel over time and space thus easing congestion on the network, and second, pricing policies are viewed as revenue generation mechanisms to raise much needed resources to invest in the transport infrastructure (e.g., Hensher and Puckett, 2007; Kockelman and Kalmanje, 2005).

The widespread interest in pricing policies has resulted in considerable attention being directed to modeling the impact of pricing policies on travel demand and network dynamics in a behaviorally realistic way. Several studies have been undertaken in the recent past with a view to developing frameworks and operational model systems capable of accurately forecasting the impacts of pricing strategies (e.g., Zhang, Mahmassani, & Vovsha, 2011). Challenges in accurately reflecting the impacts of pricing strategies on travel demand stem from the complex interactions and adjustments involved in the formation and execution of activity-travel schedules in time-sensitive networks. A pricing policy may impact the generation of activities, the manner in which activities (and therefore, trips) are chained together, destination choice, mode choice, time of day choice, route choice, task allocation among household members, and solo and joint activity-travel engagement by household members. All of these activity-travel choices are intertwined in complex ways that are not yet completely understood. As a result, modeling changes in activity-travel behavior in response to a pricing policy, while accounting for the myriad time-space interactions and constraints that shape activity-travel patterns, remains a complex and challenging task (Pendyala, 2005). Although emerging tour-based models (Vovsha and Bradley, 2006) attempt to reflect the impacts of pricing policies by carrying logsum terms (representing accessibility measures) through a series of nests in a nested logit model system, such models often lack the treatment of time as a continuous entity which is critical to accurately reflecting changes in activity-travel demand in the presence of time-space prism constraints. Moreover, there has been limited progress thus far in the integration of continuous-time activity-travel behavior models with dynamic network models, which is needed to fully encapsulate the range of activity-travel modifications that a pricing policy may bring about. Focusing the modeling effort largely on the demand side or the network side, without a tight coupling between the two enterprises, raises the risk of not being able to adequately capture travel behavior impacts in a holistic fashion.

With a view to contributing towards modeling pricing in the planning process, this chapter presents an integrated modeling framework of demand and supply that is enhanced to reflect the impacts of pricing policies on activity-travel behavior and network dynamics in a prism-constrained behavioral paradigm. The enhancements to the modeling framework are intended to help make an integrated demand-supply model responsive to pricing policies even if some or all of the individual choice models that comprise the demand model do not include price or cost as explanatory variables. Although the framework and the extensions to it can be applied in the context of any type of pricing policy, the application in this chapter focuses on a system-wide pricing strategy such as a mileage based fee, VMT (vehicle miles traveled) tax, or enhanced fuel tax. The chapter includes discussions on how the framework can be easily applied in the context of parking pricing strategies, subarea/cordon pricing, or corridor-based tolling or pricing strategies – some or all of which may vary by time of day.

The remainder of this chapter is organized as follows. The next section presents a description of the integrated modeling framework. The third section describes how the integrated modeling framework has been extended to be sensitive to pricing policies and reflect changes in activity-travel behavior while accounting for network dynamics. The fourth section describes the case study application scenario. The fifth section presents results from the case study application. The sixth and final section offers concluding thoughts and directions for future developments.

INTEGRATED DEMAND-SUPPLY MODELING FRAMEWORK

The development of integrated models of travel demand and network supply has been a topic of much interest in the profession (Timmermans, 2003; Hatzopoulou, Hao, & Miller, 2011; Balmer, Axhausen, & Nagel, 2006; Zhang et al., 2011). With advances in the development and implementation of microsimulation-based activity-travel demand models on the one hand, and dynamic traffic assignment and simulation models on the other, considerable interest has emerged in integrating these model systems with a view to capture behavioral dynamics in time-dependent networks at the level of the individual traveler (Rossi, 2010; Castiglione et al., 2012). A number of implementations have tied activity-based travel

microsimulation models with dynamic traffic assignment models in a sequential paradigm (e.g., Lin, Eluru, Waller, & Bhat, 2008; Kitamura, Kikuchi, Fujji, & Yamamoto, 2005). In a sequential linkage, the activity-based travel model and the dynamic traffic assignment model are run separately and linked together through input-output data flows and typical feedback loops (that are similar to those seen in four step travel demand models).

While these frameworks are convenient to implement, they fall short on a couple of counts. First, they do not ensure consistency in the representation of activity-travel patterns that emerge at the end of the simulation. In a dynamic context, activity-travel patterns may be viewed as evolving over the course of a day, subject to a number of time-space and household constraints that individuals encounter. When an individual undertakes a trip, the arrival time at a destination is determined by network conditions prevailing at the time that the trip was undertaken. If an individual is delayed due to congestion on the network, then activity-travel decisions subsequent to the late arrival may be impacted. The individual may choose to curtail the duration of the activity, forego an activity due to time-space prism constraints, alter the destination for a subsequent activity, and reallocate tasks to another household member. Thus, it is important to ensure that arrival times at destinations reflect actual network conditions experienced by the traveler, and activity-travel decisions are sensitive to and consistent with arrival events. For example, the start time of an activity cannot be prior to arrival time at the location where the activity will be pursued. Inconsistencies of this nature are liable to creep into sequential integrated model implementations.

Second, the sequential frameworks do not allow the modeling of the impacts of network disruptions that may occur due to unplanned or planned events. Network disruptions may occur for a short period of the day (say, a crash blocks a lane of traffic for one hour). The impact of such disruptions on activity-travel demand can only be reflected by modeling activity-travel decisions as a function of prevailing network conditions experienced by travelers. Using network skims from a prior iteration of a sequentially integrated model system would provide completely erroneous destination arrival times and provide no indication of the impact of the network disruption on activity-travel characteristics. In order to model the impacts of network disruptions, and the potential benefits of operational congestion mitigation strategies (such as traveler information systems), there needs to be a tighter coupling between the demand and supply model systems wherein the two models constantly communicate with one another and thus inform one another of prevailing conditions at each time step of the simulation.

In view of the limitations of sequential integrated modeling paradigms, Kitamura, Kikuchi, & Pendyala (2008) proposed a dynamic event-based integrated modeling framework that has been recently fully operationalized by Pendyala et al. (2012). The model framework, called Sim-TRAVEL (Simulator of Transport, Routes, Activities, Vehicles, Emissions, and Land), is depicted in Figure 1. Complete details about the modeling framework and operation are provided elsewhere

(Pendyala et al., 2012) and hence only a brief description is provided here.

In this framework, activity-travel demand is modeled along the continuous time axis with each simulation time step one minute in duration. The activity-travel demand model simulates activity-travel choices within each simulation time interval (minute). This involves determining the type of activity (purpose) that a person will pursue, where the person will pursue the activity (destination), the mode of transportation, and the departure time (minute of the day). In any given time interval (minute), only a small fraction of the population of a region will depart on a trip. The activity-based model determines the set of individuals who will embark on a trip in any given time step and the key attributes for the trip. The activity-travel demand model passes this set of trips to the dynamic traffic assignment model, which in turn, routes and simulates the trips on the network. The routing and simulation process is based on prevailing network conditions that exist at the time that the trip is being executed on the network; the arrival time is therefore governed by prevailing network conditions. In each time step (minute), the dynamic traffic assignment model returns to the activity-travel demand

Figure 1. Integrated Demand-Supply Modeling Framework in SimTRAVEL

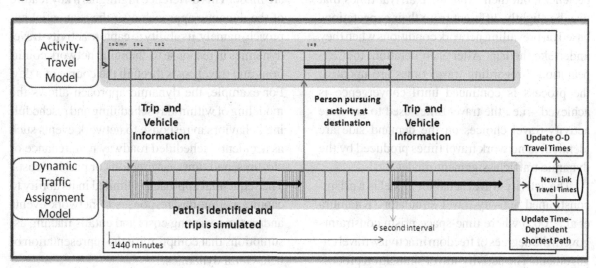

model, the set of trips that have arrived at their intended destination. For all individuals who have arrived at their destination, the activity-travel demand model then simulates subsequent activity-travel choices subject to time-space prism constraints. Thus, in each minute (simulation time step) of the day, the activity-travel demand model passes a set of departing trips to the dynamic traffic assignment model and the dynamic traffic assignment model passes back a set of arriving trips to the demand model. This minute-by-minute communication between the model systems ensures that arrival times are determined based on prevailing network conditions and that activity-travel decisions are based on actual arrival times experienced by travelers. At the end of a 1440 minute simulation, the model system compiles time-dependent origin-destination travel time matrices that will form the basis of activity-travel choices in the subsequent iteration. Thus, activity-travel choices are made based on "expected" travel times (represented by travel times from the previous iteration), while arrival times are determined by actual prevailing network conditions (within the current iteration). In essence, this framework is attempting to replicate the process whereby individuals make activity-travel decisions based on their expectations of network travel times (gathered through past experience), but then experience arrival times that may be slightly different from their expectations based on prevailing network conditions when they undertake the trip. After each iteration, the "expectations" regarding travel times are updated; the process is continued until convergence is achieved – i.e., the travel times used to generate activity-travel choices on the demand side are identical to network travel times produced by the dynamic traffic assignment model.

The activity-travel behavior model is a prism-constrained activity-travel simulator (Kitamura et al., 2005) where time-space prism constraints govern the degrees of freedom in activity-travel engagement. The activity-travel simulation process begins with the generation of time-space prisms

for each individual based on their working status, childcare and chauffeuring responsibilities, and school hours. The time-space prism generation step yields an activity skeleton showing mandatory activity periods that are blocked and open time-space prisms in which activities and travel may be undertaken. Violations of time-space prism constraints are allowed under extreme circumstances (say, a person may be late to work due to unexpected congestion on the network). Participation in activities and the time allocated to activities is directly constrained by available time in the time-space prism. Similarly, destination choice is also constrained by the available action space in the time-space prism. The prism-constrained framework for modeling activity-travel behavior can be leveraged to model the impacts of pricing policies on travel behavior.

It can be seen that the dynamic approach to integration of the activity-travel demand model and the dynamic traffic assignment model constitutes a continuous-time network-sensitive microsimulation framework for simulating the activity-travel engagement behaviors of households and individuals. Unlike the sequential integration approach, the activity-travel patterns that are generated at the end of the dynamic process are emergent in nature and consistent with network conditions that prevail at the time activity-travel decisions are made. This difference highlights a key feature of the dynamic approach over the sequential approach, namely, its ability to capture activity-travel dynamics in response to changing network conditions and travel costs through the course of a day. For example, the dynamic approach allows the modeling of within-day scheduling and rescheduling behaviors in response to network events such as accidents, scheduled roadway maintenance or closures, and time-varying tolls or parking costs. The sequential approach is limited in its ability to capture within day responses to network events and/or time-varying costs and entails making assumptions that compromise the representation of behavioral dynamics.

There are several key considerations in the context of the implementation of a dynamic event-based integrated model system of this nature. These include convergence properties, convergence criteria on the demand and supply side, the adoption of rule-based heuristics to ensure within-person and within-household consistency in activity-travel patterns, and modifications to the framework to simulate the impacts of temporary network disruptions. A detailed discussion of these issues is beyond the scope of this chapter and the reader is referred to Pendyala, Chiu, Hickman, & Waddell (2009) and Pendyala et al. (2012) for a commentary on these issues.

ENHANCEMENT OF MODELING FRAMEWORK TO REFLECT PRICING IMPACTS

As mentioned earlier, there may be instances where activity-travel choice models do not necessarily include price or cost as an explanatory variable. While tour-based nested logit models purport to reflect pricing effects through the use of logsum terms, they do not completely reflect the evolutionary process by which activity-travel patterns emerge in response to network conditions within a time-space prism constrained paradigm. In addition, they do not explicitly model activity durations (time use patterns), which is desirable from the standpoint of modeling activity-travel demand in response to changing network conditions along the continuous time axis. While activity-travel choice models often include travel time as an explanatory variable, there may be situations where cost is not included as an explicit explanatory variable. In order to accommodate for such instances, and reflect the impact of pricing on activity generation, the modeling framework described in the previous section is enhanced as described below.

In the activity-travel simulation framework, activities are generated (i.e., a discretionary activity is undertaken) if the individual has time available in the time-space prism prior to the

onset of the next constraint (represented by a fixed activity such as work). In addition, the set of destinations that a person can visit is limited by the time available in the prism. For example, say a person has completed an activity at 8:00 AM, and the next prism constraint (such as beginning time of work) is at 9:00 AM. At the end of the activity (at 8:00 AM), the person has one hour available in the prism. If the travel time from the current location to the next fixed activity location is less than one hour, then the person presumably has time to pursue another activity prior to the next fixed activity. The activity type choice model in the simulator generates an activity (of a certain purpose). Then, the simulator scans all possible destinations where the activity may be pursued subject to the constraint that the individual must be able to reach the next fixed activity at the appointed time. Any destination that does not satisfy this condition is not included in the choice set. If the time-space prism expands (say, due to an improvement in level of service), then new activities may be generated and/or a larger destination choice set becomes available because of the expanded action space. If the time-space prism contracts (say, due to a deterioration in level of service), then the time available in the open prism may not be sufficient to pursue additional activities (thus resulting in suppression of trips) and/or the destination choice set shrinks due to a contracted action space.

In the modified SimTRAVEL framework, the travel time measure that is used to determine if sufficient time is available in the prism to pursue an additional activity (prior to the onset of the next fixed activity), and generate the feasible destination choice set, is modified to represent a generalized travel time measure that includes the time equivalent of cost. This generalized travel time measure is also used to simulate the actual destination chosen for an activity. Thus, on the demand side, any pricing policy can be converted to a time equivalent (based on a value of time) to construct a generalized travel time variable that influences activity-travel choices. On the network side, however, the actual network travel times are used to simulate destination arrival times with a view to accurately reflecting vehicular movements on the network. However, changes in activity generation and destination choice will alter vehicular flows on the network thus resulting in changes in network conditions relative to a situation where there is no pricing policy.

For purposes of constructing the generalized travel time measure, every individual (adult) within a household is assumed to share the same value of time, reflecting that income is more of a household-level characteristic than a person-level characteristic. As no mode choice model has been implemented in the current version of Sim-TRAVEL (it is a highway-only implementation without transit modes), a value of time could not be derived from a mode choice model. Therefore, values of time were derived based on household income. This is a simplification adopted in this application for demonstration purposes; in real applications, values of time may be derived from a mode choice model or from a value of time distribution furnished by an econometric model that accounts for individual heterogeneity (observed and unobserved). An approximate household wage rate, ω_h, is calculated for each household h by converting annual household income to a value in units of dollars per minute. To do this, it is assumed that there are 250 working days in a year and six working hours per day (to account for full time and part time workers). Thus,

$$\omega_h \ (\$ \ / \ min) = Annual \ Income_h \ (\$) \times \frac{1}{250 \ (days)} \times \frac{1}{6 \ (hr \ / \ day)} \times \frac{1}{60 \ (min \ / \ hr)}$$

$$(1)$$

The value of time is treated as a fraction of the wage rate; this fraction is a parameter that is user defined and can be varied to examine the sensitivity of the model results to assumptions regarding the value of time in relation to the wage rate. For this particular study, the value of time is assumed to be one-third of the wage rate if there is at least one worker in the household, and assumed to be

one-half of the wage rate if there is no worker in the household. The value of time is divided by the number of workers (or number of adults, if there is no worker in the household) to obtain an individual (person-level) value of time in dollars per minute. Thus, the value of time, τ_i^h, for an individual i in a household h with n_w^h ($n_w^h > 0$) workers is:

$$\tau_i^h \ (\$ \ / \ min) = \frac{1}{3} \times \omega_h \times \frac{1}{n_w^h} \qquad (2)$$

The value of time, τ_i^h, for an individual i in a household h with no workers ($n_w^h = 0$) and n_a^h ($n_a^h > 0$) adults is:

$$\tau_i^h \ (\$ \ / \ min) = \frac{1}{2} \times \omega_h \times \frac{1}{n_a^h} \qquad (3)$$

Suppose a pricing policy equivalent to a fee of q dollars per mile of travel is levied. Then, the value of time can be used to derive a travel time equivalent of the additional cost of driving per mile of travel. This time equivalent of cost for an individual i in a household h, ν_i^h, may be derived as:

$$\nu_i^h \ (min \ / \ mile) = \frac{1}{\tau_i^h \ (\$ \ / \ min)} \times q \ (\$ \ / \ mile)$$

$$(4)$$

The generalized travel time for any origin-destination pair, γ_i^h, may then be computed as a sum of the actual travel time between the origin-destination pair, t, and the time equivalent of the additional cost (price) of traveling between the origin-destination pair of interest (which varies for each person). Thus, for an origin-destination pair separated by a distance, δ:

$$\gamma_i^h \ (min) = t \ (min) + \nu_i^h \ (min \ / \ mile) \times \delta \ (mile)$$

$$(5)$$

In the enhanced SimTRAVEL framework, this generalized travel time measure is used to determine remaining time in the prism, in constructing the feasible destination choice set (as generalized travel time is greater than travel time, the action space – and consequently, the destination choice set will shrink), and in choosing the destination for an activity. The use of the generalized travel time in determining remaining time available in the prism (prior to the onset of the next activity) represents the equivalent of shrinking the time-space prism and hence activity generation will be impacted. At this time, no mode choice model is implemented within SimTRAVEL and hence no modal shifts are reflected in the application.

On the network side, actual network travel times are used to determine traveler arrival time at destinations. If a destination that is substantially closer in distance is chosen (because of the pricing policy), then the arrival time at the destination is likely to be earlier than if the traveler had chosen a farther away destination in the absence of any pricing policy. This is likely to result in a larger amount of residual time being available in the time-space prism; even though generalized travel time is used to determine whether additional activities may be undertaken within available time in the prism, it is possible that the additional time available in the prism (due to early arrival at a closer destination) will result in no appreciable decrease in activity generation (unless the price levied is extremely high).

CASE STUDY DEMONSTRATION

The enhanced SimTRAVEL framework was applied to study the impact of a system-wide pricing policy such as a mileage-based fee or increase in fuel tax. The price is represented in a dollars per mile basis consistent with the enhanced formulation described earlier. The framework can be easily customized to accommodate cordon or corridor based pricing strategies that vary by time of day;

in such applications, the generalized travel time measures will be computed for specific origin-destination pairs that are impacted by the pricing strategy as opposed to all origin-destination pairs (as is the case in the application presented in this chapter). Moreover, since the framework already accommodates time-varying skims (literally on a minute-by-minute basis if desired), the model system is capable of accommodating time-varying or dynamic pricing strategies.

The case study demonstration site is located in the Maricopa County (Greater Phoenix) region in Arizona. Due to data limitations (on the land use front) and in the interest of reducing computational burden, the case study site is limited to a three-city region in the southeast Maricopa County. The three city region encompasses the cities of Chandler, Gilbert, and Queen Creek that together have a population of about 500,000 people residing in 170,000 households. The simulation exercise for this chapter utilizes a five percent sample in the interest of rapid computational time. Due to land use data limitations, all individuals residing in the three city area were assigned (through a series of location choice models in the land use model component) to work and school locations within the three city area. It should be noted that this is not completely realistic as many individuals residing in these cities have work locations beyond the boundaries of the subregion (in cities such as Tempe, Phoenix, Scottsdale, and Mesa). Moreover, the effects of congestion are not fully reflected in these simulation results, partly because only a five percent sample is used for simulation purposes, and more importantly because all of the other background trips (made by people residing in other cities of the Maricopa County region) are not captured in the simulation. There are about 13-14 million trips made by all of the other residents of Maricopa County; in the absence of simulating those trips, congestion effects are not fully reflected in the simulation. However, for purposes of this study, the primary interest lies in demonstrating the ability of the simulation model to reflect the impacts of pricing policies on activity-travel patterns; doing so under free-flow conditions on the network does not necessarily diminish the value of the demonstration.

The model system is run for a variety of scenarios. The base scenario is one where there is no pricing policy. The pricing scenarios include 20 cents per mile, 50 cents per mile, 1 dollar per mile, 2 dollars per mile, and a very high charge of 5 dollars per mile. The intent of the exercise was to see how the model reflected changes in activity-travel patterns in response to a range of pricing levels and whether the estimates of impacts were reasonable given the body of evidence on price elasticities of travel. The study focuses exclusively on adult trips including all trips that adults make for purposes of chauffeuring children. Child trips are simulated, but not considered in this impact assessment because children are not likely to have direct control of their travel choices and are not likely to make decisions regarding willingness to pay for accessing destinations in the event of a pricing policy implementation.

RESULTS OF MODEL APPLICATION

This section presents the results of the model application. Within the scope of this chapter, it would be impossible to furnish comprehensive results on all activity-travel characteristics for a number of demographic segments. As such, only a few illustrative output statistics are reported and discussed in this chapter with a view to demonstrate the types of indicators that the model is reporting at a broad and aggregate level. It should be noted that, even though this chapter is reporting broad aggregate outputs (because those are easy to interpret), the model system is a disaggregate microsimulation based system capable of simulating and reporting changes in travel behavior at the level of the individual traveler. As the simulator was applied in free flow conditions, multiple iterations of the dynamic integrated model did not have to be executed. This in turn helped bring about efficiencies in the model run times.

Table 1 shows the results of the simulation for the entire sample of individuals that was carried through each simulation scenario. There are a total of 24853 people in the simulation, of which 16596 are adults 18 years of age or older. The statistics reported in this table are derived based

Table 1. Trip Length Distribution Under Alternative Pricing Scenarios

Trip Length (miles)	Pricing Scenario (price per mile)					
	Baseline	20 Cents	50 Cents	1 Dollar	2 Dollars	5 Dollars
< 0.5	0.7%	1.1%	1.5%	2.0%	2.7%	4.4%
≥ 0.5 and < 1.0	1.4%	2.3%	3.2%	4.3%	5.9%	9.3%
≥ 1 and < 2	3.3%	5.1%	7.1%	9.3%	12.4%	18.1%
≥ 2 and < 5	16.4%	21.3%	26.3%	31.3%	36.9%	42.7%
≥ 5 and < 10	29.8%	31.3%	31.0%	29.7%	26.3%	18.5%
≥ 10 and < 15	21.0%	18.8%	16.5%	13.3%	9.8%	5.0%
≥ 15	27.5%	20.1%	14.4%	10.1%	5.9%	2.2%
Average Trip Length	*12.0*	*9.9*	*8.4*	*7.1*	*5.8*	*4.0*
Vehicle Miles of Travel (VMT)	*980116*	*815443*	*696745*	*593976*	*477795*	*309201*
Reduction in VMT (relative to baseline)		*-164674*	*-283372*	*-386141*	*-502322*	*-670916*

on activity-travel demand simulated for the entire set of 24853 individuals. This table focuses on trip distance and vehicle miles of travel because those are key measures of travel often targeted by pricing strategies. The statistics reported in the table are consistent with expectations and behaviorally intuitive. In response to the pricing strategy, it is found that the percent of trips less than five miles in length progressively increases as the pricing level increases. Conversely, the percent of trips more than five miles in length progressively decreases as the pricing level increases. This is consistent with the notion that a pricing strategy shrinks the action space and leads to individuals choosing destinations which are closer to their trip origins. The average trip length progressively decreases; the average trip length in the baseline scenario is about 12 miles per trip and there is a continuous decreasing trend until average trip length is just about 4 miles per trip in the very high price scenario (5 dollars per mile). Given that a 10 mile trip would cost 50 dollars in this scenario, it is not unreasonable to expect average trip lengths to be under five miles in this scenario. Even a four-mile trip would cost travelers 20 dollars under this pricing scenario. The reductions in vehicle miles of travel (VMT)

are similarly consistent with other trends seen in the table.

Table 2 presents trip duration distributions under different pricing levels. The results are closely mirror the trends seen in Table 1 and are behaviorally intuitive and consistent with expectations. As the level of pricing increases, individuals are pursuing trips that are shorter in duration. The proportions of trips ten minutes or less in duration are progressively increasing with corresponding reductions in the proportions of trips that are greater than 10 minutes in duration. As expected, trip lengths (seen in Table 1) and trip durations are decreasing at almost the same rate with increasing levels of pricing. For example, in the 5 dollar per mile scenario, trip lengths and trip durations both drop to about one-third of the corresponding values in the no-pricing baseline scenario.

Table 3 presents statistics on a per-capita basis for the non-worker demographic segment. There were a total of 9250 non-workers among the 24853 persons in the simulation. Statistics for these 9250 individuals were compiled and analyzed on a per-capita basis to obtain deeper insights into the person-level changes that may be happening as a result of a pricing policy for a specific demo-

Table 2. Trip Duration Distribution Under Alternative Pricing Scenarios

Trip Duration (minutes)	Pricing Scenario (price per mile)					
	Baseline	20 Cents	50 Cents	1 Dollar	2 Dollars	5 Dollars
< 10	31.7%	41.1%	50.0%	59.2%	69.3%	83.5%
≥ 10 and < 20	36.4%	35.1%	32.5%	28.2%	23.0%	13.5%
≥ 20 and < 30	19.0%	15.5%	12.0%	9.0%	5.9%	2.4%
≥ 30 and < 50	10.8%	7.3%	5.0%	3.3%	1.7%	0.1%
≥ 50 and < 70	1.9%	0.9%	0.5%	0.3%	0.1%	0.0%
≥ 70 and < 100	0.3%	0.1%	0.1%	0.0%	0.0%	0.0%
≥ 100	0.0%	0.0%	0.0%	0.0%	0.0%	0.0%
Average Trip Duration	*17.0*	*14.2*	*12.2*	*10.3*	*8.3*	*5.8*
Vehicle Hours of Travel (VHT)	*23137*	*19455*	*16729*	*14291*	*11505*	*7378*
Reduction in VHT (relative to baseline)		*-3682*	*-6408*	*-8846*	*-11632*	*-15759*

Table 3. Person-level Activity-Travel Attributes for Non-workers

	Pricing Scenario (price per mile)					
	Baseline	20 Cents	50 Cents	1 Dollar	2 Dollars	5 Dollars
Daily Time Allocation Per-capita						
Time Spent on Activities						
Home	1231	1240	1248	1254	1263	1288
Work	0	0	0	0	0	0
School	0	0	0	0	0	0
Maintenance	70	74	75	75	76	69
Discretionary	33	32	32	33	32	30
Pick Up	2	3	5	6	8	7
Drop Off	4	4	4	5	6	6
OH-Other	14	14	14	15	14	13
Total activity duration	*1354*	*1367*	*1378*	*1388*	*1400*	*1413*
Time Spent on Travel						
Home	35	29	24	20	16	10
Work	0	0	0	0	0	0
School	0	0	0	0	0	0
Maintenance	27	24	19	16	12	8
Discretionary	8	6	5	4	3	2
Pick Up	3	3	2	2	2	1
Drop Off	4	3	3	3	2	1
OH-Other	4	3	3	2	2	1
Total travel time expenditure	*82*	*69*	*58*	*47*	*36*	*23*
Trip Rates by Purpose						
Home	1.8	1.8	1.8	1.8	1.7	1.6
Work	0.0	0.0	0.0	0.0	0.0	0.0
School	0.0	0.0	0.0	0.0	0.0	0.0
Maintenance	1.5	1.6	1.6	1.5	1.5	1.4
Discretionary	0.4	0.4	0.4	0.4	0.4	0.4
Pick Up	0.2	0.2	0.2	0.2	0.2	0.1
Drop Off	0.2	0.2	0.2	0.2	0.2	0.1
OH-Other	0.2	0.2	0.2	0.2	0.2	0.2
Total Trip Rate	*4.4*	*4.4*	*4.3*	*4.3*	*4.2*	*3.7*
Total Trips	*40321*	*40383*	*39981*	*39707*	*38656*	*34452*

graphic segment of interest. The non-worker demographic segment was examined because it has more degrees of freedom (not bound by rigid work schedules and locations) and no simplifying assumptions were made with respect to possible activity locations for non-workers (for workers and children, the work and school locations were artificially constrained to fall within the three city simulation area, which is not necessarily realistic of actual location patterns). In the table, it can be seen that travel time expenditures show a steady decrease as the pricing levels increase (middle block of the table). The total daily travel time expenditure decreases from about 82 minutes of travel per day per person to a mere 23 minutes per person per day under the highest pricing scenario of 5 dollars per mile. Decreases in travel time expenditures are found to occur across the board for all trip purposes.

What is interesting to note is that activity durations either increase or hold steady across the pricing scenarios. As expected, in-home stay duration increases as pricing levels increase; in response to pricing policies, people travel less and the extra time is naturally spent at home. However, there is no reduction in out-of-home activity duration or time allocation. All of the reduction in travel time expenditure is allocated to in-home stay, and the out-of-home activity time allocation remains largely untouched. It appears as though people are largely attempting to fulfill their activities (albeit at closer destinations) and spending about the same amount of time at the destinations (activities). This is quite plausible as participating in the activity per se does not entail a price and hence there is no need to adjust the activity duration (outside home). In fact, in the absence of constraints, non-workers could allocate slightly higher durations to activity engagement if they so desired, but the simulation does not indicate that non-workers do that.

An examination of daily trip rates shows modest decreases in trip rates in response to increases in pricing levels. The drop in per-capita trip rate is quite modest even for medium level pricing strategies, and more dramatic drops are seen only at the highest level of pricing fee of 5 dollars per mile. Trip rates largely remain unchanged for small increases in pricing levels, and this explains why activity time expenditures also remain largely unchanged. Given that activity durations remain largely unchanged and trip rates show modest drops, it appears that activity duration per out of home episode creeps up slightly as the

pricing level increases. This phenomenon is a manifestation of the behavioral paradigm that is implemented within the activity-travel simulator. When an individual travels to a destination that is close by (in response to a pricing policy), then he/she will have a longer available time-space prism to pursue the activity. Thus, from a pure activity engagement perspective, the individual experiences more relaxed constraints and is able to spend longer durations at activities without incurring any additional cost or violating time-space prism constraints (even non-workers may have such prism constraints due to child chauffeuring and child care responsibilities). However, satiation effects may limit the amount of time that people will allocate to activity engagement outside the home; as a result the time allocation to activity engagement remains mostly unchanged and the increase in in-home activity time allocation virtually accounts for all of the decrease in travel time expenditure. It appears that people are much more prone to adjusting destination choice as opposed to activity generation (i.e., their activity agenda). These findings are quite consistent with expectations and potentially reflective of the hierarchy of activity-travel choices that people follow; when confronted with a higher cost (say, due to a fuel price hike), people are likely to alter destinations and reduce miles of travel before actually eliminating activities and suppressing activity generation (Ye, Pendyala, & Gottardi, 2007; Saad, 2008).

CONCLUSION AND DISCUSSION

This chapter presents a continuous time integrated modeling methodology that is capable of reflecting the impacts of pricing policies on activity-travel behavior and network dynamics. The integrated microsimulation model system, called SimTRAVEL, involves the tight coupling of a continuous time activity-based travel behavior model with a dynamic traffic assignment and simulation model. The activity-based travel model simulates activity-travel patterns over the course of a day while explicitly recognizing time-space prism constraints and interactions that govern traveler choices. This effort is motivated by the widespread interest in developing microsimulation modeling tools capable of reflecting changes in activity-travel behavior and network performance in response to pricing policies; such modeling tools would not only provide robust forecasts of pricing impacts, but would also allow rigorous social equity and environmental justice analysis as impacts can be assessed for any demographic segment or subpopulation of interest.

In the SimTRAVEL framework, activity-travel decisions are simulated along the continuous time axis in response to actual network conditions experienced by travelers. The activity-travel demand model and the dynamic traffic assignment model communicate with one another on a minute-by-minute basis so that each model knows the prevailing conditions associated with the other. This minute-by-minute communication protocol allows activity-travel choices to be simulated based on actual destination arrival times experienced by travelers; this ensures perfect consistency in the simulated activity-travel patterns and provides the ability to simulate the impacts of a variety of dynamic strategies aimed at enhancing network performance. In order to apply the framework in a pricing policy context, a generalized travel time measure that converts the levied price to equivalent travel time based on an individual's value of time, and adds it to the actual network travel time, is defined. The generalized travel time measure is used in simulating activity-travel choices within the demand model; using this price-enhanced travel time measure means that time available within a time-space prism (to pursue activities) would be diminished, action spaces would contract (thus constraining choice sets), and destinations that are closer in proximity will be chosen. Thus, the framework accounts for impacts of pricing policies on both activity generation and destination choice (besides mode choice, where travel cost routinely appears as an explanatory variable).

On the network side, actual network travel times resulting from the modified activity travel patterns (after the implementation of a pricing policy) are used to determine arrival times at destinations. Thus, the model system captures the dynamics associated with behavioral response to pricing policies on both the demand and supply side while ensuring consistency in the simulation of the activity-travel patterns.

The model is applied to a subregion of the Greater Phoenix metropolitan area in Arizona to demonstrate the feasibility of applying the model and the sensitivity of the model to pricing measures. The results of the model application effort show that vehicle miles of travel decrease substantially as the pricing level increases; however, activity generation (trip frequency) shows more modest decreases particularly at low pricing levels. It is found that vehicle miles of travel and vehicle hours of travel decrease to a greater degree than trip frequencies. It is likely that, in response to a price increase, people adjust their miles of travel (destination choice) wherever possible and avoid eliminating activities from their agenda or schedule. Activities need to be accomplished – the groceries have to be purchased, children have to be chauffeured to and from school, errands must be completed, and social visits and recreational activities are valuable to the well-being of people. Rather than eliminate activities, individuals are likely to try and reduce distances traveled to neutralize the effect of a mileage based pricing strategy. Destinations that are closer in distance are chosen for activities, and errands may be consolidated where possible to bring about efficiencies in travel (thus contributing to a modest decrease in trip frequencies). These findings are consistent with the changes in activity-travel patterns that people said they implemented in response to the high gas prices of the summer of 2008 (Saad, 2008).

The results of the simulation exercise are quite consistent with elasticity estimates (from real-world pricing contexts) reported in the literature. An examination of the elasticity estimate for vehicle miles of travel in this simulation exercise suggests that its value is about -0.14, i.e., a one percent increase in price brings about a 0.14 percent decrease in vehicle miles of travel. This value is remarkably consistent with values reported in the literature where the elasticity of vehicle miles of travel with respect to price is often reported in the range of -0.05 to -0.25 (Burris, 2003; Olszewski and Xie, 2005; Puget Sound Regional Council, 2008; Polak and Meland, 1994; Espey, 1998; Goodwin, Dargay, & Hanley, 2004). Elasticity estimates for trip frequencies (as opposed to vehicle miles of travel or distance traveled) are somewhat harder to glean from the literature. Within this simulation exercise, elasticity estimates are quite non-linear with the elasticity of trip frequency with respect to price dramatically increasing as price increases. At the highest price levels considered in the simulation (2 dollars per mile to 5 dollars per mile), the elasticity of trip frequency with respect to price is -0.07, which is somewhat in line with the value reported in Goodwin et al. (2004) who indicate that a 10 percent increase in fuel price brings about a one percent decrease in volume of traffic (which may or may not correlate exactly with trip frequency). At lower price levels considered in the simulation, the elasticity of trip frequency with respect to price is considerably smaller, and in the absence of reliable elasticity estimates in the literature (for trip frequency), it is difficult to assess the validity of the model predictions. In general, it has been reported that travel demand is quite inelastic to price (Albert and Mahalel, 2006) and the results of the simulation exercise reported in this study are consistent with that observation. Moreover, the findings are consistent with earlier studies which show that travelers first tend to adjust activity-travel attributes that are easier to change (less constrained), such as destination choice, vehicle type choice, or time of day choice, prior to adjusting more constrained attributes such as activity agenda, mode choice, auto ownership, and longer term residential and work location choice (Ye et al., 2007).

The research presented in this chapter demonstrates the applicability of an integrated model of activity-travel demand and dynamic traffic assignment system for analyzing behavioral impacts of a pricing policy. The study effort, however, has several limitations offering a number of fruitful directions for further research. First, the simulation exercise was performed on a sample of the population without fully reflecting the impacts of congestion on activity-travel demand. It would be of value to conduct a full-population simulation to see how the interplay of congestion and pricing effects would impact activity-travel behaviors at the disaggregate and aggregate levels. Second, sensitivity to pricing was introduced by formulating a simplified generalized travel time measure based on the level of pricing and the value of time derived from the household income. This simplification was introduced to account for the absence of cost variables in the model specifications and is not an ideal mechanism to reflect the impacts of pricing signals on behavioral choices. Future research efforts should be aimed at implementing rigorous methodologies founded on microeconomic principles to reflect behavioral impacts of pricing. Third, the pricing policy modeled in this research is a system-wide static pricing scenario primarily affecting the planning of activities and trips. However, the true value of the dynamic approach to demand-supply model integration may be revealed in the context of dynamic time-varying pricing policy scenarios. The key feature of the dynamic approach utilized in the research is the ability to capture within day activity-travel dynamics in response to changing network conditions and travel costs. Future research efforts should therefore extend the current study to consider and model the impact of dynamic pricing policies on the full range of activity-travel behaviors.

ACKNOWLEDGMENT

The authors gratefully acknowledge the support of the Federal Highway Administration (FHWA) Exploratory Advanced Research Program (EARP) whose funding under contract DTFH61-08-C-00010 made this research possible. Thanks are also due to two anonymous referees who provided valuable review comments. The authors are, however, solely responsible for any errors and omissions.

REFERENCES

Albert, G., & Mahalel, D. (2006). Congestion tolls and parking fees: A comparison of the potential effect on travel behavior. *Transport Policy*, *13*(6), 496–502. doi:10.1016/j.tranpol.2006.05.007.

Balmer, M., Axhausen, K. W., & Nagel, K. (2006). An agent-based demand-modeling framework for large-scale microsimulations. *Transportation Research Record: Journal of the Transportation Research Board*, *1985*, 125–134. doi:10.3141/1985-14.

Burris, M. W. (2003). Application of variable tolls on congested toll road. *Journal of Transportation Engineering*, *129*(4), 354–361. doi:10.1061/(ASCE)0733-947X(2003)129:4(354).

Castiglione, J., Grady, B., Lawe, S., Roden, D., Patnam, K., Bradley, M., & Bowman, J. (2012, May). *Sensitivity testing of the SHRP2 C10A DaySim-TRANSIMS model system in Jacksonville, Florida*. Paper presented at the 4th TRB Conference on Innovations in Travel Modeling. Tampa, FL.

Espey, M. (1998). Gasoline demand revisited: An international meta-analysis of elasticities. *Energy Economics*, *20*(3), 273–295. doi:10.1016/S0140-9883(97)00013-3.

Goodwin, P., Dargay, J., & Hanley, M. (2004). Elasticities of road traffic and fuel consumption with respect to price and income: A review. *Transport Reviews*, *24*(3), 275–292. doi:10.1080/0144164042000181725.

Hatzopoulou, M., Hao, J. Y., & Miller, E. J. (2011). Simulating the impacts of household travel on greenhouse gas emissions, urban air quality, and population exposure. *Transportation*, *38*(6), 871–887. doi:10.1007/s11116-011-9362-9.

Hensher, D. A., & Puckett, S. M. (2007). Congestion and variable user charging as an effective travel demand management instrument. *Transportation Research Part A, Policy and Practice*, *41*(7), 615–626. doi:10.1016/j.tra.2006.07.002.

Kitamura, R., Kikuchi, A., Fujii, S., & Yamamoto, T. (2005). An overview of PCATS/DEBNetS micro-simulation system: Its development, extension, and application to demand forecasting. In R. Kitamura, & M. Kuwahara (Eds.), *Simulation Approaches in Transportation Analysis: Recent Advances and Challenges* (pp. 371–399). New York: Springer. doi:10.1007/0-387-24109-4_14.

Kitamura, R., Kikuchi, A., & Pendyala, R. M. (2008). *Integrated, dynamic activity-network simulator: Current state and future directions of PCATS-DEBNetS*. Paper presented at the 2nd TRB Conference on Innovations in Travel Modeling. Portland, OR.

Kockelman, K. M., & Kalmanje, S. (2005). Credit-based congestion pricing: A policy proposal and the public's response. *Transportation Research Part A, Policy and Practice*, *39*(7-9), 671–690. doi:10.1016/j.tra.2005.02.014.

Lin, D.-Y., Eluru, N., Waller, S. T., & Bhat, C. R. (2008). Integration of activity-based modeling and dynamic traffic assignment. *Transportation Research Record: Journal of the Transportation Research Board*, *2076*, 52–61. doi:10.3141/2076-06.

Olszewski, P., & Xie, L. (2005). Modelling the effects of road pricing on traffic in Singapore. *Transportation Research Part A, Policy and Practice*, *39*(7-9), 755–772. doi:10.1016/j.tra.2005.02.015.

Pendyala, R. M. (2005). Modeling pricing in the planning process. In *Proceedings of the Expert Forum on Road Pricing and Travel Demand Modeling*. Washington, DC: Office of the Secretary of Transportation, US Department of Transportation.

Pendyala, R. M., Chiu, Y.-C., Hickman, M., & Waddell, P. (2009). *SimTRAVEL: A simulator of transport, routes, activities, vehicles, emissions, and land*. Washington, DC: Federal Highway Administration, Exploratory Advanced Research Program.

Pendyala, R. M., Konduri, K. C., Chiu, Y.-C., Hickman, M., Noh, H., & Waddell, P. et al. (2012). Integrated land use – Transport model system with dynamic time-dependent activity-travel microsimulation. *Transportation Research Record. Journal of the Transportation Research Board*, *2303*, 19–27. doi:10.3141/2303-03.

Polak, J., & Meland, S. (1994). An assessment of the effects of the Trondheim toll ring on travel behaviour and the environment. In *Proceedings of First World Congress on Applications of Transport Telematics and Intelligent Vehicle Highway Systems*. Paris, France: IEEE.

Puget Sound Regional Council. (2008). *Traffic choices study – Summary report*. Seattle, WA: Puget Sound Regional Council.

Rossi, T. F. (2010). *Partnership to develop an integrated, advanced travel demand model and a fine-grained, time-sensitive network in the Sacramento region*. Paper presented at the 3rd TRB Conference on Innovations in Travel Modeling. Tempe, AZ.

Saad, L. (2008). Majority now cutting back elsewhere to afford gas: Appeal of fuel-efficient cars is surging among Americans. *USA Today/Gallup Poll*. Retrieved July 29, 2012, from http://www.gallup.com/poll/107203/Majority-Now-Cutting-Back-Elsewhere-to-Afford-Gas.aspx

Timmermans, H. J. P. (2003). *The saga of integrated land use-transport modeling: How many more dreams before we wake up?* Paper presented at the 10th International Conference on Travel Behaviour Research, International Association for Travel Behaviour Research (IATBR). Lucerne, Switzerland.

Vovsha, P., & Bradley, M. (2006). Advanced activity-based models in context of planning decisions. *Transportation Research Record: Journal of the Transportation Research Board*, *1981*, 34–41. doi:10.3141/1981-07.

Ye, X., Pendyala, R. M., & Gottardi, G. (2007). An exploration of the relationship between mode choice and complexity of trip chaining patterns. *Transportation Research Part B: Methodological*, *41*(1), 96–113. doi:10.1016/j.trb.2006.03.004.

Zhang, K., Mahmassani, H. S., & Vovsha, P. (2011). *Integrated nested logit mode choice and dynamic network micro-assignment model platform to support congestion and pricing studies, the New York metropolitan case*. Paper presented at the 90th Annual Meeting of the Transportation Research Board. Washington, DC.

KEY TERMS AND DEFINITIONS

Activity-Based Travel Model: A model in which the activities and trips undertaken by residents of a region are simulated at the level of the individual traveler along the continuous time axis while recognizing the derived nature of travel demand.

Dynamic Traffic Assignment Model: A model in which individual trips are routed and vehicular movements are simulated in regular time steps through the network is capable of reflecting dynamics. The model recognizes the time-dependent nature of shortest paths.

Integrated Model: This is a model system in which multiple models are brought together in a unifying framework. The models communicate with one another in a seamless fashion with appropriate data exchanges and feedback loops to bring about consistency in representation of traveler behaviors.

Generalized Travel Cost: The generalized travel cost is a measure of impedance reflecting the burden associated with traveling between an origin-destination pair. The generalized travel cost includes not only out-of-pocket travel cost but also the time cost of travel and any other measures of separation translated into equivalent monetary units.

Policy Sensitivity: The ability of models to reflect traveler response and behavioral changes in the event of a policy implementation is key to their usefulness in practice. Policy sensitivity reflects the extent to which models are able to fulfill this role.

Traveler Behavior: Measures of travel demand that reflect how, where, when, why, and how much people travel during the course of any time period of interest.

Chapter 6
An Effective Methodology for Road Accident Data Collection in Developing Countries

Muhammad Adnan
NED University of Engineering and Technology, Pakistan

Mir Shabbar Ali
NED University of Engineering and Technology, Pakistan

ABSTRACT

Underreporting of road accidents has been widely accepted as a common phenomenon. In many developing countries this remains a critical problem as inappropriate information regarding road accidents does not provide a base to analyse its root causes. Therefore, effectiveness of implemented interventions are always questionable. In Pakistan, responsibility of collecting initial information regarding road accidents lies with the Police Department; however, reported figures are reflecting underestimation of the situation. This chapter reports the effectiveness of prevailing approaches for recording accident information in developing countries like Pakistan, India and Bangladesh, etc. Furthermore, it presents a unique methodology that has been adopted in Karachi for recording road accident information through an institute established on the notions of public-private partnership. Various features of that unique data collection mechanism are presented along with the discussion of some success stories, where the collected data has contributed significantly in improving road safety conditions.

INTRODUCTION

World Health Organization (WHO) in its statistical report mentioned that 1.3 million people annually die all over the world in road crashes (Peden et al, 2004). It has been reported in the literature that in developing countries fatalities due to road crashes are three to four times more than in the developed world (Bener et al 2003; Mohan and Tiwari 2005). In many developing countries road safety has not given prime importance due to lack of political will. However, development of infrastructure and policies that suits motorized traffic has been given significant consideration in almost all developing countries and due to this rapid increase in vehicle ownership has been observed. One such study reported that annual increase in vehicle ownership in developing nations of Asia is 12-18% which resulted in a dramatic increase in the number and rate of accidents. The situa-

DOI: 10.4018/978-1-4666-4920-0.ch006

tion in developing country like Pakistan is even worse as it has been reported that overall increase in motorization is about 410% between the years 2001 to 2005. This is because of the motorization friendly policies of the Pakistan Government that has allowed commercial banks to introduce car financing in almost all major urban areas at affordable terms to even those individuals whose income level lies in an average category (Aizaz 2007). This heavy motorization resulted in serious deterioration of road safety conditions which is evident from various informal surveys.

The deteriorating condition in road safety aspects demands serious endeavours for its improvement. Proper analysis of root causes of road accident is dependent on rich information of the data set. In developed part of the world, accident information has been gathered on scientific notions, where various institutes co-operate with each other for development of the refined database. For example, in UK, Department for Transport publishes national level reports and statistics on country-wide road accidents. On similar notions, US census bureau collectively publish various documents on safety aspects of US roads. Cuerden et al (2008) conducted a study for Department for Transport, UK, on site information gathering system for road accident to improve the quality of the data set for better analysis of accident causes. These kind of collective information gathering units along with the involvement of academics for proper guidance of essential aspects of accident information are scarce in developing nations. One such example has been mentioned for Abu Dhabi region by Khan et al (2004) regarding the accident record mechanism, in which police personnel are involved in primary data collection on prescribed questionnaire. Khan et al (2004) further reviewed the accident data collection mechanism in some advanced countries, and indicated that in majority of the countries police is collecting primary information regarding accident data, however, in advanced countries due to the proper vehicle registration and driver information databases, the accident record is then linked with these da-

tabases, so the highway departments then have all the essential information required to carry out accident analysis. In developing nations, lack in proper co-ordination among various agencies is the major cause of in-sufficient information related to road accidents, on top of it due to the complexity involved in procedural requirements, less severe accidents are not reported at all (Kumar et al 2010). This situation largely contributes in high percentage of underreporting of road accidents.

Over the years it has been seen that in developed part of the world, Non Governmental Organizations (NGOs) can initiate road safety activities which the public authorities have problem to address due to variety of reasons. For example, access to private funding or co-operation of communities and individuals etc. In developed world NGOs role can be defined as a supplement and extension of the government efforts. However, in developing countries their role is much critical, sometimes they are providing such essential services that in developed countries governmental agencies and institution would provide. Under these circumstances, NGOs in the developing world are acting as a main contributor to economic development, essential services, employment and the budget. Because of the non serious attitude at the part of government institutions, in many countries NGOs are came up with the plan to supplement activities related to road accident data collection and its analysis.

On the above lines, this chapter discusses state-owned accident data collection mechanism prevailing in developing countries such as India, Bangladesh and Pakistan along with the discussion of roles NGOs are playing in road safety improvement in these countries. The chapter then reports a unique methodology of accident data collection system that was introduced in 2007 in Karachi Metropolis (A largest metropolitan city of Pakistan, reported as sixth largest metropolitan city in the world). This chapter further discuses an operational model of the institute, which is involved in the accident data collection in Karachi.

ACCIDENT DATA COLLECTION MECHANISM IN DEVELOPING NATIONS

This section reports data collection mechanism of road accidents in some developing nations such as India, Bangladesh and Pakistan. Furthermore, based on the data collection mechanism prevailing in these nations, this section highlights key features of their road safety situation.

Road Accident Data–India

The major commonality between the developing countries regarding road accidents is a phenomenon of highly under reporting of accidents, and India is no exception. This is the main reason for significant differences in the figures and facts obtained from various sources. The Ministry of Road Transport and Highways of Indian Government has been the responsible for gathering accident statistics from all over India. Usually, the basic information collection is still the job of local police, and then this information is gathered on a state basis, and then transferred to the national authority. The recent program of Indian Road Accident Data (IRAD) under the initiative of UN-ESCAP (United Nations' Economic and Social Commission for the Asia and Pacific), the ministry is regularly publish accident statistics. The report published in 2011, indicated that between 1970 and 2010, the number of accidents increased by 4.4 times with 9.3 times increase in fatalities and 7.5 times increase in the number of persons injured, while there was an increase of 82 times in the number of registered motor vehicles and more than three times increase in the road network of India. The available figures are significantly alarming. Civil Society and other stakeholders realized this situation, and as a result significant number of Non Governmental Organisations (NGOs) is listed who are working for the cause of improvement of road

safety. However, it has been seen that majority of those NGOs has limited their focus only on awareness campaigns among different sectors of society through different means (Guler 2008).

Government functionaries in India have followed a positive approach to work with these NGOs. For example, in the city of Bangalore, road safety is very much led by the local Police. The Police are using the revenue from the traffic fines for road safety improvements and they are addressing a number of key issues with support from many responsible stakeholders (Sudhir and Sameera, 2006). Under these conditions there is much lesser burden on NGOs and therefore their role is quite similar to those working in developed countries. However, there exist some states within India, where government functionaries are completely idle regarding road safety conditions. These are the regions where NGOs can play vital role with a larger responsibilities. Among the major road safety related NGOs working in India, ArriveSAFE, Headlight, International Road Federation (India Chapter), Foundation for Road safety, IRTE (Institute of Road Traffic Education) and GRSP (Global road safety partnership) are making a significant impact on improvement of road safety conditions. In developing countries, for successful operations of NGOs it is necessary that a key figure of the society is running its affairs or at least strongly associated. Sometimes, influential character of this figure help out in removing hindrances and obstacles for carrying out key tasks to suffice the goals of the program/ project. However, in a long run of any NGO this may have a negative impact as in less developed countries it is often seen that NGOs are suffering from the leadership bailout and staff turnover as a result of the lack of institutionalization and overdependence on the founder (Guler 2008). IRTE and GRSP have done significant work on this aspect and ensure that association of key figures with the organization does not harm staff development.

Road Accident Data–Bangladesh

Bangladesh is a South Asian country that ranks one of the poorest in the world in terms of per capita income. In Bangladesh fatality rates per 10,000 vehicles are about 86 persons (Ross, 1998), which is 33% higher than India. About 20 percent of road accident occurred in metropolitan cities viz. Dhaka, Chittagong, Khulna and Rajshahi (Hoque, 1991). According to Hoque (2004) road safety improvement efforts in Bangladesh seriously suffer from several serious drawbacks. Among the various problems; lack of funding and other resources, unwillingness of the government authorities, unavailability of professional agency, insufficient inter-agency coordination, inadequate personnel, lack of trained traffic police for effective enforcement and traffic regulations, absence and inadequate dissemination of road safety research are the prominent reasons for road safety conditions.

In Bangladesh as well, primary data collection regarding road accidents lies with the police department, and then information are transferred to various departments for further compilation of statistics. It seems that there are some gaps in co-ordination mechanism for proper data management, because several researchers have indicated various agencies for road accident statistics such as Police Head Quarters, Bangladesh Bureau of Statistics, Bangladesh Road Transport Authority and Road and Highway Department. Alam et al (2011) reported accident statistics from police records, and concluded that accidents and fatalities have increased from 1.14 to 3.87 and 0.41 to 2.98 per 100,000 population respectively in year 2007 compared with 1997. The national authorities such as National Road Safety Council (NRSC) has taken variety of steps to come up with the road safety improvement plan, however, due to their limited role in decision making, they have not been supported well by key stakeholders. Having the realization of the state of the problems, NGOs are becoming active in the area

of road safety in Bangladesh. Bangladesh Rural Advancement Committee (BRAC) and Centre for Rehabilitation of the Paralyzed (CRP) are two leading NGOs working towards betterment of road safety; however, their focus is very wide as they tackle many other issues such as economic development, injustice in the society, Gender issues, environment and health etc. It has been seen that BRAC has done a significant amount of work on various aspects of road safety such as from research to community awareness projects. This NGO is following a norms common in professional NGOs of the developed world. Governing board comprises of many key individuals from national and international organizations (such as Amnesty International). It can be easily asserts from the setting of the organization that in terms of leadership availability, BRAC is sustainable and will continue to grow its activities further. Additional feature of the operational model of this institute is its special emphasis on transparency and accountability. Clear policies and procedures which are well documented, transparent definition of various levels of authorities and proper staff supervision have made this organization distinct from the others.

Road Accident Data–Pakistan

In Pakistan, like many developing countries, issue of road safety has not been the prime agenda or priority of the government. International donor agencies such as World Bank and ADB have provided funding for various country-wide transportation projects but there is no exclusive project for road safety issue despite the current demanding situation. In year 2006, Government of Pakistan has established a National Road Safety Secretariat (NRSS) to improve road safety situation, however, the impact of this institute has been quite low because of lack of funding and professional manpower, unavailability of true records of road accidents and inadequate co-ordination among different government functionaries.

Road accident data collection is the responsibility of the police department, and the information is further processed at city and provincial level for onward transmission to national authorities. This suggests that the prevailing system is as usual as followed in other parts of the world. However, lack of government interest and institutional co-ordination, the quality of data is such that it is not providing useful information for further analysis (Aizaz 2007). Aizaz (2007) further indicated that less than 10% of Road traffic crashes are reported in Pakistan as suggested by the police records compared with local hospitals records. Based on this, it is the prime aim of the NRSS to establish a road safety data bank with a mechanism to update of the data base on regular basis. However, this has not been a reality due to lack of political will in this cause.

The review of data collection mechanism of developing nations such as India, Bangladesh and Pakistan, suggested that the basic accident data collection responsibility is lies with the police department. However, depending on the strength of the co-ordination among various government functionaries and availability of required resources in terms of funding, the richness is introduced in the basic data, and it will become more useful when national authorities are using it for policy making. In India, situation is much better; however, both in Bangladesh and Pakistan, lack of useful data is hampering the progress towards road safety improvement. Role of NGOs is appreciable in these circumstances as they are working well to introduce programmes through which, general awareness has been created, and in some regions results are significant. The next section presents a unique methodology for accident information collection system, the model followed in Karachi metropolis has been successful and it delivered number of fruitful results.

NGO BASED DATA COLLECTION– KARACHI CASE STUDY

Lack of political will and other issues because of which road safety situation is worsened in developing nations has been realised strongly by development funding agencies such as WHO and Asian Development Bank (ADB), as a result these agencies have shifted their focus towards regional Non-Governmenatal Organisations (NGOs). This has been evident from the fact that between 1973 and 1988 only 6% of World bank-financed projects involved NGOs, however, from 1994 onwards this percentage has increased up to 50% (Ellevest, 1997). Furthermore, in 2009, WHO arranged a global meeting of NGO's advocating for road safety with a view point that these organizations have a key role to play in generating political commitment to addressing deaths and injuries on the world's roads. In current state, there are various NGOs working in Pakistan having different agenda but no one devoted its focus to the road safety issue in any urban region of Pakistan. Recently, in year 2007, a centre has been established based on public-private partnership with a name of Road Traffic Injury research and Prevention Centre (RTIR & PC) in Karachi, Pakistan. This section elaborates the purpose, operational model, and outcomes of several projects carried out by this centre.

RTIR & PC Objectives

The need for the establishment of this centre was identified by the doctors as they monitor a large number of patients coming in the hospitals due to the accidents which causes significant increase in accident fatality rate. This centre was developed with a purpose of providing solutions and interventions based on the analytical study of road crashes and pressurize government functionaries for their implementation. To fulfil this objective, a data collection mechanism was also devised as there were large discrepancies noted with the accident records available from Police department. It was later found out that in year 2008 police data indicated around 1004 road accident fatalities for the whole province of Sindh (which comprises of many urban cities) and RTIR & PC statistics indicated 1185 fatalities for the Karachi region only. This provides enough justification for inclusion of data collection mechanism in its primary tasks. Other objectives of the centre include proposal development after analysis of collected data for improvement in road safety conditions and then lobbying for their successful implementation with the civic agencies and stakeholders (Adnan et al 2010).

Data Collection Methodology

The methodology followed for accident data collection is explained in this sub-section. The RTIR & PC follow a method, which doesn't involve government functionaries or police department. The method include direct interview of accident victims, on a prescribed form that contain 20 different items, in hospitals where team of interviewers were deployed for 7 days a week and 24 hours of the day. In case of fatal accident, data collectors gather information from ambulance drivers, relatives or eye witnesses or family members of the victims. Occasionally, hospital and police record is also used to gather the required information, in cases where no source of information is available to the deployed team. The members of survey team are trained on various aspects of the information gathering procedure, and they are well worse with the different terminologies used in the form. In total, five major hospitals have been chosen where survey team consists of 6 members have been deployed on 8 hour shift basis. The hospitals from which data collection is carried out include Jinnah Post Graduate Medical Centre (JPMC), Agha Khan University (AKU), Civil Hospital Karachi (CHK), Abbasi Shaheed Hospital (ASH) and Liaqat National Hospital (LNH), Karachi. RTIR & PC manages the filled

data forms and digitize them to form a complete database. There are several checks performed at this stage, for example, comparison with the media reports, logical consistency of the filled items in the form and records from medico-legal register of the hospitals. The cell is working efficiently for almost 6 years, since its inception in year 2007. Figure 1 presents the data collection and compilation mechanism of the RTIR & PC.

As the general characteristics of the accident data collection is such that it required efforts on sustainable basis. Any effort that is not sustainable for longer period of time would not render fruitful results. This has been noted earlier at the time of establishment of the centre, and key volunteers from medical and engineering academics are involved as prime stakeholders to take care of the affairs of the centre. Representative from NED University of Engineering and Technology and Aga Khan University Hospital has laid the foundation for the centre in terms of required technical support. This is necessary because through institutional involvement, the overall organisational framework of the centre will be less dependent on its founders; as a result of this long term sustainability can be ensured. Furthermore, the government authorities have been portrayed as a key player in overall management of the system, but it is not the case. Regular meetings are arranged with the relevant government functionaries, and based on the findings these functionaries are informed about the condition of road safety in the entire city. With these continuous efforts authorities are now listening, and found supportive of the ideas presented in front of them regarding different aspects of road safety. The motivational factor behind the positive attitude of the government functionaries is that every intervention was carried out by providing all the credit to these agencies with limited request of funding for implementation. This was done just to gain support from government officials for smoothly carrying out various operations of the centre. At initial level, financing of the centre was sup-

Figure 1. Data collection and compilation mechanism of RTIR & PC

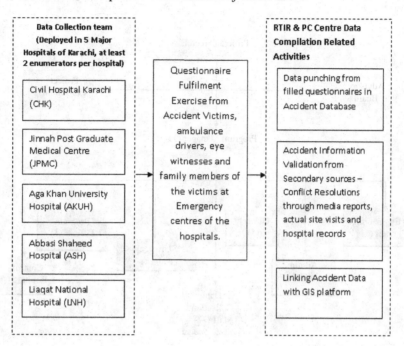

ported through Corporate Social Responsibility (CSR) funding budget of Indus Motors Pvt. Ltd. However, as the system progresses and development of data bank producing some fruitful results, WHO has shown interest in the project and since 2011 WHO is providing funds for data collection. The centre publishes annual reports that are well circulated in all institutions, which contain the summary of the data in the form of tables and graphs. These reports help in advocating the case of poor road safety conditions in the city. Figure 2 presents the overall organisation of RTIR & PC, in order to fulfil its objectives.

Glimpse of the Collected Data

Table 1 provides number of injury and fatal accidents recorded at trauma centre (RTIR & PC) and police department for Karachi region only. It can be seen that there is significant amount of differences present especially in years where data is available from police department. The results in the table indicate the requirement of such centre all over Pakistan for appropriate facts and figures related to road accidents.

Figure 3 presents the accident distribution over all age groups, young age group individuals have been found more vulnerable compared to other age groups. This is mostly due to lack of proper enforcement and ignorance at the part of parents as they are allowing teenage kids to drive auto vehicles especially motorcycles. Table 2 describe the accidents distribution over gender groups, which clearly indicates that females involvement is significantly lesser compared with males, despite of almost equal population distribution overall. The main reason of this trend is due to the cultural norms followed in the society, where females are mostly comfortable as housewives or nonworking class and highly dependent on males.

SUCCESS STORIES

RTIR & PC this centre has possess many success stories, despite of its young age. By the

Figure 2. Organisational framework of RTIR & PC, number in brackets represents staff

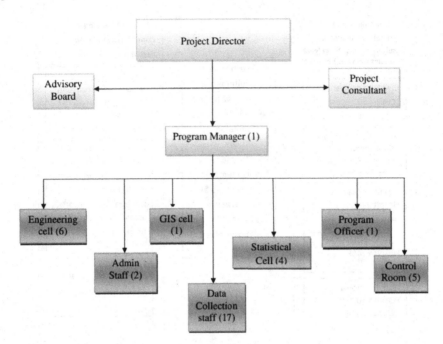

Table 1. Comparison of accidents from RTIR & PC and police department

	2007	2008	2009	2010	2011
Trauma Injury	34707	31312	29763	30340	31139
Police Injury	0	0	0	1099	940
Trauma Fatal	892	1185	1288	1227	1161
Police Fatal	0	0	0	491	466

Figure 3. Accident distribution over age groups

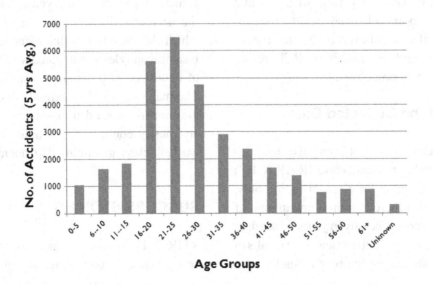

Table 2. Accident distribution over gender

Gender	2007	2008	2009	2010	2011
Male	31634	29353	27031	26678	27693
Female	3973	3144	4020	4889	4607

efforts of different task teams, road safety audits and major accident investigations has been performed on major arterials of Karachi including Shahrah-e-Usman Ramz, Chaudary Fazal Ellahi road, Korangi road, Korangi Industrial Road, Jail Chowrangi etc. Based on these studies several low cost solutions have been proposed which are implemented with the support of civic agencies. The after intervention studies at these spots show considerable reduction in fatalities and severity of accidents. For example, in the case of New Preedy Street (see Figure 4), at a particular point where pedestrians movement are significantly high, road curve was very sharp due to which the location could not able to suffice proper safe sight distance requirements (Saqib et al 2010). This finding was disseminated to relevant civic

agencies; some specific traffic signs were posted as a short term solution that resolved the issue to a significant extent.

In addition to above, Shaheed-e-Millat expressway was identified as a black spot location, as frequency of road accident was very high. The major problem at that location was perceived as unavailability of speed calming devices and absence of barriers which separates the two way traffic. These measures were proposed by the team of RTIR & PC and for its implementation efforts are made through continuous advocating and raising the voice in this aspect at various meetings and media reports. This resulted in improvement of this section of the expressway, and now it is included in the list of safer roads. Figure 5 presents the current condition of this road after some low cost interventions.

CONCLUSION

This chapter reports the effectiveness of prevailing approaches for recording accident information in

Figure 4. New preedy street improvement

Figure 5. Shaheed-e-millat expressway interventions

the developing countries like, Pakistan, India and Bangladesh etc. Furthermore, this chapter presents a unique methodology that has been adopted in Karachi for recording road accidents data by forming a institution named as Road Traffic Injury Research and Prevention Centre (RTIR & PC) in 2007, which is based on public-private partnership and having its major funding from national and international donor agencies. The main characteristics of this methodology that it is a need based method in the context of developing nations, which not only record accident information, but also provide support details for better investigation of causes of accidents. Another feature of this method is that information is gathered (based on a specified questionnaire) in emergency wards of hospitals, directly from the victims in case of injury accidents or from the persons who are direct witness of fatal accidents (in most of the cases these persons brought victims in hospitals). The special attribute of gathering road accident information is that it is not a cross sectional activity (i.e. a point in time activity), for appropriate analysis of accidents it is required that data collection process should be at least spanning over few years. This implies that any attempt of gathering road accident information should be sustainable over a longer period of time. This sustainability of the data collection process followed in RTIR & PC is ensured through well-built internal organisational structure, supported with a panel comprises of local professionals that include road safety researchers from academia, practicing traffic and road safety engineers and relevant medical practitioners from major hospitals that frequently meets to monitor progress and discuss important findings from the collected data. This chapter also discusses some success stories of RTIR & PC in improving road safety condition of the Karachi city over the last four years since its inception, which are all well supported with evidences from the data. On the basis of these successes, it is recommended that the similar framework can be employed in other parts of Pakistan as well as in other developing nations to improve level of road accidents information and consequently overall road safety conditions.

ACKNOWLEDGMENT

Authors of this chapter like to thank NED University of Engineering and Technology and RTIR & PC, Karachi for providing necessary data, support and facilities to formulate this chapter.

REFERENCES

Adnan, M., Ali, M. S., Qadir, A., & Sheeraz, K. (2011). Increasing effectiveness of road safety interventions- An operational model for developing countries. In *First International Forum of Traffic Safety,* (pp. 221-235). Univeristy of Damam.

Aizaz, A. (2007). Road safety in Pakistan. *National Road Safety Secretariat, Ministry of Communications, Government of Pakistan.* Retrieved April 1, 2013, from http://www.unescap.org/ttdw/common/Meetings/TIS/EGM%20Roadsafety%20Country%20Papers/Pakistan_Roadsafety.pdf

Alam, M. S., Mahmud, S. M., & Hoque, M. M. (2011). Road accidents trends in Bangladesh: A comprehensive study. In Noor, Amin, Bhuiyan, Chowdhury and Kakoli (Eds.), *4th Annual Paper Meet and 1st Civil Engineering Congress* (pp. 172-181), Dhaka, Bangladesh: IEEE.

Bener, A., Abu-Zidan, F. M., Bensiali, A. K., Al-Mulla, A. A., & Jadaan, K. S. (2003). Strategy to improve road safety in developing countries. *Saudi Medical Journal, 24*(6), 603–608. PMID:12847587.

Cuerden, R., Pittman, M., Dodson, E., & Hill, J. (2008). *The UK on the spot accident data collection study – Phase II report.* London: Department of Transport.

Ellevest, L. A. (1997). The role of NGOs in road safety. *Road safety in Bangladesh.* Retrieved April 1, 2013, from http://www.rhd.gov.bd/Documents/ExternalPublications/WorldBank/TransSectPub/contents/documents/B21.pdf

Faizo, J., Hoque, M. M., & Tiwari, G. (1998). Fatalities of heterogeneous traffic in large south Asian cities. In *Proceeding of the Third International Symposium on Highway Capacity,* (pp. 423-436). Copenhagen: Danish road Directorate.

Guler, E. (2008). How to improve NGO effectiveness in development? A discussion on lessons learned. *NGO MANGER.* Retrieved April 1, 2013, from http://www.ngomanager.org/dcd/2_Organisational_Development/Capacity_building/NGO_Effectiveness.pdf

Hoque, M. M. (1991). *Accident investigation for the safety improvement of Dhaka-Aricha highway: A section of Asian highway.* Dhaka, India: Department of Civil Engineering, Bangladesh University of Engineering & Technology.

Hoque, M. M. (2004). The road to road safety, issues and initiative in Bangladesh. *Regional Health Forum, 8*(1), 39-51.

Khan, M. A., Al Kathairi, A. S., & Garib, A. M. (2004). *A GIS based traffic accident data collection, referencing and analysis framework for Abu Dhabi.* Paper Presented in CODATU XI: World Congress: Towards More Attractive Urban Transportation. Bucarest, Romania.

Kumar, R., Ali, M. S., & Ahmed, A. (2010). An appraisal of signal free corridor in Karachi via empirical study of road accidents and pedestrian movement concerning road crossing. In *Proceedings of the 3rd International Conference on Infrastructural Engineering in Developing Countries* (pp. 379-388). NED University of Engineering and Technology.

Mohan, D., & Tiwari, G. (2005). Road safety in low income countries: Issues and concern regarding knowledge transfer from high income countries. In G. Tiwari, D. Mohan, & N. Muhlard (Eds.), *The way Forward- Transportation Planning and Road Safety* (pp. 122–135). MacMillian India Press.

Peden, M., Scurfield, R., Sleet, D., Mohan, D., Hyder, A. A., Jarawan, E., & Mathers, C. D. (2004). *World report on road traffic injury prevention.* Geneva: World Health Organization.

Saqib, M., Sheeraz, K., & Farooqui, R. (2010). Development of guidelines for road safety audit in Pakistan: Case studies. In *Proceedings of the 3rd International Conference on Infrastructural Engineering in Developing Countries* (pp. 237-288). NED University of Engineering and Technology.

Sudhir, M., & Sameera, K. (2006). Bangalore: Silicon city or black city? *ArriveSafe Organizations.* Retrieved April 1, 2013, from http://www.arrivesafe.org/pdfs/Bangalore-Silicon_Capital_or_Black_City.pdf

KEY TERMS AND DEFINITIONS

Developing Country: A country in which living of standards is low for majority of its residents, and having underdeveloped industrial base.

Non Governmental Organizations: These are organizations which are legally allowed to work independently from government with the objective to work for betterment of the society.

Road Accident: A crash or collision on a section of road which affects vehicle(s) or driver(s) or other road users due to many contributory factors.

Road Accident Data Collection: A process of obtaining road accident information and its compilation for extracting meaningful results after its analysis on scientific notions.

Road Accident Fatality Rate: The ratio of deaths in an area to the population of that area due to road accidents; expressed per 1000 per year

Road Safety Improvement Plan: List of Actions or measures, derived after careful investigation and analysis of road accident data, for improvement of road safety condition of the region

RTIR & PC: Road Traffic Injury Research & Prevention Center, developed in Karachi with a purpose to improve road safety condition of Karachi.

Under Reporting of Road Accident: Road Accident not formally informed to the agencies responsible for collecting and maintaining road accident records, in many circumstance it involve dealing with Police.

Chapter 7
Traffic Safety Implications of Travel Demand Management Policies:
The Cases of Teleworking and Fuel Cost Increase

Ali Pirdavani
Hasselt University, Belgium

Tom Brijs
Hasselt University, Belgium

Tom Bellemans
Hasselt University, Belgium

Bruno Kochan
Hasselt University, Belgium

Geert Wets
Hasselt University, Belgium

ABSTRACT

Travel Demand Management (TDM) consists of a variety of policy measures that affect the transportation system's effectiveness by changing travel behavior. Although the primary objective to implement such TDM strategies is not to improve traffic safety, their impact on traffic safety should not be neglected. The main purpose of this study is to investigate differences in the traffic safety consequences of two TDM scenarios: a fuel-cost increase scenario (i.e. increasing the fuel price by 20%) and a teleworking scenario (i.e. 5% of the working population engages in teleworking). Since TDM strategies are usually conducted at a geographically aggregated level, crash prediction models that are used to evaluate such strategies should also be developed at an aggregate level. Moreover, given that crash occurrences are often spatially heterogeneous and are affected by many spatial variables, the existence of spatial correlation in the data is also examined. The results indicate the necessity of accounting for the spatial correlation when developing crash prediction models. Therefore, Zonal Crash Prediction Models (ZCPMs) within the geographically weighted generalized linear modeling framework are developed to incorporate the spatial variations in association between the Number Of Crashes (NOCs) (including fatal, severe, and slight injury crashes recorded between 2004 and 2007) and a set of explanatory variables. Different

DOI: 10.4018/978-1-4666-4920-0.ch007

exposure, network, and socio-demographic variables of 2200 traffic analysis zones in Flanders, Belgium, are considered as predictors of crashes. An activity-based transportation model is adopted to produce exposure metrics. This enables a more detailed and reliable assessment while TDM strategies are inherently modeled in the activity-based models. In this chapter, several ZCPMs with different severity levels and crash types are developed to predict the NOCs. The results show considerable traffic safety benefits of conducting both TDM scenarios at an average level. However, there are certain differences when considering changes in NOCs by different crash types.

INTRODUCTION

Urbanization and population growth together with employment and motor vehicle growth largely affect the road transportation system's performance. To diminish the negative impacts, different policy measures and strategies have been applied by authorities. These programs and strategies that promote more efficient use of transportation systems are generally called TDM strategies (Litman, 2003). TDM strategies consist of several policies and strategies which aim to overcome transportation problems by means of mode shift (e.g. using public transportation instead of cars, biking for short distance trips or carpooling), travel time shift (e.g. avoiding traffic peak-hours by leaving home/ the work place earlier or later) or travel demand reduction (e.g. teleworking) (VTPI, 2012). In general, TDM strategies are implemented to improve transportation systems' efficiency. However, their potential secondary impacts such as the effect on traffic safety or environmental effects should not be overlooked.

On the other hand and for many years, researchers have attempted to investigate road safety by predicting the NOCs based on patterns they learned from crashes that occurred in the past. From an ethical point of view, this reactive approach is not acceptable because it requires several years of crashes to occur in order to identify and treat safety problems. Therefore, providing a more proactive approach, capable of evaluating road safety at the planning-level is essential. In the last few years, researchers and practitioners have increasingly applied this proactive approach. In

this regard, dealing with traffic safety in a proactive manner and at the planning level requires the ability to integrate a crash predicting context into TDM strategies.

The main contribution of this study is, therefore, to couple ZCPMs with two TDM scenarios; namely the fuel-cost increase and the teleworking scenario that are simulated in an activity-based transportation model called FEATHERS (Forecasting Evolutionary Activity-Travel of Households and their Environmental RepercussionS) (Janssens, Wets, Timmermans, & Arentze, 2007). This is carried out to evaluate the traffic safety effects of conducting such TDM strategies by means of a simulation-based analysis of the impact on the travel demand in Flanders, Belgium. This way, the behavioral impact of TDM scenarios in terms of traffic demand is incorporated in the analysis. By assigning traffic demand to the road network and using this information at zonal level, the impact of responses to TDM, such as changes in trip planning, route choice and modal choice are incorporated in the analysis. This study is an assessment exercise which independently illustrates different impacts of a 20% increase in fuel-related costs and a simulation of 5% teleworking population on traffic safety.

It is necessary to indicate that the activity-based FEATHERS model (Bellemans et al., 2010), models the transportation demand of a population that is aware of the state of the transportation network. Hence, the assumed travel times during the activity-travel planning phase are in correspondence with the travel times obtained after assigning the total traffic demand to the road network (this is achieved through iteration). This means that the model is a steady state model and that no transients are modeled. Moreover, the model is a short term model in the sense that it does not assume a shift in the composition of the vehicle fleet or changes in the location of businesses and/ or the location choice for living, since they occur at a far slower time scale than the adaptation of travel behavior triggered by changing fuel cost or promoting teleworking.

The structure of this chapter is as follows. Initially, the relevant literature will be reviewed. Then the activity-based model which is used in this study will be briefly introduced. In the next sections, the data preparation and the TDM scenario evaluation process will be demonstrated. Finally, the results of this evaluation will be shown followed by the final conclusions and discussion.

BACKGROUND

In this section the relevant literature concerning the fuel-cost increase and the teleworking scenarios will be reviewed.

Fuel-Cost Increase Scenario

Fuel-related costs are major components of each motor vehicle's operating expenses. By increasing the fuel price as a TDM strategy, people tend to travel less by car, and instead use public transportation, carpool, or shift towards slow modes (i.e. biking and walking), etc. Thus, traffic crashes are expected to decrease as a result of a reduction in the number of car kilometers traveled. Grabowski and Morrisey (Grabowski & Morrisey, 2004) reported a relatively stable number of fatal motor vehicle crashes despite new traffic safety laws and vehicle innovations over a period of time. Their explanation was that the price of gasoline declined, which resulted in more vehicle kilometers traveled (VKT) and potentially more fatalities. Chi et al. (2010) also investigated

the impact of gasoline price changes on different types of crashes at a more disaggregated level for different ages and genders. In their reactive approach, they developed models to predict traffic crashes based on explanatory variables like exposure, gasoline price, alcohol consumption, seat belt usage, etc. Their study concluded that an increase in gasoline price has both short-term and intermediate-term effects on reducing total traffic crashes. One of the longer-term effects of a fuel cost increase is the change of the fleet composition to more fuel-economic vehicles, which can partially compensate the increased fuel price by an increased fuel efficiency. In the literature it is described (Goodwin, Dargay, & Hanly, 2004; Litman, 2010) that the fuel price elasticity of fuel consumption ranges from -0.25 to -0.6, the elasticity of fuel efficiency ranges from 0.3 to 0.4 and the vehicle mileage elasticity ranges from –0.1 to -0.3. Given the fact that increasing fuel price has a direct impact on VKT reduction, it can be expected that crash frequency also tends to decrease.

Teleworking Scenario

"Teleworking" is a general term used when applications of telecommunication systems substitute for actual travel to the work place. Teleworking is one of the most popular and effective components of commute trip reduction programs (Litman & Fitzroy, 2012). Teleworking can significantly reduce participating employees' commute travel and consequently the total distance traveled.

The most immediate and direct impacts of teleworking are a decrease in travel demand and consequently a reduction of total distance traveled. Previous research has evaluated these impacts from individual and global points of views; i.e. some studies focused on the changes of only telecommuters' behavior and their travel pattern (individually) whereas other studies investigated the effects of a telecommuting strategy on a more global level (Choo, Mokhtarian, & Salomon,

2005; Choo & Mokhtarian, 2007; Dissanayake & Morikawa, 2008; Henderson & Mokhtarian, 1996; Kochan, Bellemans, Cools, Janssens, & Wets, 2011; Koenig, Henderson, & Mokhtarian, 1996; Mokhtarian & Varma, 1998; Nilles, 1996; Vu & Vandebona, 2007).

Based on the literature, it can be concluded that although teleworking seems to decrease the amount of VKT significantly, individual estimations by different studies tend to vary strongly. This uncertainty was also reported by Choo et al. (2005) who claimed that a wide range of answers can be obtained to the question of "what impact on travel?". They concluded that although teleworking has a statistically significant impact on reducing travel demand, the magnitude of this impact would not be very extraordinary.

The main focus of this chapter is not to assess the magnitude of the impact of teleworking on distance traveled, however, it is important to assure that the estimates of our study are reasonable and in line with the findings of other studies. This is important in view of the fact that these estimates are the main input of the ZCPMs and, therefore, we would like to avoid any possible bias in the results of our policy assessment.

Kochan et al. (2011) studied the effects of teleworking on total distance traveled in Flanders, Belgium. It was reported that in 2002, in Flanders, the total distance traveled decreased by 1.6% when the proportion of teleworkers that telework on a working day was 3.8% (Kochan et al., 2011). These results are in line with the findings of literature. Therefore, our study will be based on the framework presented in Kochan et al. (2011), although we simulate that 5% of the working population engages in teleworking instead of 3.8%.

In general, it can be concluded that the cause-effect relationship between fuel-cost increase or teleworking and a reduction in VKT is well-established in the literature. Moreover, the relation between different types of exposure metrics (e.g. number of trips or VKT) and crashes has also been reported and well documented in lit-

erature (Abdel-Aty, Siddiqui, & Huang, 2011a; Hadayeghi, Shalaby, & Persaud, 2010a; G. R. Lovegrove, 2005; Naderan & Shahi, 2010; Pirdavani, Brijs, Bellemans, Kochan, & Wets, 2012, 2013). Although exposure might not be the direct cause of crash occurrence, it is the major predictive variable to estimate the number of crashes. Moreover, strategies that reduce travel demand or distance traveled, or cause a modal shift towards a safer mode (e.g. from car to public transportation) are known to reduce the NOCs (Litman & Fitzroy, 2012; Litman, 2006; G. R. Lovegrove & Litman, 2008). Therefore, it is plausible to utilize the association between the TDM scenarios and the number of crashes so as to evaluating the traffic safety impacts of such TDM strategies.

METHODOLOGY

Crash prediction models (CPMs) can be developed at different levels of aggregation, for instance, at the local level (i.e. road section or intersection) or at the regional level (e.g. traffic analysis zones (TAZ)). Recently, crash analyses at a regional level receive more and more attention. Several studies examined the association of a collection of zone-level factors such as traffic patterns, socio-demographic and socio-economic variables, land use patterns and weather conditions with crashes, aggregated by a specific spatial scale (Aguero-Valverde & Jovanis, 2006; Amoros, Martin, & Laumon, 2003; Hadayeghi, Shalaby, & Persaud, 2003, 2007; Hadayeghi et al., 2010a; Hadayeghi, Shalaby, & Persaud, 2010b; Huang, Abdel-Aty, & Darwiche, 2010; G. R. Lovegrove & Litman, 2008; G. R. Lovegrove & Sayed, 2006; Noland & Oh, 2004; Noland & Quddus, 2005; Pirdavani et al., 2012, 2013; Quddus, 2008; Wier, Weintraub, Humphreys, Seto, & Bhatia, 2009). Macro-level crash analyses can provide important information, enabling cross-sectional comparisons between different zones, or identifying safety problems in specific zones (Huang et al., 2010). Furthermore, it is indispensable to take traffic safety into account already during the planning stage of transportation projects. To do so, traffic safety impacts of different transportation project alternatives should be compared and assessed. This can be accomplished by associating the NOCs with a number of factors which have zone-level characteristics (Huang et al., 2010).

Moreover, TDM strategies are usually performed and evaluated at geographically aggregated levels rather than merely at the level of individual intersections or road sections. Therefore, the impact of adopting a TDM strategy on transportation or traffic safety should also be evaluated at a level higher than the local consequences. Local level CPMs mostly aim to predict the safety effects of infrastructural improvements and are not typically designed to evaluate traffic safety impacts of TDM strategies. Thus, the application of CPMs at a higher aggregation level will be more practical (Tarko, Inerowicz, Ramos, & Li, 2008).

The application of CPMs at TAZ level has been initially introduced by Levine at al. (1995) and further extended by several other researchers (Amoros et al., 2003; Noland & Oh, 2004; Noland & Quddus, 2004; Aguero-Valverde & Jovanis, 2006; Quddus, 2008; Wier et al., 2009; Huang et al., 2010) by examining the association of a collection of network infrastructure variables, socio-demographic and socio-economic variables and weather conditions with the NOCs in TAZs. The results of these studies indicated that traffic volume, VKT, vehicle hours traveled (VHT), trip production/attraction, number of intersections, number of lanes, road length and road density, network capacity, urbanization degree, income and education levels, employment rate and population size are among the most significant predictors of crashes.

Although most of the above-mentioned studies were trying to demonstrate their potential as a proactive road safety predictive tool, so far not much attention has been paid to the application of these models to evaluate the effects of TDMs on traffic safety. There are very few attempts at estimating the road safety impacts of a specific TDM strategy. In a study conducted by Lovegrove and Litman (G. R. Lovegrove & Litman, 2008), they assumed the effect of implementing these strategies on different explanatory variables of the CPMs. Based on these assumptions the expected NOCs were calculated for each TDM strategy. It was concluded that a smart growth strategy of more compact and multi-modal land use development patterns may increase traffic safety by means of reducing crash frequency per capita by 20% and 29% for total and severe crashes respectively. An et al. (2011) found VHT, the number of intersections and the number of households with low income levels to be correlated with the NOCs in TAZs. After running two add-capacity projects and applying the results in their developed ZCPMs for the do-nothing scenario and both project scenarios, total crashes for both projects were estimated to decrease respectively by 0.1% and 0.06% when compared with the do-nothing scenario.

As can be seen from the literature, exposure is the most important predictor of crashes. Therefore, having a more informative measure of exposure is expected to result in better crash prediction. When a TDM scenario is performed, it basically changes the exposure compared with the null scenario. Thus, it is essential to predict the exposure metrics as accurately as possible. Activity-based models help with this as they are able to simulate the scenarios and in this case, they model the decision process of individuals with respect to the changes in fuel price or teleworking. This is the key advantage of activity-based transportation models rather than making educated guesses about the impact of TDM policies on travel demand in order to obtain exposure. In the next section, the activity-based model is briefly introduced and its contribution to the TDM scenario evaluation process is described.

Impact of TDM Scenarios on Traffic Demand

Traditionally, travel was assumed to be the result of four subsequent decisions which were modeled separately, also referred to as four-step models. More recently, several studies claim that travel plays a rather isolated role in these models and the reason why people undertake trips is completely neglected (Arentze & Timmermans, 2004). This gave rise to a new framework of models, called activity-based transportation models. The main difference between four-step models and activity-based transportation models is that the latter try to predict interdependencies between several facets of activity profiles (Davidson et al., 2007). The major advantage of activity-based models is that they deal with participation of various types of activities during a day. Moreover, a microsimulation approach which considers a high behavioral realism of individual agents is often adopted in these types of models (Kochan et al., 2011). Interactions between family members like using household vehicles, sharing household responsibilities or performing joint activities affect people's travel behavior. Four-step models that ignore such links are expected to misstate people's responses to TDM strategies in some circumstances. Therefore, it can be concluded that activity-based models are capable of treating TDM strategies and policy issues more effectively compared to four-step models (Vovsha & Bradley, 2006).

FEATHERS Framework

The FEATHERS framework (Janssens et al., 2007) was developed to facilitate the development of activity-based models for travel demand in Flanders, Belgium. The scheduling engine that is currently implemented in the FEATHERS

framework is based on the scheduling engine of the ALBATROSS system (Arentze & Timmermans, 2004). The real-life representation of Flanders is embedded in an agent-based simulation model which consists of over six million agents, each agent representing one member of the Flemish population. A sequence of 26 decision trees are used in the scheduling process and decisions are based on a number of attributes of the individuals (e.g. age, gender), the households (e.g. number of cars) and the geographical zones (e.g. population density, number of shops). For each agent with its specific attributes, the model simulates whether an activity (e.g. shopping, working, leisure activity, etc.) is going to be carried out or not. Subsequently, location, transport mode (available modes in FEATHERS are "car driver", "car passenger", "public transportation" and "slow mode" including pedestrians and cyclists) and duration of the activity are determined, taking into account the attributes of the individual (Kochan, Bellemans, Janssens, & Wets, 2008). Traffic demand is subsequently assigned to the road network in such a way that an equilibrium is established between transportation demand and supply (Bellemans et al., 2010), which results in a time-dependent traffic state on the road network. In order to run, calibrate and validate the activity-based model, three major types of data are required (Kochan, et al., Forthcoming); data describing the environment (e.g. population density, level of service of the transportation networks), a synthetic population which is simulated and finally activity-travel data originating from a representative sample of the population from which people's behavior is derived.

Implementation of Fuel-Cost Increase Scenario in FEATHERS

An important asset of activity-based models is their integrated approach towards activities and travel. Due to this approach, it can be taken into account that certain trips, which are linked to activities that are not so flexible (e.g. work activities) are less likely to be altered under changing traffic system conditions than others (e.g. leisure activities). In addition, activity-based models are not only able to predict a change in the demand for travel, but they also predict shifts between different modes of transport and the reallocation of activities due to the imposed measures. Providing a structured approach to agent-based modeling of activities and travel for individuals, the FEATHERS framework is able to account for TDM strategies. For instance, when applying a fuel cost increase scenario, FEATHERS can predict the impact on the number of trips (NOTs), modal shift and changes in trip time and length. Price changes can have an impact on different facets of travel, affecting the NOTs people undertake, their destination, route, mode, travel time, type of vehicle (including size, fuel efficiency and fuel type) and parking location and duration. Therefore, in order to predict the impact of price changes like fuel price, the scheduling engine has to be structured to account for those changes. In this scheduling engine, price and cost parameters are incorporated in the decision trees related to activity selection, timing, trip-chaining, location and mode choices. The extended decision trees or parametric action decision trees combine conventional decision trees and parametric action assignment rules yielding a model that is sensitive for travel-costs scenarios (Arentze & Timmermans, 2005).

In this study, fuel-related cost is assumed to increase by 20% as a result of an increase in fuel price. We consider the short term effect and can as such neglect the rebound effect caused by a changing fuel economy of the fleet (i.e. the fuel economy is considered to remain constant, which results in the reduction of fuel consumption to be equal to the reduction of the VKT). One might question how the impact of this global fuel price increase will be sensible at a smaller scale level, like zonal level. As mentioned earlier, each zone has its own characteristics; i.e. the level of income, availability of public transportation, major activity

types, etc. are different from zone to zone. These differences result in different travel behavior and more specifically different mode choice behavior by the inhabitants of each zone. Therefore, despite the fact that the fuel price increase is applied globally, its impact is dissimilar from zone to zone.

Implementation of Teleworking Scenario in FEATHERS

In contrast to trip-based and tour-based models, activity-based models are sensitive to institutional changes in society in addition to land-use and transportation-system related factors (Arentze & Timmermans, 2005). Such changes are related to work times and work durations of individuals and opening hours of stores or other facilities for "out-of-home" activities. To account for teleworking scenario, the scheduler in FEATHERS first starts with an empty schedule or diary and evaluates whether work activities will be undertaken or not. If there will be any work activity, then the number of work activities (1 or 2 work activities), their starting times, durations and also the time in-between the work activities (in case 2 work activities are performed) will be estimated. In a second step the locations of the work activities are determined. The system sequentially assigns locations to the work activities in order of scheduling position. This is carried out by systematically consulting a fixed list of specific decision trees (Kochan et al., 2011). After the locations of the work activities are determined, the teleworking scenario gets involved. A dedicated procedure samples employees as teleworkers according to a preset distribution. The proportion of working population that is selected to telework on any given working day is 5%. After selecting the teleworkers, their work location(s) will be replaced by their home address and their schedules will be updated with this new information. This way teleworkers stay at home during their working episode. Now that the teleworking scenario is enforced, the scheduler returns back to normal scheduling and proceeds with the next decision steps, which are selection of work related transport modes (only for non-teleworkers), inclusion and time profiling of non-work fixed and flexible activities, determination of fixed and flexible activity locations and finally determination of fixed and flexible activity transport modes. More information about this procedure can be found in (Kochan et al., 2011).

Data Preparation

The study area in this research is the Dutch-speaking region in northern Belgium, Flanders. Flanders has over 6 million inhabitants, or about 60% of the population of Belgium. As already mentioned before, an activity-based model within the FEATHERS framework is applied on the Flemish population to derive travel demand. FEATHERS produces the traffic demand by means of origin-destination (OD) matrices. These OD matrices include the number of trips for each traffic mode at different disaggregation levels (i.e. age, gender, day of the week, time of day and motive). This traffic demand is then assigned to the Flemish road network to obtain detailed exposure metrics at the network level. To carry out this assignment, the user equilibrium method was selected. The fundamental nature of equilibrium assignment is that travelers will strive to find the shortest path (e.g. minimum travel time) from origin to destination, and network equilibrium occurs when no traveler can decrease his travel effort by shifting to a new path. This is an optimal condition, in which no user will gain from changing travel paths once the system is in equilibrium. Exposure metrics are then geographically aggregated to the TAZ level. This has been carried out at the zonal level, comprising 2,200 TAZs in Flanders. The average size of TAZs is 6.09 square kilometers with a standard deviation of 4.78 square kilometers. In addition, a set of socio-demographic and road network variables were collected for each TAZ. The crash data used in this study consist of a geocoded set of fatal and injury crashes that occurred during the period 2004 to 2007. Table 1 shows a list of variables, together with their definition and descriptive statistics, which are used in developing the ZCPMs presented in this study.

Motivation for Conducting Spatial Analysis

The most common modeling framework for ZCPMs is the GLM framework (Abdel-Aty, Siddiqui, & Huang, 2011b; Aguero-Valverde & Jovanis, 2006; Amoros et al., 2003; An et al., 2011; De Guevara, Washington, & Oh, 2004; Hadayeghi et al., 2007; Hadayeghi, Shalaby, Persaud, & Cheung, 2006; Hadayeghi et al., 2003; Hadayeghi, 2009; Lord & Mannering, 2010; G. R. Lovegrove & Sayed, 2006; G. R. Lovegrove, 2005; G. Lovegrove & Sayed, 2007; Naderan & Shahi, 2010; Noland & Oh, 2004; Noland & Quddus, 2004; Pirdavani et al., 2012, 2013). Within a GLM framework, fixed coefficient estimates explain the association between the dependent variable and a set of explanatory variables. In other words, a single model is fitted on the observed data for all locations (e.g. TAZs). However, not surprisingly different spatial variation, which is often referred to as "spatial non-stationarity", may be observed for different variables especially where the study area is relatively large. Neglecting this spatial variation may deteriorate the predictive power of ZCPMs and also has impacts on the significance of explanatory variables.

Checking for the existence of spatial correlation of dependent and explanatory variables can be carried out by means of different statistical tests such as "Moran's autocorrelation coefficient" commonly referred to as Moran's I (Lee & Wong, 2001). Moran's I is an extension of the Pearson product-moment correlation coefficient to a univariate series. It may be expected that in the

Table 1. Selected variables to develop ZCPMs

	Variable	Definition	Average	Min	Max	SD
Dependent variables	CCFS	total Car-Car/Fatal and Severe injury crashes observed in a TAZ	2.82	0	21	3.06
	CCSL	total Car-Car/Slight injury crashes observed in a TAZ	19.22	0	199	20.77
	CSFS	total Car-Slow mode/Fatal and Severe injury crashes observed in a TAZ	1.36	0	16	2.08
	CSSL	total Car-Slow mode/Slight injury crashes observed in a TAZ	10.07	0	202	17.81
Exposure variables	NOTs Car	average daily number of car trips originating/arriving from/at a TAZ	2765.8	0	18111.4	2869.8
	NOTs Slow	average daily number of slow-mode trips originating/arriving from/at a TAZ	1082.2	0	9134	1352.2
	Motorway VKT	average daily vehicle kilometers traveled on motorways in a TAZ	27471.82	0	946152.8	84669.53
	Other Roads VKT	average daily vehicle kilometers traveled on other roads in a TAZ	26662.85	0	303237.6	28133.04
Network variables	Capacity	hourly average capacity of links in a TAZ	1790.1	1200	7348.1	554.6
	Intersection	total number of intersections in a TAZ	5.8	0	40	5.9
	Urban	Is the TAZ in an urban area? "No" represented by 0 "Yes" represented by 1	0	0	1	-[a]
	Suburban	Is the TAZ in a suburban area? "No" represented by 0 "Yes" represented by 1	0	0	1	-
Socio-demographic variables	Income Level	average income of residents in a TAZ described as below: "Monthly salary less than 2249 Euro" represented by 0 "Monthly salary more than 2250 Euro" represented by 1	1	0	1	-
a: Data not applicable						

existence of spatial patterns, close observations are more likely to be similar than those far apart. Moran's *I* can be formulated as follows:

$$Moran's\,I = \frac{n}{SumW}\frac{\sum_{i=1}^{n}\sum_{j=1}^{n}w_{ij}\left(x_i - \bar{x}\right)\left(x_j - \bar{x}\right)}{\sum_{i=1}^{n}\left(x_i - \bar{x}\right)^2}$$

(1)

where n is the number of cases (number of TAZs in our study), $\bar{x}$ is the mean of x_i's, w_{ij} is the weight between cases i and j, and SumW is the sum of all w_{ij}'s:

$$SumW = \sum_{i=1}^{n}\sum_{j=1}^{n}w_{ij}$$ (2)

The value of Moran's *I* varies from -1 representing complete spatial dispersion to 1 indicating

full spatial clustering. Table 2 shows the Moran's *I* values for the selected variables used in the model construction. It is evident that all of the selected variables show significant spatial clustering. Table 2 also includes the significance level of Moran's *I* values by means of Z-scores. Z-scores can be derived as follows:

$$Z\left(MI_i\right) = \frac{O\left(MI_i\right) - E\left(MI_i\right)}{SD\left(MI_i\right)}$$ (3)

Where $Z(MI_i)$ is the Z-score of Moran's *I* of variable *i*, $O(MI_i)$ is the Observed Moran's *I* of variable i, $E(MI_i)$ is the expected Moran's *I* of variable i and $SD(MI_i)$ is the standard deviation of Moran's *I* of variable i. The results presented in Table 2 indicate the necessity of considering spatial autocorrelation when developing crash prediction models.

Table 2. Moran's I Statistics for Dependent and Selected Explanatory Variables

Variable	Observed Moran's *I*	Z-Score	Spatial Status
CCFS	0.091	16.17	Non-stationary
CCSL	0.173	30.928	Non-stationary
CSFS	0.140	25.074	Non-stationary
CSSL	0.219	39.242	Non-stationary
log(NOTs Car)	0.177	31.606	Non-stationary
log(NOTs Slow)	0.222	39.648	Non-stationary
log(Motorway VKT)	0.067	12.016	Non-stationary
log(Other Roads VKT)	0.101	18.042	Non-stationary
Capacity	0.121	21.54	Non-stationary
Intersection	0.199	35.556	Non-stationary
Urban	0.437	78.088	Non-stationary
Suburban	0.239	42.539	Non-stationary
Income Level	0.187	33.318	Non-stationary
CCFS: Car-Car/Fatal and Severe injury crashes CCSL: Car-Car/Slight injury crashes CSFS: Car-Slow mode/ Fatal and Severe injury crashes CSSL: Car-Slow mode/Slight injury crashes			

Model Construction

Inclusion of spatial variation in traffic safety studies has been considered by several researchers. However, there are different spatial modeling techniques that can be applied. Autologistic models, conditional autoregressive models, simultaneous auto-regression models, spatial error models, generalized estimating equation models, Full-Bayesian spatial models and Bayesian Poisson-lognormal models are some of the most employed techniques to conduct spatial modeling in traffic safety (Aguero-Valverde & Jovanis, 2006, 2008; Flahaut, 2004; Guo, Wang, & Abdel-Aty, 2010; Huang et al., 2010; Levine et al., 1995; Miaou,

Song, & Mallick, 2003; Quddus, 2008; Siddiqui, Abdel-Aty, & Choi, 2012; C. Wang, Quddus, & Ison, 2009; X. Wang & Abdel-Aty, 2006). The output of these models are still fixed variable estimates for all locations, however spatial variation is taken into account.

Another solution for taking spatial variation into account is developing a set of local models, so called geographically weighted regression (GWR) models (Fotheringham, Brunsdon, & Charlton, 2002). These models rely on the calibration of multiple regression models for different geographical entities.

The GWR technique can be adapted to GLM models (i.e. extend GLM models) and form geographically weighted generalized linear models (GWGLMs) (Fotheringham et al., 2002). GW-GLMs are able to model count data (such as the number of crashes) while simultaneously accounting for spatial non-stationarity. Hadayeghi et al. (2010b) used the GWR technique in conjunction with the GLM framework using the Poisson error distribution. They developed different GWGLM models to associate the relationship between crashes and a set of predictors. The comparison between GLMs and GWGLM models revealed that the GWGLM models clearly outperform the GLMs since they are capable of capturing spatially dependent relationships.

Reviewing the literature for different model forms showed that the following GLM model has been widely used in different studies (Abdel-Aty et al., 2011b; An et al., 2011; Hadayeghi, 2009; G. R. Lovegrove, 2005; Pirdavani et al., 2012):

$$E(C) = \hat{a}_0 \times (Exposure)^{\hat{a}_1} \times e^{\sum_{i=2}^{n} \hat{a}_i x_i} \quad (4)$$

where; E(C) is the expected crash frequency, $\hat{a}_0, \hat{a}_1$ and $\hat{a}_i$ are model parameters, is the exposure variable (e.g. VKT or NOTs) and x_i's are the other explanatory variables. Logarithmic transformation of Equation (4) when considering only one exposure variable yields:

$$ln\left[E(C)\right] = ln(\hat{a}_0) + \hat{a}_1 ln(Exposure) + \\ \hat{a}_2 x_2 + \hat{a}_3 x_3 + \ldots + \hat{a}_n x_n \quad (5)$$

The Geographically Weighted form of Equation (5) would be:

$$in\left[E(C)(i_i)\right] = in(\hat{a}_0(i_i)) + \hat{a}_1(i_i) in \\ (Exposure) + \hat{a}_2(i_i) x_2 + \ldots + \hat{a}_n(i_i) x_n \quad (6)$$

The output of these models will be different location-specific estimates for each case (here each TAZ). All variable estimates are functions of each location (here the centroid of each TAZ), representing the x and y coordinates of the ith TAZ's centroid.

To account for severity of crashes, different models are developed at different severity levels; i.e. "fatal + severe injury" and "slight injury" crashes. Moreover, TDM scenarios have different safety impacts on different road users. For instance, if implementing a TDM scenario results in transferring individuals out of private vehicles to non-motorized modes, the safety level of car users might be improved, but injury risk for pedestrians or cyclists is expected to increase. Therefore, to address this issue, crashes are further disaggregated into two types namely "Car-Car" and "Car-Slowmode" crashes ("Slowmode" comprises pedestrians and cyclists) and different models are fitted for these different crash types. Hence, four GWGLM models are developed to associate the relationship between crash frequency and the explanatory variables. These models are constructed using a SAS macro program (Chen & Yang, 2012). The selected models are shown in Table 3 represented by the minimum, maximum, 1st quartile, median and 3rd quartile of the parameter estimates.

Traffic Safety Evaluation Process

Road crashes are known to be a function of two components; exposure and risk. By implementing the TDM scenarios, the risk component is kept constant and only the exposure factor will be changed. To compute the changes in exposure, OD matrices for the null scenario and both the fuel-cost increase and the teleworking scenarios were derived from FEATHERS for scenario evaluation. After assigning the travel demand to

Table 3. Model Estimates for the Final Chosen ZCPMs

Coefficients	Model #1 (CCFS) Estimates	Model #2 (CCSL) Estimates	Model #3 (CSFS) Estimates	Model #4 (CSSL) Estimates
(Intercept)	-9.763, -2.692 (-6.517, -5.569, -4.445)[a]	-7.356, -3.077 (-5.611,-4.944,-4.196)	-11.797, -5.453 (-7.889,-7.317,-6.833)	-10.897, -3.994 (-6.574,-6.075,-5.63)
log(NOTs Car)	-0.035, 0.632 (0.093, 0.184,0.268)	0.194, 0.622 (0.352, 0.424,0.479)	-	-
log(NOTs Slow)	-	-	0.484, 1.222 (0.616, 0.745,0.838)	0.621, 1.165 (0.794, 0.917,1.008)
log(Motorways VKT)	-0.036, 0.047 (-0.002, 0.013,0.022)	-0.022, 0.041 (0.001, 0.011,0.018)	-0.073, 0.023 (-0.04, -0.02,-0.007)	-0.054, 0.044 (-0.019,-0.008,0.004)
log(Other Roads VKT)	0.169, 0.669 (0.348, 0.42,0.465)	0.171, 0.632 (0.296, 0.342,0.395)	-0.05, 0.511 (0.163, 0.239,0.311)	0.0243, 0.361 (0.133,0.178,0.229)
Capacity	2.8 e-5, 1.003e-3 (3.3e-4,4.5e-4,6.3e-4)	6.5 e-6, 9.8e-4 (3.5e-4,4.8e-4,6.3e-4)	-4.2e-4, 8.2e-4 (3.3e-5,1.6e-4,3.5e-4)	-7.02e-4, 6.06e-4 (-8.4e-5,4.2e-5,1.9e-4)
Intersection	-0.0296, 0.0611 (0.007,0.019,0.029)	-0.0096, 0.0484 (0.017,0.022,0.026)	-0.063, 0.086 (0.003,0.012,0.023)	-0.0523, 0.056 (0.005,0.015,0.027)
Income level	-	-0.467, 0.637 (-0.185,-0.109,0.053)	-0.562, 1.97 (-0.25,-0.129,0.089)	-0.658, 2.525 (-0.209,-0.078,0.062)
Urban	-1.829, -0.017 (-0.89,-0.68,-0.37)	-	-	-0.193, 1.216 (0.359,0.619,0.86)
Suburban	-0.85, 0.138 (-0.4,-0.29,-0.147)	-	-	-0.219, 0.841 (0.165,0.325,0.409)
PCC[b]	0.735	0.907	0.789	0.952

a: minimum, maximum, (1st quartile, median, 3rd quartile) of the parameter estimates.
b: The Pearson Correlation Coefficient (PCC) between observed and predicted crash values.

the road network, all required variables become available to set up the evaluation task. Now, the final ZCPMs (see Table 3) are applied and crashes are predicted for each TAZ. The traffic safety evaluation can then be conducted by comparing the NOCs predicted by the final ZCPMs for the null and both the fuel-cost increase and the teleworking scenarios. Figure 1 depicts the conceptual framework of the traffic safety evaluation process in more detail.

VALIDATION AND SENSITIVITY ANALYSIS

GWR models aim at identifying spatial heterogeneities in regression models of georeferenced data. The spatial variability of the estimated local regression coefficients is usually examined to verify whether the underlying data shows signs of local deviations from a global regression model. In this regard, mapping the spatial GWR coefficient patterns associated with each variable may reveal some useful information. This approach, however, ignores possible dependencies among the local coefficient estimates linked with different variables. These dependencies can be expressed

Figure 1. Conceptual framework of the traffic safety evaluation process

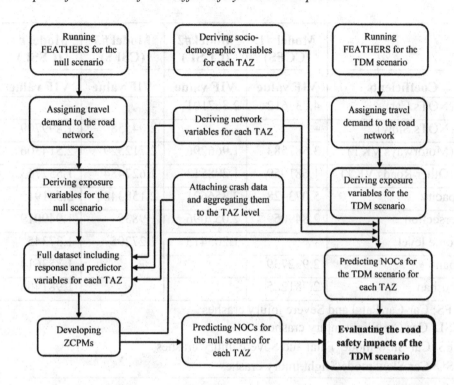

as the correlation between several sets of local coefficient estimates associated with different variables at all locations. Strong dependencies among the local coefficient estimates imply the fact that coefficients are not uniquely defined and as such, any convincing interpretation cannot be derived (Wheeler & Tiefelsdorf, 2005).

Due to the greater complexities of the GWR estimation procedure that conceivably causes interrelationships among the local estimates, it is essential to check for multicollinearity among local coefficient estimates. There are frequently used exploratory tools available to discover possible multicollinearity, such as bivariate scatter plots or bivariate correlation coefficients. However, a more statistically oriented measure that adopts a simultaneous view to identify multicollinearity is the variance inflation factor (VIF). The VIF quantifies the severity of multicollinearity. It provides an index that measures how much the variance of an estimated regression coefficient is

increased because of collinearity. Analyzing the magnitude of multicollinearity is carried out by considering the size of the VIF. As a common rule of thumb, 10 is defined (Kutner, Nachtsheim, & Neter, 2004) as a cut off value meaning that if the VIF is higher than 10 then multicollinearity is high. VIF values among local coefficient estimates of models are shown in Table 4. These results suggest that multicollinearity among local coefficient estimates is not a problem in any of the developed models meaning that the estimations and the choice of predictor variable are reliable.

Due to the nature of GWR models which are location specific models, validation cannot be accomplished by conventional methods (e.g. k-fold cross-validation). Unlike traditional regression modeling in which a general model is fitted on a training dataset and validated on a test dataset, GWR models are a series of local models, there-fore, the concept of training and testing cannot be applied in the context of GWR models. However,

Table 4. VIF Among Local Coefficient Estimates of GWR Models

Coefficients	Model #1 (CCFS) VIF value	Model #2 (CCSL) VIF value	Model #3 (CSFS) VIF value	Model #4 (CSSL) VIF value
log(NOTs Car)	4.737612	2.867101	-	-
log(NOTs Slow)	-	-	2.04558	1.899709
log(Motorways VKT)	3.587583	1.966296	2.712529	2.514306
log(Other Roads VKT)	1.681959	1.298513	1.627484	1.557763
Capacity	5.073428	2.356621	2.158348	2.541915
Intersection	2.849059	2.057096	1.9835	1.949019
Income level	-	1.205415	1.27295	1.37345
Urban	2.932739	-	-	1.853614
Suburban	2.781285	-	-	1.981406
CCFS: Car-Car/Fatal and Severe injury crashes CCSL: Car-Car/Slight injury crashes CSFS: Car-Slow mode/ Fatal and Severe injury crashes CSSL: Car-Slow mode/Slight injury crashes				

a new framework is proposed in this research by which the sensitivity of the prediction power of fitted models is checked. To this end, the whole dataset is randomly divided into 10 segments. In each round of model fitting one segment is left out, therefore, there will be 9 different models fitted for each single data point (here TAZ). Each of these models are developed by using the derived information from the neighboring TAZs. In this case, neighboring TAZs are changed in each round of model fitting for each TAZ. Robustness of the prediction models can be confirmed by checking the variability of predictions derived from 9 different models that are fitted for each TAZ. In case of having an acceptable low variation in predictions, it could be concluded that models are not sensitive to presence/absence of specific vicinity TAZs. Moreover, a low variation in predictions further confirms the presence of spatial correlation and the right choice of bandwidth, meaning that

missing information of left out TAZs are properly substituted by presence of other TAZs that have similar characteristics to the excluded TAZs. Comparing predictions of different local fitted models revealed a high predictive accuracy, substantiating the robustness of models.

RESULTS

Before describing the traffic safety impact of the two TDM scenarios, it would be beneficial to have a look at the changes made to the more traffic-related attributes playing a role in the whole chain. As described before, increasing fuel-related costs will affect and increase the total travel expenses of motor vehicle trips or motivating teleworking will allow a certain percentage of working population to work from home. In the case of the fuel-cost increase scenario, people will start comparing the relative costs of travelling and may consider a shift to other available transportation modes. For instance, short-distance trips can be substituted by public transportation (e.g. bus or tram) or by slow modes (i.e. biking or walking), while long-distance trips may shift towards public transportation (e.g. train) or be substituted by carpooling. In the case of the teleworking scenario, many trips are cancelled and teleworkers are staying at home. However, it is possible that the remaining scheduled trips (except work related trips) of teleworkers still need to be performed. These trips are often short-distance trips and are usually carried out by public transportation (e.g. bus or tram) or slow modes (i.e. biking or walking).

Comparing OD matrices derived from the activity-based model for the null and both the fuel-cost increase and the teleworking scenarios enables us to perceive any changes in NOTs for different modes and will also allow us to figure

out if any mode shift has occurred. Changes in NOTs are shown in Figure 2. The results of these comparisons revealed that the fuel-cost increase scenario has a mixed effect in changing the NOTs, while the teleworking scenario reduces the NOTs for all types of travel mode.

Predictably, in the fuel-cost increase scenario the total number of predicted "Car-Car" crashes decreases compared to the null scenario. This is due to reduced car exposure as the main predictor of these types of crashes. On the contrary and as a result of an increase in Slowmode NOTs, for "Car-Slowmode" crashes a slight increase is observed for both "fatal + severe injury" and "slight injury" crashes. Furthermore, in the teleworking scenario and as a result of reduced exposure for both car and Slowmode NOTs, the total predicted NOCs for all types of crashes decreases compared to the null scenario. Figure 3 depicts changes in NOCs for all types of crash-

Figure 2. Changes in travel demand after implementing the two TDM scenarios

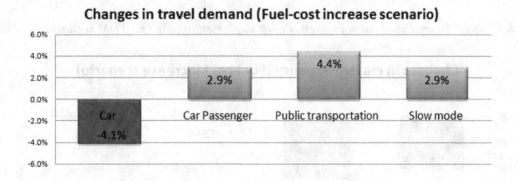

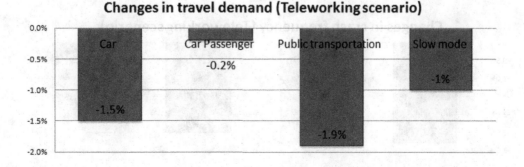

es and for both the fuel-cost increase and the teleworking scenario.

To have a better insight into the distributional changes in NOCs, Figure 4 represents the violin plots of changes in NOCs after the fuel-cost increase and the teleworking scenarios' implementation. The violin plot is a synergistic combination of the box plot and the density trace (Hintze & Nelson, 1998). These plots retain much of the information of box plots (except for the individual outliers), besides providing information about the distributional characteristics of the data. In these plots, the wider the violin, the more data points are associated to that value. Moreover, the white dots indicate the median; black boxes show the upper and lower quartile and the vertical black lines denote the upper and lower whiskers.

In the development of "Car-Slowmode" models, both car and Slowmode-related exposure variables were used. Following the implementation of the fuel-cost increase scenario and as a result of mode shift, the number of car trips decreased whereas the number of Slowmode trips increased. However, these mode shifts are not always similar in all TAZs; i.e. more urbanized areas have a higher number of mode shifts and consequently more Slowmode-related crashes are predicted to occur in these areas. For a better understanding, Figure 5 depicts the population distribution in Flanders per each TAZ where major cities are highlighted with circles. An illustration of changes in the NOCs for all TAZs may present a better understanding on how different TAZs are affected by the fuel-cost increase scenario. In Figure 6, the changes in the predicted NOCs are displayed for each TAZ. Figure 6 reveals that the reductions in CCFS and CCSL crashes are greater for urban areas and generally smaller for TAZs close to the Flemish borders. As explained earlier, CSFS and CSSL crashes are predicted to increase in more urbanized areas; this is evident from the corresponding maps in Figure 6 where concentrations of red dots stand for the major cities in Flanders.

Following the implementation of the teleworking scenario, the total number of car and Slowmode

Figure 3. Changes in predicted crash frequency after implementing the two TDM scenarios

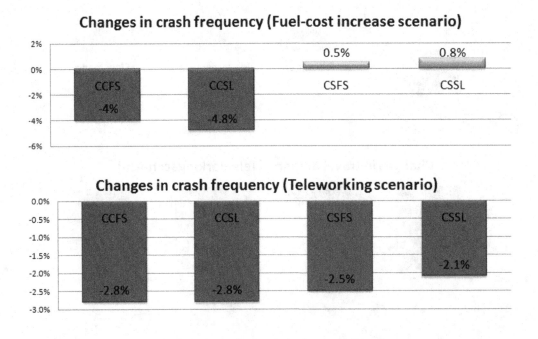

Figure 4. Violin plots of changes in crash occurrence after TDM scenarios implementation

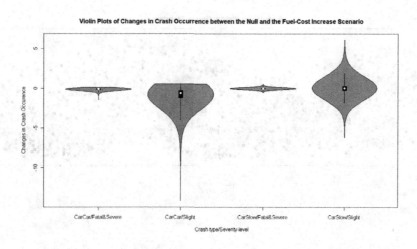

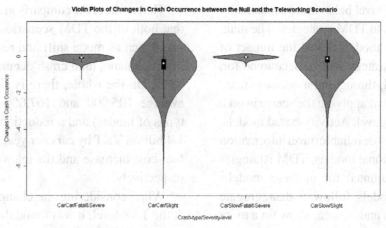

trips decreased. However, these changes are not always similar in all TAZs. In fact, in more urbanized areas, the NOTs reduce more heavily and, therefore, also the NOCs reduce more rapidly. This can be explained by the fact that most of the commuters commute to urbanized areas. An illustration of changes in the NOCs for all TAZs may present a better indication on how different TAZs are affected by the teleworking scenario. In Figure 7, the changes in the predicted NOCs are displayed for each TAZ. Figure 7 reveals that the reductions in CCFS and CCSL crashes are greater for urban areas. As explained earlier, CSFS and CSSL crashes are also predicted to decrease more substantially in more urbanized areas; this

is evident from the corresponding maps in Figure 7 where concentrations of blue dots stand for the major cities in Flanders.

CONCLUSION AND DISCUSSION

In this study, the traffic safety impacts of two TDM scenarios (i.e. the fuel-cost increase and the teleworking scenario) are evaluated. To this end, ZCPMs are coupled with the activity-based model, FEATHERS. Based on the results of the analyses, the following conclusions can be drawn:

Activity-based transportation models provide an adequate range of in-depth information

Figure 5. Population distribution per TAZ and the position of major urban areas in Flanders

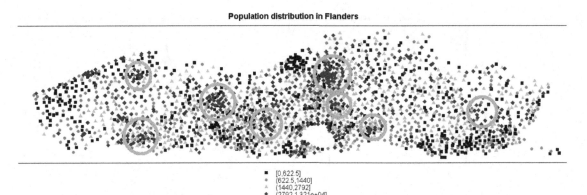

about individuals' travel behavior to realistically simulate and evaluate TDM strategies. The main advantage of these models is that the impact of applying a TDM strategy will be accounted for, for each individual, throughout a decision making process instead of applying the scenario on a general population level. Activity-based models, therefore, provide more reliable travel information since, unlike traditional models, TDM strategies are inherently accounted for in these models. Activity-based models follow a disaggregate modeling approach and as such, allow for a more detailed analysis of the reduction of travel demand due to the implementation of TDM scenarios.

In crash analysis, predictor variables are often found to be spatially heterogeneous especially when the study area is large enough to cover different traffic volume, urbanization and socio-demographic patterns. The results of the analysis confirm the presence of spatial correlation of dependent and different explanatory variables which are used in developing crash prediction models. This was examined by computing Moran's *I* statistics for the dependent and selected explanatory variables. The results reveal the necessity of considering spatial correlation when developing crash prediction models.

The results of the comparison analysis revealed that both of the TDM scenarios have many impacts such as mode shift and reductions of total travel demand, total crash occurrence, VKT and VHT. On the whole, there is a reduction of on average 105,000 and 167,000 daily trips (all types of modes) and a reduction of nearly 5 and 1.4 billion VKT by cars per year as a result of the fuel-cost increase and the teleworking scenario, respectively.

When considering the changes in the NOCs at the TAZ level, it was found that the maximum reduction of "Car-Car" crashes and the maximum increase of "Car-Slowmode" crashes were both observed in urban areas (i.e. cities) after implementing the fuel-cost increase scenario. It can be concluded that in cities, in contrast to other areas, there is a higher likelihood of finding an alternative mode for cars. In contrast, the TAZs in less urbanized regions and the TAZs nearby the borders usually lack good public transportation services. Therefore, it is expected that we will not see many trips shift from cars to other modes in less urbanized areas and consequently there is a more stable traffic safety situation in these TAZs despite conducting the fuel-cost increase scenario. For the teleworking scenario, it turns out that

Figure 6. Changes in NOCs in each TAZ after the fuel-cost increase scenario implementation

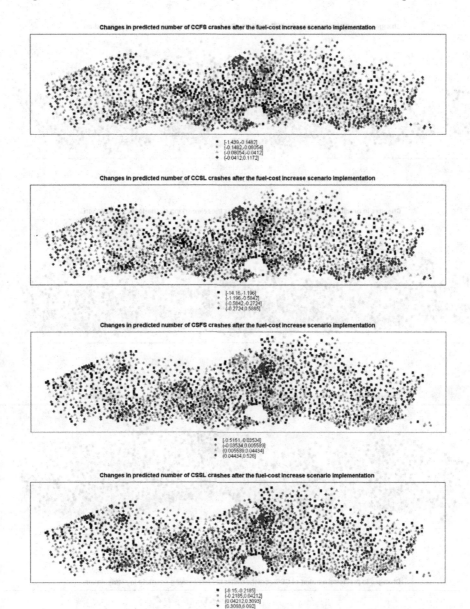

especially urbanized areas (cities) benefit most from a general reduction of "Car-Car" and "Car-Slowmode" crashes. This can be due to the fact that most of businesses that allow their employees to telework are generally located in cities.

In summary, adopting a fuel-cost increase policy can generally be recommended from the road safety point of view and due to its positive impacts on crash frequency reduction. However, the slight negative effect on the traffic safety level of vulnerable road users requires special attention. These negative impacts can be diminished by improving cycle paths infrastructure, improving public transportation efficiency, etc. Moreover, it should be noticed that these positive impacts are fully realizable, only in the short term. In the

Figure 7. Changes in NOCs in each TAZ after the teleworking scenario implementation

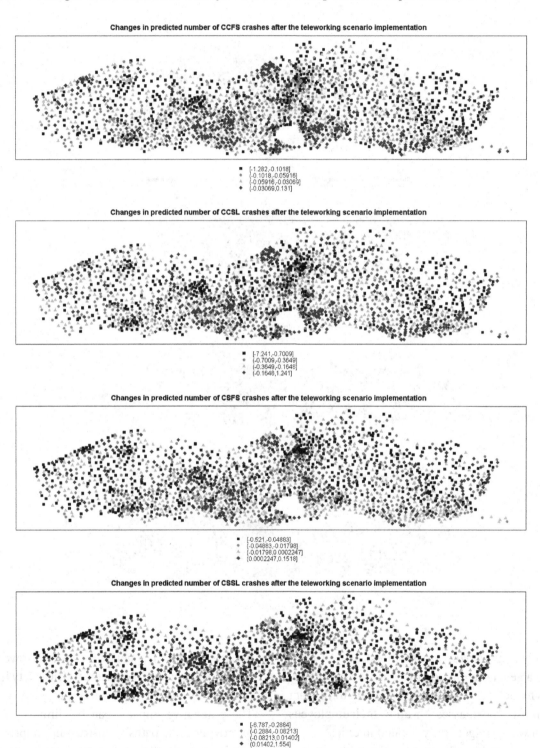

long run and due to the shift in the composition of the vehicle fleet or changes in the location of businesses and/or the location choice for living, these positive impacts might erode. Hence, fuel-cost increase strategies should be considered as short term effective TDM policies, with respect to their road safety impacts.

Crashes are known to be a function of two components; exposure and risk. It is therefore likely that a fuel price increase will impact people's driving behavior and their speed choice; i.e. drivers might try to reduce their fuel consumption by driving more slowly. As a result, it can be assumed that the risk component will also decrease after the fuel-cost increase scenario implementation. In this study however, only the changes in the exposure component were taken into account, whereas the risk component was assumed to be constant. This might be a limitation of this study. If we were to include the risk component in this study as well, however, the traffic safety benefits might be expected to be even larger than predicted in this study.

Due to the observed mixed effects of TDM scenarios on the safety levels of different road users, decision makers and road engineers are strongly recommended to make a distinction between different road users when carrying out any safety assessment. Moreover, combined policies might complement each other and accordingly, desired safety benefits might be realized with more confidence. Another policy related issue that needs further exploration is the safety assessment of other TDM policies; i.e. assessment of an aging population, a public transportation level-of-service improvement and their combination with the studied policies in this research are on the list of the future research agenda.

Moreover, the real power of activity-based models has not yet been fully incorporated. In this study, the methodology relied on the aggregate daily traffic information. Activity-based models are however capable of providing disaggregate travel characteristics by differentiating between many household and person characteristics like gender, age, number of cars, etc. Hence, different types of disaggregation based on time of day, age, gender and motive are on the list of potential future research in order to take full advantage of the output of activity-based models.

REFERENCES

Abdel-Aty, M., Siddiqui, C., & Huang, H. (2011a). *Zonal level safety evaluation incorporating trip generation effects*. Paper presented at the Transportation Research Board (TRB) 90th Annual Meeting. Washington, DC.

Abdel-Aty, M., Siddiqui, C., & Huang, H. (2011b). *Integrating trip and roadway characteristics in managing safety at traffic analysis zones*. Paper presented at the Transportation Research Board (TRB) 90th Annual Meeting. Washington, DC.

Aguero-Valverde, J., & Jovanis, P. P. (2006). Spatial analysis of fatal and injury crashes in Pennsylvania. *Accident; Analysis and Prevention*, *38*(3), 618–625. doi:10.1016/j.aap.2005.12.006 PMID:16451795.

Aguero-Valverde, J., & Jovanis, P. P. (2008). Analysis of road crash frequency with spatial models. *Transportation Research Record: Journal of the Transportation Research Board*, *2061*(1), 55–63. doi:10.3141/2061-07.

Amoros, E., Martin, J. L., & Laumon, B. (2003). Comparison of road crashes incidence and severity between some French counties. *Accident; Analysis and Prevention*, *35*(4), 537–547. doi:10.1016/S0001-4575(02)00031-3 PMID:12729817.

An, M., Casper, C., & Wu, W. (2011). *Using travel demand model and zonal safety planning model for safety benefit estimation in project evaluation*. Paper presented at the Transportation Research Board (TRB) 90th Annual Meeting. Washington, DC.

Arentze, T. A., & Timmermans, H. J. P. (2004). ALBATROSS – Version 2.0 – A learning based transportation oriented simulation system. Eindhoven, The Netherlands: EIRASS (European Institute of Retailing and Services Studies)..

Bellemans, T., Kochan, B., Janssens, D., Wets, G., Arentze, T., & Timmermans, H. (2010). Implementation framework and development trajectory of FEATHERS activity-based simulation platform. *Transportation Research Record: Journal of the Transportation Research Board*, *2175*(1), 111–119. doi:10.3141/2175-13.

Chen, V. Y.-J., & Yang, T.-C. (2012). SAS macro programs for geographically weighted generalized linear modeling with spatial point data: Applications to health research. *Computer Methods and Programs in Biomedicine*, *107*(2), 262–273. doi:10.1016/j.cmpb.2011.10.006 PMID:22078167.

Chi, G., Cosby, A. G., Quddus, M. A., Gilbert, P. A., & Levinson, D. (2010). Gasoline prices and traffic safety in Mississippi. *Journal of Safety Research*, *41*(6), 493–500. doi:10.1016/j.jsr.2010.10.003 PMID:21134515.

Choo, S., & Mokhtarian, P. L. (2007). Telecommunications and travel demand and supply: Aggregate structural equation models for the US. *Transportation Research Part A, Policy and Practice*, *41*(1), 4–18. doi:10.1016/j.tra.2006.01.001.

Choo, S., Mokhtarian, P. L., & Salomon, I. (2005). Does telecommuting reduce vehicle-miles traveled? An aggregate time series analysis for the U.S. *Transportation*, *32*(1), 37–64. doi:10.1007/s11116-004-3046-7.

Davidson, W., Donnelly, R., Vovsha, P., Freedman, J., Ruegg, S., & Hicks, J. et al. (2007). Synthesis of first practices and operational research approaches in activity-based travel demand modeling. *Transportation Research Part A, Policy and Practice*, *41*(5), 464–488. doi:10.1016/j.tra.2006.09.003.

De Guevara, F. L. D., Washington, S., & Oh, J. (2004). Forecasting crashes at the planning level: Simultaneous negative binomial crash model applied in Tucson, Arizona. *Transportation Research Record: Journal of the Transportation Research Board*, *1897*(1), 191–199. doi:10.3141/1897-25.

Dissanayake, D., & Morikawa, T. (2008). Impact assessment of satellite centre-based telecommuting on travel and air quality in developing countries by exploring the link between travel behaviour and urban form. *Transportation Research Part A, Policy and Practice*, *42*(6), 883–894. doi:10.1016/j.tra.2007.12.006.

Flahaut, B. (2004). Impact of infrastructure and local environment on road unsafety: Logistic modeling with spatial autocorrelation. *Accident; Analysis and Prevention*, *36*(6), 1055–1066. doi:10.1016/j.aap.2003.12.003 PMID:15350882.

Fotheringham, A. S., Brunsdon, C., & Charlton, M. (2002). *Geographically weighted regression the analysis of spatially varying relationships*. West Sussex, UK: John Wiley & Sons Ltd.

Goodwin, P., Dargay, J., & Hanly, M. (2004). Elasticities of road traffic and fuel consumption with respect to price and income: A review. *Transport Reviews*, *24*(3), 275–292. doi:10.1080/0144164042000181725.

Grabowski, D. C., & Morrisey, M. A. (2004). Gasoline prices and motor vehicle fatalities. *Journal of Policy Analysis and Management*, *23*(3), 575–593. doi:10.1002/pam.20028.

Guo, F., Wang, X., & Abdel-Aty, M. (2010). Modeling signalized intersection safety with corridor-level spatial correlations. *Accident; Analysis and Prevention*, *42*(1), 84–92. doi:10.1016/j.aap.2009.07.005 PMID:19887148.

Hadayeghi, A. (2009). *Use of advanced techniques to estimate zonal level safety planning models and examine their temporal transferability.* (PhD thesis). Department of Civil Engineering, University of Toronto, Toronto, Canada.

Hadayeghi, A., Shalaby, A., & Persaud, B. (2003). Macrolevel accident prediction models for evaluating safety of urban transportation systems. *Transportation Research Record: Journal of the Transportation Research Board, 1840*(1), 87–95. doi:10.3141/1840-10.

Hadayeghi, A., Shalaby, A., & Persaud, B. (2007). Safety prediction models: Proactive tool for safety evaluation in urban transportation planning applications. *Transportation Research Record: Journal of the Transportation Research Board, 2019*(1), 225–236. doi:10.3141/2019-27.

Hadayeghi, A., Shalaby, A., & Persaud, B. (2010a). Development of planning-level transportation safety models using full Bayesian semiparametric additive techniques. *Journal of Transportation Safety & Security, 2*(1), 45–68. doi:10.1080/19439961003687328.

Hadayeghi, A., Shalaby, A. S., & Persaud, B. N. (2010b). Development of planning level transportation safety tools using geographically weighted poisson regression. *Accident; Analysis and Prevention, 42*(2), 676–688. doi:10.1016/j.aap.2009.10.016 PMID:20159094.

Hadayeghi, A., Shalaby, A. S., Persaud, B. N., & Cheung, C. (2006). Temporal transferability and updating of zonal level accident prediction models. *Accident; Analysis and Prevention, 38*(3), 579–589. doi:10.1016/j.aap.2005.12.003 PMID:16414003.

Henderson, D. K., & Mokhtarian, P. L. (1996). Impacts of center-based telecommuting on travel and emissions: Analysis of the Puget Sound demonstration project. *Transportation Research Part D, Transport and Environment, 1*(1), 29–45. doi:10.1016/S1361-9209(96)00009-0.

Hintze, J. L., & Nelson, R. D. (1998). Violin plots: A box plot-density trace synergism. *The American Statistician, 52*(2), 181–184. doi: doi:10.1080/00031305.1998.10480559.

Huang, H., Abdel-Aty, M., & Darwiche, A. (2010). County-level crash risk analysis in Florida. *Transportation Research Record: Journal of the Transportation Research Board, 2148*(1), 27–37. doi:10.3141/2148-04.

Janssens, D., Wets, G., Timmermans, H. J. P., & Arentze, T. A. (2007). *Modelling short-term dynamics in activity-travel patterns: Conceptual framework of the feathers model.* Paper presented at the 11th World Conference on Transport Research. Berkeley, CA.

Kochan, B., Bellemans, T., Cools, M., Janssens, D., & Wets, G. (2011). *An estimation of total vehicle travel reduction in the case of telecommuting: Detailed analyses using an activity-based modeling approach.* Paper presented at the European Transportation Conference. Glasgow, UK.

Kochan, B., Bellemans, T., Janssens, D., & Wets, G. (2008). *Assessing the impact of fuel cost on traffic demand in flanders using activity-based models.* Paper presented at the Travel Demand Management TDM. Vienna, Austria.

Kochan, B., Bellemans, T., Janssens, D., & Wets, G. (2013). Validation of an activity-based traffic demand model for flanders implemented in the feathers simulation platform. In *Computational Intelligence for Traffic and Mobility.* Atlantic Press. doi:10.2991/978-94-91216-80-0_6.

Koenig, B. E., Henderson, D. K., & Mokhtarian, P. L. (1996). The travel and emissions impacts of telecommuting for the state of California telecommuting pilot project. *Transportation Research Part C, Emerging Technologies*, *4*(1), 13–32. doi:10.1016/0968-090X(95)00020-J.

Kutner, M. H., Nachtsheim, C. J., & Neter, J. (2004). *Applied Linear regression models* (4th ed.). New York: McGraw-Hill..

Lee, J., & Wong, D. W. S. (2001). *Statistical analysis with ArcView GIS*. New York: John Wiley & Sons, Inc.

Levine, N., Kim, K. E., & Nitz, L. H. (1995). Spatial analysis of Honolulu motor vehicle crashes: II: Zonal generators. *Accident; Analysis and Prevention*, *27*(5), 675–685. doi:10.1016/0001-4575(95)00018-U PMID:8579698.

Litman, T. (2003). The online TDM encyclopedia: Mobility management information gateway. *Transport Policy*, *10*(3), 245–249. doi:10.1016/S0967-070X(03)00025-8.

Litman, T. (2006). *Mobility management traffic safety impacts*. Paper presented at the Transportation Research Board (TRB) 85th Annual Meeting. Washington, DC.

Litman, T. (2010). *Changing vehicle travel price sensitivities: The rebounding rebound effect*. Victoria Transport Policy Institute. Retrieved from http://www.vtpi.org

Litman, T., & Fitzroy, S. (2012). *Safe travels: Evaluating mobility management traffic safety impacts*. Victoria Transport Policy Institute. Retrieved from http://www.vtpi.org

Lord, D., & Mannering, F. (2010). The statistical analysis of crash-frequency data: A review and assessment of methodological alternatives. *Transportation Research Part A, Policy and Practice*, *44*(5), 291–305. doi:10.1016/j.tra.2010.02.001.

Lovegrove, G., & Sayed, T. (2007). Macrolevel collision prediction models to enhance traditional reactive road safety improvement programs. *Transportation Research Record: Journal of the Transportation Research Board*, *2019*(1), 65–73. doi:10.3141/2019-09.

Lovegrove, G. R. (2005). *Community-based, macro-level collision prediction models*. (Doctoral thesis). University of British Columbia, Vancouver, Canada.

Lovegrove, G. R., & Litman, T. (2008). *Using macro-level collision prediction models to evaluate the road safety effects of mobility management strategies: New empirical tools to promote sustainable development*. Paper presented at the Transportation Research Board (TRB) 87th Annual Meeting. Washington, DC.

Lovegrove, G. R., & Sayed, T. (2006). Macro-level collision prediction models for evaluating neighbourhood traffic safety. *Canadian Journal of Civil Engineering*, *33*(5), 609–621. doi:10.1139/l06-013.

Miaou, S.-P., Song, J. J., & Mallick, B. K. (2003). Roadway Traffic Crash Mapping: A Space-Time Modeling Approach. *Journal of Transportation and Statistics*, *6*(1), 33–57.

Mokhtarian, P. L., & Varma, K. V. (1998). The trade-off between trips and distance traveled in analyzing the emissions impacts of center-based telecommuting. *Transportation Research Part D, Transport and Environment*, *3*(6), 419–428. doi:10.1016/S1361-9209(98)00018-2.

Naderan, A., & Shahi, J. (2010). Aggregate crash prediction models: Introducing crash generation concept. *Accident; Analysis and Prevention*, *42*(1), 339–346. doi:10.1016/j.aap.2009.08.020 PMID:19887176.

Nilles, J. M. (1996). What does telework really do to us? *World Transport Policy and Practice*, *2*(1-2), 15–23.

Noland, R. B., & Oh, L. (2004). The effect of infrastructure and demographic change on traffic-related fatalities and crashes: A case study of Illinois county-level data. *Accident; Analysis and Prevention, 36*(4), 525–532. doi:10.1016/S0001-4575(03)00058-7 PMID:15094404.

Noland, R. B., & Quddus, M. A. (2004). A spatially disaggregate analysis of road casualties in England. *Accident; Analysis and Prevention, 36*(6), 973–984. doi:10.1016/j.aap.2003.11.001 PMID:15350875.

Noland, R. B., & Quddus, M. A. (2005). Congestion and safety: A spatial analysis of London. *Transportation Research Part A, Policy and Practice, 39*(7-9), 737–754. doi:10.1016/j.tra.2005.02.022.

Pirdavani, A., Brijs, T., Bellemans, T., Kochan, B., & Wets, G. (2012). Developing Zonal Crash Prediction Models with a Focus on Application of Different Exposure Measures. *Transportation Research Record: Journal of the Transportation Research Board, 2280* (-1), 145-153. doi:10.3141/2280-16.

Pirdavani, A., Brijs, T., Bellemans, T., Kochan, B., & Wets, G. (2012). Developing Zonal Crash Prediction Models with a Focus on Application of Different Exposure Measures. Transportation Research Record: Journal of the Transportation Research Board, 2280 (-1), 145-153. doi:10.3141/2280-16., doi:10.1016/j.aap.2012.04.008 PMID:23200453.

Quddus, M. A. (2008). Modelling area-wide count outcomes with spatial correlation and heterogeneity: An analysis of London crash data. *Accident; Analysis and Prevention, 40*(4), 1486–1497. doi:10.1016/j.aap.2008.03.009 PMID:18606282.

Siddiqui, C., Abdel-Aty, M., & Choi, K. (2012). Macroscopic spatial analysis of pedestrian and bicycle crashes. *Accident; Analysis and Prevention, 45*, 382–391. doi:10.1016/j.aap.2011.08.003 PMID:22269522.

Tarko, A., Inerowicz, M., Ramos, J., & Li, W. (2008). Tool with road-level crash prediction for transportation safety planning. *Transportation Research Record: Journal of the Transportation Research Board, 2083*(1), 16–25. doi:10.3141/2083-03.

Vovsha, P., & Bradley, M. (2006). Advanced activity-based models in context of planning decisions. *Transportation Research Record: Journal of the Transportation Research Board, 1981*(1), 34–41. doi:10.3141/1981-07.

VTPI. (2012). *Online TDM encyclopedia.* Victoria Transport Policy Institute. Retrieved from http://www.vtpi.org/tdm/index.php

Vu, S. T., & Vandebona, U. (2007). *Telecommuting and its impacts on vehicle-km travelled.* Paper presented at the International Congress on Modelling and Simulation, University of Canterbury, Christchurch, New Zealand.

Wang, C., Quddus, M. A., & Ison, S. G. (2009). Impact of traffic congestion on road accidents: A spatial analysis of the M25 motorway in England. *Accident; Analysis and Prevention, 41*(4), 798–808. doi:10.1016/j.aap.2009.04.002 PMID:19540969.

Wang, X., & Abdel-Aty, M. (2006). Temporal and spatial analyses of rear-end crashes at signalized intersections. *Accident; Analysis and Prevention, 38*(6), 1137–1150. doi:10.1016/j.aap.2006.04.022 PMID:16777040.

Wheeler, D., & Tiefelsdorf, M. (2005). Multicollinearity and correlation among local regression coefficients in geographically weighted regression. *Journal of Geographical Systems, 7*(2), 161–187. doi:10.1007/s10109-005-0155-6.

Wier, M., Weintraub, J., Humphreys, E. H., Seto, E., & Bhatia, R. (2009). An area-level model of vehicle-pedestrian injury collisions with implications for land use and transportation planning. *Accident; Analysis and Prevention*, *41*(1), 137–145. doi:10.1016/j.aap.2008.10.001 PMID:19114148.

KEY TERMS AND DEFINITIONS

Activity-Based Transportation Model: An activity-based transportation model is a class of transportation forecasting models that predict travel demand based on activities conducted by individuals. These models often consist of a number of decision trees that are used in the scheduling process. These decisions are usually made based on a number of attributes of individuals, households and geographical entities.

Crash Prediction Models: Crash prediction models are statistical models by which the number of expected crashes is predicted given a set amount of input data such as infrastructure, traffic, socio-demographics etc.

Fuel-Cost Strategy: Fuel-related costs are major components of each motor vehicle's operating expenses. By increasing the fuel price as a TDM strategy, people tend to travel less by car, and instead use public transportation, carpool, or shift towards other modes.

Geographically Weighted Generalized Linear Models: GWGLMs are extensions of GLMs by which local spatial regression models are developed to incorporate the spatial variations in association between the number of crashes and a set of predictor variables.

Road Safety: Road safety refers to a set of measures and methods that intend to reduce the risk of road users.

Travel Demand Management: Travel demand management refers to a number of strategies that result in more efficient transportation systems by means of travel demand reduction, travel time shift and mode shift.

Teleworking Strategy: Teleworking is one of the most popular and effective components of commute trip reduction programs and refers to the use of telecommunication systems in substitute of physical travel to the work place.

ENDNOTES

CCFS: car-car/fatal and severe injury

CCSL: car-car/slight injury

CPMs: crash prediction models

CSFS: car-slow mode/fatal and severe injury

CSSL: car-slow mode/slight injury

FEATHERS: Forecasting Evolutionary Activity-Travel of Households and their Environmental Repercussions

GLM: generalized linear modeling

GWGLMs: geographically weighted generalized linear models

GWR: geographically weighted regression

NOCs: number of crashes

NOTs: number of trips

OD: origin-destination

TAZ: traffic analysis zone

TDM: travel demand management

VHT: vehicle hours traveled

VIF: variance inflation factor

VKT: vehicle kilometers traveled

ZCPMs: zonal crash prediction models

Chapter 8
Evaluation of Spatio–Temporal Microsimulation Systems

Christine Kopp
Fraunhofer Institute for Intelligent Analysis and Information Systems (IAIS), Germany

Luca Pappalardo
ISTI-CNR, Italy & University of Pisa, Italy

Bruno Kochan
University of Hasselt, Belgium

Salvatore Rinzivillo
ISTI-CNR, Italy

Michael May
Fraunhofer Institute for Intelligent Analysis and Information Systems (IAIS), Germany

Daniel Schulz
Fraunhofer Institute for Intelligent Analysis and Information Systems (IAIS), Germany

Filippo Simini
University of Bristol, UK

ABSTRACT

The increasing expressiveness of spatio-temporal microsimulation systems makes them attractive for a wide range of real world applications. However, the broad field of applications puts new challenges to the quality of microsimulation systems. They are no longer expected to reflect a few selected mobility characteristics but to be a realistic representation of the real world. In consequence, the validation of spatio-temporal microsimulations has to be deepened and to be especially moved towards a holistic view on movement validation. One advantage hereby is the easier availability of mobility data sets at present, which enables the validation of many different aspects of movement behavior. However, these data sets bring their own challenges as the data may cover only a part of the observation space, differ in its temporal resolution, or not be representative in all aspects. In addition, the definition of appropriate similarity measures, which capture the various mobility characteristics, is challenging. The goal of this chapter is to pave the way for a novel, better, and more detailed evaluation standard for spatio-temporal microsimulation systems. The chapter collects and structure's various aspects that have to be considered for the validation and comparison of movement data. In addition, it assembles the state-of-the-art of existing validation techniques. It concludes with examples of using big data sources for the extraction and validation of movement characteristics outlining the research challenges that have yet to be conquered.

DOI: 10.4018/978-1-4666-4920-0.ch008

INTRODUCTION

Modeling individual movement behavior is a complex task and requires thorough validation throughout the modeling process. The complexity of spatio-temporal microsimulation systems originates mainly from the vast solution space of individual movements in geographic space and time. The size of the solution space is closely linked to the spatial and temporal resolution of the microsimulation, which is typically predetermined by the application. The outcome of a microsimulation is a complete mobility model for a given region, time period and population. Based on a synthetic population it provides a detailed schedule about who moves when and where using which mode of transport. This comprehensive information makes the validation of spatio-temporal microsimulation systems challenging.

In current practice the evaluation of microsimulations relies on a partial evaluation of mobility characteristics. Most often a comparison with traffic counts is performed as e.g. in (Gao et al., 2010; Horni et al., 2009; Meister et al., 2010). Traffic counts have the advantage that they can be comparably easy obtained. However, traffic counts do not contain origin-destination information and are typically available for vehicular traffic only. Thus, they cover only a small aspect of individual movement. In addition, most traffic counts are available for major roads only and are therefore not representative for the whole street network.

In other words, traffic counts are a vital source for the validation of microsimulation systems but their application is limited to a subset of model characteristics.

The example of traffic counts illustrates that a new holistic validation concept for spatio-temporal microsimulation systems is needed. Only a validation which considers a broad set of mobility characteristics can ensure that the outcome of a microsimulation is a truthful reproduction of reality. The required variety of validation data to implement such a concept is just becoming available due to the advancement of information and communication technology. Thus, we are at the right moment of time to animate the discussion about a new validation standard. In addition, research on spatio-temporal data mining and analysis has made tremendous advances during the past decade. As a result, a rich set of preprocessing, feature extraction, indexing and data mining methods are available to exploit and handle spatio-temporal data.

The validation of microsimulation systems is a manifold task. In general, the validation workflow of the modeling process can be divided into three parts, namely *input data* validation, *internal model* validation and *external model* validation (see *Figure 1*). Input data validation ensures that the model is build using high-quality data. Usually, the provided input data comes from secondary data sources and has originally been collected for a different purpose. For this reason

Figure 1. Quality cycle in microsimulation systems

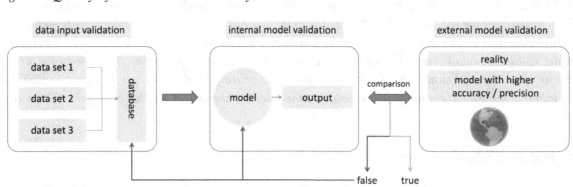

it is important to show in a first validation step that the input data is an appropriate source for the goal of the overall modeling process. Internal model validation measures how well the model can predict its input data, i.e. how reliable a predictive model will perform on (unseen) training data. A high internal quality is a prerequisite for the external quality of the model. If the input data of the model is difficult to predict, this is likely to be the case also for unknown data. In addition, as microsimulation systems typically rely on non-deterministic algorithms, the variability of the model is subject to internal model validation. Finally, during external model validation the model output is compared to either independent real world data or other model results with known high quality. This step ensures the final quality of the model results. If the model outcome meets a given quality standard the process of modeling is finished. Otherwise, either the input data or the modeling process are subject to change and to a repeated validation, leading to a validation cycle.

In this chapter we attempt to compile a comprehensive overview on the state-of-the-art of validating spatio-temporal microsimulation systems. We provide a structured review on the various aspects of movement data evaluation and give practical insights into challenging problems based on real-world examples. More detailed, Section *Properties of Mobility Data* recapitulates general properties of mobility data that influence the comparability of mobility data sets. Section *Data Input and External Model Validation* describes mobility characteristics and validation techniques that are commonly used to compare two mobility data sets while Section *Internal Model Validation* focuses on the estimation of internal model quality. In Section *Validation Use Cases* we provide real-world examples outlining the challenges of comparing mobility data sets. Finally, the *Conclusion* summarizes the vital points of this chapter and draws a roadmap for the further advancement of evaluating spatio-temporal microsimulation systems.

PROPERTIES OF MOBILITY DATA

Due to the manifold techniques to record mobility information, mobility data sets can differ in various aspects. In order to make valid statements about the similarity or dissimilarity of two data sets it is therefore essential to have a clear understanding of the delimitation of each set with respect to its spatial, temporal and population dimension. In this section we will discuss these dimensions as well as different properties of mobility data sets. The properties include the observation space, sampling coverage and resolution. In addition, we consider missing data properties because they can influence the representativeness of a data set. Note that our grouping of mobility properties results mainly from our experience in practice. A partially differing compilation is, for example, chosen in (Andrienko et al., 2013).

Dimensions of Mobility Data

Mobility is inherently connected to three basic dimensions: space, time and population. Geographic space defines *where* movement takes place, time defines *when* movement takes place and the population or object dimension specifies *who* is moving. In this section we will give a short introduction to all three dimensions, summarized from (Andrienko at al., 2008; Körner, 2012).

Commonly, we refer to geographic space as the three-dimensional Euclidean space that co-rotates with Earth and is centered at its center of mass, i.e. the physical space we observe in everyday life. In order to specify the position of an object in physical space, spatial reference systems such as the Cartesian or Geographic reference system are used. Typically, the spatial component of mobility data is specified using two-dimensional geographic coordinates, i.e. the longitude and latitude of the moving object's positions.

Time is a one-dimensional extent which describes the ordering and duration of events. Today Coordinated Universal Time (UTC) is used as standard temporal reference system to refer to a specific moment in time. UTC uses the Gregorian calendar to reference days. It further divides a day into hours, minutes and seconds. Due to the Earth's rotation and its revolution around the sun, we perceive a natural structure of time into cycles. Over the year we observe the change of seasons, our working activity is typically organized by a weekly cycle, and our day/night rhythm repeats every 24 hours. Be aware that those cycles are nested and form hierarchies as e.g. year/month/day-in-month or year/week-in-year/day-in-week. Such hierarchies are especially relevant for the validation of mobility data because the data sets belong often to different time periods, and the aggregation of data into time cycles provides the only way for comparison.

The population dimension specifies of which entities the movements are observed. Entities may be animate (e.g. persons, animals) or inanimate (e.g. parcels, airplanes). As this book is placed in the area of transportation research, we tailor the following description to humans. Persons have numerous sociodemographic characteristics such as their gender, age, occupation or income. Sociodemographic characteristics are known to influence movement behavior (Curtis & Perkins, 2006; Scheiner, 2010). For example, the age determines whether we can travel independently by ourselves or whether we are allowed to drive a car while the occupation determines whether we have regular work trips. Another important variable that influences mobility is the place of living (Curtis & Perkins, 2006; Schwanen et al., 2005). For example, the trip length and preferred mode of transport varies between urban and rural areas.

In addition to the three basic dimensions that characterize movement, the movement itself can be described by physical and semantic properties. For example, movement possesses speed, acceleration, direction and turn characteristics. In addition, it has some means of transportation and is conducted with some specific activity in mind (e.g. when going to work).

Together the four dimensions provide a good way to structure properties of mobility data sets, which we will discuss next.

Observation Space

The observation space delimits the spatial, temporal, population and movement dimensions for which the comparison shall be made. More precisely, in the spatial dimension it restricts the region in which the movement is observed. Typically, this is a city, community or even larger administrative area. In addition, the spatial observation may be restricted to a specific type of geographic objects. For example, instead of monitoring continuous space, we may observe movement only on the street network. Furthermore, we could observe only highways or the pedestrian area of a city.

In the temporal dimension the observation space defines the time moment, time interval or time cycle in which the movement takes place. If a data set consists of raw measurements it typically refers to a specific time period, e.g. the month January 2013. Often data sets are already aggregated to a specific time cycle, e.g. an average week. In such cases it is still important to know how the cycle relates to the greater time hierarchy. Is it, for example, an average week in January (with slippery roads in the northern hemisphere) or in June (holiday season), and which year does it represent (e.g. 1980)? Furthermore, an observation may be restricted to selected time intervals within, e.g. we may observe only the working days of a week or the daytime between 6 and 20 o'clock.

The population observation space defines the set of persons whose movements are studied. It is closely connected to the data collection process. If a survey is conducted, the population typically represents the residents of a defined area, e.g. the inhabitants of a city or country. Further attributes may be used in the selection process. For example, only persons above 18 years of age or persons who commute to work could be considered. This definition has the advantage that it is compatible with many official statistics. However, as geographic space is not a closed system, it lacks the mobility of externals visiting the area as e.g. commuters, freight carriers or tourists. In contrast, the population may comprise all persons travelling in a certain area as observed, for example, when using induction loops for traffic monitoring.

Finally, mobility data may be limited to certain mobility characteristics. For example, GPS tracking devices may be installed into the car of a person and record only vehicular movement. Induction loops have a similar effect as they monitor only motorized traffic. The studied movement may also be related to certain activities only as, for example, shopping, working or vacation.

Sampling Coverage

The sampling coverage is closely related to the observation space. As it is typically not possible to monitor the complete observation space, the data set is only a sample of the spatial, temporal and population dimension. Samples are generally characterized by their distribution and size. Both characteristics are important to know because they determine the representativeness and sampling error of a data set with respect to the observation space.

In the spatial dimension sampling processes are most visible when a decision about the placement of (a limited number of) stationary sensors has to be made. Examples of such sensors are induction loops, light barriers, cameras, WiFi or Bluetooth scanners which count the number of passing vehicles or persons. Note that those sensors are typically placed at strategic points with high traffic volume and may therefore not be representative for the observation space. Similar problems can arise if mobile sensors are used. Although each person moves in space and records data for various locations, a really large sample is needed for a complete coverage of the street network. For example, Hecker et al. (2010) analyzed a data set with 42,780 test persons of mixed GPS and

CATI (Computer Assisted Telephone Interview) records of up to seven days in Germany. The trajectories covered barely 26.7% of the German street network. Andrienko et al. (2013) identify yet another bias inherent to event-based mobility data. The authors have analyzed sequences of geo-referenced Flickr data. Naturally people take pictures of interesting places, which are therefore over-represented in the data set. In order to detect abnormalities in the spatial sampling coverage a first step is to plot the data on a map. Co-location of data with certain geographic objects (e.g. highways, points of interest) or clearly delineated sectors with/without data indicate a spatial sampling bias. However, as mobility is not equally distributed in geographic space further analyses may be required to detect irregularities.

In the temporal dimension the sampling coverage defines how frequent measurements are taken. As time is a uniform quantity in one dimension, the analysis of its distribution and sample size is easier than in the spatial dimension. Andrienko et al. (2013) distinguish between the analysis of the length and regularity of time intervals between measurements, the coverage of the observation interval as well as of relevant time cycles. If the time interval between two measurements is short enough to permit a good interpolation of an object's position, the authors call the data quasi-continuous. Elsewise, it is considered episodic. For example, GPS data with a time interval of one second between measurements is quasi-continuous. Call detail records (CDR), which accumulate only during a user's phone activity, are episodic. Both examples illustrate also the difference between regular and irregular measurement techniques. Regular measurements guarantee a homogeneous coverage of the temporal observation space. However, only in combination with frequent measurements, a representative temporal sample can be formed. Consider, for example, traffic counts which are observed for five minutes at noon every day. Because movement activity varies over time, it is not obvious how to relate these measurements to the movement activity of a whole day. Without an assumption about a relationship between noon and daily (or day-of-week) traffic, we would even not be able to make assumptions about the weekly or yearly variation of traffic outside of the observed five minute time intervals. Thus it is important to cover all relevant time cycles within the temporal observation space sufficiently. In order to analyze the temporal coverage of a data set, Andrienko et al. (2013) propose to plot histograms or the cumulative distribution function of either the number of measurements or the time interval between consecutive measurements for different time cycles.

Spatio-temporal microsimulations have the scope to model population movement. Therefore, the sampling coverage of input or validation data must typically be representative for some national population. As mobility data sets are often secondary data sources only, a variety of sampling biases can arise. As mentioned in (Körner et al., 2012) a first cause of sampling bias is the different affinity of people to either the companies or devices collecting mobility data. On the one hand, companies (e.g. mobile network providers) target specific customer groups. Their data collection is therefore biased towards those sociodemographic groups. On the other hand, data collection relies increasingly on the usage of mobile devices (e.g. CDR, Bluetooth). However, mobile devices are not equally distributed and used within the population, but show a clear bias towards the young generation. A second cause for a biased population sample is the uncontrolled relationship between persons and data collection devices. A person may carry multiple tracking devices (e.g. mobile phone(s), tablet) and thus be included several times. Similarly, an observed device may be shared by one or more persons (e.g. a car) and therefore represent multiple users. The assessment whether a data set contains a population bias is a complex task because most secondary mobility data sets contain only numeric identifiers due to privacy reasons. In such a case expert knowledge as well as good

reasoning capabilities are required for the analysis (Andrienko et al., 2013).

Finally, a sample bias may also be introduced by selection processes in the dimension of movement characteristics. For example, Bluetooth scanners require up to ten seconds to detect all devices within their range. In consequence, Bluetooth-enabled devices that pass the sensor range with a high velocity have a smaller probability to be detected than slow-moving devices (Gurczik at al., 2012; Schmietendorf, 2011). In addition, a sample bias may be introduced during data preprocessing. For example, when cleaning GPS data, points above or below a certain velocity or trips below a given lengths may be removed as noise. An empirical detection of such biases is hard because it is not obvious for which type of bias to look in the first place. Therefore, it is important to have a good understanding of the data collection process and the performed preprocessing steps.

Resolution

We use the term resolution to refer to the level of aggregation or the amount of detail in a data set. In the population dimension the smallest possible measurement unit is a single person, which corresponds to the natural resolution of microsimulations. However, input and test data sets may not be that fine-grained. For example, sociodemographic characteristics are typically aggregated for larger geographic areas in order to be privacy-preserving. Similarly, movement information may be available only in aggregated form or without sociodemographic references. In some mobility data sets identifiers are routinely changed so that the association to a specific unit is lost over time.

The spatial resolution of a data set can vary between a few centimeters and several kilometers depending on the monitoring technology used to collect the data. For example, GPS data has a very high resolution while CDR data may relate to very large GSM cells in suburban areas. However, also the spatial resolution of microsimulations can vary. Some systems perform a simulation on the level of the street network as, for example, MATSim (Balmer et al., 2006) while other systems operate on the level of traffic analysis zones as, for example, FEATHERS (Bellemans et al., 2010).

In the temporal dimension the resolution of a data set corresponds to the time span of a single measurement. For example, traffic counts are typically aggregated at the level of hours while most data sets containing time stamps have a resolution of seconds or milliseconds. The temporal resolution is often confused with the temporal sampling rate. However, a data set may have a very low sampling rate (e.g. one GPS point every hour) while the temporal resolution of the measurement is very high (e.g. a timestamp of the format JJJJ-MM-DD:hh:mm:ss).

The resolution of movement characteristics can vary in a broad range. For categorical variables (e.g. type of activity, mode of transportation) the resolution depends on the employed ontology or classification system. For derived numeric movement characteristics (e.g. speed, acceleration) the resolution depends on the aggregation level of the spatial and temporal dimension.

Missing Data

Missing data typically originates from uncontrolled events or processes during data collection and extends over all dimensions of mobility data. For example, technical devices may be defective or the human recollection of movement incomplete. Missing data pose a problem to data evaluation for several reasons. First, the amount of missing data may be so high, that an exclusion of incomplete data records would strongly reduce the data set. Second, summary statistics may be considered for a given time interval. If the missing data is ignored (i.e. substituted with zero values) an underestimation of movement behavior will be induced. Third, a relationship between the absence of data and the mobility behavior of a person may

exist (Körner, 2012). For example, people between 30 and 39 years of age show with an average of 53 kilometers per day the highest mobility while teenagers travel around 30 kilometers per day and people above 74 years travel only 16 kilometers on average (Bundesministerium für Verkehr, Bau und Stadtentwicklung, 2010). If certain characteristics of such groups relate to the intensity of missing data, for example, elder persons may be more reliable to carry a GPS device than teenagers, the pattern of missing data is not any more at random. Therefore it is important to detect and analyze a data set for missing data as e.g. proposed in (Körner, 2012; Andrienko et al., 2013; Hecker et al., 2010).

DATA INPUT AND EXTERNAL MODEL VALIDATION

In general, the validation process of model input data does not differ from the validation process of model output data. In both cases various characteristics of the data set in question have to be assured by comparison against external data sources. Both times we are interested in mobility characteristics of a given population. Thus we have the common task to compare mobility characteristics between two mobility data sets, which is the main topic of this section. We will start by an introduction to general measures for the comparison of categorical and numerical data sets. Next, we give a systematic overview on the various mobility characteristics that can be used to describe mobile behavior. We will structure this part according to movement characteristics considering single movement positions, differences between movement positions (e.g. length and distance) and sequential dependencies between movement positions. In this way we increase the spatio-temporal complexity of the observed characteristic step by step. Finally, we will discuss the state-of-the-art of external model validation.

General Measures for Comparing Categorical and Numerical Variables

Due to the wide spectrum of movement characteristics, a number of different error or distance measures can be applied for the comparison of two mobility data sets. In general, each measure is based on a particular definition of error or distance, and its estimate will thus reflect the characteristic features and properties of the underlying error/distance function. Therefore, there is no absolute best measure, and the validation method has to be chosen considering the features that one wishes to evaluate and the characteristics of the data sets. In most cases it is recommendable to use several measures in order to have a comprehensive picture of the error/distance.

In this section we will introduce general measures for the comparison of (one or many) pairwise observations as well as for the comparison of distributions of numerical and/or categorical data. For a comprehensive overview we refer the reader to (Hyndman and Koehler, 2006) and (Cha, 2007).

Let $A=(a_1, a_2, ..., a_n)$ and $B=(b_1, b_2, ..., b_n)$ denote two data sets with pairwise observations. For all error measures we will assume that data set B contains the ground truth. If the data is categorical the error is typically specified as average of the 0-1 loss, i.e.

$$Err = \sum_{i=1}^{n} l(a_i, b_i) \Big/ n$$

with

$$l(a_i, b_i) = \begin{cases} 0 & if\ a_i = b_i \\ 1 & else \end{cases}.$$

The error can be further analyzed using a confusion matrix. The rows of a confusion matrix represent the ground truth while the columns represent values of the second (predicted) data set. All coinciding data records are located in the diagonal of the table. *Table 1* shows a fictitious example of a confusion matrix for evaluating a model that predicts the mode of transportation.\

In total the ground truth data set contains 23 objects. The confusion matrix shows that of the eight actual cars the system predicted five as cars and three as public transport. Of the six public transports it predicted three correctly, two as cars and one as bike, and of the bikes it predicted eleven correctly and two as public transport. We can see from the matrix that the system in question has trouble distinguishing between cars and public transport but distinguishes well between bike and other types of the mode of transport.

For numeric data the most commonly applied error measures are mean absolute error (MAE), mean absolute percentage error (MAPE) and root mean square error (RMSE). They are defined as follows:

$$MAE = \sum_{i=1}^{n} \left| a_i - b_i \right| \Big/ n,$$

$$MAPE = \left(\sum_{i=1}^{n} \left| \frac{a_i - b_i}{b_i} \right| \Big/ n \right) \cdot 100\%,$$

$$RMSE = \sqrt{\sum_{i=1}^{n} \left(a_i - b_i \right)^2 \Big/ n}.$$

In addition to error functions, also various distance functions can be applied to measure the

Table 1. Example of a confusion matrix

		Data Set A		
		car	public transport	bike
	car	5	3	0
Data Set B	public transport	2	3	1
	bike	0	2	11

(dis)similarity between pairwise observations. Most well-known is the Minkowski distance:

$$d_M = \sqrt[p]{\sum_{i=1}^{n} \left| a_i - b_i \right|^p}$$

which results in the Manhattan distance for $p=1$, the Euclidean distance for $p=2$ and the Chebyshev distance for $p=\yen$. In the Minkowski family the weight of large individual errors increases with increasing p, amounting to the maximum absolute pairwise difference for $p=\yen$. One way to reduce the effect of large errors is to apply, for example, the Lorentzian distance:

$$d_L = \sum_{i=1}^{n} \ln(1 + \left| a_i - b_i \right|).$$

For visual inspection, numerical pairwise observations can also be depicted in a scatter plot. The closer the points are to the diagonal representing equal values, the more similar are both data sets. The linear dependence between the data sets can be quantified using e.g. Pearson's correlation coefficient.

For the comparison of distributions, methods for categorical, discrete and continuous data exist. One way to treat categorical distributions is to view the two frequency values of each category as a pairwise observation and to apply the above described methods for numeric data. Another way of comparison is to perform a statistical test to assess how likely both data sets origin from the same statistic population. For categorical data the chi-squared test for homogeneity can be used for this purpose.

Discrete valued distributions can be treated similar to categorical distributions. However, due to their numerical nature, we can derive and compare further moments of the distribution as, for example, its mean, variance or skewness. The mean of two data sets can be compared using, for

example, a two-sample t-test or Z-test whereas the variance can be compared using the F-test (under the assumption of normally distributed data).

Finally, continuous valued distributions can be compared using the Kolmogorov-Smirnov test for homogeneity. Similar to discrete valued distributions, we can compare the mean, variance or skewness of the distributions. In addition, the distribution may be discretized and treated similar to categorical distributions.

Evaluating the Distribution of Movement Positions

In this section we consider count-based evaluations of movement characteristics that describe the population's whereabouts for given instances in time, space or a combination of both. We will begin with general statistics related to the population and the population's movements. Afterwards we will consider their spatial, temporal and spatio-temporal distribution. General count-based population and mobility statistics are the:

- Distribution of sociodemographic attributes.
- Distribution of activities.
- Distribution of trips.
- Distribution of mode of transport.

Sociodemographic attributes that are closely related to a person's mobility are, for example, age, gender, occupation or income. It is important to compare not only the distribution of each single attribute but also their joint probability distribution. Activities are typically the cause for mobility. For example, we travel to work, go shopping or to the cinema. An interesting mobility characteristic is therefore the distribution of trip activities, stating the percentage of trips that are made for a specific purpose. In addition, we can consider the distribution of activities within the population. Which percentage of the population performs a certain activity? How often is an activity performed on average? Körner (2012) defines a family of quantities that can be used for the evaluation of such questions. Similarly we can analyze the number of trips or home-based tours, and (the split of) the mode of transport (e.g. on foot, by bike, by car or public transport).

Next, we consider the *spatial* distribution of the population at a given moment or interval of time

- Using a specific mode of transportation.
- Travelling with a specific speed.
- Performing specific activities.

The spatial distribution of the population becomes visible, for example, in the traffic volume. The traffic volume states the average or total number of passing vehicles or persons in a given time interval, e.g. an hour or a day. When derived from local sensors (e.g. induction loops, camera systems, Bluetooth), the traffic volume is available only for a selected set of locations. However, data mining techniques can be used to predict traffic frequencies for sites without sensors (May et al., 2008a, May at el., 2008b). Traffic counts can also be derived from GPS trajectory data as investigated in (Pappalardo et al., 2013). In such a case the geographic coverage of measurements increases, however, only a sample of passer-bys is recorded. Traffic counts can further be differentiated according to the mode of transport or the speed class. In addition, differences between the spatial distribution of counts and other numeric characteristics (e.g. speed) can be quantified by calculating pairwise differences between the values of each location. For visualization the spatial distribution of the values or their differences can be depicted on a map using e.g. a color encoding similar to (Andrienko & Andrienko, 2010). In addition to the distribution of the population when travelling, the distribution of the population during the performance of activities can be analyzed. Similar to traffic counts, the number of visitors at

train stations, shops etc. can be compared. While those visits are of short duration and show a high variability, we can also analyze the distribution of long-term activity locations as the home or work place. Depending on the spatial aggregation unit, statistics about the number of persons living or working in a given street, sector or city may be compared.

In the following we analyze the *temporal* distribution of the population at a certain location or in a certain area

- Using a specific mode of transportation.
- Travelling with a specific speed.
- At the begin/end of certain activities.
- At the begin/end of a trip.

The temporal usage of a location can be measured by continuously monitoring the time of passage of moving objects. Depending on the data source, a stream of events or an already aggregated count for a series of time intervals may be given. If one or both of the time series are discretized, the data sets have to be adapted to contain the same regular intervals of time. The temporal distribution can further be differentiated according to a specific mode of transport, speed class or average speed. In addition to the temporal distribution of movements, the temporal distribution of activities or trips can be compared using their start or end time. For a visual comparison of temporal distributions, a temporal histogram as shown in (Andrienko & Andrienko, 2010) can be used. Note that the temporal distribution of passages may also be gained from GPS trajectory data as described in (Schreinemacher et al., 2012). Here again the problem arises that only a sample of passers-by are observed and the data may be sparse in time or space.

Finally, a joint comparison of mobility characteristics in the *spatial and temporal* dimension can be made. Due to the high complexity of spatio-temporal data, such a comparison typically relies on a sequential aggregation in space and time. For example, the data can be first divided into a set of time moments or intervals. For each time slice a measure comparing the spatial distribution of two data sets is computed. The computation is repeated for each time slice and then summarized in a graph by its mean or variance. Similarly, the data set can be divided by locations first. For each location a comparison of the temporal distribution is performed. Subsequently, the results are aggregated over all locations. A spatio-temporal comparison can also be aided by visualization. For example, a geographic map containing temporal mosaic diagrams as in (Andrienko & Andrienko, 2010) is able to show the full variation of some variable (or the difference between two data sets) in space and time. However, such maps are very complex because of their high information density. Visual analysis can then be aided by classifying similar situations. For example, Schreinemacher et al. (2012) cluster street segments according to the temporal distribution of passages. The street segments were then colored according to their types in order to identify spatial relationships. If a set of speed profiles is already given, each location can be assigned to its most similar profile. Spatio-temporal differences between two data sets can then be observed by visualizing the spatial distribution of the assigned profiles. Andrienko et al. (2012) performed a clustering the other way around. They determined the spatial distribution of visitors for a run of 30 minute time intervals and subsequently clustered the spatial distributions. For such a comparison of two data sets, a set of spatial distributions has to be given in advance, according to which a classification of time intervals can be made in both data sets. The results can then be compared in a time graph.

Evaluating the Distribution of Differences between Movement Positions

In this section we consider movement characteristics that are derived from the difference of two positions in either space or time, namely length and duration. In the most simple form, we can compile the total length (duration) of all trips performed in a given period of time, e.g. one year. The total sum can be further differentiated according to the used mode of transportation or the traversed type of street. For example, we can calculate the total number of kilometers (hours) travelled by car on highways. Instead of the total number, we can also compare the distribution or averages of the length (duration) with respect to different categories or a combination of them:

- Persons.
- Trips.
- Locations.
- Activities.

For example, the distribution or average trip length (duration) per person and day is a very characteristic information about a population's movement behavior. Those statistics can also be calculated for single trips. Next, we can calculate the length (duration) to reach specific locations. Imagine, for example, that a shop is interested to determine the catchment area of its customers or a city council wants to estimate how far (long) incoming or outgoing commuters travel daily to reach their work location. Further, the length (duration) that people are willing to travel to perform certain activities can be compared. For activities we can additionally compute their duration. So far we have considered absolute values of movement characteristics. Another interesting feature is the relative value of the length (duration) of a route compared to the shortest possible route (in space or time). Such a comparison is especially useful if a traffic assignment step is performed during the microsimulation in order to map the movement between zonal areas to the street network. While time is a one-dimensional extent, movement takes place in three-dimensional Euclidean space. In order to measure the spatial extent (spread) of a person's mobility, typically the radius of gyration (ROG) is used. The radius of gyration r_g is defined as:

$$r_g = \sqrt{\frac{1}{n} \sum_{i=1}^{n} (p_i - p_c m)^2}$$

with

$$p_{cm} = \frac{1}{n} \sum_{i=1}^{n} p_i$$

Hereby represent the positions recorded for a given user. In the mobility context, is a two-dimensional vector describing latitude and longitude of a user's movements.

Similar to the previous section, we can evaluate the spatial and temporal distribution of the above characteristics. When choosing the spatial dimension, the movement characteristics are typically attached to the place of living of a person or the targeted activity location. For example, from national statistics as (Bundesministerium für Verkehr, Bau und Stadtentwicklung, 2010) it is known that the average number of kilometers travelled per person and day of people that live in large cities is shorter than of people living in suburban areas. In the temporal dimension movement characteristics are typically attached to the start or end time of an activity or trip. This allows to compare, for example, whether two data sets contain the same characteristic variation of the trip length (duration) over the day or between week days and weekends.

Evaluating Sequential Dependencies between Movement Positions

In this section we describe characteristics that originate from the sequence of movement positions. In general, we can distinguish between the physical and semantic representation of movement sequences. In the first case a trajectory consists of the sequence of passed or visited geographic locations. In the second case a trajectory is a sequence of activities as, for example, "home → work → shopping → home".

The most common representation of movement dependencies between *geographic locations* is an origin-destination (OD) matrix. An OD matrix states for each pair of start and end locations the number of performed trips in a given time interval. Such a matrix can also be evaluated for a specific mode of transport (e.g. for the railroad network) or for specific trip purposes (e.g. home-work trips). Comparing only the OD distribution of the start and end location of trips, however, does not guarantee that the "right" route choice has been made. Therefore, we can compare the OD distribution for movement positions within a trip. If the movement is mapped to the street network we can calculate an OD matrix for each passed street segment from those trips which pass the segment. Having derived a single error value from the OD matrix comparison for each segment, a color-encoded map or average error value can be computed. Another way to compare local movement behavior is the calculation of flows between neighboring areas or street segments. Given a movement trajectory, its sequential information is discarded with exception to the very next step, i.e. we create a Markov chain from the data. Such flows describe, for example, turning probabilities at cross roads or hand-over information of GSM cells. If we extend such flows to contain several steps, we obtain movement rules as, for example, given that a person moves from A→ B then the probability of moving to C is 25%. The detection of movement patterns, however, is a complex task.

One possibility is to find frequent sub-trajectories in the data sets as proposed by Giannotti et al (2007). Another possibility is to build a compact model of the location dependencies using e.g. Bayesian Networks (Liebig et al., 2009).

In the case of *semantic trajectories*, we have to find an appropriate measure to compare activity-travel sequences. First and foremost the goodness-of-fit measure has to be able to consider the different dimensions of activity-travel patterns. However, another critical point is that the measure should also be able to compare sequential information. The Sequence Alignment Method (SAM) is an appropriate measure as it complies with all of the above aspects. Introduced by Wilson (1998) in time use research, SAM has the right properties for working out comparisons between predicted and observed activity-travel patterns. SAM works by calculating a distance between the predicted and observed string of activity-travel information. Unlike the Euclidean distance, a specific distance is computed by determining the amount of effort it takes in order to make the two strings equal. To calculate the total amount of effort, a series of possible operations are performed on the strings. This way strings can be made equal by using so-called 'identity', 'substitution', 'insertion' and 'deletion' operations. The distance calculated this way is then taken as the measure of dissimilarity between the strings. However a shortcoming of this approach is that SAM can only handle one-dimensional strings. This means that SAM can analyze similarities for specific attributes of activity-travel patterns, such as activity type, mode choice, location choice, etc. but not the inter-relationships between elements of different attributes. Therefore, a multidimensional extension of the traditional SAM was developed (Joh, 1999). In this way multidimensional activity-travel patterns can be compared. However, the comparison relies only on the sequential activity information. For the inclusion of temporal information, further, sophisticated similarity measures have yet to be developed. Nevertheless, similarly to

physical movement sequences, we can also extract and evaluate Markov probabilities and rules from the activity-travel sequences.

State-of-the-Art of External Model Validation

The validation of spatio-temporal microsimulations with external data sources depends strongly on the availability of data sources in the modeling region. Typically, three or four different aspects of the data can be evaluated. In the following we will provide a cross section of common microsimulation evaluations based on the MATSim and FEATHERS simulation systems. Most often, a validation of the traffic volume, trip length and trip duration over a given time interval or a 24 hour time cycle is performed. For example, Gao et al. (2010) evaluate the average trip duration and length per hour of day, the aggregated traffic volume for two 4 hour time periods as well as the average speed on highways for two 2 hour time intervals during peak traffic. They summarize the results using (temporal) histograms, scatter plots, relative differences, RMSE and regression analysis. Horni et al. (2009) focus in their work on the evaluation of leisure and shopping trips. They provide histograms about the average shopping trip length and duration. In addition, they provide histograms to compare the distribution of the length of shopping trips. The authors also evaluate the number of shopping activities per location and provide a map showing the locations with either the largest positive or negative differences for two configurations of the microsimulation. An evaluation of traffic counts is performed using scatter plots as well as box plots. the latter show the absolute and relative differences over a 24 hour time cycle. Meister et al. (2010) target the evaluation of the mode of transport split. They provide histograms showing the cumulative model split for increasing trip length and duration. In addition, they visualize the deviation of the share of public transport for 5 x 5 km grid cells on a map. Similar to the previous authors, a temporal histogram and box plot are used to show the absolute and relative deviation of traffic counts in a 24 hour time interval. Kochan (2012) takes a broader view on the evaluation of mobility characteristics. The author also evaluates traffic counts and travel lengths. For traffic counts he uses Person's correlation coefficient, and for travel lengths he calculates the total vehicle kilometers traveled per year. In addition, the author performs a comparison of trip start times and the distribution of trip origin-destination pairs. For the former he uses a temporal histogram over a 24 hour cycle. For the latter the author provides a scatter plot and calculates the coefficient of determination of a linear regression model.

The provided literature review shows that many different mobility characteristics are considered during evaluation. The validations included count-based evaluations of trips and activities. Evaluations of different modes of transport and speed were performed as well as differences between movement positions. Typically, the temporal distribution over a day was considered, and values for different locations provided to show the distribution in space. Yet, the selection also shows that a uniform evaluation standard is missing. Many characteristics are shown in temporal histograms without an explicit quantification of the error. This makes it hard to set up a validation benchmark to enable the comparison of results across different simulation platforms and data sets. In addition, most validations focus on either spatial or temporal characteristics. Combinations of both dimensions as well as the evaluation of dependencies and sequential information are greatly missing. Finally, all validations lack a holistic view on validation and concentrate only on few movement characteristics.

INTERNAL MODEL VALIDATION

The internal validation of transport demand models tests the ability of the model to predict travel behavior. It is typically performed on the level of model components and requires comparing the model predictions with information other than that used in estimating the model. If the model output and the independent data are in acceptable agreement, the model can be considered validated. As microsimulation systems typically rely on non-deterministic algorithms, the variability of a model is also subject to internal model validation. In this section we will first introduce general techniques for the validation of model components and model variability. Afterwards we discuss a practical example of internal model validation in the case of an activity-based transportation model inside the FEATHERS framework (Bellemans et al., 2010).

Validation on the Level of Model Components

Different techniques exist regarding internal model validation. A widely known approach is the so-called cross-validation method (Kohavi, 1998). This technique is generally used in prediction tasks when one wants to investigate how reliable the model performs in actual practice. The task hereby is to learn a model from data that is at one's disposal as, for example, a travel survey. Such a model may be a regression model or a decision tree or any other decision support tool obtained by means of a learning algorithm. The difficulty of evaluating a predictive model is that it may possess strong prediction potency on the training data set, but might do worse in predicting unseen data. This phenomenon is also called overfitting. Cross-validation avoids overfitting by separating the data set into two parts: one is used to train or develop the model, and the other part is used to validate the model. In ordinary cross-validation the training and validation data sets cross-over in sequential steps such that each data record has the opportunity to be in the validation set once. In practice various procedures exist for cross-validation of a model, namely: hold-out validation, k-fold cross-validation and leave-one-out cross-validation.

In hold-out validation a common way is to divide the available data set into two non-overlapping fractions: one for training and the other for validation. The test data is held out and not being used during the training phase. This way hold-out validation prevents that training data and test data overlap each other, yielding an estimation of higher accuracy for the generalization performance of the learning algorithm. A well-known drawback of this approach is that this procedure does not make use of all the data at hand and that secondly the outcomes are highly dependent on the choice for the training and validation data sets.

In *k*-fold cross-validation the data is first subdivided into *k* equal-sized data parts or so-called folds. Next, *k* repetitions of training and validation steps are carried out such that within each repetition another fold of the data is held-out for validating the model while the *k*-1 folds left are used for learning. An advantage of this approach is its accurate performance estimation, however, the overlapping of training sets between repetitions is a drawback.

The last validation technique discussed here, leave-one-out cross-validation (LOOCV) is a special application of the traditional *k*-fold cross-validation where *k* equals the total number of records in the data set. In each iteration step all data records except one single record are used for training and the model is tested afterwards based on that single record. The model accuracy estimation accomplished by means of LOOCV is almost unbiased.

Validation of Model Variability

Activity-based models of travel demand using a micro-simulation approach inevitably include stochastic error that is caused by the statistical

distributions of random components. Indeed, for making choices based on decision trees the transport demand system needs to make choices by means of randomly picking out a choice alternative based on the probability distribution in the decision tree nodes. As a result, running a traffic micro-simulation model several times with the same inputs will obtain different outputs. Analysis of the impacts on the model outputs thereby is one of the vital steps in the model development and validation. In order to take the variation of outputs in each model run into account, a common approach is to run the model multiple times and to use the average value of the results. The concept of confidence interval can then be applied with the purpose of determining the required minimum number of model runs to ensure at least a certain percentile of zones in the concerned study area reach stability i.e., with a certain level of confidence that the obtained average value of each of these zones can only vary within an acceptable interval. However, how many runs are really needed in order to reach stability depends strongly on the kind of activity-based transport demand model under concern.

Example of a Model Components Validation

In this section we present a concrete example of a hold-out validation for an activity-based transport demand model implemented in the FEATHERS framework (Bellemans et al., 2010). We first provide a short description of the FEATHERS framework and the activity-based transport model inside FEATHERS in order to sketch the validation context. Subsequently we discuss the results of the model components validation.

The FEATHERS framework is a versatile system that facilitates the development and maintenance of activity-based models for transport demand. For this purpose FEATHERS provides all necessary tools to develop and maintain activity-based models in a particular study area. Currently, the FEATHERS framework incorporates the core of the ALBATROSS Activity-Based scheduler (Arentze et al., 2005). This scheduler assumes a sequential decision process consisting of 26 decision trees that intends to simulate the way individuals build daily schedules. The output of the model consists of predicted activity schedules. They describe for a given day which activities are conducted, at what time (start time), for how long (duration), where (location) and, if travelling is involved, the transport mode used and the chaining of trips. The activity-based model inside FEATHERS uses a CHAID-based decision tree induction method (Kass, 1980) to derive decision trees from activity diary data. The following example validation therefore describes the quality of the resulting trained decision trees for each step in the decision process model. Most decision trees involve a choice between discrete alternatives, for example, the transport mode. However, activity duration and activity start time decisions are modeled as a continuous choice and therefore a continuous decision tree is constructed for each of these kinds of choices.

We tested the predictive performance of the decision tree models using a hold-out sample, i.e. only a subset of the data was used during training to build the model. For each decision step, a random sample of 70% of the cases (training set) was used to build the decision trees. The other subset of 30% of the cases (test set) was presented as unseen data to the models for the validation. The accuracy of each discrete choice decision tree was calculated as percentage of correct predictions while the accuracy of continuous valued decision trees was evaluated using MAPE (see Section *General Measures for Comparing Categorical and Numerical Variables*).

In order to make a better judgment about the predictive ability of the discrete choice decision trees, we additionally calculated a null-model for each decision tree. A null-model is defined as a model that randomly selects a choice alternative. The performance of a null-model can simply be

derived by dividing 100 by the number of choice alternatives. By comparing the null-models with the respective decision trees the relative performance of each tree can be determined, i.e. it becomes possible to see whether or not the decision trees are vigorous enough to score better then the null-models.

As stated before the activity-based model inside of FEATHERS consists of 26 decision trees. However, for illustration purposes, we show the validation of only a selection of decision trees. The predictive performance of the selected decision trees on the training and validation sets are presented in *Table 2*. As can be seen all selected trees perform better then the null-models where a random choice alternative is being selected. Indeed, when looking, for example, at the first tree, which predicts whether or not a work activity is included in an activity-travel schedule, it can clearly be seen that its performance is much better than of its equivalent null-model. The null-model indicates that it would correctly predict choices in 50% of the cases while the accuracy on the test set is 77.8% indicating that the tree correctly predicts choices in almost 78% of the cases. Based on *Table 2* it can also be concluded that the degree of overfitting for the selected decision trees, i.e. the difference between the training and the validation set is low. Therefore it can be underlined that the transferability of the model, with regard to the selected trees, to a new set of cases is satisfactory. Keeping the first decision tree as an illustration again, it shows that the training and the test set accuracy differ only by about 0.1% meaning that the decision tree that was estimated with the training set clearly performed well on the unseen test set.

For all continuous valued decision trees in *Table 2* the MAPE, determined on the validation and test set, is shown. As can be seen, the MAPE for each decision tree is approximately the same for the training and validation set, implying that the decision trees perform well in case of unseen data cases. However, values differ much across

Table 2. Predictive performance of discrete (D) and continuous (C) decision trees (A dash (-) in the table indicates that the respective error measure is not applicable)

Choice	Tree Type	Nr of Choice Alternatives	Null Model (%)	CMA Training Set (%)	CMA Test Set (%)	MAPE Training Set (%)	MAPE Test Set (%)
Inclusion of work episode	D	2	50.0	77.9	77.8	-	-
Total duration of work episodes	C	-	-	-	-	27.9	26.4
Timing of work episodes	C	-	-	-	-	11.8	12.9
Work location, in/out home	D	2	50.0	63.1	61.4	-	-
Transport mode work episodes	D	4	25.0	65.3	62.1	-	-
Inclusion of fixed episode	D	2	50.0	87.2	86.8	-	-
Duration of fixed episodes	C	-	-	-	-	140.1	154.0
Timing of fixed episodes	C	-	-	-	33.3	34.6
Inclusion of flexible episode	D	2	50.0	79.6	78.8	-	-
Duration of flexible episode	D	3	33.3	41.8	39.5	-	-
Timing of flexible episode	D	6	16.6	49.5	47.4	-	-
Location, same as previous	D	3	33.3	60.0	59.1	-	-
Location, distance-size class	D	25	4.0	8.9	7.7	-	-
Transport mode non-work episodes	D	4	25.0	52.7	49.8	-	-

all trees. This is caused by the fact that the nature of the different choices to be determined is very diverse. For example, the duration of work episodes tend to be rather stable as opposed to the duration of fixed episodes (e.g. bring/get activity). Nevertheless, overall the continuous decision trees perform quite well.

The example above demonstrated the application of the hold-out validation technique in case of an activity-based transport model inside FEATHERS, however other validation techniques discussed previously may be considered as well.

VALIDATION USE CASES

In today's world mobility surveys are still the main source to gather data as input for mobility models. Unfortunately the implementation of a survey does have some significant disadvantages. It is usually time-consuming and connected with costs. For this reason surveys are often restricted in the number

of participants, space or time. In consequence, it is often hard to build a comprehensive mobility model that offers detailed information for a large geographical area for a longer period of time given the input data.

In contrast to surveys, more and more big data is available for analysis. In most cases the data is not tailored to the use in mobility models. Yet, it offers a high potential to describe mobility of daily life. Two of the most common big data sources are GPS and GSM. For this reason we will explore the evaluation of mobility characteristics based on both big data sources in this section. This is done by two examples. In the first example we compare a GPS data set in a central region of Italy with a GSM data set of a European country. This evaluation is done by an indirect cross-data set validation were we compare derived statistics from two distinct data sets portraying the same phenomenon. In the second example both data sets are collected in parallel in the greater area of Lausanne, Switzerland.

EVALUATING GPS AND GSM DATA IN THE REGION OF PISA

Radius of Gyration

In this section we present a cross-data set validation using GPS and GSM data. The employed GPS data set contains information of approximately 9.8 million different car travels from 159,000 cars with on-board GPS devices. The GSM data was collected by a European mobile phone carrier for billing and operational purposes. With respect to the dimensions of mobility data discussed in Section *Properties of Mobility Data*, both data sets differ in several aspects. Regarding the *observation space*, the GPS data refers to trips performed during one month (May 2011) in an area corresponding to a region in central Italy (a 250 km x 250 km square). In contrast, the mobile phone data covers an entire European country and a period of observation of six months. Moreover, with respect to the population, the car travel data set represents a 2% sample of the overall population of cars in Italy, while the mobile phone data set covers users of a major European operator (100,000 users). The *Resolution* of the GPS data is higher than of the GSM data, providing very detailed information about the spatio-temporal position of users, with an average sampling rate of a few seconds. Conversely, information provided by the GSM data set is not very accurate in terms of space and time because an individual may be anywhere within a tower's reception area, which can span up to tens of square miles. Since call patterns are bursty, for most of the time we do not know the actual position of the user.

Despite its low resolution, mobile phone data is very appropriate to study general mobility. It usually includes all possible means of transportation. In contrast, GPS data may refer only to a particular kind of mobility. For example, our study data set contains only car traces because the GPS devices were installed into the cars. The fact that one data set contains aspects missing in the other data set makes the two types of data suitable for an external validation of patterns emerging from human mobility behavior. We do not expect to observe the exact same behavior in both data sets, but the same tendencies and laws behind the movement patterns.

The example of external validation we discuss in this section has been analyzed in detail by Pappalardo et al. (2013). The authors investigate whether known general mobility patterns found in GSM data by González et al. (2008) also apply to car travel. Based on the GPS data set described earlier, they computed main mobility measures used in literature, such as the radius of gyration (see Section *Evaluating the Distribution of Differences between Movement Positions*) and compared it to the GSM data set. The distribution of the radius of gyration across the GPS data set resulted in a power law with an exponential cutoff: $P(r_g) \sim (r_g + r_o)^{-b} \exp(-r_g/t)$ with $r_o = 5.54$, $b = 1.13$ and $t = 39.76$ (see *Figure 2* left). Though the parameters differed from the earlier estimated parameters $r_o = 5.8$, $b = 1.65$ and $t = 350$ (see *Figure 2* (b)) by González et al. (2008), the type of the curve agrees with the previously found results. The results confirm that the vast majority of individuals tend to travel within small distances, whereas some of them carry out very long journeys. The results further strengthen the insight that a huge heterogeneity exists in the characteristic travel distance of people. Moreover, the variability seems to be independent from the spatial observation space (a region with GPS data vs. a whole country with GSM data) and temporal observation space (one month for GPS, six months for GSM). As we see in the GPS plot of *Figure 2* (a), there is a difference between the predicted behavior and the observed behavior for people with a radius of less than ~5 km. This is presumably due to the sampling coverage, since people tend to cover small distances by foot, bike, or bus, resulting in a low probability to find such travels in the car data set. This is a phenomenon we do not observe in GSM data, since the data covers all types of travel.

Figure 2. Distribution of the radius of gyration; left: computed on the GPS data set (source: Pappalardo et al., 2013); right: computed on the GSM data set (source: González et al., 2008)

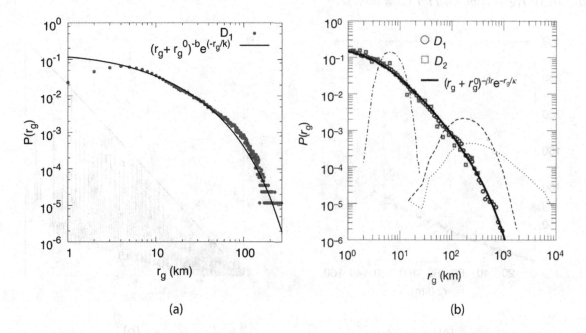

(a)   (b)

Another interesting characteristic of individual mobility is the most frequent location L_1, i.e. the zone where a person can be located with highest probability when not moving, most likely the home or work place. Estimating L_1 in GSM data is rather immediate: it is the tower from which the user performs the highest number of calls. Working with GPS car traces is more complex because the data does not provide explicit information about the visited locations of a user but only of the used parking sites. In order to solve the problem Pappalardo et al. (2013) applied the Bisecting K-means clustering algorithm (Tan et al., 2005) on the sets of origin and destination points of the sub-trajectories. The most frequent location L_1 does not necessarily coincide with the center of mass p_{cm} of movement positions, which is used in the calculation of the radius of gyration. Pappalardo et al. (2013) therefore calculated the distance $d(p_{cm}, L_1)$ between both locations and related it to the previously extracted radius of gyration. The results are depicted in *Figure 3* for

the GPS data (left) as well as the GSM data (right). In both data sets the distance tends to grow with the radius of gyration. However, the GSM data shows an interesting "trail" emerging for higher radius of gyration that requires further investigation. The strong correlation between the two variables is interesting and presumably due to the systematic nature of human motion. Indeed, if a person travels arbitrarily in any direction from and to the same preferential location, the distance between the center of mass and the most frequent location will tend to zero, and the radius of gyration will have no relation with it. On the contrary, since each vehicle follows systematic travels among few preferred places, the center of mass is pulled by these trips towards the mean point of the frequent locations. Therefore, the more a vehicle travels away from its L_1, the more the center of mass tends to be distant from the most frequent location. This outcome in both data sets suggests that the center of mass is not adequate to describe a realistic barycenter of individual

Figure 3. Correlation between the radius of gyration r_g and the distance between the center of mass and the most frequent location of users $d(p_{cm}, L_1)$; left: computed on GSM data set (source: Pappalardo et al., 2013); right: computed for GSM data set

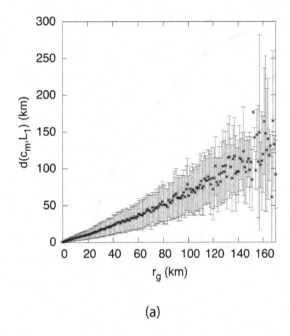

(a)

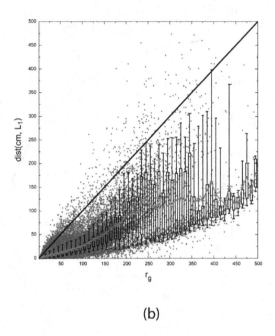

(b)

mobility, especially in the case of users with a large radius of gyration.

In the last example the comparison between GPS and GSM is made only visually. In a future analysis the values will also be compared numerically. In order to do so we need first to properly choose the size of the bin used to sample users, second to choose an appropriate function to describe the correlation and third to fit the data to it.

Traffic Counts

Consider a data sample representing movements of individuals such as, for example, the GPS car travel data set introduced above. A comparison with the ground truth, i.e. the movements of cars of the *whole* population within the urban area, would be very useful both for validation and for traffic prediction purposes. Although in general it is very difficult to obtain a whole population

describing a particular phenomenon, nowadays many sensing technologies are available that provide streets-based traffic counts.

In (Pappalardo et al., 2013) the authors use a data set containing logs from Variable Message Panels (VMP) to assess the generality of analytical results obtained from the GPS data set. VMPs are devices situated in the entry gates of the city of Pisa with the purpose of counting all entering vehicles. The information provided by VMPs has a coarse population resolution because it does not tell *which* cars pass the devices but only *how many* vehicles pass through the gates. In terms of observation space, the two data sets cover the same time period (although the VMPs cover a larger temporal extent). The VMPs are constrained on specific positions over the road network. Thus, exploiting the spatial precision of GPS data, all vehicle trajectories were intersected with the VMP locations. As for the temporal accuracy, the VMPs provide an aggregated count of vehicles on an

Figure 4. Traffic sensed by a VMP device and GPS traffic volume at one entry gate in Pisa

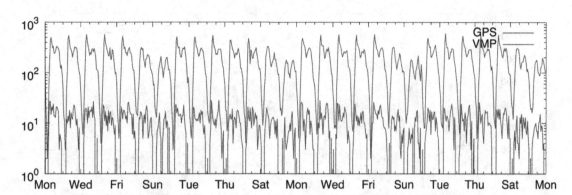

hourly basis. The determined VMP passages in the GPS data were therefore aggregated hour by hour. *Figure 4* shows the hourly frequency counts of the VMP and GPS data of one gate in a time graph. It can be clearly seen that there is a good match between the curves, which essentially differ for a scaling factor. This is due to a different sampling coverage of the two data sets: VMPs are able to count any vehicle passing, whereas the GPS data set contains only traces of a subset of all vehicles.

In order to perform a scaling between the VMP and GPS traffic counts, the authors applied a discrete wavelet transform (DWT). A DWT is a mathematical tool that projects a time series onto a collection of orthonormal basis functions and produces a set of coefficients, capturing information from the time series at different frequencies and distinct times. From the coefficients the authors build a model to scale the traffic counts obtained from the GPS data sample to the full population. *Figure 5* shows the real VMP series along with the scaled GPS signal and the measured relative error at a selected VMP location. The error is low when the GPS traffic is high. During the night hours the relative error tends to grow since there are too few circulating GPS vehicles, but the absolute error is still negligible. However, for a traffic manager it is crucial to have a precise estimation during the rush hours in order to design

ad hoc intervention options to avoid congestions, a situation for which our reconstruction provides a very high precision.

Evaluating Mobile Phone Data in the Region of Lausanne

In our second example we explore GPS and GSM data in the area around Lausanne, Switzerland. The data was collected during the Lausanne Data Collection Campaign, which was carried out by the Nokia Research Center (NRC). During this campaign the NRC equipped about 200 people living around Lake Geneva with smartphones (Nokia N95). Each smartphone, equipped with multiple sensors, collected a wide range of data generated by each participant. All data was continuously collected for about one year. In 2011 a data set of 38 persons was released to the research community (http://research.nokia.com/page/12000).

The data set itself consists of both social and geographic data. This includes information about the GPS Position and the GSM-Cell-ID in which a mobile phone activity, like calls and SMS, took place. With respect to the dimensions of mobility data discussed in Section *Properties of Mobility Data*, the data set covers a large temporal observation space (one year), but is limited in its spatial observation space (area around Lausanne). Especially the population sample (38 participants)

Figure 5. Comparison between real and scaled GPS signal at a single gate in Pisa

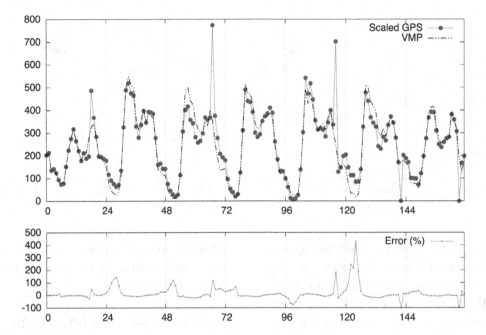

covers only a very small part of the Lausanne population. The resolution of the GPS data is, like in the first example, higher than that of the GSM data. GSM only produces a record in the data set if the phone of a participant is interacting with the mobile network of the operator. GPS, on the other side, is producing a record every second if the quality of the satellite connection allows it. Another point to mention is that in this second example the GPS data is not limited to a particular kind of mobility (e.g. cars) since the GPS data origins from smart phones, which were carried around by the participants all day long.

This combination of GPS and GSM data makes the data set very interesting, because it gives the rare opportunity to compare GSM data with ground truth information about the mobility of a person. For this reason we evaluated the usability of mobile phone data for the extraction of mobility quantities. In the following we present an excerpt of our results published in (Schulz et al., 2012). In particular we were interested in measurement quantities that help to enrich and improve existing mobility models. Two of the analyzed quantities are presented in the following.

Travel Distance

In the first analysis we compared the travel distance based on the GPS and GSM data sets. The GPS data include the distance between any two consecutive GPS points excluding those points inside of a stop as well as the travel distance considering only the centroid coordinates of stop locations. Against it, the GSM data set contains the average daily travel distance between consecutive GSM activities predicated on the estimated GSM-cell centroids. See the Table 3.

The results in *Table 3* show that the distance calculated from GSM activity data is only a half of the travel distance measured by GPS. This is s sign that GSM Data cannot characterize the real daily travel. On the other hand, if the travel distance is reduced to distance calculated from GPS stops,

Table 3. Comparison of average daily travel distances (in km)

GPS Sequence	GPS Stops	GSM Activity
39.10	19.22	18.56

both measurements are similar. This leads us to the second analysis, which is about the identification of frequent activity locations.

Activity Locations

In our second analysis we took a closer look at frequent stop locations. These are defined as locations where people stay over a longer period of time to do some activities, like work, school or sports. For this reason we can also call those stops activity locations. After identifying those locations from the GPS data, we conducted two analyses. In the first one we determined the proportion of GSM activities that take place within typical activity locations. In the second one we analyzed the number of stop locations that can potentially be detected through GSM activity data. In both cases more than 2/3 respectively 50% of all frequent activity locations could be detected. In sum this means that GSM activity data is a good source to identify and analyze activity locations. On the other hand it also means that GSM activities mostly tell us about where people stay, not where they move, which is consistent with our analysis about the travel distance.

CONCLUSION

The increasing interest in spatio-temporal microsimulation systems as well as the diversity of available spatio-temporal data sets call for a new evaluation standard for microsimulation systems. On the one hand, the standard has to direct researchers and practitioners towards a holistic view on movement validation. On the other hand, it has to broaden the scope of validation methods to seize the potential of new mobility data sources. This chapter compiles a comprehensive overview on the state-of-the-art of validating spatio-temporal microsimulation systems by providing a systematic overview about properties of movement data, mobility characteristics, commonly used similarity measures and validation schemes. A cross section of the state-of-the-art shows that an explicit quantification of the external model error is often missing, which restrains the comparison of results across different simulation platforms and data sets. In addition, most evaluations are limited to a small set of mobility characteristics, focusing typically on either spatial or temporal characteristics. Furthermore, comparisons are typically performed on the level of persons, trips, activities or movement sequences. The validation of movement characteristics based on group patterns (e.g. convergence, moving clusters), however, has not been considered in the literature so far. The major reason for this practice is the complexity of movement data and the limited availability of external validation data. The former problem requires a tight interaction between the mobility mining research community and the transportation research community in order to turn currently complex analysis methods into standard tools that are generally available. The latter problem is likely to decrease with the increasing availability of big data sources. However, big data sets bring their own challenges as the data may cover only a part of the observation space, differ in its temporal resolution or be not representative in all aspects. Our validation examples using real-world application data show that differing data properties often hinder a direct comparison, and additional research efforts have to be invested into the development of data harmonization techniques. In summary, the validation of spatio-temporal microsimulation systems is a complex task and vital research area which holds many challenging research questions for future work.

REFERENCES

Andrienko, G., & Andrienko, N. (2010). A general framework for using aggregation in visual exploration of movement data. *The Cartographic Journal*, *47*(1), 22–40. doi:10.1179/00087040 9X12525737905042.

G. Andrienko, N. Andrienko, P. Bak, D. Keim, & S. Wrobel (Eds.). (2013). *Visual analytics of movement*. Berlin: Springer.

Andrienko, N., Andrienko, G., Pelekis, N., & Spaccapietra, S. (2008). Basic concepts of movement data. In *Mobility, Data Mining and Privacy*. Berlin: Springer. doi:10.1007/978-3-540-75177-9_2.

Andrienko, N., Andrienko, G., Stange, H., Liebig, T., & Hecker, D. (2012). Visual analytics for understanding spatial situations from episodic movement data. *Künstliche Intelligenz*, *26*(3), 241–251. doi:10.1007/s13218-012-0177-4.

Arentze, T., & Timmermans. (2005). *ALBATROSS 2: A learning-based transportation oriented simulation system*. Eindhoven, The Netherlands: European Institute of Retailing and Services Studies.

Balmer, M., Nagel, K., & Raney, B. (2006). Agent-based demand modeling framework for large scale micro-simulations. *Transportation Research Record*, *1985*, 125–134. doi:10.3141/1985-14.

Bellemans, T., Kochan, B., Janssens, D., Wets, G., & Arentze, T., & Timmermans. (2010). Implementation framework and development trajectory of the feathers activity-based simulation platform. *Transportation Research Record: Journal of the Transportation Research Board*, *2175*, 111–119. doi:10.3141/2175-13.

Bundesministerium für Verkehr. Bau und Stadtentwicklung. (2010). *Mobilität in Deutschland 2008, abschlussbericht*. Retrieved from http://www.mobilitaet-in-deutschland.de

Cha, S.-H. (2007). Comprehensive survey on distance/similarity measures between probability density functions. *International Journal of Mathematical Models and Methods in Applied Sciences*, *4*(1), 300–307.

Curtis, C., & Perkins, T. (2006). *Travel behaviour: A review of recent literature* (Working Paper No. 3). Brisbane, Australia: Curtin University.

Gao, W., Balmer, M., & Miller, E. J. (2010). Comparisons between MATSim and EMME/2 on the greater Toronto and Hamilton area network. *Transportation Research Record. Journal of the Transportation Research Board*, *2197*, 118–128. doi:10.3141/2197-14.

Giannotti, F., Nanni, M., Pinelli, F., & Pedreschi, D. (2007). Trajectory pattern mining. In *Proceedings of the 13th ACM SIGKDD International Conference on Knowledge Discovery and Data Mining (KDD'07)*, (pp. 330-339). ACM.

González, M. C., Hidalgo, C. A., & Barabási, A.-L. (2008). Understanding individual human mobility patterns. *Nature*, *453*(7196), 779–782. doi:10.1038/nature06958 PMID:18528393.

Gurczik, G., Junghans, M., & Ruppe, S. (2012). *Conceptual approach for determining penetration rates for dynamic indirect traffic detection*. ITS World Congress.

Hecker, D., Stange, H., Körner, C., & May, M. (2010). Sample bias due to missing data in mobility surveys. In *Proceedings of the 2010 IEEE International Conference on Data Mining Workshops (ICDMW'10)*, (pp. 241-248). IEEE.

Horni, A., Scott, D. M., Balmer, M., & Axhausen, K. W. (2009). *Location choice modeling for leisure and shopping with MATSim: Utility function extension and validation results*. Paper presented at the 9th Swiss Transport Research Conference. Bern, Switzerland.

Hyndman, R. J., & Koehler, A. B. (2006). Another look at measures of forecast accuracy. *International Journal of Forecasting, 22,* 679–688. doi:10.1016/j.ijforecast.2006.03.001.

Joh, C-H., Arentze, T., Hofman, F., & Timmermans. (1999). Activity pattern similarity: Towards a multidimensional sequence alignment. In *Proceedings of the IATBR Conference.* Austin, TX: IATBR.

Kass, G. V. (1980). An exploratory technique for investigating large quantities of categorical data. *Applied Statistics, 29,* 119–127. doi:10.2307/2986296.

Kochan, B. (2012). *Implementation, validation and application of an activity-based transportation model for Flanders.* Hasselt, Belgium: University of Hasselt.

Kohavi, R., & Provost, F. (1998). *Glossary of terms: Machine learning.* Boston: Kluwer Academic Publishers.

Körner, C. (2012). *Modeling visit potential of geographic locations based on mobility data.* (PhD Thesis). University of Bonn, Bonn, Germany. Retrieved from http://hss.ulb.uni-bonn. de/2012/2811/2811.htm

Körner, C., May, M., & Wrobel, S. (2012). Spatio-temporal modeling and analysis – Introduction and overview. *Künstliche Intelligenz, 26*(3), 215–221. doi:10.1007/s13218-012-0215-2.

Liebig, T., Körner, C., & May, M. (2009). Fast visual trajectory analysis using spatial Bayesian networks. In *Proceedings of the 2009 IEEE International Conference on Data Mining Workshops (ICDMW'09),* (pp. 668-673). IEEE.

May, M., Hecker, D., Körner, C., Scheider, S., & Schulz, D. (2008a). A vector-geometry based spatial kNN-algorithm for traffic frequency predictions. In *Proceedings of the 2008 IEEE International Conference on Data Mining Workshops (ICDMW '08),* (pp. 442-447). IEEE.

May, M., Scheider, S., Rösler, R., Schulz, D., & Hecker, D. (2008b). Pedestrian flow prediction in extensive road networks using biased observational data. In *Proceedings of the 16th ACM SIGSPATIAL International Conference on Advances in Geographic Information Systems (ACM GIS '08),* (pp. 1-4). ACM.

Meister, K., Balmer, M., Ciari, F., Horni, A., Rieser, M., Waraich, R. A., & Axhausen, K. W. (2010). *Large-scale agent-based travel demand optimization applied to Switzerland, including mode choice.* Paper presented at the 12th World Conference on Transportation Research. New York, NY.

Pappalardo, L., Rinzivillo, S., Qu, Z., Pedreschi, D., & Giannotti, F. (2013). Understanding the patterns of car travels. *The European Physical Journal. Special Topics, 215,* 61–73. doi:10.1140/epjst/e2013-01715-5.

Scheiner, J. (2010). Social inequalities in travel behaviour: Trip distances in the context of residential self-selection and lifestyles. *Journal of Transport Geography, 18*(6), 679–690. doi:10.1016/j.jtrangeo.2009.09.002.

Schmietendorf, G. (2011). *Verkehrsdatenerfassung mit bluetooth-detektion: Möglichkeiten und grenzen.* (Diploma Thesis). TU Dresden, Dresden, Germany. Retrieved from http://elib. dlr.de/72017/1/Diplomarbeit_final_fin_ende.pdf

Schreinemacher, J., Körner, C., Hecker, D., & Bareth, G. (2012). Analyzing temporal usage patterns of street segments based on GPS data – A case study in Switzerland. In *Proceedings of the 15th AGILE International Conference on Geographic Information Science (AGILE'12)*. AGILE.

Schulz, D., Bothe, S., & Körner, C. (2012). Human mobility from GSM data - A valid alternative to GPS? In *Proceedings of the Mobile Data Challenge Workshop*. ACM.

Schwanen, T., Dijst, M. J., & Dieleman, F. M. (2005). The relationship between land use and travel patterns: Variations by household type. In K. Williams (Ed.), *Spatial Planning, Urban Form and Sustainable Transport*. Aldershot, UK: Ashgate.

Tan, P. N., Steinbach, M., & Kumar, V. (2005). *Introduction to data mining*. Reading: Addison Wesley.

Wilson, C. (1998). Analysis of travel behoviour using sequence alignment methods. In *Proceedings of the 7th Annual Meeting of the Transportation Research Board*. Washington, DC: Transportation Research Board.

KEY TERMS AND DEFINITIONS

Big Data: Data sets of large volume, high velocity and high variety

Error Measure: States the difference between a measured value and its true value

Evaluation: Assessing the quality of some object based on objective measures

GPS: GLOBAL Positioning System

GSM: GLOBAL System for Mobile Communications

Microsimulation: Computational model on the level of individuals

Mobility Characteristic: Characteristics related to the movement of a person

Spatio-Temporal Data: Data related to time and space

Chapter 9
Activity–Based Travel Demand Forecasting Using Micro–Simulation:
Stochastic Error Investigation of FEATHERS Framework

Qiong Bao
Hasselt University, Belgium

Tom Bellemans

Hasselt University, Belgium

Bruno Kochan
Hasselt University, Belgium

Davy Janssens
Hasselt University, Belgium

Geert Wets
Hasselt University, Belgium

ABSTRACT

Activity-based models of travel demand employ in most cases a micro-simulation approach, thereby inevitably including a stochastic error that is caused by the statistical distributions of random components. As a result, running a transport micro-simulation model several times with the same input will generate different outputs. In order to take the variation of outputs in each model run into account, a common approach is to run the model multiple times and to use the average value of the results. The question then becomes: What is the minimum number of model runs required to reach a stable result? In this chapter, systematic experiments are carried out by using the FEATHERS, an activity-based micro-simulation modeling framework currently implemented for Flanders (Belgium). Six levels of geographic detail are taken into account, which are building block level, subzone level, zone level, superzone level, province level, and the whole Flanders. Three travel indices (i.e., the average daily number of activities per person, the average daily number of trips per person, and the average daily distance travelled per person), as well as their corresponding segmentations with respect to socio-demographic variables, transport mode alternatives, and activity types are calculated by running the model 100 times. The results show that application of the FEATHERS at a highly aggregated level only requires limited model runs. However, when a more disaggregated level is considered (the degree of the aggregation here not only refers to the

DOI: 10.4018/978-1-4666-4920-0.ch009

size of the geographical scale, but also to the detailed extent of the index), a larger number of model runs is needed to ensure confidence of a certain percentile of zones at this level to be stable. The values listed in this chapter can be consulted as a reference for those who plan to use the FEATHERS framework, while for the other activity-based models the methodology proposed in this chapter can be repeated.

INTRODUCTION

Travel demand modeling was first developed in the late 1950s as a means to do highway planning. The four-step model, as the exemplification of the conventional trip-based approach, is the primary tool for forecasting future demand and performance of regional transportation systems (McNally, 2007). However, traditional trip-based approaches consider the trip as the unit of analysis, and the trip chains made by an individual are treated as separate, independent entities in the analysis, which often leads up to failure of recognizing the existence of linkages among trips. In some instances, the forecasts of trip-based approaches have proved to be inaccurate due to such an inappropriate representation of travel behaviour relationships (Jones et al., 1990). In the 1970s, the activity-based approach emerged, which explicitly recognizes and addresses the inability of conventional trip-based approach to reflect underlying human behaviour in general, and travel behaviour in particular. The approach is a richer, more holistic framework in which travel is analyzed as daily or multi-day patterns of behaviour related to and derived from differences in lifestyles and activity participation among the population (Kitamura, 1988). A full activity-based model of travel demand predicts which activities (activity participation) are conducted where (destination choice), when (timing), for how long (duration), which chain of transport modes is involved (mode choice), travel party (travel arrangements and joint activity participation) and which route is chosen (route choice), subject to personal, household, spatial, temporal, institutional and space-time constraints. (Rasouli & Timmermans, 2012, pp. 63-64) In the following 1990s, a rapid growth of

interest in activity-based analysis has led up to the development of several practical models, including RAMBLAS (Veldhuisen et al., 2000a), CEMDAP (Bhat et al., 2004), FAMOS (Pendyala et al., 2005), ALBATROSS (Arentze and Timmermans, 2000; 2004), and FEATHERS (Bellemans et al., 2010). The main contribution of these activity-based models is to "offer an alternative to the four-step models of travel demand, better focusing on the consistency of the sub-models and proving increased sensitivity to a wider range of policy issues" (Janssens et al., 2008, p. 71).

However, the activity-based models, focusing on activity-travel generation and activity scheduling decisions, use in most cases a micro-simulation approach, in which heterogeneity and randomness are fundamental characteristics since they simulate individual activity patterns by drawing randomly from marginal and conditional probability distributions that are defined for the various choice facets that make up an activity pattern (Kitamura et al., 2000; Timmermans et al., 2002; Arentze and Timmermans, 2005). As a result, running a traffic micro-simulation model several times with the same inputs will obtain different outputs due to the random number seed used in each run. In order to address practitioners' concerns about this variation, it is natural to run the traffic micro-simulation model multiple times, estimate the effects of stochastic error by analysing the variation of the outputs between the runs, and use the average value of these outputs for further analysis. The question then becomes: what is the minimum number of runs required to reach a stable result (i.e., with a certain level of confidence that the obtained average value can only vary within an acceptable interval)? In this respect, several relevant studies have been carried out, such as Benekohal and Abu-Lebdeh (1994), Hale (1997), Veldhuisen et al. (2000b), Vovsha et al. (2002), Castiglione et al. (2003), Horni et al. (2011), and Cools et al. (2011). In particular, Castiglione et al. (2003) investigated the extent of random variability in the San Francisco model by running the model 100 times at three levels of geographic detail, namely zone level, neighborhood level, and county-wide level. The analysis was then conducted by showing how quickly the mean values of output variables such as the number of trips per person converge towards the final mean value (after 100 runs) as the number of simulation runs increases. However, only two zones and neighborhoods were considered in that study, which to a large extent limits the generalization of the conclusions drawn in that paper. In this chapter, we focus on the same issue but look for the answer one step further, which is to find the minimum number of model runs needed to enable at least a certain percentile of zones at different levels of geographic detail to reach a stable result. Systematic experiments are carried out by using the FEATHERS, an activity-based micro-simulation modeling framework currently implemented for Flanders (Belgium). By running the model 100 times, three travel indices, i.e., the average daily number of activities per person, the average daily number of trips per person, and the average daily distance travelled per person, as well as their corresponding segmentations with respect to socio-demographic variables, transport mode alternatives, and activity types, are calculated, based on the six different geographical levels of Flanders.

The remaining of this chapter is structured as follows. In Section 2, we briefly introduce the FEATHERS framework and the levels of geographic detail of Flanders, followed by the detailed elaboration of the experiment execution in Section 3. In Section 4, the analysis results are presented and further discussed. The chapter ends with conclusions in Section 5.

FEATHERS FRAMEWORK FOR FLANDERS

FEATHERS (The Forecasting Evolutionary Activity-Travel of Households and their Environmental RepercussionS) (Bellemans et al., 2010) is a micro-simulation framework particularly developed to facilitate the implementation of activity-based models for transport demand forecast. Currently, the framework has been implemented for the Flanders region of Belgium, in which a sequence of 26 decision trees, derived by means of the chi-squared automatic interaction detector (CHAID) algorithm, is used in the scheduling process, and decisions are based on a number of attributes of the individual (e.g., age, gender), of the household (e.g., number of cars), and of the geographical zone (e.g., population density, number of shops). For each agent (i.e., person) with its specific attributes, the model simulates whether an activity (e.g., shopping, working, leisure activity, etc.) is going to be carried out or not. Subsequently, the location, transport mode and duration of the activity are determined, taking into account the attributes of the individual. Based on the estimated schedules or activity travel patterns, travel demand can then be extracted and assigned to the transportation network. Currently, the FEATHERS framework is fully operational at six levels of geographic detail of Flanders, i.e., Building block (BB) level, Subzone level, Zone level, Superzone level, Province level, and the whole Flanders level. Figure 1 illustrates the hierarchy of the geographical layers with different granularities.

In recent years, a number of applications have been carried out upon the FEATHERS platform (see e.g., Kochan et al. (2008), Kusumastuti et al. (2010), and Knapen et al. (2012)). However, like other activity-based models, the FEATHERS framework is based on micro-simulation approach. Stochastic error thereby inherently exists, which requires systematic investigation with the purpose

Figure 1. Six levels of geographic detail of Flanders used in the FEATHERS

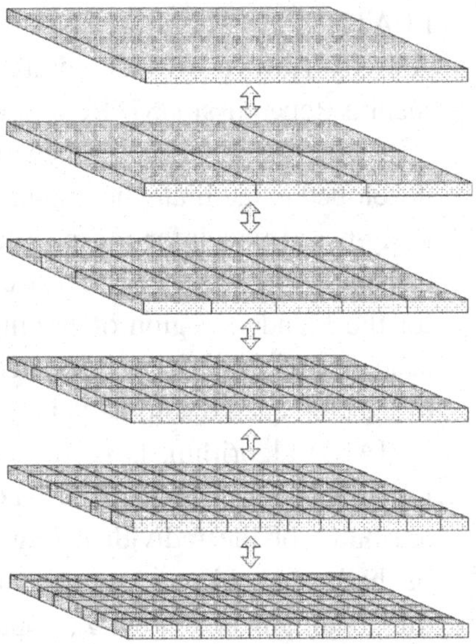

Geographical Level	Number of zones	Average area (km²)
Flanders	1	13709.24
Province	6	2284.87
Superzone	327	41.93
Zone	1145	11.97
Subzone	2386	5.75
BB	10521	1.30

of better understanding the variability of simulation results and facilitating the further development of this modeling framework.

METHODOLOGY

To estimate the impact of micro-simulation error of the FEATHERS framework at all of the six levels of geographic detail of Flanders, 100 successive model runs are performed in this study based on a 10% fraction of the study area population. By considering only a fraction of the full population, computation time is kept within acceptable limits, but it still takes around 18 hours for a single model run at the BB level, the most disaggregated geographical scale.

After each model run, the prediction file, containing the whole activity travel pattern or schedule information for each agent, is generated, based on which the three travel indices (i.e., the average daily number of activities per person, the average daily number of trips per person, and the average daily distance travelled per person) can be computed. Moreover, segmentations of these travel indices based on socio-demographic variables, transport mode alternatives, as well as activity types can be obtained.

Recall the main objective of this study, which is to determine the minimum number of model runs needed to ensure a certain percentile of zones at different geographical levels to reach a stable result concerning the travel indices (i.e., with a certain level of confidence that the obtained average index value of each of these zones can only vary within an acceptable interval). Accordingly, the concept of confidence interval (*CI*) is adopted in this study, and the following equation is applied (Dowling et al., 2004):

$$CI_{(1-\alpha)\%} = 2 \times t_{(1-\alpha/2),N-1} \frac{s}{\sqrt{N}} \qquad (1)$$

where $CI_{(1-\alpha)\%}$ represents $(1-\alpha)\%$ confidence interval for the true average value; α is the probability of the true average value not lying within the confidence interval; $t_{(1-\alpha/2),N-1}$ is the Student's *t*-statistic for the probability of a two-sided error summing to α with *N-1* degrees of freedom; N is the required number of model runs; and s denotes the estimated standard deviation of the results.

For the experiment, a 95% level of confidence is selected and the desired confidence interval, which acts as the predefined stable condition, is set as a 10% fraction of the final average value (after 100 runs) of the index (X) under study, i.e., $CI \leq 0.1 \times \bar{X}_{100}$, where $\bar{X}_{100} = \sum_{i=1}^{100} X \big/ 100$. Also, the standard deviation of the results among 100 runs is used as the estimation of s.

Now, by using Eq. (1), an iterative process is applied for each zone to estimate the required minimum number of model runs in terms of the corresponding index under study. In short, it is necessary to iterate until the estimated number of model runs N matches the number of repetitions assumed when looking up the Student's *t*-statistic. In this way, the minimum number of FEATHERS runs needed to ensure a certain percentile of zones at different geographical levels to achieve stable results with respect to the corresponding index can be derived.

Furthermore, by considering the socio-demographic variables gender (two categories: male and female) and age (five categories: 18-34 years, 35-54 years, 55-64 years, 65-74 years, and 75+ years) as well as four types of transport modes (i.e., car as driver, car as passenger, slow mode, and public transport) and four types of activities (i.e., home-related activity, work-related activity, shopping activity, and touring activity), the required minimum number of FEATHERS runs with respect to these segmentations can be obtained, respectively.

RESULTS AND DISCUSSION

In this section, the results of the experiment on the average daily number of activities per person, the average daily number of trips per person, and the average daily distance travelled per person, as well as their related segmentations at all the geographical levels of Flanders are presented and discussed.

Travel Indices

According to Eq. (1), the required minimum number of FEATHERS runs for each zone at all the geographical levels can be calculated based on the predefined stable condition. Figure 2 illustrates the minimum number of model runs needed to enable different percentiles of zones of each geographical level to reach the stability with respect to the average daily number of activities per person, the average daily number of trips per person, and the average daily distance travelled per person, respectively.

In general, the required minimum number of runs for the daily distance travelled is larger than that for the daily number of trips, which is in turn larger than that for the daily number of activities, especially for the lower geographical levels, such as the BB level, the Subzone level, and the Zone level. This can be mainly accounted for by the fact that in the FEATHERS framework, the type of activities is firstly scheduled, followed by the determination of activity locations. The stochastic error is therefore accumulated by executing each of the above procedures.

Moreover, for all the three indices, with a decrease in the geographical aggregation level, the required minimum number of model runs to enable the certain percentile of zones to achieve the predefined stable condition is increasing, which means that relative to a highly aggregated geographical level, it is more difficult for a lower level to make the same percentile of zones reach stability. In other words, with a certain number of

Figure 2. The required minimum number of model runs for different percentiles of stable zones at six geographical levels on three travel indices

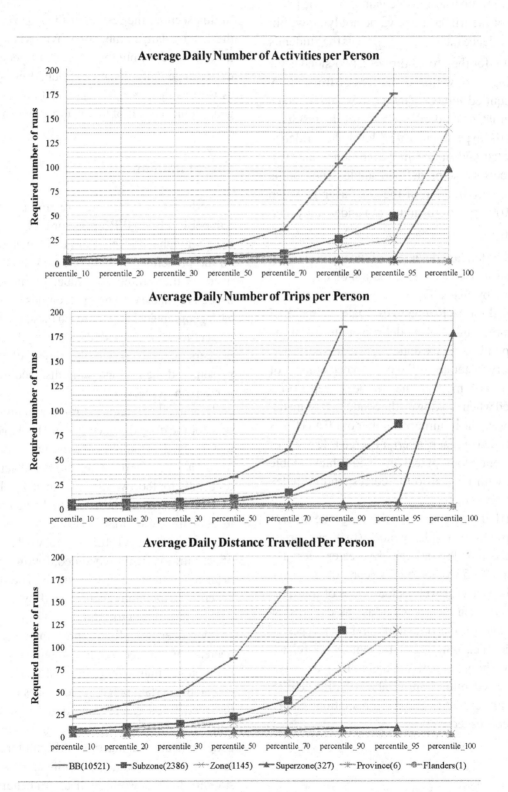

model runs, a lower geographical level can only guarantee a smaller percentile of zones to reach stable status. Taking the daily number of trips as an example, at both the Flanders and the province levels, the sample mean of this index has negligible variation, thereby only a limited number of runs (less than 5) is needed to ensure all the zones in these levels to be stable. When it comes to the Superzone level, also few runs are needed if only 95% of the zones are required to be stable. However, if the stability of all the zones at this level are required to reach the stable state, the number of model runs has to be increased dramatically, which is around 180 runs. The situation becomes worse when even lower geographical levels are taken into account. At the final BB level, 180 model runs can only ensure 90% of the zones to be stable, and within 100 runs, only around 70% of the zones can be guaranteed in terms of their stability. It is therefore a dilemma to choose between on the one hand more detailed exploration and on the other hand more reliable results. One compromising solution is to set another relatively achievable confidence interval condition for the zones with high variation, especially when these zones are not involved in the study area.

Segmentations

In order to illustrate the impact of segmentations of the population on the required number of model runs, the above travel indices are disaggregated based on socio-demographic variables (gender and age), transport mode alternatives, as well as different activity types. The results are presented and discussed in the following sections.

Gender

Figure 3 illustrates the results of gender segmentation related to the average daily number of trips per person and the average daily distance travelled per person. As can be seen, the required minimum number of model runs for either male or female is a little bit larger than that of the overall travel indices for each percentile due to the classification by gender. Moreover, the female group needs a relatively larger number of runs for each percentile of zones to reach the predefined stability than the male group, especially for the lower geographical levels. It can be partly attributed to the fact that as a whole the female group in Flanders generates a relatively smaller number of trips and distance travelled than the male group.

Age

When age categories are considered with respect to the same travel indices analyzed in Section 4.2.1, the required minimum number of model runs for different percentiles is significantly increased, especially at the highly disaggregated geographical levels. Whereas at the Flanders and the Province levels, less than 5 runs are needed for both indices, even when the full percentile is under requirement (see Tables 1 and 2). Moreover, concerning the lower geographical levels, it is interesting to see that the required number of runs for the first two age categories (i.e., 18-34 years and 35-54 years) is apparently less than that for the following two age categories (i.e., 55-64 years and 65-74 years), which is further less than that of the last age category, i.e., over 75 years. This dissimilarity between different age groups can be explained by the fact that the first two age groups involve a larger population in Flanders than the age groups 55-64 years and 65-74 years, which also involve a larger population than the eldest age group. Such a situation potentially increases the instability of the index under concern with respect to the elder age group because less population normally implies a lower number of trips and distance travelled as well.

Figure 3. The required minimum number of model runs for different percentiles of stable zones at six geographical levels by gender on average daily number of trips and distance travelled per person

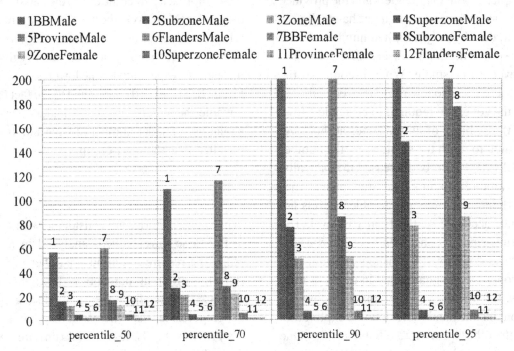

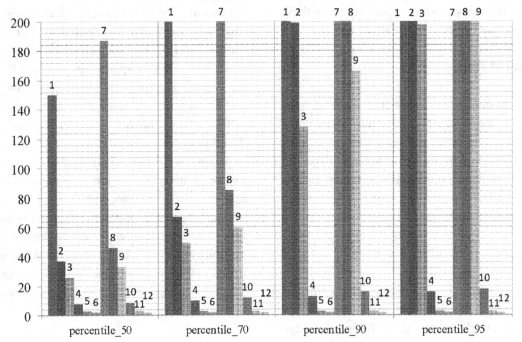

Table 1. The required minimum number of model runs for different percentiles of stable zones at 6 geographical levels by age on average daily number of trips per person

BB (10521)	Nr. of Persons	Required Minimum nr of Runs				Subzone (2386)	Nr. of Persons	Required Minimum nr of Runs			
		p_50	p_70	p_90	p_100			p_50	p_70	p_90	p_100
18-34	119657	81	161	>200	>200	18-34	119657	26	47	138	>200
35-54	181022	59	113	>200	>200	35-54	181022	17	31	84	>200
55-64	67781	143	>200	>200	>200	55-64	67781	53	94	>200	>200
65-74	63261	186	>200	>200	>200	65-74	63261	70	129	>200	>200
75+	47409	>200	>200	>200	>200	75+	47409	127	>200	>200	>200
Zone (1145)	Nr. of persons	required minimum nr of runs				Superzone (327)	Nr. of persons	required minimum nr of runs			
		p_50	p_70	p_90	p_100			p_50	p_70	p_90	p_100
18-34	119657	20	36	98	>200	18-34	119657	7	8	10	42
35-54	181022	13	23	61	>200	35-54	181022	5	6	8	>200
55-64	67781	41	77	>200	>200	55-64	67781	10	13	21	>200
65-74	63261	52	103	>200	>200	65-74	63261	13	17	26	>200
75+	47409	91	180	>200	>200	75+	47409	23	30	45	>200
Province (6)	Nr. of persons	required minimum nr of runs				Flanders (1)	Nr. of persons	required minimum nr of runs			
		p_50	p_70	p_90	p_100			p_50	p_70	p_90	p_100
18-34	119657	2	2	3	3	18-34	119657	--	--	--	2
35-54	181022	2	2	2	2	35-54	181022	--	--	--	2
55-64	67781	3	3	3	3	55-64	67781	--	--	--	2
65-74	63261	3	3	3	3	65-74	63261	--	--	--	2
75+	47409	3	3	3	3	75+	47409	--	--	--	3

Note: In this table, p_50 represents percentile 50. Similar definitions hold for p_70, p_90, and p_100.

At the Flanders level, there is only one geographical zone, therefore the concept of p_50, p_70 and p_90 is not applicable.

Transport Modes

In addition to the socio-demographical variables, research on the mode split is also important from the practitioner's point of view. In this study, four different transport modes, i.e., car as driver, car as passenger, slow mode, and public transport are considered. The results are shown in Table 3 and Table 4. We find that the most frequently used transport mode in Flanders, i.e., the car as driver, needs the lowest number of model runs to reach the predefined stable condition for both the trip and the distance related indices at any geographical level and for any required percentile of zones. On the contrary, the public transport appears to be the mode with the highest variation since the largest number of model runs are needed to achieve the predefined confidence interval.

Activity Types

Concerning the activity-related index, the FEATH-ERS framework defines 10 different activity types. The results of four common activity types in our daily life are listed in Table 5. They are home-related activity, work-related activity, shopping activity, and touring activity, respectively. Regardless of the most stable geographical levels, i.e., the Flanders and Province levels, home-related activity needs a lower number of model runs to reach stability in comparison with work-related activity, which in turn requires fewer runs with respect to shopping activity. Touring activity, however, requires the highest number of model runs among these four types. Such an ordering appears to be quite consistent with the frequency of these activities taking place in our daily life.

Table 2. The required minimum number of model runs for different percentiles of stable zones at 6 geographical levels by age on average daily distance travelled per person

BB (10521)	Nr. of Persons	Required Minimum nr of Runs				Subzone (2386)	Nr. of Persons	Required Minimum nr of Runs			
		p_50	p_70	p_90	p_100			p_50	p_70	p_90	p_100
18-34	119657	>200	>200	>200	>200	18-34	119657	69	124	>200	>200
35-54	181022	158	>200	>200	>200	35-54	181022	41	77	>200	>200
55-64	67781	>200	>200	>200	>200	55-64	67781	156	>200	>200	>200
65-74	63261	>200	>200	>200	>200	65-74	63261	>200	>200	>200	>200
75+	47409	>200	>200	>200	>200	75+	47409	>200	>200	>200	>200
Zone (1145)	Nr. of persons	required minimum nr of runs				Superzone (327)	Nr. of persons	required minimum nr of runs			
		p_50	p_70	p_90	p_100			p_50	p_70	p_90	p_100
18-34	119657	50	97	>200	>200	18-34	119657	13	16	22	127
35-54	181022	29	56	156	>200	35-54	181022	9	10	15	>200
55-64	67781	113	>200	>200	>200	55-64	67781	25	34	54	>200
65-74	63261	166	>200	>200	>200	65-74	63261	38	49	76	>200
75+	47409	>200	>200	>200	>200	75+	47409	70	95	149	>200
Province (6)	Nr. of persons	required minimum nr of runs				Flanders (1)	Nr. of persons	required minimum nr of runs			
		p_50	p_70	p_90	p_100			p_50	p_70	p_90	p_100
18-34	119657	3	3	3	3	18-34	119657	--	--	--	2
35-54	181022	3	3	3	3	35-54	181022	--	--	--	2
55-64	67781	3	3	3	3	55-64	67781	--	--	--	2
65-74	63261	3	3	4	4	65-74	63261	--	--	--	3
75+	47409	4	4	4	5	75+	47409	--	--	--	3

Note: In this table, p_50 represents percentile 50. Similar definitions hold for p_70, p_90, and p_100.

At the Flanders level, there is only one geographical zone, therefore the concept of p_50, p_70 and p_90 is not applicable.

CONCLUSION

In this chapter, we investigated the effect of stochastic error in FEATHERS, an activity-based micro-simulation travel demand modeling framework currently implemented for Flanders (Belgium), in which six levels of geographic detail were taken into account. The concept of confidence intervals was applied with the purpose of determining the required minimum number of model runs to ensure at least a certain percentile of zones in each geographical level to reach the predefined stability.

By successively running the activity-based model inside FEATHERS 100 times based on a 10% fraction of the full population, the variation

of three travel indices including the average daily number of activities per person, the average daily number of trips per person, and the average daily distance travelled per person, as well as their corresponding segmentations with respect to socio-demographic variables (gender and age), transport mode alternatives, and activity types, were estimated. The results indicated a consistent phenomenon, i.e., for a given percentile of zones, the index under study at a higher aggregated level was normally easier than at a lower level to achieve the predefined stable condition. Here, the degree of the aggregation not only referred to the size of the geographical scale, but also to the detailed extent, i.e., the segmentation of the population, of the index under study.

Table 3. The required minimum number of model runs for different percentiles of stable zones at 6 geographical levels by transport modes on average daily number of trips per person

BB (10521)	Required Minimum nr of Runs				Subzone (2386)	Required Minimum nr of Runs			
	p_50	p_70	p_90	p_100		p_50	p_70	p_90	p_100
Car as Driver	62	119	>200	>200	Car as Driver	16	29	87	>200
Car as Passenger	>200	>200	>200	>200	Car as Passenger	74	136	>200	>200
Slow Mode	184	>200	>200	>200	Slow Mode	47	88	>200	>200
Public Transport	>200	>200	>200	>200	Public Transport	161	>200	>200	>200
Zone (1145)	required minimum nr of runs				Superzone (327)	required minimum nr of runs			
	p_50	p_70	p_90	p_100		p_50	p_70	p_90	p_100
Car as Driver	12	22	54	>200	Car as Driver	5	6	7	>200
Car as Passenger	50	99	>200	>200	Car as Passenger	13	17	24	>200
Slow Mode	35	68	174	>200	Slow Mode	9	12	17	>200
Public Transport	112	>200	>200	>200	Public Transport	25	33	50	>200
Province (6)	required minimum nr of runs				Flanders (1)	required minimum nr of runs			
	p_50	p_70	p_90	p_100		p_50	p_70	p_90	p_100
Car as Driver	2	2	2	2	Car as Driver	--	--	--	2
Car as Passenger	3	3	3	3	Car as Passenger	--	--	--	2
Slow Mode	3	3	3	3	Slow Mode	--	--	--	2
Public Transport	3	3	3	3	Public Transport	--	--	--	3

Note: In this table, p_50 represents percentile 50. Similar definitions hold for p_70, p_90, and p_100.

At the Flanders level, there is only one geographical zone, therefore the concept of p_50, p_70 and p_90 is not applicable.

Concerning the geographic scales, only a limited number of model runs was required at the highly aggregated levels (such as the whole Flanders and the province levels) to ensure all the zones (i.e., the 100 percentile) in these levels to be stable with respect to all the indices and their segmentations. However, when it came to the BB level, the most disaggregated geographical level in this study, more than 200 model runs were usually required to enable all the zones to satisfy the stable condition for any index. And within 100 runs, normally only 70% or even 50% of the zones could guarantee stable model results. It is therefore a dilemma to choose between more detailed exploration and more reliable results. One compromising solution is to set another relatively achievable confidence interval condition for the zones with high variation, especially when these zones are not involved in the study area.

With regard to the different segmentations of the population, it was found that the required number of model runs was relatively lower for the particular target segments which potentially involved more trips or activities. Specifically, the male group which generated a relatively larger number of trips and distance travelled in Flanders needed a relatively lower number of model runs than the female group in order to reach the predefined stability for each percentile of zones. Also, the required number of runs for the younger age categories (i.e., 18-34 years and 35-54 years) apparently seemed to be lower than that for the other higher age categories (i.e., 55-64 years, 65-74 years, and over 75 years). Furthermore, the most frequently used transport mode in Flanders, i.e., the car as driver, required the lowest number of model runs, when compared with the other transport modes, in order to satisfy the predefined

Table 4. The required minimum number of model runs for different percentiles of stable zones at 6 geographical levels by transport modes on average daily distance travelled per person

BB (10521)	Required Minimum nr of Runs				Subzone (2386)	Required Minimum nr of Runs			
	p_50	p_70	p_90	p_100		p_50	p_70	p_90	p_100
Car as Driver	139	>200	>200	>200	Car as Driver	33	61	188	>200
Car as Passenger	>200	>200	>200	>200	Car as Passenger	143	>200	>200	>200
Slow Mode	>200	>200	>200	>200	Slow Mode	>200	>200	>200	>200
Public Transport	>200	>200	>200	>200	Public Transport	>200	>200	>200	>200
Zone (1145)	required minimum nr of runs				Superzone (327)	required minimum nr of runs			
	p_50	p_70	p_90	p_100		p_50	p_70	p_90	p_100
Car as Driver	24	44	119	>200	Car as Driver	7	9	12	>200
Car as Passenger	100	190	>200	>200	Car as Passenger	22	31	44	>200
Slow Mode	160	>200	>200	>200	Slow Mode	34	49	74	>200
Public Transport	173	>200	>200	>200	Public Transport	38	50	79	>200
Province (6)	required minimum nr of runs				Flanders (1)	required minimum nr of runs			
	p_50	p_70	p_90	p_100		p_50	p_70	p_90	p_100
Car as Driver	3	3	3	3	Car as Driver	--	--	--	2
Car as Passenger	3	3	3	3	Car as Passenger	--	--	--	2
Slow Mode	3	3	3	4	Slow Mode	--	--	--	3
Public Transport	3	3	4	4	Public Transport	--	--	--	3

Note: In this table, p_50 represents percentile 50. Similar definitions hold for p_70, p_90, and p_100.

At the Flanders level, there is only one geographical zone, therefore the concept of p_50, p_70 and p_90 is not applicable.

stable condition for both the trip and the distance related indices. Finally, concerning the index of activity, home-related activity as the most frequently executed activity in our daily life needed a lower number of model runs to reach stability when compared with the other activity types.

With the growth of micro-simulation in travel demand modeling, analysis of the variance of the simulation results becomes particularly important due to the highly stochastic nature of such systems. The results obtained in this chapter can thus be consulted as a reference for those who plan to use the FEATHERS framework, while for the other activity-based models, the methodology proposed in this chapter to calculate the minimum number of model runs can be repeated. In the future, more aspects could be investigated. First of all, the

impact of the population fraction on the stochastic error should be studied. New insights could probably be gained by repeating the experiment based on the full population instead of the 10% fraction used in this study. Moreover, based on the model outputs, other valuable travel indices could be taken into account as well, such as the index on travel time. Also, traffic assignment could be performed by loading the model outputs onto the corresponding road network. Thus, the variation of the vehicle kilometres travelled could be investigated. In addition, apart from looking at the stochastic micro-simulation error in FEATHERS (as well as other activity-based travel demand models), exploration on other potential uncertainty due to phenomena like input variability and model specification is also worthwhile.

Table 5. The required minimum number of model runs for different percentiles of stable zones at 6 geographical levels by activity types on average daily number of activities per person

BB (10521)	Required Minimum nr of Runs				Subzone (2386)	Required Minimum nr of Runs			
	p_50	p_70	p_90	p_100		p_50	p_70	p_90	p_100
Home-related Activity	11	19	53	>200	Home-related Activity	5	7	14	>200
Work-related Activity	58	113	>200	>200	Work-related Activity	16	28	85	>200
Shopping Activity	175	>200	>200	>200	Shopping Activity	44	79	>200	>200
Touring Activity	>200	>200	>200	>200	Touring Activity	191	>200	>200	>200
Zone (1145)	required minimum nr of runs				Superzone (327)	required minimum nr of runs			
	p_50	p_70	p_90	p_100		p_50	p_70	p_90	p_100
Home-related Activity	4	5	10	68	Home-related Activity	3	3	3	51
Work-related Activity	12	22	60	>200	Work-related Activity	5	6	7	>200
Shopping Activity	31	60	151	>200	Shopping Activity	9	11	15	>200
Touring Activity	133	>200	>200	>200	Touring Activity	28	40	57	>200
Province (6)	required minimum nr of runs				Flanders (1)	required minimum nr of runs			
	p_50	p_70	p_90	p_100		p_50	p_70	p_90	p_100
Home-related Activity	2	2	2	2	Home-related Activity	--	--	--	2
Work-related Activity	2	2	2	2	Work-related Activity	--	--	--	2
Shopping Activity	3	3	3	3	Shopping Activity	--	--	--	2
Touring Activity	3	3	3	3	Touring Activity	--	--	--	2

Note: In this table, p_50 represents percentile 50. Similar definitions hold for p_70, p_90, and p_100.

At the Flanders level, there is only one geographical zone, therefore the concept of p_50, p_70 and p_90 is not applicable.

REFERENCES

Arentze, T. A., & Timmermans, H. J. P. (2000). *Albatross: A learning-based transportation oriented simulation system*. Eindhoven, The Netherlands: European Institute of Retailing and Services Studies.

Arentze, T. A., & Timmermans, H. J. P. (2004). A learning-based transportation oriented simulation system. *Transportation Research Part B: Methodological, 38*(7), 613–633. doi:10.1016/j.trb.2002.10.001.

Arentze, T. A., & Timmermans, H. J. P. (2005). Representing mental maps and cognitive learning in micro-simulation models of activity-travel choice dynamics. *Transportation, 32*, 321–340. doi:10.1007/s11116-004-7964-1.

Arentze, T. A., Timmermans, H. J. P., Janssens, D., & Wets, G. (2008). Modeling short-term dynamics in activity-travel patterns: From Aurora to Feathers. In *Proceedings of Transportation Research Record Conference* (pp. 71-77). Transportation Research Record.

Bellemans, T., Janssens, D., Wets, G., Arentze, T. A., & Timmermans, H. J. P. (2010). Implementation framework and development trajectory of Feathers activity-based simulation platform. *Transportation Research Record: Journal of the Transportation Research Board, 2175*, 111–119. doi:10.3141/2175-13.

Benekohal, R. F., & Abu-Lebdeh, G. (1994). Variability analysis of traffic simulation outputs: Practical approach for TRAF-NETSIM. *Transportation Research Record: Journal of the Transportation Research Board, 1457*, 198–207.

Bhat, C. R., Guo, J. Y., Srinivasan, S., & Sivakumar, A. (2004). A comprehensive microsimulator for daily activity-travel patterns. In *Proceedings of the Conference on Progress in Activity-Based Models*. Maastricht, The Netherlands: Academic Press.

Castiglione, J., Freedman, J., & Bradley, M. (2003). Systematic investigation of variability due to random simulation error in an activity-based microsimulation forecasting model. *Transportation Research Record: Journal of the Transportation Research Board, 1831*, 76–88. doi:10.3141/1831-09.

Cools, M., & Kochan, B. Bellemans, T. Janssens, D., & Wets, G. (2011). Assessment of the effect of microsimulation error on key travel indices: Evidence from the activity-based model FEATHERS. In *Proceedings of the 90th Annual Meeting of the Transportation Research Board*. Washington, DC: Transportation Research Board.

Dowling, R., Skabardonis, A., & Alexiadis, V. (2004). Traffic analysis toolbox: Vol. III. *Guidelines for applying traffic microsimulation modeling software (Publication FHWA-HRT-04-040)*. Washington, DC: U.S. Department of Transportation.

Hale, D. (1997). How many NETSIM runs are enough? *McTrans Newsletter, 11*(3), 4–5.

Horni, A., Charypar, D., & Axhausen, K.W. (2011). Variability in transport microsimulations investigated with the multi-agent transport simulation MATSim. *Arbeitsberichte Verkehrs- und Raumplanung, 692*.

Jones, P., Koppelman, F., & Orfeuil, J.-P. (1990). Activity analysis: State-of-the-art and future directions. In P. Jones (Ed.), *Developments in Dynamic and Activity-based Approaches to Travel Analysis* (pp. 34–55). Aldershot, UK: Gower.

Kitamura, R. (1988). An evaluation of activity-based travel analysis. *Transportation, 15*, 9–34. doi:10.1007/BF00167973.

Kitamura, R., Chen, C., Pendyala, R. M., & Narayanan, R. (2000). Micro-simulation of daily activity-travel patterns for travel demand forecasting. *Transportation, 27*, 25–51. doi:10.1023/A:1005259324588.

Knapen, L., Kochan, B., Bellemans, T., Janssens, D., & Wets, G. (2012). Activity-based modeling to predict spatial and temporal power demand of electric vehicles in Flanders, Belgium. *Transportation Research Record: Journal of the Transportation Research Board, 2287*, 146–154. doi:10.3141/2287-18.

Kochan, B., Bellemans, T., Janssens, D., & Wets, G. (2008). Assessing the impact of fuel cost on traffic demand in Flanders using activity-based models. In *Proceedings of Travel Demand Management*. Vienna, Austria: Travel Demand Management.

Kusumastuti, D., Hannes, E., Janssens, D., Wets, G., & Dellaert, B. G. C. (2010). Scrutinizing individuals' leisure-shopping travel decisions to appraise activity-based models of travel demand. *Transportation, 37*, 647–661. doi:10.1007/s11116-010-9272-2.

McNally, M. G. (2007). The four step model. In *Handbook of Transport Modelling*. London: Elsevier Science.

Pendyala, R. M., Kitamura, R., Kikuchi, A., Yamamoto, T., & Fujji, S. (2005). FAMOS: Florida activity mobility simulator. In *Proceedings of the 84th Annual Meeting of the Transportation Research Board*. Washington, DC: Transportation Research Board.

Timmermans, H. J. P., Arentze, T. A., & Joh, C.-H. (2002). Analysing space-time behavior: New approaches to old problems. *Progress in Human Geography*, *26*(2), 175–190. doi:10.1191/0309132502ph363ra.

Veldhuisen, K., Timmermans, H. J. P., & Kapoen, L. L. (2000a). Ramblas: A regional planning model based on the micro-simulation of daily activity travel patterns. *Environment & Planning A*, *32*, 427–443. doi:10.1068/a325.

Veldhuisen, K. J., Timmermans, H. J. P., & Kapoen, L. L. (2000b). Microsimulation model of activiy patterns and traffic flows: Specification, validation tests, and Monte Carlo error. *Journal of the Transportation Research Board*, *1706*, 126–135. doi:10.3141/1706-15.

Vovsha, P., Petersen, E., & Donnelly, R. (2002). Microsimulation in travel demand modeling: Lessons learned from the New York best practice model. *Journal of the Transportation Research Board*, *1805*, 68–77. doi:10.3141/1805-09.

KEY TERMS AND DEFINITIONS

Activity-Based Models: A class of models that predict for individuals where, when, and how specific activities (e.g., work, leisure, shopping, ...) are conducted, subject to the individual interactions and spatio-temporal constraints.

Confidence Interval: A type of interval estimate of a population parameter and is used to indicate the reliability of an estimate.

FEATHERS: The Forecasting Evolutionary Activity-Travel of Households and their Environmental Repercussions.

Geographic Level: Predefined areas or zones at a specific scale.

Micro-Simulation: A category of computerized analytical tools that perform highly detailed analysis of activities such as highway traffic flowing through an intersection through a population.

Percentile: The value of a variable below which a certain percent of observations fall.

Stochastic Error: The error that is random from one measurement to the next. It is, in effect, a symbol of the inability to model all the movements of the dependent variable.

Chapter 10
A Driver's Mind:
Psychology Runs Simulation

Marco Lützenberger
Technische Universität Berlin, Germany

ABSTRACT

Over the last decade, traffic simulation frameworks have advanced into an indispensible tool for traffic planning and infrastructure management. For these simulations, sophisticated models are used to "mimic" traffic systems in a lifelike fashion. In most cases, these models focus on a rather technical scope. Human factors, such as drivers' behaviours are either neglected or "estimated" without any proven connection to reality. This chapter presents an analysis of psychological driver models in order to establish such a connection. In order to do so, human driver behaviour is introduced from a psychological point of view, and state-of-the-art conceptualisations are analysed to identify factors that determine human traffic behaviour. These factors are explained in more detail, and their appliances in human behaviour models for traffic simulations are discussed. This chapter does not provide a comprehensive mapping from simulation requirements to particular characteristics of human driver behaviour but clarifies the assembly of human traffic behaviour, identifies relevant factors of influence, and thus, serves as a guideline for the development of human behaviour models for traffic simulations.

INTRODUCTION

Computer aided traffic simulation is a mighty tool. Currently, there are many professional simulation frameworks available that are able to simulate traffic in a life-like fashion. These frameworks predict road traffic in many ways. As an example, traffic simulations are frequently used to predict the effects of infrastructure changes, such as additional traffic lanes or entirely new roads on the overall traffic situation. Furthermore, traffic simulations are frequently used to predict the ef-

fects of 'logical' changes, such as adapted traffic light circuits or altered right of ways.

As opposed to practical approaches–where ideas are directly implemented in the real traffic system–traffic simulations allow to predict effects without really affecting the traffic system per se. Changes to the traffic system frequently entail additional stress-factors for traffic participants and also increase the accident probability since traffic participants are confronted with a new situation. Mistakes in planning may also result in heavy congestion, and–last but not least–practical

DOI: 10.4018/978-1-4666-4920-0.ch010

experiments usually involve major costs–a factor that is significantly reduced by computer-aided predictions.

The potential to decrease investments has significantly fostered the development of sophisticated and highly realistic simulation frameworks. The operation principle of these frameworks varies from implementation to implementation and highly depends on the application's scope.

As an example, there are so called *macroscopic* simulation frameworks that focus on the traffic flow 'as a whole' and neglect individuals. These simulation frameworks frequently apply fluid dynamics in order to predict traffic movements. As opposed to that, *microscopic* traffic simulation frameworks simulate the movements of each single vehicle. For this purpose, efficient and quick longitudinal- and lateral models are used.[1]

Nevertheless, when it comes to road traffic, there seems to be no parameter more essential than the driver itself. The question what actually happens on the road is not only determined by physics of motion, but also by the perception and attitudes of the drivers and external conditions (Lützenberger et al., 2011; Lützenberger et al., 2012).

There are some approaches that use conceptualisations of driver behaviour for traffic simulations (e.g., Ehlert et al., 2001; Krajzewicz, 2010; Fellendorf & Vortisch, 2010; Sykes, 2010; Beuck et al., 2008, to name but a few). In most cases, an agent-based model is used as a foundation. The reason for the appliance of agent-based technics is the nature of the multi-agent system paradigm, which considers autonomous, reactive, proactive, and socially competent entities as intelligent agents (Wooldridge & Jennings, 1995)–this system description, almost naturally fits for simulated traffic participants.

Considering traffic participants as intelligent agents simplifies the entire development of traffic participant models as the agent community provides many tools, concepts and methodologies for the conceptualisation and implementation of agent-based software. The problem, however, is that it is inherently difficult to find a formal model for the behaviour of human beings. Most approaches make assumptions about such behaviour, nevertheless, a calibration that validates hypothesised behaviour structures against empirical data, is generally lacking. The reason for this is simple–it is difficult to perform such evaluation. Human behaviour is highly individual and where a model fits for some behaviour characteristics, the same model may totally fail for others.

But how can one learn about the requirements for a valid conceptualisation of human driver behaviour? This question is easily answered: If one wants to learn about a particular domain, it is always a good idea to refer to where there is a lot of experience. Whenever it comes to human behaviour, there are practically no other research domains with more experience than human factor psychology. In fact, the history of traffic-related psychology even outnumbers the history of computer-aided traffic simulations. The first serious work dates back as far as 1938 (Vaa, 2001; Carsten, 2007), when Gibson and Crooks (1938) presented their formal description of safe driving behaviour.

Currently, there are many psychological driver conceptualisations available, each one trying to capture and to explain the traffic behaviour of human beings, and each one with a particular focus on particular aspects of the driving task.

The Structure of this Chapter

This chapter aims to present and to analyse the most popular psychological driver conceptualisations in order to derive requirements for simulation models of drivers (or traffic participants, in more general terms) and to serve as a guideline for the development of human behaviour models for traffic simulations.

It is not the intention to provide a complete overview over psychological approaches–such endeavour is way beyond the scope of a single chapter. For a more comprehensive overview, the interested reader is referred to fundamental literature, such as Michon (1985), Hale et al. (1990), Ranney (1994), Keskinen et al. (2004), Engström & Hollnagel (2007), Peters & Nilsson (2007), or Carsten (2007). Instead of providing a broad overview, this survey focuses on approaches that are currently used as psychological models for human traffic behaviour. Nevertheless, in order to provide some background to psychological approaches, the chapter starts by presenting the origin of our current understanding of driver behaviour.

The work of Michon (1985) significantly shaped this understanding. It was Michon who first identified the inapplicability of monolithic behaviour conceptualisations and proposed a hierarchically ordered approach, including different levels of driver behaviour, each one with different intentions and objectives. It was the same work that helped a stagnating branch of psychology, namely human factor research in driver behaviour, to gain new momentum.

This chapter comprises three parts. The first part explains where our current understanding of human driver behaviour comes from and provides some background about psychological driver conceptualisations. In the second part, contemporary driver conceptualisations are analysed and the most important characteristics about each model are emphasised and compared. In the third part, these characteristics are discussed and requirements for computer-simulated traffic behaviour are derived.

A BIT OF HISTORY

It is commonly agreed (Vaa, 2001; Carsten, 2007) that the work of Gibson and Crooks (1938) can be considered as the first serious work in the domain of driver behaviour research. In the following years, there have been many developments that culminated in the 1960s. In the 1970s, the community somehow lost some of its momentum, which was surprisingly especially in view of the

'cognitive revolution' that had 'swept the superordinate domain of psychology at the same time (Michon, 1985).

Although there have been many approaches and ideas, the community of driver research somehow failed to agree on 'joint model', which was commonly accepted by the broad majority. Developments were somehow isolated–having no connection among each other. In 1984, the community reacted. The organising committee of the *General Motors Symposium* engaged John A. Michon, a luminary of psychological driver research, to identify reasons for the lacking progress.

In order to do so, Michon used a comprehensive description of human driver behaviour that he defined earlier (Michon, 1976) and respectively analysed the capability of existing approaches to 'comprehend' his understanding of human driver behaviour. I present Michon's description of human driver behaviour in the following.

A Description of Human Driver Behaviour

The basic idea of Michon's description of human driver behaviour is that human mobility is always surrounded by a social as well a technological environment and that any kind of behaviour in this environment can be considered as interaction between the human being and its environment. Michon (1976) distinguishes between four *Behavioural Levels* of interaction between human beings and the transport and traffic system, in which the former respectively occurs in a different role and with different intentions. Humans may either occur as an active road user, as a transportation consumer, as an active social being, or as a psycho-biological organism. The four levels of behaviour are illustrated in Table 1.

Following Michon (1976), human behaviour in traffic environments serves not only one but many purposes and goals simultaneously. Human beings do not act in one but in many different roles at the same time. On the one end, humans

Table 1. Behavioural levels relative to the hierarchical structure of problem solving tasks in traffic and transport environments (adapted from Michon 1985, after Michon, 1976)

	Behavioural Level			
	I	**II**	**III**	**IV**
Human Quality as a Problem Solver	Road user	Transportation Consumer	Social Agent	Psycho-biological organism
Problem to be solved	Vehicle Control	Trip making	Activity pattern (Communication)	Satisfaction of basic needs
Task environment	Road	Road network (Topographical structure)	Socio-economic structure	Nature (environment)
Task aids	Vehicles, signs, etc.	Transport mode	Transport system	'Culture', Technology

may occur as psycho-biological organisms, trying to satisfy basic needs. On the other hand, humans occur as active road users, attempting to control their vehicle.

Michon (1976) argues that–due to the different roles in which human beings act–any reasonable conceptualisation of human driver behaviour has to account for different levels of behaviour as well. Furthermore, Michon (1976) identified some form of interaction between the different levels. Behaviour on the lower levels can be influence by behaviour on the higher levels and vice versa. Michon (1976) described the connection and the arrangement of the identified levels of behaviour as a 'nested hierarchy'.

It was Michon's objective to identify shortcomings of existing driver conceptualisations. In order to do so, he used his understanding of human driver behaviour and compared the capabilities of existing approaches to hold for such form of behaviour. This analysis is summarised in the following.

John A. Michon–What Do We Know, What Should We Do?

In order to provide some structure to his analysis, Michon (1985) defined a classification system for driver behaviour models and respectively analysed the most popular approaches of each model cat-

egory. In total, his classification system comprises two dimensions. The first dimension, distinguishes between *Behavioural Models* and *Psychological Models*. While the former can be considered as 'input-output-oriented' models, the latter category implies some internal state of the driver.

The second dimension, distinguishes between *Functional Models* and *Taxonomic Models*. Taxonomic models can be considered as inventories of facts as well as relations between those. Relations, which hold between these facts, are those of sets, such as super- and subordination, identity, sequential relations, as well as measures on sets, such as proportions, likelihood or generalised distance. As opposed to the rather static expressiveness of taxonomic models, functional models always define a dynamic interaction between their constituting components. The two-dimensional driver behaviour classification system (Michon, 1985) is illustrated in Table 2.

Based on the proposed dimensions, Michon (1985) identified five categories of driver behaviour conceptualisations, namely *task analysis models*, *trait models*, *mechanistic models*, *adaptive control models* and *motivational models*. In the following the particular characteristics of each model type are explained in more detail. Furthermore, the most popular approaches of each category are mentioned.

Table 2. Michon's two-dimensional driver behaviour classification system (adapted from Michon, 1985, Figure 3, p. 490)

	Taxonomic	Functional
Behavioural (Input-Output)	Task Analyses	Mechanistic Models
		Adaptive Control Models
Psychological (Internal State)	Trait Models	Motivational Models

Task Analysis Models

In psychological terms, task analysis describes the mental subdivision of a superior task into a set of analytical sub-tasks. Transferred to the domain of driving behaviour, task analysis can be understood as the decomposition of the driving task into tasks and subtasks. Task analysis models consist of three different types of descriptions. Firstly, facts about the driving tasks, the so-called *Task Requirements* are defined. Secondly, behavioural requirements, the so-called *Performance Objectives* are specified. Finally, the ability requirements (or *Enabling Objectives*), which are required to perform the conceptualised task, are described.

One of the most popular task analysis models is that of McKnight & Adams (1970a, also McKnight & Adams (1970b); McKnight & Hundt (1971)). The model describes the driving task by means of 45 major tasks, which are further subdivided into more than 1.700 elementary tasks. The model served as a foundation for many other approaches, such as for Molen (1981), who extended the work of McKnight & Adams (1970a) in order to account for pedestrian behaviour. Perchonok (1972) additionally incorporated principles of performance failures. Another popular example for a task analysis model is the approach of Quenault (1967, also Quenault et al. (1968)). In fact, the approach attempts to combine task analysis and trait models

and can thus be considered as a mechanism for systematic observation under unrestrained driving conditions.

Trait Models

In psychological terms, the trait theory is an approach, which deals with the analysis of the human personality (Kassin, 2003). As the name indicates, the trait theory particularly focuses on the human measurement process of traits. Those are usually defined as habitual patterns of human behaviour, of human thoughts or of human emotions. The trait theory was adapted from psychology and used as foundation for many driver conceptualisations. One essential aspect that all driver behaviour trait models do have in common is the basic assumption, that it is possible to identify the accident-prone driver by means of well-designed tests (Peters & Nilsson, 2007).

The development of trait models was mainly driven by Conger et al. (1959), who compared drivers, which were responsible for accidents to those without accident records in terms of psychiatry, psychology and functionality. Another popular trait model of driver behaviour is the approach of Fleishman (1967, also Fleishman (1975)). The model can be considered as factorial model, which accounts for perceptual, cognitive and motor skills. In his work Fleishman (1967) argues that such skills are a result of combinations of elementary traits, such as reaction speed or spatial orientation. Another approach worth mentioning is the work of Shaw & Sichel (1971). The model is based on mechanisms that were commonly used for industrial control procedures, as for instance the measurement time intervals between accidents. The model is based on the idea, that parameters between two critical incidents will remain stationary as long as the underlying generating processes do not change. Changes in personality variables, however, may alter the average interval between successive incidents.

Mechanistic Models

Mechanistic Models are based on the idea, that it is possible to capture the dynamics of complex systems by understanding the constituting parts of such systems and the coupling between these atomic elements. Therefore, mechanistic models are grounded on the quite strict assumption that platoons of cars behave as an incompressible fluid. Mechanistic models are frequently used within the area of car following.

Two popular mechanistic models are those of Greenberg (1959) and Edie & Foote (1960). The models are quite similar and describe car-moving processes as a problem of hydrodynamics. One key assumption of both models is that deceleration processes of vehicles may trigger capacity problems for the following vehicles, which may travel as shockwaves through entire vehicle platoons. Another popular example for a mechanistic model is the work of Alberti & Belli (1978), who describe a Boltzmann-like model, which is based on a statistical approach. Another interesting approach is that of Herman et al. (1959). The approach is the first one to relax the strict assumption of mechanistic models that car platoons have to be considered as incompressible fluids. The authors additionally conceptualised mind of the driver and thus increased the expressiveness of their model to account for the dynamics of human driving behaviour.

Adaptive Control Models

These models focus explain how drivers adapt to the dynamics of the surrounding environment or to the controlled vehicle (Peters & Nilsson, 2007). Adaptive control models can be subdivided into *servo-control models* and information *flow control models* (Michon, 1985). While the former category addresses continuous tracking, the latter focuses on discrete decision-making of the conceptualised drivers.

Servo-Control Models

Servo-control models act upon input signals, which may either evolve from the lateral position of a vehicle on the road or from the road curvature (Michon, 1985). Furthermore, servo-control models are grounded on the assumption that drivers intend to minimise the difference between a reference state (e.g. a target state) and the current state (Engström & Hollnagel, 2007). Usually, servo-control models are used in order to model lateral and longitudinal vehicle control in constrained situations. Higher level aspects, such as decision making, planning or motivational aspects are not considered. Servo-control models are also frequently referred to as Manual Control Models (Engström & Hollnagel, 2007).

Most servo-control models are based on the conceptual framework of adaptive dynamic, which was presented by Weir & McRuer (1968, also McRuer & Weir (1969)). The framework was improved several times (McRuer et al., 1977).

Information Flow Control Models

The development of information flow control models began in the 1950s, when it was discovered, that air traffic controllers had difficulties in handling simultaneous messages (Hale et al., 1990). The basic idea of information flow control models is that human cognition can be modelled as sequences of logically separated computational steps, including perception, decision and response selection (Engström & Hollnagel, 2007). The separation of phases made it possible to assign limited capacities to the different action stages and thus to account for limitations in the attention and the performance of human beings. Information flow control models had a considerable impact on multiple task sharing theories and were frequently used in order to understand interactions of a driver with driver support systems while driving.

One popular example for an information flow control model is the work of Kidd & Laughery (1964). The model may be considered as an inventory of human factors data, which are connected in a sequential and task-dependent fashion. The model allows for the dynamic simulation of the driver's and the vehicle's behaviour and can be used in order to obtain information about critical manoeuvres in various road configurations and for various vehicle dynamics.

Motivational Models

Motivational models describe the driving task as a dynamic regulation of risk (Engström & Hollnagel, 2007). As opposed to behavioural models, the focus of motivational models is on the self-paced nature of driving. Motivational models are frequently used in order to capture the dynamical adaptation of drivers to varying driving conditions. For this purpose, utilities and trade-offs are used in order to describe why drivers prefer one decision to another (Carsten, 2007). Belonging to the category of psychological models, motivational models also define attitudes and controlling factors by means of internal states a subjective risk.

Compared to behavioural models, motivational models introduce more factors that permit prediction. As a consequence, they should be more subject to parameterisation and verification (Carsten, 2007), yet, following Ranney (1994), such empirical testing has not generally taken place.

One popular example for a motivational model is *Wilde's Risk Homeostasis Theory* (Wilde, 1978; Wilde, 1982; Wilde & Murdoch, 1982), which is based on the assumption that drivers attempt to establish a balance between what happens on the road and their level of acceptable subjective risk. A similar–though, more advanced–driver conceptualisation was proposed by Näätänen & Summala (1974, also Näätänen & Summala, 1976). The model is based on the assumption that the perceived risk in traffic depends on the probability of hazardous events and the importance

of the consequences of that event. Fishbein & Ajzen (1975, also Ajzen & Fishbein, 1977) presented a motivational model that relates beliefs and attitudes on the one hand and intentions and behaviour on the other hand. Their model is able to comprehend planned- as well as intentional behaviour of the drivers. Finally, Fuller (1984) presented a motivational model that incorporates successful aspects of all other motivational models that were mentioned above. The model has been formulated in terms of avoidance learning and accounts–among other things–for the defensive driving concept.

Michon (1985) analysed driver behaviour models from the above-mentioned categories and respectively identified shortcomings. None of the examined approaches was able to capture and to reproduce his understanding of driver behaviour. He criticised taxonomic models to not account for the dynamic relations between their individual elements and mechanistic models for having to much focus on the physics of vehicles and too little on the behaviour of the driver. His hopes were on functional models rather than on taxonomic ones. It was his opinion, that the structural composition–and especially the dynamic interaction between constituting model components–as well as the comprehensive description of internal states could be used to capture the dynamics of human driver behaviour. Yet, he also mentioned several shortcomings of functional models. In the case of servo-control models, he identified shortcomings in the perception mechanism, as the examined approaches were not able to account for tasks that were beyond following the road. He criticised information flow control models to not account for behavioural aspects of the conceptualised drivers and also to neglect high-level aspects of human behaviour. Finally he criticised motivational models to fail in providing details on cognitive procedures and learning. As the main problem, he identified the intentional character of motivational models and the fact the analysed models put a focus on the results of cognitive functions, namely beliefs, emotions and intentions, rather than on the cognitive functions themselves.

In more general terms, Michon (1985) criticised that the examined models were either bottom up approaches, neglecting higher level aspects of the driving task, or–in the case of top down approaches–fail to explain the architecture of internal models, which drivers have to hold in their mind. It was his opinion that controlling the vehicle is only one of the tasks a driver has to perform in traffic environments and that a more comprehensive consideration of driving is generally required, not least because many traffic-related problems originate from a background other than driving.

In order to counter the problems Michon (1985) proposed the *Hierarchical Control Model*. The Hierarchical Control Model was one of the first driver conceptualisations, which was not entirely focused on the driving task, but considered driving from a larger point of view. The model got widely accepted (Keskinen et al., 2004) and was subsequently used as a foundation for many state-of-the-art driver conceptualisations. Event today–a quarter of a century later–the original structure of Michon's Hierarchical Control Model can be recognised in many state-of-the-art approaches. The Hierarchical Control Model is presented in the following.

The Hierarchical Control Model

Instead of defining human traffic behaviour as a monolithic construct, Michon (1985) used a hierarchically ordered structure of different levels of driver behaviour. The Hierarchical Control Model distinguishes between three levels of behaviour, namely the *strategic level* (planning), the *tactical level* (manoeuvring) and the *operational level* (control). Michon (1985) defined the different levels of behaviour as follows:

The Strategic Level can be considered as the planning of an intended trip. In this stage, the trip goals are determined and a route is being calculated. Furthermore, the driver selects his means of travel and performs a cost-risk-analysis.

The Manoeuvring Level refers to tactical exercise manoeuvres of the drivers. Actions which are performed on the manoeuvring level, such as obstacle avoidance, lane change manoeuvres, gap acceptance, turning, or overtaking have to be in compliance with the goals which have been set at the level above. However, theses goals may also be adapted as a result to some manoeuvres, which were performed on this level.

The Control Level considers fundamental car controlling processes, such as controlling speed, following the road and keeping the car on the road.

Michon (1985) argued, that the behavioural levels should define an information flow control structure that enables control to shift in a timely manner. Hence, Michon (1985) defined an interaction between the three levels of behaviour and allowed the outcome of lower levels to change goals and criteria, which have been defined at a higher level.

The Hierarchical Control Model was one of the first approaches that defined human driver behaviour as a hierarchically ordered structure of different behavioural levels, each one serving different goals and purposes. A driver's decisions do not only affect the particular level on which the decisions were made, but gradually affect other levels and thus determine the driver's entire behaviour. The Hierarchical Control Model had a major influence on the entire psychological research community and determined the development of driver conceptualisations significantly (Keskinen et. al, 2004). In the following years, there were many attempts to clarify the nature of the levels of behaviour that Michon proposed.

After the origin of hierarchically ordered driver behaviour conceptualisations was presented, this chapter continues by presenting state-of-the-art approaches of human factor research in driver behaviour. In doing so all factors that are relevant for human traffic behaviour are collected. These factors should be considered for simulation models of traffic participants.

HUMAN DRIVER BEHAVIOUR–A STATE OF THE ART

This analysis distinguishes between three categories of driver conceptualisations. *Hierarchical Structures* roughly maintain the original structure of Michon's Hierarchical Control Model, but refine individual behaviour phases or provide more detailed descriptions of involved processes. *Multi-Dimension Hierarchies* extend the one-dimensional hierarchy of Michon's original model by further dimensions and thus realise advanced concepts such as different levels of experience and automation. Finally, *Cognitive Approaches* combine principles of cognitive models with those of hierarchical structures.

Advances in Hierarchical Structures

This first category roughly maintains the original structure of Michon's Hierarchical Control Model. Approaches in this category usually refine certain model aspects, or add further levels of behaviour.

The Hierarchical Risk Model for Traffic Participants

The first approach that fits into the category of `classical hierarchical structures' is that of van der Molen & Bötticher (1988, also Bötticher & van der Molen (1988)). The authors developed a hierarchical driver behaviour model that comprises the same hierarchy as Michon's Hierarchical Control Model. It was their intention to extend Michon's work to additionally take behaviour alternatives and subjective probabilities–such as utility aspects–into account. Furthermore, it was their intention to describe perceptual, judgemental and decision processes of traffic participants at all levels of behaviour. Another key aspect is the connection of the driver's behaviour to its physical environment. For their work, van der Molen and Bötticher followed Michon's guidelines for the development of a comprehensive driver model

(Michon, 1985) and defined a dynamic interaction between the different levels of driver behaviour. Interaction between the strategic level behaviour and the tactical level behaviour was realised by so called *Strategic Plans*. Interaction between tactical- and the operational behaviour was accomplished by so called *Manoeuvring Plans*. The approach of van der Molen and Bötticher has a close resemblance to Michon's original model. Nevertheless, some differences can be observed as well. To start with, the Hierarchical Risk Model for Traffic Participants provides a significant refinement of the driver's strategic level behaviour specification. Motivational factors, expectations and even judgements were included in the strategic decision making process. Another important extension to Michon's approach is the additional connection between the drivers' strategic decision-making and their perception. Such connection implies some interdependency between the driver's strategic behaviour and his environment.

Keskinen's Hierarchical Levels of Behaviour

The approach of Keskinen (1996) can be considered as an extension to Michon's original model. Nevertheless, instead of refining individual behaviour levels, Keskinen advanced Michon's work by extending the level hierarchy. Altogether, Keskinen (1996) defined four levels of driver behaviour. At the *Vehicle Manoeuvring* level, drivers account for the controlling of speed, the vehicle's direction and its position. This level is closely related to Michon's control level. One hierarchy above, at the *Mastering Traffic Situations* level, drivers adapt to the demands of the present traffic situation. This level complies with Michon's manoeuvring level. On the next higher level, drivers deal with *Goals and Context of Driving*. At this level of behaviour, drivers consider their purpose, their environment their social context and their company. This level is similar to that of

Michon's strategic level behaviour, yet, the explicit consideration of the driver's environment was not described by Michon and can be considered as an extension in terms of strategic behaviour. Finally, Keskinen defined as an entirely new level atop of the drivers' strategic level behaviour, namely the *Goals for Life and Skills for Living* level. Keskinen et al. (2004) argue that such additional level is able to cover the area of personality and motives and expresses behaviours that are 'less congruent with the norms of the society' (p. 18). As an example for behaviour, which typically evolves from the additionally defined level, consider young male drivers, which often suffer from a lack of control of their driving behaviour and thus frequently cause violations against traffic regulations.

Regarding this model two aspects have to be mentioned. To start with, Keskinen defined an explicit connection between the driver's strategic level behaviour and his environment. He established such connection in order to account for an interaction between external factors and the driver's (strategic-level) decision-making. A similar feature was defined in the model of van der Molen and Bötticher (1988). Secondly, an additional level of behaviour was defined in order to account for aspects that may affect a human's driving behaviour without being explicitly related to the driving itself. Factors such as motives, the driver's lifestyle or the driver's gender or age may fall into this category. The model's capability to include external factors for strategic decision-making was already practically used. It was successfully applied in the European project GADGET (Christ, 2000) in order to explain the behaviour of drivers that are aware of alternative transport modes (Panou et al., 2007).

The analysis of approaches that fall under the umbrella of 'classical hierarchical structures' ends at this point. The bottom line is that there were only few approaches that maintained the original structure of the Hierarchical Control Model. The main reason for this is the multi-dimensional nature of human traffic behaviour. Behaviour occurs not only on one, but on many dimensions. As a con-

sequence, many researchers proposed approaches that extend Michon's work by further dimensions. The most popular *Multi-Dimension Hierarchies* are presented in the following.

Multi-Dimension Hierarchies

Michon's work provided new impetus to the domain of human factor research in driver behaviour. His idea to consider driver behaviour as hierarchically ordered levels was an entirely new way of thinking. The previous section emphasised that the original model was not comprehensively extended. The reason for this is that most researchers were convinced that human behaviour comprises not only one, but many dimensions such as experience, automation or emotions, to name but a few. In order to account for these additional factors of human behaviour, multi-dimension hierarchies extend Michon's 'vertical' arrangement by further 'horizontal' dimensions. These approaches are presented in the following.

The Matrix of Tasks

The first work that falls into this category was presented by Hale et al. (1990). The authors combined the principles of Michon's hierarchy with those of Rasmussen (1986), who was convinced that human behaviour (in general) has many distinct levels, which are somehow hierarchically ordered. Instead of focusing on driver behaviour, Rasmussen embraced a larger view and generalised the Hierarchical Control Model to account for all kinds of human performance. In his *Three-Level-Model*, Rasmussen (1986) considers human operative performance as a combination of *knowledge-based*, *rule-based* and *skill-based* behaviour. While knowledge-based behaviour can be considered as conscious problem solving, rule-based behaviour refers to the application of learned rules and skill-based behaviour refers to automated skills, which require no cognitive processing.

Michon and Rasmussen both identified a dynamic interaction among behaviour activities of different levels of the driving task. Yet, neither of them actually provided a specification of this interaction.

A specification was done by Hale et al. (1990), who solved the problem, by defining a mapping from Rasmussen's performance levels to Michon's levels of driving behaviour. To define such mapping, Rasmussen's levels of operative performance had to be applied to the driving task. Hale et al. (1990) defined such application as follows:

Knowledge-Based Behaviour is applied when the driver is either located in difficult environmental conditions or in an unfamiliar traffic. Furthermore, knowledge-based behaviour is applied in case the driver's skills are not fully developed.

Rule-Based Behaviour refers to the standard interaction with other road users. It is also applied when automatic routines are transferred to a new system (e.g. driving an unfamiliar car type).

Skill-Based Behaviour is applied in all familiar traffic situations. As opposed to the other phases, this kind of behaviour requires no cognitive processing.

Based on the above-mentioned understanding of knowledge-, rule- and skill based behaviour in traffic conditions, Hale extended the Hierarchical Control Model by a second dimension, namely Rasmussen's taxonomy. The *Matrix of Tasks* (Hale et al., 1990) in which Michon's driving tasks were related to Rasmussen's taxonomy is illustrated in Table 3.

Exceeding the capabilities of each model for itself, the combined approach allowed for a conceptualisation of the driver's expertise and his familiarity with the situation. Tasks of skilled drivers for instance are located on the diagonal that runs from the upper left to the lower right matrix cell in the table. Cells aside this diagonal either reflect differences in the driver's experience or differences in the driver's familiarity with the situation. Tasks of novice drivers, for instance, are mainly clustered in the top right quadrant.

The work of Hale became widely accepted and provided new impetus in developing a comprehensive model of driving behaviour (Ranney, 1994). The reason for the model's success was twofold. First, Hale's model accounted for automaticity, which is not limited on individual levels of behaviour, but comprises the entire hierarchy, including strategic-, manoeuvring- and control level behaviour. As an example, for the increased expressiveness of Hale's approach consider the shifting of gears. Following Michon (1985), the shifting of gears can be classified as control level behaviour. Using Hale's model it is possible to distinguish between inexperienced drivers, which apply knowledge-based behaviour for the shifting of gears and experienced drivers, which may accomplish the same task with skill-based action patterns. Consider navigation as another example. Following Michon (1985), navigation can be considered as strategic level behaviour. Using Hale's model it is possible to distinguish between novice drivers, which apply knowledge-based behaviour, and experienced drivers, which use skill-based actions for navigating through familiar environments.

Table 3. The Matrix of Tasks. A combination of Rasmussen's three levels of human operative behaviour and Michon's Hierarchical Control Model (adapted from Hale et al., 1990, Figure 1, p. 1383)

	Planning	**Manoeuvre**	**Control**
Knowledge	Navigation in strange town	Controlling a skid on icy roads	Learner on first lesson
Rule	Choice between familiar routes	Passing other cars	Driving an unfamiliar car
Skill	Home/work travel	Negotiating familiar junctions	Road holding round corners

The second reason for the popularity of Hale's work is the additional support of motivational aspects on different levels of behaviour. In reality, the purpose and the importance of a trip may influence a driver throughout his journey. Yet, situations, which are encountered 'en route', may trigger short-term goals that motivate tactical problem solving and lead to the same outcome. As an example, consider a driver who has selected a route and a departure time that ensures a leisurely and uneventful drive. The presence of extreme slow traffic ahead, may motivate even this driver to speed up and to pass.

The Filter Model of Risky Behaviour and Road Accidents

The second multi-dimensional conceptualisation of human driver behaviour that is presented here was proposed by Summala (1996). The *Drivers Task Cube* describes a driver's tasks by means of three dimensions. In the first dimension, a functional hierarchy comprises vehicle choice, trip decisions, navigation, guidance, and vehicle control. In the second dimension, a functional taxonomy distinguishes between enclosed capabilities, such as lane keeping, headway control or obstacle avoidance. Finally, in the third dimension, three psychological processing levels were defined.

Instead of a solid model, the Drivers Task Cube can be considered as description, or a list of important variables (Keskinen et al., 2004). Shortly after his model was published, Summala (1997) concluded that motivational factors should have a more important role. As a consequence, Summala developed the *Multiple Sieve Model* or the *Filter Model of Risky Behaviour and Road Accidents* as an extension of the Drivers Task Cube and additionally accounted for motives and emotions of drivers.

The GADGET Matrix

The third approach that is presented here was proposed by Hatakka et al. (1997). The *GADGET-Matrix* model extends Michon's original hierarchy by further dimensions. On the vertical dimension, the authors distinguish between four levels of driving behaviour, namely:

- **Goals for life and skills for living:** This level of driver behaviour comprises a driver's attitudes, such as his lifestyle, his social background, his gender or his age.
- **Driving goals and context:** This level comprises the strategic-level planning of a trip. Things, such as where, when and with whom one is driving are considered here.
- **Mastery of traffic situations:** This level resembles Michon's manoeuvring level and can be considered as regular driving in a given context.
- **Vehicle manoeuvring:** Complies with Michon's car control level. On this level, the driver's focus is mainly on the vehicle.

The above-mentioned categories should be familiar, already as those were presented when the approach of Keskinen (1996) was described. Both, the GADGET-Matrix and the approach of Keskinen were developed in symbiosis within the same project: the European project *GADGET* (Christ, 2000). However, in order to cover high-order aspects of driver behaviour the original vertical dimension was extended by three horizontal columns, namely *knowledge and skills*, *risk-increasing factors* and *self-assessment*. These additional columns are described in the following:

- **Knowledge and Skills:** Can be considered as routines and information that are required for driving under regular conditions.

- **Risk-Increasing Factors:** Can be considered as traffic or life related factors, which are associated with a higher risk.
- **Self-Assessment:** Is the level on how good a driver is able to reflect his own driving skills and motivations.

As dictated by the nature of hierarchical driver models, decisions on the upper levels are able to affect the drivers' lower level behaviour. The GADGET-Matrix emphasises, that high-level aspects, such as a driver's attitudes, his lifestyle or his personal values are able to affect strategic-level decision-making. The two cells, which express this connection, are illustrated in Table 4.

The Drivability Model

The next multi-dimensional approach that is presented here is the *DRIVABILITY* model, which was proposed by Bekiaris et al. (2003). The DRIVABILITY model cannot be considered as a real multi-dimensional driver hierarchy model, but rather as a combination of a classical hierarchy and a multi-dimensional one. Yet, as the approach identifies several factors, which may simultaneously distract a driver's behaviour, the DRIVABILITY model is presented in this section. The fundamental assumption of the DRIVABILITY model is that driver behaviour evolves over time as a result to several permanent and temporary contributors. The most important contributors are:

Individual Resources can be physical, social, psychological and mental conditions of the conceptualised driver.

The Knowledge & Skills Level describes not only the driver's training and his experience, but also knowledge in general. The reason for this is that basic education may influence a driver's motivation and his behaviour. Furthermore, this contributor also comprises the driver's self-awareness for his own skills.

Environmental Factors describes the driver's surrounding. In addition to the status of his vehicle, this may also comprise traffic hazards, the weather condition, or the general traffic situation.

Workload & Risk Awareness are the two common denominators between the driver resources and his environmental status. The driver's risk awareness is further influenced by his risk perception, by his level of attention and possibly by driver support systems.

When looking at the DRIVABILITY model, it becomes clear that the driving process can be affected by no less than five factors. With regards to of computer simulations, contributor I, II and III are particularly interesting. Following Bekiaris et al. (2003), Individual Resources such as cognition, perception and stress are able to affect a driver's actions. Furthermore, Knowledge and Skills influence a driver's decisions. Finally, Environmental Factors, such as traffic-, or weather conditions, the visibility level or traffic hazards do have the same capability.

Table 4. Two cells of the GADGET-Matrix, indicating the connection between a driver's goals for life and his strategic behaviour (adapted from Hatakka et al., 1997)

	Knowledge and Skills	
	Goals for Life and Skills for Living	**Driving Goals and Context**
Awareness about:	- Relation between personal tendencies and driving skills - Lifestyle/life situation - Peer group norms - Motives - Personal values	- Effects of journey goals - Planning and choosing routes - Effects of social pressure by passengers inside the car

The Adaptive Control of Thought-Rational

An approach that is very similar to that of Bekiaris et al. (2003) is that of Salvucci et al. (2001). The Adaptive Control of Thought-Rational, or ACT-R, combines cognitive, perceptual and motor dimension and focuses on highway driving with moderate traffic. In fact, ACT-R cannot only be considered as a multi-dimensional driver conceptualisation, but also as a cognitive approach, yet, due to its resemblance to the approach of Bekiaris et al. (2003), the approach is presented in this section.

The ACT-R approach comprises two central models, namely the ACT-R Architecture and ACT-R Driver Model. The ACT-R architecture (Anderson et al., 2004) defines how the decision making process of the driver is accomplished.

The model is rather low-level and is based on the brain structures and information processing steps of human beings. In total, the decision making process is influenced by four factors, namely the Intentional Module, the Declarative Module, the driver's Visual Module and by his Manual Module. While the former two can be considered as attitudes of the driver without any connection to external factors, the latter two modules are directly connected to the External World.

Observations, for instance, are done with the Visual Module and may comprise the driver's decision making. Actions on the other hand are executed with the driver's Manual Module and may affect the External World.

The second constituting model of the ACT-R approach is the ACT-R driver model (Salvucci et al., 2001). The ACT-R driver model defines the driving process to comprise three different tasks: to control, to monitor and to decide. As opposed to Michon's suggestion, the authors do not distinguish between different levels of behaviour. The ACT-R approach emphasises that a driver's decisions are subject to his personal attitudes as well as to external influences. It is also important

to mention that the driver's actions are able to affect his environment (Anderson et al., 2004).

Above, the most relevant driver conceptualisations that extended the Hierarchical Control Model by at least one further dimension were presented. As opposed to attempts that only refine the vertical structure of the Hierarchical Control Model, there were considerably more efforts to add further dimensions. These additional dimensions were used to capture aspects of automation and to conceptualise varying skills of the conceptualised drivers.

In the following state-of-the-art approaches from the domain of cognitive driver psychology are analysed.

Cognitive (Hierarchical) Approaches

Michon (1985) stated that the driver conceptualisations he analysed, have failed to keep up with the '*cognitive revolution that 'swept psychology in the past fifteen years*' (p. 485). One conclusion of his work was that cognitive approaches have the greatest potential to serve as a comprehensive driver conceptualisation. As a consequence to that, many research groups tried to combine cognitive approaches–where behaviour was only monolithically described–with Michon's idea of hierarchical structures. The most popular models of this category are presented in the following.

A Common Mental Environment Model – The ACME Driver Model

The *A Common Mental Environment–Driver* Model, or *ACME-Driver* Model, was presented by Krajzewicz & Wagner (2002). For their work, the authors utilised a well-known psychological paradigm, which was invented by Atkinson & Shiffring (1968).

This original model distinguishes between three different types of memory, namely the *Sensoric Input Register*, the *Short-Term Memory* and the *Long-Term Memory*. The main difference between the memory types is the period of time that collected information stay available.

Krajzewicz & Wagner (2002), however, extended the original model by another concept, which was proposed by Tulving (1972), who additionally distinguishes between three types of the long-term memory. Where the episodic memory stores information about single situations from the human's life, the semantic memory is used to save common or logically expressible rules like rules of algebra. Finally, the procedural memory contains non-verbalisable information about movements. Both, the sensoric input register and the long-term memory are considered for the cognitive computation. This process is done in the short-term memory of the conceptualised driver.

In their model, Krajzewicz & Wagner (2002) define no explicit behaviour hierarchy. The authors argue that the ACME-Driver model is not able to reproduce the complete cognition of a human but focuses on particular aspects only.

The ACME-Driver model defines connections between the short-term memory and the long-term memory and between the short-term memory and the sensoric input register. These connections underline the importance of external factors and long-term aspects such as experiences and strategies for the outcome of cognitive processes. As a matter of fact, the ACME-Driver model is one of the few psychological works that was actually implemented within a traffic simulation framework, namely the SUMO framework (Krajzewicz, 2010).

The Contextual Control Model

The *Contextual Control Model*, or *COCOM*, was presented by Hollnagel (1993, also Hollnagel & Woods (2005)). The model is based on the *Perceptual Cycle* (Neisser, 1976) and considers the controller as well as the controlled system as a *Joint Cognitive System* rather than focusing on both entities in isolation. The central concept of the

COCOM model is the so-called *Construct-Action-Event Cycle*, which describes on how a controller selects his actions based on his knowledge or his assumptions about the situation in which the action takes place. The construct-action-event cycle also provides a concept to describe the consequences of the selected actions on the controlled system. That is, the selected actions generate new events, which are–together with external disturbances– again perceived by the controller.

The COCOM approach provides many configuration options, as for instance to adjust the time which is available for each decision making process. Nevertheless, the approach does not account for different levels of behaviour, although it was developed after Michon (1985) proposed his guidelines. The authors recognised that the capabilities of the model were limited and extended their approach by hierarchically ordered behaviour structures. The refined model is presented in the following.

The Extended Control Model

The Extended Control Model, or E*COM* (Hollnagel & Woods, 2005; Engström & Hollnagel 2007) was developed as an extension to the COCOM in order to account for the required distinction between different levels of driving behaviour. The ECOM combines its predecessor, the CO-COM with the hierarchical organisation that was proposed by Michon (1985) and addresses the deficiency of many related models to account for the dynamic aspects of driving and to capture the simultaneous relations between control processes of different levels of driving behaviour (Engström & Hollnagel, 2007).

The ECOM distinguishes between four levels of behaviour, namely the tracking, the regulating, the monitoring and the targeting. On the targeting level the driver sets general goals of the driving task. These goals constitute the input for the next level, the monitoring level, on which the driver attempts to control the state of the joint vehicle-driver system relative to the driver's environment. Among others, the monitoring level comprises tasks like monitoring properties of the traffic environment (such as speed limits) or the location and the condition of the vehicle. On the regulating level, the driver deals with conscious processes, such as keeping desired safety margins to other traffic elements. Finally, on the tracking level, the driver performs momentary and automated corrections to external disturbances, such as wind gusts.

The analysis of the COCOM and the ECOM clearly emphasises necessity of different levels of behaviour. While the COCOM had no such feature, the ECOM can be considered as a vertical extension to the hierarchical pattern, which was proposed by Michon (1985).

Observations

So far, psychological works that are currently used to describe and to explain human driver behaviour were presented. Most of the works that were presented were somehow shaped by the trendsetting work of Michon (1985). Two aspects mirror the resemblance to Michon's model. First, the consideration of different levels of behaviour and secondly, the comprehensive support for the cognitive abilities of drivers.

The above-presented analysis emphasised that approaches from the first category generally extend the original version of the Hierarchical Control Model. The Hierarchical Risk Model for Traffic Participants (van der Molen & Bötticher, 1988), for instance, can be considered as a refinement of the Hierarchical Control Model. The authors used Michon's original structure, but defined an additional connection between the drivers' perception and their strategic-level behaviour. This connection can be found in other approaches as well (e.g., Bekiaris et al. (2003), Anderson et al. (2004), Krajzewicz & Wagner (2002), Engström & Hollnagel (2007)). The conclusion is that such connection is highly relevant when it comes to human driver behaviour. Beyond that, a driver's

strategic-level behaviour is always connected to his environment. As an example consider a driver with a high affinity for public transport who might change his means of transportation when confronted with extreme weather conditions (e.g. freezing rain, or heavy snowfalls) near a metro station and available parking (Lützenberger et al., 2012). Furthermore, van der Molen & Bötticher (1988) refined the internal aspects of the original Hierarchical Control Model by elementary sub-processes, namely perceptual, judgemental and decision processes. Although this was a necessary step towards a better understanding of human driver behaviour, the refinement was heavily criticised by Michon (1989) and even by the authors themselves (van der Molen & Bötticher, 1988). The problem was the lacking definition of the internal processes of each elementary sub-process. Due to this deficiency, the model was referred to as 'an empty one' (van der Molen & Bötticher, 1988, p. 538). Finally, the authors accounted for motivational aspects that may affect a driver's short- and long-term behaviour. Motivational factors can be found in most analysed approaches (e.g., Summala (1997); Hatakka et al. (1997); Bekiaris et al. (2003)). These factors are significantly determine a driver's behaviour.

Nevertheless, the Hierarchical Risk Model for Traffic Participants was not the only approach that underlined the importance to distinguish between different levels of behaviour. Keskinen (1996) substantiated this thesis and introduced an additional top-level hierarchy, namely Goals for Life and Skills for Living. Following Keskinen (1996), external factors, such as the driver's perception, are able to affect a driver's behaviour. As opposed to the van der Molen and Bötticher (1988) this kind of distraction affects the driver's selection of alternative transport modes, only.

The analysis of Multi-Dimension Hierarchies emphasised that the original structure of the Hierarchical Control Model was generally maintained, however, researchers extended this hierarchy by further dimensions in order to account for sophisticated abilities of human behaviour, such as experience, skills and automation.

The Matrix of Tasks (Hale et al., 1990), for instance, integrates the level of expertise of conceptualised drivers as a horizontal dimension. This extension allows to distinguish between the levels of automation that are assigned to the decision-making process on each level of behaviour. However, the model is generally considered to be on a 'conception level', as it neither refines decision-making processes nor provides concepts for factors that evolve from the driver's environment and affect those in their actions.

Where Hale et al. (1990) used two dimensions for the conceptualisation of human driver behaviour, Summala (1996) added another–a third–dimension. In a first dimension, different levels of behaviour are hierarchically ordered. This dimension follows Michon's approach, though, extends the original hierarchy by more general aspects, such as the choice of the vehicle. Regarding this model it has to be mentioned that Summala (1996) explicitly extended the strategic level behaviour and thus underlines the importance of high-level aspects for the driving behaviour of human beings. Furthermore, the difference between the Drivers Task Cube (Summala, 1996) and its successor, the Multisieve Model (Summala, 1997) substantiates the requirement for motivational factors. Those were explicitly included since Summala recognised that motives and emotions are able to affect a driver on each level of behaviour, including the strategic one.

As opposed to that, the GADGET-Matrix (Hatakka et al., 1997) does not explicitly allow motivational factors to influence drivers on each level of behaviour. Hatakka et al. (1997) distinguish between different levels of behaviour, though, motives and personal values affect the uppermost levels, only. Nevertheless, due to the hierarchical arrangement of the GADGET-Matrix disturbances on the upper levels implicitly affect the lower levels and thus determine the operational levels as well.

Bekiaris et al. (2003) used a similar approach. The DRIVABILITY-Model defines several contributors that are able to affect drivers during the driving process. A driver's decisions may be affected by: individual resources, knowledge and skills, environmental factors, as well as his risk awareness and his workload. The DRIVABILITY-Model, however, defines no hierarchical architecture and arranges the contributors in one single dimension. The reason for this is that the DRIVABILITY-Model focuses on a higher level of behaviour, only. The model can be considered as a specification of Michon's strategic level behaviour, rather than a comprehensive behaviour conceptualisation. Again, it has to be mentioned that, following Bekiaris et al. (2003), strategic level behaviour is a subject to knowledge and skills, environmental factors, the driver's risk awareness and his workload.

The ACT-R (Anderson et al., 2004) works in a similar way and defines similar dependencies. Again, there is no explicit consideration for different levels of behaviour. The reason for this is the same reason as in the approach of Bekiaris et al. (2003): The ACT-R focuses on a particular level of behaviour. As opposed to the DRIVABILITY-Model, the ACT-R, focuses on a lower level of behaviour. Nevertheless, the authors clearly underline the necessity for a connection between the driver's actions and his personal attitude as well as external factors.

Finally, the analysis of cognitive approaches emphasised a close resemblance to the two other categories that were presented in this chapter. Hierarchies, internal factors such as motivations and emotions as well as external factors such as the environment or the drivers' social state were included. In fact, this kind of convergence is no surprise, but rather an indication for the requirements a comprehensive solution.

To start with, the ACME-Driver Model (Krajzewicz & Wagner, 2002) considers experiences and sensor input for the decision-making process of drivers. There is no distinction between different levels of behaviour, though, the model focuses on a particular level, only. The reason for this limitation is of a pragmatic nature. Above it was already indicated that ACME-Driver model is used in order to generate the behaviour for the SUMO traffic simulation framework (Krajzewicz, 2010). This framework, however, focuses on the operational levels, only. Lower (as well as upper) levels are neglected and the authors argue that the ACME-Driver model was never intended to be a comprehensive solution, but focuses on very particular aspects of driving. Nevertheless, the connection between the driver's perception and their operational behaviour is clearly emphasised by the model, which explicitly accounts for such relation in order to mimic short-term behaviour, such as breaking manoeuvres, in a lifelike fashion.

The same applies for the COCOM approach (Hollnagel, 1993), where a driver's actions are considered to be a result to external events or disturbances as well as to the driver's knowledge or situation-related assumptions. The approach was advanced in order to account for different levels of behaviour. The ECOM (Engström & Hollnagel, 2007) comprises the same microscopic control cycle as the COCOM, however, the driver's decision-making comprises four of such cycles, each one responsible for the decision-making on a particular level of behaviour, and each one with different goals, plans, targets and objectives, and respectively influencing the lower level of behaviour.

Above, the most relevant state-of-the-art approaches were analysed in order to identify factors that determine human driver behaviour. In the following this work is concluded by discussing the requirements of these factors for the development of driver models for traffic simulations.

CONCLUSION

The approaches that were analysed above were developed independently from each other. Nevertheless, despite the separated development, most authors used Michon's guidelines (Michon, 1985) for the development of their own approach and thus accounted for similar behavioural factors. The resulting models somewhat converged in their expressiveness and it was possible to identify four key factors, namely the hierarchical arrangement of different behaviour levels, a connection between the driver's behaviour and his environment, the importance of internal aspects such as emotions and motives, and the driver's level of familiarity and automatisms.

In the following these factors are presented in more detail in order to clarify their exact nature, to outline their dependencies and to provide a guideline for the development of human behaviour models for traffic simulations.

Behaviour levels and their hierarchical arrangement: To start with, most presented models (Engström & Hollnagel, 2007; Hale et al., 1990; Hatakka et al., 1997; Keskinen, 2004; Summala, 1996; Summala 1997; van der Molen & Bötticher, 1988) understand human driver behaviour as a hierarchically ordered structure, where several levels of behaviour interact in a flowing transition, respectively allowing the outcome of lower levels to change goals and criteria that have been defined at a higher level. Most approaches roughly maintain the hierarchical arrangement that was originally proposed by Michon (1985). In more detail, Michon (1985) distinguishes between strategic-, manoeuvring-, and control level behaviour. Strategic level behaviour can be considered as a 'high-level skill', by which humans plan intended trips, determine trip goals, select routes and perform cost-risk-analyses. Strategic-level behaviour can be influenced by higher-level considerations, such as the Goals for Life and Skills for Living level that was proposed by Keskinen et al. (2004), or by the targeting level that was proposed by Engström & Hollnagel (2007). Also, strategic-level compensations affect lower-levels of driver behaviour, including tactical exercise manoeuvres such as obstacle avoidance, lane change manoeuvres, gap acceptance, turning or overtaking.

Environmental Factors: A driver's behaviour is closely connected to his environment. This connection was not defined in Michon's model, though, most state-of-the-art approaches (Bekiaris et al., 2003; Engström & Hollnagel, 2007; Hale et al., 1990; Hollnagel, 1993; Keskinen et al., 2004; Krajzewicz & Wagner, 2002; Salvucci et al., 2006; van der Molen & Bötticher, 1988) clearly emphasise the necessity of such connection. It has to be mentioned that the effects of external factors comprise the entire behavioural hierarchy of the driver and not only the lower levels, where such dependency is somehow obvious. As an example for an effect of the environment on a driver's manoeuvring-behaviour consider the sudden breaking of a preceding vehicle, which causes a pursuer to adapt his velocity in the same way, in order to avoid an accident. However, the analysis clearly showed that external factors also affect the upper levels of behaviour. Above, this connection was explained by means of a driver with a high affinity for public transport that might change his means of transportation when confronted with extreme weather conditions (e.g. freezing rain, or heavy snowfalls) near a metro station and available parking (Lützenberger et al., 2012). As another example, consider the occurrence of congestion that may cause isolated drivers[2] to avoid critical road sections and to deviate from their originally selected strategy (Lützenberger et. al, 2012).

The analysis clearly shows that there has to be a connection between the drivers' strategic-level decision making and their environment. Thus, any reasonable simulation model for strategic-level traffic behaviour has to define such connection. Most existing simulation frameworks, however, define such connection only for the lower levels of behaviour.

Emotion and Motives: Since these factors evolve directly from the driver, both factors are summarised under the term 'internal factors'. Most examined approaches (Bekiaris et al., 2003; Hale et al., 1990; Hatakka et al., 1997 Salvucci et al., 2006; Summala, 1997; van der Molen & Bötticher, 1988) account for internal factors and define a dependency between the driver's mental state and their behaviour. Again, this dependency comprises the entire behavioural hierarchy, such that emotions may affect a driver's route selection, its breaking or lane-changing behaviour and finally its technical procedures such as shifting the gear.

Familiarity and Automatisms: The last aspect to mention is the concept of familiarity and automatisms. In chronological terms, Hale et al. (1990) were the first to expand Michon's vertical arrangement by horizontal factors and thus described human driver behaviour by means of more than one dimension. On The vertical axis, Hale et al. (1990) maintained Michon's behaviour hierarchy, though, in horizontal terms, differing levels of automatisms and situation familiarity were added. The survey that was presented in this chapter emphasised the relevance of these concepts as most examined approaches (Hatakka et al., 1997; Krajzewicz & Wagner, 2002; Summala, 1996; Summala, 1997) account for familiarity and automatisms.

To sum up, the survey that was done in this chapter emphasised that there are four factors that are determining for human driver behaviour. These factors include i) different levels of behaviours which are vertically arranged, ii) environmental factors that affect each level of behaviour iii) emotion and motives, or internal factors that evolve from the driver itself and affect its behaviour on each level, iv) aspects of familiarity and automatisms that account for a driver's level of expertise and its skills.

It is difficult to provide a general that connects the above-mentioned factors to a category of questions that are supposed to be answered by means of a simulation model for human driver behaviour. Nevertheless, the above characterisation aims to facilitate the development of such models in two aspects. First, the listing helps to determine weather or not particular capabilities of human behaviour features are required for the own approach. Secondly, the detailed explanation of each factor clarifies their nature and their dependencies and thus facilitates the development of human behaviour models for traffic simulations.

REFERENCES

Ajzen, I., & Fishbein, M. (1977). Attitude-behavior relations: A theoretical analysis and review of empirical research. *Psychological Bulletin, 84*(5), 888–918. doi:10.1037/0033-2909.84.5.888.

Alberti, E., & Belli, G. (1978). Contributions to the boltzmann-like approach for trafficflow - A model for concentration dependent driving programs. *Transportation Research, 12*(1), 33–42. doi:10.1016/0041-1647(78)90105-3.

Anderson, J. R., Bothell, D., Byrne, M. D., Douglass, S., Lebiere, C., & Qin, Y. (2004). An integrated theory of the mind. *Psychological Review, 111*, 1036–1060. doi:10.1037/0033-295X.111.4.1036 PMID:15482072.

Atkinson, R. C., & Shiffring, R. M. (1986). Human memory: A proposed system and its control processes. In The Psychology of Learning and Motivation: Advances in Research and Theory (pp. 89-195). Academic Press, Inc.

Barcelló, J. (2010). Models, traffic models, simulation and traffic simulation. In *Fundamentals of traffic simulation* (pp. 1–62). Berlin: Springer. doi:10.1007/978-1-4419-6142-6_1.

Bekiaris, E., Amditis, A., & Panou, M. (2003). Drivability: A new concept for modelling driving performance. *Cognition Technology and Work, 5*, 152–161. doi:10.1007/s10111-003-0119-x.

Beuck, U., Nagel, K., Rieser, M., Strippgen, D., & Balmer, M. (2008). Preliminary results of a multi-agent traffic simulation for berlin. In *The Dynamics of Complex Urban Systems* (pp. 75–94). Berlin: Physica-Verlag HD. doi:10.1007/978-3-7908-1937-3_5.

Bötticher, A. M. T., & van der Molen, H. H. (1988). Predicting overtaking behaviour on the basis of the hierarchical risk model for traffic participants. In *Road User Behaviour - Theory and Research* (pp. 48–65). Berlin: Van Gorcum.

C. Cacciabue (Ed.). (2007). *Modelling driver behaviour in automotive environments - Critical issues in driver interactions with intelligent transport systems*. Berlin: Springer.

Carsten, O. (2007). From driver models to modelling the driver: What do we really need to know about the driver? In *Proceedings of Cacciabue* (pp. 105–120). Cacciabue. doi:10.1007/978-1-84628-618-6_6.

Christ, R. (2000). *Gadget final report: Investigations on influences upon driver behaviour - Safety approaches in comparison and combination (Technical report)*. GADGET Consortium.

Conger, J. J., Gaskill, H. S., Glad, D. D., Hassel, L., Rainey, R. V., Sawrey, W. L., & Turrell, E. S. (1959). Psychological and psychophysical factors in motor vehicle accidents - Follow-up study. *Journal of the American Medical Association, 169*(14), 1581–1587. doi:10.1001/jama.1959.03000310033008 PMID:13640905.

Edie, L. C., & Foote, R. S. (1960). Effect of shock waves on tunnel traffic flow. In *Proceedings of Highway Research Record*. Washington, DC: National Research Record Council.

Ehlert, P. A. M., & Rothkrantz, L. J. M. (2001). A reactive driving agent for microscopic traffic simulations. In *Proceedings of the 15th European Simulation Multiconference,* (pp. 943-949). Prague, Czech Republic: SCS Publishing House.

Engström, J., & Hollnagel, E. (2007). A general conceptual framework for modelling behavioural effects of driver support functions. In *Proceedings of Cacciabue* (pp. 61–84). Cacciabue. doi:10.1007/978-1-84628-618-6_4.

Fellendorf, M., & Vortisch, P. (2010). Microscopic traffic flow simulator visim. In *Proceedings of Barceló* (pp. 63–94). Barceló.

Fishbein, M., & Ajzen, I. (1975). *Belief, attitude, intention, and behavior: An introduction to theory and research*. Reading, MA: Addision-Wesley Pub. Co..

Fleishman, E. A. (1967). Performance assessment based on an empirically derived task taxonomy. *Human Factors*, 9(4), 349–366. PMID:5584850.

Fleishman, E. A. (1975). Toward a taxonomy of human performance. *The American Psychologist*, 30(12), 1127–1149. doi:10.1037/0003-066X.30.12.1127.

Fuller, R. (1984). A conceptualization of driving behavior as threat avoidance. *Ergonomics*, 27(11), 1139–1155. doi:10.1080/00140138408963596 PMID:6519053.

Gibson, J. J., & Crooks, L. E. (1938). A theoretical filed-analysis of automobile-driving. *The American Journal of Psychology*, 51(3), 453–471. doi:10.2307/1416145.

Greenberg, H. (1959). An analysis of traffic flow. *Operations Research*, 7(1), 79–85. doi:10.1287/opre.7.1.79.

Hale, A. R., Stoop, J., & Hommels, J. (1990). Human error models as predictors of accident scenarios for designers in road transport systems. *Ergonomics*, 33(10-11), 1377–1387. doi:10.1080/00140139008925339.

Hatakka, M., Keskinen, E., Katila, E., & Laapotti, S. (1997). Do psychologists have something to offer in driver training, driver improvement and selection? In *Assessing the driver*. Rot-Gelb-Grün Braunschweig.

Herman, R., Montroll, E. W., Potts, R. B., & Rothery, R. W. (1959). Traffic dynamics: Analysis of stability in car following. *Operations Research*, 7(1), 86–106. doi:10.1287/opre.7.1.86.

Hollnagel, E. (1993). *Human reliability analysis: Context and control*. New York: Academic Press, Inc..

Hollnagel, E., & Woods, D. D. (2005). *Joint cognitive systems - Foundations of cognitive systems engineering*. Boca Raton, FL: CRC Press. doi:10.1201/9781420038194.

Kassin, S. (2003). *Psychology* (4th ed.). New York: Prentice Hall.

Keskinen, E. (1996). Why do young drivers have more accidents? *Junge Fahrer und Fahrerinnen*, 52, 42–53.

Keskinen, E., Hatakka, M., Laapotti, S., Katila, A., & Peräaho, M. (2004). Driver behaviour as a hierarchical system. In *Traffic Transport Psychology: Theory and Application* (pp. 9–23). London: Elsevier.

Kidd, E. A., & Laughery, K. R. (1964). *A computer model of driving behavior: The highway intersection situation* (Report no. VJ-1843-V-1) Buffalo, NY: Cornell Aeronautical Laboratories.

Krajzewicz, D. (2010). Traffic simulation with SUMO – Simulation of urban mobility. In *Proceedings of Barceló* (pp. 269–294). Barceló. doi:10.1007/978-1-4419-6142-6_7.

Krajzewicz, D., & Wagner, P. (2002). ACME (a common mental environment)-driver a cognitive car driver model. In *Proceedings of the 16th European Simulation Multiconference on Modelling and Simulation* (pp. 689-693). SCS Europe.

Lützenberger, M., Ahrndt, S., Hirsch, B., Masuch, N., Heßler, A., & Albayrak, S. (2012). Reconsider your strategy – An agent-based model of compensatory driver behaviour. In *Proceedings of the 15th Intelligent Transportation Conference (ITSC 2012)*. Anchorage, AK: IEEE.

Lützenberger, M., Masuch, N., Hirsch, B., Ahrndt, S., Heßler, A., & Albayrak, S. (2011). The BDI driver in a service city. In *Proceedings of the 10th International Conference on Autonomous Agents and Multiagent Systems (AAMAS'11)*. Taipei, Taiwan: IFAAMAS.

McKnight, A. J., & Adams, B. B. (1970a). Driver education task analysis: Volume I: Task descriptions. Humand Resources Research Organization.

McKnight, A. J., & Adams, B. B. (1970b). Driver education task analysis: Volume II: Task analysis methods. Humand Resources Research Organization.

McKnight, A. J., & Hundt, A. (1971). Driver education task analysis: Volume III: Instructional objectives. Human Resources Research Organization.

McRuer, D. T., Allen, R. W., Weir, D. H., & Klein, R. H. (1997). New results in driver steering control models. *Human Factors*, *19*(4), 381–397.

McRuer, D. T., & Weir, D. H. (1969). Theory of manual vehicular control. *Ergonomics*, *12*(5), 599–633. doi:10.1080/00140136908931082 PMID:5823971.

Michon, J. A. (1976). The mutual impacts of transportation and human behaviour. In *Transportation planning for a better environment* (pp. 221–236). Plenum Press. doi:10.1007/978-1-4615-8861-0_18.

Michon, J. A. (1985). A critical view of driver behavior models: What do we know, what should we do? In *Human Behavior and Traffic Safety* (pp. 487–525). Plemun Press. doi:10.1007/978-1-4613-2173-6_19.

Michon, J. A. (1989). Explanatory pitfalls and rule-based driver models. *Accident; Analysis and Prevention*, *21*(4), 341–353. doi:10.1016/0001-4575(89)90025-0 PMID:2669785.

Näätänen, R., & Summala, H. (1974). A model for the role of motivational factors in driver's decision-making. *Accident; Analysis and Prevention*, *6*, 243–261. doi:10.1016/0001-4575(74)90003-7.

Näätänen, R., & Summala, H. (1976). *Road-user behavior and traffic accidents*. North-Holland Publishing Company.

Neisser, U. (1976). *Cognition and reality - Principles and implications of cognitive psychology*. W. H. Freeman and Company.

Panou, M., Bekiaris, E., & Papakostopoulos, V. (2007). Modelling driver behaviour in European Union and international projects. In *Proceedings of Cacciabue* (pp. 3–25). Cacciabue. doi:10.1007/978-1-84628-618-6_1.

Perchonok, K. (1972). *Accident cause analysis - Final report*. National Technical Information Service.

Peters, B., & Nilsson, L. (2007). Modelling the driver in control. In *Proceedings of Cacciabue* (pp. 85–104). Cacciabue.

Quenault, S., Pryer, P., & Golby, C. (1968). *Age group and accident rate - Driving behaviour and attitudes*. Road Research Laboratory.

Quenault, S. W. (1967). *Driver behaviour - Safe and unsafe drivers*. Road Research Laborator.

Ranney, T. A. (1994). Model of driving behavior: A review of their evolution. *Accident; Analysis and Prevention*, *26*(6), 733–750. doi:10.1016/0001-4575(94)90051-5 PMID:7857489.

Rasmussen, J. (1986). *Information processing and human-machine interaction: An approach to cognitive engineering*. London: Elsevier Science Ltd..

Salvucci, D. D., Boer, E. R., & Liu, A. (2001). Toward an integrated model of driver behavior in a cognitive architecture. *Transportation Research Record*, *1779*, 9–16. doi:10.3141/1779-02.

Shaw, L., & Sichel, H. S. (1971). *Accident proneness - Research in the occurrence, causation, and prevention of road accidents*. New York: Pergamon Press.

Summala, H. (1996). Accident risk and driver behaviour. *Safety Science, 22*(1-3), 103–117. doi:10.1016/0925-7535(96)00009-4.

Summala, H. (1997). Hierarchical model of behavioural adaptation and traffic accidents. In *Traffic Transport Psychology: Theory and Application* (pp. 41–52). New York: Pergamon.

Sykes, P. (2010). Traffic simulation with paramics. In *Proceedings of Barceló* (pp. 131–172). Barceló.

Tulving, E. (1972). Episodic and semantic memory. In Organization of Memory, (pp. 381-403). Academic Press, Inc.

Vaa, T. (2001). Cognition and emotion in driver behaviour models: Some critical viewpoints. In *Proceedings of the 14th ICTCT Workshop*, (pp. 48-59). ICTCT.

van der Molen, H. H., & Bötticher, A. M. T. (1988). A hierarchical risk model for traffic participants. *Ergonomics, 31*(4), 537–555. doi:10.1080/00140138808966698.

van der Molen, H. H., Rothengatter, J., & Vinjé, M. (1981). Blueprint of an analysis of the pedestrian's task-i: Method of analysis. *Accident; Analysis and Prevention, 13*(3), 175–191. doi:10.1016/0001-4575(81)90004-X.

Weir, D. H., & McRuer, D. T. (1968). A theory for driver steering control of motor vehicles. *Highway Research Record, 247*, 7–39.

Wilde, G. J. (1978). Theorie der risikokompensation der unfallverursachung und praktische folgerungen für die unfall verhütung. *Hefte zur Unfallheilkunde, 130*, 134–156. PMID:659134.

Wilde, G. J. (1982). The theory of risk homeostasis: Implications for safety and health. *Risk Analysis, 2*(4), 209–225. doi:10.1111/j.1539-6924.1982.tb01384.x.

Wilde, G. J., & Murdoch, P. A. (1982). Incentive systems for accident-free and violation-free driving in the general population. *Ergonomics, 25*(10), 879–890. doi:10.1080/00140138208925048 PMID:7173151.

Wooldridge, M., & Jennings, N. R. (1995). Intelligent agents: Theory and practice. *The Knowledge Engineering Review, 10*(2), 115–152. doi:10.1017/S0269888900008122.

ADDITIONAL READING

Barcelló, J. (2010). Models, traffic models, simulation and traffic simulation. In Barcelló, J. (Ed.). Fundamentals of traffic simulation (pp. 1-62). Springer Berlin/Heidelberg.

Carsten, O. (2007). From driver models to modelling the driver: What do we really need to know about the driver? In Cacciabue (2007) (pp. 105-120).

Engström, J., & Hollnagel, E. (2007). A general conceptual framework for modelling behavioural effects of driver support functions. In Cacciabue (2007) (pp. 61-84).

Hale, A. R., Stoop, J., & Hommels, J. (1990). Human error models as predictors of accident scenarios for designers in road transport systems. *Ergonomics, 33*(10-11), 1377–1387. doi:10.1080/00140139008925339.

Keskinen, E., Hatakka, M., Laapotti, S., Katila, A., & Peräaho, M. (2004). Driver behaviour as a hierarchical system. In T. Rothengatter, & R. D. Huguenin (Eds.), *Traffic Transport Psychology: Theory and Application* (1st ed., pp. 9–23). Elsevier.

Lützenberger, M., Ahrndt, S., Hirsch, B., Masuch, N., Heßler, A., & Albayrak, S. (2012). Reconsider your strategy – An agent-based model of Compensatory Driver Behaviour. In *Proceedings of the 15th Intelligent Transportation Conference (ITSC 2012)*, Anchorage, AK, USA (pp. 340-346). IEEE.

Lützenberger, M., Masuch, N., Hirsch, B., Ahrndt, S., Heßler, A., & Albayrak, S. (2011). The BDI Driver in a Service City. In *Proceedings of the 10th International Conference on Autonomous Agents and Multiagent Systems (AAMAS'11)*, Taipei, Taiwan (pp. 1257-1258). IFAAMAS.

Michon, J. A. (1985). A critical view of driver behavior models: What do we know, what should we do? In L. Evans, & R. C. Schwing (Eds.), *Human Behavior and Traffic Safety* (pp. 487–525). Plenum Press. doi:10.1007/978-1-4613-2173-6_19.

Peters, B., & Nilsson, L. (2007). Modelling the driver in control. In Cacciabue (2007) (pp. 85-104).

Ranney, T. A. (1994). Model of driving behavior: A review of their evolution. *Accident; Analysis and Prevention, 26*(6), 733–750. doi:10.1016/0001-4575(94)90051-5 PMID:7857489.

KEY TERMS AND DEFINITIONS

Driver Behaviour: The capability of drivers to solve problems and to compensate disturbances that may either evolve from the driver's environment or from the driver itself.

External Factors: Factors that may distract a driver's behaviour and that evolve from the environment of the driver. Good examples for external factors are sever weather conditions, congestion or alternative modes of transport (e.g., bus or metro stations).

High-Level Driving Behaviour: A driver's capability to solve problems that are not entirely related to the driving task. The planning of an intended trip, including route selection, transport mode choice or navigation are good examples for high-level driving behaviour.

Internal Factors: Factors that may distract a driver's behaviour and that evolve from the driver himself. Good examples for internal factors are emotions or the driver's attitude

Multi-Agent System: A group of loosely coupled and interacting software agents

Software Agent: A software program that acts autonomously and enjoys one or more of the following characteristics: reactive, proactive and socially competent

Traffic Simulation Framework: A software package that allows to configure, to execute, to monitor and to evaluate traffic simulations.

ENDNOTES

[1] For a comprehensive introduction into applied models and the principles of traffic simulations, the reader is referred to Barceló (2010).

[2] In the most cases drivers that are familiar with the place.

Chapter 11
Large–Scale Agent–Based Models for Transportation Network Management under Unplanned Events

Yunjie Zhao
SUNY Buffalo, USA

Adel W. Sadek
SUNY Buffalo, USA

ABSTRACT

The focus of this chapter is on issues surrounding the development and applications of large-scale agent-based traffic models. Following a brief overview of Agent-Based Modeling and Simulation (ABMS) applications in transportation modeling, the chapter proceeds to describe the authors' continued efforts and experiences with the development, calibration, validation, and application of a regional agent-based traffic model of the Buffalo-Niagara metropolitan area. The model is developed using the TRansportation ANalysis SIMulation System (TRANSIMS), an open-source, agent-based suite of transportation models. A unique feature of the chapter is its focus on unplanned or extreme events, such as severe snowstorms and major incidents on the freeways, and how the models may be calibrated and applied under such situations. The chapter concludes by summarizing the main lessons learned from the Buffalo case study and providing suggestions for future research.

INTRODUCTION

As an example of a complex adaptive system, the behavior of surface transportation systems emerges as a result of interactions among the human element, the physical system and the environment. These interactions result in a very complex, dynamic behavior, which is very hard to predict.

This is particularly true during emergencies, such as natural or man-made disasters, where the occurrence of the extreme event adds another layer of complexity and results in unexpected system performance. Given the complexity of predicting the emergent behavior of transportation systems, Agent-based Modeling and Simulation (ABMS) principles, and advanced simulation platforms,

DOI: 10.4018/978-1-4666-4920-0.ch011

are needed for the analysis and evaluation of transportation performance during such events.

A quick review of the transportation research literature in the last twenty to thirty years may lead one to conclude that the application of ABMS principles and ideas in transportation modeling has a relatively long history. However, such a conclusion must be qualified by making the following observations. First, while the transportation community may not have always used the term "ABMS" to refer to models where agent-based modeling principles were utilized, such principles have been utilized to model both the transportation demand as well as supply sides. Second, until very recently, there has been a disconnection and lack of integration between agent-based transportation demand and agent-based supply models. Moreover, because the demand and supply models were often developed independently, the definition of agents between the demand and supply models is often inconsistent. Finally, very few modeling attempts have been aimed at using ABMS to model or understand the impact of extreme or unplanned events (e.g. a natural or man-made disaster such as an earthquake, a terrorist attack or a severe snow storm) on the transportation system.

This chapter will describe the authors' continued efforts and experiences with the development, calibration, validation and application of a regional agent-based traffic model of the Greater Buffalo-Niagraa metropolitan area. The model was developed using the TRansportation ANalysis SIMulation System (TRANSIMS), an open-source, agent-based suite of transportation models originally developed by Los Alamos National Lab (LANL), and one of the few models which offer a consistent definition of an agent throughout both the demand and supply side modeling phases. A unique feature of the current effort is its focus on unplanned or extreme events, such as severe snow storms and major incidents on the freeways, and how the models may be calibrated and/or applied under such situations.

Specifically, the chapter is divided into the following sections. Section two provides a *very brief* overview of ABMS applications in transportation modeling on both the demand and supply sides. A subsection is included which describes previous research related to the application and calibration of agent-based transportation models to modeling extreme and unplanned events. Section three discusses the specific case of the development and calibration of the Buffalo-Niagara TRANSIMS model. Section four presents how the impact of inclement weather (specifically snow storms) on traffic flow was modeled and captured by calibrating TRANSIMS Cellular-Automata (CA) traffic simulation model. Section five then describes how the TRANSIMS model was used to study the impact of various freeway incident scenarios, as well as the compounded effect of these incidents and inclement weather, on the transportation system performance in the Buffalo Niagara region. The chapter concludes by summarizing the main lessons learned from the Buffalo case study, and provides suggestions for future research.

AGENT-BASED MODELING IN TRANSPORTATION

ABMS is a modeling paradigm that aims at "describing a system from the perspective of its constituent units" (Bonabeau, 2002). It is a "bottom-up" modeling approach which starts with the individual components of the system (i.e. agents) and defines their potential interactions. The macro-level behavior of the system then results from the myriad interactions among its constituent units. Toroczkai and Eubank (2006) define an agent as an entity that has the following properties: (1) an agent's state as defined by a set of variables corresponding to the agent's state space; (2) a perception of the state of the environment in which the agent operates; (3) a set of allowable actions; (4) a set of strategies that help the agent select an action based on its own state and its perception of the environment; (5) a set of utility functions which define the agent's aspirations, goals or desires; and (6) a multivariate objective function which the agent seeks to optimize. ABMS is particularly appropriate for studying the behavior of transportation systems where the behavior emerges from interactions among the system's components.

ABM Applications in Transportation Demand Modeling

For nearly thirty years, the traditional, four-step trip-based approach to transportation modeling has dominated the planning process. However, this process, which consists of the steps of trip generation, trip distribution, modal split and trip assignment, is plagued with many limitations. This has led to an active stream of recent researches that examine alternative paradigms for modeling travel demand, by incorporating more behaviorally realistic methodologies. Among the most significant of those alternative paradigms is the activity-based approach, which constitutes a valid example of ABM applications in travel demand modeling.

As pointed out by Davidson et al. (2007), activity-based models possess the following three distinct features: (1) a modeling approach which views travel as derived from the daily activities undertaken by travelers; (2) using tours as the unit of modeling, instead of trips, which helps preserve consistency across trips (see Figure 1); and (3) utilizing a micro-simulation modeling approach at a fully-disaggregate level. The earliest group of activity-based models was utility theory models with time budget constraints (Becker, 1965; DeSerpa, 1971). In the late 1980s and the 1990s, the activity-scheduling approach was proposed (e.g. Ben-Akivai et al., 1996). Since then, several other activity-based models have emerged, and while it is impossible to review or categorize all such models here given space limitations and given the focus of this chapter, a few representative

examples include the ALBATROSS (A Learning Based Transportation Oriented Simulation System) model by Arentze and Timmermans (2004); time allocation models (Meloni et al. 2004; Bhat 2005); the Florida Activity Mobility Simulator (Pendyala, Kitamura, Kikuchi, Yamamoto, & Fujii, 2005), and the Comprehensive Econometric Micro-simulator for Daily Activity-travel Patterns or CEMDAP (Bhat et al. 2006).

ABM and Transportation Supply Modeling

In addition to agent-based modeling approaches to demand modeling, state-of-the-art microscopic traffic simulation models can also be very well regarded as examples of agent-based models. In a microscopic traffic simulation model, the agent is typically the driver vehicle unit or DVU. The agents decide their speeds, accelerations/decelerations, lanes in which to drive based on their own states (i.e. position, current speed) and their perceptions of the environment (i.e. headway to other cars). In addition, the agents select their travel route so as to minimize their travel time or a generalized cost function which serves as the objective function. Examples of well-known agent-based microscopic traffic simulation models include PARAMICS (Quadstone 2004), VISSIM (PTV-AG, 2004), AIMSUN (Barcelo & Ferrer, 1998) and TRANSIMS (Los Alamos National Lab (LANL), 2004), which is utilized in the study described in this chapter.

Historically, computer simulation of traffic systems can be traced back to the 1950s when Gerlough (1955) first utilized a general-purpose discrete variable computer to simulate freeway traffic. Recently, traffic simulation models have become much more sophisticated, compared to their earlier predecessors. This increased sophistication is in at least three different areas: (1) the modeling methodology applied; (2) the level of detail; and (3) the scope of the transportation system modeled. In terms of modeling method-

Figure 1. An example of a trip chain

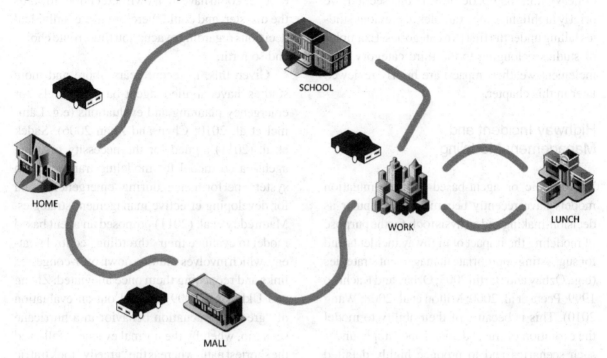

olinglies, while earlier simulation models were based on macroscopic relationships among the key parameters of traffic flow (i.e. flow, speed and density), nowadays and thanks to the recent advances in computer hardware and software, a truly microscopic, *agent-based* modeling approach, based on either car-following or cellular automata models, is quite feasible.

With respect to the level of detail, state-of-the-art traffic simulators track travel on a person-by-person, and second-by-second (and even a fraction of a second) basis. They also model such details as lane channelization, lane connectivity, the operations of traffic signals, etc. Finally, from the viewpoint of the scope or scale of the transportation systems modeled, whereas historically, the majority of microscopic traffic simulation models focused on small-scale networks, a handful of recent studies have attempted developing large-scale microscopic or agent-based models of regional transportation networks (i.e. the network of a metropolitan area or a given city). Examples

of such studies include (Rakha et al. 1998; Bert et al. 2005; Jha et al. 2004; Lee et al. 2001; Smith et al. 2008; Lawe et al. 2009; Krajzewicz et al. 2006; Meister et al. 2010).

Transportation Modeling and Extreme or Unplanned Events

While the majority of previous studies involving the development, calibration and applications of transportation models have focused on normal traffic and network conditions, there are nevertheless several examples in the literature that address the cases of extreme or unplanned events. Broadly speaking, these studies can be classified into the following groups: (1) studies that have focused on quantifying the impact of highway incidents on network operations and the advantages of traffic diversion or re-routing during such scenarios; (2) studies that focused on modeling network evacuations; and (3) studies that quantified and/or modeled the impact of inclement weather (e.g. snow or heavy rain) on traffic flow. In this section, we briefly highlight some examples of previous studies falling under the first two categories. Examples of studies belonging to the third category (i.e., inclement weather impact) are briefly reviewed later in this chapter.

Highway Incident and Management Modeling

Microscopic or agent-based traffic simulation models have recently become quite popular as decision-making and analysis tools for the purpose of modeling the impact of highway incidents and for suggesting appropriate management strategies (e.g., Ozbay and Bartin 2003; Ozbay and Kachroo 1999; Peeta et al. 2000; Milton et al. 2008; Wang 2010). This is because of their ability to model the evolution of travel demand and supply under such scenarios and to produce highly detailed information about the performance of the complex transportation system during such events A representative example of such studies is the one by Dia and Gondwe (2008) which demonstrated the feasibility of using microscopic traffic simulation to study incident impacts from both a traffic flow and emissions points of view. In addition, the researchers of that paper also conducted some interesting evaluation studies of select traffic management strategies, including ramp metering, Variable Message Signs (VMS) and Variable Speed Limit respectively.

Network Evacuation Modeling

In general, most previous efforts in that regard have followed the conventional four-step travel demand forecasting model (see Pel et al. 2012 for a comprehensive overview). As a top-down aggregate approach, however, the four-step process is incapable of capturing individual travel behavior under an emergency condition. The ability to capture individual is exactly the strength of the agent or activity-based model, where each agent or evacuee could have their own perceptions towards the disaster, and could therefore make individual decisions regarding evacuation time, route choice and so forth.

Given this, in recent years, more and more studies have applied agent-based models for emergency planning and evaluations (e.g. Lämmel et al. 2010; Chen and Zhan 2006). Sadek et al. (2011) argued for the necessity of using agent-based model for modeling transportation system performance during emergencies and for developing effective management strategies. Madireddy et al. (2011) proposed an agent based model to evaluate their "throttling" control strategy, which involves shutting down over-congested links and reopening them once alleviated. Zhang and Ukkusuri (2009) carried out an evaluation of "greedy" evacuation behavior in a hurricane scenario, whereby the normal evacuees followed the shortest path, whereas the "greedy" took traffic congestion into consideration when developing their evacuation plans.

In terms of the capabilities of existing agent- or activity- based models for emergency applications, Henson and Gaulias (2006) conducted a comprehensive review of 46 agent-based models and assessed their appropriateness for homeland security applications. They pointed out that only a few models met the spatial and temporal needs of homeland security applications. Among the models reviewed was the TRANSIMS model utilized in this chapter, and which is presented as a potential candidate for satisfying some of the needs of emergency applications.

THE BUFFALO-NIAGARA TRANSIMS MODEL

As opposed to previous transportation simulation studies which have typically modeled single transportation corridors, or relatively small transportation sub-networks, the focus of the research described in this chapter is on modeling a *regional* metropolitan area of a size that has traditionally been modeled only using the ubiquitous four-step planning process, not in a detailed agent-based or microscopic traffic simulation model as this study attempts. The *regional* scope of the model thus allows for evaluating the impact of unplanned events on transportation system performance in a holistic and system-wide fashion. For example, when assessing the impact of a highway accident on a freeway facility, a regional agent-based model allows the analyst to thoroughly investigate the effectiveness of traffic diversion or re-routing strategies and whether the alternate routes have sufficient surplus capacity to handle the diverted traffic.

Besides the *regional* scope of the model, another unique advantage of the Buffalo-Niagara model is its temporal extent and resolution. Specifically, the model tracks travel on a person-by-person and second-by-second basis for a full 24-hour time period. This in turn allows for investigating how the timing of an unplanned event (i.e., whether it occurs during the peak or off-peak time periods) may influence or determine its likely impact. It also allows for investigating the interplay between supply and demand during such extreme or unplanned events.

The Buffalo-Niagara Case Study

The Buffalo-Niagara Falls Metropolitan Statistical Area, located at the eastern end of Lake Erie in Western New York State, is a metropolitan area with a population of around 1,140,000 in 2010, making it the second largest metropolitan area in New York State. The area is well known for its winter weather and lake-effect snow events, which makes it an ideal choice for studying issues surrounding the calibration and application of large-scale agent-based models to inclement weather (specifically snow) scenarios, as investigated by the current research. In terms of travel patterns and characteristics, the region includes a worldwide major tourist attraction (Niagara Falls),

and several major highway connections including: (1) Interstate 90 from the east (Rochester, Albany, and Boston); (2) Interstate 90 from the southwest (Erie, Cleveland, and Chicago); (3) U.S. 219 from the south; and (4) Queen Elizabeth Way (QEW) and Route 405 from the west and north (points in Ontario including Hamilton and Toronto). Moreover, the area is home to three heavily-used and congested US-Canada border crossings with a substantial number of truck movements.

TRANSIMS

TRANSIMS, which was initially developed by Los Alamos National Lab (LANL), is an integrated, open-source set of transportation planning models designed to provide a number of capabilities that go beyond the traditional "four-step" modeling process. The model is one of the very few *person-based* simulators currently available, and combines detailed modeling of traffic flow dynamics with the ability to model traveler behavior. In general, TRANSIMS has the following four functional components or modules.

- **Population Synthesizer:** Creates a synthetic population of the modeled region using census data. This synthetic population is then input into the Activity Generator.
- **Activity Generator:** Uses data from travel diaries to assign travel activities to each synthetic household based on socio-economic similarities between the households included in the travel diary sample and the synthetic households. The activity generator creates travel tours, which encompass all travel legs from a home base until the traveler returns to the home base once again.
- **Route Planner:** Or router, chooses the best route for travel activity based on the shortest travel time as calculated either by the micro-simulator or by link delay functions. The resulting output is a set of *time-*

dependent route plans: specific routes for each trip. Trips may be on highway or transit networks. The router operates at a greater level of time-of-day detail than is typical in 4-step models, typically using congested link travel times at 15-minute intervals.

- **Micro-Simulator:** Executes the route plans and simulates traffic flow dynamics using a Cellular Automata (CA) traffic model. The micro-simulator then calculates the resulting travel times and feeds those back into the route planner. This iterative process is continued until the system approximates "equilibrium".

Because TRANSIMS simulates individual trips, and their interactions (traffic congestion) with other trips, the model is capable of tracking travel on a *person by person and second by second* basis. TRANSIMS's disaggregate nature and micro-simulation capabilities thus allow for a continuous time representation, and provide a significant advantage over the typical four-step methodology, which only accommodates a limited number of discrete time intervals. In addition, the TRANSIMS network is typically much more detailed than the typical four-step network, and captures salient aspects of the traffic system including signal operations, queue formation and dissipation, lane changes, and gap acceptance behavior.

From a demand modeling standpoint, it should be noted that while TRANSIMS is designed to allow for using an activity-based approach to transportation demand modeling (using its Population Synthesizer and Activity Generator), the model's Router and Micro-simulator modules can still be applied using standard trip tables (i.e. Origin-Destination (O-D) matrices). This provides for a cost-effective approach for regional planning organizations to take advantage of the increased resolution of the TRANSIMS micro-simulator, while primarily depending upon standard O-D matrices with which they have dealing for several

years. Implementing only TRANSIMS's Router and Micro-simulator, using O-D matrices, for a given area is typically referred to as a "Track 1" TRANSIMS implementation. "Track 1" TRANSIMS implementation is the focus of the current study, which uses standard trip tables, along with information about the diurnal distribution of trips in order to generate the activity list or trip plans.

Development History of the Buffalo-Niagara TRANSIMS Model

Work on the development of the Buffalo-Niagara TRANSIMS model took place in two phases. The first phase, which was completed in 2009, was conducted by a research team from the Volpe National Transportation Systems Center. That first study was more of a feasibility scoping study whose main focus was to assess the feasibility of developing a pilot TRANSIMS model by piecing together existing data from various sources. Because of its feasibility character and the extremely labor intensive nature of the network development and debugging process, only a small sub-network (see Figure 2) was modeled in great detail in TRANSIMS micro-simulator by the Volpe study. The Router, however, was implemented for the whole region.

In 2009, a subsequent study was undertaken by University at Buffalo (UB) researchers to build on the Volpe's model and further extend the scope of the micro-simulated area. This second phase is what is described in the current chapter. Figure 2 also shows the extended micro-simulator sub-area scope. Specifically, the expanded sub-network covers a 756 kilometer square (292 mile square) area, and is made up of 2185 nodes and 3037 links. Approximately 1.6 million trips (after calibration) are generated and simulated during a 24-hr period. This makes the area among the largest networks reported in the literature to be micro-simulated using a detailed agent-based model.

Figure 2. Original and expanded micro-simulation subarea of buffalo and niagara region

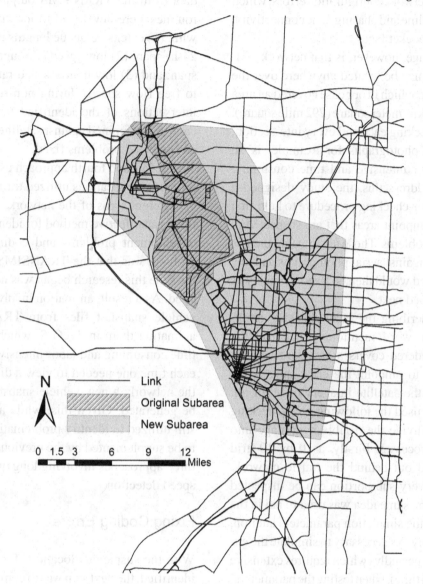

Model Refinement

The TRANSIMS suite of models includes a routine, called TransimsNet, which is designed to aid in the migration from a four-step transportation planning network (which basically is a link-node database) to a TRANSIMS network which naturally has to contain much more detailed information about the transportation network geometry and configuration. TransimsNet employs

default logic to generate the additional required information (e.g. where to place signals and stop signs, where to add pocket lanes, how the lanes connect at an intersection). In many cases, and especially at complex intersections, the results from the TransmisNet generated network may not agree with the real-world situation. This in turn may lead to problematic areas in the model which might result in poor performance of the network and even total traffic gridlock. The most common problems are network configuration errors, which include signal time and phasing, lane connectivity, and incorrect pocket lanes.

The challenge, however, is that network coding problems may be located anywhere over the whole network, which in our case covered an area as large as 756 kilometer square (292 mile square). Given this, checking each and every intersection, against aerial photographs for example, is an extremely labor intensive and time consuming process. To address this, the study designed a systematic error-checking procedure to help first identify and pinpoint areas that are suspected to have coding problems. Those areas would then be later checked against aerial photographs and any errors identified would then be fixed manually as will be described next.

Before describing the error-checking methodology, it was worth mentioning that since the network considered covers a very large area it is impractical to pinpoint the error spots when comparing to the satellite imagery once for all. Therefore, we used the following error-checking procedure to divide the troubleshoot stage into several sub-processes. Firstly, a 10 by 10 grid mask was laid out behind the traffic network. In this way, every sub-portion can be inspected one by one. The same idea was used to aid in the calibration of the simulation parameters later on, since it is not always necessary to simulate the entire network repeatedly (which requires extensive computational time), when testing the parameters' sensitivity. As long as the tested subarea included diverse transportation facility types (e.g., both arterials and freeways), it could be utilized, as a representative of the bigger model, to gain insight into the sensitivity of the model's results to changes in the model's parameters.

Error Checking Procedure

The following four approaches were utilized to help locate network bottlenecks and grid lock, in an efficient manner. By reading and screening

data from the TRANSIMS output files, simple routines were developed to identify those links with: (1) extensive queue lengths throughout the 24-hr span; (2) low speeds throughout the 24-hr span; and (3) low hourly speed ratio (compared to free flow speed) during non-rush hour. The intersections of the identified links were then carefully examined against satellite imagery, and any detected problems fixed.

The last and fourth approach used to pinpoint problematic locations utilized traffic animations of different areas of the network. While animation is an effective method for identifying model development problems and coding errors, the problem was that the TRANSIMS visualizer at the time this research began was not fully developed. As a result, animation involved generating vehicle snapshot files from TRANSIMS and animating them in ArcGIS, which was a rather time consuming and labor intensive effort, since each time one needed to view a different part of the network, a new vehicle snapshot file had to be generated. Given this, while animation was still utilized to identify problematic areas, it had to be supplemented by the previously mentioned three approaches involving long queues and low speed detection.

Fixing Coding Errors

With the suspicious locations for coding errors identified, the next step was to compare the coded configuration and settings against aerial photographs and other information to ensure validity. Below, we give examples for some of the problems encountered and how they were fixed.

Missing Pocket Lanes: One common problem, which resulted from the inability of the Transim-sNet default logic to always exactly match the real geometric configuration, was missing pocket lanes at intersections, which typically resulted in significant gridlock at those intersections. Following the confirmation of the right configuration from the aerial photograph, the identified missing pocket lanes were added.

Missing Roads: Another challenge resulted from the fact that in a large-scale transportation model, the local or residential streets are typically not included or modeled. This leads to a network capacity that is less than the real-world capacity especially if there is a large fraction of trips that use the local street network. We will address this problem when discussing how the model's demand was calibrated later in this chapter.

Fixing Intersections: Other common examples of problems were that intersections whose configuration did not accurately reflect reality and had to be fixed. This often resulted because the TRANSIMS network was originally based on the four-step planning network, and which was later enriched with more details by the TransmisNet module. In the four-step planning model, intersection configurations are sometimes simplified, and this led to some problems when the simple configuration was used in conjunction with the micro-simulator.

Calibration

Calibrating and validating traffic simulation models generally involve comparing the simulated model volumes to real-world field counts to either adjust model parameters or to validate the model results before application. However, the excessive computational requirements of running the Buffalo-Niagara TRANSIMS model caused simulation runs of the model to take more than 30 hours on a dual-core desktop. This precluded the use of parameter calibration procedures such as Genetic Algorithms (GA) or other kinds of heuristic search approaches that historically have been used to help calibrate microscopic simulation models (Smith et al., 2008). Moreover, with heuristic approaches, calibrated parameter values lack a true explicit physical meaning and multiple sets of values for those parameters could yield similar results. Given the aforementioned limitations, our

approach in this study focused on a high-level calibration process that strived to get the model results closer to real-world observations. In doing so, a total of 162 hourly count station volume data were used. Those count stations can be classified as the follows:

- **Toll Stations:** These are toll-based counts from the four international bridges (Lewiston-Queenston, Whirlpool, Rainbow and Peace) in the region. They provide limited classification data for the tolled direction (the direction entering Canada from the US) on the international bridges.
- **Federal Highway Administration (FHWA) counts:** These are classification counts based on axle counts and supplied by the New York State Department of Transportation (NYSDOT) and the Greater Buffalo-Niagara Regional Transportation Council (GBNRTC).
- **Length Counts:** These are length-based counts from the New York State Thruway Traffic Data System.
- **Non-Classified:** These are non-classification counts that provide volumes by hour of day.

Initial Model Validation

As a first step toward validating the extended model developed in this study, comparisons were made between: (1) the field counts (referred to herein as NYSDOT results); (2) the simulated volumes from original TRANSIMS model developed by Volpe (referred to hereafter as Router since the original model utilized Router for the network parts outside the small micro-simulated subarea); and (3) the current study's extended TRANSIMS model (referred to hereafter as the TRANSIMS model).

The key observations from the initial validation phase can be summarized as follows:

1. The TRANSIMS model showed a much closer match to the NYSDOT field data compared to the original TRANSIMS router, especially when the peak hour volume are relatively high. This agrees with intuition since the router, similar to other four-step planning models, uses a link travel time function to propagate traffic which cannot accurately capture phenomena such as queue formation and dissipation. TRANSIMS micro-simulator on the other hand is capable of reflecting such phenomena.

2. The hourly summations of all the link counts indicated a consistent overestimated traffic flow. This was a clear indication that the travel demand assumed for the model appeared to be too high.

3. When classifying the validation results based upon the road functional classification type, the extended TRANSIMS model appear to perform significantly better compared to the original Router results on freeways and collectors.

Parameter Calibration

As discussed above, the initial validation results seemed to point out that the assumed demand appeared to be on the high side. This was further confirmed by the observation that when the model was run with the assumed demand, not only the simulated counts were higher than the field, but also almost 20% of all the trips were being "lost". In TRANSIMS, "lost" trips refer to those which could not be completed and had to be removed from the simulation.

For those "lost" trips, TRANSIMS reports a problem, and classifies this problem as either: (1) a "wait" problem, where a vehicle for example waited too long at an intersection and had to be removed to avoid gridlock; (2) a "departure time" problem, where a traveler could not leave within the time window allowed for the trip's start time because of congestion or gridlock for example;

and (3) an "arrival time" problem, where a traveler arrived too late to his destination. The fact that 20% of the trips were being lost also seemed to indicate that the capacity of the modeled network was not enough to handle the assumed demand especially during peak hours.

The study's first step toward calibrating the model was to try to reduce the number of the lost trips. In an attempt to achieve this, the study first adjusted some of the model's parameters, which were thought to have an impact on the number of the lost trips. Three of the key parameters which were explored in this study are:

1. **The MAXIMUM_WAITING_TIME parameter:** Which defines when vehicles waiting will be removed from the simulation (to avoid gridlock) and reported as a "waiting time problem";

2. **The MAX_ARRIVAL_TIME_VARIANCE parameter:** Which defines the incremental time period, beyond the expected arrival time of a given trip, at which a vehicle still en-route will be removed from the simulation and reported as "an arrival time problem".

3. **The MAX_DEPARTURE_TIME_VARIANCE parameter:** Which defines the incremental time period, beyond the scheduled departure time for a given, at which a vehicle unable to leave the parking lot at the beginning of the trip (because of congestion) will be removed and "a departure time problem" will be reported.

As should be obvious, the types of reported TRANSIMS problems are inter-related. For example, if the value of the MAXIMUM_WAITING_TIME time were increased from its default value of 360 seconds to say 3600 seconds, all the waiting time problems would be resolved. However, if this was done, the arrival time would increase due to increased waiting time, and as a result, there would be many more arrival time problems. In other words, there is a tradeoff between these two problems.

Several trial runs were made, each time varying the values of those parameters in an effort to reduce the number of "lost" trips. While some combinations helped in reducing the number of lost trips, in most of those cases, the threshold values specified would not be acceptable from a practical standpoint (e.g. most travelers would not tolerate arriving one hour or more late to their destinations). This once again seems to confirm the suspicion that the main source of the problems is that the assumed demand exceeds the capacity of the modeled network. This issue will be addressed next.

Demand Calibration

As previously mentioned, the observation that the simulated link volumes were larger than the field counts, coupled with the large number of wait and arrival time problems, seemed to imply that the number of the vehicles on the network exceeded its capacity. It is our hypothesis that one big reason behind this is that, the transportation network modeled within the TRANSIMS micro-simulation only included the major roads that were modeled in the region's four-step model. This meant that many of the local and collector roads were not included, and as a result the modeled network had a lower traffic-carrying capacity than the real-world network, because it was missing several links. This is also especially true because, in the original four-step network, some of the flow occurs on centroid connectors, while in TRANSIMS, traffic is loaded directly from activity locations onto the roads (typically arterials and some collectors) that are part of the model. There was therefore a need to adjust or calibrate the demand to get the model results closer to the field observations. To do this, field traffic counts from a total of 193 count stations within the subarea were utilized, and several comparisons were then made between the simulated results,

after demand adjustment or calibration, and the field counts as described below.

Scenario One: 80% Demand

Based on the observation that the summation of all the hourly counts for the 193 links was about 80% of the simulated volume, the demand was reduced to 80% of its original level. As a result, the average percent error was reduced from its original value of 65% to 29%, but was still slightly on the high side. Moreover, a comparison of the diurnal distribution (i.e., the distribution of traffic volumes over the 24 hours of the day) showed discernible difference between the simulated and field distributions. This suggested that not only the demand level needed to be adjusted, but also the diurnal distribution needed some calibration, as described next.

Scenario Two: 77% Demand and Diurnal Distribution Adjustment

The diurnal distribution calibration is a time-consuming recursive process. One problem is that many trips start in a given hour and end in a different hour, which may cause some discrepancies if the assumed diurnal distribution is based on field counts, which was the case in our TRANSIMS model. The reason behind this is that the diurnal distribution in TRANSIMS is used to define when a trip starts, whereas the field counts typically capture a trip at one point throughout the course of that trip. Consider, for instance, a trip that starts at 8:50 am and reaches its destination at 9:15 am. The trip starts during the 8:00 – 9:00 am time interval, but ends during the 9:00 – 10:00 am interval. Therefore if the traffic count occurred on a link close to the trip's destination, the count would lead us to assume that the trip started somewhere in the 9:00 – 10:00 am trip, whereas in reality the trip belongs to the previous hourly interval. This could easily result in shifting the simulated results to the right as discussed next.

To further calibrate the demand, we considered the case of a demand level equal to 77% of the base demand level, since the results from the previous section showed that 80% demand was still on the high side. However, when the results from that scenario were plotted against the field data, it was found that the simulated counts curve (MSim shown in red) was very similar to the field count curve (NYSDOT shown in blue), but shifted to the left by one hour as shown in Figure 3 (a). We postulated that this shift was due to the fact that the diurnal distribution assumed for TRANSIMS was based on field counts and thus suffered from the "delay" or "lag" effect just described. To address this, the diurnal Distribution was shifted accordingly, and this helped significantly improve the results, as shown in Figure 3 (b).

Validation

For validation, previous researches have suggested numerous measures based on comparing simulated and field counts, including percentage error, T-test, U-statistic, Regression, GEH statistic and mean absolute error (MAE). Among those, regression analysis appears to be the most suited for validating large-scale simulation models because it is not as sensitive to volume variations as other statistics. In this study, both regression analysis and the MAE method were used. Regression was conducted for both the hourly volume and cumulative volume for the entire subarea (i.e. utilizing data from all 162 count stations).

With the 77% demand and the diurnal distribution adjustment, the overall model results closely matched the field counts. Moreover, the number of "lost trips" was dramatically reduced to as low as 0.1% of the total. The validation results were quite promising. Table 1 shows the MAE values for select hours during the day. As can be seen, the simulation model performed quite well (MAE

Figure 3. (a) NYSDOT vs. TRANSIMS before Diurnal distribution calibration (b) afterwards

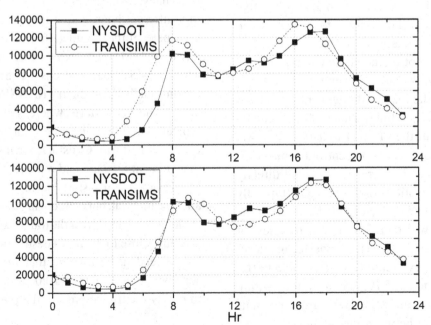

Table 1 MAE Comparison between Field and Simulation

Hr	Field	Simulation	MAE
8	102009	91827	10%
9	100874	106302	5%
16	114617	107494	6%
17	125962	123089	2%
18	126661	120440	5%
19	96056	99665	4%
20	74224	73728	1%

< 10%) during both morning and afternoon rush hours (8:00-10:00, 16:00 – 21:00). As a further demonstration of the close match between the adjusted model's simulated volumes and the field counts, regression analysis was conducted for both the hourly volume and cumulative volume for the entire subarea. The coefficient of correlation, R^2 was equal to 0.958 for the hourly volume and to 0.998 for the cumulative volume (as shown in Figure 4). Additional volume comparisons were performed for individual links; these are not included here because of space limitations.

CALIBRATING THE MODEL FOR INCELEMENT WEATHER EVENTS

With the TRANSIMS model extended, validated and calibrated, the study then proceeded to investigate how to calibrate the agent-based model to better reflect the impact of inclement weather (particularly snow events) on traffic flow. Specifically, the study's objective was to modify the TRANSIMS micro-simulator to allow for capturing such an impact. As is well known, inclement weather (such as rain, sleet, snow, or fog) can have several negative effects on transportation system, i.e. decreased network capacity, pavement traction, limited visibility and so forth. In response, drivers adapt to such changes, which in turn results in a different set of driving behavior parameters (e.g., driving speed, reaction time and lane changing maneuver) and vehicle dynamics parameters (e.g., acceleration and deceleration frequency and magnitude). To capture the impact of inclement weather on traffic flow in the model therefore, additional calibration and tuning was needed. In this section, we first review previous studies on the topic of quantifying the impact of

Figure 4. NYSDOT vs. simulation (a) hourly volume and (b) cumulative volume

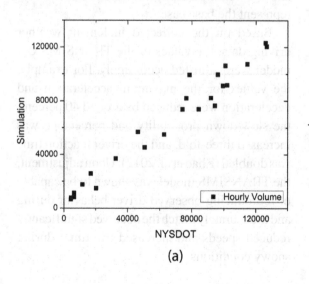

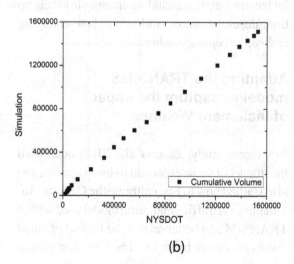

(a)

(b)

inclement weather on traffic flow, followed by a description of how a large scale agent-based model can be adapted to capture the impact of inclement weather (Zhao et al. 2012).

Related Work

In the past decades, a number of researchers have been contributing to quantifying the inclement weather impact on the traffic flow. These studies considered both macroscopic, and to a lesser degree, microscopic impacts of inclement weather on traffic. Studies which focused on macroscopic impacts attempted to quantify the changes in macroscopic traffic flow parameters, such as capacity (Agarwal et al. 2005; Transportation Research Board, 2000), traffic flow/volume (Hanbali and Kuemmel 1993) and travel time/speed (Kyte et al. 2001; Stern et al. 2003; Transportation Research Board 2000) caused by inclement weather events. The common research methodology is to categorize the weather events (e.g., light, moderate or heavy rain) and to conduct the statistical analysis on the impact based on those categorizations. Alternatively, microscopic impact studies (Colyar et al. 2003; Hranac et al. 2006; Rakha et al. 2010; Sterzin 2004) focused on changes in individual driver behavior during inclement weather, including changes in acceleration, deceleration, car-following, lane-changing and gap acceptance behavior.

Adapting the TRANSIMS model to capture the Impact of Inclement Weather

In a recent study, Zhao et al. (2012) quantified the impact of snow events on freeway speeds, and also studied how to best calibrate the Cellular Automata (CA) traffic simulation model used within TRANSIMS to better reflect the impact of snow events on driver behavior. The first step was to identify the model's parameters that could potentially be adjusted to better reflect driver behavior during inclement weather. Among the parameters identified were: (1) the maximum acceleration and deceleration rates; (2) the slowdown probability and percentage; (3) driver reaction time; and (4) look ahead distance, lane and time factors. With those parameters identified, the second step was to collect field data on driver behavior during inclement weathers to shed light onto how the parameters should be adjusted.

To do this, a probe vehicle was equipped with a GPS receiver connected to a laptop that logged the second-by-second information provided by the GPS including the time stamp, the vehicle co-ordinates, the vehicle speed and heading. Longitudinal acceleration was calculated by differentiating vehicle speed. Lateral acceleration was calculated by multiplying yaw rate (calculated by differentiating vehicle heading) by vehicle speed. During the course of the study, a total of eight representative routes distributed throughout the Buffalo-Niagara metropolitan area were selected for data collection. Whenever inclement weather (specifically snow) would hit, the equipped vehicle would be used to collect driving data on one or more of those routes. Normal driving data for clear and dry weather conditions was also collected to represent the base case.

Based on the collected inclement weather driving data, the values of the TRANSIMS CA model were adjusted accordingly. For example, the values for the maximum acceleration and deceleration were reduced by around 40 percent, the slow-down probability and percentage was increased three-fold, and the driver reaction time was doubled (Zhao et al. 2012). Upon adjustment, the TRANSIMS model was shown to be capable of reproducing observed driver behavior during and to accurately match the observed significantly reduced speeds and increased trip times during snowy conditions.

MODEL APPLICATIONS

This section describes a few examples of possible applications of the calibrated agent-based model to demonstrate its utility and the range of transportation systems planning and management applications that can now be addressed thanks to its increased resolution and regional scope. Specifically, three examples are provided. The first example focuses on quantifying the reduction in the overall network capacity of the Buffalo-Niagara transportation system during inclement weather and the maximum demand level the network can sustain under such conditions. The second example focuses on evaluating the impact of various freeway incident scenarios that differ in terms of severity, duration and time of occurrence, and the benefits of providing real-time traffic and route guidance information under such scenarios. Finally, the third example looks at the compounded effect of incidents and inclement weather conditions.

Network Capacity under Inclement Weather

This first application of the Buffalo-Niagara agent-based model focuses on determining: (1) whether the impaired network would be able to sustain the typical travel demand load in the region; and (2) the likely increase in average network travel time, within the micro-simulated area, as a result of inclement weather. To simulate this scenario, the TRANSIMS model was run with the CA model's parameters adjusted to reflect driver behavior during inclement weather as previously described. The results are summarized in Figure 5, where it can be seen that under the snow storm event model, there were around 90,000 trips that could not be completed (i.e. lost trips in TRANSIMS) because of excessive waiting or failing to reach their destination within the allowable time window. It can also be seen that the network was only able to accommodate around 88% of the normal weather

demand. To be noted, the 88%, 90%, 95%, 100% are additional demand adjustment factors applied on top of the 77% traffic demand introduced in the model Calibration Section. This underlines the importance of implementing travel demand management procedures, which strive to reduce cut down on demand, during inclement weather if acceptable performance levels of the network are to be maintained. Figure 5 also shows that that inclement weather has resulted in an increase in the average trip travel time from 9.48 minutes under normal weather conditions to around 13.50 minutes. This in turn points out to the benefits of real-time traveler information provision so that travelers could plan accordingly.

Freeway Incident Impact Modeling and the Benefits of Transportation Information Provision

In this second example, the TRANSIMS model was used to evaluate and analyze several scenarios involving a major incident on one of the key freeways or limited access highways in the region (e.g. I-90, I-290 or I-190). The scenarios differed in terms of the incident-related attributes assumed. Those attributes included: (1) the time of the day at which the incident occurs; (2) the incident severity level in terms of the number of highway lanes blocked; and (3) the duration of the incident. The intent of the analyses was to first demonstrate the potential applications of the TRANSIMS model in evaluating such scenarios and recommending a course of action. Moreover, the analyses provided some invaluable insight into the likely impact of system performance at regional levels and the benefits of intelligent transportation systems (ITS) mitigation strategies such as traveler information provision. In terms of traveler information provision, the study evaluated whether providing travel information, via for example Variable Message Signs (VMS), improved traffic congestion, and if so, what the magnitude

Figure 5. Number of incomplete trips and average travel time for 100%, 95%, 90% and 88% demand respectively

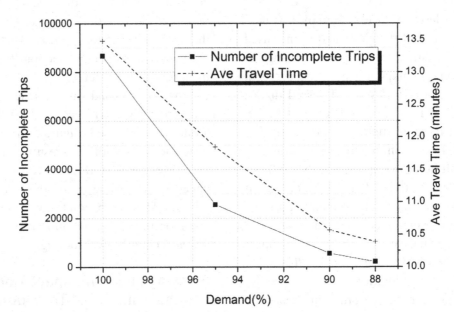

Scenario Design and Assumptions

of the improvement, from both an individual user perspective as well as a system-wide basis, was.

Before describing the scenarios simulated and the results obtained, it is worth noting that the regional agent-based model developed herein offered clear advantages over other state-of-the-practice methods such as queuing analysis, macroscopic simulation model or shock wave analysis. Thanks to its high-level of detail, coupled with the regional scope of the system modeled, the Buffalo-Niagara model offered: (1) realistic modeling of network configuration and traffic flow dynamics at the incident scene instead of just assuming a certain capacity reduction value on the impacted link as is the case with macroscopic models; (2) accurate modeling of driving behavior and maneuvers (e.g. modeling the merging and weaving maneuvers as drivers upstream notice the incident site); (3) the ability to capture the delay for individual vehicles as well as the total system-wide or aggregate delay; and (4) the ability to capture the *system-wide* impact of the incident and any associated traffic management strategy such as diverting traffic onto alternate routes (Kamga et al. 2011).

In total, sixteen scenarios were designed with the levels of four key variables varied as the followings: (1) incident time: 9:00 -10:00 am (peak) versus 12:00 -13:00 pm (off-peak); (2) incident duration of 30 min and 60 min; (3) incident severity varying from one lane blocked to two blocked lanes; and (4) the traffic management strategy changing from providing VMS traffic diversion information to not providing such information.

To eliminate other potential factors which affect driving behavior, such as excessive weaving behavior due to on ramps and off ramps, the incident simulation site selected was a 3-lane, 2.9-mile long, fairly straight freeway segment on I-90. For the scenarios involving information provision through VMS, it was assumed that drivers would be immediately notified of the increased travel time due to the incident via the VMS system. It was further assumed that drivers are aware of the congestion level and travel time associated with an alternate route. The aforementioned assumptions are justifiable on the grounds of a well-designed

ITS system, where real-time traffic information is available to drivers who could then make route decisions based on this information. For example, the Wisconsin Driver Survey showed that 84.7% of drivers would be willing to take an alternate route if they were forewarned of an upcoming incident along their current route (Ran et al. 2004).

Results

The evaluation results of the sixteen different scenarios considered yielded some useful insight into the likely impact of incidents and the effectiveness of the different mitigation strategies. Among the key observations made were the followings:

Impact of Minor Incidents: The simulation results indicated that low severity incidents (i.e. incidents blocking only one lane out of the three lanes or those lasting for 30 minutes or less) did not show a significant increase in the travel time along the impacted incident site. This was the case whether the low severity incident occurred during the peak or off-peak period. The same observation was also true for slightly more severe incidents (i.e. incidents blocking two out of the three lanes available) that happen during *off-peak periods*. For that case, the increase in the segment's travel time was less than 5%.

Impact of Medium-severity Incidents during Peak Hours: As opposed to medium-severity incidents (i.e. those blocking two lanes for 60 minutes) which occur during off-peak hours, medium severity incidents that occur during peak hours do have a significant impact on travel time. Specifically, for an incident that occurred at 9:00 am (the morning peak period), blocked two lanes and lasted for 60 minutes, the segment's travel time increased from its base level of approximately 2 minutes to more than 30 minutes.

Impact of Information Provision: To evaluate the likely impact of information provision and traffic re-routing during incidents, the scenario described in the last paragraph (i.e. an incident occurring at 9:00 am, blocking two lanes and

lasting for 60 minutes) was simulated assuming the presence of VMS with accurate information about travel time along the incident-impacted segment and the alternate routes, and assuming drivers' rerouting in response to the provided information. It was observed that when drivers re-routed in response to the travel information provided, the delay along the impacted segment was significantly reduced compared to the case when they did not. Specifically, the segment's travel time with re-routing was about 10 minutes compared to more than 30 minutes for the case without VMS and rerouting. Additionally, the total incident delay with re-routing was approximately $1/8^{th}$ of its value for the case of no re-routing.

Because of re-routing, however, the traffic volumes increased on the alternate routes as shown on Figure 6. As can be clearly seen from Figure 6, while the VMS managed to eliminate the extreme congestion on the I-90 segment (indicated by the solid black line on the left side of Figure 6), the volumes increased on the alternate route. However, that increase did not lead to any significant congestion problems or any sort of gridlock as was the case on the freeway when traffic was not re-routed. For less severe incidents (those blocking only one lane and/or lasting for less than 30 minutes), VMS was found to have little or no effect, indicating that if the incident site is cleared quickly, there is no need to apply a detour.

The Ability of the Model results to Capture Incident-related Traffic Patterns: Figure 7 plots the fundamental diagram curves (i.e. the speed vs. volume and the volume vs. density plots) for both the incident scenarios as well as the incident-free scenarios. As can be clearly seen, the incident scenarios can be easily distinguished from normal conditions. This demonstrates the ability of the agent-based model to accurately reflect traffic conditions during incidents, and suggests that model may even be used to train, develop and test automated incident detection algorithms for a real-time freeway management system, in the absence of adequate field data.

Figure 6. Density diagram for the incident site and surrounding arterial: no re-routing (left) and re-routing (right)

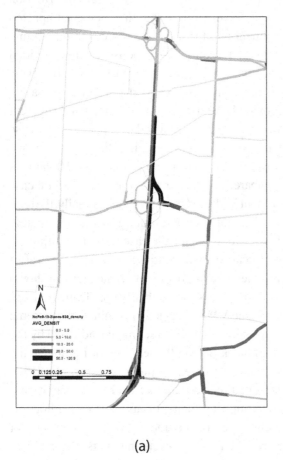

(a)

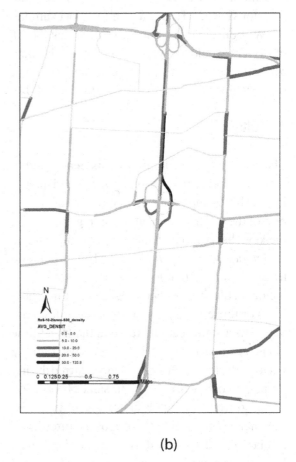

(b)

Multiple Hazard Scenario or Incidents during Inclement Weather Conditions

The agent-based Buffalo-Niagara model was also used to evaluate and analyze scenarios where more than one type of transportation extreme event or hazard occurred at the same time (we refer to those as multiple hazard scenarios). For example, inclement weather is often accompanied by a likely increase in accident frequency or risk. In addition, the impact of an accident occurring during inclement weather is likely going to be more severe than when the accident occurs during normal or dry weather. Until now, very few

studies have attempted to evaluate the impact of combinations of hazards on transportation system performance. This study addressed that gap by evaluating the impact on the transportation system performance of scenarios involving combinations of inclement weather (i.e. heavy snow) and freeway capacity-reducing incidents.

Figure 8 is provided as an example of the type of analyses that are now possible with the TRAN-SIMS model, thanks to its calibration to allow for capturing the impact of inclement weather on driver behavior and traffic flow. Specifically, the Figure compares the travel time along the 2.9 mile freeway segment considered in conjunction with the incident scenarios for the following four cases.

Figure 7. Fundamental diagram: volume-speed (top) and volume-density (bottom)

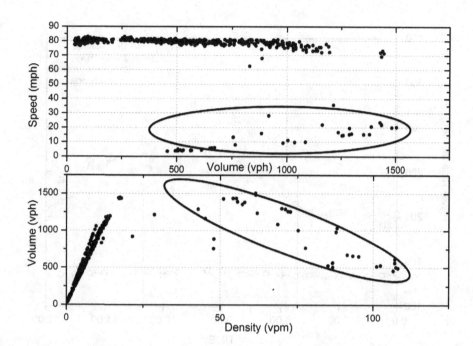

The first case is a dry/good weather scenario but with no incidents (the solid black triangle line). The second is a dry weather with a low-severity incident blocking one lane and lasting for half an hour that occurs at 9:00 am (during the peak period) showed as a hollow inverted triangle line. The third is a snowy day without any incident (the hollow square line), while the forth is a combination of inclement weather and incident (same severity as the good weather incident) shown as the circle line.

A number of observations can be made in relation to Figure 8. As can be seen, inclement weather has a significant impact on increasing the segment's travel time throughout the whole day. Whereas the typical, dry weather travel time for that segment ranged between 134 and 140 seconds, the travel time under the snowy conditions for which the TRANSIMS micro-simulator was calibrated, ranged between 180 to more than 300 seconds, even in the absence of any capacity-reducing incidents. Second, whereas low-severity incidents had no significant impact on the

segment's travel time during normal weather conditions, the combination of inclement weather and a low severity incident during peak hours significantly increased the segment's travel time to around 360 seconds, which is approximately 40% more than the travel time during inclement weather but with no incidents.

CONCLUSION

This chapter has described the authors' continued efforts and experiences with the development, calibration, validation and application of a regional agent-based traffic model of a medium-sized metropolitan area with the goal of shedding light on the challenges, lessons learned and the opportunities of regional agent-based transportation models. Specifically, the chapter highlighted efficient procedures for identifying network coding errors, and described how one might go about validating and calibrating such complex models so as to achieve a good match between the model's

Figure 8. Travel time comparison between peak hour, off peak hour and no incident under inclement weather

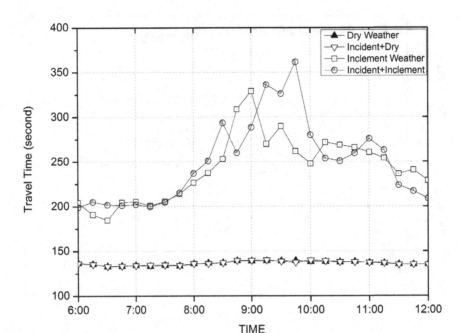

simulated results and the field counts. A unique feature of the research described herein is its focus on not only calibrating the model for normal conditions, but also on how the traffic model's parameters may be adjusted so as to reflect driver behavior during inclement weather conditions. The chapter has also presented example applications that take advantage of the high-fidelity level of the model, its agent-based nature, and its calibration for unplanned or extreme events. Specifically, three examples were described that addressed: (1) quantifying the reduction in overall network capacity during inclement weather; (2) evaluating the impact of various freeway incident scenarios and the utility of information provision; and (3) assessing the compounded effect of both incidents and inclement weather conditions. The followings will summarize some of the main conclusions and observations made during the course of the study, organized by the different stages of the study. In that regard, it should be noted that while some of the study's conclusions may be specific to the case

study considered and the agent-based modeling software utilized (i.e., TRANSIMS), others are more generic in nature and transcend the specific case study or modeling software.

TRANSIMS Model Development, Validation and Calibration Main Conclusions

Among the main conclusions derived from this part of the study are:

- While TransimsNet provides for a very efficient and practicable way to jump-start the development of a TRANSIMS network from a four-step planning model network, the default logic of TransimsNet may not capture all of the real-world geometric details especially at complex intersections. Complex intersection configurations thus need to be manually checked against the real-world and any identified problems must be fixed in order to avoid model gridlock.

- The most common problems when using TransimsNet to generate an enriched transportation network are problems related to missing pocket lanes and complex intersections.

- The fact that modeled transportation networks typically do not include local and residential streets is likely to resulted in a reduced capacity compared to that of the real-world network and may require reducing the modeled demand in order to avoid gridlock

Impact of Inclement Weather on Traffic

The main conclusions derived from the part of the study are:

- From a microscopic standpoint, driving under inclement weather appears to be associated with a much higher frequency of acceleration and deceleration maneuvers compared to normal weather conditions. In addition, the magnitude of the vehicle acceleration and deceleration is typically significantly lower than normal driving.

- Through the proper adjustment of the model parameters, the TRANSIMS model appears to be capable of simulating freeway traffic under the inclement weather with well-tuned parameters in a microscopic level.

Emergency Scenarios Evaluation

The main observations made during this part of the research included:

- Incidents blocking only one lane out of the three lanes and/or those lasting for 30 minutes or less do not appear to have a significant impact on travel time along the im-

pacted incident site. This is also true more severe incidents (i.e. incidents blocking two out of the three lanes available) that happen during *off-peak periods*.

- Incidents blocking two out of three lanes on a freeway, lasting for 60 minutes or more, and occurring during peak hours lead to a dramatic increase in travel time.

- For medium severity incidents, the provision of real-time travel and dynamic route guidance information appear to be quite beneficial in terms of significantly reducing incident-related delay.

- The compounded effect of freeway incidents and inclement weather can lead to a significant increase in travel time, and is more likely to result in a massive network break down. This is due to the congestion caused by freeway incidents and the vulnerability brought by inclement weather.

There are several future research directions which the researchers are currently pursuing to further advance the research described in this chapter. Two of those directions are:

- **Studying the impact of inclement weather on travel demand:** While this study focused on modeling only the impact of inclement weather on driving behavior, future research should address how inclement weather affects travel demand and the resulting traffic volumes. The researchers how begun this process by analyzing archived hourly traffic volume counts from the NYS Thruway Authority.

- **Exploring other applications of the TRANSIMS model:** The TRANSIMS model developed in this study and in the earlier Volpe study is an invaluable planning and research asset which could be used to evaluate a number of interesting scenarios. For example, we have recently used the model to evaluate the likely environmental benefits of routing traffic based on the least fuel consumption or the least emissions route (i.e. green routing) (Guo et al. 2013). In the future, the researchers plan to use the model to evaluate other and new applications, including weather-responsive traffic management applications, as well as sustainable transportation strategies and policies.

REFERENCES

Agarwal, M., Maze, T. H., & Souleyrette, R. (2005). *Impact of weather on urban freeway traffic flow characteristics and facility capacity*. Academic Press.

Arentze, T. A., & Timmermans, H. J. P. (2004). A learning-based transportation oriented simulation system. *Transportation Research Part B: Methodological, 38*(7), 613–633. doi:10.1016/j. trb.2002.10.001.

Barcelo, J., & Ferrer, J. L. (1998). *AIMSUN2: Advanced interactive microscopic simulation for urban networks*. Academic Press.

Becker, G. S. (1965). A theory of the allocation of time. *The Economic Journal, 75*(299), 493–517. doi:10.2307/2228949.

Ben-Akivai, M., Bowman, J., & Gopinath, D. (1996). Travel demand model mystem for the information era. *Transportation, 23*(3), 241–266. doi:10.1007/BF00165704.

Bert, E., Torday, A., & Dumont, A. (2005). Calibration of urban network microsimulation models. In *Proceedings of 5th Swiss Transport Research Conference*. Ascona, Switzerland: Swiss Transport Research.

Bhat, C. R. (2005). A multiple discrete–continuous extreme value model: Formulation and application to discretionary time-use decisions. *Transportation Research Part B: Methodological, 39*(8), 679–707. doi:10.1016/j.trb.2004.08.003.

Bhat, C. R., Guo, J., Srinivasan, S., Pinjari, A., Eluru, N., Copperman, R., & Sener, I. N. (2006). *The comprehensive econometric microsimulator for daily activity-travel patterns (CEMDAP)*. Austin, TX: The University of Texas at Austin.

Bonabeau, E. (2002). Agent-based modeling: Methods and techniques for simulating human systems. *Proceedings of the National Academy of Sciences of the United States of America, 99*(3), 7280–7287. doi:10.1073/pnas.082080899 PMID:12011407.

Chen, X., & Zhan, F. B. (2006). Agent-based modelling and simulation of urban evacuation: Relative effectiveness of simultaneous and staged evacuation strategies. *The Journal of the Operational Research Society, 59*(1), 25–33. doi:10.1057/palgrave.jors.2602321.

Colyar, J., Zhang, L., & Halkias, J. (2003). Identifying and assessing key weather-related parameters and their impact on traffic operations using simulation. In *Proceedings of the ITE Institute of Transportation Engineers (ITE) Annual Meeting*. Seattle, WA: ITE.

Davidson, W., Donnelly, R., Vovsha, P., Freedman, J., Ruegg, S., & Hicks, J. et al. (2007). Synthesis of first practices and operational research approaches in activity-based travel demand modeling. *Transportation Research Part A, Policy and Practice, 41*(5), 464–488. doi:10.1016/j.tra.2006.09.003.

DeSerpa, A. C. (1971). A theory of the economics of time. *The Economic Journal, 81*(324), 828–846. doi:10.2307/2230320.

Dia, H., & Gondwe, W. (2008). Evaluation of incident impacts on integrated motorway and arterial networks using traffic simulation. In *Proceedings of the 29th Australasian Transport Research Forum*. Australiasian Transport Research.

Gerlough, D. L. (1955). *Simulation of freeway traffic on a general-purpose discrete variable computer. Los Angeles, CA*. Los Angeles: University of California.

Guo, L., Huang, S., & Sadek, A. W. (2013). An evaluation of likely environmental benefits of a time-dependent green routing system in the greater Buffalo-Niagara region. *Journal of Intelligent Transportation Systems: Technology, Planning and Operations*.

Hanbali, R. M., & Kuemmel, D. A. (1993). Traffic volume reductions due to winter storm conditions. *Transportation Research Record*, 1387.

Henson, K. M., & Gaulias, K. G. (2006). Preliminary assessment of activity analysis and modeling for homeland security applications. *Transportation Research Record: Journal of the Transportation Research Board*, 1942, 23–30. doi:10.3141/1942-04.

Hranac, R., Sterzin, E., Krechmer, D., Rakha, H., & Farzaneh, M. (2006). *Empirical studies on traffic flow in inclement weather (FHWA-HOP-07-073)*. Academic Press.

Jha, M., Gopalan, G., Garms, A., Mahanti, B., Toledo, T., & Ben-Akiva, M. (2004). Development and calibration of a large-scale microscopic traffic simulation model. *Transportation Research Record*, 1876, 121–131. doi:10.3141/1876-13.

Kamga, C. N., Mouskosb, K. C., & Paaswell, R. E. (2011). Methodology to estimate travel time using dynamic traffic assignment (DTA) under incident conditions. *Transportation Research Part C, Emerging Technologies*, 19(6), 1215–1224. doi:10.1016/j.trc.2011.02.004.

Krajzewicz, D., Bonert, M., & Wagner, P. (2006). The open source traffic simulation package SUMO. In *Proceedings of RoboCup 2006 Infrastructure Simulation Competition*. Bremen, Germany: RoboCup.

Kyte, M., Khatib, Z., Shannon, P., & Kitchener, F. (2001). The effect of weather on free-flow speed. Transportation Research Board, 1776, 60–68.

Lämmel, G., Grether, D., & Nagel, K. (2010). The representation and implementation of time-dependent inundation in large-scale microscopic evacuation simulations. *Transportation Research Part C, Emerging Technologies*, 18(1), 84–98. doi:10.1016/j.trc.2009.04.020.

Lawe, S., Lobb, J., Sadek, A. W., Huang, S., & Xie, C. (2009). TRANSIMS implementation in Chittenden County, Vermont. *Transportation Research Board Record*, 2132, 113–121. doi:10.3141/2132-13.

Lee, D., Yang, X., & Chandrasekar, P. (2001). Parameter calibration for PARAMICS using genetic algorithm. In *Proceedings of the 80th Annual Transportation Research Board Meeting*. Transportation Research Board.

Los Alamos National Lab (LANL). (2004). *TRANSIMS: Transportation analysis simulation system: Version 3.0 (LA-UR-00-1724)*. Los Alamos, NM: TRANSIMS.

Madireddy, M., Medeiros, D. J., & Kumara, S. (2011). An agent-based model for evacuation traffic management. In *Proceedings of the 2011 Winter Simulation Conference*. Winter Simulation.

Meister, K., Balmer, M., Ciari, F., Horni, A., Rieser, M., Waraich, R., & Axhausen, K. (2010). Large-scale agent-based travel demand optimization applied to Switzerland, incling mode choice. In *Proceedings of the 12th World Conference on Transportation Research*, (Vol. 1). Transportation Research.

Meloni, I., Guala, L., & Loddo, A. (2004). Time allocation to discretionary in-home, out-of-home activities and to trips. *Transportation, 31*(1), 69–96. doi:10.1023/B:PORT.0000007228.44861.ae.

Milton, J. C., Shankar, V. N., & Mannering, F. L. (2008). Highway accident severities and the mixed logit model: An exploratory empirical analysis. *Accident; Analysis and Prevention, 40*(1), 260–266. doi:10.1016/j.aap.2007.06.006 PMID:18215557.

Ozbay, K., & Bartin, B. (2003). Incident management simulation. *Simulation, 79*(2), 69–82. doi:10.1177/0037549703253494.

Ozbay, K., & Kachroo, P. (1999). *Incident management in intelligent transportation systems*. Artech House Intelligent Transportation Systems Library.

Peeta, S., Ramos, J. L., & Pasupathy, R. (2000). Content of variable message signs and on-line driver behavior. *Transportation Research Record: Journal of the Transportation Research Board, 1725*(1), 102–108. doi:10.3141/1725-14.

Pel, A. J., Bliemer, M. C. J., & Hoogendoorn, S. P. (2012). A review on travel behaviour modelling in dynamic traffic simulation models for evacuations. *Transportation, 39*(1), 97–123. doi:10.1007/s11116-011-9320-6.

Pendyala, R. M., Kitamura, R., Kikuchi, A., Yamamoto, T., & Fujii, S. (2005). Florida activity mobility simulator: Overview and preliminary validation results. *Transportation Research Record: Journal of the Transportation Research Board, 1921*(1), 123–130. doi:10.3141/1921-14.

PTV-AG. (2004). Vissim microscopic traffic and transit simulation user manual - V.3.70. Author.

Quadstone, L. T. D. (2004). *Quadstone paramics v5. 0 modeller user guide*. Scotland, UK: Author.

Rakha, H., Van Aerde, M., Bloomberg, L., & Huang, X. (1998). Construction and calibration of a large-scale microsimulation model of the Salt Lake area. *Transportation Research Record, 1664*, 93–102. doi:10.3141/1644-10.

Rakha, H., Zohdy, I., Park, S., & Krechmer, D. (2010). *Microscopic analysis of traffic flow in inclement weather – Part 2 (FHWA–JPO–11–020)*. Academic Press.

Ran, B., Barrett, B., & Johnson, E. (2004). *Evaluation of variable message signs in Wisconsin: Driver survey*. Academic Press.

Sadek, A. W., Zhao, Y., Huang, S., Fuglewicz, D., Hulme, K., & Qiao, C. (2011). Advanced transportation simulation modeling for transportation system evaluation and management during emergencies. *Journal of Homeland Security on Catastrophes and Complex Systems: Transportation*.

Smith, M. C., Sadek, A. W., & Huang, S. (2008). Large-scale microscopic simulation: Toward an increased resolution of transportation models. *Journal of Transportation Engineering, 134*(7), 273–281. doi:10.1061/(ASCE)0733-947X(2008)134:7(273).

Stern, A., Shah, V., Goodwin, L., & Pisano, P. (2003). *Analysis of weather impacts flow in metropolitan Washington D.C.* Washington, DC: Academic Press.

Sterzin, E. D. (2004). *Modeling influencing factors in a microscopic traffic simulator*. Cambridge, MA: MIT.

Toroczkai, Z., & Eubank, S. (2006). Agent-based modeling as a decision-making tool. In *Proceedings of Frontiers of Engineering: Reports on Leading-Edge Engineering from the 2005 Symposium*. Washington, DC: The National Academies Press.

Transportation Research Board. (2000). *Highway capacity manual*. Washington, DC: National Research Council.

Wang, F.-Y. (2010). Parallel control and management for intelligent transportation systems: Concepts, Architectures, and applications. *IEEE Transactions on Intelligent Transportation Systems, 11*(3), 630–638. doi:10.1109/TITS.2010.2060218.

Zhang, B., & Ukkusuri, S. V. (2009). Agent-based modeling for household level hurricane evacuation. In *Proceedings of the 2009 Winter Simulation Conference* (pp. 2778–2784). Winter Simulation.

Zhao, Y., Sadek, A. W., & Fuglewicz, D. P. (2012). Modeling inclement weather impact on freeway traffic speed at the macroscopic and microscopic levels. *Journal of the Transportation Research Board Record, 2272*.

Chapter 12
Agent-Based Modeling for Carpooling

Luk Knapen
Hasselt University, Belgium

Ansar-Ul-Haque Yasar
Hasselt University, Belgium

Sungjin Cho
Hasselt University, Belgium

Tom Bellemans
Hasselt University, Belgium

ABSTRACT

Modeling activities and travel for individuals in order to estimate traffic demand leads to large scale simulations. Most current models simulate individuals acting in a mutually independent way except for the use of the shared transportation infrastructure. As soon as cooperation between autonomous individuals is accounted for, the individuals are linked to each other in a network structure and interact with their neighbours in the network while trying to achieve their own goals. In concrete traffic-related problems, those networks can grow very large. Optimization over such networks typically leads to combinatorially explosive problems. In this chapter, the case of providing optimal advice to combine carpooling candidates is considered. First, the advisor software structure is explained; then, the characteristics for the carpooling candidates network derived for Flanders (Belgium) are calculated in order to estimate the problem size.

INTRODUCTION

Modeling activities and travel for individuals in order to estimate traffic demand, leads to large scale simulations. Most current models simulate individuals acting in a mutually independent way except for the use of the shared transportation infrastructure (road and transit capacity use). In many cases those tools scale (i) linearly with respect to daily agenda generation for mutually independent agents and (ii) quadratically with the number of travel analysis zones (TAZ) due to the use of origin-destination (OD) pair based flow and impedance matrices.

DOI: 10.4018/978-1-4666-4920-0.ch012

As soon as cooperation between individuals is accounted for, the need for agent-based simulation arises because (i) on one hand individuals have their own goals and plans and (ii) on the other hand they need to communicate, coordinate and negotiate to achieve their goals. This results in rapidly increasing problem complexity (combinatorial explosion). Agent-based simulations are known not to scale well. However, some problems raise questions that can be answered using this technique only.

This chapter focuses on the specific transportation related problem of *carpooling for commuters*. This case has been chosen because the study of scalability questions requires a well defined problem (and application context) in order to apply the results of mathematical and computer science research. The concept of *shared trip execution* is diverse. First the context is sketched both by analysing the essential phenomena relevant to cooperation and by showing a selection of existing advisory services available to candidate carpoolers today. Then, the principle of operation for a *commuter trip matching advisory service* is described. In order to analyse the behaviour of such advisor, it can be exercised by virtual community implemented by an agent-based simulator. The objectives are (i) analysing the advisor behaviour in order to tune the built-in machine learning mechanism and (ii) evaluating the transient phenomenon between initial deployment and the state in which the required critical mass of users has been attained. The last section presents initial results calculated from schedules generated by the FEATHERS activity-based model for the six million population in Flanders.

Carpooling is a form of cooperation while executing a daily agenda hence requiring coordination between people. In actual practice, carpooling and similar concepts can be supported by intelligent advisory systems for trip matching. Evaluating the operational fitness of such systems in the testing phase requires an active community of users. This chapter focuses on the use of an agent-based model to exercise the advisory system under test.

Carpooling as a Specific Instance of Cooperation

Carpooling has been the subject of investigation since it is a travel mode that can help to mitigate adverse effects caused by high transportation demand.

Carpooling implies cooperation. Most models for transportation demand either operate at aggregate levels (like the well known four step models (FSM)) or consider microsimulated actors to be mutually independent, except for the space they occupy on the road network while traveling. Carpooling is a phenomenon where cooperation is essential. Modeling actor interactions generates new challenges for research. Many cooperation problems require some form of combinatorial optimization. In the DataSIM project, the problem of carpooling was introduced in order to study the scalability of microsimulators involving interacting individuals.

This chapter concentrates on carpooling for commuting which means long term cooperation on periodic trips in the european context. The relationship between HOV lane advantages and carpooling is not considered because it is not relevant for the situation in the study area of DataSIM (Flanders, Belgium).

Advisory Services

It is assumed that people looking for carpooling partners first explore their own social network consisting of family members, neighbors, colleagues and acquintances. When no partner can be found in this way, individuals start consulting public services like websites for global exploration.

Nowadays a diverse set of advisory websites for carpooling is available. Those websites can be distinguished by the *services supplied*, by the integrated *automatic matching mechanism* used (if any) and the set of parameters used in the matching process (characteristics and preferences for the individual, trip times, routes driven), by the *business model* for payment handling, by the *types of co-traveling* supported (carpooling, van-sharing, ridesharing, ...) covered and by the *target user community* addressed (individuals or companies). A categorization is given below (see table in appendix).

Several of those websites contain *matching services* which means that they can suggest specific trips to be combined in a carpool. From a business point of view, this matching mechanism needs a minimum level of accuracy since wrong advice would decrease customer confidence and hence customer loss. Advisors that make use of statistical methods and machine learning techniques, need a sufficient amount of data to get trained. Either training is performed once, using a dataset specified a priori, or a feedback mechanism is provided for periodic retraining.

This chapter focuses on the problem of testing a carpooling advisory system. Testing cannot be performed by a real customer community because, due to the built-in statistics based algorithms, a large customer-tester community and a long period of test-mode operation would be required and any wrong advice could chase away some customers. We consider a setup where the operational service is tested using a virtual community implemented by an agent-based simulator.

Research Questions

Research questions in the domain of *cooperation modeling* include:

- Can microsimulation reveal factors relevant to carpooling and other forms of cooperation in transportation systems? In other words: how do schedule adaptation (replanning) and time pressure influence decisions to cooperate?
- What conditions need to be fulfilled before people start cooperating? What are the effects of decreased flexibility, increased mutual dependency, time pressure and

monetary savings on cooperation-related decisions? How do mutual dependency and schedule inflexibility depend on the fraction of the population that is prepared to cooperate? I.o.w. does a critical fraction exist beyond which cooperation inhibiting factors disappear?

- Is there a way to determine an upper bound for traffic participation by carpooling using microsimulators?
- What kind of problems are expected to occur when using agent-based modeling on a large scale (nation-wide, millions of agents)? What is the minimal size of an agent community to analyze realistic cooperation problems in transportation? What is the maximal size that is computationally feasible when negotiation between agents is to be modeled?
- How to test the quality of trip matching advice delivered by websites dedicated to carpooling?
- How to evaluate the evolution of the operations and the quality of the delivered advice (transient phenomena before the critical participation level has been reached)?

BACKGROUND – LITERATURE OVERVIEW

Several aspects of cooperation on trips (co-traveling) and carpooling have been investigated in the literature. Papers report on research concerning

- Factors that significantly influence the decision to carpool; those have been investigated by panel survey research (revealed and stated preference research on incentives and inhibiting factors).
- Business models for advisory systems.
- Aspects of mutual payments in carpooling context.

- Behavioural models for individuals including activity selection, schedule timing, rescheduling due to unexpected events, distribution of tasks among related agents (including model specification, parameter estimation and algorithm design).
- The routing problem for co-traveling.
- Extraction of carpooling opportunities from large sets of GPS trajectories.

Several papers report research on existing carpooling projects analysing business models, influencing factors and motives for the service providers. Other research concentrates on behavioural models and on factors that significantly determine carpooling related decisions. Since many of the aspects mentioned above are essential for the operation of a carpooling advisor, they are briefly discussed in the subsections below. The topics found in literature have been subdivided into three classes. First we discuss some papers covering basic forms of car sharing and papers that identify influencing factors and estimate their effect on the intention to carpool. The second subsection presents an overview of the current state of research performed to derive operational simulation models once influence factors have been identified. The third subsection lists research efforts focusing on specific components required to complete a simulator. An elaborated overview has been given in order to show the complexity of the design of an operational advisor, the multitude of design options and the mutual incompatibility of some of them.

Concepts and Influencing Factors

(Murray, Chase, Kim, & McBrayer, 2012) investigates how US-based public transit providers integrate vanpooling in their program. The report presents results from a survey conducted among 41 agencies. Aspects like the business model, fares, incentives, customer feedback and the use of several technologies (website, Facebook, Twitter)

are surveyed and results are presented in tables. Of the respondents, 28 are public transit agencies. The most prominent reason for an agency to add a ridesharing program to their services, is to help solving the *last mile* problem. It was found that most agencies use a variety of performance measures to determine whether the amount spent on ridesharing is worthwhile. Several concepts (carpooling, vanpooling, slugging) are investigated. (Burris et al., 2012) reports on a study of *slugging* (casual ridesharing). It explains the concept, tries to elicit determining factors but is superficial and anectdotical and does not provide clear conclusions. (Buliung, Soltys, Habel, & Lanyon,2009) uses data extracted from a webservice that facilitate connections between potential carpoolers. The service is free and open to the public. The data are used to analyze the carpool formation and use process. The paper aims at investigating (i) the staging of the carpool process (evolution in time of waiting, formation, starting) (ii) describing geographical patterns of demand (iii) and testing the hypothesis that the carpool formation and use process is sensitive to individual characteristics, residential spatial context, the individual's mobility status and the attitudes toward cost, the environment, and the value of time (VOT). The paper presents a comprehensive list of related research on incentives to encourage carpooling, socio-economic characteristics, the effect of size of the potential list of carpoolers, the behavioural process and spatial factors. Age, gender and spatial accessibility to potential co-travelers, are found to be important factors. One of the inhibitors for co-traveling is the mutual dependency. In order to overcome unexpected or emergency situations, *Guaranteed Ride Home (GRH)* programs are provided as an inexpensive insurance policy. (Menczer, 2007) discusses GRH programs for commuters in the context of public transit, carpooling and vanpooling. Eligibility (legal aspects), payments, program rules, market organisation, average cost per claim, amount of claims are analysed and discussed. The program costs are concluded to be low.

The study described in (Trasarti, Pinelli, Nanni, & Giannotti, 2011) processing GPS traces for specific individuals. Similar trips are extracted (based on space and time-of-day). A *routine* is defined as a sufficiently large set of similar traces. A *profile* is a set of routines. A *representative* of a routine is the *medoid* of the routine. *Routine containment* is a relation specifying that the endpoints of the contained routine are sufficiently close to the some points on the routine representative of the container routine. If a routine is contained in another one, then the profiles are *sharable*. The concepts of profiling are applied to the carpooling problem. Based on the assumption that the passenger walks for a given maximal distance to a location where (s)he is picked up by a driver, an upper bond for carpooling is determined using travel profiles.

From Model Design, Simulation and Parameter Estimation to Operational Systems

Another line of research focuses on modeling co-operation, both on activities and on trip execution. (Cho et al., 2012) discusses communication and coordination, negotiation and social networks in an agent-based model to simulate carpooling behaviour. (Bellemans et al., 2012) focuses on a case where one large manufacturing plant dominates the traffic in a moderately sized city. In such case one can envisage to organize carpooling via the employer. The authors propose to use an agent-based model to exercise the matching service to extensively test the operational software before actual deployment. The paper also suggests to make use of big-data (recorded GPS trajectories and GSM traces) to learn the traffic patterns to support high quality matching advice.

Rescheduling or schedule adaptation is essential while cooperating and is part of the negotiation process. Rescheduling aspects have been studied mostly in the context of unexpected events. The *Aurora* model was introduced in (Joh, 2002) that explores an heuristic to find good solutions for the activity-travel rescheduling problem which is a combinatorial optimization having a large search space. (Joh, 2003) shows how to estimate the parameters for the *Aurora* model S-shaped utility as a function of activity duration. A parameter estimation method is developed, tested on synthetic data and evaluated. (Nijland, Arentze, Borgers, & Timmermans, 2009) estimates some of the parameters required by the *Aurora* model. It describes the setup of a survey and comments the *mixed logit* model results as well as the limitations of the method used. The results consist of probability for schedule adaptations in case of unexpected time shortage. (Arentze, Pelizaro, & Timmermans, 2005) presents an overview of the *Aurora* activity-based model for schedule generation and adaptation. People are simulated as individual agents. A comprehensive model has been specified describing the insertion, repositioning, deletion and substitution of activities as well as changing locations, trip chaining options and transport modes. Models of this level of detail are required to integrate carpooling concepts in a simulator. In this paper *Aurora* is used in an experimental setup to study schedules consisting of work activities and *green activities* in several scenarios.

(J. Guo, Nandam, & Adams, 2012) lists characteristics of Computational Process Models (CPM) and their assumed shortcomings (dichotomous classification of activities: fixed/flexible, dichotomous classification of decision making process: pre-day-planning/on-day-rescheduling, plan completion and certainty (as opposed to partial activity attribute planning). A data collection method to acquire data to uncover the (re)planning process is presented. The paper does not handle the problem of converting recorded survey data into parameters of an operational model.

In (Ronald, 2012) the author develops an agent based model capable of negotiations in the activity planning and scheduling phases and focusing on cooperation while executing discretionary social activities. The model simulates activity travel behaviour over a one week period. The agents negotiate about the kind of social activity to jointly execute, the location and timing.

(Knapen, Yasar, et al., 2013) introduces the problem of carpooling by commuters. An advisory mechanism for candidate carpoolers based on commuter trip matching is proposed. In order to determine the optimal advice, the success probability for the required negotiation is determined from individuals socio-economic profiles, time and route similarity functions. As a first case, bipartite matching is considered. (Knapen, Keren, et al., 2013) extends the model to the general case where each individual can function either as a driver or a passenger, can negotiate and cooperate with any other individual in carpools only limited by car capacity. This leads to finding an optimal general *allocation* problem in a graph.

(Kamar & Horvitz, 2009) investigates a mechanism to build an online application where knowledge about trips comes available in realtime and is used to advice people about *ridesharing*. It makes use of recorded GPS traces to find out which users can be paired. GPS trails had been collected over 5 years for a community of employees all working for a single company. Agents are assumed to be rational. Extra time and fuel are accounted for. The payment method is analyzed extensively: the authors opt for a VCG (Vickrey–Clarke–Groves) based method optimized over the set of cooperating partners only (for computational efficiency reasons). *Ridesharing* supply and demand are posted to a software system. People make bids to the system. The system tries to determine the optimal set partitioning (set cover problem). The paper presents interesting notes about price determination and about the concepts of dealing with the complete population or with local groups when it comes to payment. The solution efficiency is calculated in terms of total cost and in terms of trip number reduction.

(Agatz, Erera, Savelsbergh, & Wang, 2010) focuses on dynamic non-recurring trips which is related to commuting carpooling but requires different solution concepts. Both maximal individual advantage and system wide optimum are considered.

(Luetzenberger, Masuch, Hirsch, Ahrndt, & Albayrak, 2011) investigate the effect of environmental conditions and plan to incorporate the agent interactions required when carpooling.

(Ghoseiri, 2012) develops a Dynamic Rideshare Optimized Matching model and solution that is aimed at identifying suitable matches between passengers requesting rideshare services with appropriate drivers available to carpool for credits and HOV lane privileges. The research develops a spatial, temporal, and hierarchical decomposition solution strategy that leads to the heuristic solution procedure. The abstract is available via http://drum.lib.umd.edu/handle/1903/13023 but the full text is not publicly available yet.

(Manzini & Pareschi, 2012) describes an interactive system to support the mobility manager operating on the LTCPP (long term car pool problem). The proposed methods and models make use of clustering analysis (CA). The basic hypothesis is that in a group the driver of the shared car turns among the participants. Clustering procedures using methods available in standard DSS (decision support system) are proposed. After clustering, for each driver a TSP is to be solved. Similarity measures are used but not discussed. The result is a GUI based interactive system that can be applied to company employees. A case study for a public service in the city of Bologna is presented. Experiments show that the overall *relative* saving in distance and time increases with the number of participants.

Finally, (dynamicridesharing.org, 2012) is a website providing information on dynamic ridesharing systems, the pitfalls and difficulties encountered while attempting to set up a successful system. The mission is to share information about development processes in order to avoid to repeat past mistakes. The website gives a clear definition of *dynamic ridesharing*, an overview of existing (non)dynamic ridesharing initiatives and a bibiliography including scientific papers, patents and links. (Gruebele, 2008) is a kind of monograph available from dynamicridesharing. org The paper, although unusual, specifies a system requirements list in a rigorous and well founded way. It contains an extensive list of definitions and a structured list of requirements. Unfortunately, it contains only one bibliography item.

(Varrentrapp, Maniezzo, & Stützle, 2002) provides an informal and formal problem statement are given for the LCPP (Longterm Car Pooling Problem). Then the soundness of the problem formulation is argued and some properties of the LCPP are proved. Finally the problem is proved to be NP-complete.

Particular Algorithms and Model Components

(Chun & Wong, 2003) describes a group negotiation protocol for agreement on agenda schedules. A group can consist of two or more agents. The negotiation mechanism is based on ideas drawn from the *A* shortest path algorithm*. Each agent is assumed to specify its most preferred option first and to specify consecutive new proposals in non-increasing order of preference. Each one uses a private (i.e. not published) utility function. The protocol initiator makes use of a proposal evaluation function that is based on the assumption that agents behave as mentioned before. Versions using preference feedback by agents and conflict resolution by initiator are reported to result in nearly optimal solutions using a quite small number of negotiation rounds. (Kothari, 2004) develops a MAS (Multi-Agent System) named *Genghis* in Jade to handle dynamic carpooling. *Genghis* is aimed at interactive use. Focus is on algorithms for *route matching* (heuristics based) and *reputation* management. Software agents operate on behalf of their interactive users, using the *Contract Net Protocol*. *Genghis* agents do not negotiate but simply provide their best offer at once (page 13, section 2.4): *offers* and *calls for proposal* are matched pairwise and a route and time based score is calculated. The thesis presents an operational prototype having limited functions, in detail. (Knapen, Keren, et al., 2012) studies the problem of finding an optimal route for co-traveling. The origin (home) and destination (work) locations are given for each individual as well as a set of carpool parkings. Each of those home, work and parking locations are possible transferia (locations where to change travel mode or to change vehicle) where one can join a carpool. Each individual declares the maximal time and/ or distance that is acceptable to move from origin to destination. The combined route (co-route) that solves the problem consist of a *join* part and a *fork* part. In the *join* tree, carpoolers enter the driver's car at several locations and times. In the *fork* tree they successively leave the car and, if not at their destination, continue their trip by other means. The paper proposes an algorithm to find the optimal solution for the *join* tree. (Lu, 2011) presents a method to find a set of shortest paths at once. The shortest path for carpooling is to be found for the case where all pick-up is at home locations and all drop-off is at work locations (hence excluding the join-fork case). The problem is characterized as a small *TSP* (traveling salesman problem) because of limited car capacity. The combinatorial problem of finding the optimal visit order is not covered by the paper. The paper focuses on the determination of the shortest path between each pair of locations in a pre-processing step. The LU algorithm is an extended A* that handles multiple destinations at once by in each step selecting the neighbour that delivers the most promising estimate. It is reported to outperform the Dijkstra algorithm when the destinations are clustered in an area whose radius is much shorter than the distance from the origin to the cluster.

CO-TRAVELING SERVICES CONTEXT

After having shown research effort reports in previous section, we now concentrate on existing operational systems available to the public. A survey of carpooling related sites on the web has been conducted in march 2013. The results are shown in this section. In order to clearly distinguish between several options that are available, key terms have been explained in the first subsection below. The second section lists the attributes that were considered to be essential for classifying the websites. The last subsection describes some examples in order to show the variety of services provided and to give an idea bout business models used.

Kinds of Cooperative Traveling – Terminology

Table 1 summarizes the most common concepts for shared trip execution.

Carpooling Website Attributes

Web-based services aimed at individuals, organisations and companies who consider cooperative traveling have been visited and analysed. The table in appendix contains an inventory of represenattive carpooling related websites. Explanations for the keywords used can be found in the glossary

in the appendix. Following attributes have been listed for each site:

Example Services: Data Extracted from Websites

1. (Enterprise Rideshare - Vanpool & Rideshare Services for Individuals, Employers & Government Agencies:, 2012) addresses both individuals and employers, provides a Guaranteed Ride Home program and considers vanpools as a natural extension of the local car rental service they provide.

2. (Carpool solutions for university and corporate networks., 2012) as a social network for ridesharing. All University of Minnesota students, staff, and faculty are eligible to sign-up for the university's private Zimride Rideshare Community. They are an example of carpooling organized via the employer or company. *"The service is active at over 125 universities. Universities pay around $10,000 per year to use the platform."* source wikipedia (http://en.wikipedia.org/wiki/Zimride).

3. Lyft is an on-demand ridesharing service owned and operated by Zimride. It focuses on safety. Every driver who applies to become a part of the community is screened for criminal offenses and driving incidents. Lyft uses strict driving requirements, performs a criminal background check, provides an ex-

Table 1. Carpooling domain definitions

Carpooling for commuting	The concept where people agree to periodically drive together for commuting (see also LCPP in the glossary in appendix)
Casual carpooling	See *Slugging*
Ride-sharing	Booking a seat in someone's vehicle for a single journey
Slugging	The practice of forming ad hoc, informal carpools for purposes of commuting. Practiced in the US where people wait in *slug lines* to be picked up by drivers who offer seats often in order to be able to use HOV lanes.
Vanpooling	Group of five or more people with similar commutes (compatible times and destinations) who share a van (often rented from a specialized vanpool service).

Table 2. Attributes used to qualify carpooling related websites

Co-travel booking time	At what time does the user book a ride ? Impulsively and infrequently (Irreg), shortly before the intended trip starts (Real-time) or well planned in advance for recurring periodic trips (Pre-time)?
Co-travel pool kind	Car-pool, Van-pool, Taxi-pool ?
Contact possibility	How to contact the co-travel partners/candidates ?
Target population segment	Which specific categories of people are focused on ?
Targets specific region	Does the website service a limited region ?
Payment method	What methods for payment are supported ?
Functions supplied	What facilities are supplied by the website ?
Person attributes	Which person attributes/preferences are registered on the website and used in the matching process ?
Trip attributes	Which trip attributes/preferences are registered on the website and used in the matching process ?
Extras delivered	What functions additional to trip/person matching does the website offer ?
Collaboration	(How) Does the website cooperate with other services (like social network sites) ?
Number of users	What is the current amount of users registered with the website ?

cess liability insurance and inspects vehicles in advance. It maintains a zero-tolerance drug and alcohol policy for community drivers. Smartphone apps for iPhone and Android are made available.

4. Car sharing and ridesharing also get combined: information extracted from Wall Street Journal (Nassauer, 2009) and (Car Sharing, an alternative to car rental and car ownership – Zipcar, 2012). When reserving a car on Zipcar, members have the option to automatically post the date, time and destination of their rental onto the Zimride website. Once transferred to the Zimride site, the user specifies her/his preferences. Zimride then finds and notifies users looking for a ride.

5. Metro Transit provides a broad range of public transportation services across King County, Washington including bus, dial-a-ride-transit (DART), door-to-door van service for people with disabilities who cannot use regular buses. It also runs a publicly owned vanpool program in the country, with

more than 1200 vans and it hosts a regional ridematch system that helps commuters form (compose) and sustain carpools and vanpools by matching trips (Metro Carpooling Made Easy, 2013)) Data to be registered on the website used for matching include (1)] (a) the maximum wait time for late riders (b) smoking indicator (c) permission for food and drink in the car (d) *music/news/nothing* radio preference.

a. *VanPool* provides the van and everything else for successful ridesharing: rider support services, maintenance, insurance, fuel, tires and training. Groups of five to fifteen people are supported.

b. *VanShare* serve to bridge the gap between a public transportation mode and a final destination.

c. MetroPool set up by Metro for small groups to experience and enjoy 100% electric vanpool and vanshare commuting.

6. (Nurminen, Pakarinen, & Hartikainen, 2011) documents a Bing Maps smartphone application to publish and/or find carpool trips to join. Using this application, a passenger can browse routes specified by selecting origin and destination locations, then select a route and send a *join* request. Users create and manage their routes/trips and carpools by accepting other users' requests; they also can send messages to carpool members and follow the driver's position on the map. By creating a carpool and assigning a route to it, an individual can declare to be ready for drive and accept the join requests. https://www.carpoolzone.smartcommute.ca/en/my/mytext.php?section=routing delivers support for co-routing. Following statements have been taken from the website. (1)] (a) "Unlike matching based simply on the distance between commuters' endpoints, route-based *ma*tching considers the entire route a commuter actually drives. This allows matching with commuters who can be picked up part-way, with minimal changes in the driver's route." (b) "Each match is scored according to its suitability for you, and matches are shown with the best at the top. Scores depend on routes and end-points." (c) "You can adjust Search Agent options including search distance, schedule flexibility, and more, to find the commuters that suit you best. The Search Agent will email you if new matches are found at a later date."

7. http://www.taxistop.be/4/carpool/4smartpool-2.htm advertizes co-routing support as follows: "Matches not based on postal codes but on a routing algorithm …] The use of underlying geographical data and routing algorithms makes it possible to refine the search process. The possibility to drop or pick someone up along the way, largely increases the chances to find a suitable partner."

COOPERATION BY CARPOOLING

On one hand carpoolers sacrifice time, schedule and route flexibility (Shewmake, 2010, p. 21). On the other hand carpooling can decrease travel costs (fuel, parking). Each actor tries to determine a feasible solution of maximal quality by negotiation after having found potential partners to carpool and after having decided which amount of schedule adaptation is acceptable for each trip considered for carpooling. A commuting carpooler commits for medium to long term cooperation and hence can be assumed to behave in a utility optimizing way. In order to build a model for cooperating individuals, the building blocks (components) mentioned below are required because carpooling introduces additional constraints on the characteristics of trips (timing, routing).

- **Schedule Adaptation:** Is required during negotiation. It requires knowledge about the (near) future because each agent needs to predict travel times that in general are departure time dependent. Part of the re-scheduling literature focuses on situations originating from unexpected events ((Roorda & Andre, 2007), (Gan & Recker, 2008), (Nijland et al., 2009), (Knapen, Muhammad, Bellemans, Janssens,2012) and (J. Y. Guo, Nandam, & Adams, 2012)).

  Rescheduling during the planning phase requires a different approach. Researchers in this field focus on the the decision process used while scheduling. In the context of negotiation to cooperate, sometimes rescheduling of previously scheduled but not yet started activities is required ((Doherty & Axhausen, 1999), (Rindt & McNally, 2002), (Doherty, Lee-Gosselin, Burns, & Andrey, 2002), (Nijland, Arentze, & Timmermans, 2008), (Auld, Mohammadian,2009), (Auld et al., 2009)).

Schedule adaptation can make use of utility maximization after selecting a suitable model specifying the (marginal) utility as a function of activity duration. (Joh, 2003) introduces S-shaped utility functions in *Aurora*. The author shows the complexity of both the use of non-monotonically decreasing marginal utility as well as the estimation of parameters for such function. *Aurora* assumes that a schedule (daily agenda) has no intermediate deadlines. Such deadlines however are essential; one of the reasons is the case mentioned above where previously completed negotiations to cooperate, are considered as hard constraints.

(Roorda & Andre, 2007) describe a stated adaptation experiment to find out how people reschedule when they are faced with an unexpected delay of one hour at a given moment. One of the results is that the required rescheduling actions are determined by the attributes of the delayed activity and not by the person attributes

All of those however focus rescheduling due to unexpected events, not due to negotiation. Furthermore, all authors assume that the marginal utility while accomplishing a task, does depend on absolute time only by the constraints stating that a particular activity shall be performed within a specific time windows.

(Knapen, Muhammad, et al., 2012) shows that schedule adaption can be implemented very efficiently when monotonic marginal utility function is used and that schedule adaptation by itself does not inhibit to build models where millions of individuals are involved.

- **Negotiation:** Is essential to cooperation both on activity (see (Ronald, Arentze, & Timmermans, 2012), (Ronald, 2012)) and on trip execution. The simplest cases are those where either (i) the individuals involved have no constraints imposed by third parties or (ii) the individuals are already involved in agreements that only impose hard (i.e. non-negotiable) constraints. Things become more complex when a candidate applies to join an existing group and as a consequence needs to negotiate with several people about a single *co-trip* to be performed. If an individual starts negotiating to cooperate with people already involved in an agreement, negotiations become mutually dependent. This can lead to very complex optimization problems.

Note also the additional difficulty caused by trip durations that depend on departure time (due to time dependent road network load and congestion). In addition, different actors can estimate future trip durations in a different way which requires additional negotiation to agree on expected travel time used to schedule the trip. If those cases are excluded, monotonically evolving algorithm like the one proposed in (Chun & Wong, 2003) can provide an efficient solution. With $N*$, each agent has non-disclosed knowledge about the set of private acceptable solutions. A total order based on preference, is assumed to exist over each private set of solutions. Each agent is assumed to propose successive options in non-increasing preference order until an agreement is reached or no more solutions are available. Note that in order to agree on departure (arrival) time, discete time-values (or discrete periods of time) need to be used since the departure (arrival) time preference function for an agent in general is not a monotonically decreasing one; hence an enumeration is required.

Two major aspects of negotiation require investigation:

1. The negotiation *process* that defines how agents interact.
2. The negotiation *outcome* prediction that is required in public advisory tools

to determine whether or not two agents who do not yet belong to each others social network, should be advised to start a negotiation. This requires quantified similarity concepts.

- **Value of Time (VOT):** Schedule adaptation only requires the abstract notion of utility. In the carpooling context however, monetary cost of a trip is involved and several quantities (including absolute time, duration, fuel cost, public transit fares) are used in negotiation. Those quantities need to be fed into a *preference* function delivering a single value. Since both monetary and duration values are included, the notion of VOT comes into play.

  (Abrantes & Wardman, 2011) presents a meta-study of VOT for travelers in the UK. 1749 valuations originating from 226 studies conducted over 48 years have been processed. The results consist of a small base set of absolute values. Values are expressed relative to car-IVT (in vehicle time). Values for cases not mentioned in the base set are expressed relative to the base values. Elasticity (e.g. VOT valuation depends on trip distance) has been covered by a set of formulas derived by a data fitting process. Concrete values for VOT to feed a simulation model, can be extracted from this study. The paper shows how VOT depends on delay by congestion, journey purpose and several other factors.

- **Incentives:** Are covered by many papers some of which focus on local situations like (Vlaamse-Overheid & Traject-2007). Many US large cities, universities and public transit providers offer carpooling/ridesharing incentive programs (Ungemah, Goodin, Dusza, & Burris, 2007). Incentives contain direct cost savings, tax benefits, HOV-lan use, parking facilities, guaranteed-ride-home and emergency-ride-home

insurance, reduced public transit fares, etc (even discounts on ski lift tickets price). Studies mentioned in section Background – Literature Overview and websites mentioned in section CO-Traveling Services Context. on one hand suggest the existence of a large range of incentive types and on the other hand the doubtful effectiveness of some of them. In order to account for those incentives in a simulation model, they need to be inventoried and in some cases a conversion factor is to be determined to derive the monetary equivalent value. Incentives can be conceptually simple but error-prone to integrate in an operational model (e.g. local fiscal or employer specific benefits).

AGENT-BASED MODEL TO EXERCISE ADVISOR SOFTWARE

In previous sections, research results on cooperation between individuals and schedule (daily agenda) adaptation has been summarized. Attributes used to classify carpooling related services available via the world wide web, have been listed and representative examples have been given. The basic components required to model cooperating individuals have been identified. Now the material supplied in previous sections will be applied to the concrete case of evaluating the operation of a web based trip matching service aimed at advising commuters looking for partners to carpool.

It is assumed that an advisory service for carpooling while commuting is to be built. People will register their periodic commuting trips: the base period typically is one week i.e. a specific pattern valid for working days is repeated after every seventh day. Considering one week periods accommodates for most situations (including part-time workers). People who are able to fulfill all their carpooling needs within their own social

Agent-Based Modeling for Carpooling

network (*local exploration*) of acquaintances, are assumed not to need the service. Others will need to explore the set of unknown carpooling candidates (*global exploration*). The *global carpooling matching service* (*GCPMS*) shall determine which trips are best suited to carpooling and provide advise by suggesting people to start a negotiation with respect to a specific periodically executed trip.

Advisor Model - Principle of Operation

In order to find carpooling companions people who did not find a suitable partner by exploring their private network, register themselves with the service. Registration implies first posting some descriptive characteristics like age, gender, education level, special interests (like music style preferences), job category, driver license availability, etc. Those qualifiers are used because it is known that continued successful cooperation between people requires a minimal level of similarity.

Secondly, people post information about each trip they periodically plan to execute: those data consist of source and destination locations, earliest and latest departure and arrival times, the maximal detour distance that is acceptable and the availability of a car (possibility to drive). Note the a particular driver license owner can be unavailable for driving on a specific day of the week because the family car on that day is in use by her/his partner.

The service shall match *periodic trip executions*, not people. A periodic trip on Wednesday from A to B leaving at about 08:30h needs to be matched with a another one having similar characteristics. Of course, the people involved shall be mutually compatible but they are not the primary subject of matching. A particular individual can periodically carpool with several people for different trips in the week (on Monday with colleague A, on Tuesday with neighbour B who differs from A). Periodic trip execution is abbreviated by *periodicTripEx* in the remainder of the text.

A *pooled trip execution* is the cooperative execution of a set of trips using a single car and a single driver. As a consequence, the route for each passenger shall be embedded in the route of the driver (*single driver constraint*).

After having found a good match (details on how to do so will be explained below) the matcher conveys its advise to the candidates involved (the owners of the matched *periodicTripEx*); they evaluate the proposal, negotiate about carpooling and possibly agree to cooperate. Note that this negotiation is not guaranteed to succeed. One of the reasons is that the individuals dispose of more information during the *negotiation process* than the service does during the *matching process*. People register only limited information in the matching service for privacy reasons and because specifying detailed information is time consuming and error prone; hence websites do not ask for it. An example is time preference for trip departure: a website allows to register a time window but does not allow for the specification of time preferences like *the sooner the better*. Because the matcher service cannot be sure about the negotiation result, the candidates convey the negotiation result back to the matcher service. This project assumes that sufficient (financial) incentives are in place in order to make this happen.

After trip execution, users can qualify each other. The *GCPMS* allows for controlled mutual evaluation of individuals with respect to timeliness and safety. Only individuals cooperating in an agreement can qualify each other. The negotiation and qualification feedback is used by a learning mechanism incorporated in the matching service. After receiving the feedback, the matching service disposes of the *PTE* and the individual's characteristics as well as of the negotiation result; those are used to train a *logit* based predictor. Please refer to Figure 1 for an high level overview of dataflows, relations and method activation.

244

Figure 1. Application context: the right hand side shows the matcher service. People register some descriptive data about themselves and trips to be executed periodically (periodicTripEx). Those constitute a graph: the edges are labeled with the probability that negotiation will succeed when the trip owners are advised to carpool. Negotiation result is fed back to train the logit predictor. The left hand side shows the entities exercising the matcher service in consecutive phases.

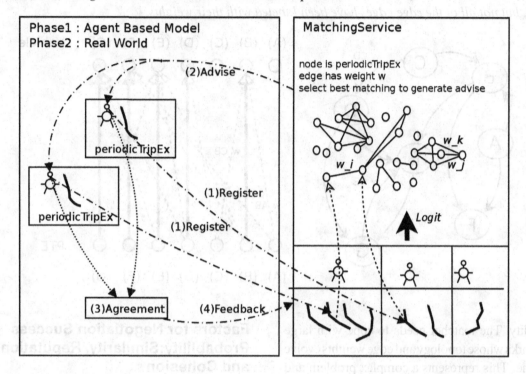

The model used for matching consists of a directed graph (see Figure 2 left part); by convention, each edge points to the *PTE* whose owner will be the driver. Each vertex corresponds to a *PTE*. A vertex for which the owner is unable to become the driver, never can be a target edge (its *indegree* equals zero). Two vertices are connected by an edge if and only if it is worth to advise the *PTE* owners to start negotiating. Every edge is labeled with the estimated probability for the negotiation to succeed. Note that

1. The set of vertices evolves over time because people register and withdraw *PTE* as time evolves and because people join and leave the carpooling candidates society (removing all their *PTE* in the latter case).

2. Edges emerge as soon as the negotiation success probability exceeds a given threshold; this can be caused by changes in the *PTE* (e.g. by relaxing the time constraints) and people characteristics respectively (e.g. by reputation changes due to partner evaluation being registered (see below)).

3. Probability estimates can change over time by re-training the predictor. Note that this can cause threshold crossing and hence edge creation or deletion.

Finally the problem size can grow large when a nation-wide service is considered. Large scale deployment probably is a necessary condition for both effective operation (delivery of advice that has a high success probability) and economic

Figure 2. The leftmost diagram shows the graph where vertices correspond to PTE (periodic trip execution) and the edges are labeled with the success probability for the negotiation (if that is sufficiently large). The rightmost part shows the same information in bipartite graph showing both PTE and vehicles . Continuous line arcs connect an PTE to the vehicle of its owner; dashed lines show potential participation as a passenger. Grey vertices correspond to PTE where the owner is prepared to drive. Some, but not all of the edge edges have been labeled with their weights.

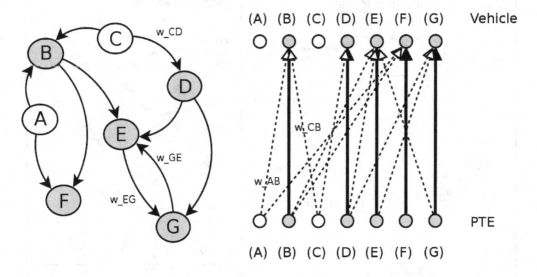

viability. The matcher needs to cope with large networks whose topology and edge weights evolve in time. This represents a complex problem and hence thorough evaluation before deployment.

An agent based model simulating the actual population behaviour, will be used to exercise the matching service for several reasons. First, performance and effectiveness need to be evaluated on a running system since they are very difficult to predict from design data only. Second, deploying such system should go flawlessly because lost customers will be reluctant to return. Finally, the system behaviour during the startup transient when only few customers already registered, is difficult to predict and hence observations made are difficult to interpret; simulation can support learning about the overall system behaviour.

Factors for Negotiation Success Probablility:Similarity, Reputation and Cohesion

The functions used to determine the input variables for the negotiation success probability estimator are briefly explained in this section and shown in Figure 4. Details can be found in (Knapen, Yasar, et al., 2013).

1. Path similarity pathSim() is a value in [0,1] assigned to an ordered pair (pte_0, pte_i) of *PTE* that indicates to what extent the OD (Origin, Destination) pairs involved in the respective trips, are compatible for carpooling in case the owner of pte_0 is assigned to be the driver. Path similarity defines a function of *PTE* that is not symmetric in its arguments. This is easily seen because the distance driven depends on the driver selection; the driver needs a detour to pick up passengers.

Figure 3. *The left hand part shows the preference function used to determine the start of a trip in the agent-based model. The right hand part shows the preference function used by the global advisor based on scarce information registered by the user.*

Preference functions for trip departure/arrival

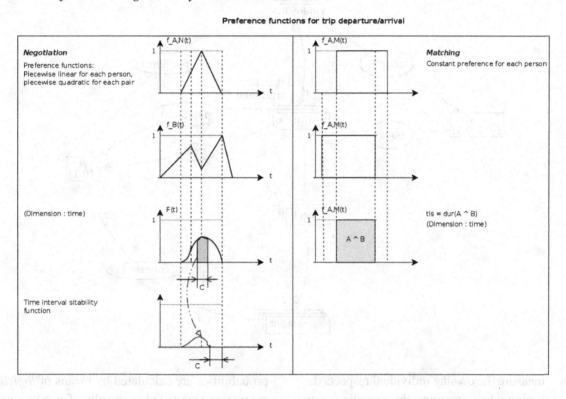

2. Profile similarity profSim() is a value in [0,1] assigned to a pair of individuals that indicates to what extent the individuals are compatible for carpooling. Profile similarity is based on socio-economic category, gender and age.

3. Time interval similarity tis() is a value in [0,1] assigned to an ordered pair of *PTE* having identical origins and identical destinations; it indicates to what extent the time intervals involved are compatible for carpooling. Compatibility for car pooling requires a minimal amount of intervals overlap (see Figure 5). Time interval similarity can be calculated only for a pair consisting of the passenger trip and the part of the driver's trip for which the route coincides with the passenger trip route (because tis() applies to trips having identical origins and destinations).

4. Safety reputation sReputation() of a driver is a value in [0,1]. Each individual has an *sReputation* value that evolves over time due to qualification by passengers (i.e. individuals who participated in an agreement where the person being evaluated was the driver). Notifications received are registered in a personal *qualifications list* with the individual they apply to; for each issuer, only the most recent qualification is kept. The *sReputation* is calculated as a weighted average of the values posted in the qualification list: the weight decreases with age of the notification and increases with the duration of the cooperation.

5. Timeliness reputation tReputation() (or accuracy reputation) is a value in the range [−0.5,0.5] assigned (by the co-travellers) to a *PTE* in an *agreement*: it indicates to what

Figure 4. Overview of functions defined on the sets (individual, PTE and agreement) used in the model. Continuous lines represent references, dashed lines represent functions

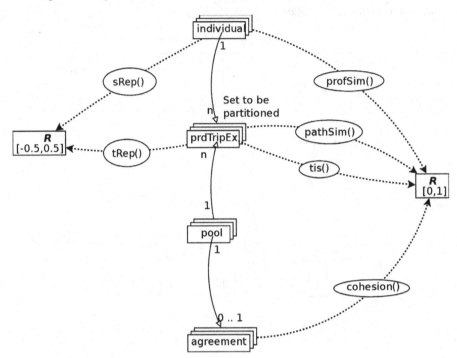

measure the owning individual respects the timing when executing the periodic trip in the *agreement*. *tReputation* is defined for both drivers and passengers. *tReputation* has been defined as a characteristic of a tuple *(PTE,agreement)* and not as a characteristic of an *individual* or of a *PTE* pte_0 because an individual can behave differently on a specific *PTE* in different agreement contexts (pools).

6. Cohesion qualifies the strength of an *agreement* using a value in [0,1] that is a function of attributes of the *agreement* only.

Weights Determination - Learning Mechanism

The weights used to label the edges in the graph, are probability values associated with the success of the negotiation process between individuals. Those

probabilities are calculated by means of *logistic regression* (logit) fed by results of negotiations that have been advised by the *carpoolMatcher*.

Figure 6 summarizes the data dependencies relevant to edge weight determination. From the point of view of the matcher service, the outcome of a negotiation process is a discrete variable with values: *success* (yes) and *failure* (no). Independent variables influencing the negotiation are continuous: *profSim, pathSim, tis, cohesion* and *sReputation*. A *logit* model is used to predict the negotiation outcome. Negotiation results fed back to the *Global CarPooling Matching Service (GCPMS)* are used to determine the coefficients for the *logit* model by linear regression.

Optimisation Problem

The *GCPMS* aim is to maximize carpooling. Hence, the advice is based on maximizing the

Figure 5. Activities ($a_{A,0}, a_{B,0},$ $a_{C,0}$) for individuals A, B and C and the associated trips. The valid departure intervals $i_{d,A}$, $i_{d,B}$, $i_{d,C}$ are shown. Note that B can choose to co-travel with A or C but A and C cannot co-travel.

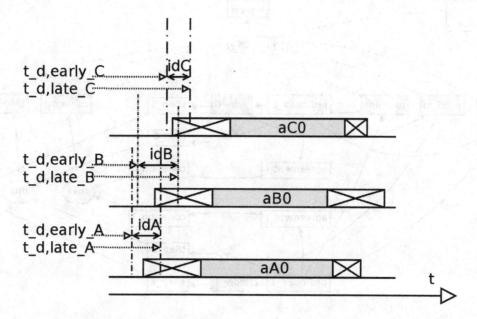

expected value for the negotiation outcomes. This can be written as a linear problem.

The problem formulation can easily be derived from the rightmost graph in Figure 2 as follows. Let $G(V,E)$ with vertex $V=V_p \cup V_v$ set and edge set E denote the bipartite graph of Figure 2. V_v denotes the set of vehicle vertices, V_p denotes the set of *PTE* vertices. A variable x_e is associated with each edge e. Value *one* (*zero*) means that the edge has (not) been selected. $P(e)$ denotes the *PTE* (source vertex) for the edge; $V(e)$ denotes the vehicle used (target vertex). $cap(v)$ denotes the vehicle capacity (defined as the number of seats, including the driver seat). Let $W(p)$ denote the vehicle owned by the owner of the *PTE p*. The weight associated to each edge that links a *PTE* to the owners vehicle, is set to zero because those links do not contribute to the objective of maximizing the number of succeeded negotiations:

$$\forall e \in E : (V(e) = W(P(e)) \Rightarrow (w_e = 0) \quad (1.1)$$

$$maximize \sum_{\epsilon \in E} w_e \cdot x_e$$

Subject to

$$\forall e \in E : x_e \leq 1 \, (1.2)$$

$$\forall p \in V_p : \sum_{\{e \in E | P(e)=p\}} x_e = 1 \, (1.3)$$

$$\forall v \in V_v : \sum_{\{e \in E | V(e)=v\}} x_e \leq cap(v) \, (1.4)$$

Equation 1.2 limits the range of the (boolean) variables. Equation 1.3 requires that each *PTE* shall be assigned to exactly one vehicle (i.e. the trip shall be executed). Equation 1.4 states the limited capacity for each vehicle. Equation 1.5 follows from the requirement that each car be driven by its owner only.

Figure 6. Dependencies between concepts used to calculated the weight for a edge connecting two periodicTripEx's

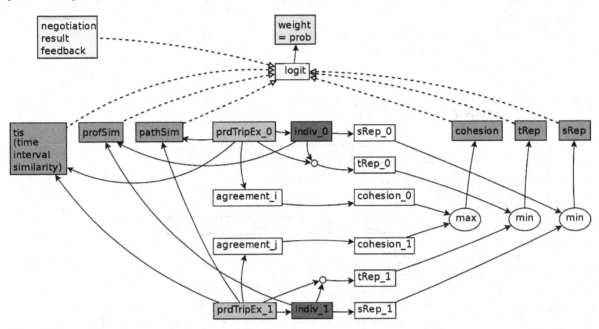

$$\forall v \in V : \left(\exists e \in E \mid \left(V\left(e\right) = v \right) \wedge \left(x_e = 1 \right) \right) \Rightarrow$$

$$\left(\exists f \in E \mid W\left(P\left(f\right) \right) = v \right) \wedge \left(x_f = 1 \right)$$

$$(1.5)$$

Equation 1.5 says that if there is a passenger in the car who possibly is not the car owner, then the car owner is in the car too.

Solving this problem in general requires *integer programming*.

Data Characteristics - Problem Size

Before taking a final decision about the method to choose, we analysed the characteristics of the graph in which to embed an optimal *allocation (pairing)*. From the output of a FEATHERS activity based simulation run for Flanders, we filtered *home-work* trips starting in a given period of time. *Profile* similarity, *path* similarity and *time interval* similarity can be calculated since the origin, destination and start time follow from the FEATH-ERS predictions (9139001 episodes). In order to

calculate time interval similarity we assume that people are prepared to shift the trip start within a time window $[t_0-20[min], t_0+10[min]]$ where t_0 denotes the originally planned time of departure. 20% of the home-work trips starting between 07:30h and 8:00h were selected randomly in order to take into account that not everyone is interested in carpooling. In travel statistics for Flanders, it can be found that about 6% of commuters make use of carpooling.

The 57053 selected trips were paired to calculate profile, path and timeInterval similarity. Since we do not know the relation between those quantities and the negotiation success probability, we assumed the probability to equal the product of the similarities. For profile similarity, we considered the same attributes as (Buliung et al., 2009): socio-economic category, gender and age. Trip pairs having a probability larger than *minProb* were selected and added as edges in the graph. For minProb=0.70 this results in 2203228 edges.

The connected components for the graph were determined. This was repeated for several *minProb* values. Table 3 shows the size (number of vertices) in the eight largest connected components in the graph. It can be seen that for probability threshold values below 0.85 the graph consists of a small amount of very large components and a set of small ones. The occurrence of two giant components is unusual. In this experiment it is caused by the use of an inappropriate high weight for the *gender* attribute in the profile similarity. The case for *minProb* 0.95 is trivial. It consists of thousands of very small components. Cases between 0.875 and 0.925 consist of (large) numbers of cases each one of which can be optimized within a feasible delay: for those cases, a parallel solution method (cluster, cloud computing) makes sense.

Table 4 summarizes network characteristics. Note the difference between the average and largest component sizes in each case. For *minProb=0.75* and lower values, the networks consist of one or a few (very large) components and hundreds of small ones. Note also the remarkable result that the completeness $\frac{nEdges}{nVertices * (nVertices - 1)}$ is of the same order of magnitude for all cases. Completeness is the ratio of the number of edges in the graph to the maximum number of edges possible for the given number of vertices.

Figure 7 shows the frequency distribution for the number of vertices in the connected components for different *minProb* values. *Fat tailed* distributions occur: most cases consist of lots of small components and a few large ones (note that the x-axis has a logarithmic scale).

Figures 8 and 9 show the distributions for the inDegree and outDegree values respectively for several minProb values. The vertex degrees are several orders of magnitudes larger than the car capacity (typically at most 4 or 5). This indicates that brute force search is infeasible because of the need to investigate large number of cases. The number of possible assignments for a specific car equals $\frac{N!}{(N - c)!c!}$ where N is the inDegree of the vertex representing a trip and c is the capacity of the trip owner's car.

Data Characteristics - Problem Size

The problem size explosion (as expected) strongly depends on the *minProb* value and we shall be prepared to solve the scalability problem. If a suf-

Table 3. Size for the eight largest connected components in the graph as a function of minProb

minProb	CS1	CS2	CS3	CS4	CS5	CS6	CS7	CS8
0,700	32096	23155	6	4	3	3	2	2
0,725	31335	22468	6	3	3	3	3	3
0,750	29969	21439	5	5	4	4	4	3
0,775	27888	19827	6	5	5	4	4	4
0,800	24688	17484	16	14	12	9	8	7
0,825	20388	14311	40	18	17	13	10	10
0,850	7154	5620	5288	3255	2459	1205	380	129
0,875	3262	2303	2053	1007	980	941	935	915
0,900	1303	601	523	265	230	219	217	175
0,925	127	120	108	62	57	55	45	38
0,950	3	3	2	2	2	2	2	2
0,975								

Table 4. Graph characteristics for as a function of minimum edge weight (probability) used

probab	nVertices	nEdges	nEdges/nVertices	completeness	Avg CompSize	nComponents
0,750	51812	1013758	19,56608508	0,000378	1036,24	50
0,760	50546	843966	16,69698888	0,000330	856,71	59
0,770	49055	695225	14,17235756	0,000289	700,79	70
0,780	47233	566821	12,00052929	0,000254	704,97	67
0,790	45193	456026	10,09063351	0,000223	551,13	82
0,800	42835	362962	8,473491304	0,000198	424,11	101
0,810	40222	286275	7,117373577	0,000177	302,42	133
0,820	37367	223161	5,972141194	0,000160	217,25	172
0,830	34088	172331	5,055474067	0,000148	176,62	193
0,840	30415	131029	4,308038797	0,000142	144,15	211
0,850	26726	97800	3,659357929	0,000137	102,79	260
0,860	22828	70830	3,10276853	0,000136	78,72	290
0,870	18810	49163	2,613662945	0,000139	54,84	343
0,880	14548	32585	2,23982678	0,000154	37,59	387
0,890	10493	20086	1,914228533	0,000182	26,77	392
0,900	6775	11205	1,653874539	0,000244	15,16	447
0,910	3825	5648	1,476601307	0,000386	9,73	393
0,920	1981	2642	1,333669864	0,000674	7,56	262
0,930	976	1116	1,143442623	0,001173	6,55	149
0,940	334	279	0,835329341	0,002508	4,12	81
0,950	45	24	0,533333333	0,012121	2,14	21

ficiently large population is available (i.e. when sufficient people registered as a customer), it makes no sense to advise people to start a negotiation in case the probability for negotiation success is below 0.85 because sufficient candidates having high negotiation success probability are available. From Table 3 and the diagram in Figure 7 we conclude that a parallel solution to the problem is useful because the problem can be reduced to a series of problems of similar size.

FUTURE RESEARCH DIRECTIONS

The trip matching advisor requires deployment of combinatorial optimization techniques in a dynamic setting. The resulting problem is hard to solve. This complexity adds to the one induced by negotiations. While agents negotiate they need to revise their private schedule (daily or weekly planning). This also has been shown to be a computationally hard problem by itself in the general case where activity resequencing is considered. As soon as cooperation on activities is added to the problem statement so that a required task can be performed by one of a set of people, another level of complexity is added. The latter is not uncommon in daily practice: e.g. bring/get (drop/pick) children at school.

Interesting research paths are: (i) determination of the critical mass of carpooling candidates required to make an advisory service effective

Figure 7. Frequency distribution for the connected components size as for several probability threshold (minProb) values. Distributions are fat tailed

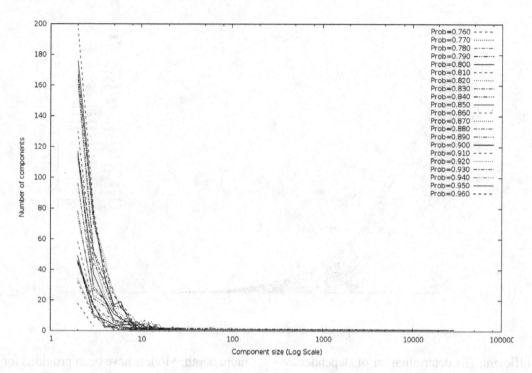

Figure 8. Frequency distribution for the vertex inDegree for several probability threshold (minProb) values

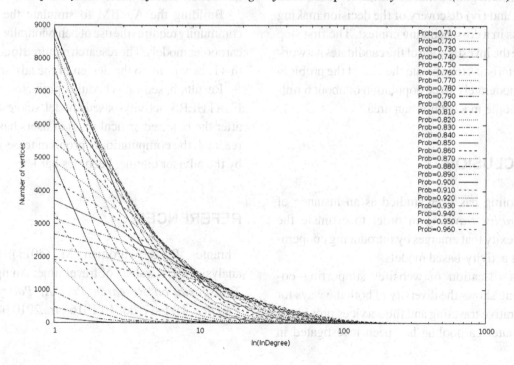

Figure 9. Frequency distribution for the vertex outDegree for several probability threshold (minProb) values

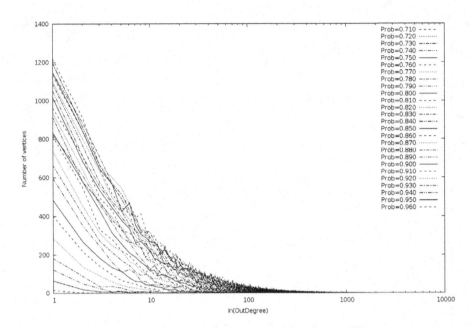

and efficient, (ii) determination of dependency of operational characteristics of a co-traveling supporting service on the spatial distribution of locations used in a particular area, (iii) finding heuristics to good solutions to the co-scheduling proble and (iv) discovery of the decision making process in a co-scheduling context. The first step will be the investigation of the candidates network characteristics to estimate the size of the problem for a moderately sized population of about 6 million people in a semi-urban area.

CONCLUSION

Carpooling has been studied as an instance of *cooperative traveling* in order to estimate the complexity that emerges by introducing cooperation in activity-based models.

Classification of websites supporting co-traveling shows the diversity of both the ways for cooperative traveling and the services provided.[1] Commuter carpooling has been investigated in more depth. Models have been provided for both (i) the engine that constitutes the core of a trip matching advisory service and for (ii) an agent-based model (AgnBM) to exercise such matching advisor for testing and evaluation.

Building the AgnBM to simulate the users community requires the use of behaviourally sound carpooler models. The research required to achieve this is beneficial to the design of the advisor too.

Results based on schedules predicted by the FEATHERS activity-based model suggest that, after the required critical mass of users has been reached, the computational problem to be solved by the advisor engine, becomes hard.

REFERENCES

Abrantes, P., & Wardman, M. (2011). Meta-analysis of UK values of travel time: An update. *Transportation Research Part A, Policy and Practice, 45*, 1–17. doi:10.1016/j.tra.2010.08.003.

Agatz, N., Erera, A., Savelsbergh, M., & Wang, X. (2010). *Sustainable passenger transportation: Dynamic ride-sharing* (Research Paper No. ERIM Report Series Reference No. ERS-2010-010-LIS). Rotterdam, The Netherlands: Erasmus University of Rotterdam.

Arentze, T., Pelizaro, C., & Timmermans, H. (2005). Implementation of a model of dynamicactivity-travel rescheduling decisions: An agent-based micro-simulation framework. In *Proceedings of CUPUM 05*. London: CUPUM.

Auld, J., Mohammadian, A., & Roorda, M. (2009). Implementation of a scheduling conflict resolution model in an activity scheduling system. In *Proceedings of the TRB 2009 Annual Meeting* (Vol. 88). Washington, DC: TRB (Transportation Research Board).

Bellemans, T., Bothe, S., Cho, S., Giannotti, F., Janssens, D., & Knapen, L. et al. (2012). *An agent-based model to evaluate carpooling at large manufacturing plants*. Niagara Falls, NY: Procedia Computer Science. doi:10.1016/j. procs.2012.08.001.

Buliung, R., Soltys, K., Habel, C., & Lanyon, R. (2009). The driving factors behind successful carpool formation and use. *Transportation Research Record*, 2118.

Burris, M., Christopher, E., DeCorla-Souza, P., Greenberg, A., Heinrich, S., & Morris, J. et al. (2012). *Casual carpooling scan report*. Washington, DC: Office of Transportation Management Congestion Management and Pricing Team Federal Highway Administration..

Car Sharing, An Alternative to Car Rental and Car Ownership – Zipcar. (2012). Retrieved from http://www.zipcar.com/

Carpool Solutions for University and Corporate Networks. (2012). Retrieved from http://www. zimride.com

Cho, S., Yasar, A., Knapen, L., Bellemans, T., Janssens, D., & Wets, G. (2012). *A conceptual design of an agent-based interaction model for the carpooling application*. Niagara Falls, NY: Procedia Computer Science. doi:10.1016/j. procs.2012.06.103.

Chun, H. W., & Wong, R. Y. (2003). N* - An agent-based negotiation algorithm for dynamic scheduling and rescheduling. *Advanced Engineering Informatics*, (17): 1–22. doi:10.1016/ S1474-0346(03)00019-3.

Doherty, S., & Axhausen, K. W. (1999). The development of a unified modeling framework for the household activity-Trave 1 scheduling process. In *Traffic and mobility: Simulation-economics-environment* (pp. 35–56). Berlin: Springer. doi:10.1007/978-3-642-60236-8_3.

Doherty, S., Lee-Gosselin, M., Burns, K., & Andrey, J. (2002). Household activity rescheduling in response to automobile reduction scenarios. *Transportation Research Record*. doi:10.3141/1807-21.

Dynamic Rideshareing. (2012). Retrieved from http://dynamicridesharing.org/

Enterprise Rideshare - Vanpool & Rideshare Services for Individuals, Employers & Government Agencies. (2012). Retrieved from http://www. enterpriserideshare.com/vanpool/en.html

Gan, L. P., & Recker, W. (2008). A mathematical programming formulation of the household activity rescheduling problem. *Transportation Research Part B: Methodological*, 42, 571–606. doi:10.1016/j.trb.2007.11.004.

Ghoseiri, K. (2012). *Dynamic rideshare optimized matching problem*. (PhD thesis). University of Maryland, University Park, MD. Retrieved from http://drum.lib.umd.edu/handle/1903/13023

Gruebele, P. (2008). *Interactive system for real time dynamic multi-hop carpooling* (Tech. Rep.). Retrieved from http://dynamicridesharing.org/

Guo, J., Nandam, S., & Adams, T. (2012). A data collection framework for exploring the dynamic adaptation of activity-travel decisions. Tampa, FL: TRB (Transportation Research Board)..

Guo, J. Y. Nandam, & Adams. (2012). *A data collection framework for exploring the dynamic adaptation of activity-travel decisions* (Tech. Rep.). Madison, WI: Department of Civil and Environmental Engineering University of Wisconsin – Madison. Retrieved from http://onlinepubs.trb.org/

Joh, C. (2002). Modeling individuals' activity–travel rescheduling heuristics: Theory and numerical experiments. *Transportation Research Board of the National Academies*, 16– 25.

Joh, C. (2003). *Estimating non-linear utility functions of time use in the context of an activity schedule adaptation model*. Lucerne, France: Academic Press..

Kamar, E., & Horvitz, E. (2009). Collaboration and shared plans in the open world: Studies of idesharing. In *Proceedings of the Twenty-First International Joint Conference on Artificial Intelligence*. Pasadena, CA: IJCAI Organization.

Knapen, L., Keren, D., Yasar, A., Cho, S., Bellemans, T., & Janssens, D. et al. (2012). *Analysis of the co-routing problem in agent-based carpooling simulation*. Niagara Falls, NY: Procedia Computer Science. doi:10.1016/j.procs.2012.06.106.

Knapen, L., Keren, D., Yasar, A., Cho, S., Bellemans, T., & Janssens, D. et al. (2013). *Estimating scalability issues while finding an optimal assignment for carpooling*. Halifax, Canada: Procedia Computer Science. doi:10.1016/j.procs.2013.06.051.

Knapen, L., Muhammad, U., Bellemans, T., Janssens, D., & Wets, G. (2012). Framework to evaluate rescheduling due to unexpected events in an activity-based model. In *Proceedings of TRB 2013 Annual Meeting*. Washington, DC: TRB.

Knapen, L., Yasar, A., Cho, S., Keren, D., Dbai, A. A., Bellemans, T., et al. (2013). Exploiting graph-theoretic tools for matching in carpooling applications. *Journal of Ambient Intelligence and Humanized Computing*.

Kothari, A. (2004). *Genghis - A multiagent carpooling system*. (B.Sc Thesis). University of Bath, Bath, UK.

Lu, Q. (2011). On pre-processing for least-cost carpooling routing in a transportation network. In *Proceedings of IARIA* (pp. 62 - 68). IARIA.

Luetzenberger, M., Masuch, N., Hirsch, B., Ahrndt, S., & Albayrak, S. (2011). Strategic behaviour in dynamic cities. In D. Weed (Ed.), *Proceedings of the 43rd Summer Computer Simulation Conference*, (pp. 148–155). IEEE.

Manzini, R., & Pareschi, A. (2012). A decision-support system for the car pooling problem. *Journal of Transportation Technologies,* (2), 85–101.

Menczer, W. (2007). Guaranteed ride home programs. *Journal of Public Transportation*, *10*(4), 131–150.

Metro Carpooling Made Easy. (2013). Retrieved from http://metro.kingcounty.gov/tops/van-car/carpool.html

Murray, G., Chase, M., Kim, E., & McBrayer, M. (2012). *Ridesharing as a complement to transit - A synthesis of transit practice*. Washington, DC: Transportation Research Board..

Nassauer, S. (2009). Zipcar plans partnership with zimride. *Wall Street Journal*. Retrieved from http://online.wsj.com/article/0,SB123915473346099771,00.html

Nijland, L., Arentze, T., Borgers, A., & Timmermans, H. J. (2009). Individuals' activity-travel rescheduling behaviour: experiment and model-base d analysis. *Environment & Planning A, 41,* 1511–1522. doi:10.1068/a4134.

Nijland, L., Arentze, T., & Timmermans, H. (2008). Multi-day activity scheduling reactions to planned activities and future events in a dynamic agent-based model of activity-travel behaviour. In *Design & decision support systems in architecture and urban planning*. Eindhoven, The Netherlands: University of Technology..

Nurminen, J., Pakarinen, K., & Hartikainen, J. (2011). *Carpool application quick guide*. Nokia. Retrieved from https://projects.developer.nokia.com/carpoolwindowsphone

Rindt, C., & McNally, M. (2002). *An agent-based activity microsimulation kernel using a negotiation metaphor* (Tech. Rep. No. UCI-ITS-AS-WP-02-7). Irvine, CA: Department of Civil & Environmental Engineering and Institute of Transportation Studies, University of California.

Ronald, N. (2012). *Modelling the effects of social networks on activity and travel behaviour*. (PhD thesis). TUE, Eindhoven, The Netherlands.

Ronald, N., Arentze, T., & Timmermans, H. J. (2012). Modeling social interactions between individuals for joint activity scheduling. *Transportation Research Part B: Methodological, 46*(2), 276–290. doi:10.1016/j.trb.2011.10.003

Roorda, M., & Andre, B. (2007). Stated adaptation survey of activity rescheduling empirical and preliminary model results. *Transportation Research Record, 2021*, 45–54. doi:10.3141/2021-06

Shewmake, S. (2010). *Can carpooling clean the air? The economics of HOV lanes, hybrid cars and the clean air act*. (Doctor of philosophy dissertation). University of California, Davis, CA.

Trasarti, R., Pinelli, F., Nanni, M., & Giannotti, F. (2011). Mining mobility user profiles for car pooling. In *Proceedings of the 17th ACM SIGKDD International Conference on Knowledge Discovery and Data Mining* (pp. 1190–1198). New York, NY: ACM. Retrieved from http://doi.acm.org/10.1145/2020408.2020591

Ungemah, D., Goodin, G., Dusza, C., & Burris, M. (2007). Examining incentives and preferential treatment of carpools on managed lane faci lities. *Journal of Public Transportation, 10*(4), 151–170.

Varrentrapp, K., Maniezzo, V., & St¨utzle, T. (2002). *The long term car pooling problem on the soundness of the problem formulation an d proof of NP-completeness* (Technical Report No. AIDA-02-03). Darmstadt, Germany: Fachgebiet Intellektik, Fachbereich Informatik, TU Darmstadt.

Vlaamse-Overheid, & Traject-NV. (2007). *Onderzoek naar hinderpalen en voorwaarden voor het succesvol promoten van carpooling* (Tech. Rep.). Vlaamse Overheid. Retrieved from http://www.mobielvlaanderen.be/studies/carpoolen02.php?a=18

KEY TERMS AND DEFINITIONS

Activity Based Model: Model of reality that predicts timing and location of daily activities for people in order to derive travel demand.

Agent Based Model: Software technique that builds solution from autonomous cooperating intelligent software agents.

Carpooling: Combining, in a structural way, spatially and temporarily similar trips for several people in order to perform them collectively using a single car. This is a form of co-traveling.

Car Sharing: The process of booking a vehicle for personal use during a limited time (similar to car renting).

DCPP: Daily Car Pool Problem: pools are formed on a daily basis. People commit to commute in a given pool for a single day.

Dial-a-Ride: (DAR, DART) is a public transport service for people whose disability or health condition prevents them from using the regular fixed-route transit services.

Emergency Ride Home: Insurance concept to return home in emergency cases without making use of the pool vehicle/driver.

FSM: Four step model.

Guaranteed Ride Home: Insurance concept to overcome carpooling return trip unavailaility.

HOV: High occupancy vehicle

LCPP: Also LTCPP: Long Term Car Pool Problem: Pools are formed for a indefinitely long time and each member in turn becomes the driver. The idea is to minimize the number of cars on the road.

Paratransit: See Dial-a-Ride.

Ridesharing: Combining specific (one-time) car trips in an ad hoc manner to perform them simultaneously using a single car.

Schedule: Agenda, list of activities to be performed by an individual in a given period of time

VOT: Value of time.

ENDNOTES

[1] The authors express their gratitude to Samaneh Hosseinzadeh Bahreini who contributed to surveying carpooling related websites.

Chapter 13
The Evolution from Electric Grid to Smart Grid

Jesus Fraile-Ardanuy
Universidad Politecnica de Madrid, Spain

Dionisio Ramirez
Universidad Politecnica de Madrid, Spain

Sergio Martinez
Universidad Politecnica de Madrid, Spain

Jairo Gonzalez
Universidad Politecnica de Madrid, Spain

Roberto Alvaro
Universidad Politecnica de Madrid, Spain

ABSTRACT

In this chapter, an overview of electric power systems is presented. The purpose is to describe the structure and operation of the power system and its evolution to the new smart grids. The first section gives an introduction about the electric grid and its evolution. Then, there is a section with a brief description of the different components of the electric power system: generation, transmission, distribution, and consumption. The third section is related to power system control, explaining why control actions are necessary in the power system to maintain the balance between supply and consumption and to keep constant the system frequency (at 50 or 60 Hz). In order to understand future applications of electric vehicles, it is important to present a fourth section related to fundamentals of the electricity markets. The chapter finishes with a description of the future power systems with high penetration of intermittent renewable energies, energy storage capacity, active demand management, and integration with telecommunication infrastructure.

INTRODUCTION TO ELECTRICAL POWER SYSTEMS

Electricity is an important form of energy due to the versatility, immediacy, and cleanness in its use. According to the International Electrotechnical Commission (1985), an electrical power system is the set of "all installations and plants provided for the purpose of generating, transmitting and distributing electricity". Although this broad definition can be applied to systems of very different size, from a simple load supplied by a hand-portable engine-generator to a complex nation-wide electrical network, this chapter focuses on interconnected networks linking generators to loads.

DOI: 10.4018/978-1-4666-4920-0.ch013

In a power plant, in general, a primary energy source (e.g., thermal energy from different kind of fuels or the sun, kinetic energy from water or the air) is converted (directly or through some successive transformations) into electrical energy. The generators are the devices at the end of the energy transformation chain in a power plant. They are mainly, but not only, rotating electrical machines. On the opposite part of the power system, the loads are the devices that make use of the electrical energy by converting it into another useful form of energy. The grid is the rest of the power system, and it comprises the lines, cables, transformers, switches, protections, and all the installations needed to convey the electrical energy from the generators to the loads. In some cases, the transmission of electrical energy is done with high voltage direct current (HVDC) links, but the majority of grids are three-phase alternating current (AC) based systems. Figure 1 shows a schematic overview with the main parts of a power system: a generator and its step-up substation, a high voltage transmission line, a distribution system with three successive step-down substations and two distribution lines, and four loads connected at different voltage levels.

Apart from its many benefits, it is important to know some general issues related to the use of electricity as a form of energy that are important to understand the technical challenges that modern power systems have to face. First, electrical energy cannot be stored in a significant amount, thus, at every time instant, the power injected into the grid by all the connected generators has to be equal to the power consumed in the rest of elements of the system, including all the losses. Second, as it covers so many basic needs, it is almost irreplaceable, what, in economic terms, means that the electricity demand is very inelastic. Third, in an electrical grid, the power flows from generators to loads cannot be directed through specific paths, they are subjected to physical laws.

The objective of this chapter is to present a general overview of electrical power systems, their components, how are they operated and controlled, and its evolution to the new smart grids, helping non-specialist readers to understand these concepts.

COMPONENTS OF THE ELECTRICAL POWER SYSTEM

As stated before, the four main parts of a power system are: generation, transmission, distribution and consumption. This section describes their main functions and components and introduces some basic tools for the analysis of power systems.

Generation of Electrical Energy

Although there are ways for direct transformation of a primary energy source into electricity, as with photovoltaic panels, the vast majority of electrical energy is generated with rotating electrical generators that are driven by a mechanical device, known as prime mover. The prime mover supplies rotational mechanical energy to the generator,

Figure 1. Schematic overview of a power system

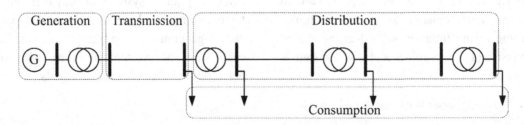

which in turn converts it into electrical energy that is injected into the grid. Different primary energy sources can be used in the prime mover, resulting into different power plant technologies, with different economic and technical characteristics. Depending on the type of prime mover, the most common power plants can be classified in:

- Steam turbine thermal plants (nuclear, coal, oil, gas, biomass, solar, geothermal).
- Combustion thermal plants (gas, Diesel, combined cycle).
- Hydraulic turbine plants (reservoir, run-of-the-river, tidal).
- Wind turbine plants.
- Photovoltaic plants.

Steam turbine thermal power plants make use of a steam turbine to drive the electrical generator that is coupled in the same shaft. In the turbine, the dry or superheated steam is expanded (its temperature and pressure decrease), thus converting the thermal energy from the steam into rotating mechanical energy. The output steam is condensed in a heat exchanger (condenser or cooling tower) to become liquid water. The water is pumped to a higher pressure and is then heated in a boiler to generate steam and reinitiate the cycle. The necessary heat may come: from a nuclear reaction, from the burning of different fossil fuels (coal, oil, gas) or biomass, from the sun, or from a geothermal source. In general, these plants are very reliable and produce relatively cheap energy, but they are polluting, with low efficiency in the energy conversion (around 35%), low flexibility (it takes several hours to change production), and there is a high variability in the price of fuel (in the case of fossil fuels).

In a combustion thermal power plant, the prime mover is an internal combustion engine: a gas turbine or a reciprocating motor. The fuel, gas or diesel fuel is burned inside the machine and the combustion gasses themselves exert a force on the blades or the pistons that, in turn, drive the electrical generator. In the case of a Diesel power plant, the prime mover is a motor similar to those used in the automotive industry. As their output power can be modified very quickly, even from a standstill, they offer high operation flexibility and are often used as backup generators in industry and buildings. Gas turbine plants are not so fast, but they are still very flexible. In the case of a gas turbine, it is also possible to reuse the exhaust gasses as the heat source for a complementary steam turbine that drives another generator, in what is called a combined cycle power plant, increasing the whole thermal-to-mechanical conversion efficiency (up to 60%), although to the price of lower operational flexibility. Combustion power plants in general require lower capital costs and construction times than steam turbine plants, but operating costs are higher due to high fuel prices.

In hydraulic power plants, the prime mover is a hydraulic turbine that transforms the energy of moving water into rotational mechanical energy. The power is proportional to the product of water flow and hydraulic head, the pressure difference between the inlet and the outlet of the turbine. In reaction turbines the pressure fall is directly converted into mechanical energy. In action turbines, the potential energy of water is first converted into kinetic energy and then transformed into rotational mechanical energy. It is possible to store hydraulic energy in reservoirs. In run-of-the-river plants, where there is no reservoir or its capacity is negligible, all the water has to be turbined as it pass or it is wasted. In pumped-storage plants, there are two reservoirs at different elevations, so the water can be pumped to store energy in off-peak demand hours and turbined to generate electricity during peak demand hours, constituting the most flexible power plants in a system.

In a wind generator, the prime mover is a wind turbine, which transforms the kinetic energy of moving air into mechanical energy to drive an electrical generator. Aggregations of wind generators form a wind plant or farm. Wind energy is a non dispatchable energy source and its production is very variable and difficult to predict with accuracy. However it is a clean and renewable energy with no fuel costs.

In photovoltaic plants there is no prime mover. The electromagnetic energy from sun radiation is directly converted into electricity in a solar panel, with similar characteristics to wind energy.

Transmission and Distribution of Electrical Energy

As previously stated, in a power system, the transmission and distribution subsystems transport the electrical energy from the generators to the loads. They include the lines, cables, transformers, switches, protections, and all the necessary installations.

The main components of the transmission system are the high voltage power lines. Their function is to transport large amounts of electrical power over long distances, from generation plants to large consuming areas. Electrical power is proportional to the product of voltage and current, thus the current is inversely proportional to the voltage for the same amount of energy transmitted. As the transmission losses associated to the current flow through a line are proportional to the square of the current, the transmission efficiency increases with higher voltage levels. Therefore, the transmission lines are operated at the highest voltage levels in a power system.

Unlike the most simplified representation of the power system shown in Figure 1 (just one line from generation to distribution), a normal transmission system is a mesh of interconnected lines, offering alternative paths for the power flows. In the event of the lost of a major component of the transmission system (a line or a transformer), the power flows are redistributed in the grid so that the energy demanded by loads can be supplied. Thus, a meshed transmission grid confers service security to the system.

Substations are the other major component of a transmission system. These installations serve different purposes: to be the interconnection nodes of lines in the grid, to perform transformation between different transmission voltage levels, to provide for line switching or sectioning, to connect reactive compensation equipment, to take electrical measurements, or to house protection equipment.

The distribution system connects the transmission system with the large amount of electricity final consumers. As there are loads with very different power consumption, the distribution grid delivers electrical energy at different voltage levels, as it is schematically shown in Figure 1 where three step-down substations are represented. The components of the distribution network are similar to those of the transmission system: lines, cables, transformers, switches, protections..., adapted to lower voltage levels. As opposed to the transmission grid, the distribution lines are connected radially, for simplicity of operation and protection. This means that there are no parallel paths simultaneously connected. However, the power lines are normally sectionalized, so they can be reconfigured off-line to offer alternative paths if needed.

Consumption of Electrical Energy

Electrical energy can be delivered to consumers by the distribution network at different voltage levels. The greater is the amount of energy consumed, the higher is the voltage level. Great industrial consumers are connected to the higher distribution voltage levels or even to the transmission grid directly. On the other side, residential consumers are connected to the lowest voltage part of the distribution system.

There is a multitude of electrical equipment that makes use of electricity, with many different characteristics and power consumption levels, from miliwatts to megawatts. The most common industrial loads include large electric motors, driving multiple kinds of machinery (fans, pumps, mills...), as the main component of their electrical energy use, but there are also some large consumers with specialized loads (arc furnaces, electrolysis…). Motors are also the main electricity consumers in commercial and residential loads, but electric heating and lighting are important too.

The aggregation of the electricity demand of a given area constitutes the power objective to be covered by the area operator (distribution or transmission operator) at every single instant in time with the available resources: energy resources but also grid capacity limits. Despite this aggregated power demand varies constantly, it has to be supplied. Fortunately its evolution can be forecast with relative accuracy so that the availability of generation can be planned in advance to the real time operation of the system. Figure 2 shows the daily evolution of the actual demand and the day ahead forecast in a power system.

Electrical Power System Analysis

As it has been shown in the previous sections, there are numerous different components in an electrical power system. Many of them (generators, loads, communication network…) constitute highly sophisticated systems by themselves, so that

the power system as a whole is amongst the most complex systems ever built. As a consequence, the design, operation and control of power systems are complicated engineering tasks that require the use of specialized analysis tools. However, with a relatively simple modeling of components, it is possible to describe the general behavior of the system and to understand the most relevant phenomena that can take place.

In the steady state operation of an AC system, voltage (u) and current (i) are sinusoidal periodic waveforms:

$$u(t) = U\sin(2\pi f\, t + \varphi_u)$$
$$i(t) = I\sin(2\pi f\, t + \varphi_i)$$

where U and I are the r.m.s. values of voltage and current, f is the system frequency, t is the time instant, and φ_u and φ_u are the initial phase angle for voltage and current. They can be represented in the complex domain as phasors U and I. If the imaginary unit is denoted by j ($j^2 = -1$):

$$\underline{U} = U\exp(j\varphi_u) = U$$
$$\underline{I} = I\exp(j\varphi_i) = I$$

Figure 2. Daily evolution of power system demand (actual and day ahead forecast)

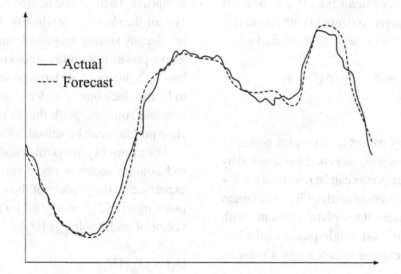

Two-terminal elements, i.e. elements having two terminals (resistors, reactors, capacitors, voltage or current sources...), are the basic components of electric circuits. *Passive elements* are those for which the time integral of the instantaneous power cannot be negative over any time interval beginning at an instant before the first supply of electric energy. A *two-terminal passive element* can be represented by its *complex impedance* ($Z = R + j X$) or *admittance* ($Y = G + j B$), so that $U = Z I$ or $I = Y U$. The instantaneous power absorbed or consumed by a generic two-terminal element can be expressed as the product of the instantaneous voltage and current:

$$p(t) = u(t) i(t) = U I[\cos(\varphi_u - \varphi_i) - \cos(4\pi ft + \varphi_u + \varphi_i)]$$

The average power consumed by the element is called *active power* or *real power* (*P*). If the phase shift between voltage and current in the element is denoted by φ (i.e., $\varphi = \varphi_u - \varphi_i$), the active power can be expressed as:

$$P = U I\cos\varphi$$

The product of the voltage and current r.m.s. values is called *apparent power* (*S*) and the term $\cos\varphi$ is called *power factor* (i.e., $P = S \cos \varphi$). If the complex conjugate is denoted with an asterisk sign (*), the *complex power* (*S*) is defined as:

$$\underline{S} = \underline{U}\,\underline{I}^* = U I = S = S\exp(j\varphi) = S\cos\varphi + jS\sin\varphi$$

The imaginary part of the complex power (*S* sin φ) is called *reactive power* and it is denoted by *Q*. So the complex power can be rewritten as: $S = P + j Q$. In power system analysis it is a common practice to represent three-phase elements with one-line diagrams and single-phase equivalent circuits, and to express quantities in a per-unit

(p.u.) system, so that all the previous expressions are formally analogous.

The *power flow*, or *load flow*, is the basic mathematical tool for the analysis of power systems. It is used in the operation of the system to know its state, in contingency analysis, as a planning tool to test how the system would work with new generating or grid elements... The power flow models the electrical behaviour of grid elements (lines, transformers, compensation equipment...) and the grid topology. From input data about the power generation and load, the primary output of a power flow is the set of voltage phasors (magnitude and phase) at all the grid nodes. And, from these, it is possible to calculate the current and the active and reactive power flows through every element of the system, i.e., the output of a power flow is the complete characterization of the electrical state of the system.

More precisely, in an electrical network, there are some points, known as *PQ buses*, in which the active and reactive powers are the known variables of the problem, as in a load node or in a substation. In the rest of the nodes (*PV buses*), there are connected generators, which define the active power injected into the grid and, in addition, the nodal voltage magnitude in order to keep acceptable operating conditions in the system, by means of the necessary reactive power generation or consumption. There is one degree of freedom in the system, the *slack bus*, in which the known variables are the bus voltage magnitude and phase. As the active power injected is an unknown variable, a bus with one or more large generators is chosen to be the slack bus, in order to accommodate the possible solution. With this in mind, the power flow problem can be solved with nodal analysis.

For a power system with *n* nodes, the complex *n*x1 column vector of nodal currents $[I_N]$ can be expressed as the product of the *n*x*n* nodal admittance matrix $[Y_N]$ multiplied by the *n*x1 column vector of nodal voltages $[U_N]$:

$$[I_N] = [Y_N]\,[U_N]$$

where I_{Ni}, the i-th element in $[I_N]$, is the phasor current entering the i-th node from the generator (or set of generators) or load connected to the bus. Similarly, U_{Ni}, the i-th element in $[U_N]$, is the i-th nodal voltage. Y_{Nij}, the element in row i and column j in $[Y_N]$, is: for $i \neq j$, minus the sum of the complex admittances of all elements that link the nodes i and j directly, and, for $i = j$, the sum of the complex admittances of all elements connected to node i, including shunt elements (reactors or capacitors intended to be connected in parallel with the network). For example, in Figure 3:

$$Y_{Nij} = -1/Z_{sij}$$

$Y_{Nii} = Y_{shi} + 1/Z_{sij} + Y_{pij} +$ the corresponding admittances for the links not shown in the figure

$Y_{Njj} = Y_{shj} + 1/Z_{sij} + Y_{pji} +$ the corresponding admittances for the links not shown in the figure .

The nodal current for a PQ node i can be expressed in terms of the complex power injected in the bus by the PQ load, $S_i = U_{Ni} I_{Ni}^*$:

$$S_i^* / U_{Ni}^* = I_{Ni}$$

Or, in terms of nodal voltages and admittances:

$$(P_i - jQ_i) / U_{Ni}^* = Y_{Ni1}U_{N1} + \cdots$$
$$+ Y_{Nii}U_{Ni} + \cdots + Y_{Nin}U_{Nn}$$

This nonlinear equation can be solved for U_{Ni} with a recursive algorithm. For example, with the Gauss method, the i nodal voltage at iteration k, $U_{Ni}^{(k)}$, can be expressed in terms of the voltages from the previous iteration, $U_{Ni}^{(k-1)}$:

$$U_{Ni}^{(k)} = [(P_i - jQ_i) / U_{Ni}^{*(k-1)} - (Y_{Ni1}U_{N1}^{(k-1)} + \cdots + Y_{Ni(i-1)}U_{Ni-1}^{(k-1)} + Y_{Ni(i+1)}U_{Ni+1}^{(k-1)} + \cdots + Y_{Nin}U_{Nn}^{(k-1)})] / Y_{Nii}$$

For power systems with a large number of buses, more advanced algorithms have to be used, as the Newton-Raphson method. Regardless of the algorithm, once the problem is solved, all node voltages are available in magnitude and phase, thus the current or power flow in every element of the system can be directly calculated from the element model and the bus voltages at both terminals of the element. For example, the

Figure 3. Detail of buses i and j of a power system and the link (line or transformer) between them. All generators and PQ loads connected to each bus are grouped in a block, and all shunt passive elements (reactors or capacitors) are represented by their equivalent shunt admittance. The link between buses is represented by its Π equivalent model (a lumped parameter circuit in which the electrical behavior of the link is modeled with one series impedance and two parallel impedances). The dotted line represents the part of a bus where other possible links (not shown in the figure) may be connected.

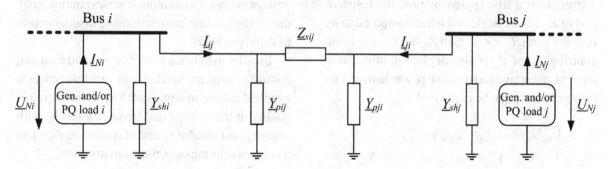

current flowing from bus i to the link between buses i and j in Figure 3 is:

$$I_{ij} = Y_{pij} U_{Ni} + (U_{Ni} - U_{Nj}) / Z_{sij}$$

As a simple example, let us consider a power system with four buses: bus 1 is the slack node, with a generator that controls the voltage at 1.03 p.u.; bus 2 is a PV node, with a generator that injects 0.5 p.u. active power and controls the voltage at 1.02 p.u.; and buses 3 and 4 are PQ nodes with complex power consumption $0.4 + j\,0.2$ p.u. and $0.6 + j\,0.4$ p.u., respectively. In addition, there is a shunt capacitor connected in bus 4 with $Y_{sh4} = j\,0.1$ p.u. There are four lines linking the buses with the following characteristics: $Z_{s12} = 0.03 + j\,0.06$ p.u., $Y_{p12} = Y_{p21} = 0.01 + j\,0.03$ p.u.; $Z_{s13} = 0.02 + j\,0.04$ p.u., $Y_{p13} = Y_{p31} = 0.01 + j\,0.02$ p.u.; $Z_{s24} = 0.02 + j\,0.04$ p.u., $Y_{p24} = Y_{p42} = 0.01 + j\,0.02$ p.u.; $Z_{s34} = 0.03 + j\,0.06$ p.u., $Y_{p34} = Y_{p43} = 0.01 + j\,0.03$ p.u. From these characteristics, the resulting elements of the nodal admittance matrix can be: $Y_{N11} = 15.02 - j\,34.95$ p.u., $Y_{N22} = 15.02 - j\,34.95$ p.u., $Y_{N33} = 14.02 - j\,31.95$ p.u., $Y_{N44} = 14.02 - j\,31.85$ p.u., $Y_{N12} = Y_{N21} = -5 + j\,15$ p.u., $Y_{N13} = Y_{N31} = -10 + j\,20$ p.u., $Y_{N14} = Y_{N41} = 0$ p.u., $Y_{N23} = Y_{N32} = 0$ p.u., $Y_{N24} = Y_{N42} = -10 + j\,20$ p.u., $Y_{N34} = Y_{N43} = -4 + j\,12$ p.u. Voltages at PQ buses from the results of the power flow are: $U_3 = 1.011$ p.u. and $U_4 = 1.002$ p.u.

In terms of power flows, the complex power leaving bus i towards bus j: can be computed as $S_{ij} = U_{Ni} I_{ij}^*$. This is a rather complicated expression, but with some simplifications, it can be used to show some general behaviour of power flows in a system. At a first approximation, the resistive part of Z_{sij} can be neglected when compared to its reactive part ($R_{sij} << X_{sij}$), so $Z_{sij} \approx j\,X_{sij}$, and if the contribution of Y_{pij} is also neglected, after some algebra, the active and reactive power leaving bus i towards bus j can be expressed as:

$$P_{ij} = U_{Ni} U_{Nj} \sin (\varphi_{UNi} - \varphi_{UNj}) / X_{sij}$$
$$Q_{ij} = U_{Ni} [U_{Ni} - U_{Nj} \cos (\varphi_{UNi} - \varphi_{UNj})] / X_{sij}$$

where U_{Ni} and φ_{UNi} denote the magnitude and phase of U_{Ni}. These expressions show that, generally speaking: active power flow depends on the phase difference between bus voltages, flowing from higher to lower phases, and reactive power flow depends on the magnitude difference between bus voltages, flowing from higher to lower voltage magnitudes.

This idea can be expressed from a different point of view. If a generator increases the active power injected in the grid, the voltage phase difference between the bus where it is connected and the rest of the buses also rises. This occurs normally in a power system as a response to an increase in load demand. Apart from the power limits of the generator, this imposes a limit in the transmission capacity, when the phase difference is 90°: $P_{ijmax} = U_{Ni} U_{Nj} / X_{sij}$.

Analogously, if the reactive power injected into a bus is raised, the voltage magnitude of the bus also rises, and vice versa. The system operator takes advantage of this behaviour for the purpose of voltage control.

POWER SYSTEM CONTROL

In electric power systems, generation and consumption must be balanced continuously due to the lack of large electricity storage capacity.

Generation can suddenly vary due to a fault in large power plants (where their generators are disconnected from the electric grid) or due to the intermittency of its primary energy source, for example in renewable energy systems such as wind or solar energy. Consumption varies continuously due to the random connection and disconnection of different loads.

In order to balance power supply and demand, control actions are needed to ensure that power is supplied to the consumers with a certain degree of quality in the voltage and frequency levels, with security and reliability and at minimum cost and an acceptable impact on the environment.

Understanding Electric Generators and their Control

As stated in the previous section, large power plants use alternators (also called synchronous generators) to convert mechanical energy from their prime movers to a.c. electrical energy as it is shown in Figure 4. These electrical machines are driven by different types of turbines and they convert this mechanical power input to three-phase electrical power output.

In order to understand how these alternators work, Figure 5 (left) shows the simplest generation machine, consisting of a stationary magnet producing a constant magnetic field (B) and a rotating winding (in this particular case, a single coil) within this magnetic field. The rotating part of this machine is called the rotor and the stationary part is called the stator.

The rotating part of this machine is called rotor and the stationary part is called stator. The rotor of this machine is rotated by the action of a turbine and a sinusoidal voltage is induced in this coil, based on the Faraday's law:

$$e = -\frac{d\varphi}{dt} = \frac{d}{dt}(B\,S\cos\omega t) = BS\omega\sin\omega t$$

Figure 4. Electric generation

Where, e is the voltage induced in the coil and ϕ is the flux through this coil. Flux depends on the coil area, S, and the rotor angular speed, ω. The frequency of this voltage is directly related to the mechanical speed, so the higher angular speed the higher frequency. The voltage amplitude is proportional to the flux and the mechanical speed.

In a real synchronous machine such as the one shown in Figure 5 (right), the magnetic field, B, is not generated by a stationary magnet but by a winding (called field winding) fed by a dc current and located in the rotor. The induced coil located in the rotor in Figure 5 (left) is also replaced by three phase ac windings located in the stator (called armature windings). The rotor of the generator is turned by the turbine, producing a rotating magnetic field, so that this magnetic field induces three-phase voltages within the stator windings.

Therefore, two different loops are necessary to control the generator: frequency can be modified by acting on the mechanical speed, and the induced voltage on the stator windings can be adjusted by modifying the magnetic field B, through the d.c. current applied to the field winding.

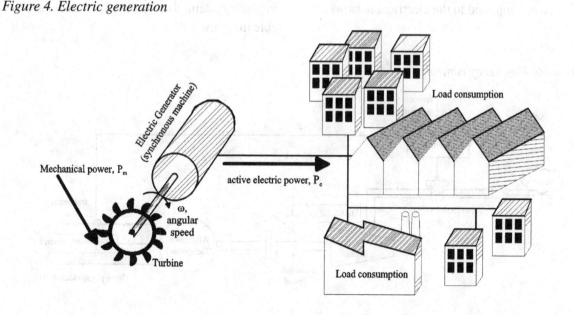

Figure 5. Electric generation fundamentals. A simple rotating coil within a uniform magnetic field (left). Synchronous machine structure (right)

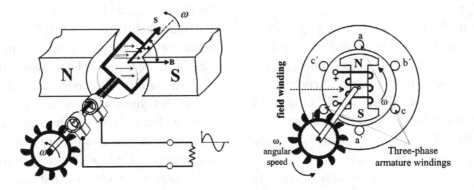

Power System Control Loops

All generators in Continental Europe must operate synchronously to match the changing electrical demand. This synchronous system is named *Union for the Coordination of Transmission of Electricity* (UCTE) system, and in this system, network frequency and voltage are kept nearly constant by two different (and almost uncoupled) control loops:

- **Voltage Regulation:** Acting on the reactive power supplied to the electrical network.
- **Frequency Control:** Acting on the active power supplied to the electrical network.

Frequency Control

At constant speed, the rotor of the alternator is driven by the turbine and there is an active power balance in the generator between the mechanical power supplied by the turbine, P_m, and the electrical active power output, P_e. In this steady state situation, the angular acceleration in this rotational system is zero, and the angular speed is kept constant (see Figure 6).

If the electric load is increased, the electrical active power demand will rise, so the rotor will reduce its angular speed and the frequency will drop. Two nested regulation loops, called primary and secondary controls, are commonly used in power systems to keep frequency under acceptable margins.

Figure 6. Frequency control

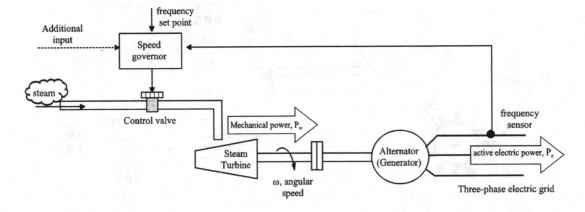

Primary Frequency Control

In this inner loop, also known as Load Frequency Control (LFC), the generator control is equipped with speed governors. This system measures the mechanical speed variation (or the frequency variation in the network) and modifies the mechanical power of the prime mover, changing the valve position to restore the active power balance (and the frequency). For stable operation, the speed governors are designed to allow the speed to drop linearly as the electric load is increased, as shown in the top part of Figure 7.

In steady state, the generator is operating at point a. If the load demand is increased in ΔP_m, then the frequency will drop, Δf, reaching a final frequency of $f_2 = f_1 - \Delta f$.

The slope of the load-frequency characteristic is called speed regulation (or droop) and it is expressed as:

$$R = -\frac{\Delta f}{\Delta P_m}$$

where:

- R is the speed regulation (droop) in per-unit system[1] (p.u.)
- Δf is the frequency change in p.u.
- ΔP_m is the change in the real power in p.u.

Now consider the case of two generators supplying the load as shown in the middle part of Figure 7. In steady state, both generators share the total active power demanded by the load at rated frequency of 50 Hz:

$$P_{m1} + P_{m2} = P_{load}$$

If the load is increased in ΔP_m, then the frequency will drop Δf. The speed governors of each generator will increase the mechanical power of the prime mover according to their drooping characteristics:

$$\Delta f = -R_1 \Delta P_{m1} \quad \Delta f = -R_2 \Delta P_{m2}$$
$$\Delta P_{m1} + \Delta P_{m2} = \Delta P_m$$

$$\Delta f = -\frac{\Delta P_m}{\dfrac{1}{R_1} + \dfrac{1}{R_2}}$$

In large power systems, with n generators connected, the equivalent speed droop will be R_{eq}:

$$\Delta f = -\frac{\Delta P_m}{\dfrac{1}{R_1} + \dfrac{1}{R_2} + \dots + \dfrac{1}{R_n}} = -R_{eq}\Delta P_m$$

In this case, interconnected generators are stiffer systems than a single generator and the frequency deviation due to a given change in load demand is much smaller than in a single power unit.

Secondary Frequency Control

If the electric load is increased, the generator will reduce its angular speed and the frequency will drop. The speed governor will detect this frequency variation and will adjust the steam valve to restore the balance between mechanical power and active power, but frequency reaches a lower final steady state value. This primary control has prevented the system frequency drop to zero, but this frequency does not reach the nominal value of 50 Hz, and a stationary error will remain.

The secondary frequency control, also known as Automatic Generation Control (AGC), will add an additional input to the governor for restoring the frequency to the reference value, as it is shown in Figure 7. Interconnected power systems are divided in different control areas. In a single area system, the restoring action is performed by adding an integral control that removes the steady-

Figure 7. Speed governor characteristics, for a single generator (top) and for two generators (middle) Secondary Control Action (bottom)

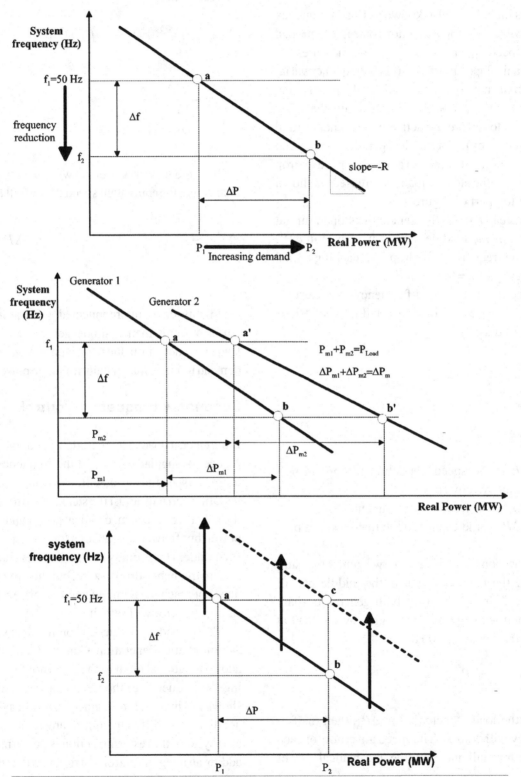

state frequency error. This second control action has a slower dynamic and it will take place after the first primary control loop has stabilized the frequency in an offset steady state value. This additional control action will raise the speed governor characteristics of the generator in steady state to the dotted line in Figure 7 (bottom), shifting the operating point from b to c.

In multiple area systems, each area has to contribute to control the system frequency and also must keep constant the power exchange agreements among different areas.

When load demand is increased in a particular area, a frequency drop occurs in the whole system and the scheduled power interchanges are modified. In this case, control action has to stabilize the system frequency, to eliminate the steady state frequency error and to restore the balance in the power interchanges among different areas. To do this, an area control error (ACE) is defined for each zone. This error is a linear combination of frequency error and power interchange error as shown in the following equation:

$$ACE_i = \sum_{j=1}^{n} \Delta P_{ij} + B_i \Delta f$$

where n is the number of areas, and ΔP_{ij} is the power interchange error between zone i and j and B_i is a frequency-bias factor of area i. Usually, this factor is chosen to be the inverse of the droop. Each generator participating in the AGC will have an ACE additional input.

Voltage Control

Power system operation must keep not only the whole system frequency within acceptable limits, but also the voltage levels in all the nodes through the voltage control.

Voltage magnitudes are controlled at local level by adjusting the injected reactive power in each grid node. Increasing the injected reactive power

will increase the voltage level in this particular bus, while increasing the reactive power absorption in a particular node will reduce its voltage level.

Voltage control in a power system can be carried out by adjusting the production (absorption) of reactive power in different parts of the electric grid. This adjustment is performed by several complementary devices:

- Automatic Voltage Regulators (AVR) in generators.
- On-load tap changer transformers.
- Static shunt capacitors and reactors.
- Static Var Compensators (SVC).
- Static Synchronous Compensators (STATCOM).

Automatic Voltage Regulator (AVR)

The Automatic Voltage Regulator (AVR) of a synchronous generator allows adjusting its terminal voltage within specific limits and controlling the reactive power flow injected in the grid. This is the primary source of reactive power in a power system. Figure 8 shows the AVR regulator principle of operation. In this feedback control system, the terminal voltage is measured and compared with the voltage set point. The action control over the error modifies the direct current fed to the field winding and, so, the generator terminal voltage.

On-Load Tap Changer Transformers

Transformers have a series of taps in their high-voltage windings[2] that allow modifying the rated turns ratio under load, to adjust the terminal voltage (Figure 9).

Static Shunt Capacitors and Reactors

Capacitor banks are connected to some buses in the electrical network aimed to inject reactive power. Shunt capacitors are used to boost voltage levels

Figure 8. Automatic Voltage Regulator

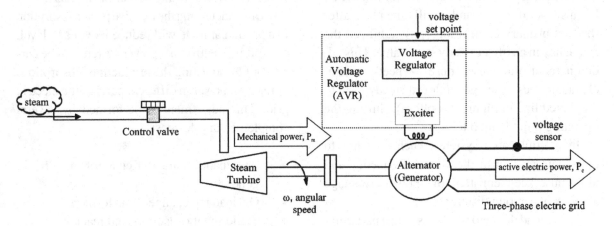

Figure 9. Transformer with on-load tap changer (left) Static Var Compensator (center) Static Synchronous Compensator (right)

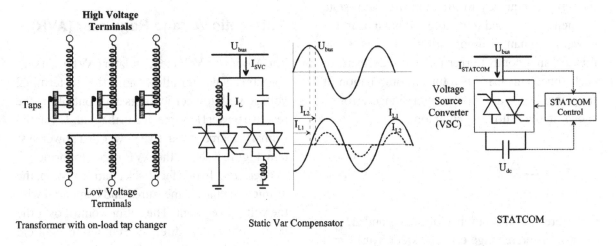

Transformer with on-load tap changer

Static Var Compensator

STATCOM

during heavy loading conditions in transmission systems and to provide power factor correction and voltage control in distribution systems. The main drawback of capacitor banks is that their reactive power output falls when the bus voltage decreases, because the reactive power depends on the square voltage.

Shunt reactors are applied to absorb reactive power from the system, limiting the maximum voltage values in long HV overhead lines. In this kind of lines, there is a significant effect of line capacitance during open circuit or light load conditions.

Static Var Compensators (SVC)

Shunt capacitors, reactors and on-load tap changer transformers provide passive control voltage, and they are connected (or disconnected) to the electric grid discretely.

Conversely, in some situations, it is necessary to continuously regulate the absorption (or generation) of reactive power. Static Var Compensators (SVCs) are static[3] systems based on power-electronics used to compensate voltage variations continuously. Ideally, these systems can adjust reactive power (lagging or leading) instantaneously with no active power consumption. Its operation can be seen as an adjustable shunt capacitor and an adjustable shunt reactor, as shown in Figure 9 (center). With SVCs a one hundred percent power factor correction can be achieved.

This system is composed by a capacitor[4] (or a reactor) which is switched in or out by antiparallel thyristors[5]. Adjusting the firing angle of each thyristor, it is possible to control the amplitude and phase of the current flowing through the capacitor (or reactor), thus adjusting the produced (or absorbed) reactive power.

Static Synchronous Compensator (STATCOM)

In a similar way, the STATCOM can provide continuously variable reactive power in response to voltage deviations. The principle of operation of this system is to synthesize three-phase sinusoidal voltages, using a Pulse Width Modulation (PWM), from a d.c. source (known as voltage-source converter, VSC). By adjusting the amplitudes of these synthesized voltages, it is possible to control the reactive power generated (absorbed) by the STATCOM.

FUNDAMENTALS OF ELECTRICITY MARKETS

In the beginning, electric utilities were vertically centralized, where companies were responsible for large power plants, part of the transmission networks and their own distribution networks and customer billings. These few companies were monopolies, not allowing customers to freely choose among different options. They were obligated to buy electricity to their local electric company. Since early 1990s, different countries around the world started to deregulate the electricity market to benefit consumers. The main objectives of this

deregulation were to get price reductions and more efficient services, making European economy more competitive.

The European Commission has been promoting the electricity liberalization since mid-1990s, reducing regulations, opening up the market to a real competition and allowing consumers and producers to agree on the final price for the electricity.

The main difference between this specific market and other liberalized business like telecommunications, transport or postal services is the difficulty to store electricity in large quantities. Furthermore, supply and demand are changing continuously so it is necessary to have a coordination agent to maintain the reliability in the whole electric power system.

In order to achieve this liberalization it was necessary to identify different activities and agents involved in the process of electricity supply, dividing the monopolistic activities from the competitive ones and avoiding that a single entity could operate in both activities at the same time.

The classic separation of the power system into generation, transmission, distribution and consumption had to be defined again and split between competitive activities (such as generation and trading) and regulated activities (such as electricity transmission).

Electric Market

Electricity can be treated as a commodity that can be separated from transmission as a service and it can be bought, sold and traded in a special market, named electricity market.

Electricity requires the use of the electric grid to connect supply and demand, respecting the technical restrictions imposed by the electric network. This electric grid has to allow the efficient electricity transmission from producers to consumers, with quality, reliability and low operating cost. As stated before, the electrical grid is hierarchized and it is divided in two different levels: high voltage transmission level and distribution level. Both levels are monopolistic activities and they have specific regulations. Typically, transmission level is owned by one company, named Transmission System Operator (TSO) and the distribution activity belongs to different distributing companies covering different parts of the territory.

It is common that European electricity markets are organized in two different parts; a financial electricity operator that is responsible for the electric system economic management and a system operator that is responsible for the electric system technical management. This system operator can be independent (ISO) or it can be the same TSO. In the last case, the system operator is also responsible for the operation and planning of the transmission network.

Market Structure

The market can be organized as a spot market, where generators and consumers match their production and demand offers and determines the energy price. The main drawback of this model

is the uncertainty about the spot price results. In order to avoid this situation, producers and consumers can sign a bilateral trade with each other. In most European countries a hybrid model is used which is a combination between spot market and bilateral agreements, where market participants choose one of the two options.

The Day Ahead Spot Market

In this market, producers submit supply bids and traders and larger consumers submit hourly demand bids for the 24 hours of the following day during the trading session. The financial market operator combines the production and consumption bids for each hour and finds the marginal price and volume as follows: Both agents (producers and consumers) place bids of volume in MWh of electricity and price for every hour of the full time period of 24 hours (for the following day) as shown in Figure 10. The sale curve has a positive slope, indicating the increased costs of providing an additional MWh. This curve depends on the electric energy mix in a country. The purchase

Figure 10. Marginal pricing scheme

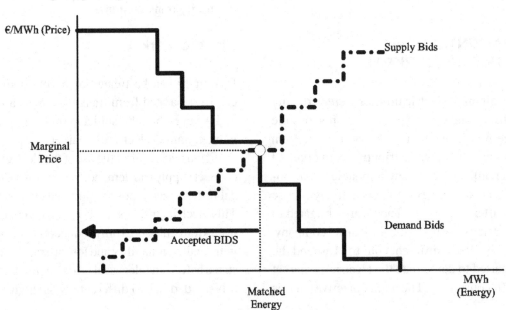

curve has a negative slope, because as prices fall down, demand increase. The marginal price for each hour is defined by the crossing point where supply and demand meet.

This means that all generators with lower operating costs than the marginal price will get benefit from selling their energy to the markets, but producers with operating costs larger than the market price will lose money if they sell energy to the market. At the same time, consumers asking for lower prices than the market price will not be able to buy.

After the marginal price and energy is evaluated, the market operator sends the provisional plan (adding the bilateral contracts) to the TSO, which checks the technical feasibility of such a trade in the electric transmission capacities. If some possible congestion problems are detected by the TSO in this phase, actions are taken to avoid them. Some producers can be taken out from the trade and be replaced by others in order to guarantee the trade technically feasible and a new marginal price and volume is evaluated.

Intraday Markets

Due to the fact that the day-ahead market is closed 12 hours before the first delivery hour, some events could happen during this time which could modify the initial production (or demand) that was traded, so intraday markets are opened to adjust trades done in previous the day-ahead market. Again, the trades on these markets are checked by the TSO to study their technical feasibility.

Ancillary Services

Electricity markets include a mechanism to maintain a continuous power balance between generation and consumption, ensuring a reliable power system. TSO needs appropriate services to deal with sudden variations from the trading based plans with enough quality and security. These tools are named ancillary or auxiliary services and they are normally divided in two parts:

- **Mandatory Services:** Where generators are required as part of their obligation to provide a certain amount of primary regulation and voltage control.
- **Optional Services:** Where generators are remunerated accordingly for different additional offered services as secondary regulation, non-spinning reserve and restoration service.

Other Costs

The final price paid by end-users can be divided in three different parts:

- The price of the energy component is determined by the wholesale electricity price and the additional retailer margin.
- Transmission costs paid for utilization of the transmission and distribution networks.
- Taxes and subsidies to incentive the investments in new technologies as wind or photovoltaic energies.

THE FUTURE POWER SYSTEMS

Introduction to Smart Grids

The Smart Grid term describes a leading edge electrical power system characterized by the wide use of measurements, communications and also by the integration of renewable sources of energy. These kinds of systems will be able to modify demand to match generation in order to achieve greater energy efficiency and promise to be a revolution in generation, distribution and electrical consumption at worldwide level.

Smart Grids have come to stay and they are the key to future Power Systems and are already attracting a lot of investments globally.

In the traditional approach to Power System management, loads are connected or disconnected without intervention from the System Operator (S.O.) or the electrical distributors. Moreover, generation has to be regulated to match consumer demand so that the S.O. has control of all the power flows throughout the electrical lines and is compelled to maintain available spinning reserves (several hundreds MW) to allow an accurate demand tracking.

Nevertheless, nowadays there are new types of energy sources connected to the grid, such as wind farms (with rated powers from 100 to 300 MW) or photovoltaic parks (100 kW to 4 MW) that generate unpredictable amounts of electric power. Also, in the near future, the growth in the use of electric vehicles (every battery car stores energy around 25 kWh and is able to deliver a power up to 150 kW peak) will lead to unmanaged bi-directional flows of electric power throughout the lines. Furthermore, storage systems based on batteries (with a max around 1 MW during 3 hours capacity), ultra-capacitors or even fuel cells (10 kW to 1 MW) will become important to the integration of renewable energies.

Thereby, in order to use Electrical Systems more efficiently and take advantage of distributed renewable sources, closer to consumers than traditional power plants, and match generation to demand, system management has to undergo a complete transformation towards the new concept of Smart Grid. To achieve this, measurements and communications between consumers and electrical distributors will become indispensable.

Among the most innovative aspects of the Smart Grids can found: distributed generation due to renewable generation, management of active demand, electrical measurements, storage systems, new type of hybrid and electric vehicles and the energy efficiency.

Distributed Generation

Smart grid technology will allow the integration of a large number of renewable resources into the distribution grid.

This will be a big advance because, for instance, the new kind of renewable generators are closer to the consumers, so the energy transportation towards the customers is much more efficient due to losses reduction. Also, in the case of isolating areas due to failures in the grid, consumers could be supplied from these generators, thereby taking advantage of the closer location of these generators to the consumers.

Nevertheless, distributed generation have a negative impact on power system stability. Also, it changes the size of fault currents and the current no longer flows unilaterally from the substation but flows into the load, so it has high impact on system operation and protection.

Active Demand Management

Load variation requirements and the intermittent nature of distributed renewable energy sources connected to the grid may, in the near future, create instability and result in overloads and grid faults.

It should be taken into account that the current regulation systems used to control Electrical Power Systems were designed some decades ago and were based on the philosophy of centralized control of generation sources and the grid. According to this philosophy, power flows from power plants towards consumers but, under the new approach, with distributed generation, the electrical power can flow in both directions.

Active demand management allows customer consumption optimization by combining the use of price curves, that may include incentives depending on the hour, and the comfort degree chosen by the customer, and in this way calculating the next day schedule to be applied to the controlled loads (for example, air conditioning).

Active demand management can also be used combined with weather forecasts to make customer power demand previsions for every day, or even actively reduce demand at moments of high consumption thus preventing grid overload.

Another feature of smart grids will be the availability of real time data on customer power consumption. This would be very helpful for carrying out a next day demand prevision; detecting irregular consumption; load planning; setting the whole consumption value or even modifying the price curve to get a better optimization of the relationship between generation and loads.

The main advantages of active demand management will be: a higher integration of renewables energies and a more efficient use of the current facilities because power flow throughout the lines will be more constant than now due to the forecasts, the control on the loads and the customers awareness. Also the integration of electric vehicles will be easier because it will be possible to carry out smart charges and discharges (delivering back energy to the grid) depending on the whole electricity demand. Other advantages are: an earlier response to line faults and lower energy dependence from abroad.

Among the disadvantages we can find: a likely reduction in consumer comfort and the need for big investments to make this technology operational.

Active demand management can be approached from several points of view:

- From the operational one: for instance, if the transmission or distribution operator detects a problem in a node or if the electrical demand cannot be satisfied, it may be necessary to limit the consumption of some customers during a certain time or even disconnect them from the grid.
- From the planning one: it requires a predictive approach and an attempt to influence consumer habits by means of economic incentives and penalties.
- From the domestic environment: by using systems that allow the smart planning of appliances, according to their priority and the daily pricing curve.

- From the social sphere: one of the key aspects is user acceptation but this implies changing their habits, acquired over years, so it will be necessary to raise the population's social awareness in relation to energy saving.

Measurements: Phasor Measurement Unit and Smart Meters

Another fundamental concept of Smart Grids is the measurements and here the key roles are played by the Phasor Measurement Unit (PMU) and the Smart Meters.

On the one hand, a system consisting of a set of PMU devices will address the synchronous measuring of electrical variables at distant points in an electrical grid, thus enabling quick action in the event of disturbance (early detection of faults, voltage drop in lines, etc.) either in super-grids (wide area transmission network covering several countries), regional transmission grids or local distribution grids.

PMU devices must be designed to have a very fast response time but, nevertheless, can be implemented in a special and dedicated device, or otherwise be an additional functionality of protection relays in substations, power plants, etc.

Every PMU must send, approximately, between ten and thirty data sets per second to the Phasor Data Concentrator (PDC) which is in charge of data concentration and data flow management received from the PMU devices in real time (from one to several dozen per PDC). Next, in the central facilities, a SCADA system presents the data of all generators and substations at constant time intervals. No wonder, therefore, that the PMU is considered one of the most important devices for the future successful development of smart grids.

On the other hand, the other important piece of measurements in the Smart Grid puzzle is the Smart Meters.

Since under the new point of view about the electricity consumption, the electricity price can vary depending on time of day, the day of the week and the months of the year (summer or winter), the customer should be able to know his own consumption and the corresponding cost to adapt his habits, by connecting or disconnecting appliances in the household. This is the function that smart meters meet in real time and that is aimed to facilitate match electrical demand and generation.

Smart meters are able to measure the customer consumption throughout the day at fixed intervals and then communicate these data wirelessly to the next stage in the smart control structure, a central computer. Also, may include measurements of surge voltages and harmonic distortion, and detect other power quality problems.

Smart meters include a wireless network interface which allow utility companies to shut off a customer's electricity over the network, known in the industry as 'remote disconnect', may be air conditioning, electric cars, etc.

Some of the benefits that Smart Meters provide to the customers are:

- Accurate and on-time consumption readings and billing.
- Better information on the consumed energy, encouraging energy savings and the energetic efficiency.
- Bidirectional communication with the client, enabling new value added services.
- Flexibility to face regulatory changes.

Use of Smart Meters is also advantageous to the electric system:

- Contribute to improve demand management with the reduction of losses and the overall optimization.
- Allow a better planning.
- Make possible to improve the electrical power system efficiency.
- Make possible the development of smart grids.

Thus, with the use of smart meters, the demand will be able to follow an increasingly variable generation (as consequence of the distributed renewable generation) and as well contribute to consumer education and better awareness of household energy usage. In this way, the user becomes an active part of the system, and can benefit from dynamic tariffs or incentives.

Storage

By using storage systems, the power curve may be smoothed and the predictability may be increased in the cases of renewable sources or punctual power demand originated by electric vehicles charges. In this way, the new kind of distributed generators and storage systems, closer than the big power plants to the consumers, will carry out a fundamental change in the classic grid. Their use will reduce the losses associated with the transport and will produce a more efficient use of energy. As tradeoff, it will appear non-manageable bidirectional power flows so that will be necessary a decentralized control system to manage them and ensure the quality and the supply.

There are several alternatives to implement a strategically distributed storage system, all around the territory. Battery banks, ultracaps or fuel cells can become in an alternative to the gas turbines and diesel generators to cover peaks, but in a distributed way. Likewise, electronic technology will allow in the near future using batteries in electric and hybrid cars as a local storage and contribute to cover peaks of power demand whereas charges will be carried out during off-peak hour or at night.

Storage systems may also contribute to offset the effect of intermittent energy sources, such as solar photovoltaic or wind power, and even may be used to provide ancillary services as frequency control and spinning reserve replacement. In addition, this reserve of energy may allow a higher response capacity to peak demand and a true real time response to the power requirement of loads.

However, in order that storage systems can perform their function, regardless of the type selected in the future, it is necessary that grid have a certain intelligence degree to manage stored energy in the way of a centralized coordination to optimize the charge and discharge processes in relation to the grid.

Storage, when used at substations and generation system levels, can provide peak shaving, load smoothing, shifting in time of the energy generated from renewable sources, voltage stabilization, spinning reserve reduction and reactive power compensation.

Used at local level, storage ensures reliable operation under islanding condition and improves the voltage control as well as provides extra energy for the electric vehicles charge.

Therefore, storage is key to Smart Grids can manage, in a fast, reliable and efficient way changes in the electric power demand.

Furthermore, storage is also an integral part of the called micro-grids. These grids are sometimes consequence of the grid structure itself (an islanding condition, for instance) but it can also appear as consequence of an electrical power supply interruption, when the supply is not reliable or the electricity price is too high. In these cases, there are also renewable generators connected to the micro-grid so that storage becomes again necessary to perform power profile smoothing.

Electric Vehicle

The emergence of electric vehicles in the energetic scenario makes indispensable to study the impact that they will produce on the electrical grid. Management of these new actors means that the control system must have a complete visualization of the overall architecture and adjust load requirements to grid status.

Vehicle to grid (V2G) technology will allow using the batteries in the vehicles like a storage system connected to the grid and deliver electric power towards the grid if necessary, what could bring important benefits for the grid control. However, as aforementioned, this will imply the arising of new no-manageable power flows throughout the electrical lines. This concept is new and it is against the classic Electrical Systems control theory, especially taking into account that the charges will be carried out in locations that can change continuously throughout the day. Accordingly, it will be necessary some kind of smart control, in this case to perform the charge scheduling management depending on to the grid status. Another issue to be considered is the additional battery aging due to V2G applications. Han, Sekyung and Han, Soobee (2013) demonstrated that this application is economically feasible.

To illustrate this application, the energy necessary to accelerate a high speed train (Talgo S102, mass 357 ton) from zero to regime speed (320 km/h) can be stored in around 20 commercial electric vehicles (Nissan Leaf, 24 kWh). Nevertheless, the electrical power needed to be delivered could be constrained by the charger technical specifications. For example, using commercial fast chargers of 50-100 kW the number of vehicles would increase up to 70-40.

Energy Efficiency

Energy efficiency is the reduction of the energy amount necessary to provide products and services, and it is aimed to significantly reduce the world's energy needs and help to control global emissions of greenhouse gases. For instance, at consumer level, it is possible to reduce the electrical consumption, improving the isolation in buildings, using highly efficient household appliances or high efficient lighting.

Indeed, in the new approach of the electrical energy usage, all the leading edge technologies used to perform a smart control of the grid would not make sense if the energy efficiency is not taken into account.

REFERENCES

Han, S., & Han, S. (2013). Economic feasibility of V2G frequency regulation in consideration of battery wear. *Energies, 6,* 748–765. doi:10.3390/en6020748.

International Electrotechnical Commisson. (2013). *Electropedia: The world's online electrotechnical vocabulary.* Retrieved from http://www.electropedia.org/

ADDITIONAL READING

Amoroso, Francesco A., & Gregorio Cappuccino. *Storage: An Indispensable Ingredient in Future Energy.* IEEE Smart Grid. Retrieved March 2013 from http://smartgrid.ieee.org/december-2012

Barrantes, Juan Antonio (Endesa, S.A.) (2012). *Smart Grids. Diseñando el sistema eléctrico del futuro.* CALIDAD, 16-19.

Blume, S. W. (2007). *Electric power system basics for the nonelectrical professional.* Hoboken, New Jersey: John Wiley & Sons, Inc. doi:10.1002/9780470185810.

Borlase, S. (2012). *Smart Grids: Infrastructure, Technology, and Solutions (Electric Power and Energy Engineering).* CRC Press.

Bouhafs, F., & Mackay, M. (2012). *Active Control and Power Flow Routing in the Smart Grid.* IEEE Smart Grid Newsletter, Dec 2012

Carvallo, A., & Cooper, J. (2011). *The Advanced Smart Grid: Edge Power Driving Sustainability.* ARTECH HOUSE.

Chapman, S. J. (2005). *Electric Machinery Fundamentals* (4th ed.). Mc Graw Hill.

Conchado, A., & Linares, P. *Gestión activa de la demanda eléctrica doméstica: beneficios y costes.* Instituto de Investigación Tecnológica, Universidad Pontificia Comillas. 2010. Retrieved March 2013 from http://www.proyectogad.com/

Feijoo, V. José Manuel (Endesa, S.A.). *La importancia de la gestión de la demanda y las redes inteligentes en la operación flexible del sistema.* Asociación empresarial eólica. Retrieved November 2010. http://www.aeeolica.org

Ferrero, R. Mario. *Gestión Activa de la Demanda Eléctrica. Observatorio Regional de la Sociedad de la Información (ORSI).* October 4, 2011. Retrieved March 2013 from http://www.orsi.jcyl.es/web/jcyl/ORSI/es/Plantilla100DetalleFeed/1262860952313/Publicacion/1284193183652/Redaccion

Gellings, C. W. (2009). *The Smart Grid: Enabling Energy Efficiency and Demand Response.* The Fairmont Press, Inc..

Gómez-Exposito, A., Conejo, A. J., & Cañizares, C. (2009). *Electric Energy Systems. Analysis and Operation.* CRC Press.

Hart, David G. *How Advanced Metering Can Contribute to Distribution Automation. IEEE Smart Grid.* Retrieved March 2013 from http://smartgrid.ieee.org/august-2012

Jamasb, T., & Pollitt, M. (2005). *Electricity Market Reform in the European Union: Review of Progress toward Liberalization & Integration.* MIT Center for Energy and Environmental Policy Research. Retrieved March 23, 2013, from http://web.mit.edu/ceepr/www/publications/working-papers/2005-003.pdf

James Momoh, J. (2012). *Smart Grid: Fundamentals of Design and Analysis. IEEE Press Series on Power Engineering.* John Wiley & Sons, Inc. doi:10.1002/9781118156117.

Keyhani, A. (2011). *Design of Smart Power Grid Renewable Energy Systems*. John Wiley-Sons.

Kundur, P. (1994). *Power system stability and control*. New York: McGraw-Hill, Inc..

Mao, Ronald and Julka, Vibhor. *Advanced Metering Infrastructure Using Wireless Broadband Networks*. IEEE Smart Grid. Retrieved March 2013 from http://smartgrid.ieee.org/march-2012

Milano, F. (2010). *Power System Modelling and Scripting*. Springer. doi:10.1007/978-3-642-13669-6.

Mohan, N. (2012). *Electric Power Systems. A First Course*. John Wiley Sons.

Padiyar, K. R. (1996). *Power System Dynamics. Stability and Control*. John Wiley and sons.

Rogers, G. (2000). *Power System Oscillations*. Kluwer. doi:10.1007/978-1-4615-4561-3.

Saadat, H. (2004). *Power System Analysis* (2nd ed.). Mc Graw Hill.

Schavemaker, P., & Van der Sluis, L. (2009). *Electrical Power System Essentials*. John Wiley Sons Soto Martos, Fernando. *Gestión activa de la demanda de energía eléctrica*. Universidad Carlos III de Madrid. Retrieved March 2010 from http://e-archivo.uc3m.es/

Sioshansi, F. P. (2011). *Smart Grid: Integrating Renewable, Distributed & Efficient Energy*. Academic Press, Elsevier.

Wood, A. J., & Wollemberg, B. F. (1996). *Power Generation, Operation, and Control* (2nd ed.). New York: John Wiley & Sons, Inc..

ENDNOTES

[1] A per-unit system is the expression of system quantities as fractions of a defined base unit quantity.

[2] These taps are located in the high-voltage windings instead of in the low-voltage windings, because the current is lower, so it is easier to switch from one tap to the other.

[3] Static means that this system has no rotating parts.

[4] In the case of using a capacitor, it is necessary to include a small inductance in series to minimize the transient current during the turning-on maneuver.

[5] A thyristor is a power electronic device acting as a semicontrolled switch. This device conducts applying current through a control terminal (firing stage) and it is blocked externally, when reversed voltage appears at its main terminals.

Chapter 14

Adding Electric Vehicle Modeling Capability to an Agent–Based Transport Simulation

Rashid A. Waraich
ETH Zurich, Switzerland

Gil Georges
ETH Zurich, Switzerland

Matthias D. Galus
ETH Zurich, Switzerland

Kay W. Axhausen
ETH Zurich, Switzerland

ABSTRACT

Battery-electric and plug-in hybrid-electric vehicles are envisioned by many as a way to reduce CO_2 traffic emissions, support the integration of renewable electricity generation, and increase energy security. Electric vehicle modeling is an active field of research, especially with regards to assessing the impact of electric vehicles on the electricity network. However, as highlighted in this chapter, there is a lack of capability for detailed electricity demand and supply modeling. One reason for this, as pointed out in this chapter, is that such modeling requires an interdisciplinary approach and a possibility to reuse and integrate existing models. In order to solve this problem, a framework for electric vehicle modeling is presented, which provides strong capabilities for detailed electricity demand modeling. It is built on an agent-based travel demand and traffic simulation. A case study for the city of Zurich is presented, which highlights the capabilities of the framework to uncover possible bottlenecks in the electricity network and detailed fleet simulation for CO_2 emission calculations, and thus its power to support policy makers in taking decisions.

DOI: 10.4018/978-1-4666-4920-0.ch014

INTRODUCTION

Battery and Plug-in Hybrid Electric Vehicles (BEV resp. PHEV) are seen by many as a key component to a future transport sector with lower greenhouse gas emissions. These vehicles do not only have a more efficient driving cycle than conventional vehicles, but also allow a diversification of energy sources for driving (MacKay, 2008). BEV and PHEV are abbreviated to electric vehicles (EV), with the exception of cases where the distinction is required.

Several governments have announced national goals regarding the number of EVs they want to have on their roads. Examples include the USA with one million EV until 2015 (White House, 2009) and Germany with the same number of vehicles until 2020 (Bundesregierung, 2009). At the time of this writing almost all major car manufacturers have either introduced a plug-in electric vehicle or are planning to do so, (see e.g. de Santiago et al., 2012).

While these numbers highlight the fact that a shift towards an era probably dominated by EVs has started, there are also many uncertainties connected with such an introduction, leading to many open questions:

Although these vehicles will require additional electricity for charging, it is not clear if the supplementary electricity can be generated in a sustainable way. Even if the required energy is coming from alternative sources, such as solar or wind power, further questions arise, such as can electricity generation match the time of electricity demand? Could the Vehicle-to-Grid (V2G) concept help in this regard, where batteries of the vehicles could act as a power reserve (Brooks, 2002; Kempton & Tomić, 2005)? Could a viable V2G model be built around ancillary services, where car batteries are used for voltage and frequency regulation (Hirst & Kirby, 1999; Kirby, 2004) and which is rewarded with a higher return than if vehicle batteries act only as power reserve (Letendre et al., 2006)? With this said however,

there is a possibility that such utilization of batteries could also reduce their life span in such a way that V2G is no longer attractive (Kramer et al., 2008).

Additional questions arise around the charging infrastructure: While PHEV in the sense of all hybrid electric vehicles can both charge their batteries from the electricity network as well have a backup gasoline tank, BEV depend on a functioning charging infrastructure system. So what is the right way to provide such an infrastructure? Which are the places where such infrastructure should be built first? Will normal charging plugs or higher powered plugs allowing for faster charging prevail? Or will future cars have swappable batteries, allowing for their energy to be replenished even faster than filling up a gasoline tank (Li et al., 2011)? In addition, do new technologies for charging, such as inductive charging along roads, which charge the vehicle during the drive (Wu et al., 2011) or solar panels mounted on top of the cars have a place as part of the overall charging infrastructure (Li et al., 2009)? As vehicles with bigger battery capacity require less public charging infrastructure, could it be the case that EV with high capacity batteries might make public charging infrastructure obsolete? Or will such a mass production of large batteries never become reality? What is the best investment for public funding, e.g. subsidizing public charging infrastructure or car batteries?

There are also many open questions which arise in relation to the electricity network: While it is often suggested (Parks et al., 2007), that EVs could charge during off-peak demand during the night, there are also studies which suggest that well-meant pricing incentives could backfire and cause more damage than good, even potentially generating new peaks (Waraich et al., 2009). They demonstrate that to solve such problems, communication technologies could be used in order to match supply and demand, in general referred to as smart charging/grid (Amin & Wollenberg, 2005). In conjunction with V2G and distributed energy generation, such technology becomes even more relevant. In this case, a building with solar panels in times of a local/temporal surplus, can feed energy into the electricity network. Furthermore, the usage of home appliances and charging of EVs could be delayed when there is an electricity shortage in the electricity network. How can such complex scenarios be modeled? While the energy increase due to electric vehicles is predicted to be small compared to the overall electricity load (Duvall et al., 2007), charging may still not be possible due to problems in the distribution network due to constraint violations at the lower level voltage network, possibly causing power line and transformer overloads (Farmer et al., 2010). How can such possible bottlenecks in the electricity network be uncovered to allow owners of the electricity network to prepare for possible future EV scenarios?

In order to study these questions, models of the electricity demand introduced by these EVs, including preferences of the drivers/owners are required, which are coupled with electricity supply models. Supply models refer to electricity network flow models, but can also include intelligent controls for matching demand and supply and electricity generation. Discussing related work in the background section, we argue that there is a lack of microscopic models related to EVs, which could help in the analysis of these problems at an adequate level of detail. Indeed, this is essential when studying where in the distribution network transformer overloading and other problems occur, such as those described in Farmer et al. (2010). In this regard, reusability plays an important role, as building complex models from scratch is a difficult task.

Based on the authors' previous work related to detailed demand and supply modeling of EVs within an interdisciplinary working environment, in this chapter a framework for EV modeling is presented. Key features of the framework include that it is open source and as such allows not only free access to its use in other projects, but also

spurs contribution of new modules, so that the wider EV research community can benefit from it. According to the best of the authors' knowledge, this is the first open-source framework supporting detailed EV demand modeling with interfaces for integration with supply models.

The rest of the chapter is structured in the following way: In the next section related work is discussed, following which the framework itself is presented, as is a case study for the city of Zurich, which exemplifies the potential application of the framework. After discussing different aspects of the case study in relation to the framework, future work is outlined. Following the conclusions, at the end of the chapter a further reading list is provided.

BACKGROUND

The Big Picture

There are numerous studies related to electric vehicles, many of which look at different countries, regions or cities, e.g. Vermont in Farmer et al. (2010) or British Columbia in Kelley et al. (2009). Some studies are based on surveys (Axsen et al., 2009), others on simulations (Knapen et al., 2012), and others look at different types of charging (Lopes et al., 2009) or placement of charging stations (Chen et al., 2013). Due to space constraints it is not possible to discuss all of the literature here. However, if one focuses solely on those contributions trying to assess the impact of EV charging on the electricity network, one can categorize the papers according to the level of detail with which they model demand and supply. The first category of papers is only concerned with an aggregate view of the problem (Hadley & Tsvetkova, 2009; Wynne, 2009). Whilst such papers do not try to model the demand and supply in much detail, they do provide system wide key figures, e.g. total energy consumption. It is clear that although such work is helpful in order to get an overview on aggregate energy demand

and CO_2 reductions, it is not able to assess exactly where in the electricity network problems might occur due to the introduction of EVs. Many such studies implicitly assume that the electricity network will be able to handle the extra load, which does not take existing power line and transformer constraints into account, as for example pointed out by Farmer et al. (2010).

When starting to refine the models, there are two strands of work, where people either try to refine the models of demand or supply side. While only few electricity demand models exist which could potentially provide detailed demand side modeling, e.g. Knapen et al. (2012), on the electricity network side, many detailed supply models are available for investigating the impact which EVs have on the distribution network (e.g. see Lopes et al., 2009).

The research gap of detailed electricity demand and supply modeling is recognized also in a recent literature review assessing the impact of PHEV on the distribution network (Green II, 2011), where the authors' first conceptual paper on this issue is strongly endorsed (Galus et al., 2009). While it is clear that the problem at hand does require detailed modeling of demand and supply side, most studies leave one out. It is the authors' contention that several reasons lie behind the scarcity of detailed modeling of both sides of the issue. These reasons will be pointed out in the following sections when comparing related work.

Related Work

As previously mentioned, many studies look at different charging schemes, vehicle-to-grid, etc. although the focus is often on aggregates. In the following three pieces of work provide a good sample of the current state of the art in this field. After discussing the work briefly, we will highlight why we think that there is a possible a gap between the requirements of the problem at hand in terms of resolution and detail and why this is still missing.

Binding & Sundstroem (2011) attempted to model both the demand and supply side of the electricity network. This includes, among others, a travel demand model and an electricity network model. The paper focuses on integration of both demand and supply and mostly stresses the performance of the simulation. The modeling of the traffic is carried out in an event-based fashion. For modeling activity and trip durations and departure times, certain distributions are used, e.g. normal and uniform distribution. Although an agent-based approach is used, there is no special emphasis on modeling of individual preferences of people or households. When making comparisons to the authors' previous work (Galus et al., 2009), they argue in favor of a fully integrated approach of the transportation and power system simulation, in order to avoid performance overheads. This point is addressed later in the present chapter.

Cui et al. (2012), is also based on an agent-based approach. Their study area is Knox County, TN, which is divided into geographical zones of around 6 square kilometers. An agent-based modeling environment called NetLogo is used to model people (Tisue & Wilensky, 2004). A vehicle ownership model is estimated based on Nested Multinomial Logit whilst they also take taste heterogeneity of different households into account. With regards to charging, they assume that people will start charging immediately, when arriving at work and back home. The level of detail of the transport model is not described in the paper, but as the charging profiles at work and home are identical, one can infer that the work duration is probably the same for all agents. This results in a repetition of the exact charging pattern at work in the morning and home in the evening.

One of the most sophisticated models for EV demand modeling is presented in Knapen et al. (2012), where the electric power demand by EVs is modeled for the region of Flanders. They use the FEATHERS (Bellemans et al., 2010) activity-based model to predict the daily schedules of people. This involves a microscopic level demand modeling and route assignment. Through simulations four different kinds of charging strategies are evaluated on an aggregated level. The average zone size in the case study is 13 square kilometers.

These three papers are among the most detailed in terms of EV demand modeling. However, from the point of view of the electricity network, more detailed demand modeling is required. For example, in the case study for the city of Zurich presented later in this chapter, each electric node covers, on average, an area of 150-200m radius. This means that in order to appropriately analyze the electricity network with regards to possible future EV charging, one must perform far more detailed and higher resolution simulations than is the case in these three papers. But why is electricity demand side modeling still happening aggregated on a system wide level? The authors think there are several reasons for this, making it a very difficult problem to solve:

The first hurdle towards a detailed demand and supply side modeling is that only an interdisciplinary approach including for example, the competences of transportation, electrical engineers, computer scientists, mechanical engineers, etc. can handle such a project. However, even if a team is able to master this hurdle, it does not necessarily mean that the EV related study has the goal of detailed modeling in mind. Furthermore, most studies focus on a specific study area. As such, it is difficult for different scientists to apply these models in other regions, as the implementation and detailed documentation of the models is often not publically available. Furthermore, as the models are often implemented for specific studies, they are not designed with extension in mind, rendering their reuse and extension difficult. It therefore seems that most studies related to EV start from scratch, although similar studies have been conducted previously.

The authors of this chapter have gone through most of the steps described above: Starting with an interdisciplinary team of transportation-, electrical-, computer science- and mechanical

engineers a detailed simulation of the city of Zurich is performed, both of the demand and supply side. In this chapter it is tried to fill the gap in the research community described above. Starting with detailed demand modeling, it is tried to generalize the authors' previous work, such that other EV researchers can possibly reuse it. Furthermore, effort is made towards publishing the work open source with documentation, thus making it possible for others to access this work. By doing so, we not only hope to vitalize detailed EV demand modeling, but also hope that some researchers will follow this practice and contribute their work, such that the whole EV research community can benefit from it.

In the following some of our preceding work with regards to the EV framework is described, before describing the framework itself.

PRECEDING WORK

Galus et al., (2009) presented for the first time, the concept that one could bring together detailed demand and supply side modeling by integrating transportation and power system simulation models. Furthermore it showed that these models could be run iteratively. The idea is that electricity could be priced with a location dependent virtual price signal using an agent-based approach, and agents could adjust their demand accordingly, such that demand and supply could be matched (Galus, 2012).

Such a test system was implemented and presented in Waraich et al. (2009b), and Galus et al., (2012b), where different scenarios are simulated including uncontrolled charging, time of use pricing and centralized smart charging. In case of smart charging a central aggregator in the system communicates to the vehicles, when they should charge, while taking inputs like parking duration, state of charge and planned trip distance into account. It successfully demonstrated that from different starting system conditions the prices do converge to a stable state, such that all vehicles can be charged. Furthermore, the simulations also show how pricing could affect the behavior of people.

These models have been further developed further, as presented in Galus et al. (2012b), where a detailed vehicle fleet (Noembrini, 2009) and an energy consumption model (Georges, 2012) is added. In the meantime, work on the demand side modeling has been extended and generalized further as a framework. Whilst some elements of the framework have been presented in the papers mentioned above, here the whole framework and its modules are presented for the first time including an application.

THE TRANSPORTATION ENERGY SIMULATION FRAMEWORK

Requirements and Reasoning behind the Framework

Before describing the Transportation Energy Simulation (TES) framework itself, the general requirements of the framework are outlined.

The framework needs to cover a wide range of applications as presented in the introduction. This means that the framework should be built modular and extendible. With such a framework, people could plug together complex scenarios themselves, e.g. by looking at the examples provided, extending simpler models and implementing new models using standardized interfaces. Furthermore, it should be possible to implement a model inside or outside the framework. This enhances the flexibility of the framework because not all libraries and tools required for an application might be available through the framework and full integration might require too much time.

A second important requirement for the framework is that one should be able to model change in behavior at a person level. It should be possible to infer how people might possibly change their behavior due to certain policy measures, e.g.

change of prices or resource availability, such as charging stations, etc. Furthermore, certain applications also require that one is also able to model preferences of individuals, for which the input can for example stem from stated preference surveys (Weis et al., 2012). Therefore, it is a requirement for the framework that people are modeled individually as agents taking decisions rather than an aggregated group.

As electricity demand by EVs is generated by people's travel demands, a transport model is needed which supports detailed spatial and temporal modeling such as MATSim-T (2013). Furthermore, the performance of such a traffic simulation is also important as one wants to be able to capture the whole daily movement of possibly millions of agents throughout the whole day.

In order for the system to be beneficial to a wider audience, it is important that the system is not only available for free, but also that the system is open source. This would be in line with the peer review process often adapted in research, so that not only the description of models can be reviewed, but also the implementations themselves.

The last requirement is probably the most important when it comes to the success of such a framework and has to do with the usability of the framework. Documentation, examples and tutorials should be available to support people and make the initial learning as simple as possible. In addition the availability of visualization tools for the simulations can facilitate the work with the framework. Although from a scientific point of view one might pay the least amount of attention to this requirement, it may well be the single most important requirement for the actual adaptation of such a framework, especially by those who are new to the field.

As mentioned earlier, the framework presented is a continuation of previous work, which uses an agent-based travel demand and traffic simulation called MATSim. In the following section the MATSim simulation is briefly described, before characterizing the TES framework and its interaction with MATSim.

MATSIM

Figure 1 shows MATSim's simulation process: Each agent in MATSim has a daily plan of trips and activities, such as going to work, school or shopping. The initial daily plans of agents are provided as input in the initial demand step together with supply models, e.g. street network and building facilities. These initial plans can be based on, for example, activity/travel diaries of people. The goal of the MATSim simulation process is to optimize the plan for each agent while respecting supply side constraints and the preferences of each agent. The plans of all agents are executed by a micro-simulation, resulting in traffic flows along network roads, which can cause traffic congestion. The execution of these plans is then scored and assigned a utility value. For example, a person with lower travel time has a higher utility than one who has a longer congested travel time. Additionally, working and other activities increase the utility. The goal of each agent is to maximize the utility of its daily plan by *replanning* it after each iteration, e.g. changing routes, working time, travel mode or location choice. In this step, either a new plan is assigned to an agent by adapting a previously executed plan, or a previously executed plan is reselected. Plans with a higher score have a higher chance of reselection, while plans with a lower score are deleted over time, as only a limited number of plans per agent are kept. This idea corresponds conceptually to mutation, selection and survival of the fittest in a co-evolutionary algorithm (Holland, 1992). This iterative process approaches a point of rest corresponding to a user equilibrium called relaxed/ optimized demand.

TES INTEGRATION WITH MATSIM

Next the interaction and integration between the TES framework and MATSim is described. The development is facilitated by the fact that MATSim itself is built in a modular fashion and as such facilitates extension. Thus, at many points in the MATSim simulation, it is possible to provide additional functionality, and as such to extend the overall simulation. This allowed the development of the framework, without having to change any of the code of MATSim itself.

Figure 2 shows how TES is plugged into MATSim. TES itself consists of several modules, which are needed for simulation of EV related scenarios, such as energy consumption or charging modules. These modules can be setup according to scenario specific constraints, before starting the TES simulation. When TES is started up, it plugs itself into MATSim at several points before the combined MATSim-TES simulation is performed itself. Although the modules are described in detail later, here a brief description of the different plug-in points between MATSim and TES is provided:

(0): This refers to the point in time, where MATSim has just been initialized. At this time TES can perform operations required for initialization of the simulation, such as defining at which locations parking charging infrastructure is available.

(1): This refers to the time just before a new iteration in MATSim is started. This is already part of the MATSim iteration loop. Here, operations, which are part of the optimization can take place, e.g. a policy change.

Figure 1. Co-evolutionary simulation process of MATSim

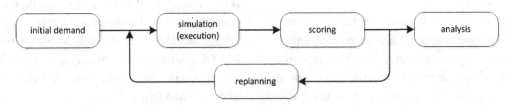

Figure 2. An overview depicting the Transportation Energy Simulation Framework and MATSim together with important integration points

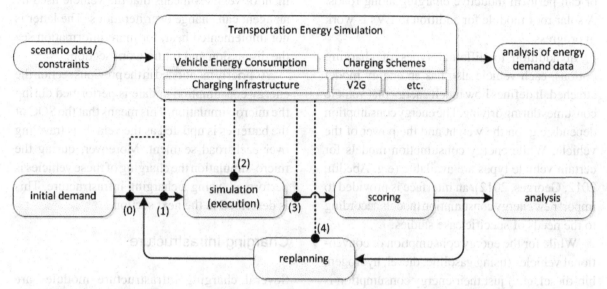

For example, if charging stations need to be priced according to demand, the price can be adapted here.

(2): During the execution of the MATSim simulation, TES can extend agent and vehicle models. For example, the energy consumption of vehicles moving along roads can be updated or vehicles can be charged according to the preferences of the agent/charging schemes.

(3): This point indicates the time when the micro-simulation execution in MATSim is over, and can be used to produce statistics of the iteration or for adapting the utility score of the agent. For example, the cost of charging can be aggregated and added to the utility score of the agent, so that the prices does influence the decision of the agent in future iterations.

(4): The plan of the agent can be adapted during the replanning step in MATSim as explained earlier. This can also be utilized to adapt choices in the context of EVs. For example, if the assignment of vehicles to people is not fixed, a vehicle owner could change the

vehicle type to maximize its utility. In this case, people with easier access to charging stations might prefer EVs, while others might prefer PHEVs or switch to a different mode.

MODULES

After providing an overview regarding how TES is integrated into MATSim above, this section describes the individual modules and features of the framework in more detail.

Vehicle Characteristics and Energy Consumption

At the time when the first simulations involving TES modules were presented, see (Waraich et al., 2009b), MATSim did not have any model to distinguish different types of vehicles. Therefore, a new system for modeling vehicle types was developed. The idea behind the modeling of vehicle type in TES is such that one can quickly switch together any type of EV. For example, one can plug together a vehicle, which supports charging at stationary plugs and has a swappable battery or can perform inductive charging along roads. A solar roof module for addition to EVs is work in progress.

In addition to different types of charging options, each vehicle also has an energy model attached. It defines how much energy that vehicle consumes during driving. The energy consumption depends e.g. on the weight and the power of the vehicle. While energy consumption models for certain vehicle types are available (e.g. Abedin, 2012; Georges, 2012), an interface is provided to import new energy consumption models according to the needs of specific case studies.

While for the energy consumption of conventional vehicles (using gasoline, diesel, hydrogen, bio-diesel, etc.) just their energy consumption is logged for later analysis as they drive, for EVs the energy consumption is modeled in more detail. For such vehicles a battery capacity needs to be defined, for which the state of charge (SOC) is updated during driving and when charging. The PHEV model, which is implemented at the time of this writing, is a series hybrid (Chan, 2007). Such vehicles use the electric drive as long as the SOC is above a minimum threshold value which is determined by battery life time considerations (e.g. 20%). Thereafter, the on-board electric generator is turned on to run the vehicle in charge sustaining mode using gasoline. This means that, on average, over a driving cycle the battery is not charged in this mode. Such vehicles have one energy consumption model for the electric drive and a second one when the on board generator is turned on. More complicated energy control strategies for PHEVs, such as those presented by Tulpule et al. (2009), can be created by implementing the application programming interfaces provided in TES in this regard.

After defining a vehicle together with its energy consumption model, the vehicle needs to be assigned to a vehicle owner. This assignment can be static or dynamic. In the first case the assignment is conducted once in the simulation and is not changed thereafter. Dynamic assignment of vehicles means that the vehicle used by an agent can change over iterations. The latter is not implemented hear, for more information see the discussion and future work section.

As briefly mentioned in the previous section the energy consumption update is performed during the micro-simulation. This means that the SOC of the batteries is updated as the vehicle is traveling over each road segment. Moreover, during the micro-simulation the charging of these vehicles is performed, using a charging infrastructure. This is described in the next section.

Charging Infrastructure

Several charging infrastructure modules are available, and their location and configuration, such as plug availability, can be defined during the initialization of the simulation. Furthermore, to facilitate a simple scenario setup, one can also easily deploy a charging infrastructure according to activity type. For example, one can define that charging is available at home with 3.5 kW and work with 11 kW.

Besides modules for plug-in charging infrastructure, a module for inductive charging has also been implemented. Vehicles equipped with such modules can charge as they drive along roads, where the corresponding technology is installed. In the first tests, which were performed using the inductive charging module (Abedin & Waraich, 2013), only one type of power is available to all vehicles. This is currently being extended, such that differences in charging capability of different vehicles can be accounted for, as described in Suh et al. (2011).

At the time of this writing, a module for optimal placement of charging stations is still work in progress. To exemplify optimal placement of charging stations, at least one application of this is planned to be available in the initial version of the framework for reference. As swapping stations and dedicated public fast charging stations are also of interest to the EV research community, ongoing work is providing interfaces and basic implementations of such modules.

Charging Schemes

A charging infrastructure alone, as defined in the previous section, is not sufficient to capture the variety of cases and scenarios, outlined in the introduction. Therefore, the simulation of the charging infrastructure and charging behavior of vehicles is controlled by so called charging scheme modules. There are several charging schemes which are available at the time of this writing in TES, although new ones are being developed.

One of the charging schemes available for stationary charging is known as uncontrolled charging (sometimes also referred to as dumb charging). It implements the simple behavior that an agent just plugs-in the vehicle whenever a charging plug is available and starts charging immediately. Such a module is implemented in TES by tracking the agent during the MATSim simulation and charging the vehicle when the vehicle arrives at a parking place where an electric plug is available.

A second charging behavior for stationary charging is available for scenarios where the price for charging changes over the day. These prices can either be fixed for the whole day in advance or vary throughout the day. A vehicle charging controller can be added to a vehicle, and it can charge the vehicle according to the desires of the agent. E.g. by specifying the time, when charging should start, which corresponds to technology already available. One such charging module is already implemented into TES. It handles the case where charging prices are known to the vehicle for the whole day. In this case, the agent tries to minimize the charging price it needs to pay while considering temporal and spatial variation of prices. This also takes planned trip throughout the day into account. If required by the investigated case study, this charging price can also be integrated into the overall utility function of the agent,

such that it has direct influence on the behavior of the agent and its various travel related choices, as presented in Waraich et al. (2009b).

As indicated in the background section, charging modules which allow for smart charging are also available in TES. Such a module can be integrated with an external power system simulation, as demonstrated in Waraich et al. (2009b). In this case it is tried to charge all vehicles, while taking electricity network constraints into account. Whereas the smart charging approach used in Waraich et al. (2009b) is based on a central entity, which controls the charging behavior of vehicles connected to the electricity network, a decentralized approach is tested in Schieffer (2010) using TES. In this case a charging module is implemented which assumes that all vehicles are provided information about the base load distribution curve and can decide independently from a central entity when to charge while trying to act in the best interest of the electricity network owner. Although it is not always possible to make the assumption that car owners would act in the best interests of the electricity network, which is possibly in conflict with their own interests, it provides a starting point for further research in this direction.

For inductive charging, at the moment only a default charging scheme is implemented, where vehicles just try to charge whenever inductive technology at roads is available. More advanced inductive charging schemes could include charging price optimization for the agent. Policies of the electricity network could also be included in some charging schemes, e.g. the inductive charging capability of a road could be turned off to shed load.

Vehicle-To-Grid (V2G)

In Galus & Andersson (2011), an early version of TES is utilized in combination with an intelligent controller for PHEV storage management. It is shown that such an approach could be utilized to balance the fluctuations in energy generation from renewable energy sources such as a wind park. In this approach only the output from the TES framework is utilized. The first integrated simulation of V2G inside TES is presented in Schieffer (2011). As this is still preliminary work for integration of V2G modules into TES, there remains a great deal of potential when it comes to extension of the framework in this regard.

Output Modules

As during the simulation all energy consumption and EV battery SOC updates are logged, it is possible to easily perform various kinds of analysis, e.g. for CO_2 emissions. Furthermore, simple graphs can also be generated, automatically summarizing results after each MATSim iteration or at the end of the simulation.

Although custom analysis outputs can be built by using interfaces provided by TES, there is still a big gap in terms of visualization of the TES simulation. While free and commercial visualization of the MATSim simulation are available (MATSim-T, 2013), those visualizers are not built with support of EV related scenarios in mind. Such visualizations could not only expedite the learning process of the framework, but also help during the implementation of new modules and debugging.

Adding Modules

Modules can interact with TES in two ways, either as modules, which are implemented inside the framework, or as external modules. While modules in TES need to be implemented in Java, communication to outside modules must happen through interfaces. If outside modules only provide input to TES or need the output from TES at the end of the simulation, the data exchange can happen through files. But if an external module needs to be invoked after each iteration, it is best to automate the invocation of the external mod-

ule, for which examples are provided with TES. Alternatively, if an external module needs to be invoked even more often, e.g. during the simulation itself, it might be advisable to re-implement such modules inside TES, as this might otherwise lead to high overheads and performance degradation, in turn leading to long run times, especially for larger scenarios.

Performance

As TES aims to be able to simulate large scenarios, with possibly millions of agents on high resolution navigation networks with millions of road segments, the performance of the simulation is very important. MATSim itself is capable of simulating such large scenarios, as demonstrated by Meister et al. (2010). This is achieved by utilizing multiple cores/processors for the micro-simulation (Dobler & Axhausen, 2011).

As TES requires many operations, which must be performed while following the agent throughout the simulation, the handling of events generated by the agent throughout the simulation needs to be fast. This has been implemented by using the concept of parallel event handling (Waraich et al., 2009a), which allows TES modules which are related to, for example, SOC management to be handled in parallel with the micro-simulation execution. This means that all presented TES modules are fully integrated within the MATSim simulation.

Modules Contributed by Other Researchers

Although the framework is not yet available publicly (planned for the end of 2013), several researchers have already contributed to its implementation besides the first author. Indeed, Abedin (2012) contributed through an energy consumption model for electric vehicles, which is based on Faria et al. (2012). Furthermore, Georges (2012) contributed with energy consumption models for small VW Golf sized vehicles, with conventional, plug-in hybrid and electric vehicle powertrains. While the model implemented by Abedin (2012) just takes the speed driven into account, the second model also takes traffic conditions into account, which is described as part of the case study later in this chapter.

Planned Modules

There are several modules for which a reference implementation is planned. Such a basic or default implementation can help to prepare the appropriate interaction and integration with other modules and other researchers can simply extend the work or re-implement modules based on clearly defined interfaces. There are several modules which are planned or which are a work in progress, such as optimization of charging station locations, a solar panel module, electricity model for buildings and adaptation of routes of agents due to swapping of batteries or performing fast charging. Such planned

modules and work in progress is described further in the future work section.

After the presentation of the TES framework in this section, which is rather abstract, the next section presents an application of the framework in order to allow the reader to develop a better understanding of how some of the modules of the framework can be utilized in practice.

CASE STUDY: CITY OF ZURICH

In this section the ARTEMIS case study for the city of Zurich is presented (Galus, Georges & Waraich, 2012), which investigates the possible impact of future EV scenarios on the electricity network of the city. The TES framework is used in conjunction with several embedded models and external modules. The interaction between the different modules and sub systems involved in the simulations is depicted in Figure 3. For the simulation several inputs are required for TES

Figure 3. Interaction of the Transportation Energy Simulation framework with MATSim and external models within the case study of the city of Zurich. External models include the Vehicle Fleet, Energy Consumption and the Power System Simulation.

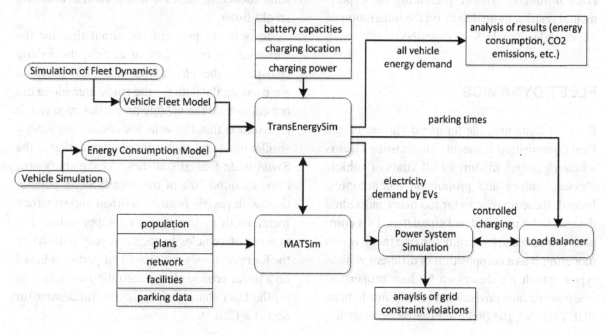

and MATSim. For TES, scenario specific information regarding the vehicle fleet and its energy consumption is provided as input. This is further described in the sections *Fleet Dynamics*, *Vehicle Energy Consumption Model* and *Scenario Overview*. For MATSim also scenario specific inputs are provided, which are described in the *Traffic Simulation Model* section. In addition, extensive information on the electricity network is needed, with is further described in the section entitled *Power System Simulation and Load Balancing*.

There are three outputs from TES, which are analyzed further: A) The spatial and temporal distribution of the energy consumption for overall energy consumption and CO_2 emissions analysis. The latter is further described in the results section. B) The electricity demand by EVs which is given to the power systems simulation as input to determine whether the required demand could be supplied by the electricity network. C) Information on EV parking times given as input to the load balancer to handle cases, where electricity network constraint violations occur. In such cases controlled charging is applied to possibly solve the problems. This is further described in the section entitled *Power System Simulation and Load Balancing*. Before presenting the experimental results, more details on the integration of the modules into TES are described.

FLEET DYNAMICS

By fleet dynamics the temporal change of the fleet composition is meant. The existing fleet is a heterogeneous mixture of all kinds of vehicle classes, shapes and propulsion technologies. Indeed, these amount to far too many individual designs to be modeled and simulated. This complexity is reduced by parameterizing the fleet and modeling it as a composition of different vehicle types, which are described by four properties: The powertrain (conventional vehicle, full-hybrid, PHEV, BEV), the fuel used (gasoline, electric),

the vehicle's power (eight categories, with most of them ranging between 50 kW and 200 kW) and the vehicle's mass (ten categories considered, most of which range between 900 kg and 2600 kg). This means that in total 320 types of vehicles were considered in the simulation. Furthermore, for modeling future years, it is considered that each year a certain number of vehicle owners change their vehicle, new people start driving and others quit using a car. Furthermore, the technology of the vehicles also changes over time. In the following it is briefly described, how considering several boundary conditions, the fleet composition of the reference years 2020, 2035 and 2050 are approximated.

Based on the Swiss federal statistics for the reference year 2010, all registered vehicles are mapped to vehicle classes according to the four vehicle properties described above. The dynamics of the fleet within a single vehicle class is modeled according to Noembrini (2009). It is assumed that certain vehicle models are renewed on an annual basis. The probability of such a change depends on the age of the vehicle. In general, the removal probability of a vehicle increases until a certain age, after which this probability drops back to zero, modeling the case that a vehicle becomes an old-timer.

In order to perform the simulation for the surroundings of the city of Zurich, the federal statistics for the vehicle types of all of Switzerland are used, as the data for the study area alone did not contain all the vehicle properties required. It is assumed that the vehicles considered have a similar mass and power distribution to that of the Swiss-wide federal statistics. As the study area covers around 20% of the overall Swiss population, with people from both urban and suburban locations, this assumption seems appropriate. The number of vehicles in each category defined by the four previously mentioned properties is based on a linear vehicle class penetration model based on the fleet characteristics from Bundesamt für Statistik (2013).

For simplicity's sake the possible growth over time of the electricity network, road network and population growth predictions are ignored and instead the data from the year 2010 is used. This means this study looks at the impact on the current electricity network based on scenarios, with increasing EV and PHEV penetration. This in turn means that the overall size of the fleet in all scenarios remains the same. The implications of this simplification and current efforts for improvement are examined further in the discussion section.

It is assumed for all scenarios that over time the market share of vehicles with regards to mass and power distribution does not change. Of course the drive technology available in the market changes as full-hybrid, PHEV and BEV enter the market replacing conventional vehicles. The probability of a drive technology change is based on the market share of EVs in 2050 according to ewz (2009), where two scenarios are distinguished with a lower and higher market penetration of BEV. Based on these scenarios, a low-EV and high-EV penetration scenario is defined, (see Figure 4).

In the low-EV penetration scenario, it is assumed that as of 2035 all conventional vehicles will have been replaced in the market by full hybrids or EVs. From 2040 onwards, even full-hybrids are replaced over time by PHEVs and BEVs. In the high-EV penetration scenario, an environment favoring EV penetration compared to the low-EV scenario is assumed and as such the BEV market share increases faster over time. Factors which could induce such an EV friendly development are faster development of battery technology, faster and ubiquitous availability of charging infrastructure, and PHEVs becoming available everywhere in the market between 2015 and 2020. Indeed, from 2015 onwards no new conventional vehicles are released into the market.

While one of these scenarios is called low-EV penetration and one high-EV penetration, this does not indicate that these scenarios mark lower or upper bound for electrified vehicle penetration. On the contrary, such naming is merely meant as a distinction between the two scenarios.

Figure 4. Market share of low-EV and high-EV penetration scenarios from 2010 to 2050 in comparison. The low- and high-EV scenarios are distinguished through the use of different colored lines. The white lines show the scenario, where EVs replace the conventional vehicles faster from the market (high penetration scenario), while the green line shows the scenario, where conventional vehicles are replaced from the market at a slightly slower rate (low penetration scenario).

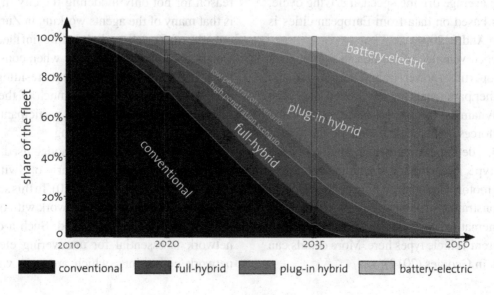

ENERGY CONSUMPTION MODEL

After describing the vehicle fleet dynamics, in this section the energy consumption models of the vehicles are characterized. The models are pre-calculated externally and then integrated into TES, as a real-time model calculation would require a lot of time, thus affecting simulation performance. The data exchange to TES is via a regression model, which allows us to calculate the energy consumption of each vehicle based on approximated traffic patterns and the technical specification of the vehicle.

Modeling energy consumption, while considering driving patterns is quite complex. Even on a free road the vehicle speed is mostly not constant, e.g. due to curves. In addition, speed fluctuations due to interaction with other traffic participants are even stronger. In order to prepare a vehicle energy consumption model, which is suitable for usage in TES, a regression is formulated, which allows to calculate the energy demand of a vehicle based on the maximum allowed driving speed on the road and the average speed driven by the vehicle. Such a simplification is needed, as the simulation within a road in the MATSim micro-simulation is not detailed enough to capture second-to-second driving patterns. However, as an unlimited number of driving profiles can lead to the same average driving speed, a driving cycle, which is based on data from European cities is adopted (André, 2004).

For each vehicle, in addition to the four vehicle properties (power train, fuel, power and mass) other parameters are considered also, such as aerodynamics, rolling resistance, gravity and inertial forces. After calculation of the forces involved, a detailed computer simulation of each vehicle type is performed, including modeling of their motors and energy conversion. Due to space constraints, it is not possible to describe the mathematical formulation of the models of the different vehicle types here. More details can be found in Georges (2012).

In order to also account for technological improvement over time of the various vehicle types, an annual energy demand reduction, which differs for each vehicle power train, is used, following the model described in Safarianova et al. (2010). This model makes the assumption that electric vehicles have less potential to improve their energy economy than conventional vehicles, as electric vehicles are already far more efficient than conventional vehicles.

A sample regression model for a compact car is shown in Figure 5. It shows for five road types with different speed limits the energy consumption depending on the average speed driven.

TRAVEL DEMAND AND TRAFFIC SIMULATION MODEL

After describing the vehicle fleet and energy consumption models, which are inputs for TES, this section describes the inputs for the MATSim simulation. Although the study area for the electricity network is only the city of Zurich, the travel and traffic simulation model contains all agents residing within 30km around a central place in Zurich (Quai Bridge). Additionally, such agents, who reside outside this 30km circle at any time of the day, are also included in the scenario. The reason for not only modeling the city of Zurich is that many of the agents working in Zurich live outside of Zurich and therefore influence the electricity demand in the city when considering EVs. Furthermore if only agents residing in the city of Zurich are modeled, much of the traffic interactions between different participants of the road network would be missing.

The MATSim demand model used in this case study is based on a scenario of Switzerland presented in Meister et al. (2010). In this scenario, a detailed navigation road network with over one million road segments is used. Such a detailed network is essential for uncovering electricity network constraints, which are only visible at

Figure 5. Energy regression model for a compact car with a conventional powertrain for the year 2012. Each line represents one discrete legal speed limit. The crosses indicate the raw-data obtained by simulation.

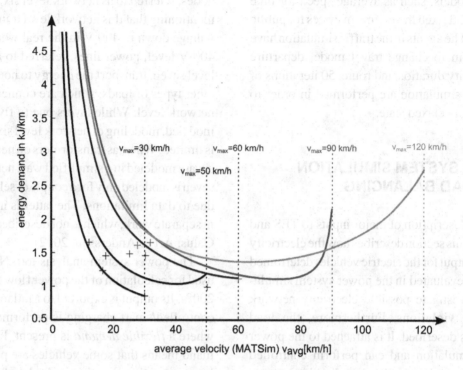

the lower layers of the distribution network. A detailed description of the generation of initial plans of the agents' is omitted here, as this is not part of the work in this case study and is presented in Meister et al. (2010). In general, the generation of these initial plans can be based on activity/travel diary data, using activity-based models of travel behavior, such as those presented by Arentze & Timmermans (2000). In addition to travel diaries, other data sources, such as GPS tracking data (Schüssler & Axhausen, 2011) or data from public transport fare cards (Lee et al., 2012) can also be utilized.

Due to the large number of scenarios and time constraints of the study, only a 10% population sample is used with around 180 000 agents. Such population sampling is common practice, where the network flow capacities and that of the infrastructure (e.g. parking) are adapted accordingly to match the sample size.

Whereas parking is often neglected in traffic simulations, e.g. in Meister et al. (2010), initial investigations towards electric demand modeling within this case study showed that this would not render results which are suitable for the detailed study at hand. If the simulation is executed without detailed information on parking, this can result in a higher demand for parking than the actual supply. This means that although in reality, an area with low parking supply would not be attractive for travel with a car, it might be attractive in the simulation, if parking supply constraints are not modeled. This problem is solved using the parking choice model presented in Waraich & Axhausen (2012), where all 300 000 parking spaces including private parking, street parking and garage parking in the city of Zurich are modeled.

The modes of transportation available in this simulation are car, public transport, bike and walk. Only car driving is simulated physically, taking road capacity and space constraints into account. The travel times of the other modes are based on simpler models, such as average speed for bike and walk and fixed travel time matrices for public transport. The agents in the traffic simulation have the freedom to change travel mode, departure time, activity duration and route. 50 iterations of the traffic simulation are performed in order to reach a near-relaxed state.

POWER SYSTEM SIMULATION AND LOAD BALANCING

After the description of major inputs to TES and MATSim this section describes how the electricity demand output for the electric vehicles determined by TES is evaluated in the power system simulation to investigate possible electricity network constraint violations. Furthermore, the load balancer is described. It is attached to the power system simulation and can perform controlled charging, meaning that it can redistribute power demand of vehicles to avoid electricity network constraint violations.

As mentioned earlier, one of the main objectives of the case study is to establish whether or not EV charging could violate physical constraints of power lines and transformers in the electricity network in Zurich. The electricity network model which is used for such analysis is provided by the utility company of Zurich (*ewz*). The electricity network model is structured into network levels. In the following the top seven layers of the electricity network are described. The first network level contains power lines at voltages from 380 kV down to 220 kV. The second level transforms the voltage, whilst the third level contains power lines of 150 kV. The fourth network level contains another voltage transformation while the fifth network level contains power lines in the voltage range of 11kV to 22 kV in Zurich. The electricity network model contains approximately 800 nodes on the fifth network level. These nodes represent the electric load of the city in the model used. Transformers are typically installed at the nodes, referred to as network level six. It is worth mentioning that this network level transforms the voltage down to 400 V in the real world. On the 400 V level, power lines, referred to as network level seven, transport the energy to households or other types of loads, which are connected at this network level. While layers one to five are fully modeled, modeling of network level six and seven is limited. Whereas transformers on network level six are modeled in a simplified way, network level seven is modeled only for a couple of selected areas due to data limitations. The latter is investigated in separate work, which is not described here, (see Galus, Art & Andersson, 2012).

The power system analysis tool NEPLAN is used for calculation of the power flow (Busarello, 2008). Its output is exported to Matlab, where the controlled/smart charging is performed in cases where a *flexible demand* is present. Flexible demand means that some vehicles are parked for a longer duration than is required to fully charge their batteries. Hence, these vehicles incorporate flexibility for when they actually have to be charged. This type of load balancing is simulated using a game theoretical, agent-based approach in Matlab. The use of agent-based modeling in TES/MATSim and in the power system simulation ensures the theoretical consistency and integration of both models. More details of this agent-based load balancing are described below.

For management of overloaded resources in the electricity network an approach based on "mechanism design" (Galus, 2012) is chosen. This allows for the optimal allocation of finite resources among competing agents. The competitive behavior of the agents for the resource is based on predefined rules, according to which the agents decide and act. Ideally, this method should lead to the result that those agents who need a resource most are willing to pay the most for it. The willingness to pay can be represented by a utility function (Aumann, 1976). Such allocation of finite resources between competing agents is applied in the case study for electricity load balancing in order to avoid overloaded power lines and transformers in the network, which can result from the additional power demand introduced from electric vehicles. The algorithm allocates power, which can be limited by the physical conditions of the electricity network, optimally among agents. Due to space constraints, the mathematical formulation of this model is not presented here. The mathematical formulation and detailed analysis can be found in Galus (2012) and Galus et al. (2012b).

SCENARIO OVERVIEW

There are four scenarios, which are investigated in this chapter. The parameters of them are shown in Table 1. Besides a base scenario of 2010, scenarios A to C are modeled. They represent scenarios with an increasingly higher availability of charging infrastructure and increasing EV market share. Moreover, within each scenario, over time the EV penetration, energy efficiency,

availability of charging infrastructure and battery capacity increases. In scenario A, only charging at home is possible. In scenario B charging with higher power is additionally available at work. Furthermore, in scenario B a faster penetration of EVs over time is assumed compared to scenario A (low- vs. high-EV penetration). In scenario C, the charging infrastructure develops at all places faster over time, including public parking spots.

Although additional experiments with higher battery sizes and charging power have been conducted as part of the case study, those are omitted due to space constraints and can be found in Galus, Georges & Waraich (2012).

TES INTEGRATION AND SIMULATIONS

After describing the different modules and data exchange involved, the present section describes in more detail how this data is integrated into TES for the simulations.

Table 1. Scenario definitions of the case study: The three scenarios A, B and C distinguish themselves in terms of market penetration by EVs, charging infrastructure and battery capacity. As various types of EVs are present in each scenario, the driving range is kept constant instead of the battery size. For measuring the driving range the New European Driving Cycle (NEDC) is used (Tzirakis et al., 2006).

	Year	Market penetration of EVs	Charging Infrastructure			Battery Capacity
			Home	Work	Public	
base scenario	2010	-	-	-	-	-
scenario A	2020	low	3.5 kW	-	-	80 km
	2035					80 km
	2050					150 km
scenario B	2020	high	3.5 kW	11 kW	-	80 km
	2035					80 km
	2050					150 km
scenario C	2020	high	3.5 kW	3.5 kW	3.5 kW	80 km
	2035		11 kW	11 kW	11 kW	80 km
	2050		11 kW	11 kW	11 kW	150 km

For each scenario run, the vehicle fleet and energy consumption regression models and battery sizes are read in from a file and vehicles are assigned to agents. This assignment of vehicles to agents in the simulation is done in a simplified way: In a preprocessing step, BEV are assigned to those agents with the lowest travel demand. All other vehicle types are assigned randomly to the rest of the vehicle drivers. The assignment of BEV in this fashion is performed to avoid BEV running out of energy during the simulation. As an average weekday is simulated, it is clear that most of those agents, who have electric vehicles, should be able to finish their day without running out of energy in their battery. It is clear that the ownership of different vehicle models is not random in reality, but instead is often based on preferences and attributes of the agents, such as income. This limitation is discussed further in the discussion section.

The setup of the charging infrastructure for the total 13 runs for the case study is facilitated by the options available for defining stationary charging. The stationary charging module allows setting the charging power at each activity location also at once as required in the case study. For charging, the uncontrolled charging scheme is used, meaning that all vehicles start charging immediately upon arrival. In the presented case study, there is no price signal for electrical charging present which might change agent behavior, as this is the case in some of the simulations presented in Waraich et al. (2013a). Therefore, to optimize the run time of the experiments, a MATSim run is performed first with 50 iterations to reach a relaxed demand. This relaxed demand is then utilized as the starting point for the different scenarios simulated with TES, such that only a single iteration is required.

The output of the simulation is then further analyzed with regards to energy and power demand as well as emissions. Furthermore, the electricity demand, SOC and parking times of the vehicles are additionally used as input to the power system simulation, so as to uncover possible electricity network constraint violations. In the following sections the results of the simulations are presented regarding energy demand, emissions and impact on the distribution network. Due to space constraints only a fraction of the overall results are presented here, for demonstration purposes only. The full results can be found in Galus, Georges & Waraich (2012) and Galus (2012).

RESULTS–ENERGY AND EMISSIONS

This section looks at the aggregated results related to energy demand and CO_2 emissions for all simulated vehicles, while in the next section the impact on the electricity network for only the city of Zurich is reported.

Although only a 10% sample is simulated, the results refer to the whole population, containing around one million vehicles. As in MATSim a one day period is simulated, the results are meant per day and have not been extrapolated to annual figures. Such an extrapolation would have been quite rough anyway, as only average weekday traffic is modeled and the traffic patterns on weekends are different from those on weekdays. Furthermore, the seasonal effect, including weather conditions would need to be taken into account, which has not been considered. This needs to be explored further, especially as the range of BEV is strongly affected, in a negative way if heating is turned on in winter. Other devices in the vehicles are also not modeled, which would require additional energy to that needed for propulsion of the vehicle.

Figure 6, shows the daily travel distance by power train and fuel. Based on the scenario definitions the fleet moves towards more usage of EVs, thus leading to an increased travel distance driven electrically. Scenarios B and C are clearly ahead of scenario A in the year 2035 in terms of usage of electric drive trains, due to the number of electrified vehicles and the charging infrastructure available. This gap is reduced in

Figure 6. Development of the distance travelled for the whole simulated fleet in scenarios A, B and C for 2010 to 2050, divided by power train and fuel. On the left side the distance, which is travelled by using a combustion engine is shown. On the right side the distance travelled using electricity is shown. As PHEV can travel using gasoline and electricity, they are present in the middle in both areas.

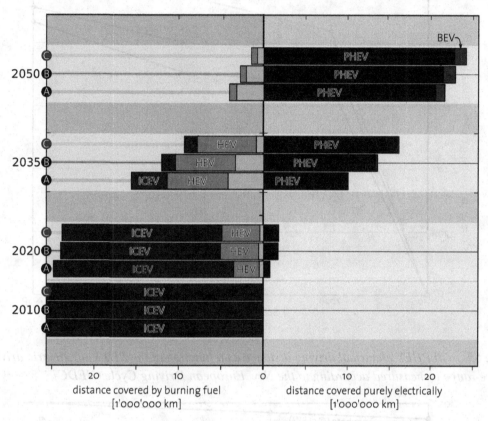

2050, as the number of EVs reaches almost the same level as in the other two scenarios.

In the year 2050, the prevalent powertrain in all scenarios is PHEV. The distance travelled electrically by PHEVs depends on many factors, including:

1. The availability of the charging infrastructure, in terms of number of locations and charging power.
2. Battery capacity: the higher the battery size, the longer a vehicle can travel electrically.
3. The efficiency of the vehicle – the more efficient the power conversion, the more the vehicle can drive electrically using the same battery size.

The influence of availability of charging infrastructure on PHEV electric drive is highlighted in Figure 7. It shows for PHEVs the percentage of the distance, which can be performed electrically for the different scenarios. One can see that home charging alone is the most important contributor for allowing PHEVs to drive using electricity and that in 2050 the gap between home charging only and a ubiquitously available charging infrastructure, adds only 10% to electrified driving.

Instead of looking at distance travelled electrically by PHEV over time, and charging station availability, one can also look at the influence of battery size in this regard. Figure 8 shows the influence of charging infrastructure and battery size on the distance travelled electrically by PHEVs. It uses the results from additional simu-

Figure 7. Share of the distance travelled by PHEVs, which is driven using electricity for the different scenarios

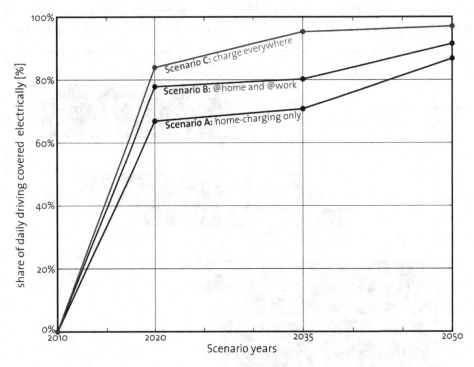

Figure 8. Share of PHEV electrical driving distance as a function of the PHEV all electric drive range. This drive range is measured according to the New European Driving Cycle (NEDC).

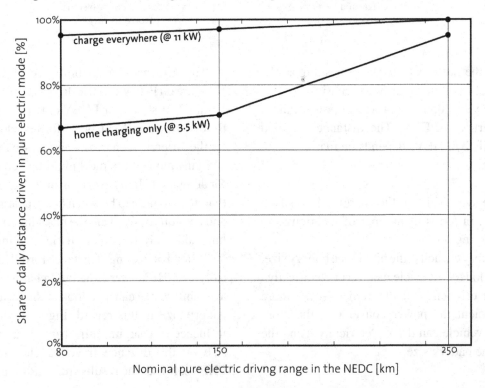

lation runs, which are not defined in Table 1, including battery sizes of more than 250 km. One of the interesting insights of Figure 8 is that one can achieve an almost complete electrification (ca. 95%) of PHEV drive in two ways: Either by equipping PHEV with smaller batteries of 80 km range and at the same time making charging infrastructure ubiquitously available or having large battery capacities of 250 km installed in the PHEVs and making charging only available at home. Furthermore, the figure also shows that if one starts with small batteries (80km range) and only home charging, a 71% electrification of the driving distances is already possible. Both Figure 7 and Figure 8 provide an overview of the some of the trade-offs involved in closing the gap between this 71% electric drive scenario and a 95/100% electric drive for PHEVs. This can help to design policies, which can best achieve such a goal, e.g. subsidizing home charging, car batteries or investment in public charging infrastructure.

After looking at different influences on the electric drive distance of PHEVs, Figure 9 gives an overview of the energy demand of the vehicle fleet between 2010 and 2050 for the three scenarios (A) to (C). The figure shows both the electrical and chemical (gasoline) energy demand. Due to the technological improvement and increasing number of EVs the total energy demand is shrinking and the electricity demand share is growing. While looking at this figure, it is important to remember that gasoline is primary energy and electricity final energy. This means, this figure cannot be utilized to assess the overall reduction of primary energy, as electricity generation depends on the electricity generation process and mix. This means the overall primary energy demand reduction in 2050 compared to base case scenario in 2010 could be far less than the 75% when looking at primary energy and electrical energy combined.

The CO_2 emissions reduction is even higher than the reduction in the total energy consumption, which is also attributed to the low emission of the

current Swiss electricity generation mix. Figure 10 shows the vehicle fleet's daily CO_2 emissions. For the electricity generation, a CO_2 intensity according to the Eco-Invent database is assumed (Frischknecht et al., 2001), taking into account the current energy generation. For the calculation of the emissions 44 g CO_2/MJ_{eq} is used for the Swiss electricity production mix and 88 g CO_2/MJ_{eq} is used for gasoline according to Eco-Invent. In this study neither the import/export, nor the change of the electricity generation mix over time is considered, thus meaning that for all scenarios the current energy mix is assumed.

While the current electricity generation CO_2 intensity in Switzerland is low, especially due to the high share of hydro (54%) and nuclear (41%) power generation (Bundesamt für Energie, 2011), in the case study it was also considered how the CO_2 emissions could develop if the power generation CO_2 intensity were to become higher. It is found that if most power were to be generated in oil and coal power plans in the future, the CO_2 reductions would probably not be significant enough to justify a shift from conventional to electric vehicles from an environmental perspective.

RESULTS–DISTRIBUTION NETWORK

In the previous sections the insights of the simulation results with regard to trade-offs between battery size, charging station availability and reduction of energy demand and CO_2 emissions have been discussed. This chapter continues the analysis of the results and looks at the impact of EV charging demand on the electricity network. Although one of the main objectives of the case study presented is to identify congestions, i.e. physical bottlenecks for the energy flow in the electricity network, due to space constraints only one of many investigated scenarios is analyzed. This analysis shows only major results while a detailed analysis can be found in Galus (2012)

Figure 9. The temporal development of the energy demand, by fuel and electricity and according to the different power trains

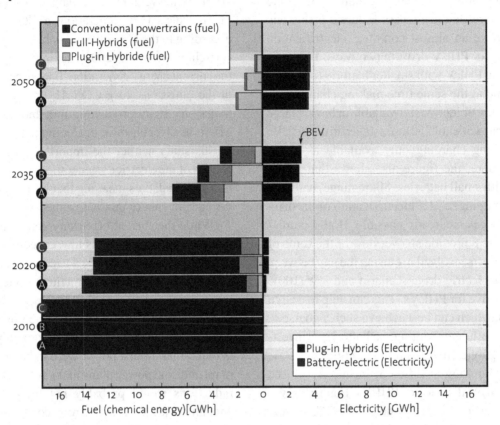

and Galus, Georges & Waraich (2012). Providing a glimpse into the large number of results, only partial findings for scenario C for year 2050, are presented. Scenario C is most interesting, as it features the highest electricity demand of electric vehicles compared to all other scenarios. In scenario C, people can charge not only at home and work, but also use a public charging infrastructure. Furthermore, the public charging infrastructure allows for faster charging than in most of the other scenarios.

Figure 11 shows the aggregated base case electricity load over the day together with the load introduced by EVs in an uncontrolled charging mode for 2050. One can see that the aggregated overall contribution of EVs to the current base load increases the peak electricity demand and also shifts the time of the peak to the early morning

hours. The peak demand also changes its shape and becomes more like a plateau at 600 MW, starting at around 09:00 a.m. and lasting until around noon. In the evening hours almost no electricity is charged inside the city. This happens because the charging infrastructure is ubiquitously available. Agents use this infrastructure frequently and charge their vehicles during the day, e.g. at work. Another reason for the low load is that agents living in the city arrive home early between 17:00 and 19:00 and typically do not travel far during the day. Hence, their need for energy to recharge the EVs is small. As only charging inside the city is considered here, most people working in Zurich but living outside the city do not influence the electricity demand in the evening. The peak load increase for 2050 is only around 10% compared to the base case scenario and not dramatic.

Figure 10. CO_2 Emissions from 2010 to 2050 for the Scenarios (A) to (C) by power train. The CO_2 intensities of the electricity are based on the average Swiss consumer mix, while the CO_2 intensities of fuel are based on that of gasoline according to the same source (ECO-INVENT, see Frischknecht et al. (2001)).

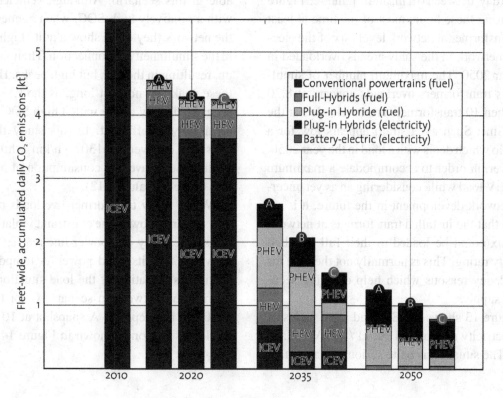

Figure 11. Aggregated load curves for the city of Zurich for uncontrolled EV charging according to scenario C in comparison with the base case 2010

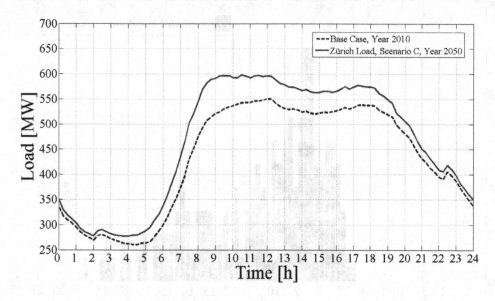

While the aggregated peak load increase is relatively small, asset overloads appear throughout the day, between 6 a.m. and 7 p.m., see Figure 12. During these hours most of the time at least one transformer at network levels six of the electricity network in the study area is overloaded in the year 2050. The maximum number of simultaneous transformers overloads appears at 8.30 am, when 10 transformers are overloaded at the same time. Such asset strain appears low for a scenario which deals with a load in the year 2050. However, in order to accommodate a maximum of the EV load while considering an as yet uncertain network development in the future, it is assumed that the installed transformers at network level six could be loaded to their full installed capacity rating. This is normally not the case for redundancy reasons which help ensuring security of supply.

Figure 13 shows the EV load at all nodes of the electricity network on the 11 / 22 kV voltage level. The situation is quite serious, as at certain nodes peaks of almost 3 MW occur. This happens due to the high charging powers which are available in this scenario. Although vehicles arrive with a relatively high SOC, when connecting to the network they often show a quite high degree in the simultaneity of connection. Their load adds up, resulting in the few, but high peaks. However these peaks do not last long, as the EVs in this scenario usually arrive with a high SOC as they are relatively efficient. In this study the EVs consume on average 130 Wh/km while other studies use an average consumption of 500 Wh/km, (see e.g. Galus 2012).

While many transformer overloads occur in this scenario, power line constraint violations are not severe. Only one power line reached a level above 60% of its rated power. A temporal and spatial visualization of the load situation of the distribution network in scenario C for the year 2050 can be prepared. A snapshot at 10 a.m. of the load situation is shown in Figure 14. Violet

Figure 12. Number of overloaded transformers on the 11 kV and 22 kV level of the electricity network

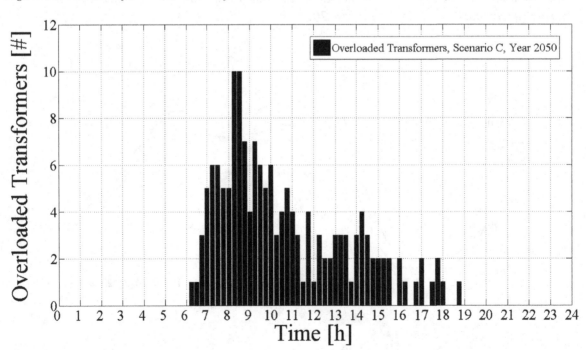

Figure 13. Development of the EV electricity demand in Scenario C in 2050 at all nodes of the 11 kV / 22 kV electricity network

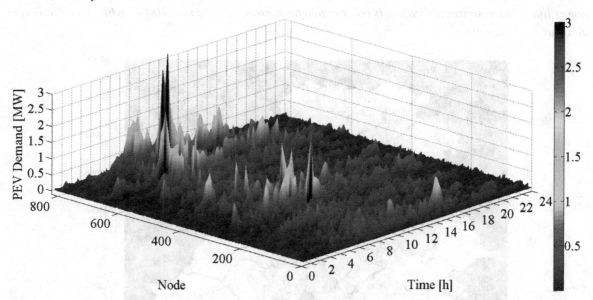

dots and links represent network assets (transformers and power lines), which are overloaded.

In order to try avoiding the transformer overloads, controlled charging is performed using the load balancer. Through controlled charging, the peak load resulting from EV charging is reduced. This is achieved by charging vehicles at later times if possible. Figure 15 shows the difference of load imposed on the electricity network of the controlled and uncontrolled charging scenario. A positive value indicates that the load in the uncontrolled charging scenario is larger than in the controlled charging case. Obviously, the load in the morning hours is reduced and shifted into evening hours by using the load balancer. However, after following the controlled charging strategy there appears a difference in the total energy charged in uncontrolled and controlled manner. The difference is not negligible and can be quantified to 2.4 MWh. This means, some EVs leave their parking lots with a SOC that is lower than their desired SOC for departure. This is due to heavily congested nodes, which do not allow, even when utilizing the complete temporal charg-

ing flexibility, to fully charge some EVs. A solution to this is to expand the network infrastructure selectively where bottlenecks arise, i.e. building more power lines and transformers. Another solution could also be to provide feedback to the vehicles which include information on temporal and special congestion in the network, e.g. through varying prices charged for electricity. This would allow vehicles to react and adapt their temporal and special charging patterns. This approach has been demonstrated successfully by Waraich et al. (2009b) and Galus et al. (2012b).

DISCUSSION

In the following, a couple of issues, especially in relation to the TES framework are discussed together with future work, following which the discussion will be directed more towards the framework itself.

Figure 14. A snapshot of the spatial distribution of electricity network resources and their utilization at 10 a.m. for the 11kV network of the city of Zurich. The dots denote transformers, while the links denote power lines. The resource utilization is color coded from green (0%) to red (100%), while violet indicates an overloaded resource.

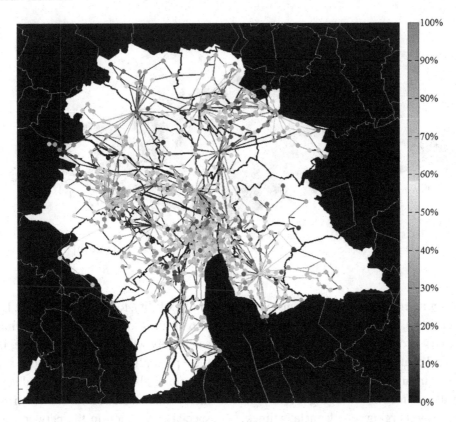

Figure 15. Shift of load due to controlled charging in Scenario C in the year 2050. Positive values indicate, that the uncontrolled EV load is bigger than the controlled load.

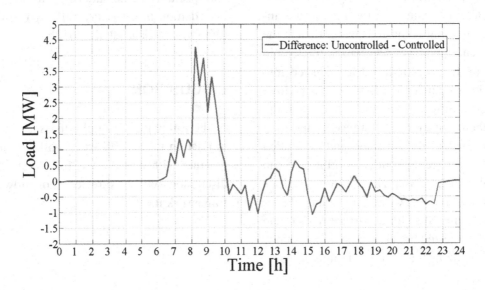

Case Study Discussion and Future Work

In the case study, several simplifications are made, of which one of the most fundamental is in relation to future scenarios, where neither the population nor road network or distribution network are updated to fit a possible future scenario. An attempt is made to improve this aspect of the MATSim scenario within a different project for Switzerland, where planned road projects and federal projections of Swiss population growth are taken into account in the simulations, (see THELMA, 2013).

A second simplification, which has been previously alluded to, is that an average working day is simulated, omitting simulations of Saturdays and Sundays, which exhibit different traffic patterns. Furthermore, seasonal changes also have impact on the energy consumption (cooling and heating), which would also need to be considered for calculating annual figures. In this regard there is clearly potential for improvement, which some of the authors hope to tackle further in THELMA (2013).

Two experimental design issues are highlighted here, regarding the number of runs conducted. It is common knowledge that a single simulation run counts as a single experiment and that one needs to perform several experiments in order to be able to report variance of simulation results. Unfortunately, this was not possible due to time constraints for the case study at hand. In order to still give a sense of the order of magnitude of variance encountered between runs, variance from previous experiments are reported here. Horni et al. (2011) reported on the variability of different MATSim runs in the region of Zurich employing a 10% population sample. The variability at street count stations for the whole day is mostly in the range of 1 to 7%, with a mean of around 4%. This variation between the runs is higher on average when looking at specific hours, with most of them in the range of 10 to 15%. The variation expected for the runs conducted in this case study

is lower, as the destination choice module used during replanning is not utilized, which is the case in Horni et al. (2011). Furthermore, Horni et al. (2011) applied a higher replanning rate of agents per iteration than that used in this or earlier studies, in order to accelerate the convergence of destination choice (20% replanning vs. 10% replanning used in this chapter). Population sampling is certainly also an additional factor contributing to increased variability of traffic volume counts, thus meaning that the variance figures reported would probably drop if population sample bigger than 10% were used.

An additional reason why repetition of the experimental runs would be required is that vehicles are assigned to people in a random fashion. While it is verified that this had only little effect on aggregate results, no such analysis was possible for the results regarding the electricity network. However, one can argue in this regard that the omission of such repeated runs does not have a significant impact on the current results: A large variance would be expected for such areas where only a small number of cars are present, such that a switch between non-EV and EV would have a big impact. However, such areas are of less importance to the electricity network results, because bottlenecks normally arise in high demand areas. In these areas the variance of demand between runs should automatically drop due to the larger number of vehicles involved.

The random assignment of vehicles to people is also not appropriate, but instead a model like that by Jäggi & Axhausen (2011), could be used to define which household is more likely to buy a certain type of car. Furthermore, neighborhood effects could also be modeled for adoption of new vehicle types, as investigated by (Axen et al., 2009) through stated and revealed choice experiments.

The assignment of BEVs to people is achieved by assigning them to those people, travelling the shortest distance over the day. There are enough such candidates, as the average daily driving range in the study area is far less than the 80km minimum battery size available to EVs (Bundesamt für

Statistik, 2013). In addition to person attributes, an improved model could also take the driving range of the vehicle into account, as part of the optimization in the simulation. A similar approach has been adapted in the simulation of Knapen et al. (2012).

In comparison with the authors' previous work (Waraich et al., 2009b), in this case study the TES framework is only used for demand modeling. Controlled charging is achieved through use of the external load balancer modules. Furthermore, the data flow in this case study is only one way from TES to the power system simulation, while an iterative interaction between TES and the power system simulation is presented in Waraich et al. (2009b). As there are no prices for electricity/ special EV parking involved in this case study, agents did not exhibit any change in behavior due to EV ownership, as has been successfully demonstrated within similar context in the past. See e.g. Waraich et al. (2009b) or Waraich & Axhausen (2012).

As mentioned in the background section, it is pointed out by Binding & Sundstroem (2011) that the degree of integration of their models is higher than present in our approach. While such tight coupling has advantages in term of performance, there is also a downside to it: For such full integration all program code needs to be developed within the same programming language which is often not possible, as the programming languages and libraries used in the different expert fields vary. By integrating loosely coupled models written by different domain experts, within the the presented case study far more advanced models could be integrated than is the case in Binding & Sundstroem (2011), e.g. for demand side modeling.

Framework Discussion

After discussing the TES framework within the context of the case study, in this section a more general discussion of the TES framework is presented.

As the target audience of the framework two major groups of users can be envisioned: Firstly interdisciplinary teams, who would like to perform case studies related to electric mobility for a specific study area. To such people the TES framework does not only provide the benefit that models developed by other researchers can be reused, but TES also provides a common platform of thinking, about how the problem at hand can be addressed, while facilitating interoperability of models.

The second target group of TES users are those who do not work within an interdisciplinary team, but would still like that their models are used beyond simple test scenarios or in case studies with narrow scope. To such users TES provides a platform, where models from various fields of expertise can be reused. This facilitates the implementation and integration of new models by such users. Furthermore, TES makes it easier for such users, that their models can be adopted by a wider audience within the research community than before.

A question which might arise in this regard is, why should people change their behavior and start providing their models for reuse to others for free, although this was not the case till now? There are several points which need to be discussed. At the moment most research is presented either in written form through scientific journals or via presentations at conferences. A platform, where research related to electric mobility can be reused, is an ideal place to advertise new related work. This could increase the reuse, visibility and impact of the work within the overall research field, which is probably one of goals of most scientific efforts. Furthermore, by having a platform with standardized interfaces, it becomes simpler to compare different models and to get feedback from other users regarding it. Also providing good documentation to modules is as such in the self-interest of the module creator, as this increases the chance that the module gets used and can improve through feedback.

While it is argued above that it should be in the self-interest of module creators to provide their modules for free, in the following it is discussed whether or not such modules must always be open source. While it is advantageous to provide a module open source in order to get detailed feedback, in some cases, people might want to provide their work to others for reuse, but not allow them to see the detailed implementation. The reason behind this might be to advertise the work to others for reuse, while still wanting to maintain a competitive research advantage. For example, one might have an extension of a module or its publication planned and one may wish to protect against other researchers doing the same extension quicker. A second reason for not providing the source code might be that one does not feel comfortable with showing the details of the source code. For both situations, instead of contributing the module source code, compiled modules can be contributed to TES instead.

Another question relates to how such a framework can be maintained over time. There is a range of possibilities when it comes to how the framework might be supported. In the minimal case, just the framework is made available to others for use and one needs to provide a way in which, people can contribute new modules and search existing ones. This could be done either by hosting those modules with documentation at the framework's website or by providing an external link to such resources.

However in order to promote the framework, one would probably need to do more than the bare minimum described above, possibly including advertising the framework to potential users and contributors whilst also providing them with help through tutorials and possible collaboration. In order to maintain the quality of new modules contributed, one might also need to provide and enforce guidelines, e.g. minimum standards regarding documentation and testing. It might also be necessary from time to time to keep the framework up to date with the most current version

of MATSim. Whilst it is tried to base the implementation of TES only on parts of MATSim, which are deemed stable, such as event handlers, there might be parts which could require an update to a newer version at the request of users. For example, if users may require more advanced features of MATSim, which are not available in the current MATSim version compatible with TES.

FUTURE WORK

Although some of the future work has already been mentioned previously, in this section work in progress and planned work for TES is described further.

It is planned to make the framework available until the end of 2013, at the URL www.tesfw.org (Transportation Energy Simulation FrameWork). This will require preparation of documentation and examples. In the longer run, it is also planned to work towards animated visualization of EVs and the provision of tools for simpler use, as mentioned earlier. Furthermore, modules which are still work in progress are also planned to be part of the framework when it is published, including optimal placement of charging stations and a module, to allow for simple extension of vehicle types to support a solar panel roof and a module for modeling the spatial and temporal intensity of the sun shine (Perez et al., 1990; Gadsden et al., 2003). Also regenerative braking, which is often present in EVs has not been modeled till now and needs to be taken up in future.

With regards to the usage of charging stations, such as fast charging and swapping stations, there are at least two strands of modeling which seem possible. The first approach is a simpler and higher performance solution, which does not adapt agent plans for rerouting to charging stations during the simulation, but changes plans only at the end of the simulation whilst keeping track of utilization constraints of charging stations and taking agent decisions into account. A second approach could adapt the plans during the execution of the micro-simulation, which would be more accurate. The downside of this approach is, that it is more complex than the first approach and tightly coupled with the MATSim micro-simulation implementation and is therefore slower than the first approach. Therefore it is more likely that the first approach will be included in the framework first.

Something, which has been entirely ignored within the TES framework until now is the energy demand of buildings and especially of homes. This seems to be especially important, as the electric vehicle is part of the energy system at home, which includes electricity generation, e.g. from the solar roof of the home/vehicle, demand response to shed load at times of overload in the electricity network, including those of home appliances (Farhangi, 2010; Robinson, 2011) and V2G. Indeed, more research in this direction is essential in order to ascertain what kind of interfaces should be provided for such modeling of these scenarios as part of the TES framework.

As mentioned previously, the assignment of vehicles can be either modeled externally or can be a part of the simulation. This would require the implementation of replanning modules, which do not only consider choice between travel modes, but also between vehicle types, especially BEV and PHEV, where travel distance and preferences of agents are taken into account, similar to the approach taken by Knapen et al. (2012).

Other things, which must also be evaluated include how electricity supply and generation modules can be best made available in TES or if this needs to be solved externally and what interfaces would be required for that. As many modules require optimization libraries for such implementation, this work needs to be facilitated by providing examples of how to use such optimization libraries in TES using Java.

CONCLUSION

In the introduction several open questions related to the electrification of driving are posed which focus on the notion that while many studies have tried to solve such problems, there is a lack of work looking into detailed and combined demand and supply side modeling. It is argued in this chapter, that such a development is present due to the lack of an environment allowing reuse of models, developed by other researchers.

In order to propose a solution to this problem, an open source framework is presented, which could bridge this gap. This is achieved by generalizing previous work beyond single case studies in the form of a framework, which will be published online. Furthermore the framework is open for extension and reuse. In this way, the framework provides a common ground for interdisciplinary work and contribution, it is hoped that the overall research of electric mobility will benefit from it.

In this chapter, also an application of the framework is presented, which looks at the impact of EV charging on the electricity network of the city of Zurich, together with environmental analysis. To the best of our knowledge, this is the first study of its kind in terms of detailed modeling and size. Using simulation experiments possible bottlenecks in the electricity network are uncovered. Furthermore, different options and trade-offs are outlined. These results can be used by the utility provider in the city of Zurich for their planning of the electricity network. Furthermore policy makers can design incentives, while taking such additional input into account.

In the complex realm of challenges and opportunities, which are present through the introduction of EVs, the presented framework can help all stakeholders involved in planning for a more sustainable future.

ACKNOWLEDGMENT

This work is supported by the ETH Research Grant TH-22 07-3, EWZ and Novatlantis. We would like to thank Prof. Andersson, Prof. Boulouchos and Dr. Noembrini for their support within the ARTEMIS project.

REFERENCES

Abedin, Z. U. (2012). *Modelling wireless charging for electric vehicles in MATSim*. (Unpublished master's thesis). TU München, Munich, Germany.

Abedin, Z.U., & Waraich. (2013). Modelling inductive charging of battery electric vehicles using an agent-based approach. *Arbeitsberichte Verkehrs- und Raumplanung, 899*.

Amin, S. M., & Wollenberg, B. F. (2005). Toward a smart grid: Power delivery for the 21st century. *IEEE Power and Energy Magazine, 3*(5), 34–41. doi:10.1109/MPAE.2005.1507024.

André, M. (2004). The ARTEMIS European driving cycles for measuring car pollutant emissions. *The Science of the Total Environment, 334*, 73–84. doi:10.1016/j.scitotenv.2004.04.070 PMID:15504494.

Arentze, T., & Timmermans, H. (2000). *Albatross: A learning based transportation oriented simulation system*. Eindhoven, The Netherlands: EIRASS.

Aumann, R. J. (1976). Agreeing to disagree. *Annals of Statistics, 4*(6), 1236–1239. doi:10.1214/aos/1176343654.

Axsen, J., Mountain, D. C., & Jaccard, M. (2009). Combining stated and revealed choice research to simulate the neighbor effect: The case of hybrid-electric vehicles. *Resource and Energy Economics, 31*(3), 221–238. doi:10.1016/j.reseneeco.2009.02.001.

Bellemans, T., Kochan, B., Janssens, D., Wets, G., Arentze, T., & Timmermans, H. (2010). Implementation framework and development trajectory of FEATHERS activity-based simulation platform. *Transportation Research Record: Journal of the Transportation Research Board, 2175*(1), 111–119. doi:10.3141/2175-13.

Binding, C., & Sundstroem, O. (2011). A simulation environment for vehicle-to-grid integration studies. In *Proceedings of the 2011 Summer Computer Simulation Conference* (pp. 14-21). IEEE.

Brooks, A. (2002). Integration of electric drive vehicles with the power grid-a new application for vehicle batteries. In *Battery Conference on Applications and Advances, 2002* (p. 239). Academic Press.

Bundesamt für Energie. (2011). *Schweizerische elektrizitätsstatistik 2001*. Retrieved April 2, 2013, from www.bfe.admin.ch

Bundesamt für Statistik. (2013). *STAT-TAB: Die interaktive statistikdatenbank*. Retrieved March 26, 2013, from www.bfs.admin.ch

Busarello, B. C. P., & Cott+ Partner AG. (2008). *NEPLAN, power system analysis*. Retrieved April 2, 2013, from www.neplan.ch

Chan, C. (2007). The state of the art of electric, hybrid, and fuel cell vehicles. *Proceedings of the IEEE, 95*(4), 704–718. doi:10.1109/JPROC.2007.892489.

Chen, T. D., Khan, M., & Kockelman, K. M. (2013). *The electric vehicle charging station location problem: A parking-based assignment method for seattle*. Paper presented at the 92nd Annual Meeting of the Transportation Research Board. Washington, DC.

Cui, X., Kim, H. K., Liu, C., Kao, S.-C., & Bhaduri, B. L. (2012). Simulating the household plug-in hybrid electric vehicle distribution and its electric distribution network impacts. *Transportation Research Part D, Transport and Environment, 17*(7), 548–554. doi:10.1016/j.trd.2012.05.011.

de Santiago, J., Bernhoff, H., Ekergård, B., Eriksson, S., Ferhatovic, S., Waters, R., & Leijon, M. (2012). Electrical motor drivelines in commercial all-electric vehicles: A review. *IEEE Transactions on Vehicular Technology, 61*(2), 475–484. doi:10.1109/TVT.2011.2177873.

Die Bundesregierung. (2009). *Nationaler entwicklungsplan elektromobilität der bundesregierung.* Bundesministerium für Bildung und Forschung.

Dobler, C., & Axhausen, K.W. (2011). Design and Implementation of a parallel queue-based traffic flow simulation. *Arbeitsberichte Verkehrs- und Raumplanung, 732*.

Duvall, M., Knipping, E., Alexander, M., Tonachel, L., & Clark, C. (2007). Environmental assessment of plug-in hybrid electric vehicles: Vol. 1. *Nationwide greenhouse gas emissions.* Palo Alto, CA: Electric Power Research Institute.

EWZ. (2009). *Randbedingungen und szenarien für elektromobilität. AG Elektromobilität.* EWZ.

Farhangi, H. (2010). The path of the smart grid. *IEEE Power and Energy Magazine, 8*(1), 18–28. doi:10.1109/MPE.2009.934876.

Faria, R., Moura, P., Delgado, J., & de Almeida, A. T. (2012). A sustainability assessment of electric vehicles as a personal mobility system. *Energy Conversion and Management, 61*, 19–30. doi:10.1016/j.enconman.2012.02.023.

Farmer, C., Hines, P., Dowds, J., & Blumsack, S. (2010). Modeling the impact of increasing PHEV loads on the distribution infrastructure. In *Proceedings of the 43rd Hawaii International Conference on System Sciences (HICSS)* (pp. 1-10). IEEE.

Frischknecht, R., Jungbluth, N., Althaus, H. J., Doka, G., Dones, R., & Heck, T. et al. (2005). The ecoinvent database: Overview and methodological framework. *The International Journal of Life Cycle Assessment, 10*(1), 3–9. doi:10.1065/lca2004.10.181.1.

Gadsden, S., Rylatt, M., Lomas, K., & Robinson, D. (2003). Predicting the urban solar fraction: A methodology for energy advisers and planners based on GIS. *Energy and Building, 35*(1), 37–48. doi:10.1016/S0378-7788(02)00078-6.

Galus, M.D., & Andersson. (2011). *Balancing renewable energy source with vehicle to grid services from a large fleet of plug-in hybrid electric vehicles controlled in a metropolitan area distribution network.* Paper presented at the Cigré 2011 Bologna Symposium. Bologna, Italy.

Galus, M. D. (2012). *Agent-based modeling and simulation of large scale electric mobility in power systems.* (Doctoral dissertation). ETH Zurich, Zurich, Switzerland.

Galus, M. D., Art, S., & Andersson, G. (2012). *A hierarchical, distributed PEV charging control in low voltage distribution grids to ensure network security.* Paper presented at the 2012 IEEE Power & Energy Society General Meeting. San Diego, CA.

Galus, M. D., Georges, G., & Waraich, R. A. (2012). *Final report of the ARTEMIS project.* Zurich, Switzerland: ETH Zürich.

Galus, M.D., Waraich, R. A., Balmer, M., Andersson, G., & Axhausen, K. W. (2009). *A framework for investigating the impact of PHEVs.* Paper presented at the International Advanced Mobility Forum 2009. Geneva, Switzerland.

Galus, M. D., Waraich, R. A., Noembrini, F., Steurs, K., Georges, G., & Boulouchos, K. et al. (2012). Integrating power systems, transport systems and vehicle technology for electric mobility impact assessment and efficient control. *IEEE Transactions on Smart Grid, 3*(2), 934–949. doi:10.1109/TSG.2012.2190628.

Georges, G. (2012). *Fleet-wide vehicular energy demand model for project ARTEMIS.* Zurich, Switzerland: ETH Zurich.

Green, R. C. II, Wang, L., & Alam, M. (2011). The impact of plug-in hybrid electric vehicles on distribution networks: A review and outlook. *Renewable & Sustainable Energy Reviews, 15*(1), 544–553. doi:10.1016/j.rser.2010.08.015.

Hadley, S. W., & Tsvetkova, A. A. (2009). Potential impacts of plug-in hybrid electric vehicles on regional power generation. *The Electricity Journal, 22*(10), 56–68. doi:10.1016/j.tej.2009.10.011.

Hirst, E., & Kirby, B. (1999). What is system control? In *Proceedings of the American Power Conference,* (pp. 639-644). APC.

Holland, J. H. (1992). *Adaptation in natural and artificial systems: An introductory analysis with applications to biology, control, and artificial intelligence*. Cambridge, MA: MIT Press.

Horni, A., Charypar, & Axhausen. (2011). Variability in transport microsimulations investigated with the multi-agent transport simulation MATSim, *Arbeitsberichte Verkehrs- und Raumplanung, 692*.

Jäggi, B., & Axhausen, K. W. (2011). *Modeling long term investment decisions in housing and transportation*. Paper presented at the 11th Swiss Transport Research Conference. New York, NY.

Kelly, L., Rowe, A., & Wild, P. (2009). Analyzing the impacts of plug-in electric vehicles on distribution networks in British Columbia. In *Proceedings of the Electrical Power & Energy Conference (EPEC)*. IEEE.

Kempton, W., & Tomić, J. (2005). Vehicle-to-grid power fundamentals: calculating capacity and net revenue. *Journal of Power Sources, 144*(1), 268–279. doi:10.1016/j.jpowsour.2004.12.025.

Kirby, B. (2004). *Frequency regulation basics and trends*. Oak Ridge National Laboratory.

Knapen, L., Kochan, B., Bellemans, T., Janssens, D., & Wets, G. (2012). Activity-based modeling to predict spatial and temporal power demand of electric vehicles in Flanders, Belgium. *Transportation Research Record: Journal of the Transportation Research Board, 2287*(1), 146–154. doi:10.3141/2287-18.

Kramer, B., Chakraborty, S., & Kroposki, B. (2008). A review of plug-in vehicles and vehicle-to-grid capability. In *Proceedings of Industrial Electronics* (pp. 2278–2283). IEEE. doi:10.1109/IECON.2008.4758312.

Lee, D.-H. Sun, & Erath. (2012). *Study of bus service reliability in Singapore using fare card data*. Paper presented at the 12th Asia Pacific ITS Forum & Exhibition. Kuala Lumpur, Malaysia.

Letendre, S., Denholm, P., & Lilienthal, P. (2006). Plug-in hybrid and all-electric vehicles: New load, or new resource? *Public Utilities Fortnightly, 144*(12), 28.

Li, S., Kolmanovsky, I. V., & Ulsoy, A. G. (2011). Battery swapping modularity design for plug-in HEVs using the augmented lagrangian decomposition method. In *Proceedings of American Control Conference (ACC)* (pp. 953-958). ACC.

Li, X., Lopes, L. A., & Williamson, S. S. (2009). On the suitability of plug-in hybrid electric vehicle (PHEV) charging infrastructures based on wind and solar energy. In *Proceedings of the Power & Energy Society General Meeting,* (pp. 1--8). IEEE.

Lopes, J. P., Soares, F. J., Almeida, P., & da Silva, M. M. (2009). Smart charging strategies for electric vehicles: Enhancing grid performance and maximizing the use of variable renewable energy sources. In *Proceedings of International Battery, Hybrid and Fuel Cell Electric Vehicle Symposium and Exhibition* (pp. 1--11). IEEE.

MacKay, D. (2008). Sustainable energy-without the hot air. Cambridge, UK: Cambridge.

MATSim-T. (2013). *Multi agent transportation simulation toolkit*. Retrieved March 26, 2013, from http://www.matsim.org

Meister, K., Balmer, M., Ciari, F., Horni, A., Rieser, M., Waraich, R., & Axhausen, K. (2010). *Large-scale agent-based travel demand optimization applied to Switzerland, including mode choice*. Paper presented at the 12th World Conference on Transportation Research. Lisbon, Portugal.

Noembrini, F. (2009). *Modeling and analysis of the Swiss energy system dynamics with emphasis on the interconnection between transportation and energy conversion*. (Doctoral dissertation). ETH Zurich, Zurich, Switzerland.

Parks, K., Denholm, P., & Markel, A. J. (2007). *Costs and emissions associated with plug-in hybrid electric vehicle charging in the Xcel energy Colorado service territory*. Golden, CO: National Renewable Energy Laboratory. doi:10.2172/903293.

Perez, R., Ineichen, P., Seals, R., Michalsky, J., & Stewart, R. (1990). Modeling daylight availability and irradiance components from direct and global irradiance. *Solar Energy, 44*(5), 271–289. doi:10.1016/0038-092X(90)90055-H.

Robinson, D. (2011). *Computer modelling for sustainable urban design: Physical principles, methods and applications*. London: Routledge.

Safarianova, S., Noembrini, F., Boulouchos, K., & Dietrich, P. (2011). *Techno-economic analysis of low GHG emission passenger cars, TOSCA project*. Zurich, Switzerland: ETH Zurich.

Schieffer, S. (2010). *To charge or not to charge? Decentralized charging decisions for the smart grid*. (Semester's thesis). ETH Zurich, Zurich, Switzerland.

Schieffer, S. (2011). *Decentralized charging decisions for the smart grid*. (Master's thesis). ETH Zurich, Zurich, Switzerland.

Schüssler, N., & Axhausen. (2011). *Combining GPS travel diaries with psychometric scales*. Paper presented at the 9th International Conference on Survey Methods in Transport. Termas de Puyehue.

Suh, N., Cho, D., & Rim, C. (2011). Design of on-line electric vehicle (OLEV). In *Global Product Development* (pp. 3–8). Berlin: Springer. doi:10.1007/978-3-642-15973-2_1.

THELMA. (2013). *Technology-centered electric mobility assessment*. Retrieved March 29, 2013, from http://www.thelma-emobility.net

Tisue, S., & Wilensky, U. (2004). Netlogo: A simple environment for modeling complexity. In *Proceedings of International Conference on Complex Systems* (pp. 16-21). ICCS.

Tulpule, P., Marano, V., & Rizzoni, G. (2009). Effects of different PHEV control strategies on vehicle performance. In *Proceedings of American Control Conference,* (pp. 3950-3955). ACC.

Tzirakis, E., Pitsas, K., Zannikos, F., & Stournas, S. (2006). Vehicle emissions and driving cycles: Comparison of the Athens driving cycle (ADC) with ECE-15 and European driving cycle (EDC). *Global NEST Journal, 8*, 282–290.

Waraich, R. A., & Axhausen, K. (2012). Agent-based parking choice model. *Transportation Research Record, 2319*, 39–46. doi:10.3141/2319-05.

Waraich, R. A., Charypar, D., Balmer, M., & Axhausen, K. W. (2009). *Performance improvements for large scale traffic simulation in MATSim*. Paper presented at the 9th Swiss Transport Research Conference. New York, NY.

Waraich, R. A., Dobler, C., Weis, C., & Axhausen, K. W. (2013). *Optimizing parking prices using an agent based approach*. Paper presented at the 92nd Annual Meeting of Transportation Research Board. Washington, DC.

Waraich, R. A., Galus, M., Dobler, C., Balmer, M., Andersson, G., & Axhausen, K. W. (2009). *Plug-in hybrid electric vehicles and smart grid: Investigations based on a micro-simulation.* Paper presented at the 12th International Conference on Travel Behaviour Research (IATBR). Jaipur, India.

Waraich, R. A., Galus, M., Dobler, C., Balmer, M., Andersson, G., & Axhausen, K. W. (2013). Plug-in hybrid electric vehicles and smart grid: Investigations based on a micro-simulation. *Transportation Research Part C, Emerging Technologies*, *28*, 74–86. doi:10.1016/j.trc.2012.10.011.

Weis, C. Vrtic, Widmer, & Axhausen. (2012). *Influence of parking on location and mode choice: A stated choice survey.* Paper presented at the 91st Annual Meeting of the Transportation Research Board. Washington, DC.

White House. (2009). *Fact sheet: US-China electric vehicles initiative.* Washington, DC: Author.

Wu, H. H., Gilchrist, A., Sealy, K., Israelsen, P., & Muhs, J. (2011). A review on inductive charging for electric vehicles. In Proceedings of Electric Machines & Drives Conference (IEMDC), (pp. 143-147). IEEE.

Wynne, J. (2009). *Impact of plug-in hybrid electric vehicles on California's electricity grid.* (Unpublished doctoral dissertation). Duke University, Durham, NC.

ADDITIONAL READING

Abedin, Z. U., & Waraich, R. A. (2013). *Modelling Inductive Charging of Battery Electric Vehicles using an Agent-Based Approach, Arbeitsberichte Verkehrs- und Raumplanung*, **899**, *IVT*. Zurich: ETH Zurich.

Chen, T. D., Khan, M., & Kockelman, K. M. (2013). *The electric vehicle charging station location problem: A parking-based assignment method for seattle.* Paper presented at the 92nd Annual Meeting of the Transportation Research Board, Washington D.C., USA.

Farhangi, H. (2010). The path of the smart grid. *Power and Energy Magazine, IEEE*, *8*(1), 18–28. doi:10.1109/MPE.2009.934876.

Galus, M. (2012). *Agent-based modeling and simulation of large scale electric mobility in power systems.* Unpublished doctoral dissertation, ETH Zurich.

Galus, M. D. Georges. G., & Waraich, R. A. (2012). Final Report of the ARTEMIS (Abating Road Emissions Through Efficient (electric) Mobility - Interactions with the electric System) project, for EWZ (text only available in German: Abschlussbericht des Projekts ARTEMIS, Schlussbericht für das Elektrizitätswerk der Stadt Zürich (EWZ)), (in German). ETH Zürich, Switzerland.

Galus, M. D., Waraich, R. A., Balmer, M., Andersson, G., & Axhausen, K. W. (2009). *A framework for investigating the impact of PHEVs.* Paper presented at the International Advanced Mobility Forum 2009, Geneva.

Galus, M. D., Waraich, R. A., Noembrini, F., Steurs, K., Georges, G., & Boulouchos, K. et al. (2012). Integrating Power Systems, Transport Systems and Vehicle Technology for Electric Mobility Impact Assessment and Efficient Control. *Smart Grid. IEEE Transactions on*, *3*(2), 934–949.

Georges, G. (2012). *Fleet-wide vehicular energy demand model for project ARTEMIS.* ETH Zurich.

Green, R. C. II, Wang, L., & Alam, M. (2011). The impact of plug-in hybrid electric vehicles on distribution networks: A review and outlook. *Renewable & Sustainable Energy Reviews*, *15*(1), 544–553. doi:10.1016/j.rser.2010.08.015.

Horni, A., Charypar, D., & Axhausen, K. W. (2011). *Variability in Transport Microsimulations Investigated With the Multi-Agent Transport Simulation MATSim, Arbeitsberichte Verkehrs- und Raumplanung, 692, IVT*. Zürich: ETH Zürich.

Kempton, W., & Tomić, J. (2005). Vehicle-to-grid power fundamentals: calculating capacity and net revenue. *Journal of Power Sources, 144*(1), 268–279. doi:10.1016/j.jpowsour.2004.12.025.

Knapen, L., Kochan, B., Bellemans, T., Janssens, D., & Wets, G. (2012). Activity-Based Modeling to Predict Spatial and Temporal Power Demand of Electric Vehicles in Flanders, Belgium. *Transportation Research Record: Journal of the Transportation Research Board, 2287*(1), 146–154. doi:10.3141/2287-18.

MacKay, D. (2008). *Sustainable Energy-without the hot air*. UIT Cambridge.

MATSim-T. (2013). Multi Agent Transportation Simulation Toolkit. Retrieved March 26, 2013, from http://www.matsim.org

Meister, K., Balmer, M., Ciari, F., Horni, A., Rieser, M., Waraich, R., & Axhausen, K. (2010). *Large-scale agent-based travel demand optimization applied to Switzerland, including mode choice*. Paper presented at the 12th World Conference on Transportation Research, Lisbon, Portugal.

Noembrini, F. (2009). *Modeling and analysis of the Swiss energy system dynamics with emphasis on the interconnection between transportation and energy conversion*. Unpublished doctoral dissertation, ETH Zurich.

Safarianova, S., Noembrini, F., Boulouchos, K., & Dietrich, P. (2011). *Techno-economic analysis of low GHG emission passenger cars, TOSCA project*. ETH Zurich.

Schieffer, S. (2010). *To charge or not to charge? Decentralized charging decisions for the smart grid*. Semester's thesis, ETH Zurich.

Schieffer, S. (2011). *Decentralized charging decisions for the smart grid*. Master's thesis, ETH Zurich.

THELMA. (2013). Technology-centered Electric Mobility Assessment, Retrieved March 29, 2013, from http://www.thelma-emobility.net

Waraich, R. A., & Axhausen, K. (2012). Agent-Based Parking Choice Model. *Transportation Research Record, 2319*, 39–46. doi:10.3141/2319-05.

Waraich, R. A., Dobler, C., Weis, C., & Axhausen, K. W. (2013) *Optimizing parking prices using an agent based approach*. Paper presented at the *92nd Annual Meeting of Transportation Research Board*, Washington D.C., USA.

Waraich, R. A., Galus, M., Dobler, C., Balmer, M., Andersson, G., & Axhausen, K. W. (2009). *Plug-in Hybrid Electric Vehicles and Smart Grid: Investigations Based on a Micro-Simulation*. Paper presented at the 12th International Conference on Travel Behaviour Research (IATBR), Jaipur, India.

Waraich, R. A., Galus, M., Dobler, C., Balmer, M., Andersson, G., & Axhausen, K. W. (2013). Plug-in Hybrid Electric Vehicles and Smart Grid: Investigations Based on a Micro-Simulation. *Transportation Research Part C, Emerging Technologies, 28*, 74–86. doi:10.1016/j.trc.2012.10.011.

Weis, C., Vrtic, M., Widmer, P., & Axhausen, K. W. (2012). *Influence of parking on location and mode choice: A stated choice survey*. Paper presented at the 91st Annual Meeting of the Transportation Research Board, Washington D.C., USA.

Chapter 15
Impacts of Electric Mobility on the Electric Grid

Jesus Fraile-Ardanuy
Universidad Politecnica de Madrid, Spain

Roberto Alvaro
Universidad Politecnica de Madrid, Spain

Dionisio Ramirez
Universidad Politecnica de Madrid, Spain

Jairo Gonzalez
Universidad Politecnica de Madrid, Spain

Sergio Martinez
Universidad Politecnica de Madrid, Spain

Luk Knapen
University of Hasselt, Belgium

Davy Janssens
University of Hasselt, Belgium

ABSTRACT

Electric mobility is becoming an option for reducing greenhouse gas emissions of road transport and decreasing the external dependence on fossil fuels. However, this new kind of mobility will introduce additional loads to the power system, and it is important to determine its effects on it. As a direct scenario from DATA SIM FP7 EU project, an application related to electric mobility and its impact on the electric grid from Flanders region is presented in this chapter. The chapter begins with a brief description of the electric transmission network for Flanders region and the electric vehicles energy requirements for different mobility zones in this region, obtained from FEATHERS, an activity-based model. In the following section, the main assumptions that allow estimating the total electricity consumption for each mobility area is presented. Once this total consumption per zone has been estimated, an algorithm to link the mobility areas with the nearest substation is developed. Finally, the impact of charging electric vehicles on the transmission substations is examined.

INTRODUCTION

Some of the major concerns of the European Commission are climate change and energy. In 2009 the EU adopted a complete package (the well-known '20-20-20' targets to be achieved in 2020) focuses in three different but related areas: promoting both renewable energies and energy efficiency, and reducing emissions. These targets are the following (http://ec.europa.eu/clima/policies/package/documentation_en.htm):

DOI: 10.4018/978-1-4666-4920-0.ch015

- Europe has to reduce greenhouse gas (GHG) emissions at least 20% below 1990 levels.
- 20% of EU energy consumption has to come from renewable resources.
- 20% reduction in primary energy use compared with projected levels has to be achieved by improving energy efficiency.

Following the initial EU lines in this theme, the European Commission presented in 2011 the "Energy Roadmap 2050" (http://ec.europa.eu/energy/energy2020/roadmap/doc/com_2011_8852_en.pdf). This document presents main solutions to achieve a goal of cutting emissions by over 80% by 2050, without disrupting energy supplies and competitiveness of the European countries.

In order to reach these objectives, it is necessary to reduce the overall emissions, mainly in transport (reducing CO_2, NO_x and other pollutants), so road transportation must be decarbonized through a high deployment of battery electric and plug-in hybrid electric vehicles (BEVs – or simply EVs- and PHEVs).

These types of vehicles will be part of the global solution for climate change but also they could be a huge problem, because the total electricity demand will grow up in the future and the charging of EVs and PHEVs will have an important impact on the electric grid, especially under uncoordinated charging conditions.

Investments in electricity networks are very expensive and costly in time; therefore it is important to anticipate the impact of a massive deployment of electric vehicles in the electric grid. At the same time, electric companies plan their electricity networks taking into account that consumptions, in different nodes of the electric grid, vary continuously in time but these loads are assumed to be static in space.

With the introduction of electric vehicles and their inherent electric mobility, there will also be a remarkable spatial variation in the electric loads that could increase the total stress on the power grid. This stress can also cause changes in the behavior of electric vehicle drivers, since they will not be able to recharge at the desired locations and at the desired times due to charging restrictions.

The main objective of the FP7 EU DataSim Project (http://www.uhasselt.be/datasim) is to provide an entirely new and highly detailed spatial-temporal micro-simulation methodology for human mobility. This methodology is based on massive amounts of big data from different sources. One of the outputs of this project is an activity-based micro-simulation model (ActBM) for traffic forecasting called Feathers, which has been used to predict spatial and temporal electrical vehicle power demand in the region of Flanders (Knapen, Luk; Kochan, Bruno; Bellemans, Tom; Janssens, Davy & Wets, Geert; 2011).

The main objective of this chapter is to study the impact of the electric vehicles' load integration on the electric grid according to a rate of market penetration and different charging scenarios by using accurate information about the spatial and temporal electric load demand due to the electric mobility.

This analysis will be useful to foresee whether the growing presence of electric vehicles could provoke technical problems in the transmission grid. In a second stage, this analysis will allow to evaluate the capacity of the electric vehicles to promote the integration of renewable energies and the availability of this type of vehicles to offer new services such as vehicle to grid applications (V2G), creating new business models. Note that, in some electricity markets, due to their specific rules, the ancillary services (frequency regulation, voltage control, etc.) have to be provided from specific nodes of the transmission grid (Bessa, Ricardo J. and Matos, Manuel A., (2010)). Hence the importance of carrying out this analysis based on a zonal approach.

In this chapter the particular case of the Flemish electric grid is studied, starting from the Activity Based models (AB models) basis, developed in Knapen, Luk; Kochan, Bruno; Bellemans, Tom;

Janssens, Davy & Wets, Geert (2011). These are behavioral models predicting activity schedule that can be used to evaluate transportation needs. This mobility analysis is transformed into electric vehicle consumptions from which their electric load demand can be obtained. The activity-based model divides the Flanders region (6 million inhabitants on 13000 km^2) in 2368 different zones with an average area of 5.5 km^2 per zone and it estimates the electric energy and power requirements for each zone of this region.

As it is explained in Knapen, L. (2011), to obtain accurate estimations for electric vehicle power demand as a function of time and location, the results of transport demand models are used. Those models deliver detailed location, timing and motivation information about trips and activities for each individual. The charging process is performed under two scenarios. In the first one, Scenario 1, people start charging as soon as possible during the low tariff period. In the second one, Scenario 2, people start charging uniformly distributed in time, adopting a decentralized smart grid strategy. Different hypothesis and classifications regarding the available vehicles, chargers and kind of vehicle user are done. Vehicles are classified in small, medium and large, based on Belgian government statistics related to conventional vehicles, and they are assigned as company car or owner car. Chargers are classified by rated power, 3.3 kW and 7.2 kW, and by the location: at home or at work. Finally, the type of trip is divided in work or no-work trip. Work trips are done either by company car or by owner car. All vehicles are charged at home, and company cars can also be charged at work in some specific scenarios.

Although the main impact of electric vehicles on the power system will initially be more important in the electric distribution network, the granularity of activity-based model prevents to analyze this impact in such detail. Therefore, main references related to the impact of electric vehicles charging on the distribution grid will be presented in the Background section.

In this chapter a higher-level analysis for a nationwide region will be performed. The electric energy and power requirements for each mobility zone will be added to the regular electric load consumption per zone. The total electricity demand for mobility zones will be fed by electric transmission substations spread throughout the Flemish region. These substations have a nominal power capacity that should not be exceeded under any load scenario. During the analysis, this condition will be checked for each substation.

At the same time, there is no one-to-one link between the mobility zones set and the substations set, because there are more mobility zones than transmission substations, so several mobility zones will be fed by the same substation. In this work, an algorithm to link mobility zones to substation will also be developed.

The chapter is structured as follows. Initially, the state of the art related to the impact of electric mobility on power systems is presented in the Background section. In the next section, Adopted Solution, a brief description about the power system of Flanders region is given. Then, the generation of the total load profiles per mobility zone is determined as well as the main assumptions that are taken into account. Finally, the assignment method to link different mobility zones to a particular substation is explained. The last section presents the case studies, simulations, and the main results. Conclusions and future works are shown in the last part of the chapter.

BACKGROUND

Research on the impact of great deployment of electric vehicles on the power system has been carried out during last years. Some authors have focused on the increment of the national generation capacity necessary to cover the extra amount of power that EV will demand when they are charging. In this case, a deep analysis of the electric network is not required. Geth, F.; K. Willekens,

K. Clement, J. Driesen, De Breucker (2010) have studied the impact of the charging of PHEVs on the production park in Belgium under different scenarios and Fraile-Ardanuy, J., S. Martínez, B. Artaloytia, D. Ramírez, M. Fuentes, C. Sánchez (2012) proposed a similar analysis for the Spanish case.

Other authors have analyzed the impact of electric vehicles on the distribution networks. As a consequence of this analysis, most of them have also proposed different charging methods to avoid (or reduce) this impact. Clement-Nyns, K., E. Haesen, J. Driesen (2010) have studied the impact on a residential distribution network for a Belgian case, analyzing the power losses and voltage deviations and proposing a coordinated charging strategy to reduce this impact. The radial network for the analysis was the IEEE 34-node Medium Voltage (MV) test feeder downscaled to 240 V to represent a residential distribution grid and the electric vehicle loads are randomly applied to different nodes in this network (no mobility information was used).

Qian, K., C. Zhou, M. Allan, J. Yuan (2011) proposed a stochastic method for predicting the EVs charging load and its effect over the distribution network. An 11-kV 38-node electric network was used to model the distribution system and this grid was used to determine the impact of EV charging load on the system load curve. Depending on the assumed market penetration rate of EVs, the daily peak demand was increased up to almost 36% for the worst-case charging scenario. Authors also studied the congestion level of the main line sections of the network, but in this particular case, only one line exceeds its rated capacity in one of the simulated scenarios.

Shao, S., M. Pipattanasomporn, S. Rahman (2009) analyzed the impact of charging EVs on a single distribution transformer under different charging scenarios. Depending on these scenarios, the transformer can be overloaded and authors proposed several solutions to prevent it.

Zhao, L., S. Prousch, M. Hübner, A. Moser (2010) analyzed the impact of charging EVs in Medium Voltage (MV) grid (with distributed generation) and various Low Voltage (LV) grids, simulating the distribution of nodal voltages and current congestions of the network lines. In this work it is demonstrated that the LV-grids limit the penetration of EVs.

Papadopoulos, P. S. Skarvelis-Kazakos, I. Grau, B. Awad, L. M. Cipcigan, N. Jenkins (2010) studied the impact of EVs on a typical UK distribution network, analyzing the voltage drops, losses in the distribution network and the distribution transformer overloading.

Most of these previous works were based on a detailed study of small-scale distribution systems. Pieltain, L.; Gomez, T.; Cossent, R.; Mateo, C.; Frías, P. (2011) have studied the increase in the investment cost on large-scale real distribution networks due to different penetration rates of EVs. In this case, investment costs can grow up to 15% and energy losses in the network can increase up to 40% during off-peak hours for a scenario with 60% of EV penetration rate.

In order to reduce range anxiety, fast charging stations should be deployed in the near future throughout cities and countries. In Yunus, K; Zelaya, H.; Reza, M. (2011) the impact of using fast charging on a distribution transformer and the voltage drops on a distribution network nodes are studied. In this case, the bus voltages dropped below the admissible limits, but authors only suggest that a necessary action must be taken to avoid this situation.

In most of these papers, an electric distribution network model is assumed and the location of the new loads due to the EV charging is done randomly, which is not realistic. It seems clear that in some areas, there may be a higher concentration of vehicles because of different reasons (there is a mall in this area, for example). This is the main reason why it is necessary to take into account more complex mobility approximations. For example, in Soares, F. J.; Peças, J. A.; Rocha, P. M.;

Moreira, C. L. (2011) a discrete-state, discrete-time Markov chain Monte Carlo simulation is used to predict EV routes in a one year period and their consumptions.

In Li, (2012) starting from a PHEV charging demand model, authors use queuing theory to describe the behavior of a great number of vehicles at an EV charging station in a residential community.

There are some papers where algorithms for the spatial-temporal localizations of electric vehicle demand are developed and constitute the main progress of the paper. Galus, M.; Waraich, R. A.; Anderson, G. (2011) and Galus, M.; Waraich, R. A.; Noembrini, F.; Steurs, K.; Georges, G.; Boulouchos, K.; Axhausen, K.; Anderson, G. (2012) have proposed an integration of agent-based transportation micro-simulation and the electricity power network. In order to have accurate mobility simulations, a realistic vehicle energy model has also been developed. The obtained mobility information, which provides detailed spatial and temporal data about PHEVs, has been integrated into the Zurich electricity medium voltage (MV) network. A study of the number of overloaded transformer substations has been performed and a hierarchical control algorithm has been developed to ensure that the transformers at different voltage levels (22 kV and 150 kV) were not overloaded. These analysis is basis of the work presented in this chapter, but with several important differences: Galus (2011) only evaluates the mobility in a city area (Zurich) and authors have available the daily load curve from real measurements of real and reactive power values for each of the 33 transformers in the 150-22 kV substations, in time intervals of 15 minutes.

The mobility analysis presented in this chapter is deeper, covering not only a city area but also the mobility of a nationwide scale. Besides, due to the lack of electric consumption information per zone, in this work it is necessary to evaluate how to share the total electric consumption in Flanders among the different mobility zones. Therefore, a process for distributing the background electric consumption among mobility areas is presented.

In Galus (2012) a charging control algorithm is proposed and it is shown that network congestion can be mitigated using adequate control signals. To demonstrate the behavior of the control system, authors model four energy hubs with generic transformer ratings, assuming that these transformers are loaded around 50% of their rating during the peak load times. A similar approach is proposed in this chapter, where some of the substation transformer rating information and load ratios are also assumed and justified.

To improve mobility studies, some authors have been working on a better modeling of electric vehicles behavior. For example, Lee, D.; Shiah, S; Lee, C.; Wang, Y. (2007) proposes a state-of-charge estimation of the residual battery capacity of an electric scooter when the battery is discharged under real dynamic conditions.

Bingham, C., Walsh, C.; Carroll, S. (2012) evaluates the impact of the driver driving style on the battery energy consumption of his/her EV. This consumption will affect the state-of-charge and the reachable range. Finally, Maia (2011) has developed an electric vehicle simulator for energy consumption studies. This tool can be integrated in the agent-based mobility model to have a more accurate mobility results.

There are some EU projects related specifically to the impact of EV in the electric grid. For example, the main objective of the Grid for Vehicle (G4V) EU project (http://www.g4v.eu) is to develop an analytical method to evaluate the impact of a large scale introduction of EV and PHEV on the grid infrastructure. Some of the partners of this project are distribution system operators (DSOs) such as Endesa (Spain), Enel (Italy), EDF (France), EDP (Portugal), RWE (Germany), etc. These partners have shared different distribution grids models to evaluate the effect of electric vehicles charging over them.

The Mobile Energy Resources in Grids of Electricity (MERGE) EU project (http://www.

ev-merge.eu) perform an assessment of the behavior of power systems with a large penetration of electric vehicles. In this case, some studies related to the estimation of the additional investment cost in the distribution networks due to penetration of EVs have been developed. Again, the project consortium is formed by a multi-disciplinary group composed by research centers, System Operators (transmission and distribution grids), regulators and automotive industry connected partners with easy access to distribution network models.

ADOPTED SOLUTION

Electricity Grid Description

As aforementioned, the impact of wide-scale electric vehicles deployment in a national electricity network will be focused in the Flemish electricity transmission network. The main data related to this network was obtained from the Belgian electricity transmission system operator (TSO). According to Annual Report 2011 of ELIA GROUP (2011), its main characteristics are:

- The system is composed by overhead and underground transmission lines. The nominal voltage transmission levels are 380 kV, 220 kV, 150 kV and 70 kV.
- In Flemish Region there are 179 Transmission substations.
- The nominal power (also called capacity) of these substations is between 40 MVA and 800 MVA. In reference (http://www.elia.be/en/grid-data/grid-development/capacity-new-generation-units) a list of 63 main Flemish transmission substations with its nominal capacity are presented.

There were no information available about the nominal capacity of the 116 Flemish Transmission substations, so due to the similarity between the Flemish electric grid and the Dutch electric grid, the nominal capacity of the rest of the Flemish transmission substations were selected based on known data of the Dutch transmission system extracted from Schavemaker, P & van der Sluis, L. (2009).

There was not, either, available information about the geographic position of each transmission substation, therefore, a very time-demanding solution was to overlap a map of the high voltage grid from Belgium on Google Earth and then locate manually each substation.

Generating Electricity Load Profiles per Mobility Zone

In order to perform an electric mobility impact analysis of on the electric grid, it is firstly necessary to know the total electricity demand in each mobility zone.

Figure 1 shows that the share of total energy demand in each zone is divided into three different components: The first part is due to the energy demand for electric vehicles that recharge in that area. The second is the domestic consumption due to households in that specific area, and the third part contains the rest of the electrical consumption (transport, industrial, etc.). The sum of the second and third components will be called *initial electric load demand per zone* and it represents the initial load demand on the power system without the contribution of the electric vehicles charging.

Electric Vehicle Load Demand per Zone

The Feathers activity-based model estimates electric energy and power requirements due to electric vehicles for each of the 2368 zones of the Flanders region; therefore the first component of the total energy demand in each zone is provided by this activity model directly.

Figure 1. Distribution of different load demand per mobility zone

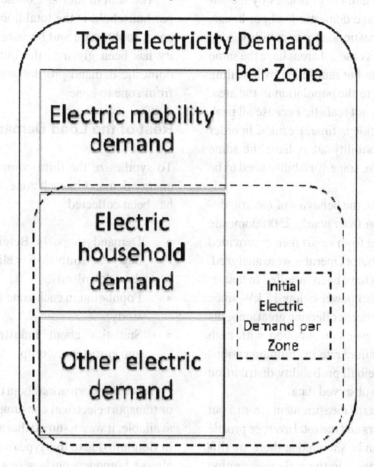

Domestic Load Demand per Zone

The second component of the total load demand per zone is the domestic demand. The process to obtain the domestic demand profile per zone was the following:

Firstly, an annual synthetic average domestic load per household in Flanders, with a quarter hour resolution (35040 measurements) provided by Flemish Regulator of the Electricity and Gas Market web site (VREG, 2012) was available and also the population in each zone provided by the activity-based mobility model. In order to evaluate the number of houses per zone, the statistics about population and demographic data was extracted from EUROSTAT website (http://epp.eurostat.

ec.europa.eu). Therefore, the number of houses per zone was determined by evaluating the quotient between the population per zone and the average number of people per house in Flanders:

$$Hz_i = \frac{Pz_i}{ANPz_i}$$

where i is the mobility zone index:

$$i \in (1, \quad 2368) \quad zones$$

Hz_i denotes the number of houses per zone, Pz_i is the population per zone and $ANPz_i$ is the average number of people per household per zone i.

Multiplying the number of houses by the annual synthetic average domestic load per house, an initial total domestic load per mobility zone was obtained. In this case, all areas have the same consumption profile but multiplied by a scaling factor proportional to the population in the area.

This situation is not realistic because all peak demands will coincide in time. Besides, in order to avoid that all mobility areas have the same consumption profile, some variability need to be added to this data.

As a second step, the behavior of electric domestic consumption from nearly 2500 domestic customers extracted from smart meters provided by a Spanish Distributor Operator were analyzed. These smart meters have been installed in households with demanded power below 15 kW since 2011, and they have been collecting great amounts of data about domestic consumption with high reliability, with a failure rate in communications less than 1%. A Weibull probability distribution function has fit the observed data.

In Figure 2-right the measurements from 5 out of 2500 smart meters and the total average profile are presented. It can be shown that there are different behavior patterns in the real consumption profiles, because not all customers consume the same energy at the same time of day. From these data, the mean and variance values per hour were evaluated. In order to use this information in Flanders, a brief comparison between the average value of the Spanish real measurements and the synthetic profile of load demand in Flanders for the same day of the year was also done (see Figure 2-left). Both profiles have similar amplitudes and there is only a two-hour shift in the evening peak demand.

Assuming the annual synthetic average domestic load per household in Flanders as an average value, new domestic demand profiles have been generated for each household in each mobility area, based on the variance evaluated in the Spanish case.

The sum of all these domestic consumptions per household is the total domestic demand per zone. In this case and because of some variability has been given to the initial data, the total domestic demand profiles are slightly different from zone to zone.

Rest of the Load Demand per Zone

To synthesize the third component of the total energy demand in each zone, the following data has been collected:

- Demand shape in Belgium for only one day (http://www.elia.be/en/grid-data/data-download).
- Population in each zone (given by mobility study).
- Statistics about industrialization (http://epp.eurostat.ec.europa.eu).

Since no information about the actual industrial or transport electrical consumption per zone was available, it was assumed that all electric demand in Belgium due to this type of loads is consumed almost homogeneously along the country with a higher ratio in areas located in Flanders. This assumption takes into account that, according to statistics about industrialization of main regions of Belgium, extracted from EUROSTAT website (http://epp.eurostat.ec.europa.eu), the Flemish region is more industrialized than the rest of the country.

Thus, the first step was to obtain the total electric demand for Flanders. This has been done by multiplying the total electric demand for the whole country, available on TSO Elia website (http://www.elia.be/en/grid-data/data-download), for a scaling factor proportional to the Flanders population.

$$Fr = \frac{Fp}{Bp}$$

Figure 2. Comparison between the average real Spanish measurements and synthetic profile load demand in Flanders (left). 2500 measurements from Spanish smart meters (right).

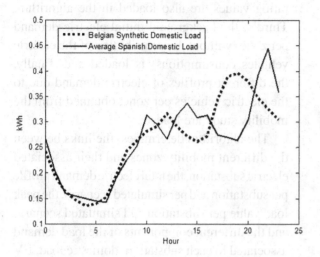
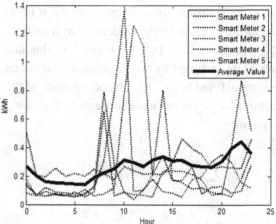

where *Fr* is the Flemish ratio, *Fp* is the Flemish population and *Bp* is the total Belgian population.

$$FTd = Fr.BTd$$

where *FTd* is the Flemish total electric demand and *BTd* represents the Belgian total electric demand. Rest of electric consumption in Flanders region, named *OFC*, is evaluated by subtracting the total electric demand in Flanders and the total electric domestic demand for all mobility zones in Flanders, named Fdd_i:

$$OFC = Ftd - \sum_{i=mobility\_zones} Fdd_i$$

A zone ratio, *Zr*, is defined as the ratio between the population per zone, *Zp*, and Flemish population, *Fp*:

$$Zr = \frac{Zp}{Fp}$$

The electric demand profile of the rest of electric load consumptions in each zone *i*, $OFCz_i$, is

obtained multiplying the zone ratio, *Zr*, by the rest of electric consumption in Flanders region, *OFC*.

$$OFCz_i = Zr.OFC$$

At this point, once the electric demand profile of the rest of load consumptions per zone is obtained ("other electric demand" part in Figure 2), it is necessary to add the other two components (energy demand due to electric vehicles per zone and domestic consumption due to households per zone) to finally obtain total energy demand per zone.

Mapping Mobility Zones and Electric Substations

To simulate the impact of charging electric vehicles on the electric grid, an assignment procedure to allocate the total electric load demand profile of each mobility zone to the nearest transmission substation has been developed based on the closest distance between the mobility area centroid and the substation location (see Figure 3). As aforementioned, there are more mobility zones than electric substations, therefore there will be several mobility zones fed by the same substation.

The following step is to calculate the centroid of each mobility zone. Each mobility zone is defined by a closed polygon defined by n vertices (x_0, y_0), (x_1, y_1), ..., (x_{n-1}, y_{n-1}), (x_n, y_n). This last vertex is assumed to be the same as the initial vertex defined by (x_0, y_0). The coordinates of the centroid (c_x, c_y) is evaluated through the following equations:

$$c_x = \frac{1}{6A} \sum_{i=0}^{n-1} (x_i + x_{i+1})(x_i y_{i+1} - x_{i+1} y_i)$$

$$c_y = \frac{1}{6A} \sum_{i=0}^{n-1} (y_i + y_{i+1})(x_i y_{i+1} - x_{i+1} y_i)$$

where A is the area of the polygon is given by:

$$A = \frac{1}{2} \sum_{i=0}^{n-1} (x_i y_{i+1} - x_{i+1} y_i)$$

The next step in the algorithm is to compute the distance between the centroid of each mobility zone and each electric substation, denoted by $dist_k$. The position of the k-substation is defined by its coordinates (sx_k, sy_k):

$$dist_k = \sqrt{\left|c_x - sx_k\right|^2 + \left|c_y - sy_k\right|^2}$$

The i mobility zone is assigned to the nearest substation, ASS_i:

$$\mathrm{ASS}_i = \min(dist_k)$$

with all the mobility zones allocated to their nearest substation, the last step is to aggregate the corresponding total electric load demand allocated to each substation.

The analysis starts loading a map of Flanders meshed in the mobility zones, as previous shown in

Knapen, L. (2011). Secondly, the geographic locations of all transmission substations and their rating values are also loaded in the algorithm. Thirdly, the background initial electric demand per zone (without the contribution of the electric vehicles consumptions) is loaded and, finally, the different profiles of electric demand due to the electric vehicles per zone, obtained from the mobility study are loaded.

The algorithm determines: the links between the different mobility zones and their associated electric substation, the total electric demand profile per substation and per simulated scenario, the peak load value per substation and simulated scenario and the different components of the load demand associated to each substation: domestic load, EV load, total aggregated, etc.

TECHNICAL RESULTS

Previous Analysis

As a previous step to the study of the impact of electric vehicles on the electric substations, the reliability of the assumptions and the work done up to this point was checked. The electric demand profile due to initial total consumptions in all the substations under this study has been analyzed.

The evaluation has been based on the comparison between the load levels simulated in each Flemish substation due to initial total consumptions and the load levels common in other electrical transmission systems. It is important to note that it has been assumed that the electric transmission grid in Belgium has no important problems respect to the load levels in the substations, and the TSO criteria to manage the electrical grid is similar to the most electrical transmission systems.

The results show a good agreement, with few exceptions that will be commented in the Conclusions section. The levels of average load in most substations due to the initial total consumptions have oscillated between 25% and 55% respect to

Figure 3. Allocating of mobility zones to the nearest substation

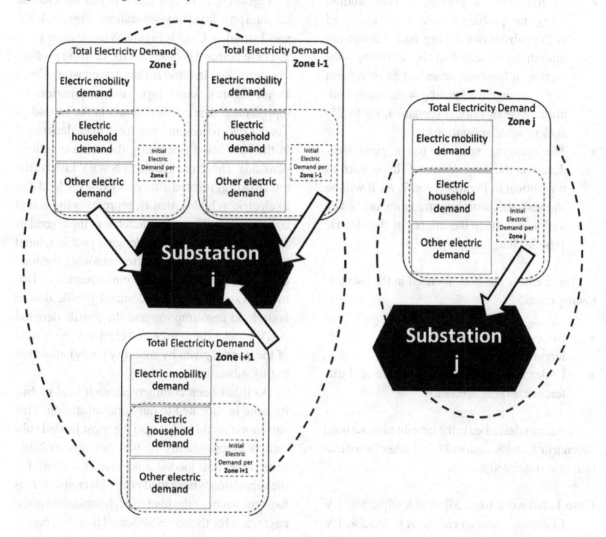

the nominal power values. These are typical levels of average load in the transformers of different electrical transmission systems (REE, 2010). Therefore, up to this point of the study, the assumptions have been considered valid.

As it was commented before, the next step to begin the study of the impact of the electric vehicle is to aggregate the electric demand profile due to electric vehicle, obtained in the mobility study, to the initial load consumptions profiles.

Simulation and Results

After simulating several charging scenarios which have been based on Knapen, L. (2011), two main conclusions are worth mentioning:

- The mobility zone with the highest electric demand does not have to be supplied by the most loaded substation neither by the substation whose load is the most increased (see Figures 4 and 5).

- At transmission grid level (the studied case), no problems have been observed in the substations, taking into account the limitations indicated in the following subsection. It has been observed an increment in the average load during some hours and, in the case of critical scenarios, up to 25-30% in some substations.

- The charging scenario has a great incidence on the power demand shape, such as it is shown in Figures 6 and 7. As it will be showed, the charging strategies are a key tool to minimize the impact of the electric vehicle charging.

The analysis has been focused in the two following cases:

- Under similar charging scenarios with different EV market share.

- Under identical EV market share and different charging scenarios.

Scenarios described in the introduction are used (Scenario 1 and Scenario 2). Vehicle electrification rate simulated are:

Case 1: No work trips, 5%. Work trips, 5%. EV Company cars can charge at work, 5%. EV Company cars cannot charge at work, 5%. (Medium EV rate penetration).

Case 2: No work trips, 10%. Work trips, 10%. EV Company cars can charge at work, 10%. EV Company cars cannot charge at work, 10%. (High EV rate penetration).

In addition, the EV can be PHEV or BEV. The BEV ratio respect to total EV is:

- Company cars, 50%
- Owner cars, 25%

Figures 4, 5, 6, 7, 8 and 9 depict the electric demand profile in some substations. Figures 4, 5, 6 and 7 simulate Case 1. Figures 8 and 9 show Case 2. These demand profiles are the demand profiles disaggregated in different kind of consumptions. In all figures, same type of consumptions is represented. The curve denoted in the legend as Total Load represents the total load demanded in the substation (including the electric vehicle demand). The curve named as Not EV Load is the total load aggregated after deducting the load due to electric vehicles, that is, represents the actual consumption. The curve denoted in the legend as Rest Of Loads is the load demand profile related to present consumptions after removing the load due to household load. The curve named as Domestic Load is the load demand profile due to household consumption and the profile denoted as EV Load is the aggregated electric vehicle load of the zones (given by mobility study) allocated to this substation.

As it has been commented, each load mobility zone is allocated to only one substation. This substation could be (or not) the most loaded substation independently of whether this mobility zone is the most loaded. Likewise, this is valid to the substation whose load is most increased. This happens because the load in each substation is the aggregated of the zones allocated to it. It is necessary, then, to analyze the effect over all substations, not only to focus the analysis on the substations from which the mobility zones with higher electric vehicles load are supplied. This effect is showed in the Figures 4, 5 y 6, where in a same charging scenario (Scenario 1), the substation that supplies the most loaded mobility zone (Figure 4) is not the most loaded substation (Figure 5) neither the substation whose load is most increased (Figure 6). In the scenario simulated, the most loaded substation is Dhanis Substation, with a peak load of 119 MW; the substation that supplies

Figure 4. Power demand shapes of the substation most loaded (Dhanis Substation, 120 MW of peak load). Scenario 1

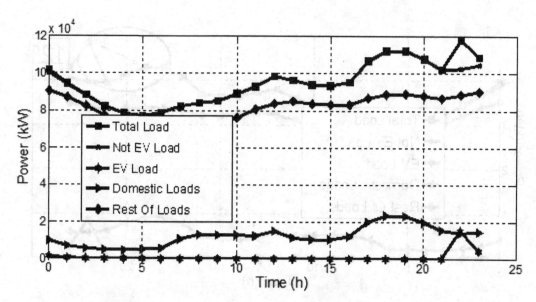

the most loaded mobility zone (2357) is Pacheco Substation, in which the load is increased in 12%, and the substation whose load is most increased is Kersbeek Substation with a total increase about 35%.

As aforementioned, the load increment in some substations could reach, in peak hours and critical scenarios, values close to 35-40% and average load values around 25% during some hours. That effect is shown in Figure 6.

In this case, the charging scenario shown in Figures 4, 5 y 6, the scenario 1 is unlikely because the charging strategy is based on all the vehicles charging in a short space of time, provoking an abrupt shape change of the demanded energy profile. The results shown in these figures represent a scenario where the electric vehicles can be charged at work or at home as early as arriving at any charge opportunity location, within the low tariff period (22h-6h). Thereby the result is an abrupt shape profile of the electric vehicle load. This behavior is not likely because not all the people will be ready to charge the vehicle at the same time (at the beginning of low tariff

period, 22h). In any case, the results under this charging scenario show that, in some cases, it could be necessary to analyze the impact of the electric vehicle charge in some substations in a deeper study.

It should be noted that, although it is not noteworthy from the point of view of system reliability and capacity to ensure the electricity supply, a generalized increment of the average load in substations and, therefore, in the lines, could increment the losses of the system and could decrease its efficiency. In addition, despite the development of more efficient electrical devices, the likely increase in the electric power demand in the rest of consumptions should be added to the electric vehicle charge.

On the other hand, in contrast to the results obtained in critical scenarios, the results under more realistic scenarios show a much lower change on the power demand profile. The energy demand profile in Scenario 1 (Figure 6) and Scenario 2 (Figure 7) are depicted. Both figures show the electricity demand profile for the same substation. In Figure 7, the simulated scenario

Figure 5. Power demand shapes of the substation that supplies the most loaded zone (Pacheco Substation).Scenario 1

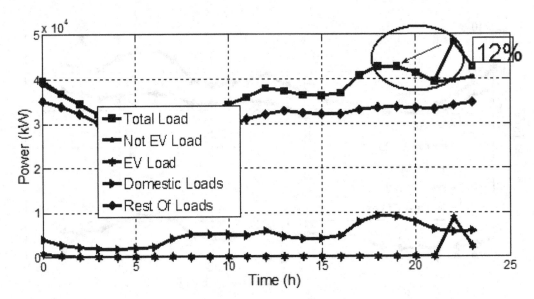

(Scenario 2) gives as result a smoother energy demand profile than in the case of the most critical scenario (Scenario 1), shown in Figure 6. As it is shown in these figures, in the more realistic scenario, the electric vehicle load demand profile is flatter, spreading the load along a wider period of time than the other scenario. In this case, all the vehicles are not charging at the same time neither in a short space of time.

Figure 6. Power demand shapes of the substation which load is the most increased (Kersbeek Substation). Scenario 1

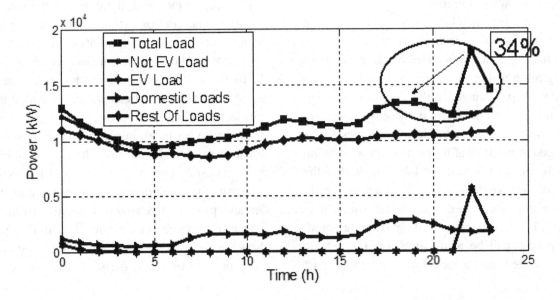

Figure 7. Power demand shapes of the substation Kersbeek Substation. Scenario 2. Case 1

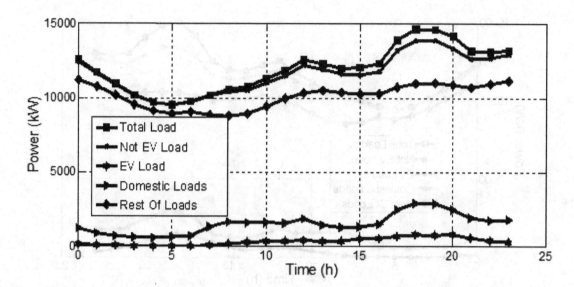

On the other hand, Figure 7 depicts a different scenario compared to the one shown in the previous figure. In this case, the electric vehicles can be charged at work or at home as early as arriving at charge opportunity location and the charging costs are not minimized (Scenario 2). This scenario is more realistic because not all people are waiting to connect the vehicle to the grid at a fixed hour. In this case, people charge the vehicle whenever they want if it is available.

Figure 8. Power demand shapes of the substation Kersbeek Substation. Scenario 1. Case 2

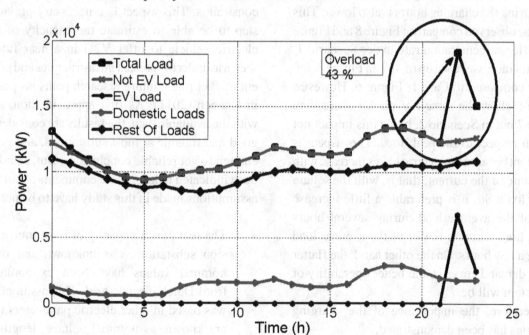

Figure 9. Power demand shapes of the substation Kersbeek Substation. Scenario 2. Case 2

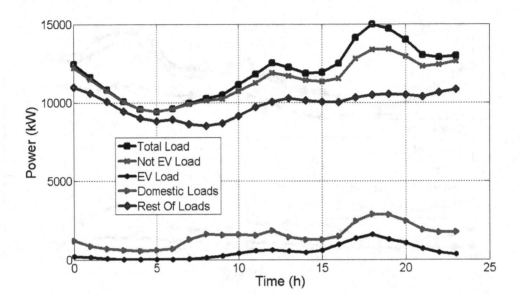

Thereby the electric vehicle load demand profile is flatter than that obtained in the other scenario because the aggregated electric vehicle charge is more spread along the day in each substation.

The peak load in this scenario is increased in 5% in contrast with the 34% increment of the scenario depicted in the Figure 6, and the average load during the charging hours is also lower. This could be observed comparing Figure 8 and Figure 6 to different penetration rate under Scenario 1. The total increase reach up to 43% in Figure 8, 8% higher compared to Case 1, Figure 6. However, Figure 9 show the same EV market share than Figure 7 but in Scenario 2, being this impact not so high respect to the peak load. This aspect is important because the electric losses increase with the square of the current; that is, with the square of the load. So, it is preferable a little increase (5%) of the average load during several hours than a high increase (34%) of the average load during a few hours. On the other hand, the flatter power demand curve is, the better operability of the system will be.

Therefore, the importance of the charging strategies has been demonstrated.

Comments

The analysis presented in this chapter gives a step forward respect to Knapen, L. (2011), where the power demand due to electric vehicle is calculated but not evaluated with respect to its interaction with the electric power systems and its technical constraints. This aspect is a necessary previous step to be able to estimate the capacity of the electric vehicle to offer V2G in a near future scenario under the present infrastructures and present market rules, future research paths proposed in Knapen (2011). As first approximation, and with the available data, the results are considered good and reliable at most substations, and good enough to get reliable conclusions. But, as it has been indicated before, some comments about the assumptions made in this study have to be noted:

- The real power capacity of most transmission substations was unknown and their nominal values have been extrapolated from Dutch electric grid. This assumption was based in other electric parameters that are known, as nominal voltage, length of the lines connected, etc. (ELIA GROUP, 2011), and that have been compared with known data of the Dutch transmission system. The nominal power ratings of about one hundred of the evaluated substations have been supposed with this assumption. The rest of power values of substations in Flanders have been collected through Belgian TSO website.

- An initial assumption to share the third component (see Figure 1) of the total electric demand per zone (the non-domestic load) has been distributed proportionally to the population in all mobility zones. This assumption could not be good in certain zones. For example, in zones where there is not a balance between population and industrial use of the land, this assumption fails. Examples are ports or zones used exclusively by industry, where there are substations that only supply electricity to these industrial zones. In this case, this assumption assigns to the non-domestic load profile a lower level than what is reasonable in this zones (remember that the non-domestic load consumption in a particular

zone is proportional to the population of this zone), being the calculated substations load, underestimated. It is also true that, in industrial zones, the impact of electric vehicles on the load profile should be lower than in residential areas, because these areas are great consumers of electricity and its electric infrastructure is robust enough to support the increment in the electric demand due to the electric vehicles. Taking into account these observations, it has been concluded that, in certain zones, more information about how the industrial consumption is distributed would be necessary to do a more reliable estimation. This problem could be observed in Figure 10, where practically the only existing consumption is due to electric vehicles. (This is not possible because this substation is located in the Antwerpen Port, and in addition, a substation without load makes no sense).

- Similar situations appear when the mobility zones are purely residential. In this case, the non-domestic load is overestimated, but the error remains on the conservative side.

Figure 10. Case of Lillo substation, which supplies the industrial zone of Antwerpen Port

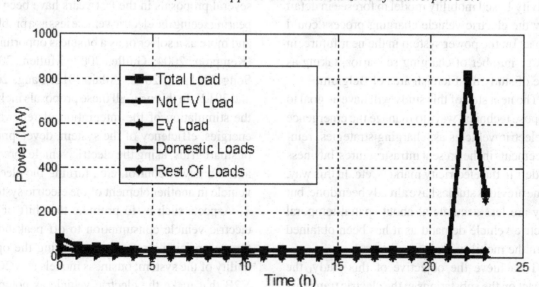

- Related to the assignment of mobility zones to the nearest substation, no real information can confirm this statement. Moreover, the possibility that one mobility zone is supplied by more than one substation is high, taking into account that the transmission grid is a mesh grid, not a radial one. In any case, from the point of view of system's operation, it is likely that the nearest substation is supporting the most part of the load in each zone. To be more precise it would be necessary to have higher access to electric grid data

Figure 8 shows the power demand shape of one of the few substations where results are not reliable. In this case, the analyzed substation is Lillo Substation, which supplies the Antwerpen port, where the total population in this particular zone is practically negligible. Therefore, the estimation of total electric load demand in this zone fails.

CONCLUSION AND FUTURE WORK

The main objective of this study is to exploit the big electric load data given by the accurate activity-based mobility model to foresee in detail how the electric vehicle charging process could impact on the power system in the near future, in a large number of charging scenarios, taking as case of study the Flemish area of Belgium.

The next step of this study will have as goal to propose technical ways to manage the emergence of electric vehicles as: charging strategies, reinforcements in the present infrastructures, business models in the electricity markets, etc. In this way, some previous studies have already been done, but they are less accurate at about spatial-temporal electric vehicle demand as it has been obtained from the mobility study.

To achieve the objective of this study, the impact on the substations in the electric transmis-sion system has been studied in a large number of charging scenarios, with the handicap of not having full access to the grid data. Under these conditions the results are not worrisome, in the way that problems related to the collapse in any node of the transmission grid have not been found.

In any case, it is important to comment that the increment in the level of the substation load reaches in some substations up to 35% in critical scenarios, raising the average load in some cases from 50% to 65%. From the TSO point of view, this increment in most substations could generate an increment of global losses of the system and is it possible that a few reinforcements in the grid (new lines) could be necessary in some particular points of the system to better manage the level of the voltage if no strategies are taken. That is an assumption that would need to be corroborated with a deeper study having higher access to the electric grid data.

Results show that with the present scenarios, the driver behavior provokes in the power system an increment in the load demand during the peak hour. This increment can be higher or lower, depending on how much critical is the scenario, but this peak is always increased.

At first, this peak increment adds more difficulties to the operability of the system. However, several proposals in the last years have been appearing seeing the electric vehicle less as a problem and more as a solver or as a business opportunity (Kempton, 2004; Guille, 2007; Mullen, 2009; Song 2011; Li, 2012; Pillai, 2012; Pang, 2010 and 2012). In this way, all these proposals include the stimulation of the integration of renewable energies, efficiency of the system, development of smart grids, using the electric vehicle for voltage and power control, etc., turning the electric vehicle in another element of the electric system.

Aspects such as to promote the shift of the electric vehicle consumption to off peak hours through pricing strategies, improving the operability of the system; business models as V2G or V2B that make the electric vehicle as potential electricity supplier or using the vehicle batteries as power storage system will be studied in the future, taking advantage of the large quantity of mobility data available at this moment.

The next step in this research will be to determine the total storage capacity available in the grid due to the possibility to store energy in the electric vehicles batteries and try to use this distributed storage capacity to provide ancillary services to the system operator.

REFERENCES

Bessa, R. J., & Matos, M. A. (2010). *The role of an aggregator agent for EV in the electricity market*. Paper presented at the 7th Mediterranean Conference and Exhibition on Power Generation, Transmission, Distribution and Energy Conversion. New York, NY.

Bingham, C., Walsh, C., & Carroll, S. (2012). Impact of driving characteristics on electric vehicle energy consumption and range. *IET Intelligent Transport Systems*, 6(1), 29–35. doi:10.1049/iet-its.2010.0137.

Clement-Nyns, K., Haesen, & Driesen. (2010). The impact of charging PHEV on residential distribution grid. *IEEE Transactions on Power Systems*, 25(1), 371–380. doi:10.1109/TPWRS.2009.2036481.

Fraile-Ardanuy, J. Martínez, Artaloytia, Ramírez, Fuentes, & Sánchez (2012). *Analysis of the impact of charging of PHEV and EV in Spain*. Paper presented at the International Conference on Renewable Energies and Power Quality (ICREPQ2012). New York, NY.

Galus, M., Waraich, R. A., & Anderson, G. (2011). *Predictive, distributed, hierarchical charging control of PHEVs in the distribution system of a large urban area incorporating a multiagent transportation simulation*. Paper presented at the 17th Power Systems Computation Conference. New York, NY.

Galus, M., Waraich, R. A., Noembrini, F., Steurs, K., Georges, G., & Boulouchos, K. et al. (2012). Integrating power systems, transport systems and vehicle technology for electric mobility impact assessment and efficient control. *IEEE Transactions on Smart Grid*, 3(2), 934–949. doi:10.1109/TSG.2012.2190628.

Geth, F. Willekens, Clement, Driesen, & De Breucker. (2010). *Impact-analysis of the charging of plug-in hybrid vehicles on the production park in Belgium*. Paper presented at the 15th IEEE Mediterranean Electrotechnical Conference MELECON. New York, NY.

Guille, C. (2009). *A conceptual framework for the vehicle to grid (V2G) implemantation*. (Thesis). University of Illinois, Urbana Champaign, IL.

Han, S. (2010). *Design of an optimal aggregator for vehicle to grid regulation service*. Paper presented at the IEEE Conference Publications on Innovative Smart Grid Technologies (ISGT). New York, NY.

HC. (2012). *Proyecto InovGrid*. Retrieved from http://www.cne.es/cne/doc/publicaciones/smart_metering/1115_4_HC_Telegestion.pdf

Kempton, W. (2004). *Vehicle to grid power implementation: From stabilizing the grid to supporting large-scale new renewable energy*. University of Delaware..

Knapen, L., Kochan, B., Bellemans, T., Janssens, D., & Wets, G. (2011). *Activity based models for countrywide electric vehicle power demand calculation*. Hasselt, Belgium: University of Hasselt. doi:10.1109/SGMS.2011.6089019.

Lee, D., Shiah, S., Lee, C., & Wang, Y. (2007). State-of-charge estimation for electric scooters by using learning mechanisms. *IEEE Transactions on Vehicular Technology*, 56(2), 544–556. doi:10.1109/TVT.2007.891433.

Li, C. T. (2012). Synergistic control of plug-in vehicle charging and wind power scheduling. *IEEE Transactions on Power Systems*. doi:10.1109/TPWRS.2012.2211900.

Li, G., & Zhang, X. (2012). Modeling of PHEV charging demand in probabilisic power flow calculations. *IEEE Transactions On Smart Grid*, 3(1), 492–499. doi:10.1109/TSG.2011.2172643.

Maia, R., Silva, M., Araújo, R., & Nunes, U. (2011). *Electric vehicle simulator for energy consumption studies in electric mobility systems*. Paper presented at the IEEE Forum on Integrated and Sustainable Transportation Systems. New York, NY.

Mullen, S. K. (2009). *Plug-in hybrid electric vehciles as a source of distributed frequency regulation*. (Dissertation). University of Minnesota, Minneapolis, MN.

Pang, C. (2010). *PHEVs as dynamically configurable dispersed energy storage for V2B uses in the smart grid*. Paper presented at the 7th Mediterranean Conference and Exhibition on Power Generation, Transmission, Distribution and Energy Conversion (MedPower 2010). New York, NY.

Pang, C. (2012). *BEVs/PHEVs as dispersed energy storage for V2B uses in the smart grid*. IEEE Transactions on Smart Grid. doi:10.1109/TSG.2011.2172228.

Papadopoulos, P. Skarvelis-Kazakos, Grau, Awad, Cipcigan, & Jenkins. (2010). *Impact of residential charging of electric vehicles on distribution networks, a probabilistic approach*. Paper presented at the 45th International Universities Power Engineering Conference (UPEC). New York, NY.

Pieltain, L., Gomez, T., Cossent, R., Mateo, C., & Frías, P. (2011). Assessment of the impact of PHEV on distribution networks. *IEEE Transactions on Power Systems*, 26(1), 206–213. doi:10.1109/TPWRS.2010.2049133.

Pillai, J. R. (2012). *Electric vehicles to support large wind power penetration in future Danish power systems*. Paper presented at the IEEE Vehicle Power and Propulsion Conference (VPPC). New York, NY.

Qian, K., Zhou, Allan, & Yuan. (2011). Modeling of load demand due to EV battery charging in distribution systems. *IEEE Transactions on Power Systems*, 26(2), 802–809. doi:10.1109/TPWRS.2010.2057456.

REE. (2010). *Informe del sistema eléctrico 2010*. Retrieved from http://www.ree.es/sistema_electrico/informeSEE-2010.asp

Shao, S. Pipattanasomporn, & Rahman. (2009). *Challenges of PHEV penetration to the residential distribution network*. Paper presented at the IEEE Power & Energy Society General Meeting. New York, NY.

Soares, F. J., Peças, J. A., Rocha, P. M., & Moreira, C. L. (2011). *A stochastic model to simulate electric vehicles motion and quantify the energy required from the grid*. Paper presented at the 17th Power System Computation Conference. New York, NY.

Song, S. (2011). *Research on coordinated dispatch of PEV charging and wind power in regional grid*. Paper presented at the 4th International Conference on Electric Utility Deregulation and Restructuring and Power Technologies (DRPT). New York, NY.

VREG. (2012). *Flemish regulator of the electricity and gas market*. Retrieved from http://www.vreg.be/verbruiksprofielen-0

Yunus, K., Zelaya, H., & Reza, M. (2011). Distribution grid impact of plug-in electric vehicles charging at fast charging stations using stochastic charging model. In *Proceedings of the 2011-14th European Conference on Power Electronics and Applications* (EPE 2011). EPE.

Zhao, L. Prousch, Hübner, & Moser. (2010). *Simulation methods for assessing electric vehicle impact on distribution grids*. Paper presented at the IEEE PES Transmission and Distribution Conference and Exposition. IEEE.

ADDITIONAL READING

Andersson, G. (2003). *Modelling and Analysis of Electric Power Systems*. Zurich: Swiss Federal Institute of Technology..

Blume, S. W. (2007). *Electric power system basics for the nonelectrical professional*. Hoboken, New Jersey: John Wiley & Sons, Inc. doi:10.1002/9780470185810.

Exposito, A. G. (2009). Electric Energy Systems. Anlaysis and Operation.CRC Press, 2009

Grigsby, L. L. (2001). *The Electric Power Engineering Handbook*. CRC Press and IEEE Press..

Kundur, P. (1994). *Power system stability and control*. New York: McGraw-Hill, Inc.

Machowski, J. (2008). *Power Systems Dynamics. Stability and Control*. John Wiley & Sons, Inc..

Members of IEEE (1996). *IEEE Recommended Practice for Energy Management in Industrial and Commercial Facilities*.

Metha, V. K. (2001). *Principles of Power Systems*. New Delhi: S. Chand and Company Ltd.

Schlabbach, J. (1999). Voltage Quality in Electrical Power Systems. Institution of Engineering and Technology, London, United Kingdom.

Shahidephour, M. (2002). *Market Operations in Electric Power System*. John Wiley and Sons, Inc. doi:10.1002/047122412X.

Vedam, S. (2009). Power Quality. VAR compensation in Power Systems. CRC Press, 2009.

Wood, A. J., & Wollemberg, B. F. (1996). *Power Generation, Operation, and Control* (2nd ed.). New York: John Wiley & Sons, Inc.

KEY TERMS AND DEFINITIONS

Electric Grid: Set of installations aimed at transporting and distributing electrical energy from power plants to consumers.

Electric Mobility: People behavior pattern in the use of electric vehicles.

Mobility Study: Study to find behavior patterns about people mobility. The result about electrical vehicle consumption has been used in this work as input data.

Smart Meter: An electrical meter able to communicate bidirectionally with the utility.

Chapter 16
Electric Vehicles in the Smart Grid

Fjo De Ridder
EnergyVille, Belgium

Reinhilde D'hulst
EnergyVille, Belgium

Luk Knapen
Hasselt University, Belgium

Davy Janssens
Hasselt University, Belgium

ABSTRACT

This chapter presents a coordination algorithm for charging electric vehicles that can be used for avoiding capacity problems in the power distribution grid and for decreasing imbalance costs for retailers. Since it is expected that the fraction of electric vehicles will exceed 50% in the next decades, charging these vehicles will roughly double the domestic power consumption. Not all parts of the grid are expected to be able to provide the required power. Good estimates of the vehicles' use (routes driven, trip duration and length, when and where cars are parked) is crucial information to test the grid. The authors have chosen to use FEATHERS, an agent-based behavioral model, to provide this information. In a first case study, charging is coordinated to prevent grid capacity problems. In a second case study, charging and discharging of electric vehicles is employed by retailers to lower imbalance costs and by vehicle owners to lower charging costs. The coordination scheme can halve the imbalance cost if only charging is considered. If, on the other hand, electric vehicles can both charge and discharge, imbalance costs can completely be avoided and some revenues can be generated. The proposed coordination algorithm is a distributed algorithm, where all sensitive information that is privately owned, such as parking times, trip information, battery management, etc. is only used by the EVs. The functioning of the proposed algorithm is illustrated by simulations. It is shown that the charging can be rescheduled so that grid capacity violations are avoided. The novelty of this work is that both spatial and temporal information is used.

DOI: 10.4018/978-1-4666-4920-0.ch016

INTRODUCTION

Global primary energy production will grow with 8 to 36% by 2035 according to (Energy Information Administration, 2010), but electricity demand grows by around 80% by 2035, requiring 5900 GW of total capacity additions. In addition, electricity generation is entering a period of transformation as investment shifts to low-carbon technologies — the result of higher fossil-fuel prices and government policies to enhance energy security and to curb emissions of CO_2. Also, the European Environment Agency (2008) again stated in its most recent Energy and Environment report that the production and consumption of energy place a wide range of pressures on the environment and on public health. At all decision bodies, both locally and at the European level, there is an increased awareness that a significant portion of the rising global demand for electric energy will be met by renewable energy sources which will significantly contribute an increasing share of the total energy supply.

In the last 20 years, a large increase in renewable energy has occurred and this transition seems not to be saturated, yet (Energy Information Administration, 2010). Both wind turbines and solar installations are widely applied. They are usually distributed over large areas and the amount of power produced is not driven by the actual consumption, but rather by the available wind or sunshine. In addition, these renewable energy sources are more difficult to predict, resulting in increasing fluctuations in energy supply and consequently in energy prices. If no measures are taken, this will ultimately result in an instable power grid. Some days too much power is produced, while on other days the production cannot meet the demands.

From an economical point of view, renewables will cause larger fluctuations on the markets. In case a lot of renewable power is predicted, prices will be low on the day-ahead market and vice versa. All deviations from what is predicted are reflected in the prices on the imbalance market. One promising solution is smart grids. The basic idea is to, partially, adapt the electricity demand to the available supply. During two public holidays in 2012 (Pentecost and 31st of December), when the industrial consumption was low, it happened that too much wind power was available on the Belgian market, resulting in negative prices for power (Elia, 2013). So wind turbines operators actually had to pay to put their produced power on the grid. So far, the opposite did not take place at large scale: during wind still days in winter, it may happen that there is not enough power available from renewable sources and that all countries in e.g. Western Europe need to import power from each other. This might result in some controlled black-outs.

In conclusion, on the one hand, centrally coordinated industrial plants are being replaced by distributed smaller plants. These small plants need to react in a controlled way to changes in demand to keep the power grid stable. On the other hand, the availability of power will change. During peak production, power will be abundantly available, while at other moments shortages may happen. A solution to both problems is to make large parts of the power grid smart by tuning the power consumption to the available power. To achieve this, devices needs to be able to communicate to the grid operators and maybe to each other. This paradigm shift, from centrally coordinated production to distributed coordinated consumption and production is called "the smart grid".

One of the candidates to operate in a smart grid is electric vehicles (EVs). Nowadays the number EVs is still negligible, but studies point out that the fraction of EVs will be 70% by 2035 (Energy Information Administration, 2010). This includes hybrid and plug-in hybrid vehicles. Typically, an EV consumes about 200 Wh/km. Assuming an average speed of 50 km/h and an average daily use of about 45', this leads to an additional consumption of about 2-4 MWh for every household equipped with an EV. In other words, the overall energy consumption will double for these households. EVs have two properties, which makes them very suited candidates for actors in the smart grid. Every car has enough computational power to run complex algorithms, which can make them smart actors in the grid. Secondly, electric vehicles have a relatively large battery system, which is not actively used most of the time and can absorb redundant 'cheap' power and can deliver power during periods of scarcity. So most of the additional hardware, necessary for the smart grid, is already present.

A benchmark for smart grid control algorithms is the PowerMatcher (Kok, 2009; De Ridder, 2011). It automatically balances demand and supply in clusters of distributed energy resources. The technology is based on multi-agent systems technology and electronic markets. Basic theories used are control theory and micro-economics, are unified in market-based control theory. This control strategy consists of two types of units. Each device that participates is represented by an agent. The agent controls the power supply to the device. Its intelligence is only limited by the inspiration of its creator. If power is traded, the agent sends a bidding function to the second type of unit, i.e. an electronic market. The bidding function represents how much power the agent is willing to trade for each price. The electronic market will try to balance demand and supply. Evidently, a consumer will buy most power if the prices are low and will try to limit its consumption, if power is sparse and thus more expensive. A production unit will try to trade as much power as possible when prices are high and less when the prices decrease. The major disadvantage of this approach is that it does not take information about the future into account: it balances the actual demand with the actual supply. If, for example, prices are and remain high, most EVs will postpone charging until their comfort settings force them to charge. If nearly all cars start to charge simultaneously, the system may become unstable.

Interesting developments are Average Optimal Controllers (AOCs). These algorithms work in three steps (Vandael, 2010; Vandael, 2012): first, all demand is aggregated. So all EVs are considered as one big battery system. Secondly, an optimal charging schedule for this averaged demand is identified. Thirdly, this optimal averaged demand is decomposed over all individual EVs. The main advantage is that the aggregation step allows managing large fleets. A possible disadvantage is that the decomposition is not necessarily optimal. However, Vandael et al. benchmarked this approach against a quadric programming implementation (2010). This AOC achieved an efficiency of 95% compared to the theoretical optimal.

For that reason, a receding horizon technique is used here (e.g. Diehl, 2002). This type of control scheme is often used in smart grid simulations and can be split up, so that every EV can solve locally its optimal charging schedule problem (e.g. Chao-Kai, 2012; Yifeng, 2012, De Ridder 2013). In this chapter, realistic simulations of drivers are combined with simulations of the power grid to estimate the impact in a few case studies. The novelty of this research is twofold. Firstly, a direct coupling is established between agent-based models, where real behavior of drivers is used to estimate the impact of EV on the future smart grid and secondly the impact of EVs on the imbalance market is examined. In addition, both temporal and geographical information are taken into account.

SETTING THE SCENE

Suppose now that we are living in 2020'ties with a lot of renewable resources and smart EVs. The smart grid might look as follows

- One way to quantify the scarcity of power is by using a variable price. During peak demand prices will be high, and vice versa.

Many markets today, like the day-ahead market, are already based on this principle of operation. When the retailer communicates the prices in advance, load synchronization may occur. This means that many devices will switch on simultaneously when prices are low, resulting in novel problems in the distribution grid. A possible solution for this problem is that the distribution system operator can alter the price of the signal. How this can be done in a fair way is explained later in this chapter.

- A second problem is related to the comfort settings of the consumer. When an electric vehicle is parked to be charged, the driver expects the battery to actually charge. Probably he or she will not accept that scheduled routes need to be adapted due to an empty battery. So the degrees of freedom of the local control devices must take the comfort settings of the consumer into account.

- When electric vehicles are massively introduced, the consumption may double, potentially leading to new investment requirements in the distribution grid. Investments in the distribution grid are relatively expensive. So a possible business case to support smart grids could be found here: it may be less expensive for the distribution grid operator to steer some devices in the distribution grid, so that grid constraints are no longer violated, than it is to upgrade parts of his power grid.

- Nowadays retailers are an intermediate partner, aggregating the consumption of their clients and buying the corresponding power on the day-ahead market or with long term contracts. To be able to do so, a retailer needs to predict, e.g. on a quarter hour basis, what the power consumption and production will be of all the customers within its portfolio. In this chapter, we consider retailers which are also Balance Responsible Parties. When a retailer's estimates are wrong and there are deviations from the predicted power consumption and production, an imbalance cost needs to be paid. The imbalance cost depends on the actual marginal costs for producing and consuming power. At larger levels of system imbalance there is additional incentive coefficients added. Variations of imbalance prices can be much larger than price variations on the day-ahead market. However, if the retailer's portfolio contains some flexible and 'smart' consumption and production devices, the retailer can use this intelligence to reduce the imbalance and hence the imbalance costs. However, the retailer can even speculate on the imbalance prices and deliberately cause an imbalance within his own portfolio (estimates deviate from actual consumption and/or production) in order to 'help' the overall system balance of the Transmission System Operator. For example, the retailer can assist the Transmission System Operator when the control area is short by creating a positive imbalance. In this case, the retailer can benefit from a negative price for his positive imbalance. In literature, companies who aggregate consumption and production in a smart grid are often called aggregators (e.g. Tian, 2013).

Charging an electric vehicle takes more time than fueling conventional cars. So we assume that people park their car, plug it onto the grid and leave it there to charge or discharge. The intelligence of the car decides when to charge, depending on the parking time, the planned trips and the cost of charging. If, in the meantime, the battery system can support the grid, it may decide to do so. This will happen of course in return of remuneration and within the comfort setting of the driver.

An EV charging coordination algorithm is developed that can be used for different objectives.

Two different objectives are discussed below. The first focus is on the distribution grid. The objective of the coordination algorithm is to deal with grid constraints whilst enabling the EVs to charge as cheap as possible. The problem focused on is load synchronization: all vehicles will initially try to charge when prices are lowest, resulting possibly in capacity problems in the grid. The scientific question answered here is 'Can smart electric vehicles prevent congestion problems in the grid by applying smart grid solutions?'

The second objective focuses on the impact of smart EVs on imbalance costs made by retailers. In brief, retailers have to estimate the future energy demand and production in their portfolio one day ahead. The retailer has to pay an imbalance price if consumers are consuming more than predicted. However, imbalance prices are much more volatile and it can be costly if a retailer has an energy shortage when imbalance prices are high. On the other hand, it may happen that imbalance prices are high and the retailer has underestimated his production or consumption. Under such circumstances additional profits can be made. In the current situation, retailers have hardly any degrees of freedom to steer their position with respect to the imbalance prices. If intelligence is incorporated in EVs, the retailer can employ the flexibility of the EVs to reposition himself with respect to imbalance costs.

PRINCIPLES OF THE COORDINATION ALGORITHMS

Distributed Control Scheme

In this paragraph the developed coordination algorithm for charging EVs is explained. The problems to be solved by the coordination algorithm can be written down as optimization problems, with the objectives to optimize being (i) minimum charging costs whilst satisfying grid constraints and comfort settings, and (ii) minimum imbalance costs for the retailer. For readers not interested in the technical details, a brief summary is given. For retailers and the distribution system operator, it is essential to have an idea about the charging schedules of the EVs. For that reason, every EV provides such a schedule for the near future (couple of hours). The EV fleet can be steered in a certain direction by adjusting a steering signal, which can naively be interpreted as a price signal. From a helicopter view, they can only adjust the price seen by the EVs. Each EV is free to react to this change. Eventually, all parties will find a balance between the schedules and constraints on the one hand and the steering signal on the other hand. The remaining of this chapter is devoted to (i) showing that this approach is identical to solving the global optimal problem (where all information is centralized); (ii) constructing local controllers for the EVs; and (iii) deriving update schemes for the steering signals.

Initially, these optimization problems are formulated as central optimization problems, i.e. a problem that can be solved when all information needed is available at hand. However, a central solver is impracticable because, firstly, the complexity of the problem increases with the amount of EVs, and calculating a central optimal solution will become impossible with lots of EVs present. Secondly, from a privacy point of view, it is not feasible to have all privacy-sensitive information available on one location. Therefore, a distributed problem formulation is derived from the central optimal problem formulation, with almost identical schedules. The advantage of having distributed solvers is that they can be implemented on the computers of the EVs and that private information is only used locally. Figure 1 illustrates the transition from a central solver to a distributed one. In the central solver all information is gathered by a central unit, which calculates the optimal scheme and sends this information back to each actor. In the distributed scheme every EV sends its power schedule to the respective parking and his retailer. Both send back a steering signal and

Figure 1. Transition from global solver to a distributed solver. Every EV, the retailer and distribution system operator solve their control problem locally. Every EV sends schedules to the retailer and distribution system operator and receives a steering signal in return.

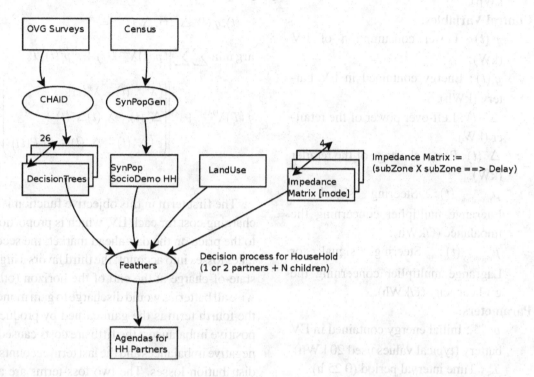

this procedure is repeated until convergence is reached. So, the most important complication is that every local solver needs to communicate its action and reaction. This communication loop needs to be iterated in every time step to reach an agreement. An important remark here is that we assume that the overall system is a cooperative system, where every actor acts in the benefit of the system. So gaming or intentionally lying is not allowed.

The variables used are defined as follows:

- **Indices:**
  - $t = \{1, ..., T\}$: Index used to number discrete time intervals (scalar value, with T typical 96).
  - $i = \{1, ..., N\}$: Index used to number EVs (N typical 50).
  - $k = \{1, ..., M\}$: Index used to number parking lots (M typical 56).

- **Environmental Variables:**
  - $c_{background}(t)$: Background consumption of households (kW).
  - $c_i(t)$: Consumption of EV (kW).
  - $SLP(t)$: Standard load profile: estimation of background consumption + EV consumption (kW).
  - $\delta_{i,k}(t)$: Parameter which is zero if EV i is consuming (driving) and one if EV is parked at parking lot k (scalar).
  - $\lambda^{DAM}, \lambda^{DAM}_{mean}$: Energy price on the day-ahead market; subscript 'mean' denotes the mean energy price over the horizon (€/kWh).
  - $\lambda^+(t)$: Energy price for left-over energy on the imbalance market (€/kWh).

○ $\lambda^-(t)$: Energy price for energy shortage on the imbalance market (€/kWh).

- **Control Variables:**
  ○ $p_i(t)$: Power consumption of EV (kW).
  ○ $q_i(t)$: Energy contained in EV battery (kWh).
  ○ $\Delta^+(t)$: Left-over power of the retailer (kW).
  ○ $\Delta^-(t)$: Power shortage of the retailer (kW).
  ○ $\mu_{\text{imbalance}}(t)$: Steering signal or Lagrange multiplier concerning the imbalance (€/kWh).
  ○ $\mu_{\text{capacity}}(t)$: Steering signal or Lagrange multiplier concerning the grid capacity (€/kWh).

- **Parameters:**
  ○ q_i^{initial} : Initial energy contained in EV battery (typical values used 20 kWh).
  ○ T_S : Time interval period (0.25 h).
  ○ ε_i : Energy losses due to charging EV (0.1 €/(kW)²/h).
  ○ ε : Energy losses due to transport (0.1 €/(kW)²/h).
  ○ $\underline{p}_i$: Lower bound for charging EV (0 if no vehicle to grid technology is present; $-\overline{p}_i$ otherwise (kW).
  ○ $\overline{p}_i$: Upper bound for charging EV (typical value 3.6 kW).
  ○ $\overline{p}_k$: Upper bound for power transport at parking lot k (typical value 14.4 kW).
  ○ $\overline{q}_i$: EV battery capacity (24 kWh).

We have chosen for an open-loop receding horizon formulation. At every time step a new optimization scheme is solved and only the first control action is applied. This is iterated for every new time step and allows the system to take new information, like the newest prediction, changes in the schedule, into account. The global optimi-

zation problem formulation, to be solved at each time interval is

$$
\left[p_i(t), q_i(t), \Delta^+(t), \Delta^-(t)\right]^* =
$$

$$
\arg\min \sum_t^T \sum_i^N \left[\left(p_i(t)\lambda^{\text{DAM}}(t) + \varepsilon_i p_i^2(t)\right)T_S\right] -
$$

$$
q_i(T)\lambda_{\text{mean}}^{\text{DAM}} + ... \left[\begin{array}{c}\left(\lambda^{\text{DAM}}(t) - \lambda^+(t)\right) \\ \Delta^+(t) - \lambda^-(t)\Delta^-(t) + \\ \varepsilon\left(\Delta^+(t) - \Delta^-(t) + SLP(t)\right)^2\end{array}\right]T_S
$$

$$(1)$$

The first term in this objective function is the charging cost for each EV, which is proportional to the price on the day-ahead market; the second takes losses into account; the third favors a higher state-of-charge at the end of the horizon (otherwise all batteries would discharge to gain money); the fourth term is the gain earned by producing positive imbalances; the fifth are costs caused by negative imbalances and the last term accounts for distribution losses. The two loss-terms are also necessary to make the problem strictly convex, which facilitates the solvers a lot, but have also a physical meaning. Losses in the transformer are typically quadratic function (Ruelens, 2013).

Subject to:

- **Conservation of Energy:**

$$
q_i(t+1) - q_i(t) = c_i(t)
$$
$$
+ p_i(t)\sum_k^M \delta_i(t) \qquad\qquad \forall t, \forall i \qquad (2)
$$

This equation links the state of charge $q_i(t)$, of the battery systems to the consumption $c_i(t)$ and (dis)charging $p_i(t)\sum_k^M \delta_i(t)$.

- **Initial State of Each EV:**

$$
q_i(1) = q_i^{\text{initial}} \qquad\qquad\qquad \forall i \, (3)
$$

This constraint ensures that the initial state of each battery equals the given value.

- **Battery Management System:** Limits of each battery system

$$0 \leq q_i(t) \leq \bar{q_i} \qquad\qquad \forall t, \forall i \quad (4)$$

The battery management systems limits the state-of-charge of each battery

- **Battery Management System:** Limits on power supply

$$\underline{p_i} \leq p_i(t) \leq \bar{p_i} \qquad\qquad \forall t, \forall i \,(5)$$

Power flowing from or to the batteries is bounded between a minimum value $\underline{p_i}$ and a maximum value $\bar{p_i}$. If discharging is not considered $\underline{p_i} = 0$, $\forall i$.

- **Limits on a Positive Imbalance:**

$$0 \leq \Delta^+(t) \leq \bar{p} \qquad\qquad \forall t \quad (6)$$

The positive imbalance must be a positive number and cannot be bigger than the limits on power supply.

- **Limit on a negative imbalance:**

$$-\bar{p} \leq \Delta^-(t) \leq 0 \qquad\qquad \forall t \qquad (7)$$

The negative imbalance must be a negative number and cannot be smaller than the lower limit on power supply.

- **Relation between imbalance, power bought on the day-ahead market and actual consumption:**

$$\Delta^+(t) + \Delta^-(t) = SLP(t) - \left(c_{\text{background}}(t) + \sum_i^N \sum_k^M p_i(t)\delta_{i,k}(t) \right) \qquad \forall t \quad (8)$$

This equation matches the actual imbalance caused by the system on the trading variables $\Delta^+(t) + \Delta^-(t)$. This constraint must be organized by the retailer.

- **Local power constraints:**

$$-\underline{p_k} \leq c_{\text{background}}(t) + \sum_i^N \sum_k^M p_i(t)\delta_{i,k}(t) \leq \bar{p_k} \quad \forall t, \forall k \quad (9)$$

If the capacity of a local parking is constraint, the accumulated power flow is bounded as well. This constraint is managed by the parking owner or distribution system operator, depending on the particular situation.

Such an overall optimization problem is difficult to solve in practice; not only in a mathematical sense, but particularly from a privacy point of view. EV drivers will, in general, not be willing to provide their travel schedules to a third party or let others take responsibility for deviations from this schedule. The battery management system is installed in the EV and the EV-constructor will not always be willing to provide this to a third party. In addition, the retailer has built up knowledge about the behavior of the imbalance prices and the day-ahead market and wants to use this knowledge at its own advantage, so also he will not be willing to share its predictions and knowledge with a third party. From a close look at the overall optimization problem, it follows that only the last two constraints are shared between the different actors. This allows us to separate the overall optimization problem into a set of local optimization problems by means of Lagrange multipliers (Boyd, 2009). The distributed problem formulation is then:

For every EV an individual optimization problem can be formulated:

$$
\left[p_i(t), q_i(t) \right]^* = \arg\min \sum_t^T
$$

$$
\left[\left(p_i(t) \left(\begin{array}{c} \lambda^{\mathrm{DAM}}(t) + \mu_{\mathrm{imbalance}}(t) + \\ \sum_k^M \delta_{i,k}(t)\mu_{\mathrm{capacity},k}(t) \end{array} \right) + \varepsilon_i p_i^2(t) \right) T_S \right]
$$

$$
- q_i(T)\lambda_{\mathrm{mean}}^{\mathrm{DAM}}
$$

$$
q_i(t+1) - q_i(t) =
$$

$$
c_i(t) + p_i(t)\sum_k^M \delta_{i,k}(t) \qquad \forall t, \forall i
$$

$$
q_i(1) = q_i^{\mathrm{initial}} \qquad \forall i
$$

$$
0 \le q_i(t) \le \overline{q}_i \qquad \forall t, \forall i
$$

$$
\underline{p}_i \le p_i(t) \le \overline{p}_i \qquad \forall t, \forall i
$$

$$
(10)
$$

This problem can be solved locally in every EV. So, the information is not seen by other parties.

The retailer's optimization problem is given by:

$$
\left[\Delta^+(t), \Delta^-(t) \right]^* = \arg\min \sum_t^T \left(\begin{array}{c} \lambda^{\mathrm{DAM}}(t) - \lambda^+ \\ (t) - \mu_{\mathrm{imbalance}}(t) \end{array} \right)
$$

$$
\Delta^+(t)T_S - \left(\lambda^-(t) - \mu_{\mathrm{imbalance}}(t) \right)
$$

$$
\Delta^+(t) + \varepsilon \left(\frac{\Delta^+(t) - \Delta^-(t) +}{SLP(t)} \right)^2 T_S
$$

subject to

$$
0 \le \Delta^+(t) \le \overline{p} \qquad \forall t
$$

$$
-\overline{p} \le \Delta^-(t) \le 0 \qquad \forall t
$$

$$
(11)
$$

and can be solved autonomously.

This set of optimization problems has common Lagrange multipliers $\mu_{\mathrm{imbalance}}(t)$ and $\mu_{\mathrm{capacity},k}(t)$. Both are estimated by a relaxation algorithm, like:

$$
\mu_{\mathrm{imbalance}}^{m+1}(t) = \mu_{\mathrm{imbalance}}^m(t) +
$$

$$
\beta \left(\begin{array}{c} SLP(t) - \left(c_{\mathrm{background}}(t) + \sum_i^N p_i(t) \right) \\ -\left(\Delta^+(t) + \Delta^-(t) \right) \end{array} \right) \qquad (12)
$$

And:

$$
\tau = \forall t \left(\begin{array}{c} t \in \{1, ..., T\}, c_{\mathrm{background}}(t) + \\ \sum_i^N \delta_{i,k}(t)p_i(t) - \overline{p}_k > 0 \text{ or } \mu_{\mathrm{capacity}}^m \neq 0 \end{array} \right)
$$

$$
(13)
$$

$$
\mu_{\mathrm{capacity},k}^{m+1}(\tau) = \mu_{\mathrm{capacity},k}^m(\tau) +
$$

$$
\beta \left(c_{\mathrm{background}}(t) + \sum_i^N \delta_{i,k}(\tau)p_i(\tau) - \overline{p}_k \right), \forall k
$$

And:

$$
\tau = \forall t \left(\begin{array}{c} t \in \{1, ..., T\}, c_{\mathrm{background}}(t) + \\ \sum_i^N \delta_{i,k}(t)p_i(t) + \overline{p}_k < 0 \text{ or } \mu_{\mathrm{capacity}}^m \neq 0 \end{array} \right)
$$

$$
(14)
$$

$$
\mu_{\mathrm{capacity},k}^{m+1}(\tau) = \mu_{\mathrm{capacity},k}^m(\tau) + \beta
$$

$$
\left(c_{\mathrm{background}}(t) + \sum_i^N \delta_{i,k}(\tau)p_i(\tau) + \overline{p} \right)
$$

With β a tuning factor (typically around 0.1 here); with $\mu_{\mathrm{imbalance}}^1(t) = 0$ and $\mu_{\mathrm{capacity},k}^1(t) = 0$, $\forall t$. The algorithm functions as follows: first, each EV calculates an optimal charging schedule, given their travel behavior, battery constraints and the day-ahead electricity price communicated from its retailer. After the EVs have communicated their optimal charging schedule to the retailer and distribution system operator, they in return calculate the imbalances and capacity, respectively, and update the steering signals/Lagrange multipliers so that his imbalance costs are minimized or the overload is reduced. The updated steering signals are communicated back to all EVs. This process is iterated until convergence is reached. In order to increase convergence speed, methods like Alternating Direction Method of Multipliers can be implemented (Boyd, 2010). An advantage of this approach is that the Lagrange multipliers indicate if the constraints are met. If a constraint cannot be met, these Lagrange multipliers will diverge. In this case, the responsible party can be warned and is able to take actions in advance.

Prediction Algorithm

These solvers need to know the prices on the day-ahead market and on the imbalance markets, the EV consumption, the background consumption and the standard load profiles in advance. For all these variables, we have used the same predictor, which is simple the hourly averaged signal over the last five days

$$x(t) = \frac{1}{P} \sum_{k=1}^{P} x(t - \frac{T}{T_s} k) \qquad (15)$$

With x the variable to be predicted and $T=24h$. This predictor has two drawbacks: (i) weekends nor holidays are taken into account here, but these can easily be taken into account if necessary; and (ii) no stochastic variability is taken into account.

Ruelens et al. (2012, 2013) have implemented a stochastic control algorithm (approximate dynamic programming (Bertsekas, 2005)) and compared the results with its deterministic counterpart. Uncertainties about the arrival and departure times are taken into account. Overall, a cost reduction of 5.6 to 8.5% is achieved.

For predicting the standard load profiles, we have used the prediction of the background consumption and added the average consumption of all EVs. This type of prediction algorithm is simple, but masks all features that will be encountered in real world situations, like prediction errors. In reality, it may be beneficial for retailers to invest in more sophisticated algorithms to make more accurate predictions.

Steering Signal

These Lagrange multipliers have an important meaning in the real world. Note first of all that they have the dimension of an energy price (€/MWh) and that all actors react to them as if it were a price (lower consumption or increase supply when the value increases and vice versa). However, these Lagrange multipliers cannot be interpreted as a pure price signal, appearing for example on the monthly bills of the consumers. Imagine for example a street with a lot of EVs, but equipped with a too small transformer, not able to supply all power. It would be unfair if the electricity price for consumers would increase, due to the grid-problem to be solved by the distribution grid operator. In fact, it is the responsibility of the grid operator to invest in the distribution grid so that the power can be delivered. If the grid operator decides that it is more beneficial to invest in a communication interface so that the flexibility of the EVs can be used to support his distribution grid, it is only fair that the EVs, which are willing to react, get a fee for offering their flexibility. So in conclusion, if the Lagrange multipliers increase, the EVs react as if the price increase, but will in fact earn something for postponing their charging schedule. Maybe consumers should receive a discount on their bill if they react to this Lagrange multiplier. For this reason, we name the Lagrange multipliers "steering signals" throughout the remaining of this chapter.

ACTIVITY BASED MODELS AND SPATIO-TEMPORAL POWER REQUIREMENT

To test the proposed algorithms, travel behavior information of the EVs is needed: the algorithms assume that all EV owners have a day-ahead knowledge on what their travel behavior will be. This information is obtained using activity based modeling. Activity-based modeling (ActBM) is a technique that predicts the daily travel agenda (schedule) for each member of a synthetic population. Most ActBM generate predictions for a single day. For each predicted activity, the ActBM specifies the activity type, start time, duration, location as well as the duration and transportation mode for the trip to reach the activity location. Activity-based models are stochastic micro simulators: planning and travel behavior for each individual is simulated. The travel demand for a given region and period of time emerge as an aggregated result from the predicted daily agendas. This allows investigating the overall effects of traffic demand management policies. Decisions taken by the individuals are influenced by the policy measures taken (e.g. service level of public transportation facility, adapted fuel cost, parking place availability). Microsimulation allows the reactions of the individuals to the changing environment, to depend on the individual's characteristics. Unfortunately, activity based are very data hungry. The activity planning and scheduling processes are complex and contain several parameters many of which cannot directly measured. Part of the required data can be found in regional governmental statistics but extensive (and expensive) travel and time use surveying is required to elicit the parameters for the decision process.

FEATHERS is an operational activity based model for the region of Flanders (Belgium); it generates schedules for a given day-of-week. FEATHERS input data consists of:

- The synthetic population for the study area. This contains socio-economic data (household composition, education level, income category, age category, gender, etc.) describing each individual so that the distributions fit the census data.
- An area subdivision into traffic analysis zones (TAZ).
- Land-use data for each TAZ. This consists of tens of attributes including number of people living in the TAZ for several age and employment categories, amount of people employed in the TAZ in several economic segments (industry, agriculture, education, distribution, hospitals, etc.).
- Impedance matrices specifying the travel time and distance between TAZ for off-peak, morning-peak and evening-peak periods and for several transportation modes (i.e. car, slow, public transport).
- A set of decision trees trained using large scale (periodic) travel surveys. Those data essentially specify individual behavior as a function of socio-economic data and partial schedule characteristics. The latter dependency is required because planning and scheduling processes build up the agenda sequentially. Example: the decision about a social visit in the evening depends on the timing and locations for the work activities already scheduled.

A schematic overview of the data flows in FEATHERS is given in Figure 2. The Flemish model is characterized by

- Synthetic population size: 6 million people.
- Number of TAZ: 2368.
- TAZ area (average value): approximately 5 km^2.
- Number of diaries in survey: approximately 8000.

Figure 2. Schematic overview of data flows in the FEATHERS activity-based simulator

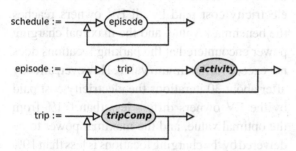

FEATHERS is built on the Albatross kernel described in (Arentze, 2004). It makes use of 26 decision trees to first predict the basic travel agenda containing mandatory periodic activities and related trips (work, school) and in a second stage the flexible activities (shopping, social visits, etc.). The decision trees are used in a fixed order. Each step determines new attributes for agenda components by stochastic sampling. The schedules are consistent at the household level (resources available to the partners). Decision trees are applied in a predefined fixed order that models the decision making process. The schedule (agenda) is constructed using several stages; these results in a chained decision process where each stage further completes the partially constructed agenda. The Albatross system is called a computational pro-

cess model (as opposed to a utility maximization model). It is a rule-based system where the rules consist of decision tree based predictions. FEATHERS output consists of a travel schedule for each member of the synthetic population. The agenda structure is given in the syntax diagram in Figure 3. For each predicted trip a tuple (origin, destination, startTime, duration, and mode) is predicted. This allows calculating expected mode-specific traffic flows in time and space; those flows are validated using traffic counts available from public traffic management services. FEATHERS predictions have been used in (Knapen, 2012) to calculate the electric power demand generated by EV charging for each TAZ in Flanders as a function of time under several EV charging behavior scenarios, EV market share and charging opportunity (at home, at work) assumptions.

The simulations to test the EV charging algorithms proposed, make use of FEATHERS predicted schedules as input data. Both the locations where EV induced electric power demand occurs and the corresponding charging time intervals are taken from FEATHERS results. Note that the distance between charging opportunities available to the individual is important

In the remaining of this chapter, we assume that the EVs "know" their owner's schedules. In

Figure 3. Syntax diagram specifying daily schedules: each episode consists of exactly one trip followed by an activity

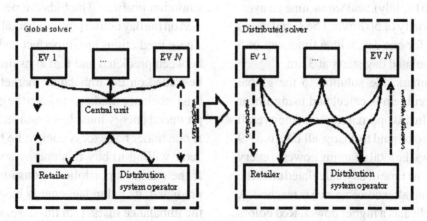

practice they initially do not have the required knowledge, but they may be able to learn it. Claessens et al. (2012) have implemented a self-learning demand side management system and were able to obtain 80% of the theoretical optimum after only 12 days of learning.

SIMULATION RESULTS

Grid Capacity

To illustrate the algorithm operation, a simulation was carried out where charging schedules were constructed for 200 EVs. From the FEATHERS predicted travel schedules for the EVs, there are 56 locations where at least one vehicle is parked during the day. Imbalances are not taken into account in this first example. The electricity tariff is assumed to be equal for all EVs, and is an hourly varying dynamic tariff. This dynamic tariff is based on the day-ahead tariffs of the Belgian Power Exchange (Belpex) (Elia, 2013). The maximum charging power of the vehicles is set to 3.6 kW. The maximum power available for charging EVs at every location is set to 14.4 kW, so only 4 EVs can charge at full power simultaneously at every location. Every vehicle is assumed to have a battery capacity of 24 kWh (Weller, 2010). The state of charge of the EV batteries at the beginning of the day is assumed to be between 90% and 100%. When the cars are driving, they consume a 200Wh/km (Tuffner, 2011, July), and we assume an average driving velocity of 50 km/h. The simulations are carried out for one day, with a time-step of 5 minutes. A simulated day starts at 3 am.

As a benchmark, the solution to the global minimization problem is calculated using linear programming. In this optimal solution, the overall cost that needs to be paid to charge all EVs is 37.9 €. Figure 4 shows the total charging power at every location versus the time of day, calculated after the first iteration, and after convergence is reached. A darker color indicates a higher power. Red colors

indicate that the capacity limit is reached. After about 100 iterations, the system converges: the electricity cost paid by all EV owners reaches the benchmark value, and the maximal charging power encountered at the parking locations does not exceed its maximum value. However, already after about 30 iterations the electricity cost paid by the EV owners differs less than 0.1% from the optimal value, and the maximal power to be delivered by the charging locations is less than 10% higher than the maximum value allowed. Figure 4 clearly shows that the algorithm forces the EVs to charge at other locations when the maximal power constraint is violated.

Power Balancing

Experimental Set-Up

We consider a street consisting of one hundred households, of which 50 are equipped with an EV. One transformer delivers power to this street. Interactions between the three different phases are ignored. Background consumption is based on in-house measured consumption of real households. The average background consumption is about 3500 kWh/year.

This set of simulations focuses on trading aspects. The business case considered consists of a retailer who can buy energy on the day-ahead market, using so-called standard load profiles. These are predictions, based on measured consumption profiles. The bids are performed at 11 AM on the day before power is actually consumed. These predictions are imperfect and mismatches between predicted and real consumption have to be traded on the imbalance market. The aim of this imbalance market is to keep the grid stable: all produced energy must be consumed somewhere. If one trader has excess energy, he has to find an actor willing to buy this energy and vice versa. If the retailer's portfolio is consuming less than predicted, its redundant energy has to be sold on the imbalance market. In this case, we say he has

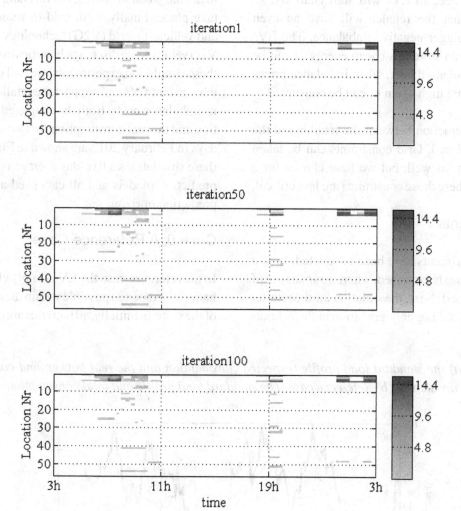

Figure 4. Total charging power at each location versus time of day at the 1st and the final iteration. A darker color indicates a higher charging power.

a positive imbalance. If the retailer's portfolio is consuming more than predicted, the difference has to be bought on the imbalance market. In this case, we speak of a negative imbalance. EVs can support the retailer here in several ways:

- When the overall grid has an energy shortage because of ill-predictions by all retailers and expensive production units are switched on, imbalance prices will be high.
  - ○ If the retailer is confronted with a local negative imbalance, he must pay a high imbalance cost. Under these

circumstances the EVs can postpone consumption or sell stored energy to lower costs.
  - ○ If the retailer has a personal positive imbalance (its portfolio is consuming less than bought on the Day-Ahead Market), the EVs can even increase this excess and increase the revenues.
- When the overall grid has sufficient energy and all costly production units are no longer producing power, the prices will be low (and can even be negative).

If the retailer has a negative imbalance, all EVs will start charging, so that the retailer will have an even bigger negative imbalance. The EVs can store this cheap energy. It can be released later, when imbalance prices are high again or can be consumed.

This interaction between the retailer and the EVs is explored. Grid constraints can be taken into account as well, but we have chosen for a situation where those constraints are less critical.

Experiments

Three experiments have been conducted. First a reference case is examined, where no smart use of EVs is applied. Next, the situation for the retailer is explored, taking only grid-to-vehicle technol-

ogy into account. Here EVs can use intelligence to decide when to charge, but discharging cannot take place. Finally, both grid-to-vehicle (G2V) and vehicle-to-grid (V2G) technology is used. In V2G vehicles can discharge batteries to the grid. In these simulation experiments, we will examine to what extent EVs can support the retailer to lower its imbalance costs. Both the estimated consumption and the real consumption for two subsequent days in February 2012 are shown in Figure 5a. In these simulations a five-day average is used in all prediction models and all cars used a four hour prediction horizon.

Case 0: A Reference Case

In the reference case the EVs simply charge their batteries as soon as possible within the constraints of the system. Initially, all batteries are completely

Figure 5. (a) the standard load profile (expected consumption and the real background consumption during 48h are shown; (b) Reference case. The standard load profile and total consumption are shown.

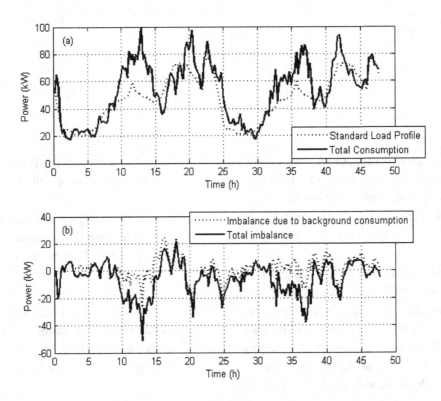

charged, so that transient effects are minimized. Results are shown in Figure 5b. The largest peak due to vehicle charging is situated between 10 and 15 h. A Second peak occurs in the evening around 20 h. Both charging peaks coincide with peaks in background consumptions. In general power prices are highest as well during these peak moments (see e.g. Figure 6a). So both the retailer and EV owner could benefit if EVs would charge at different moments. In addition, if capacity problems are present in the distribution grid, these EVs will only make the problem worse.

Case 1: Grid-to-Vehicle Technology

In this experiment, EVs can decide autonomously when to charge. Discharging is still not possible. The decision to charge depends on the day-ahead market price, which is fixed in advance, and on the imbalance price (both are shown in Figure 6a). In brief, each EV compares the actual prices with its predicted prices. If the actual prices are low, it will charge. If this causes higher imbalance costs for the retailer, he will communicate this to the EVs by means of changing the Lagrange multi-

Figure 6. Grid-to-vehicle technology. The day-ahead market price and imbalance price are shown above. In the middle, the standard load profile and total consumption are shown. The resulting imbalance with and without EV correction is shown.

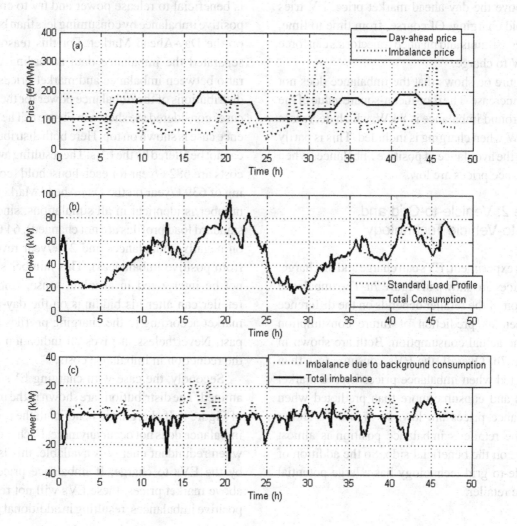

pliers. This is interpreted by the EV as a change in the price signal. Figure 6b shows the standard load profile and the actual consumption. EVs will charge when (i) when the actual imbalance prices are below the actual Day-Ahead Market prices and when the batteries can be charged. If the background consumption is below the standard load profile, the EVs consume the redundant power themselves, so that the imbalance is as low as possible. Under opposite conditions, EVs consume as less as their comfort settings allow; i.e. if the background consumption creates redundant energy, imbalance is maintained. If the background consumption exceeds the standard load profile, the EVs have no means to react and this imbalance is costly. When imbalance prices are above the day-ahead market price, EV tries to avoid charging. Of course, from time to time, local constraints and planned trajectories can force the EV to charge.

Figure 6c shows that the imbalance does not really increase. The root-mean-square value of the background imbalance is 8 kW, which decreases to 6 kW when charging is included. This is partly due to the avoidance of positive imbalances when imbalance prices are low.

Case 2: Vehicle-to-Grid and Grid-to-Vehicle Technology

In this experiment, EVs can charge and discharge. All prices are shown in Figure 7a. The imbalance position of the retailer depends on the difference between its prediction of future consumption and the actual consumption. Both are shown in Figure 7b. Overall, the EVs consume less than predicted when imbalance prices exceed market prices and consume more than predicted when imbalance prices are low. In *Figure 7*c shows that the retailer's imbalance position is almost always on the beneficial side. So the addition of vehicle-to-grid technology has a large potential for the retailer.

Note that (i) compared to the previous cases imbalances are larger (root-mean-square value of 10 kW compared to 8 kW for the charging only case), but are price driven, so all parties profit from it; (ii) compared to the situation where EVs cannot discharge, the EV's batteries are often low on energy, since selling this energy during peak moments is always beneficial.

Comparison between the Three Cases

From an economical point of view two distinct situations can be identified. If the imbalance price is below the market price, it is beneficial to charge EVs and cause a negative imbalance. If the imbalance price is above the DAM price, it is beneficial to release power and try to create a positive imbalance by consuming less than bought on the Day-Ahead Market. For this reason, we separated the imbalance data according to the ratio between imbalance and market prices. The distributions of the imbalance power for the three cases considered are shown in Figure 8. The reference case is shown on top. Here both distributions cannot be altered by the EVs. The resulting average costs are 682 €/year for each household (consisting of 639 €/year on the Day Ahead Market (this number is identical in all simulations, since the standard load profiles are not changed), 64 €/year on negative imbalances and 21 €/year revenues from positive imbalances). This number should not be interpreted in absolute sense, since the retailer can alter his biddings on the day-ahead market according to the charging profiles in the past. Nevertheless, it gives an indication about the reduction in imbalance costs.

Secondly, the case with charging EVs is examined. The distributions are shown in the middle of Figure 8. If charging is beneficial, the positive imbalance does not occur anymore. Each moment when redundant energy is available, this is used by the EVs to charge. If imbalance prices are above market prices, these EVs will not react to positive imbalances, resulting in additional gains.

Figure 7. Grid-to-vehicle and vehicle-to-grid technology. The day-ahead market price and imbalance price are shown above. In the middle, the standard load profile and total consumption are shown. The resulting imbalance with and without EV correction is shown.

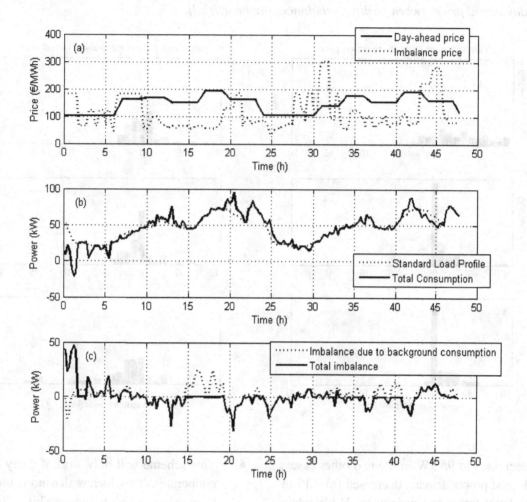

In summary, if EVs can change their charging schedule, depending on the price and imbalance costs, the latter are reduced by with 60% to 24 €/year. The revenue due to positive imbalances remained unchanged at 17 €/year.

Thirdly, if EVs can charge and discharge, the distribution is significantly altered, as can be seen in Figure 8. If imbalance prices are low, many EVs will charge, resulting in a negative imbalance position for the retailer. If imbalance prices are high, many EVs will discharge and the tail of the distribution points upwards. So the imbalance market can now be used to generate some revenue instead of being a cost factor. Negative imbalance

costs remained 21 €/year, but positive imbalance revenues are two times higher (45 €/year). Again this number should be interpreted with caution, since only 48 h are simulated. During this period a part of the energy stored in the battery is traded.

A secondary effect of smart EVs is peak shaving. Prices on the day-ahead market often coincide with a peak in background consumption (see e.g. Figure 6 or Figure 7). If EVs avoid charging during expensive moments, the peak demand decreases indirectly as well, which has a positive effect on power losses and the life-time of transformers? The maximum accumulated power demand in this simulation is 100 kW in the reference case

Figure 8. Probability distributions for the imbalances under the three simulation experiments. The left column shows the distributions when imbalance prices are under the day-ahead prices (when negative imbalances are beneficial). The right column shows the distributions when imbalance prices are higher than day-ahead prices (when positive imbalances are beneficial).

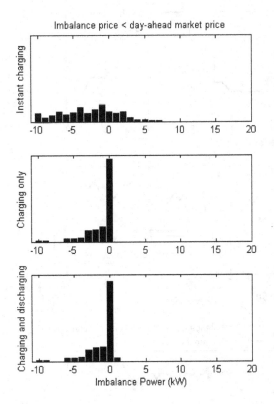
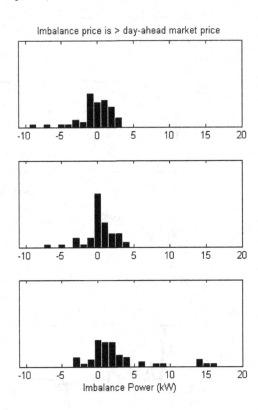

and decreases to 95 kW in the two other cases. The lowest power demand decreased from 17 to 15 kW for charging and inversed to -21 kW when discharging is allowed.

DISCUSSION

General Remarks

A mathematical method is proposed which merges the objectives of the different actors. The method is fast and distributed and can take common constraints into account. However, if coordination algorithms like the one proposed here are applied in real world circumstances, several aspects have to be taken care of

- This scheme will only work if every actor cooperates. This means that no actor can change his process to increase his individual profit, without lowering the overall profits. So as long as all actors accept to act together, the overall optimal solution can be found. If some EVs would start "gaming" and lie for example about their schedules (in order to increase their personal profit), other EVs and the retailer should start taking this into account. Reaching an optimal solution would become a difficult task under such conditions. Establishing a system where every actor is cooperating may seem a difficult task, but in theory many power markets are based on such rules, including the Belgian day-ahead market, the Belpex.

- A related problem is the fact that predictions about future prices, imbalances and trajectories are imperfect. The EV may expect sometimes that prices will decrease even more in the future and decides not to charge now, but to charge at this future moment. If this prediction is wrong, the charging/discharging is no longer optimal. However, with the actual information at hand, these schedules are the best solution possible.
- An advantage of the market structure proposed here is that flexibility can be assigned to both the retailer and the distribution system operator and eventually to a third player as well. If all flexibility would have been assigned in advance to one of the parties, the others cannot make use of it to foster their business or to avoid costs.

A similarity with the current day-ahead market exists: grid constraints may alter the optimal match between power producers and consumers; initially retailer and producers send bid functions to the day ahead market without taking net constraints into account. The optimal economical match can be computed, but is not always feasible from a physical point of view. Before allocations are sent back to the actors on the day-ahead market, load flow calculations are performed to check if the trades are physically possible. In our procedure, the steering can also change the initial solution if grid- or other constraints are violated. The advantage of this coordination mechanism is that local constraints are solved locally and that constraints are taken into account in real time (and not ad-hoc).

- As was mentioned earlier, these steering signals cannot be interpreted as pure price signals. So in the end each EV should be compensated for offering its flexibility to the retailer or distribution system operator.

This can be a fixed fee or can be proportional to the amount of energy shifted in time or to some other agreement made between the actors.

So overall the proposed coordination mechanism has a lot of similarities with the existing day-ahead markets.

Computations and Communication

All computations were performed on an ordinary laptop (Intel® Core™ i5-2520 M CPU @ 2.50 GHz, 4 GB RAM and a 64 bit operating system). All computations were finished in a couple of hours. Of course this is not yet a realistic environment, since in a real situation all computations are distributed over many different machines. On the one hand, this has the advantage that the computation speed may be a lot higher (due to parallelization of the computation). On the other hand, many communication issues may appear, slowing down the process.

Applied in real cases, communication between the EVs, retailers and distribution system operators will become critical. This communication aspects falls beyond the scope of this chapter. However, several research groups focus on those aspects. Mets (2012) studied the effects of lost messages. A disadvantage of the method proposed in this paper, is that optimal values are only reached through a series of iterations. This increases the amount of communication. However, this has some advantages too: in case communication messages are lost, the local solvers can continue working with outdated information. This makes the distributed control scheme more robust with respect to communication problems. Deconinck (2010) studied the dependability of the information infrastructure of a smart grid. They used overlay networks to deal with nodes that appear and disappear, as well as with the dynamic nature of the power values these nodes represent in a smart grid. It allows EVs to autonomously react to changes in their local environment while interacting with their peers for control applications.

A different problem is divergence of the steering signal. Under certain conditions no feasible solution does exist. In these cases, the common constraints can never be met. As a consequence, the steering signals will diverge and approach ultimately infinity. A practical solution to detect such divergence is by monitoring both the number of iterations and changes in the steering signals from one iteration to another. Both depend heavily on the tuning parameter β. For that reason it is difficult to formulate general rules.

In these examples, the maximum number of iterations is set to 20. All simulations presented here were designed to be feasible and did converge within 20 iterations.

Summary: Practical Implementation in the Grid

EVs cannot simply be viewed as energy storage devices. EVs are also used to transport people and goods. No EV owner will accept that trips have to be rescheduled due to empty batteries. For this reason the most crucial boundary condition for estimating the impact of EVs on the power markets and grids are the behavioral models mimicking the EV owners. To get good estimates about trip distances, parking times and places, FEATHERS is used. FEATHERS is an activity based model, which generates travel schedules for a single day. Today, the fraction of EVs is still negligible, so our only mean to explore their impact on the grid is by simulations. A realistic activity based model is thus required to estimate the potential of active use of EVs in a smart grid context. In the simulations performed here, we did not take feedbacks into account. Maybe some people will reschedule depending on the electricity prices ("I will go shopping 20 minutes later, my EV is very

active now."). Maybe some people will have two cars: a combustion engine car for long trips and an EV for short trips or combine both types in a hybrid car. Under such conditions, larger risks can be taken, since the schedules can always be realized. Under such conditions, the electricity markets may have an impact on the choices people make and thus on the decisions made by FEATHERS. So in conclusion, in future studies activity based models will probably play an active role in simulation about future smart grids.

A pragmatic question is how the technological principles explained here can find their way to the real world. Nowadays retailers have a typical imbalance cost of about 10-15%. These numbers are not likely to change much when EVs are introduced, as can be seen in the reference case. However, the imbalance costs can be reduced to 1% if EVs charge smart and can be turned into a 4% profit if EVs can charge and discharge. Averaged out over one year, a typical household will have a cost of 639 € on the day-ahead market, a cost for negative imbalance of 64 € on the imbalance market and a profit of 21 € for positive imbalances under current conditions, but with an EV. If smart charging is applied, the day-ahead market costs remain the same, but the negative imbalance costs are reduced by a third to 24 €. EVs which cannot discharge cannot profit from opportunities on the positive side of the imbalance market. As a result, the profit remains at 17 € for this typical household. If EV can charge and discharge smart, the negative imbalance costs cannot further be reduced and remain at 21 €, but the profits for positive imbalances increase to 45 €, which is about twice the imbalance costs. Given these numbers retailers may become interested in steering EVs and possibly other devices to get rid of imbalance costs.

A second possibility exists for the distribution system operator. If the distribution grid is not strong enough to serve all consumers, some consumption can be postponed until the pressure on the grid decreases. This is illustrated in the first example. It is very well possible that their business case is induced by the retailers. If retailers are able to steer some of the consumption, many devices will switch on simultaneously when e.g. prices are low. This effect, called load-synchronization, may result in demand peaks, which cannot be covered by the infrastructure. This leads to two possibilities. Either the distribution system operator invests in its infrastructure or he will buy some of the available flexibility to steer some devices away from these peaks.

CONCLUSION

EVs all have enough computational power on board to install artificial intelligence, communication and control software to support the power grid. In this chapter we have developed a distributed control algorithm and examined two business cases. In order to gain realistic results, three different concepts are combined. Firstly, information about the behavior of the EV owners, like: which trips are planned? When and where will the cars be parked? How many cars are parked together? ... are retrieved from an activity based model, FEATHERS. The actual fuel consumption and battery capacity are based on today's state-of-the-art technology. Secondly, detailed information about the exact topology and structure of the distribution grid in Flanders is not available. For that reason, we did not take variations in the distribution grid into account and focused on only a few zones. The third component is the intelligence of the smart grid. An algorithm is proposed for constructing EV charging schedules, taking into account a maximum charging power constraint at each charging location and the individual energy consumption of each EV. The charging schedules are constructed day-ahead, given a (time-dependent) electricity price, and given a known trip schedule for the following day. The algorithm is a price-based demand response algorithm, and is based on a dual decomposition technique. A first advantage of the proposed approach is that geographical information is included in the coordination method, and constraints of charging at different locations are taken into account. Vehicle owners are given an incentive to charge at other locations when power constraints at the charging location are violated. A second advantage is that the calculations are performed in a distributed way, to put the responsibility for constructing charging schedules only at the EV side. This contrasts with approaches where all, possibly privacy sensitive, information to form vehicle schedules needs to be gathered in one central location. Thirdly, convergence of the proposed algorithm is guaranteed for not-strictly convex utility functions for the EVs. The functioning of the algorithm has been illustrated in two applications. Evidently, nowadays the number of EVs is too small for these problems to occur and the practical implementation of this coordination algorithm falls beyond the scope of this research.

EPILOGUE

Last Sunday, June 16th 2013, was a sunny day. Solar panels, widely installed in Belgium, produced that much power that it could no longer be consumed in the country. It had to be exported to our neighboring countries, resulting in negative prices on the day-ahead market (up to − 200 €/MWh). In the afternoon unexpected clouds appeared. All large traders in solar power had to take positions on the imbalance market, where prices increased up to 150 €/MWh. If EVs, equipped with intelligence, had been present, they could have bought power, be paid for it, and sell it a couple of hours later for three times the average market price. EVs may still be rare today, the problems on the electricity grid are already out there.

ACKNOWLEDGMENT

The research leading to these results has received funding from the European Union Seventh Framework Programme (FP7/2007-2013) under grant agreement nr. 270833.

REFERENCES

Arentze, T. A., & Timmermans, H. J. (2004). A learning-based transportation oriented simulation system. *Transportation Research Part B: Methodological, 38*(7), 613–633. doi:10.1016/j.trb.2002.10.001.

Bellemans, T., Kochan, B., Janssens, D., Wets, G., Arentze, T., & Timmermans, H. (2010). Implementation framework and development trajectory of FEATHERS activity-based simulation platform. *Transportation Research Record, 2175*, 111–119. doi:10.3141/2175-13.

Boyd, S., Parikh, N., Chu, E., Peleato, B., & Eckstein, J. (2010). Distributed optimization and statistical learning via the alternating direction method of multipliers. *Foundations and Trends in Machine Learning, 3*(1), 1–122. doi:10.1561/2200000016.

Boyd, S., & Vandenberghe, L. (2009). *Convex optimization.* Cambridge, UK: Cambridge University Press..

Chao-Kai, W., Jung-Chieh, C., Jen-Hao, T., & Pangan, T. (2012). Decentralized plug-in electrical vehicle charging selection algorithm in power systems. *IEEE Transactions on Smart Grids, 3*(4), 1779–1789. doi:10.1109/TSG.2012.2217761.

Claessens, B., Vandael, S., Ruelens, F., & Hommelberg, M. (2012). Self-learning demand side management for a heterogeneous cluster of devices with binary control actions. [*rd* *IEEE PES Innovative Smart Grid Technologies Europe*] [IGST Europe] [. IEEE.]. *Proceedings of, 2012*, 3.

De Ridder, F., D'Hulst, R., Knapen, L., & Janssens, D. (2013). Applying an activity based model to explore the potential of electrical vehicles in the smart grid. *Procedia Computer Science, 19*, 847–853. doi:10.1016/j.procs.2013.06.113.

De Ridder, F., Hommelberg, M., & Peeters, E. (2011). Demand side integration: Four potential business cases and an analysis of the 2020 situation. *European Transactions on Electrical Power, 21*(6), 1902–1913. doi:10.1002/etep.529.

Deconinck, G., Labeeuw, W., Vandael, S., Beitollahi, H., De Craemer, K., Duan, R., et al. (2010). Communication overlays and agents for dependable smart power grids. In Proceedings of Critical Infrastructure (CRIS). CRIS.

Diehl, M., Bock, H. G., Schlöder, J. P., Findeisen, R., Nagy, Z., & Allgöwer, F. (2002). Real-time optimization and nonlinear model predictive control of processes governed by differential-algebraic equations. *Journal of Process Control, 12*(4), 577–585. doi:10.1016/S0959-1524(01)00023-3.

Elia. (2013). Retreived March 5, 2013 from http://www.elia.be/en/grid-data/data-download

Energy Information Administration. (2010). *International energy outlook 2010.* Paris, France: International Energy Agency..

European Environment Agency. (2008). *Energy and environment report 2008.* Retrieved March 5, 2013, from http://www.eea.europa.eu/publications/eea_report_2008_6

He, Y., Venkatesh, B., & Guan, L. (2012). Optimal scheduling for charging and discharging of electrical vehicles. *IEEE Transactions on Smart Grids, 3*(3), 1095–1105. doi:10.1109/TSG.2011.2173507.

Knapen, L., Kochan, B., Bellemans, T., Janssens, D., & Wets, G. (2012). Using activity-based modeling to predict spatial and temporal electrical vehicle power demand in Flanders. *Transportation Research Record, 2287*, 146–154. doi:10.3141/2287-18.

Kok, K., Scheepers, M., & Kamphuis, R. (2009). Intelligence in electricity networks for embedding renewables and distributed generation. In *Intelligent Infrastructures*. Dordrecht, The Netherlands: Springer. doi:10.1007/978-90-481-3598-1_8.

Mets, K., D'hulst, R., & Develder, C. (2012). Comparison of intelligent charging algorithms for electric vehicles to reduce peak load and demand variability in a distribution grid. *Journal of Communications and Networks*, *114*(6), 672–681. doi:10.1109/JCN.2012.00033.

Ruelens, F., Leterme, W., Vandael, S., Claessens, B. J., & Belmans, R. (2013). *Day-ahead and real-time planning method of a flexibility aggregator*. IEEE Transactions on Smart Grids..

Ruelens, F., Vandael, S., Leterme, W., Claessens, B. J., Hommelberg, M., Holvoet, T., & Belmans, R. (2012). Demand side management of electric vehicles with uncertainty on arrival and departure times. [*rd* *IEEE PES Innovative Smart Grid Technologies Europe*] [*IGST Europe*] [. IEEE.]. *Proceedings of the*, *2012*, 3.

Tian, L., Qi, K., & Jing, A. (2013). Sitting and sizing of aggregator controlled park for plug-in hybrid electric vehicle based on particle swarm optimization. *Neural Computing & Applications*, *22*(2), 249–257. doi:10.1007/s00521-011-0687-2.

Tuffner, F., & Kintner-Meyer, M. (2011). *Using electric vehicles to mitigate imbalance requirements associated with an increased penetration of wind generation*. Paper presented at the IEEE Power and Energy Society General Meeting. New York, NY.

Vandael, S., Boucké, N., Holvoet, T., De Craemer, K., & Deconinck, G. (2011). Decentralized coordination of plug-in hybrid vehicles for imbalance reduction in a smart grid. In *Proceedings of 10th Int. Conf. On Autonomous Agents and Multiagent Systems – Innovative Applications Track (AAMAS 2011)*. AAMAS.

Vandael, S., Boucké, N., Holvoet, T., & Deconinck, G. (2010). Decentralized demand side management of plug-in hybrid vehicles in a smart grid. In *Proceedings of the First International Workshop on Agent Technologies for Energy Systems (ATES 2010)*, (pp. 67-74). ATES.

Vandael, S., Claessens, B., Hommelberg, M., Holvoet, T., & Deconinck, G. (2013). A scalable three-step approach for demand side management of plug-in hybrid vehicles. *IEEE Transactions on Smart Grids*, *4*(2), 720–728. doi:10.1109/TSG.2012.2213847.

VandenBos, G., Knapp, S., & Doe, J. (2001). Role of reference elements in the selection of resources by psychology undergraduates. *Journal of Bibliographic Research*, *5*, 117–123.

Weller, H. (2010). Smart battery management systems. In *Proceedings of the Joint EC /EPoSS / ERTRAC Expert Workshop 2010*. Retrieved on March 5, 2013, from http://www.green-cars-initiative.eu/workshops/joint-ec-epossertrac-expert-workshop-2010-on-batteries

Chapter 17
Grid and Fleet Impact Mapping of EV Charge Opportunities

Niels Leemput
KU Leuven, Belgium

Frederik Geth
KU Leuven, Belgium

Juan Van Roy
KU Leuven, Belgium

Johan Driesen
KU Leuven, Belgium

Sven De Breucker
VITO, Belgium

ABSTRACT

This chapter assesses the impact of different technical solutions and their impact on the ability of a fleet of plug-in hybrid electric vehicles to drive in electric mode as much as possible. The technical solutions covered in this chapter to attain this objective include: charging at low and medium power; charging at home, at work, and at other locations; and using fleets with small, medium, and large battery sizes. The driving behavior of the fleet is modeled using an availability analysis based on statistical data from Flanders and The Netherlands. The fleet itself is based on data of the Flemish vehicle segmentation, while the electric consumption of each segment is determined based on realistic vehicle data and driving cycles. This data is combined into different scenarios for which the utility factor, the energy consumption, the grid impact, and the battery utilization is investigated. Based on these scenario guidelines concerning the appropriate charge power at different locations and the distribution of charge locations, the expected grid impact and utility factor of different fleets are formulated.

INTRODUCTION

A whole range of electric vehicles (EVs) is introduced into the market in the present and the near-term future (Michaeli et al., 2011). Electric propulsion offers possibilities to reduce the consumption of greenhouse gas emitting fuels, e.g. gasoline and diesel (Tanaka, 2009). Furthermore, the local concentrations of harmful pollutants are reduced, due to the absence of tailpipe emissions (Duval and Knipping, 2007).

EVs, both battery electric vehicles (BEVs) and plug-in hybrid electric vehicles (PHEVs), are charged with energy supplied through the electric power system. The increasing EV fleet size will impact the power system in terms of power consumption, load patterns, etc. It is generally concluded that uncoordinated charging of

DOI: 10.4018/978-1-4666-4920-0.ch017

EVs will significantly impact the grid voltage because of the simultaneity between the residential load peak and the plugging in of the vehicles when arriving at home, which starts the charge process (Clement et al., 2010). The impact of EVs on lower levels of the power system has also extensively been discussed, e.g. by Huang et al. (2012) and Pudjianto et al. (2012). The impact for a household is significant, due to the relatively high energy and power consumption compared to other household loads.

Coordinated EV charging may avoid these grid problems, while respecting the primary objective of EVs, namely to provide a mobility service. Mobility behavior offers flexibility towards the charging of the EV, due to the long standstill times of vehicles, on average above 90% in Belgium, and relatively low distances driven, 41 km/day on average in Belgium (Mobiel Vlaanderen, 2013). The flexibility is determined by the EV users, by indicating the departure time of the next trip and required range, and by the battery (State of Charge, maximal (dis)charge current and voltage). This flexibility can be used to include an additional objective, to determine a unique charging pattern. A significant amount of research has already been performed on coordinated EV charging (Leemput et al., 2011). Generally, it is concluded that charging coordination strategies can reduce the impact on the power system, by making more efficient use of the capacity in the system (Heydt, 1983)(Lopes et al., 2011). Typically, the proposed coordination strategies optimize the charging behavior for objectives, such as minimal charging cost, valley filling, peak shaving and maximal penetration of intermittent renewable energy sources.

Although *smart charging*, such as defined by (Lopes et al., 2011), will have a beneficial impact on congestion management (Tran-Quoc et al., 2007), the mitigation of imbalance with increasing penetrations of intermittent RES (Tuffner et al., 2011) and other ancillary services (Rebours et al., 2007), the roll-out of electric vehicles has already started, while the wide-spread implemen-

tation of coordinated vehicle charging has not. This implies that uncoordinated charging will remain the conventional charging mechanism in the near-term future. Furthermore, the charging infrastructure should have a low cost in the initial roll-out phase of electric vehicles, to allow for a broad and widespread implementation (Cuellar and Gartner, 2012). In a later phase, the charging of the vehicles can gradually switch from uncoordinated charging to coordinated charging, whenever a sufficient amount of EVs is available to validate the benefits of coordinated charging. Additionally, locally high concentrations of EVs may occur before there is a significant penetration rate on the regional/national level (Huang et al., 2012). In that case, local grid constraints can be corrected with the implementation of grid interactive chargers, e.g. equipped with voltage droop control (Rei et al., 2010), while coordinated charging can achieve a socially fair solution in a later phase.

However, before coordinated charging can take place, significant infrastructure upgrades are required. As these upgrades come at a cost, the economic benefits of cost-optimal EV charging cannot be realized with all coordination strategies. For example, the time-of-use coordination strategy (Lyon et al., 2012) does not appear to justify investing in the smart grid infrastructure required to implement real-time pricing. Even though the vehicle-to-grid (V2G) potential is investigated in this chapter, this does not imply that the current state of battery cycle life justifies its implementation. For example, when considering coordinated EV charging for grid supporting objectives, the economic impact of increasing the battery lifetime through a suitable charging strategy, which benefits the vehicle owner, is approximately two times higher than savings due to coordinated bi-directional energy trading for cost minimization, which benefits the power system operators (Lunz et al., 2012). Thus, it is unlikely that vehicle owners will be prepared to participate in a coordination mechanism with V2G capability, because it provides them less benefits than a charging strategy that increases battery lifetime. The scope within which the benefits and drawbacks of coordinated charging are considered should thus not be solely limited to the vehicles or the grid, but should take the whole system into consideration.

In this chapter, the grid impact of a fleet of plug-in hybrid electric vehicles (PHEVs) is discussed. The driving behavior of the vehicles is based on an availability model. Furthermore, the vehicles are subdivided into different categories, based on their size (subcompact, compact/midsize and large) and current driving patterns. The analysis provides information on the driven distance and the location of the vehicle when standing still (at home, work, shopping, recreation, etc.), which determines when the vehicles can be charged. The analysis is based on actual mobility behavior from the Netherlands and Flanders and includes information on the number of trips per day, the distance and duration distribution of the trips and the trip motifs. A distinction is made between week and weekend days.

Three different battery capacity scenarios are investigated. Each vehicle will be given a battery capacity in each scenario, which is different for small, middle-class and large vehicles. The scenarios cover a fleet of PHEVs with a first set of small and a second set of medium-sized battery capacities, with capacities based on current PHEVs. A third set of batteries is based on capacities found in current battery electric vehicles.

Furthermore, different charge scenarios are investigated in which the number of charge opportunities increases from only at home to charging at home and work and to charging at home, work and additional charge spots at other locations. The charge power level is restricted to a low power mode 2 case and medium power mode 3 case. As these already provide a large utility factor, fast charging is not considered here.

Based on this information, different charge strategies are determined. The resulting impact on the power system is assessed, e.g. the impact

of being able to charge at different locations in which vehicles typically are standing still: home, workplace, etc. The investigated grid impact includes the peak power and the power consumption at the residential grid, at work and at the other locations, as well as the energy available for down-regulation (G2V service) and up-regulation (V2G service). Voltage and current impacts, e.g. line currents and nodal voltage deviations, are dependent on the specific distribution grid layout. Because many different layouts occur, these impacts are not discussed here. When the vehicles are connected to the grid, the fleet can provide grid services by altering the charge power. It is determined to which extent the fleet is able to provide ancillary services, which will depend on the battery capacities.

BACKGROUND

The electric infrastructure for charging the EVs is essential for a successful roll-out. A big advantage is that the basic supply infrastructure, the electricity grid, is already in place. Charge infrastructure can be categorized according to the charge power it can provide to the vehicle. A higher charge power will result in shorter charge times to obtain an equally high electric drive range. To correlate the charge time to its resulting driving range, the concept of "charge speed" is used.

The power consumption of EVs is expressed in watt-hours per kilometer (Wh/km), which is an electric equivalent for fuel consumption commonly expressed as liters per 100 kilometer (l/100 km) for conventional vehicles. A typical EV consumes about 150-300 Wh/km. Suppose this vehicle would be charged with a charge power of 1,000 W, this results in an increase of the drive range of 3.3-6.6 km for each hour of charging. Thus, the charge speed can be expressed as 3.3-6.6 km$_{range}$/h$_{charge}$, which would require 7.6-15.2 hours of charging to obtain a driving range of 50 km. The charge speed gives a good indication of the mobility limitations related to the available charge power.

The International Electrotechnical Commission (IEC) created an international standard for conductive charge systems for EV charging, IEC 61851-1 (IEC, 2010). In this standard, different charge modes with specific maximal power ratings, are included:

- **Mode 1:** Charge current up to 16 A, single-phase or three-phase is possible. The vehicle is grid connected through a standard socket. A resistor between the power indicator and the ground provides the resistive coding, which informs the EV on the maximal power rating.
- **Mode 2:** Charge current up to 32 A, single-phase or three-phase is possible. The vehicle is grid connected through a standard socket with an in-cable protection device. This also provides the control pilot signal, which informs the EV on the maximal power rating.
- **Mode 3:** Dedicated charge infrastructure that has a fixed grid connection, currents up to 63 A are possible. The control pilot signal is provided by the charge infrastructure.
- **Mode 4:** DC-fast charging up to 400 A. This mode uses a high-power off board charger.

EVs typically come with an adapter cable that has an inlet-compatible connector on the one side, and a domestic socket on the other side. As a result, every domestic socket can be considered as charging infrastructure. The cable and its safety features determine whether it is mode 1 or mode 2 charging compatible. The extensive availability of domestic sockets offer widespread charge opportunities. Mode 1 charging is not allowed in several countries, including the USA, because of the limited safety features provided in this mode. Therefore, the focus lies on mode 2 charging for charging through a standard socket.

Even though charging currents in mode 2 up to 32 A are allowed, they are typically limited to a current of less than 16 A, where 10 A appears to be commonly used in Europe (Ricaud & Vollet, 2010). This is to avoid tripping of the fuse of the electric installation, taking into account that other appliances may be connected to the same power circuit in a typical household installation. Therefore, the charge time is relatively long in this charge mode. Even if a specific circuit could provide higher currents, this is not possible, because the socket cannot adapt the control pilot signal.

Mode 3 charging has the advantage that the available power supply can be used more effectively, because the electric vehicle supply equipment (EVSE) provides the control pilot signal. This results in a shorter charging time, because typically more than 10 A of charge current is available on the dedicated circuit the mode 3 charge unit is connected to. However, mode 3 charging has some disadvantages. Dedicated infrastructure is required, which results in fewer charge opportunities compared to mode 2 charging. Therefore, it must be considered whether the advantages of mode 3 charge infrastructure outweigh the disadvantages. E.g. for charging at home, the investments in mode 3 charge infrastructure, allowing to charge at 6.6 kW, might be superfluous if the vehicle is parked at home for sufficiently long times to charge the battery with mode 2.

Recent years saw the commercial introduction of several electric vehicles intended for mass-production such as the Mitsubishi i-MiEV (2009), the Nissan Leaf (2010), the Renault Kangoo and Fluence Z.E. (2011) and Ford Focus EV (2012 US-market, 2013 Europe). These vehicles have a battery capacity ranging between 16 and 24 kWh, limiting the range in real-life conditions to approximately 100 km. In order to tackle the range limitations, manufacturers propose PHEVs. Chevrolet introduced the Volt (with a 16 kWh battery in the initial version) in 2011, while Fisker introduced the more exclusive Karma (20 kWh battery). 2012 saw the introduction of the Volvo

V60 PHEV (12 kWh battery), Toyota Prius PHV (4.4 kWh battery) and Ford C-Max Energi (7.6 kWh battery, 2012 US-market, 2014 Europe). The roll-out of PHEVs continues in 2013 as Honda releases the Accord PHEV (6.7 kWh battery), Ford the Fusion Energi (7.6 kWh battery, 2013 US-market, 2014 Europe) and Mitsubishi the Outlander (12 kWh battery).

The PHEV has clearly gained acceptance with a broad range of car manufacturers. The battery capacity ranges between 4.4 and 20 kWh, accordingly the electric range will also differ strongly in between these different vehicles. Some of these vehicles are capable of pure electric drive even at highway speeds, such as the Volt, the Karma and both Fords. These vehicles are referred to as regular PHEVs or just PHEVs, while those PHEVs which are only capable of pure electric drive at lower speeds are called blended-mode PHEVs. Examples of the latter are the Prius PHV which switches to hybrid mode above 90 km/h and the Volvo V60 PHEV which switches to hybrid mode above 100 km/h. The drive train architectures also show a broad pallet of technologies. The Karma is a pure series hybrid vehicle. The Honda Accord and Mitsubishi Outlander allow a direct drive mode similar to parallel hybrids, while the Volvo V60 is an axle-split parallel hybrid. Both Fords and the Prius have an adapted series-parallel hybrid drive train commonly found in their hybrid models. The Volt has adopted a series-parallel hybrid drivetrain with additional clutches to allow both electric-only and range-extended driving modes.

FLEET MODELING

In order to model the driving behavior of vehicles in Flanders, statistical data of the Flemish fleet are used for the category segmentation of vehicles and for the mobility behavior. The driving and charging behavior of a fleet of PHEVs is modeled by the availability model (De Caluwé, 2008). For each vehicle in the fleet, it determines when it is driving, when it is at home, at work or another location. In Clement et al. (2010, 2011), Van Roy et al. (2010), an availability model based on Dutch data was used to analyze the impact of charging and discharging plug-in hybrid electric vehicles on a distribution grid. This availability model has been further improved and adapted with recent Flemish data on travel behavior (Mobiel Vlaanderen, 2013). In the Flemish Mobility Study, commissioned by the Flemish government, the people ($\geq$ 6 years old) surveyed were asked to keep track of all their trips (all transport means), thereby collecting the following data:

- Transportation means: car, bike, bus etc.
- Number of trips per day.
- Distance.
- Duration.
- Motif.
- Departure and return times.

Other data required for the availability model are taken from the Belgian automotive and cycle federation (Febiac, 2013), Statistics Belgium (FOD Economie-Statbel, 2013), the Federal Public Service Mobility and Transport (FOD Mobiliteit en Vervoer, 2013) and the Flemish Environmental Agency (de Geest, 2011).

In 2009, the Flemish vehicle fleet consisted of 3,093,843 passenger vehicles (de Geest, 2011). More than half of the households have only one vehicle. The average number of vehicles per household is 1.1. Therefore, only one vehicle per household is assumed in the model. The model can be run for any number of vehicles and days, on a one-minute time resolution. The model makes a distinction between work and non-work trips. Also, a distinction is made between week and weekend days, since the travel behavior is different. Intraweek variations are not taken into account, due to the lack of data to do so. About 75% of all vehicle trips of Flemish people are less than 15 km (Mobiel Vlaanderen, 2013). For the Flemish Mobility Study, people had to keep track of the motif of each trip. Here, the categorization of the non-work trips are limited to the following motifs:

- Business trips,
- Visits,
- Shopping,
- Education,
- Recreation.
- Other, e.g. doctor visit, picking up someone etc.

Number of Vehicle Trips

On average there are 3.14 trips per day per person by all transport means, of which about 65% occur by car (as driver and/or passenger). A trip is defined as the combination of outward and return journey, since about 73.4% of trips are limited to one activity and returning back home (Mobiel Vlaanderen, 2013). Considering the total distance travelled, passenger vehicles take about 71% of the average daily travelled kilometers. About 34% of this distance is for work trips. Of these 3.14 trips, 1.47 trips occur as driver of a vehicle. Considering an average of 2.3 inhabitants (FOD Economie-Statbel, 2013) and assuming one vehicle per household in Flanders, this results in 3.39 trips per day per vehicle. On weekdays, the number of trips per day per vehicle is 3.6. During the weekend this drops to 2.85 trips per day per vehicle.

Duration of Vehicle Trips

The Flemish Mobility Study provides data for the duration, which indirectly provides information on the distance, of an average vehicle trip (Mobiel Vlaanderen, 2013). This duration should be adapted to take into account:

- The difference between week and weekend days: 3.6 versus 2.85 trips per vehicle per day.

- The difference in trip durations of each motif: some motifs have longer/shorter trip distances than the average trip. Therefore, scale factors for the distance of the different motives are used. Work, business and education trips need a scale factor of 1.37, 1.92 and 1.13 respectively as these trips are longer than the average trip. Visits and recreation are on par with the average trip and have a scale factor of 0.99 and 1 respectively, while shopping and other trips are shorter than the average trip with a scale factor of 0.51 and 0.76 respectively.

Work Trips

Work trips and other trips are treated separately in the model, since the priority of the work trips is the highest. Only business trips may overlap during the trip to work and the presence at work. Trips to and from work are typically periodical and predictable. It is important to model these trips to a high degree of accuracy, because work trips represent a significant part of the total mobility behavior of the vehicles.

The average distance from home to work in Flanders is 18.82 km. Figure 1 shows the distribution of the distance to the workplace. About 82% of people live less than 30 km from their work. The distance of the trip to work for a vehicle is fixed for vehicle-by-vehicle.

A fixed work shift is assigned to each vehicle. This fixed work shift can occur during the day, night, morning, evening or can be a part-time shift. The probability for a day shift work trip is the largest at 73.3%, followed by a 12.5% probability of a part-time work shift and 6.8% for a night shift work trip, while the probability of a work trip for a morning and evening shift is equal to 3.7% (De Caluwé, 2008). Depending on the work shift, a different distribution function for the departure and return hour is used.

Similar to the distance to work and the work shift, the departure and return hour are fixed. This

Figure 1. Number of working people and vehicle use in function of distance to work

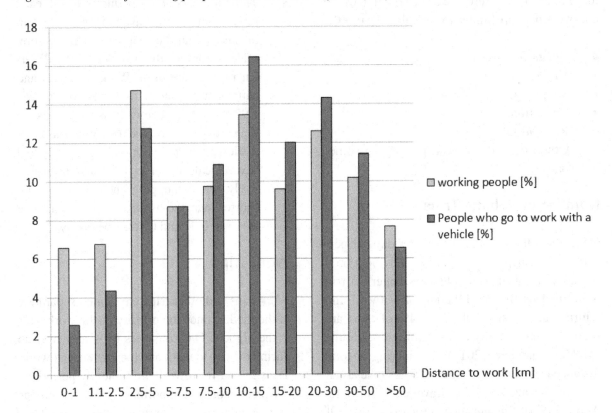

Table 1. Probability for non-working trips

Motive	Weekday [%]	Weekend day [%]
Business	8.54	2.07
Visits	12.50	19.38
Shopping	23.82	28.45
Education	10.52	0.82
Recreation	23.56	32.42
Others	21.06	16.86

is an acceptable assumption, since about 82% of the population has fixed working hours (Mobiel Vlaanderen, 2013). However, to introduce some variation between the different days, a uniform probability distribution function is used to determine the exact minute of departure and return within the one-hour period. It is assumed that the return trip occurs within 24 h.

Other Trips

Different motifs are available for non-work trips, each with a specific probability of occurrence during week and weekend days, as summarized in Table 1. For each motif, the Flemish Mobility Study provides a distribution function for the departure and return times. The distribution function of the return times is not given as a function of the departure times. Furthermore, a probability distribution of the total activity duration is not available. This could result in less reliable results (e.g. picking up someone takes a whole day, even if the distance is limited) and therefore, the availability model performs a minor adjustment to the original data, to obtain more realistic results.

The other trips are divided in two categories, one with a variable activity duration and one with a fixed activity duration. For the variable activity duration motifs, OVG provides a distribution function for the departure and return times. For the fixed duration motifs, only the distribution function for the departure times is used.

- Business, education and recreation trips are modeled as variable activity duration trips. The probability distribution functions for both the departure and return hours are used. It is assumed that education trips end the same day.
- Visits, shopping and other trips are modeled as fixed activity duration trips. The total duration of the activity, trip and presence at the activity, is fixed. Only the probability distributions for the departure time are used. The activity duration for visits, shopping and other is fixed at 180, 120 and 60 min respectively.

As mentioned earlier, the work trips are scheduled first. Afterwards, the characteristics of the other trips are defined. Regarding the scheduling of the other trips, business trips and the other motifs are treated differently. Business trips may overlap with work trips, there is no overlap between trips with other motifs, trips to work and the time at work. These trips will be placed daily before or after work. These non-work trips are allowed to overlap with each other, e.g. shopping after a visit.

Results of the Availability Model

Figure 2 shows the average percentage of a fleet of 100 vehicles on the road for work trips and other trips, respectively for weekdays (a) and weekend days (b). It is shown that on average more vehicles are on the road during the week compared to the weekend since there are on average more trips per day during the week. However, on average less than 10% of the fleet is on the road simultaneously. This is comparable with the result from Huang and Infield (2009), where also maximally 10% of the vehicles is on the road simultaneously. There

is a clear morning and evening peak during the week, which occurs due to the working trips, since most of the people work in normal day shifts and part-time shifts.

Figure 2 shows for week (c) and weekend (d) days how many vehicles are at home, at work and at another location. The latter one includes the presence at another activity and driving to the activity or work and back. On average, a minimum of 15% of the fleet is at home during a weekday and about 35% in the weekend. The amount of vehicles at home is at its maximum during the night, with more than 95% parked at home. During the evening and night, only a few vehicles are parked at work.

Segmentation of Vehicles

On average, the annual vehicle distance is about 15,000 km per Belgian vehicle travelled in Belgium. However, there is a large sensitivity of the vehicle segmentation and vehicle fuel oils in the current vehicle fleet to the annual vehicle kilometers traveled.

Gasoline cars drive on average 8,545 km per year, while diesel cars have an average of 19,340 kilometers traveled per year (de Geest, 2011; Febiac, 2013). Further on, the vehicles are divided in different vehicle segments, based on the present vehicle characteristics. This does not imply that a future fleet will use the same fuels, however it is assumed that mobility behavior will not change in the near future. In Flanders, the share of diesel vehicles is 60%, versus 40% for gasoline vehicles. The fraction of liquefied petroleum gas vehicles (LPG, less than 1%) in the current fleet is neglected (Febiac, 2013; FOD Mobiliteit en Vervoer, 2013). Table 2 gives the distribution of the vehicles and the average yearly distance traveled according to the fuel type and engine displacement in each category.

Three vehicle types are used to differentiate between subcompact, e.g. Mitsubishi i-MiEV (Mitsubishi, 2013) and Smart Electric Drive

Figure 2. Top: Average number of vehicles (as % of the fleet) on the road for work and other trips during (a) week and (b) weekend days. Bottom: Average number of vehicles (as % of the fleet) at home, at work or at another location (another activity or driving to/from an activity and work) during (c) week and (d) weekend days. Both fleets with all (100%) and no (0%) vehicles used for work trips are shown.

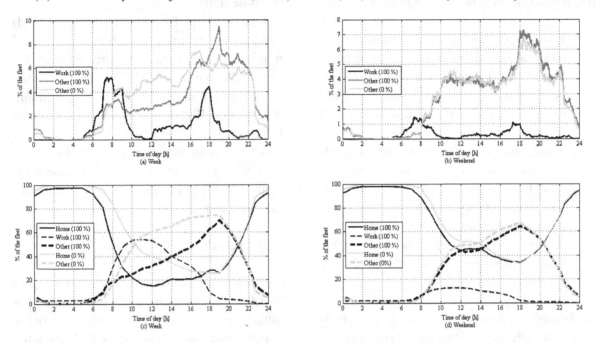

Table 2. Segmentation of the vehicles according to the engine displacement (Mobiel Vlaanderen, 2013)

	Distribution of Vehicles [%]			Average Distance of Vehicles [km]	
Engine	Gasoline	Diesel	Engine	Gasoline	Diesel
<1.4 l	22.64	4.86	<1.4 l	7,960	18,045
1.4-2.0 l	14.36	44.40	1.4-2.0 l	9,095	19,565
>2.0 l	3.00	10.74	>2.0 l	10,335	18,955
Total	40.00	60.00	Fleet average	8,545	19,340

(Smart, 2013), compact/midsize, e.g. Chevrolet Volt (Chevrolet, 2013) and Nissan Leaf (Nissan, 2013), and large vehicles, e.g. Eruf Stormster (Eruf, 2009) and Toyota RAV4 EV (Toyota, 2013b). It is modeled that the three vehicle types coincide with the engine displacement categories (Van Roy et al., 2011). 58.76% of the vehicles belong to the compact/midsize segment. Subcompact cars make up the second largest segment at 27.5% of all vehicles, while the large car segment only represents 13.74% of all vehicles. In the ef-

ficiency model, a representative specific power consumption for each vehicle segment is determined.

Efficiency Model

The specific power consumption (kWh/km) of EVs is required as a parameter to calculate the SOC of batteries. A large range of values is available in literature. Here, this parameter is calculated for different realistic driving cycles and vehicles.

The calculations are based on the battery model used by Tant et al. (2013), with an AC to DC efficiency of 90%.

The power consumption is calculated with physical parameters of the vehicles (weight, size, drag coefficient, etc.) and drive cycles (urban, extra-urban or highway). The resulting forces on the vehicle are calculated: the air friction, rolling resistance, inertial resistance and slope resistance. The model also includes regenerative braking and 500 W of auxiliary power consumption (Van Roy et al., 2011).

A representative drive cycle is composed with three American test cycles. The American cycles are preferred to the artificial European cycles for emission testing, since they are based on real traffic behavior (EPA, 2013). The three driving cycles are combined to calculate the average specific power consumption of each vehicle segment. The driving cycles include the New York City Cycle (NYCC), representing stop-and-go urban traffic with a low average speed, the Federal Test Procedure (FTP), representing extra-urban traffic, and the Highway Fuel Economy Driving Schedule (HWFET), representing highway driving. For Flanders, the distribution of driven kilometers for each cycle type is 23.72% NYCC, 39.82% FTP and 36.46% HWFET (FOD Mobiliteit en Vervoer, 2013). As the focus of the analysis is on the grid impact of the charging of the vehicles, the grid-side power consumption is calculated, i.e. including the efficiency of the charger.

Besides the power consumption calculated in Van Roy et al. (2011), the following parameters were not yet included in the calculations: ambient temperature, wind, altitude, road grade and surface, etc. Therefore, an extra correction factor of 15% on the power consumption is used (EPA, 2006).

Based on this vehicle model, the discussed parameters and combination of driving cycles the average power consumption of the different vehicle segments is:

- **Small Vehicles:** 201 Wh/km,
- **Middle-Class Vehicles:** 233 Wh/km,
- **Large Vehicles:** 334 Wh/km.

ASSUMPTIONS

In this section, the different assumptions for the simulations are discussed: charge opportunity cases, battery capacity scenarios and charge modes. A fleet of 100 PHEVs will be used for all of these cases.

Charge Cases

Four different charge cases are discussed, as summarized in Table 3, with an increasing opportunity to charge in each subsequent case. In the first charge case the vehicles are only able to charge at home, whereas in the second case they are able to charge at home and at work. In the third case vehicles are able to charge at home, at work and 25% of the other locations (e.g. at friends, the supermarket and during recreational activities). The fourth case is similar to the third

Table 3. Summary of the charge cases

Case 1a	Mode 2 charging, only at home
Case 1b	Mode 3 charging, only at home
Case 2a	Mode 2 charging at home and at work
Case 2b	Mode 3 charging at home and at work
Case 3a	Mode 2 charging at home, at work and at 25% of other locations
Case 3d	Mode 3 charging at home, at work and at 25% of other locations
Case 4a	Mode 2 charging at home, at work and at 50% of other locations
Case 4b	Mode 3 charging at home, at work and at 50% of other locations

case, but the opportunity to charge at other locations is increased to 50%.

For each of the four charge cases, charging is considered to occur without coordination. Thus, vehicles charge when they are grid connected, until the battery is completely recharged or until the next trip occurs. For standstill times shorter than 15 min, it is assumed charging does not take place. The driving pattern for 100 EVs is simulated with the discussed availability and efficiency model, on a one-minute resolution. The number of simulated EV patterns is limited, due to computational limitations. Because the residential load profiles, to which the residential charging profile of the EVs will be added, are different for every day of the year, the driving pattern will be simulated for a one-year period. Furthermore, their energy requirements are calculated, based upon the efficiency model and the distribution of the vehicle segments in the Flemish fleet.

Charge Modes

Two charge modes and charge power ratings are taken into consideration. First a 2.1 kW mode 2 charger is discussed, followed by a 6.6 kW mode 3 charger. Both modes use an on-board battery charger.

Mode 2 charging is carried out from a common single or three-phase household socket with an In Cable Control and Protection Device (IC-CPD) integrated into the charge cable. The IC-CPD incorporates a residual current device (RCD), protective earth (PE) monitoring and a pilot control (communication) function (Mathoy, 2008). Current ratings of mode 2 charging commonly range between 6 and 16 A, with a maximum of 32 A. Typically, a fixed maximum charge current of 10 A is chosen for mode 2 chargers in Europe, as the 16 A maximum rating of most sockets can cause overload in the household wiring (Ricaud & Vollet, 2010). A maximum charge current of 10 A results in a charge power of 2.1 kW when

the voltage is at its lowest allowable value, i.e. at 90% of the 230 V nominal value in continental Europe (CENELEC, 2010).

Mode 3 charging is carried out on charge stations that are directly connected to the grid, through a dedicated circuit. The connection between the charge infrastructure and the vehicle occurs through a specific plug/socket, that also communicates the allowable charge current rating to the vehicle. In accordance with IEC 61851 (IEC, 2010), the current and voltage rating can range from a single-phase 16 A/230 V connection up to a three-phase 63 A/400 V connection. Communication, fault current and over-current protection and power interruption are all located in the charge station. The medium power charging at 6.6 kW can either be realized with a single-phase connection of 32 A at 90% of 230 V, or a three-phase connection of 11 A at 90% of the 400 V line voltage.

The utility factor (UF, the proportion of electrically driven distances) and power consumption for both charge modes, each with a specific charge power, are calculated. This allows to assess to which degree the more expensive mode 3 charger contributes to an increased UF and peak power. For each of the three battery scenarios, the charge cases as summarized in Table 3, will be discussed in the following sections.

Battery Capacity Scenarios

The vehicles in the simulation are modeled as plug-in hybrid electric vehicles (PHEVs). This means that all mobility requirements are met, even if the battery is depleted. Thus, no adaptation of mobility behavior is modeled. The PHEVs are assumed to drive on battery power as long as their battery is not depleted. In contrast to blended-mode PHEVs, the combustion engine is not required to kick in for heavy acceleration or at high speeds. Consequently, the combustion engine only runs when the battery is depleted.

In this chapter, three battery capacity scenarios are investigated. In each scenario the distribution of the vehicle segments remains identical, i.e. as mentioned in the segmentation of the vehicles. The power consumption of the different segments remains as established in the efficiency model. This implies that the additional weight of the larger battery on the power consumption is not taken into account.

Three battery capacity scenarios are defined as follows. Battery scenario 1 is based on PHEVs with a small battery capacity. The nominal battery capacity of the subcompact, compact/midsize and large vehicle segment is 5, 7.5 and 10 kWh respectively. Current PHEVs which suit this battery scenario are the Toyota Prius PHV with a 4.4 kWh battery (Toyota, 2013a), the Ford C-Max Energi (Ford, 2013) with a 7.6 kWh battery and Volvo V60 plug-in hybrid (Volvo, 2013) with a 12 kWh battery.

Battery scenario 2 is based on PHEVs with a medium battery capacity. The nominal battery capacities of the vehicle segments are doubled in comparison with the previous scenario to 10, 15 and 20 kWh. Current PHEVs which suit this battery scenario are the Chevrolet Volt (Chevrolet, 2013) with a 16.5 kWh battery and the Fisker Karma (Fisker, 2013) with a 20 kWh battery.

Battery scenario 3 is based on PHEVs with a large battery capacity. The battery capacities of the vehicle segments are doubled in comparison with the second scenario to 20, 30 and 40 kWh. Currently such battery capacities are not available in PHEVs, but similar values can be found in all-electric vehicles such as the Nissan Leaf (Nissan, 2013) with a 24 kWh battery and Tesla Model S (Tesla, 2013) with a 40 kWh battery.

Discharging common lithium batteries to an extreme low SOC limits the power output and such a high depth of discharge (DOD) may impact the battery lifetime. Some manufacturers allow a relatively high DOD, e.g. the Renault Fluence ZE uses 22 of the 25.87 kWh nominal capacity (Renault, 2011), resulting in a DOD of 85%. Other manufacturers are more conservative, e.g. the Chevrolet Volt uses 10.8 of the 16.5 kWh (Chevrolet, 2013), keeping the SOC between 19.5 and 85%. Here, it is assumed that only 80% of the nominal battery capacity is used, resulting in a DOD of 80%.

These charging and fleet scenarios are useful to assess the influence of the increased charge opportunities and different battery capacities on the UF of the vehicles and power consumption. Furthermore, the sensitivity of the UF for the different charge and fleet scenarios can be compared. This allows decision makers and fleet owners to determine whether they should invest in more charge opportunities, in larger battery capacities or a combination of both.

RESULTS

In this section, the results are summarized and discussed for a fleet of 100 PHEVs. First, the mobility behavior and the resulting power consumption are discussed, followed by the impact of the different scenarios on the electric power consumption and the utility factor (UF).

Power Consumption and Driven Distances

For each of the scenarios, the mobility behavior of the vehicles is identical. The cumulative distribution function of the daily driven distances and daily power consumption is illustrated in Figure 3, for a fleet of 100 vehicles for which either none (0%) or all (100%) of the vehicles are used for work trips. The power consumption is what the vehicles need for propulsion, which is identical for each scenario. The cumulative distribution function shows that days with long driven distances, and the resulting high power consumption, are rare. The distinction between the vehicles used for work (100%) and the ones never used for work (0%) is significant. The work vehicles drive longer daily

Figure 3. (a) Cumulative distribution of the daily driven distances and (b) power consumption, both for fleets in which no (0%) and all (100%) of the vehicles are used for work trips

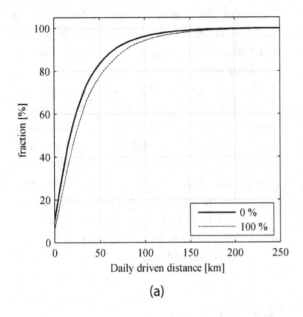

(a)

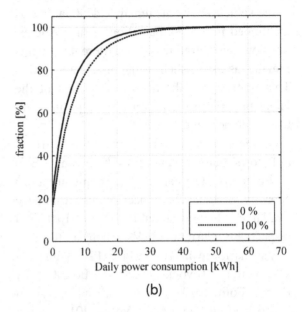

(b)

distances and therefore they have a higher daily power consumption. For the set of mobility profiles used in this chapter, the average daily driven distance and power consumption are respectively 36 km and 7.6 kWh.

These results suggest that for a large battery capacity scenario, for which the battery capacity is significantly larger than the average daily power consumption, a further increase in battery capacity will only marginally increase the UF. Furthermore, there is the sensitivity to the charge opportunities and the charge power rating. More charge locations and a higher charge power rating will increase the UF. Therefore, the impact of these factors is discussed in the following sections.

Impact of EV Charging on the Residential Power Profile

The impact of the vehicles on the residential power profile is discussed and illustrated in this subsection. Different power profiles are discussed, as summarized in Figure 4, for a fleet in which all

Figure 4. Legend of the power profiles, for a fleet in which all vehicles are used for work trips

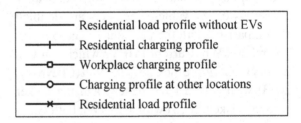

vehicles are used for work trips. Figure 5 includes the power profile for charging at home (residential), at work and at other locations. The results for battery scenario 1 are illustrated in Figure 5, for a fleet of 100 vehicles in which all vehicles are used for work trips, for 1 weekday out of the year. The yearly peak charge power for the different cases is summarized in Table 4 for the fleet of 100 vehicles in which either none (0%) or all (100%) vehicles are used for work trips. The resulting residential peak power, which is the sum of the residential and vehicle charging profile, is summarized in Table 5. The residential profile for 100 households is calculated as the sum of 100 synthetic household

Figure 5. Power profiles of 100 households with an electric vehicle for battery scenario 1, for a fleet in which all vehicles are used for work trips

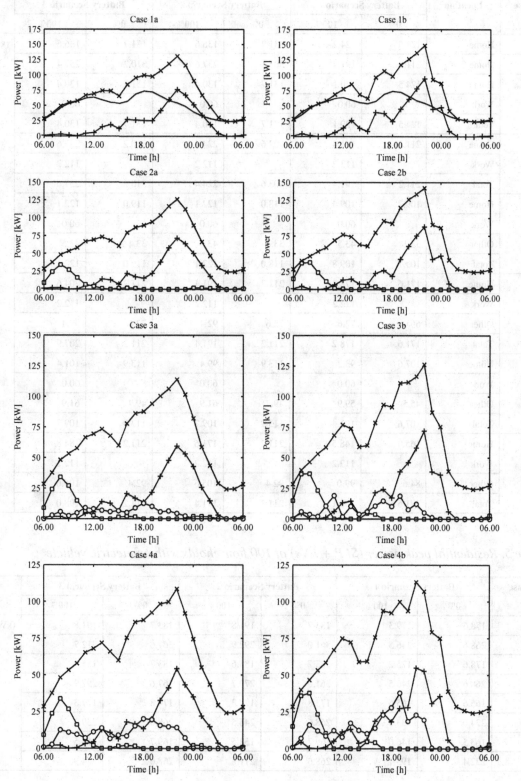

Table 4. Peak charge power of 100 vehicles

Case	Location	Battery Scenario 1		Battery Scenario 2		Battery Scenario 3		
		0%	100%	0%	100%	0%	100%	
1a	Home	124.5	124.2	131.7	136.6	131.7	136.6	(kW)
1b	Home	211.2	191.4	303.6	237.6	310.2	257.4	
2a	Home	124.5	120.1	131.7	130.4	131.7	130.4	
	Work		60.0		60.0		60.0	
	Total	124.5	120.1	131.7	130.4	131.7	130.4	
2b	Home	211.2	191.4	303.6	224.4	310.2	237.6	
	Work		112.2		112.2		112.2	
	Total	211.2	191.4	303.6	224.4	310.2	237.6	
3a	Home	109.7	109.4	118.0	122.1	119.0	122.1	
	Work		60.0		60.0		60.0	
	Other	33.1	43.5	33.4	43.5	33.4	43.5	
	Total	109.7	109.8	118.0	122.1	119.0	122.1	
3b	Home	171.6	178.2	211.2	191.4	211.2	204.6	
	Work		112.2		112.2		112.2	
	Other	66.0	72.6	72.6	92.4	72.6	92.4	
	Total	171.6	178.2	211.2	191.4	211.2	207.9	
4a	Home	107.6	93.2	113.9	99.4	113.9	101.4	
	Work		60.0		60.0		60.0	
	Other	45.5	59.9	49.7	61.9	49.7	61.9	
	Total	107.6	101.4	113.9	109.7	113.9	109.7	
4b	Home	165.0	148.5	211.2	171.6	211.2	184.8	
	Work		112.2		112.2		112.2	
	Other	84.6	99.0	92.4	105.6	92.4	105.6	
	Total	171.6	155.1	211.2	191.4	211.2	198.0	

Table 5. Residential peak power (SLP + EVs) of 100 households with an electric vehicle

Case	Battery Scenario 1		Battery Scenario 2		Battery Scenario 3		
	0%	100%	0%	100%	0%	100%	
1a	178.6	179.3	183.7	191.8	183.7	191.8	(kW)
1b	268.6	246.5	361.0	292.9	367.6	312.7	
2a	178.6	175.2	183.7	185.6	183.7	185.6	
2b	268.6	246.5	361.0	279.7	367.6	292.9	
3a	165.6	165.6	173.8	177.3	174.8	177.3	
3b	224.0	233.3	268.6	246.5	268.6	259.7	
4a	163.5	146.0	169.7	154.5	169.7	154.5	
4b	222.4	193.7	268.6	211.8	268.6	224.9	

load profiles (SLPs) that are representative for the Flemish region (VREG, 2013). The SLP is different for each day of the year.

When charging is restricted to mode 2 residential charging (case 1a), the peak charge power is 1.24 kW/vehicle in battery scenario 1, while this slightly increases to 1.3-1.4 kW/vehicle in battery scenario 2 and 3. The peak charge power at home remains near the same level when charging at work is possible (case 2a) in all battery scenarios. However, the largest reduction is achieved when charging at other locations is possible. When 25% of the other locations provide charge opportunities (case 3a), the residential peak charge power is reduced to 1.1 kW/vehicle in battery scenario 1 and 1.2 kW/vehicle in the battery scenario 2 and 3. When 50% of the other locations provide charge opportunities (case 4a), the residential peak charge power is reduced to 1 kW/vehicle in all battery scenarios. The charging peak power at work for mode 2 charging is 0.6 kW/vehicle in all battery scenarios. Case 3a results in a peak charge power at the other locations of some 0.3-0.4 kW/vehicle, rising to some 0.5-0.6 kW/vehicle in case 4a. The total peak power is also reduced from 1.2-1.4 kW/vehicle to 1-1.1 kW/vehicle with an increase of the charge opportunities.

In case of mode 3 charging at 6.6 kW, the peak charge power when charging is restricted to residential charging (case 1b) increases to 1.9 kW/vehicle in battery scenario 1, and respectively 2.4 and 2.6 kW/vehicle in battery scenario 2 and 3. The peak power at home remains near the same level in the first battery scenario and slightly decreases in the other battery scenarios when charging at work becomes possible. As in the mode 2 charge case, the peak power at home is further reduced when more charge opportunities at work and at other locations become available, as in case 3b and 4b, but the peak power remains significantly above the level of the mode 2 charge cases. For example, when 50% of the other locations provide charge opportunities, the residential peak charge power is reduced to 1.5 kW/vehicle in the

battery scenario 1 and 1.7-1.8 kW/vehicle in battery scenario 2 and 3. The peak charge power at work increases from 0.6 kW/vehicle in the slow charging scenario to 1.1 kW/vehicle with mode 3 charging in all battery scenarios. Charging at the other locations at medium charge power results in an increased peak charge power between 0.7 and 1.1 kW/vehicle, depending on the scenario. The total peak power also remains above the level of the slow charge case even with an increase of the charge opportunities.

In the case of uncoordinated charging, the higher charge power of mode 3 charging vs. mode 2 charging has a significant influence on the peak power used at home. Charging at work has little to no influence on the peak power at home. Only when charging at other locations is available, the peak power at home decreases. The difference between battery scenario 2 and 3 is negligible, but the difference of these two scenarios with battery scenario 1 is significant. The lower charge power of mode 2 charging proves beneficial for the residential and total peak power, in all three battery scenarios. The difference between the different battery scenarios is very small with mode 2 charging, even though the larger batteries need more time to recharge.

Thus, the results indicate that the residential grid impact of vehicle charging is reduced with an increasing amount of charge opportunities elsewhere. This means that, with an increasing amount of EVs being introduced, the impact on the residential grid can be mitigated if these vehicles have a significant amount of charge opportunities elsewhere.

In Table 5 the total residential peak power is shown for 100 households, combining the conventional load as described by the SLP and the additional load of the EVs. As the charge power of the EVs is significant, the conclusions regarding the impact of the amount of charge opportunities and the level of the charge power remain valid. In absence of the vehicles, the peak power consumption of the 100 households is approximately 85 kW.

Utility Factor and Power Consumption

The UF strongly depends on both the available charging locations and the battery capacity scenario. In battery scenario 1, the mean UF is about 65% when only charging at home is possible, rising to about 70% when charging at work is available and increasing to some 80% when charging at work is added and 50% of the other locations are available to charge the EVs. The impact of the charge power on the mean UF is small, compared to the impact of an increasing amount of charge opportunities.

In battery scenario 2, the mean UF is about 85% when only charging at home is possible, slightly increasing to about 87% when charging at work is available and increasing above 92% when charging at work is added and 50% of the other locations are available. The difference with battery scenario 1 is a significant 20 pp when only charging at home is available, but this decreases to 10 pp when more charge opportunities become available. In the third battery scenario the mean UF is already 96% in case 1a and 1b. The mean UF increases 10 pp compared to the second battery capacity scenario and 30 pp compared to the small battery capacity scenario when only charging at home is available. As the mean UF is already very high, the impact of a rise in charge opportunities or power level remains low in battery scenario 3.

For case 1 and case 2, the sensitivity of the UF to the charge mode is insignificant, due to the relatively long standstill times of the vehicles at home and at work. Basically, the charging is spread out more over the time the vehicle is standing still at these locations anyway. Thus, the PHEV user can decide whether the benefit of a mode 3 charging unit compared to mode 2 charging, namely having a higher charging speed, outweighs the added cost of a mode 3 charging unit. When taking into account that some PHEVs have a charge power rating that is limited to 3.3 kW, e.g. Chevrolet Volt (Chevrolet, 2013), the increase in charging time

for mode 2 charging compared to mode 3 is 60% instead of 200%, thereby reducing the benefit of mode 3 charging significantly.

The average yearly power consumption per vehicle, as summarized for all cases in Table 6, varies between 1.7 and 2.6 MWh in battery scenario 1. The power consumption at home drops from 1.7 to 2 MWh to about 1.1 to 1.3 MWh when the number of charge opportunities increases. The power consumption at work is about 400 kWh when available for the work vehicles, and does not depend on the availability of other charge opportunities or on the charge level. The power consumption at the other locations ranges between 400 and 1,000 kWh.

In battery scenario 2, the total yearly power consumption per vehicle ranges between 2.3 and 3.0 MWh. The power consumption at home once again decreases when other charge opportunities are available and drops from between 2.3 and 2.7 MWh to between 1.4 and 1.6 MWh, when the number of charge opportunities increases. The power consumption at work slightly increases to about 450 kWh. As the distance to work does not change and most batteries are fully charged before leaving to work, this result is expected. The power consumption at the other locations also slightly increases and ranges between 420 and 1,100 kWh. Similar results can be found in battery scenario 3, for which the total power consumption ranges between 2.6 and 3.3 MWh. The power consumption at work further increases to levels above 500 kWh but never reaches the levels attained at home or at the other charge locations. The power consumption at the other locations remains at the level of battery scenario 2. The extended battery capacity does not result in an increased electrically driven distance as the charge power at the other locations is already fully utilized.

To have an indication on the utilization of the battery capacity in the fleet, the yearly electric power consumption of the fleet is divided by the battery capacity of the entire fleet. For example, a utilization factor of 365 would mean that the

Table 6. Vehicle yearly power consumption for the different cases

Case	Location	Battery Scenario 1		Battery Scenario 2		Battery Scenario 3		
		0%	100%	0%	100%	0%	100%	
1a	Home	1,705.7	1,943.0	2,271.6	2,678.4	2,617.1	3,158.7	(kWh)
1b	Home	1,741.6	2,022.3	2,298.1	2,739.9	2,631.7	3,212.2	
2a	Home	1,705.7	1,778.4	2,271.6	2,376.3	2,617.1	2,695.9	
	Work		398.5		461.7		536.3	
	Total	1,705.7	2,176.9	2,271.6	2,838.0	2,617.1	3,232.2	
2b	Home	1,741.6	1,833.5	2,298.1	2,417.9	2,631.7	2,774.0	
	Work		405.4		463.8		483.2	
	Total	1,741.6	2,238.9	2,298.1	2,881.7	2,631.7	3,257.2	
3a	Home	1,434.8	1,557.9	1,875.0	2,054.2	2,139.4	2,316.3	
	Work		391.8		450.8		511.6	
	Other	466.8	398.1	494.4	420.6	503.0	430.8	
	Total	1,901.6	2,347.9	2,369.4	2,925.6	2,642.5	3,258.7	
3b	Home	1,410.2	1,554.0	1786.5	1,983.5	2,011.6	2,246.3	
	Work		397.5		451.1		468.2	
	Other	551.2	485.6	629.3	555.8	648.3	573.0	
	Total	1,961.4	2,437.1	2,415.8	2,990.5	2,659.9	3,287.5	
4a	Home	1,198.0	1,356.7	1,536.3	1,764.7	1,734.2	1,974.6	
	Work		385.2		440.7		490.5	
	Other	865.3	761.3	913.8	802.5	927.5	817.0	
	Total	2,063.3	2,503.2	2,450.2	3,007.9	2,661.7	3,282.2	
4b	Home	1,144.7	1,315.0	1,393.0	1,619.1	1,536.5	1,802.7	
	Work		389.6		439.4		455.1	
	Other	991.4	904.7	1,113.0	1,026.0	1,144.1	1,054.2	
	Total	2,136.1	2,609.3	2,506.0	3,084.4	2,680.5	3,312.0	

battery capacity of the fleet is fully used 365 times during the year, thus on average once a day. A higher battery utilization is beneficial for the user as this corresponds to a higher return on investment on the battery. The utilization factors are summarized in Table 7.

Significant differences are visible for the different battery scenarios. Battery scenario 1 has the highest utilization factor, which increases with an increasing amount of charge opportunities. For some scenarios for the work vehicles, this number even exceeds 365. Thus, the battery capacity is used more than once a day on average,

because the effective EV battery capacities are slightly lower than the average daily power consumption of the vehicles. When there are plenty of charge opportunities, the battery capacity is intensively used.

For battery scenario 2 and 3, the battery capacity is relatively large compared to the average daily power consumption. The UF is already high in case 1a and 1b, and an increase in charge opportunities does not significantly influence the UF. Consequently, the battery utilization does not increase significantly with an increasing amount of charge opportunities.

Table 7. Battery utilization for the different cases

Case	Battery Scenario 1		Battery Scenario 2		Battery Scenario 3	
	0%	100%	0%	100%	0%	100%
1a	255	288	170	198	98	117
1b	260	300	172	203	98	119
2a	255	323	170	210	98	120
2b	260	332	172	213	98	121
3a	284	348	177	217	99	121
3b	293	361	180	222	99	122
4a	308	371	183	223	99	122
4b	319	387	187	228	100	123

Grid Services

In this section, the impact of a PHEV fleet on the grid is investigated and expressed in terms of the grid connection availability at different locations, energy stored in the batteries of the fleet (V2G potential) and potential power consumption by charging the batteries of the fleet (G2V potential). These values provide information to assess the interaction with the power system, in terms of energy requirements and charging flexibility. This becomes even more important in the envisioned future power system, which contains a significant amount of intermittent renewable energy sources (Budischak et al., 2013).

The grid connection availability and V2G-G2V potential are important indicators to assess to which extent the fleet of PHEVs can deliver such ancillary services as extra power for peak load demand, load shifting or even spinning reserves (Lopes et al., 2011). These indicators will also become increasingly important for aggregators. These aggregators group the PHEVs into larger clusters and they need to know to which degree the PHEVs under their control are able to deliver grid services such as secondary frequency control (Almeida et al., 2010). Other ancillary services such as voltage support in distribution grids (Rei et al., 2010) are beyond the scope of this research.

The grid connection availability is defined here as the fraction of the fleet that is grid connected for all but 60 minutes of the year, which is 99.99% of time. Vehicles are grid connected when they are standing still at a location with a charge opportunity for more than 15 minutes. The grid connection availability at home is 13% for a fleet in which no vehicles are used for work trips, and 6% for a fleet in which all vehicles are used for work trips. Extending the charge opportunity to charging at work (case 2a and 2b), the grid connection availability increases from 6 to 18% for the fleet in which all vehicles are used for work trips (100%). If 25% the other locations are also available (case 3), the grid connection availability rises to respectively 29 and 32% for fleets in which either none (0%) or all (100%) of the vehicles are used for work trips. For a 50% availability of charge opportunities at other locations, these numbers rise to respectively 47 and 49%.

The average minimum of grid connected energy for a fleet of 100 PHEVs is summarized in Table 8, i.e. the grid connection availability is already taken into account. This energy is always available for up-regulation or V2G services. As can be seen, for the same charge case, the available energy increases with the battery capacity. As the battery capacity doubles in each battery scenario, while the UF and thus consumed energy increases far less, the available energy of the fleet increases, because the average SOC of the batteries is higher in the subsequent battery scenarios. For the first battery scenario this results in a minimum available energy of some 210-250 kWh for the 100 vehicle fleet when many charge opportunities are present, but this can drop to 30-60 kWh when only charging at home is possible. In the second battery scenario, the minimum available energy ranges between 60 (case 1, only at home) and 470 kWh (case 4, home/work/50% others) depending on the available charge opportunities, while this ranges between 130 and 960 kWh for the third battery scenario. The increase in charge opportunities strongly increases the available energy, because of the increase in grid connection availability, combined with the increase of the average SOC. The increase in charge opportunities has a much higher impact than the increase in charge power, due to the increased grid connection availability.

The energy availability of a fleet of vehicles used for work trips (100%) is 61.8 kWh for case 1a and battery scenario 2. However, for case 2a and battery scenario 1, thus with half of the battery capacity compared to scenario 2, the same fleet has a higher energy availability of 76.7 kWh. When comparing case 2a with 1b for each battery scenario, which have approximately the same UF, the energy availability increases with a factor 2.45-2.8, depending on the battery scenario. From a grid point of view, an increased number of charge points/opportunities, results in a much larger available energy reserve, while the consumed energy only slightly increases. Take for instance the example of the battery scenario 2 (10/15/20 kWh); The average energy consumed per vehicle of the fleet is some 2.3 to 2.7 MWh/yr in case 1a and 2.5 to 3 MWh/yr in case 4a, but the minimum available energy increases from 60 to 120 kWh for a 100 vehicle fleet in case 1a to some 420 kWh in case 4a. Thus, the energy available for V2G services strongly increases with the number of charge opportunities, while the average size of the battery capacity of the fleet also has an important impact.

The energy availability for fully charged vehicles are summarized in Table 9. These results give an indication on the amount of vehicles at each moment that are already fully charged, but remain grid connected. This fraction of the fleet is unable to participate in down-regulation, i.e. these vehicles cannot charge to consume excess energy available in the grid. Obviously, these numbers are lower than in Table 8. The most important lesson learned from Table 9 is the difference between the a and b cases. Here, the influence of the charge power on the available flexibility is significant, because an increase in charge power reduces the time to get fully charged and increases the number of vehicles that becomes unavailable for down-regulation.

Table 8. Energy availability (99.99%) for a fleet of 100 vehicles

Case	Battery Scenario 1		Battery Scenario 2		Battery Scenario 3		
	0%	100%	0%	100%	0%	100%	
1a	60.5	30.4	122.6	61.8	265.6	126.2	(kWh)
1b	67.5	31.1	136.8	63	281.9	127.0	
2a	60.5	76.7	122.6	170	265.6	361.9	
2b	67.5	91.1	136.8	184.1	281.9	373.4	
3a	124.1	136.8	255	300.9	511.7	625.8	
3b	139.7	157.6	278.1	338.2	593	667.0	
4a	208.1	202.8	423.2	423.2	896.4	937.7	
4b	213.2	245	461.7	471.4	908	959.4	

Table 9. Energy availability (99.99%) of fully charged vehicles for a fleet of 100 vehicles

Case	Battery Scenario 1		Battery Scenario 2		Battery Scenario 3		
	0%	100%	0%	100%	0%	100%	
1a	36	20	68	40	136	64	(kWh)
1b	58	26	112	52	224	104	
2a	36	48	68	88	136	176	
2b	58	76	112	148	224	296	
3a	70	70	160	168	320	304	
3b	120	134	244	256	472	512	
4a	132	116	280	236	504	456	
4b	198	202	392	392	792	768	

When calculating the G2V potential of the fleet in the different cases, the minimum available charge energy of the fleet which is present for 99.99% of time turns out to be near zero for all cases. This is caused by the long duration of the grid connection availability when almost all vehicles are charging at home, and some at work, at the end of the night and all batteries are simultaneously fully charged. As all batteries are fully charged, the fleet is unable to accept any additional charge energy for down-regulation.

Table 10 gives the minimum available charge energy which is present for 75% (left) and 95% (right) of time. In this table, all cases with a charge power of 6.6 kW (b-cases) are omitted as the available charge energy for down-regulation is already near zero in most of these cases. The available charge energy for the vehicles not used for work (0%) is already negligible in battery scenario 1

and much smaller than for the vehicles used for work (100%) in the other battery scenarios. An increase of the charge opportunities from only at home to at home and work causes the available charge energy to increase significantly. The impact is very low when other charge opportunities become available, because even though the grid connection availability increases, the average SOC of the fleet also increases strongly.

The minimum available charge energy, valid for 75% of time, remains very low, between 11 and 22 kWh for battery scenario 2 and between 25 and 41 kWh for battery scenario 3. The minimum available charge energy, valid for 95% of time, is much lower; only those vehicles used for work have a charge energy margin in battery scenario 2, while there is none in the first battery scenario. Only battery scenario 3 provides some charge energy margin in all cases. When compar-

Table 10. Charging energy availability for a fleet of 100 vehicles (left: 75% availability/right: 95% availability)

Case	Battery Scenario 1		Battery Scenario 2		Battery Scenario 3		
	0%	100%	0%	100%	0%	100%	
1a	1.0/0	1.6/0	5.7/0	8.6/0.2	17.5/4.5	**25.5/5.2**	
2a	1.0/0	6.4/0	5.7/0	16.6/5.1	17.5/4.5	**35.4/14.3**	(kWh)
3a	2.8/0	8.2/0	9.2/0.2	20.2/5.3	22.8/7.5	**40.8/18.7**	
4a	3.7/0	9.4/0	11.3/0.3	22.2/4.9	25.1/8.8	**41.5/19.9**	

ing Table 10 with Table 8, it becomes obvious that the available charge energy for G2V services is negligible in comparison to the available discharge energy V2G services; In the first battery scenario the minimum available discharge energy is some 200 to 250 kWh, while there is no charge energy. In the third battery scenario the minimum available discharge energy is some 900 kWh, while the charge energy is a very low 10 to 20 kWh. This implies that the implementation of a frequency droop control on the charge equipment can be relied upon to provide up-regulation by injecting the energy stored in the batteries of the fleet, but not to provide down-regulation by storing energy in the batteries of the fleet, as there is a high probability that the fleet is already fully charged.

CONCLUSION

The results of the simulations indicate that mode 2 charging is able to supply energy to meet a significant amount of the mobility requirements. More than two thirds of the distances (70%) can be driven electrically when mode 2 charging is possible at home and at the workplace for the scenario with the smallest battery capacities (5/7.5/10 kWh), and this fraction even increases to more than 85% for higher battery capacities. An increase of the charge opportunities at other locations will further increase this fraction. Also, an increase of the charge opportunities decreases the residential grid impact, because the consumed charge energy and peak charge power at home are reduced.

The available charge power has a limited impact on the utility factor. At locations for which sufficient charging time is available, the small (5/7.5/10 kWh) and medium capacity (10/15/20 kWh) batteries will be fully charged with mode 2 charging at 2.1 kW. Only at locations other than home or work, the increased charge power results in an improvement of the yearly average charged energy per vehicle with about 100 to 150 kWh

for the small batteries and even up to 200 kWh for the medium capacity batteries, as the available charge time is lower at these locations. Thus, for home and workplace charging, mode 2 charging infrastructure appears to provide sufficient energy to fulfill typical mobility requirements. Furthermore, as the initial roll-out of EVs and PHEVs will rely on uncoordinated charging, the grid impact of the mode 2 charger on the residential grid is much smaller. The maximum average charge power is some 1.4 kW/vehicle, while this doubles to 3 kW/vehicle when mode 3 charging at 6.6 kW is used at home.

The results of the smallest battery capacity scenario support the increasingly popular assumption that a carefully chosen set of small battery capacities is sufficient to obtain a high utility factor for a fleet of plug-in hybrid electric vehicles. With the assumptions of the availability model, the small batteries, ranging between 5 and 10 kWh nominal capacity, are sufficient to obtain a mean utility factor between 64% and 82%. A decisive factor in obtaining those high utility factors is the availability of charge opportunities. Charging at home and at work will result in mean utility factors up to 70%. To obtain an extra 10 pp mean utility factor, charge opportunities at other locations are required.

For the smallest battery capacity scenario, the yearly average energy charged at home reaches a maximum of about 2 MWh per vehicle and declines to less than 1.5 MWh when more charging locations become available, while the utility factor increases. The average yearly energy charged at work is about 400 kWh, for vehicles used for work trips, in all circumstances. The energy charged at the other locations is significantly higher than at work, although the available charge time is much lower. This is caused by the fact that the batteries are fully charged before leaving to work and only experience a limited discharge while driving from home to work.

With medium capacity batteries (10/15/20 kWh), the supposition that the availability of charge opportunities is a decisive factor in the utility factor of the PHEV fleet, remains valid. Although the utility factor is already high when only charging at home is available, i.e. 84%, this can be increased to 94% when more charge opportunities become available. An increase of the charge power has little effect on the charged energy at home and at work, but at the other locations the increase in charge power results in an increase of the average yearly charged energy of about 130 kWh to 200 kWh per vehicle. The average utility factor is already high in the small battery scenario, nevertheless a significant improvement of about 10 to 20 pp can be achieved by the use of medium capacity batteries. The difference becomes smaller as more charge opportunities become available.

Practically, this calls for a well-chosen user-specific battery capacity in the small to medium sized range, combined with ample charge opportunities and possibly mode 3 chargers at the locations other than at home and at work. The total yearly average charged energy reaches about 3 MWh per vehicle. Depending on the charge opportunities, this energy is fully consumed at home and drops to 1.5 MWh with an increase of the charge opportunities at other places.

For high battery capacities (20/30/40 kWh), the utility factor is very high in all circumstances. This implies that the user has to make a significant investment in the larger battery which does not result in equally higher utility factors. Therefore, the return on investment of the additional battery capacity is very low. Despite this drawback, the high capacity battery can be beneficial for those people who cover large distances (near 80 km) on a daily basis. Those people who are unable to predict to which degree the daily driven distance will alter during the lifespan of the vehicle, might also benefit from a larger battery capacity.

The available energy for V2G services for up-regulation for the entire 100 vehicle fleet can be as low as 30 to 60 kWh in the small battery scenario when only charging at home is available. This sharply increases to some 80 kWh for the 100% work vehicles scenario when charging

at work becomes available, but can increase to 200 kWh when other charge locations become available. The available discharge energy doubles when the fleet switches to medium capacity batteries (10/15/20 kWh) in all charge opportunity scenarios, with a fleet maximum of some 400 to 500 kWh. The increased availability of charge locations thus proves to be beneficial for the grid as both the available energy for reserves increases and the charge power at home decreases. From a grid point of view the medium capacity batteries are also beneficial as the available energy doubles.

Unfortunately, the minimum G2V services of the fleet for down-regulation can be almost non-existent as the batteries are fully charged near the end of the night. This prevents the vehicles from storing any excess energy available in the grid. Some G2V grid services for down-regulation can be provided by the vehicles used for work trips with medium capacity batteries (10/15/20 kWh) when the requested availability is reduced from 99.99% to 95% of time. These vehicles are able to provide some 5 kWh of down-regulation per fleet of 100 vehicles.

REFERENCES

Almeida, P. M. R., Lopes, J. A. P., Soares, F. J., & Vasconcelos, M. H. (2010). *Automatic generation control operation with electric vehicles.* Paper presented at the Bulk Power System Dynamics and Control Symposium. Rio de Janeiro, Brazil.

Budischak, C., DeAnna, S., Thomson, H., Mach, L., Veron, D. E., & Kempton, W. (2013). Cost-minimized combinations of wind power, solar power and electrochemical storage, powering the grid up to 99.9% of the time. *Journal of Power Sources*, 225(1), 60–74. doi:10.1016/j.jpowsour.2012.09.054.

CENELEC. (2010). Voltage characteristics of electricity supplied by public electricity networks. *CENELEC Std. EN*, *50*, 160.

Chevrolet Volt. (2013). Retrieved March 14, 2013, from http://media.gm.com/media/us/en/chevrolet/vehicles/volt/2013.html

Clement, K., Haesen, E., & Driesen, J. (2010). The impact of plug-in hybrid electric vehicles on a residential distribution grid. *IEEE Transactions on Power Systems*, *25*(1), 371–380. doi:10.1109/TPWRS.2009.2036481.

Clement, K., Haesen, E., & Driesen, J. (2011). The impact of vehicle-to-grid on the distribution grid. *Electric Power System Research Journal*, *81*(1), 371–380.

Cuellar, A., & Gartner, J. (2012). *Electric vehicle charging equipment (Research Report)*. London: Navigant Research.

De Caluwé, E. (2008). *Potentieel van demand side management, piekvermogen en netondersteundende diensten geleverd door plug-in hybride elektrische voertuigen op basis van een beschikbaarheidsanalyse*. (Unpublished master's thesis). KU Leuven, Leuven, Belgium.

de Geest, C. (2011). *MIRA achtergronddocument 2010, transport (Technical Report)*. Erembodegem, Belgium: Vlaamse Milieumaatschappij.

Duvall, M., & Knipping, E. (2007). *Environmental assessment of plug-in hybrid electric vehicles (Technical report)*. Palo Alto, CA: Electric Power Research Institute.

EPA. (2006). *Fuel economy labeling of motor vehicles: Revisions to improve calculation of fuel economy estimates (EPA420-R-06-017)*. Washington, DC: U.S. Environmental Protection Agency.

EPA. (2013). *Dynamometer drive schedules*. Retrieved March 18, 2013, from http://www.epa.gov/nvfel/testing/dynamometer.htm

eRUF Stormster. (2009). Retrieved June 1, 2012, from www.ruf-automobile.de/en/en-aktuelles-eruf.php

Febiac. (2013). Retrieved March 14, 2013, from http://www.febiac.be

Fisker Karma. (2013). Retrieved March 14, 2013, from http://onward.fiskerautomotive.com/en-us

FOD Economie-Statbel:Algemene Directie Statistiek en Economische Informatie. (2013). Retrieved March 14, 2013, from http://statbel.fgov.be

FOD Mobiliteit en Vervoer. (2013). Retrieved March 14, 2013, from http://www.mobilit.fgov.be

Ford C-MAX Energi. (2013). Retrieved March 14, 2013, from http://www.ford.com/cars/cmax/trim/energi/

Heydt, G. T. (1983, May). The impact of electric vehicle deployment on load management strategies. *IEEE Transactions on Power Apparatus and Systems*, *102*(5), 1253–1259. doi:10.1109/TPAS.1983.318071.

Huang, S., & Infield, D. (2009). *The potential of domestic electric vehicles to contribute to power system operation through vehicle to grid technology*. Paper presented at the 44th Int. Universities Power Engineering Conference. New York, NY.

IEC. (2010). *Electric vehicle conductive charging system - Part 1: General requirements (IEC 61851-1)*. Geneva, Switzerland: International Electrotechnical Commission.

Kempton, W., & Tomic, J. (2005). Vehicle-to-grid power fundamentals: Calculating capacity and net revenue. *Journal of Power Sources*, *144*(1), 268–279. doi:10.1016/j.jpowsour.2004.12.025.

Leemput, N., Van Roy, J., Geth, F., Tant, P., Claessens, B., & Driesen, J. (2011). *Comparative analysis of coordination strategies for electric vehicles*. Paper presented at the 2nd IEEE PES International Conference and Exhibition on Innovative Smart Grid Technologies Europe. Manchester, UK.

Lopes, J. A. P., Soares, F. J., & Almeida, P. M. R. (2011). Integration of electric vehicles in the electric power system. *Proceedings of the IEEE, 99*(1), 168–183. doi:10.1109/JPROC.2010.2066250.

Lunz, B., Yan, Z., Gerschler, J. B., & Sauer, D. U. (2012). Influence of plug-in hybrid electric vehicle charging strategies on charging and battery degradation costs. *Energy Policy, 46*, 511–519. doi:10.1016/j.enpol.2012.04.017.

Lyon, T. P., Michelin, M., Jongejan, A., & Leahy, T. (2012). Is smart charging policy for electric vehicles worthwhile? *Energy Policy, 41*, 259–268. doi:10.1016/j.enpol.2011.10.045.

Mathoy, A. (2008). *Definition and implementation of a global EV charging infrastructure (Final Report)*. Gams, Switzerland: Brusa Elektronik.

Michaeli, I., Reenock, C., & Kapoor, D. (2011). *Electric vehicles: Perspectives on a growing investment theme*. Retrieved from http://www.ceres.org/resources/reports/electric-vehicles-report

Mitsubishi i-MiEV. (2008). Retrieved March 14, 2013, from http://www.mitsubishi-motors.com/special/ev/

Mobiel Vlaanderen: Onderzoek Verplaatsingsgedrag Vlaanderen. (2013). Retrieved March 14, 2013, from http://www.mobielvlaanderen.be/ovg/

Nissan Leaf. (2013). Retrieved March 14, 2013, from http://www.nissanusa.com/electric-cars/leaf/

Rebours, Y. G., Kirschen, D. S., Trotignon, M., & Rossignol, S. (2007). A survey of frequency and voltage control ancillary services - Part 1: Technical features. *IEEE Transactions on Power Systems, 22*(1), 350–357. doi:10.1109/TPWRS.2006.888963.

Rei, R., Soares, F. J., Almeida, P. M. R., & Lopes, J. A. P. (2010). *Grid interactive charging control for plug-in electric vehicles*. Paper presented at the 13th International IEEE Conference on Intelligent Transportation Systems. Funchal, Portugal.

Renault Fluence ZE. (2011). Retrieved March 26, 2013, from http://www.media-renault.eu/fluence-ze/

Ricaud, C., & Vollet, P. (2010). *Connection system on the recharging spot: A key element for electric vehicles*. Retrieved March 14, 2013, from http://www.evplugalliance.org/en/doc/

Smart Electric Drive. (2013). Retrieved March 14, 2013, from http://www.smart-electric-drive.com/

Tant, J., Geth, F., Six, D., Tant, P., & Driesen, J. (2013). Multiobjective battery storage to improve PV integration in residential distribution grids. *IEEE Transactions on Sustainable Energy, 4*(1), 182–191. doi:10.1109/TSTE.2012.2211387.

Tesla Model S. (2013). Retrieved March 14, 2013, from http://www.teslamotors.com/models

Toyota Prius Plug-in Hybrid. (2013). Retrieved March 14, 2013, from http://www.toyota.com/prius-plug-in

Toyota RAV4 EV. (2013). Retrieved March 14, 2013, from http://www.toyota.com/rav4ev

Tran-Quoc, T., Braun, M., Marti, J., Kieny, C., Hadjsaid, N., & Bacha, S. (2007). *Using control capabilities of DER to participate in distribution system operation*. Paper presented at 2007 IEEE Power Tech. Lausanne, Switzerland.

Tuffner, F., & Kintner-Meyer, M. (2011). *Using electric vehicles to mitigate imbalance requirements associated with an increased penetration of wind generation*. Paper presented at IEEE Power and Energy Society General Meeting. New York, NY.

Van Roy, J., Leemput, N., De Breucker, S., Geth, F., Tant, P., & Driesen, J. (2011). *An availability analysis and energy consumption model for a flemish fleet of electric vehicles*. Paper presented at the 2011 European Electric Vehicle Congress. Brussels, Belgium.

Van Roy, J., & Vogt, K. (2010). *Analyse van verschillende batterijcapactiteiten voor plug-in hybride elektrische voertuigen*. (Unpublished master's thesis). KU Leuven, Leuven, Belgium.

Volvo V60 Plug-in Hybrid. (2013). Retrieved March 14, 2013, from http://www.volvocars.com/intl/campaigns/v60-plugin-hybrid/Pages/v60-plug-in-hybrid.aspx

VREG. (2013). *Verbruiksprofielen*. Retrieved March 14, 2013, from http://www.vreg.be/verbruiksprofielen-0

ADDITIONAL READING

Andersen, P. H., Mathews, J. A., & Rask, M. (2009). Integrating private transport into renewable energy policy: The strategy of creating intelligent recharging grids of electric vehicles. *Energy Policy*, *37*(7), 2481–2486. doi:10.1016/j.enpol.2009.03.032.

Andersson, S. L., Elofsson, A. K., Galus, M. D., Göransson, L., Karlsson, S., Johnsson, F., & Andersson, G. (2010). Plug-in hybrid electric vehicles as regulating power providers: Case studies of Sweden and Germany. *Energy Policy*, *38*(6), 2751–2762. doi:10.1016/j.enpol.2010.01.006.

Dallinger, D., Krampe, D., & Wietschel, M. (2011). Vehicle-to-Grid Regulation Reserves Based on a Dynamic Simulation of Mobility Behavior. *IEEE Transactions on Smart Grids*, *2*(2), 302–313. doi:10.1109/TSG.2011.2131692.

Farmer, C., Hines, P., Dowds, J., & Blumsack, S. (2010, Jan.). *Modeling the Impact of Increasing PHEV Loads on the Distribution Infrastructure*. Presented at the 43rd Hawaii International Conference on System Sciences, Kuaui, HI.

Galus, M. D., Zima, M., & Andersson, G. (2010). On integration of plug-in hybrid electric vehicles into existing power system structures. *Energy Policy*, *38*(11), 6736–6745. doi:10.1016/j.enpol.2010.06.043.

Green, R. C., Wang, L., & Alam, M. (2011). The impact of plug-in hybrid electric vehicles on distribution networks: A review and outlook. *Renewable & Sustainable Energy Reviews*, *15*(1), 544–553. doi:10.1016/j.rser.2010.08.015.

Masoum, A. S., Deilami, S., Moses, P. S., & Abu-Siada, A. (2010, Oct.). *Impacts of Battery Charging Rates of Plug-in Electric Vehicle on Smart Grid Distribution Systems*. Paper presented at the IEEE PES Innovative Smart Grid Technologies Conference Europe, Gothenburg, Sweden.

Michaeli, I., Reenock, C., & Kapoor, D. (2011, Feb.). *Electric Vehicles: Perspectives on a Growing Investment Theme*. Retrieved from Citi Investment Research & Analysis website: http://www.ceres.org/resources/reports/electric-vehicles-report

Papadopoulos, P., Skarvelis-Kazakos, S., Grau, I., Cipcigan, L. M., & Jenkins, N. (2010, Sept.). *Predicting Electric Vehicle Impacts on Residential Distribution Networks with Distributed Generation*. Presented at the IEEE Vehicle Power and Propulsion Conference, Lille, France.

Rotering, N., & Ilic, M. (2011). Optimal Charge Control of Plug-In Hybrid Electric Vehicles in Deregulated Electricity Markets. *IEEE Transactions on Power Systems*, *26*(3), 1021–1029. doi:10.1109/TPWRS.2010.2086083.

Sioshansi, R., & Miller, J. (2011). Plug-in hybrid electric vehicles can be clean and economical in dirty power systems. *Energy Policy, 39*(10), 6151–6161. doi:10.1016/j.enpol.2011.07.015.

Skerlos, S. J., & Winebrake, J. J. (2010, Feb.). Targeting plug-in hybrid electric vehicle policies to increase social benefits. *Energy Policy, 38*(2), 705–708. doi:10.1016/j.enpol.2009.11.014.

Srivastava, A. K., Annabathina, B., & Kamalasadan, S. (2010). The Challenges and Policy Options for Integrating Plug-in Hybrid Electric Vehicle into the Electric Grid. *The Electricity Journal, 23*(3), 83–91. doi:10.1016/j.tej.2010.03.004.

Tanaka, N. (2011, June). *Technology roadmap: Electric and plug-in hybrid electric vehicles.* Retrieved from International Energy Agency website: http://www.iea.org/papers/2011/EVn PHEVn Roadmap.pdf

Wang, J., Liu, C., Ton, D., Zhou, Y., Kim, J., & Vyas, A. (2011). Impact of plug-in hybrid electric vehicles on power systems with demand response and wind power. *Energy Policy, 39*(7), 4016–4021. doi:10.1016/j.enpol.2011.01.042.

KEY TERMS AND DEFINITIONS

BEV: Battery Electric Vehicle.

DOD: Depth of Discharge.

EV: Electric Vehicle, combines PHEVs and BEVs.

EVSE: Electric Vehicle Supply Equipment.

G2V: Grid-to-Vehicle.

PHEV: Plug-in Hybrid Electric Vehicle.

SLP: Synthetic Load Profile.

SOC: State of Charge.

UF: Utility Factor, the proportion of electrically driven distances.

V2G: Vehicle-to-Grid.

Compilation of References

Abdel-Aty, M., Siddiqui, C., & Huang, H. (2011a). *Zonal level safety evaluation incorporating trip generation effects*. Paper presented at the Transportation Research Board (TRB) 90th Annual Meeting. Washington, DC.

Abdel-Aty, M., Siddiqui, C., & Huang, H. (2011b). *Integrating trip and roadway characteristics in managing safety at traffic analysis zones*. Paper presented at the Transportation Research Board (TRB) 90th Annual Meeting. Washington, DC.

Abedin, Z. U. (2012). *Modelling wireless charging for electric vehicles in MATSim*. (Unpublished master's thesis). TU München, Munich, Germany.

Abedin, Z.U., & Waraich. (2013). Modelling inductive charging of battery electric vehicles using an agent-based approach. *Arbeitsberichte Verkehrs- und Raumplanung, 899*.

Abrantes, P., & Wardman, M. (2011). Meta-analysis of UK values of travel time: An update. *Transportation Research Part A, Policy and Practice, 45*, 1–17. doi:10.1016/j.tra.2010.08.003.

Adnan, M., Ali, M. S., Qadir, A., & Sheeraz, K. (2011). Increasing effectiveness of road safety interventions-An operational model for developing countries. In *First International Forum of Traffic Safety,* (pp. 221-235). Univeristy of Damam.

Agarwal, M., Maze, T. H., & Souleyrette, R. (2005). *Impact of weather on urban freeway traffic flow characteristics and facility capacity*. Academic Press..

Agatz, N., Erera, A., Savelsbergh, M., & Wang, X. (2010). *Sustainable passenger transportation: Dynamic ride-sharing* (Research Paper No. ERIM Report Series Reference No. ERS-2010-010-LIS). Rotterdam, The Netherlands: Erasmus University of Rotterdam.

Aguero-Valverde, J., & Jovanis, P. P. (2006). Spatial analysis of fatal and injury crashes in Pennsylvania. *Accident; Analysis and Prevention, 38*(3), 618–625. doi:10.1016/j.aap.2005.12.006 PMID:16451795.

Aguero-Valverde, J., & Jovanis, P. P. (2008). Analysis of road crash frequency with spatial models. *Transportation Research Record: Journal of the Transportation Research Board, 2061*(1), 55–63. doi:10.3141/2061-07.

Aizaz, A. (2007). Road safety in Pakistan. *National Road Safety Secretariat, Ministry of Communications, Government of Pakistan*. Retrieved April 1, 2013, from http://www.unescap.org/ttdw/common/Meetings/TIS/EGM%20Roadsafety%20Country%20Papers/Pakistan_Roadsafety.pdf

Ajzen, I., & Fishbein, M. (1977). Attitude-behavior relations: A theoretical analysis and review of empirical research. *Psychological Bulletin, 84*(5), 888–918. doi:10.1037/0033-2909.84.5.888.

Alam, M. S., Mahmud, S. M., & Hoque, M. M. (2011). Road accidents trends in Bangladesh: A comprehensive study. In Noor, Amin, Bhuiyan, Chowdhury and Kakoli (Eds.), *4th Annual Paper Meet and 1st Civil Engineering Congress* (pp. 172-181), Dhaka, Bangladesh: IEEE.

Albert, G., & Mahalel, D. (2006). Congestion tolls and parking fees: A comparison of the potential effect on travel behavior. *Transport Policy, 13*(6), 496–502. doi:10.1016/j.tranpol.2006.05.007.

Alberti, E., & Belli, G. (1978). Contributions to the boltzmann-like approach for trafficflow - A model for concentration dependent driving programs. *Transportation Research, 12*(1), 33–42. doi:10.1016/0041-1647(78)90105-3.

Almeida, P. M. R., Lopes, J. A. P., Soares, F. J., & Vasconcelos, M. H. (2010). *Automatic generation control operation with electric vehicles.* Paper presented at the Bulk Power System Dynamics and Control Symposium. Rio de Janeiro, Brazil.

Amin, S. M., & Wollenberg, B. F. (2005). Toward a smart grid: Power delivery for the 21st century. *IEEE Power and Energy Magazine, 3*(5), 34–41. doi:10.1109/MPAE.2005.1507024.

Amoros, E., Martin, J. L., & Laumon, B. (2003). Comparison of road crashes incidence and severity between some French counties. *Accident; Analysis and Prevention, 35*(4), 537–547. doi:10.1016/S0001-4575(02)00031-3 PMID:12729817.

An, M., Casper, C., & Wu, W. (2011). *Using travel demand model and zonal safety planning model for safety benefit estimation in project evaluation.* Paper presented at the Transportation Research Board (TRB) 90th Annual Meeting. Washington, DC.

Anagnostopoulos, T., Anagnostopoulos, C., & Hadjiefthymiades, S. (2011). Mobility prediction based on machine learning. Mobility Data Management, (2), 27-30.

Anderson, J. R., Bothell, D., Byrne, M. D., Douglass, S., Lebiere, C., & Qin, Y. (2004). An integrated theory of the mind. *Psychological Review, 111,* 1036–1060. doi:10.1037/0033-295X.111.4.1036 PMID:15482072.

André, M. (2004). The ARTEMIS European driving cycles for measuring car pollutant emissions. *The Science of the Total Environment, 334,* 73–84. doi:10.1016/j.scitotenv.2004.04.070 PMID:15504494.

Andrienko, G., Andrienko, N., Rinzivillo, S., Nanni, M., Pedreschi, D., & Giannotti, F. (2009). Interactive visual clustering of large collections of trajectories. In Proceedings of IEEE VAST. IEEE.

Andrienko, G., & Andrienko, N. (2010). A general framework for using aggregation in visual exploration of movement data. *The Cartographic Journal, 47*(1), 22–40. doi:10.1179/000870409X12525737905042.

Andrienko, G., Andrienko, N., Bak, P., Keim, D., & Wrobel, S. (Eds.). (2013). *Visual analytics of movement.* Berlin: Springer..

Andrienko, G., Andrienko, N., Rinzivillo, S., Nanni, M., Pedreschi, D., & Giannotti, F. (2009). Interactive visual clustering of large collections of trajectories. In *Proceedings of Visual Analytics Science and Technology.* IEEE. doi:10.1109/VAST.2009.5332584.

Andrienko, N., Andrienko, G., Pelekis, N., & Spaccapietra, S. (2008). Basic concepts of movement data. In *Mobility, Data Mining and Privacy.* Berlin: Springer. doi:10.1007/978-3-540-75177-9_2.

Andrienko, N., Andrienko, G., Stange, H., Liebig, T., & Hecker, D. (2012). Visual analytics for understanding spatial situations from episodic movement data. *Künstliche Intelligenz, 26*(3), 241–251. doi:10.1007/s13218-012-0177-4.

Arentze, T. A., & Timmermans, H. J. P. (2004). ALBATROSS – Version 2.0 – A learning based transportation oriented simulation system. Eindhoven, The Netherlands: EIRASS (European Institute of Retailing and Services Studies)..

Arentze, T. A., Timmermans, H. J. P., Janssens, D., & Wets, G. (2008). Modeling short-term dynamics in activity-travel patterns: From Aurora to Feathers. In *Proceedings of Transportation Research Record Conference* (pp. 71-77). Transportation Research Record.

Arentze, T., & Timmermans. (2005). *ALBATROSS 2: A learning-based transportation oriented simulation system.* Eindhoven, The Netherlands: European Institute of Retailing and Services Studies.

Arentze, T., Pelizaro, C., & Timmermans, H. (2005). Implementation of a model of dynamic activity-travel rescheduling decisions: An agent-based micro-simulation framework. In *Proceedings of CUPUM 05.* London: CUPUM.

Arentze, T. A., Timmermans, & Hofman. (2007). Population synthesis for microsimulating travel behavior. *Transportation Research Record,* (11): 85–91. doi:10.3141/2014-11.

Arentze, T. A., & Timmermans, H. J. (2004). A learning-based transportation oriented simulation system. *Transportation Research Part B: Methodological, 38*(7), 613–633. doi:10.1016/j.trb.2002.10.001.

Arentze, T. A., & Timmermans, H. J. P. (2000). *Albatross: A learning-based transportation oriented simulation system*. Eindhoven, The Netherlands: European Institute of Retailing and Services Studies..

Arentze, T. A., & Timmermans, H. J. P. (2004). A learning-based transportation oriented simulation system. *Transportation Research Part B: Methodological*, *38*(7), 613–633. doi:10.1016/j.trb.2002.10.001.

Arentze, T. A., & Timmermans, H. J. P. (2005). Representing mental maps and cognitive learning in micro-simulation models of activity-travel choice dynamics. *Transportation*, *32*, 321–340. doi:10.1007/s11116-004-7964-1.

Arentze, T., & Timmermans, H. (2000). *Albatross: A learning based transportation oriented simulation system*. Eindhoven, The Netherlands: EIRASS..

Ashbrook, D., & Starner, T. (2003). Using gps to learn significant locations and predict movement across multiple users. *Personal and Ubiquitous Computing*, *7*(5), 275–286. doi:10.1007/s00779-003-0240-0.

Atkinson, R. C., & Shiffring, R. M. (1986). Human memory: A proposed system and its control processes. In The Psychology of Learning and Motivation: Advances in Research and Theory (pp. 89-195). Academic Press, Inc..

Auld, J. Mohammadian, & Wies. (2008). *Population synthesis with control category optimization*. Paper presented at the 10th International Conference on Application of Advanced Technologies in Transportation. Athens, Greece.

Auld, J. Mohammadian, & Wies. (2010). *An efficient methodology for generating synthetic populations with multiple control levels*. Paper presented at the the 89th Annual Meeting of the Transportation Research Board. Washington, DC.

Auld, J., Mohammadian, A., & Roorda, M. (2009). Implementation of a scheduling conflict resolution model in an activity scheduling system. In *Proceedings of the TRB 2009 Annual Meeting* (Vol. 88). Washington, DC: TRB (Transportation Research Board).

Aumann, R. J. (1976). Agreeing to disagree. *Annals of Statistics*, *4*(6), 1236–1239. doi:10.1214/aos/1176343654.

Axsen, J., Mountain, D. C., & Jaccard, M. (2009). Combining stated and revealed choice research to simulate the neighbor effect: The case of hybrid-electric vehicles. *Resource and Energy Economics*, *31*(3), 221–238. doi:10.1016/j.reseneeco.2009.02.001.

Balmer, M., Axhausen, K. W., & Nagel, K. (2006). An agent-based demand-modeling framework for large-scale microsimulations. *Transportation Research Record: Journal of the Transportation Research Board*, *1985*, 125–134. doi:10.3141/1985-14.

Balmer, M., Nagel, K., & Raney, B. (2006). Agent-based demand modeling framework for large scale micro-simulations. *Transportation Research Record*, *1985*, 125–134. doi:10.3141/1985-14.

Baraglia, R., Frattari, C., Muntean, C. I., Nardini, F. M., & Silvestri, F. (2012). A trajectory-based recommender system for tourism. In Proceedings of AMT, (pp. 196-205). AMT.

Barcelló, J. (2010). Models, traffic models, simulation and traffic simulation. In *Fundamentals of traffic simulation* (pp. 1–62). Berlin: Springer. doi:10.1007/978-1-4419-6142-6_1.

Barcelo, J., & Ferrer, J. L. (1998). *AIMSUN2: Advanced interactive microscopic simulation for urban networks*. Academic Press..

Barth, D., Bellahsene, S., & Kloul, L. (2012). Combining local and global profiles for mobility prediction in lte femtocells. In Proceedings of MSWiM'12 (pp. 333-342). MSWiM.

Barthelemy, J., & Cornelis, E. (2012). *Synthetic populations: review of the different approaches*. CEPS/INSTEAD..

Becker, G. S. (1965). A theory of the allocation of time. *The Economic Journal*, *75*(299), 493–517. doi:10.2307/2228949.

Beckman, R. J., Baggerly, & McKay. (1996). Creating synthetic baseline populations. *Transportation Research Part A, Policy and Practice*, *30*(6), 415–429. doi:10.1016/0965-8564(96)00004-3.

Bekiaris, E., Amditis, A., & Panou, M. (2003). Drivability: A new concept for modelling driving performance. *Cognition Technology and Work*, *5*, 152–161. doi:10.1007/s10111-003-0119-x.

Bellemans, T., Bothe, S., Cho, S., Giannotti, F., Janssens, D., & Knapen, L. et al. (2012). *An agent-based model to evaluate carpooling at large manufacturing plants*. Niagara Falls, NY: Procedia Computer Science. doi:10.1016/j.procs.2012.08.001.

Bellemans, T., Janssens, D., Wets, G., Arentze, T. A., & Timmermans, H. J. P. (2010). Implementation framework and development trajectory of Feathers activity-based simulation platform. *Transportation Research Record: Journal of the Transportation Research Board, 2175,* 111–119. doi:10.3141/2175-13.

Bellemans, T., Kochan, B., Janssens, D., Wets, G., Arentze, T., & Timmermans, H. (2010). Implementation framework and development trajectory of FEATHERS activity-based simulation platform. *Transportation Research Record: Journal of the Transportation Research Board, 2175*(1), 111–119. doi:10.3141/2175-13.

Ben-Akivai, M., Bowman, J., & Gopinath, D. (1996). Travel demand model mystem for the information era. *Transportation, 23*(3), 241–266. doi:10.1007/BF00165704.

Benekohal, R. F., & Abu-Lebdeh, G. (1994). Variability analysis of traffic simulation outputs: Practical approach for TRAF-NETSIM. *Transportation Research Record: Journal of the Transportation Research Board, 1457,* 198–207.

Bener, A., Abu-Zidan, F. M., Bensiali, A. K., Al-Mulla, A. A., & Jadaan, K. S. (2003). Strategy to improve road safety in developing countries. *Saudi Medical Journal, 24*(6), 603–608. PMID:12847587.

Bert, E., Torday, A., & Dumont, A. (2005). Calibration of urban network microsimulation models. In *Proceedings of 5th Swiss Transport Research Conference*. Ascona, Switzerland: Swiss Transport Research.

Bessa, R. J., & Matos, M. A. (2010). *The role of an aggregator agent for EV in the electricity market*. Paper presented at the 7th Mediterranean Conference and Exhibition on Power Generation, Transmission, Distribution and Energy Conversion. New York, NY.

Beuck, U., Nagel, K., Rieser, M., Strippgen, D., & Balmer, M. (2008). Preliminary results of a multi-agent traffic simulation for berlin. In *The Dynamics of Complex Urban Systems* (pp. 75–94). Berlin: Physica-Verlag HD. doi:10.1007/978-3-7908-1937-3_5.

Bhat, C. R., Guo, J. Y., Srinivasan, S., & Sivakumar, A. (2004). A comprehensive microsimulator for daily activity-travel patterns. In *Proceedings of the Conference on Progress in Activity-Based Models*. Maastricht, The Netherlands: Academic Press.

Bhat, C. R. (2005). A multiple discrete–continuous extreme value model: Formulation and application to discretionary time-use decisions. *Transportation Research Part B: Methodological, 39*(8), 679–707. doi:10.1016/j.trb.2004.08.003.

Bhat, C. R., Guo, J., Srinivasan, S., Pinjari, A., Eluru, N., Copperman, R., & Sener, I. N. (2006). *The comprehensive econometric microsimulator for daily activity-travel patterns (CEMDAP)*. Austin, TX: The University of Texas at Austin..

Binding, C., & Sundstroem, O. (2011). A simulation environment for vehicle-to-grid integration studies. In *Proceedings of the 2011 Summer Computer Simulation Conference* (pp. 14-21). IEEE.

Bingham, C., Walsh, C., & Carroll, S. (2012). Impact of driving characteristics on electric vehicle energy consumption and range. *IET Intelligent Transport Systems, 6*(1), 29–35. doi:10.1049/iet-its.2010.0137.

Black, J. A., & Salter, R. T. (1975). A statistical evaluation of the accuracy of a family of gravity models. *Proceedings - Institution of Civil Engineers, 2*(59), 1–20. doi:10.1680/iicep.1975.3839.

Bogorny, V., Heuser, C. A., & Alvares, L. O. (2010). A conceptual data model for trajectory data mining. In Proceedings of GIScience. GIScience..

Bonabeau, E. (2002). Agent-based modeling: Methods and techniques for simulating human systems. *Proceedings of the National Academy of Sciences of the United States of America, 99*(3), 7280–7287. doi:10.1073/pnas.082080899 PMID:12011407.

Bötticher, A. M. T., & van der Molen, H. H. (1988). Predicting overtaking behaviour on the basis of the hierarchical risk model for traffic participants. In *Road User Behaviour - Theory and Research* (pp. 48–65). Berlin: Van Gorcum..

Bowman, J. L., & Ben-Akiva, M. E. (1996). *Activity based travel forecasting*. Paper presented at Activity-Based Travel Forecasting Conference. New Orleans, LA.

Boyd, S., Parikh, N., Chu, E., Peleato, B., & Eckstein, J. (2010). Distributed optimization and statistical learning via the alternating direction method of multipliers. *Foundations and Trends in Machine Learning*, *3*(1), 1–122. doi:10.1561/2200000016.

Boyd, S., & Vandenberghe, L. (2009). *Convex optimization*. Cambridge, UK: Cambridge University Press..

Brockmann, D., Hufnagel, L., & Geisel, T. (2006). The scaling laws of human travel. *Nature*, *439*(462). PMID:16437114.

Brooks, A. (2002). Integration of electric drive vehicles with the power grid-a new application for vehicle batteries. In *Battery Conference on Applications and Advances, 2002* (p. 239). Academic Press.

Budischak, C., DeAnna, S., Thomson, H., Mach, L., Veron, D. E., & Kempton, W. (2013). Cost-minimized combinations of wind power, solar power and electrochemical storage, powering the grid up to 99.9% of the time. *Journal of Power Sources*, *225*(1), 60–74. doi:10.1016/j.jpowsour.2012.09.054.

Buliung, R., Soltys, K., Habel, C., & Lanyon, R. (2009). The driving factors behind successful carpool formation and use. *Transportation Research Record*, 2118.

Bundesamt für Energie. (2011). *Schweizerische elektrizitätsstatistik 2001*. Retrieved April 2, 2013, from www.bfe.admin.ch

Bundesamt für Statistik. (2013). *STAT-TAB: Die interaktive statistikdatenbank*. Retrieved March 26, 2013, from www.bfs.admin.ch

Bundesministerium für Verkehr. Bau und Stadtentwicklung. (2010). *Mobilität in Deutschland 2008, abschlussbericht*. Retrieved from http://www.mobilitaet-in-deutschland.de

Burbey, I. (2011). Predicting future locations and arrival times of individuals. (PhD thesis). Virginia Polytechnic Institute and State University, Blacksburg, VA.

Burris, M. W. (2003). Application of variable tolls on congested toll road. *Journal of Transportation Engineering*, *129*(4), 354–361. doi:10.1061/(ASCE)0733-947X(2003)129:4(354).

Burris, M., Christopher, E., DeCorla-Souza, P., Greenberg, A., Heinrich, S., & Morris, J. et al. (2012). *Casual carpooling scan report*. Washington, DC: Office of Transportation Management Congestion Management and Pricing Team Federal Highway Administration..

Busarello, B. C. P., & Cott+ Partner AG. (2008). *NE-PLAN, power system analysis*. Retrieved April 2, 2013, from www.neplan.ch

Cacciabue, C. (Ed.). (2007). *Modelling driver behaviour in automotive environments - Critical issues in driver interactions with intelligent transport systems*. Berlin: Springer..

Car Sharing, An Alternative to Car Rental and Car Ownership – Zipcar. (2012). Retrieved from http://www.zipcar.com/

Carpool Solutions for University and Corporate Networks. (2012). Retrieved from http://www.zimride.com

Carsten, O. (2007). From driver models to modelling the driver: What do we really need to know about the driver? In *Proceedings of Cacciabue* (pp. 105–120). Cacciabue. doi:10.1007/978-1-84628-618-6_6.

Castiglione, J., Grady, B., Lawe, S., Roden, D., Patnam, K., Bradley, M., & Bowman, J. (2012, May). *Sensitivity testing of the SHRP2 C10A DaySim-TRANSIMS model system in Jacksonville, Florida*. Paper presented at the 4th TRB Conference on Innovations in Travel Modeling. Tampa, FL.

Castiglione, J., Freedman, J., & Bradley, M. (2003). Systematic investigation of variability due to random simulation error in an activity-based micro-simulation forecasting model. *Transportation Research Record: Journal of the Transportation Research Board*, *1831*, 76–88. doi:10.3141/1831-09.

Ceci, M., Appice, A., & Malerba, D. (2010). Time-slice density estimation for semantic-based tourist destination suggestion. In Proceedings of ECAI (pp. 1107-1108). ECAI.

CENELEC. (2010). Voltage characteristics of electricity supplied by public electricity networks[]. CENELEC.]. *CENELEC Std. EN, 50,* 160.

Chan, C. (2007). The state of the art of electric, hybrid, and fuel cell vehicles. *Proceedings of the IEEE, 95*(4), 704–718. doi:10.1109/JPROC.2007.892489.

Chao-Kai, W., Jung-Chieh, C., Jen-Hao, T., & Pangan, T. (2012). Decentralized plug-in electrical vehicle charging selection algorithm in power systems. *IEEE Transactions on Smart Grids, 3*(4), 1779–1789. doi:10.1109/TSG.2012.2217761.

Chapin, F. S. (1974). *Human activity patterns in the city: Things people do in time and in space.* New York, NY: Wiley..

Cha, S.-H. (2007). Comprehensive survey on distance/similarity measures between probability density functions. *International Journal of Mathematical Models and Methods in Applied Sciences, 4*(1), 300–307.

Chen, T. D., Khan, M., & Kockelman, K. M. (2013). *The electric vehicle charging station location problem: A parking-based assignment method for seattle.* Paper presented at the 92nd Annual Meeting of the Transportation Research Board. Washington, DC.

Chen, L., Lv, M., & Chen, G. (2010). A system for destination and future route prediction based on trajectory mining. *Pervasive and Mobile Computing, 6*(6), 657–676. doi:10.1016/j.pmcj.2010.08.004.

Chen, V. Y.-J., & Yang, T.-C. (2012). SAS macro programs for geographically weighted generalized linear modeling with spatial point data: Applications to health research. *Computer Methods and Programs in Biomedicine, 107*(2), 262–273. doi:10.1016/j.cmpb.2011.10.006 PMID:22078167.

Chen, X., & Zhan, F. B. (2006). Agent-based modelling and simulation of urban evacuation: Relative effectiveness of simultaneous and staged evacuation strategies. *The Journal of the Operational Research Society, 59*(1), 25–33. doi:10.1057/palgrave.jors.2602321.

Chevrolet Volt. (2013). Retrieved March 14, 2013, from http://media.gm.com/media/us/en/chevrolet/vehicles/volt/2013.html

Chi, G., Cosby, A. G., Quddus, M. A., Gilbert, P. A., & Levinson, D. (2010). Gasoline prices and traffic safety in Mississippi. *Journal of Safety Research, 41*(6), 493–500. doi:10.1016/j.jsr.2010.10.003 PMID:21134515.

Choo, S., & Mokhtarian, P. L. (2007). Telecommunications and travel demand and supply: Aggregate structural equation models for the US. *Transportation Research Part A, Policy and Practice, 41*(1), 4–18. doi:10.1016/j.tra.2006.01.001.

Choo, S., Mokhtarian, P. L., & Salomon, I. (2005). Does telecommuting reduce vehicle-miles traveled? An aggregate time series analysis for the U.S. *Transportation, 32*(1), 37–64. doi:10.1007/s11116-004-3046-7.

Cho, S., Yasar, A., Knapen, L., Bellemans, T., Janssens, D., & Wets, G. (2012). *A conceptual design of an agent-based interaction model for the carpooling application.* Niagara Falls, NY: Procedia Computer Science. doi:10.1016/j.procs.2012.06.103.

Christ, R. (2000). *Gadget final report: Investigations on influences upon driver behaviour - Safety approaches in comparison and combination (Technical report).* GADGET Consortium..

Chun, H. W., & Wong, R. Y. (2003). N* - An agent-based negotiation algorithm for dynamic scheduling and rescheduling. *Advanced Engineering Informatics,* (17): 1–22. doi:10.1016/S1474-0346(03)00019-3.

Claessens, B., Vandael, S., Ruelens, F., & Hommelberg, M. (2012). Self-learning demand side management for a heterogeneous cluster of devices with binary control actions.[*rd IEEE PES Innovative Smart Grid Technologies Europe][IGST Europe][.* IEEE.]. *Proceedings of, 2012,* 3.

Clement, K., Haesen, E., & Driesen, J. (2010). The impact of plug-in hybrid electric vehicles on a residential distribution grid. *IEEE Transactions on Power Systems, 25*(1), 371–380. doi:10.1109/TPWRS.2009.2036481.

Clement, K., Haesen, E., & Driesen, J. (2011). The impact of vehicle-to-grid on the distribution grid. *Electric Power System Research Journal, 81*(1), 371–380.

Colyar, J., Zhang, L., & Halkias, J. (2003). Identifying and assessing key weather-related parameters and their impact on traffic operations using simulation. In *Proceedings of the ITE Institute of Transportation Engineers (ITE) Annual Meeting*. Seattle, WA: ITE.

Conger, J. J., Gaskill, H. S., Glad, D. D., Hassel, L., Rainey, R. V., Sawrey, W. L., & Turrell, E. S. (1959). Psychological and psychophysical factors in motor vehicle accidents - Follow-up study. *Journal of the American Medical Association, 169*(14), 1581–1587. doi:10.1001/jama.1959.03000310033008 PMID:13640905.

Cools, M., & Kochan, B. Bellemans, T. Janssens, D., & Wets, G. (2011). Assessment of the effect of micro-simulation error on key travel indices: Evidence from the activity-based model FEATHERS. In *Proceedings of the 90th Annual Meeting of the Transportation Research Board*. Washington, DC: Transportation Research Board.

Corona, N. (2013). Un metodo per la predizione della locazione futura mediante la profilazione degli utenti. (Master thesis). University of Pisa, Pisa, Italy.

Cuellar, A., & Gartner, J. (2012). *Electric vehicle charging equipment (Research Report)*. London: Navigant Research..

Cuerden, R., Pittman, M., Dodson, E., & Hill, J. (2008). *The UK on the spot accident data collection study – Phase II report*. London: Department of Transport..

Cui, X., Kim, H. K., Liu, C., Kao, S.-C., & Bhaduri, B. L. (2012). Simulating the household plug-in hybrid electric vehicle distribution and its electric distribution network impacts. *Transportation Research Part D, Transport and Environment, 17*(7), 548–554. doi:10.1016/j.trd.2012.05.011.

Curtis, C., & Perkins, T. (2006). *Travel behaviour: A review of recent literature* (Working Paper No. 3). Brisbane, Australia: Curtin University.

Davidson, W., Donnelly, R., Vovsha, P., Freedman, J., Ruegg, S., & Hicks, J. et al. (2007). Synthesis of first practices and operational research approaches in activity-based travel demand modeling. *Transportation Research Part A, Policy and Practice, 41*(5), 464–488. doi:10.1016/j.tra.2006.09.003.

De Caluwé, E. (2008). *Potentieel van demand side management, piekvermogen en netondersteunende diensten geleverd door plug-in hybride elektrische voertuigen op basis van een beschikbaarheidsanalyse*. (Unpublished master's thesis). KU Leuven, Leuven, Belgium.

de Geest, C. (2011). *MIRA achtergronddocument 2010, transport (Technical Report)*. Erembodegem, Belgium: Vlaamse Milieumaatschappij..

De Guevara, F. L. D., Washington, S., & Oh, J. (2004). Forecasting crashes at the planning level: Simultaneous negative binomial crash model applied in Tucson, Arizona. *Transportation Research Record: Journal of the Transportation Research Board, 1897*(1), 191–199. doi:10.3141/1897-25.

De Ridder, F., D'Hulst, R., Knapen, L., & Janssens, D. (2013). Applying an activity based model to explore the potential of electrical vehicles in the smart grid. *Procedia Computer Science, 19*, 847–853. doi:10.1016/j.procs.2013.06.113.

De Ridder, F., Hommelberg, M., & Peeters, E. (2011). Demand side integration: Four potential business cases and an analysis of the 2020 situation. *European Transactions on Electrical Power, 21*(6), 1902–1913. doi:10.1002/etep.529.

de Santiago, J., Bernhoff, H., Ekergård, B., Eriksson, S., Ferhatovic, S., Waters, R., & Leijon, M. (2012). Electrical motor drivelines in commercial all-electric vehicles: A review. *IEEE Transactions on Vehicular Technology, 61*(2), 475–484. doi:10.1109/TVT.2011.2177873.

Deconinck, G., Labeeuw, W., Vandael, S., Beitollahi, H., De Craemer, K., Duan, R., et al. (2010). Communication overlays and agents for dependable smart power grids. In Proceedings of Critical Infrastructure (CRIS). CRIS.

Deming, W. E., & Stephan. (1940). On the least squares adjustment of a sampled frequency table when the expected marginal totals are known. *Annals of Mathematical Statistics, 11*(4), 427–444. doi:10.1214/aoms/1177731829.

DeSerpa, A. C. (1971). A theory of the economics of time. *The Economic Journal, 81*(324), 828–846. doi:10.2307/2230320.

Dia, H., & Gondwe, W. (2008). Evaluation of incident impacts on integrated motorway and arterial networks using traffic simulation. In *Proceedings of the 29th Australasian Transport Research Forum*. Australiasian Transport Research.

Die Bundesregierung. (2009). *Nationaler entwicklungsplan elektromobilität der bundesregierung*. Bundesministerium für Bildung und Forschung..

Diehl, M., Bock, H. G., Schlöder, J. P., Findeisen, R., Nagy, Z., & Allgöwer, F. (2002). Real-time optimization and nonlinear model predictive control of processes governed by differential-algebraic equations. *Journal of Process Control*, 12(4), 577–585. doi:10.1016/S0959-1524(01)00023-3.

Dissanayake, D., & Morikawa, T. (2008). Impact assessment of satellite centre-based telecommuting on travel and air quality in developing countries by exploring the link between travel behaviour and urban form. *Transportation Research Part A, Policy and Practice*, 42(6), 883–894. doi:10.1016/j.tra.2007.12.006.

Dobler, C., & Axhausen, K.W. (2011). Design and Implementation of a parallel queue-based traffic flow simulation. *Arbeitsberichte Verkehrs- und Raumplanung, 732*.

Doherty, S., & Axhausen, K. W. (1999). The development of a unified modeling framework for the household activity-Travel scheduling process. In *Traffic and mobility: Simulation-economics-environment* (pp. 35–56). Berlin: Springer. doi:10.1007/978-3-642-60236-8_3.

Doherty, S., Lee-Gosselin, M., Burns, K., & Andrey, J. (2002). Household activity rescheduling in response to automobile reduction scenarios. *Transportation Research Record*. doi:10.3141/1807-21.

Domenico, D. Lima, & Musolesi. (2012). Interdependence and predictability of human mobility and social interactions. In Proceedings of the Mobile Data Challenge 2012. IEEE.

Dowling, R., Skabardonis, A., & Alexiadis, V. (2004). Traffic analysis toolbox: Vol. III. *Guidelines for applying traffic microsimulation modeling software (Publication FHWA-HRT-04-040)*. Washington, DC: U.S. Department of Transportation..

Duvall, M., Knipping, E., Alexander, M., Tonachel, L., & Clark, C. (2007). Environmental assessment of plug-in hybrid electric vehicles: Vol. 1. *Nationwide greenhouse gas emissions*. Palo Alto, CA: Electric Power Research Institute..

Dynamic Ridesharing . (2012). Retrieved from http://dynamicridesharing.org/

Edie, L. C., & Foote, R. S. (1960). Effect of shock waves on tunnel traffic flow. In *Proceedings of Highway Research Record*. Washington, DC: National Research Record Council..

Ehlert, P. A. M., & Rothkrantz, L. J. M. (2001). A reactive driving agent for microscopic traffic simulations. In *Proceedings of the 15th European Simulation Multiconference,* (pp. 943-949). Prague, Czech Republic: SCS Publishing House.

Elia. (2013). Retreived March 5, 2013 from http://www.elia.be/en/grid-data/data-download

Ellevest, L. A. (1997). The role of NGOs in road safety. *Road safety in Bangladesh*. Retrieved April 1, 2013, from http://www.rhd.gov.bd/Documents/ExternalPublications/WorldBank/TransSectPub/contents/documents/B21.pdf

Energy Information Administration. (2010). *International energy outlook 2010*. Paris, France: International Energy Agency..

Engström, J., & Hollnagel, E. (2007). A general conceptual framework for modelling behavioural effects of driver support functions. In *Proceedings of Cacciabue* (pp. 61–84). Cacciabue. doi:10.1007/978-1-84628-618-6_4.

Enterprise Rideshare - Vanpool & Rideshare Services for Individuals, Employers & Government Agencies . (2012). Retrieved from http://www.enterpriserideshare.com/vanpool/en.html

Eom, J. K. (2007). Introducing a spatial-temporal activity-based approach for estimating travel demand at KTX stations. In *Proceedings of the 2007 Autumn Conference of Korean Society for Railway,* (pp. 730-739). IEEE.

EPA. (2006). *Fuel economy labeling of motor vehicles: Revisions to improve calculation of fuel economy estimates (EPA420-R-06-017)*. Washington, DC: U.S. Environmental Protection Agency..

EPA. (2013). *Dynamometer drive schedules*. Retrieved March 18, 2013, from http://www.epa.gov/nvfel/testing/dynamometer.htm

eRUF Stormster . (2009). Retrieved June 1, 2012, from www.ruf-automobile.de/en/en-aktuelles-eruf.php

Espey, M. (1998). Gasoline demand revisited: An international meta-analysis of elasticities. *Energy Economics*, *20*(3), 273–295. doi:10.1016/S0140-9883(97)00013-3.

European Environment Agency. (2008). *Energy and environment report 2008*. Retrieved March 5, 2013, from http://www.eea.europa.eu/publications/eea_report_2008_6

EWZ. (2009). *Randbedingungen und szenarien für elektromobilität. AG Elektromobilität*. EWZ..

Faizo, J., Hoque, M. M., & Tiwari, G. (1998). Fatalities of heterogeneous traffic in large south Asian cities. In *Proceeding of the Third International Symposium on Highway Capacity,* (pp. 423-436). Copenhagen: Danish road Directorate.

Farhangi, H. (2010). The path of the smart grid. *IEEE Power and Energy Magazine*, *8*(1), 18–28. doi:10.1109/MPE.2009.934876.

Faria, R., Moura, P., Delgado, J., & de Almeida, A. T. (2012). A sustainability assessment of electric vehicles as a personal mobility system. *Energy Conversion and Management*, *61*, 19–30. doi:10.1016/j.enconman.2012.02.023.

Farmer, C., Hines, P., Dowds, J., & Blumsack, S. (2010). Modeling the impact of increasing PHEV loads on the distribution infrastructure. In *Proceedings of the 43rd Hawaii International Conference on System Sciences (HICSS)* (pp. 1-10). IEEE.

Febiac . (2013). Retrieved March 14, 2013, from http://www.febiac.be

Fellendorf, M., & Vortisch, P. (2010). Microscopic traffic flow simulator visim. In *Proceedings of Barceló* (pp. 63–94). Barceló..

Fishbein, M., & Ajzen, I. (1975). *Belief, attitude, intention, and behavior: An introduction to theory and research*. Reading, MA: Addision-Wesley Pub. Co.

Fisker Karma . (2013). Retrieved March 14, 2013, from http://onward.fiskerautomotive.com/en-us

Flahaut, B. (2004). Impact of infrastructure and local environment on road unsafety: Logistic modeling with spatial autocorrelation. *Accident; Analysis and Prevention*, *36*(6), 1055–1066. doi:10.1016/j.aap.2003.12.003 PMID:15350882.

Fleishman, E. A. (1967). Performance assessment based on an empirically derived task taxonomy. *Human Factors*, *9*(4), 349–366. PMID:5584850.

Fleishman, E. A. (1975). Toward a taxonomy of human performance. *The American Psychologist*, *30*(12), 1127–1149. doi:10.1037/0003-066X.30.12.1127.

FOD Economie-Statbel:Algemene Directie Statistiek en Economische Informatie . (2013). Retrieved March 14, 2013, from http://statbel.fgov.be

FOD Mobiliteit en Vervoer. (2013). Retrieved March 14, 2013, from http://www.mobilit.fgov.be

Ford C-MAX Energi. (2013). Retrieved March 14, 2013, from http://www.ford.com/cars/cmax/trim/energi/

Fotheringham, A. S., Brunsdon, C., & Charlton, M. (2002). *Geographically weighted regression the analysis of spatially varying relationships*. West Sussex, UK: John Wiley & Sons Ltd.

Fraile-Ardanuy, J. Martínez, Artaloytia, Ramírez, Fuentes, & Sánchez (2012). *Analysis of the impact of charging of PHEV and EV in Spain*. Paper presented at the International Conference on Renewable Energies and Power Quality (ICREPQ2012). New York, NY.

Frischknecht, R., Jungbluth, N., Althaus, H. J., Doka, G., Dones, R., & Heck, T. et al. (2005). The ecoinvent database: Overview and methodological framework. *The International Journal of Life Cycle Assessment*, *10*(1), 3–9. doi:10.1065/lca2004.10.181.1.

Fuller, R. (1984). A conceptualization of driving behavior as threat avoidance. *Ergonomics*, *27*(11), 1139–1155. doi:10.1080/00140138408963596 PMID:6519053.

Furletti, B., Gabrielli, L., Rinzivillo, S., & Renso, C. (2012). Identifying users profiles from mobile calls habits. In *Proceedings of UrbComp12*. UrbComp. doi:10.1145/2346496.2346500.

Gadsden, S., Rylatt, M., Lomas, K., & Robinson, D. (2003). Predicting the urban solar fraction: A methodology for energy advisers and planners based on GIS. *Energy and Building*, *35*(1), 37–48. doi:10.1016/S0378-7788(02)00078-6.

Gaffney, S., & Smyth, P. (1999). Trajectory clustering with mixture of regression models. In *Proceedings of the 5th International Conference on Knowledge Discovery and Data Mining (KDD'99)*, (pp. 63-72). ACM.

Galus, M. D. (2012). *Agent-based modeling and simulation of large scale electric mobility in power systems*. (Doctoral dissertation). ETH Zurich, Zurich, Switzerland.

Galus, M. D., Art, S., & Andersson, G. (2012). *A hierarchical, distributed PEV charging control in low voltage distribution grids to ensure network security*. Paper presented at the 2012 IEEE Power & Energy Society General Meeting. San Diego, CA.

Galus, M. D., Waraich, R. A., Balmer, M., Andersson, G., & Axhausen, K. W. (2009). *A framework for investigating the impact of PHEVs*. Paper presented at the International Advanced Mobility Forum 2009. Geneva, Switzerland.

Galus, M., Waraich, R. A., & Anderson, G. (2011). *Predictive, distributed, hierarchical charging control of PHEVs in the distribution system of a large urban area incorporating a multiagent transportation simulation*. Paper presented at the 17th Power Systems Computation Conference. New York, NY.

Galus, M.D., & Andersson. (2011). *Balancing renewable energy source with vehicle to grid services from a large fleet of plug-in hybrid electric vehicles controlled in a metropolitan area distribution network*. Paper presented at the Cigré 2011 Bologna Symposium. Bologna, Italy.

Galus, M. D., Georges, G., & Waraich, R. A. (2012). *Final report of the ARTEMIS project*. Zurich, Switzerland: ETH Zürich..

Galus, M., Waraich, R. A., Noembrini, F., Steurs, K., Georges, G., & Boulouchos, K. et al. (2012). Integrating power systems, transport systems and vehicle technology for electric mobility impact assessment and efficient control. *IEEE Transactions on Smart Grid*, *3*(2), 934–949. doi:10.1109/TSG.2012.2190628.

Gan, L. P., & Recker, W. (2008). A mathematical programming formulation of the household activity rescheduling problem. *Transportation Research Part B: Methodological*, *42*, 571–606. doi:10.1016/j.trb.2007.11.004.

Gao, W., Balmer, M., & Miller, E. J. (2010). Comparisons between MATSim and EMME/2 on the greater Toronto and Hamilton area network. *Transportation Research Record. Journal of the Transportation Research Board*, *2197*, 118–128. doi:10.3141/2197-14.

Georges, G. (2012). *Fleet-wide vehicular energy demand model for project ARTEMIS*. Zurich, Switzerland: ETH Zurich..

Gerlough, D. L. (1955). *Simulation of freeway traffic on a general-purpose discrete variable computer. Los Angeles, CA*. Los Angeles: University of California..

Geth, F. Willekens, Clement, Driesen, & De Breucker. (2010). *Impact-analysis of the charging of plug-in hybrid vehicles on the production park in Belgium*. Paper presented at the 15th IEEE Mediterranean Electrotechnical Conference MELECON. New York, NY.

Ghoseiri, K. (2012). *Dynamic rideshare optimized matching problem*. (PhD thesis). University of Maryland, University Park, MD. Retrieved from http://drum.lib.umd.edu/handle/1903/13023

Giannotti, F., Nanni, M., & Pedreschi, D. (2006). Efficient mining of temporally annotated sequences. In Proceedings of SDM. SDM.

Giannotti, F., Nanni, M., Pinelli, F., & Pedreschi, D. (2007). Trajectory pattern mining. In *Proceedings of the 13th ACM SIGKDD International Conference on Knowledge Discovery and Data Mining (KDD'07)*, (pp. 330-339). ACM.

Giannotti, F., Nanni, M., Pedreschi, D., Pinelli, F., Renso, C., Rinzivillo, S., & Trasarti, R. (2011). Unveiling the complexity of human mobility by querying and mining massive trajectory data. *The VLDB Journal*, *20*(5), 695–719. doi:10.1007/s00778-011-0244-8.

Gibson, J. J., & Crooks, L. E. (1938). A theoretical filed-analysis of automobile-driving. *The American Journal of Psychology*, *51*(3), 453–471. doi:10.2307/1416145.

Gidofalvi, G., & Dong, F. (2012). When and where next: Individual mobility prediction. In Proceedings of MobiGIS '12, (pp. 57-64). MobiGIS..

González, M. C., Hidalgo, C. A., & Barabási, A.-L. (2008). Understanding individual human mobility patterns. *Nature, 453*(7196), 779–782. doi:10.1038/nature06958 PMID:18528393.

Goodwin, P., Dargay, J., & Hanly, M. (2004). Elasticities of road traffic and fuel consumption with respect to price and income: A review. *Transport Reviews, 24*(3), 275–292. doi:10.1080/0144164042000181725.

Grabowski, D. C., & Morrisey, M. A. (2004). Gasoline prices and motor vehicle fatalities. *Journal of Policy Analysis and Management, 23*(3), 575–593. doi:10.1002/pam.20028.

Greenberg, H. (1959). An analysis of traffic flow. *Operations Research, 7*(1), 79–85. doi:10.1287/opre.7.1.79.

Green, R. C. II, Wang, L., & Alam, M. (2011). The impact of plug-in hybrid electric vehicles on distribution networks: A review and outlook. *Renewable & Sustainable Energy Reviews, 15*(1), 544–553. doi:10.1016/j.rser.2010.08.015.

Gruebele, P. (2008). *Interactive system for real time dynamic multi-hop carpooling* (Tech. Rep.). Retrieved from http://dynamicridesharing.org/

Guille, C. (2009). *A conceptual framework for the vehicle to grid (V2G) implemantation*. (Thesis). University of Illinois, Urbana Champaign, IL.

Guler, E. (2008). How to improve NGO effectiveness in development? A discussion on lessons learned. *NGO MANGER*. Retrieved April 1, 2013, from http://www.ngomanager.org/dcd/2_Organisational_Development/Capacity_building/NGO_Effectiveness.pdf

Guo, J., Nandam, S., & Adams, T. (2012). A data collection framework for exploring the dynamic adaptation of activity-travel decisions. Tampa, FL: TRB (Transportation Research Board)..

Guo, L., Huang, S., & Sadek, A. W. (2013). An evaluation of likely environmental benefits of a time-dependent green routing system in the greater Buffalo-Niagara region. *Journal of Intelligent Transportation Systems: Technology, Planning and Operations*.

Guo, F., Wang, X., & Abdel-Aty, M. (2010). Modeling signalized intersection safety with corridor-level spatial correlations. *Accident; Analysis and Prevention, 42*(1), 84–92. doi:10.1016/j.aap.2009.07.005 PMID:19887148.

Guo, J. Y., & Bhat. (2007). Population synthesis for microsimulating travel behavior. *Transportation Research Record*, (12): 92–101. doi:10.3141/2014-12.

Gurczik, G., Junghans, M., & Ruppe, S. (2012). *Conceptual approach for determining penetration rates for dynamic indirect traffic detection*. ITS World Congress.

Hadayeghi, A. (2009). *Use of advanced techniques to estimate zonal level safety planning models and examine their temporal transferability*. (PhD thesis). Department of Civil Engineering, University of Toronto, Toronto, Canada.

Hadayeghi, A., Shalaby, A. S., & Persaud, B. N. (2010b). Development of planning level transportation safety tools using geographically weighted poisson regression. *Accident; Analysis and Prevention, 42*(2), 676–688. doi:10.1016/j.aap.2009.10.016 PMID:20159094.

Hadayeghi, A., Shalaby, A. S., Persaud, B. N., & Cheung, C. (2006). Temporal transferability and updating of zonal level accident prediction models. *Accident; Analysis and Prevention, 38*(3), 579–589. doi:10.1016/j.aap.2005.12.003 PMID:16414003.

Hadayeghi, A., Shalaby, A., & Persaud, B. (2003). Macrolevel accident prediction models for evaluating safety of urban transportation systems. *Transportation Research Record: Journal of the Transportation Research Board, 1840*(1), 87–95. doi:10.3141/1840-10.

Hadayeghi, A., Shalaby, A., & Persaud, B. (2007). Safety prediction models: Proactive tool for safety evaluation in urban transportation planning applications. *Transportation Research Record: Journal of the Transportation Research Board, 2019*(1), 225–236. doi:10.3141/2019-27.

Hadayeghi, A., Shalaby, A., & Persaud, B. (2010a). Development of planning-level transportation safety models using full Bayesian semiparametric additive techniques. *Journal of Transportation Safety & Security, 2*(1), 45–68. doi:10.1080/19439961003687328.

Hadley, S. W., & Tsvetkova, A. A. (2009). Potential impacts of plug-in hybrid electric vehicles on regional power generation. *The Electricity Journal, 22*(10), 56–68. doi:10.1016/j.tej.2009.10.011.

Hägerstraand, T. (1970). What about people in regional science? *Papers in Regional Science, 24*, 7–24. doi:10.1111/j.1435-5597.1970.tb01464.x.

Hale, A. R., Stoop, J., & Hommels, J. (1990). Human error models as predictors of accident scenarios for designers in road transport systems. *Ergonomics, 33*(10-11), 1377–1387. doi:10.1080/00140139008925339.

Hale, D. (1997). How many NETSIM runs are enough? *McTrans Newsletter, 11*(3), 4–5.

Han, S. (2010). *Design of an optimal aggregator for vehicle to grid regulation service.* Paper presented at the IEEE Conference Publications on Innovative Smart Grid Technologies (ISGT). New York, NY.

Hanbali, R. M., & Kuemmel, D. A. (1993). Traffic volume reductions due to winter storm conditions. *Transportation Research Record, , 1387.*

Han, S., & Han, S. (2013). Economic feasibility of V2G frequency regulation in consideration of battery wear. *Energies, 6*, 748–765. doi:10.3390/en6020748.

Hatakka, M., Keskinen, E., Katila, E., & Laapotti, S. (1997). Do psychologists have something to offer in driver training, driver improvement and selection? In *Assessing the driver.* Rot-Gelb-Grün Braunschweig..

Hatzopoulou, M., Hao, J. Y., & Miller, E. J. (2011). Simulating the impacts of household travel on greenhouse gas emissions, urban air quality, and population exposure. *Transportation, 38*(6), 871–887. doi:10.1007/s11116-011-9362-9.

HC. (2012). *Proyecto InovGrid.* Retrieved from http://www.cne.es/cne/doc/publicaciones/smart_metering/1115_4_HC_Telegestion.pdf

Hecker, D., Stange, H., Körner, C., & May, M. (2010). Sample bias due to missing data in mobility surveys. In *Proceedings of the 2010 IEEE International Conference on Data Mining Workshops (ICDMW'10),* (pp. 241-248). IEEE.

Henderson, D. K., & Mokhtarian, P. L. (1996). Impacts of center-based telecommuting on travel and emissions: Analysis of the Puget Sound demonstration project. *Transportation Research Part D, Transport and Environment, 1*(1), 29–45. doi:10.1016/S1361-9209(96)00009-0.

Hensher, D. A., & Puckett, S. M. (2007). Congestion and variable user charging as an effective travel demand management instrument. *Transportation Research Part A, Policy and Practice, 41*(7), 615–626. doi:10.1016/j.tra.2006.07.002.

Henson, K. M., & Gaulias, K. G. (2006). Preliminary assessment of activity analysis and modeling for homeland security applications. *Transportation Research Record: Journal of the Transportation Research Board, 1942,* 23–30. doi:10.3141/1942-04.

Herman, R., Montroll, E. W., Potts, R. B., & Rothery, R. W. (1959). Traffic dynamics: Analysis of stability in car following. *Operations Research, 7*(1), 86–106. doi:10.1287/opre.7.1.86.

He, Y., Venkatesh, B., & Guan, L. (2012). Optimal scheduling for charging and discharging of electrical vehicles. *IEEE Transactions on Smart Grids, 3*(3), 1095–1105. doi:10.1109/TSG.2011.2173507.

Heydt, G. T. (1983, May). The impact of electric vehicle deployment on load management strategies. *IEEE Transactions on Power Apparatus and Systems, 102*(5), 1253–1259. doi:10.1109/TPAS.1983.318071.

Hintze, J. L., & Nelson, R. D. (1998). Violin plots: A box plot-density trace synergism. *The American Statistician, 52*(2), 181–184. doi: doi:10.1080/00031305.1998.10480559.

Hirst, E., & Kirby, B. (1999). What is system control? In *Proceedings of the American Power Conference,* (pp. 639-644). APC.

Holland, J. H. (1992). *Adaptation in natural and artificial systems: An introductory analysis with applications to biology, control, and artificial intelligence.* Cambridge, MA: MIT Press..

Hollnagel, E. (1993). *Human reliability analysis: Context and control.* New York: Academic Press, Inc.

Hollnagel, E., & Woods, D. D. (2005). *Joint cognitive systems - Foundations of cognitive systems engineering*. Boca Raton, FL: CRC Press. doi:10.1201/9781420038194.

Hoque, M. M. (2004). The road to road safety, issues and initiative in Bangladesh. *Regional Health Forum, 8*(1), 39-51.

Hoque, M. M. (1991). *Accident investigation for the safety improvement of Dhaka-Aricha highway: A section of Asian highway*. Dhaka, India: Department of Civil Engineering, Bangladesh University of Engineering & Technology..

Horni, A., Charypar, D., & Axhausen, K. W. (2011). Variability in transport microsimulations investigated with the multi-agent transport simulation MATSim. *Arbeitsberichte Verkehrs- und Raumplanung, 692*.

Horni, A., Scott, D. M., Balmer, M., & Axhausen, K. W. (2009). *Location choice modeling for leisure and shopping with MATSim: Utility function extension and validation results*. Paper presented at the 9th Swiss Transport Research Conference. Bern, Switzerland.

Hranac, R., Sterzin, E., Krechmer, D., Rakha, H., & Farzaneh, M. (2006). *Empirical studies on traffic flow in inclement weather (FHWA-HOP-07-073)*. Academic Press..

Huang, S., & Infield, D. (2009). *The potential of domestic electric vehicles to contribute to power system operation through vehicle to grid technology*. Paper presented at the 44th Int. Universities Power Engineering Conference. New York, NY.

Huang, Z., & Williamson, P. (2001). *Comparison of synthetic reconstruction and combinatorial optimisation approaches to the creation of small-area microdata* (Working Paper, 2001/2). Liverpool, UK: Department of Geography, University of Liverpool.

Huang, H., Abdel-Aty, M., & Darwiche, A. (2010). County-level crash risk analysis in Florida. *Transportation Research Record: Journal of the Transportation Research Board, 2148*(1), 27–37. doi:10.3141/2148-04.

Hyndman, R. J., & Koehler, A. B. (2006). Another look at measures of forecast accuracy. *International Journal of Forecasting, 22*, 679–688. doi:10.1016/j.ijforecast.2006.03.001.

IEC. (2010). *Electric vehicle conductive charging system - Part 1: General requirements (IEC 61851-1)*. Geneva, Switzerland: International Electrotechnical Commission..

International Electrotechnical Commisson. (2013). *Electropedia: The world's online electrotechnical vocabulary*. Retrieved from http://www.electropedia.org/

Jäggi, B., & Axhausen, K. W. (2011). *Modeling long term investment decisions in housing and transportation*. Paper presented at the 11th Swiss Transport Research Conference. New York, NY.

Janssens, D., Wets, G., Timmermans, H. J. P., & Arentze, T. A. (2007). *Modelling short-term dynamics in activity-travel patterns: Conceptual framework of the feathers model*. Paper presented at the 11th World Conference on Transport Research. Berkeley, CA.

Jeung, H., Liu, Q., Shen, H. T., & Zhou, X. (2008). A hybrid prediction model for moving objects. In Proceedings of ICDE '08 (pp. 70-79). ICDE.

Jha, M., Gopalan, G., Garms, A., Mahanti, B., Toledo, T., & Ben-Akiva, M. (2004). Development and calibration of a large-scale microscopic traffic simulation model. *Transportation Research Record, 1876*, 121–131. doi:10.3141/1876-13.

Joh, C. (2002). Modeling individuals' activity–travel rescheduling heuristics: Theory and numerical experiments. *Transportation Research Board of the National Academies, 16*– 25.

Joh, C-H., Arentze, T., Hofman, F., & Timmermans. (1999). Activity pattern similarity: Towards a multidimensional sequence alignment. In *Proceedings of the IATBR Conference*. Austin, TX: IATBR.

Joh, C. (2003). *Estimating non-linear utility functions of time use in the context of an activity schedule adaptation model*. Lucerne, France: Academic Press..

Joh, C. H., Kim, C. S., & Song, H. M. (2008). An activity-based analysis of heavy-vehicle trip chains. *Journal of the Economic Geographical Society of Korea, 11*(2), 192–202.

Jones, P., Koppelman, F., & Orfeuil, J.-P. (1990). Activity analysis: State-of-the-art and future directions. In P. Jones (Ed.), *Developments in Dynamic and Activity-based Approaches to Travel Analysis* (pp. 34–55). Aldershot, UK: Gower..

Jovicic, G. (2001). *Activity-based travel demand modeling-A literature study*. Copenhagen: Denmark's Transport Forskning & The Danish Transport Research Institute..

Juyoung Kang, H.-S. Y. (2010). A frequent pattern based prediction model for moving objects. *IJCSNS, 10*(3), 200–205.

Kamar, E., & Horvitz, E. (2009). Collaboration and shared plans in the open world: Studies of idesharing. In *Proceedings of the Twenty-First International Joint Conference on Artificial Intelligence*. Pasadena, CA: IJCAI Organization.

Kamga, C. N., Mouskosb, K. C., & Paaswell, R. E. (2011). Methodology to estimate travel time using dynamic traffic assignment (DTA) under incident conditions. *Transportation Research Part C, Emerging Technologies, 19*(6), 1215–1224. doi:10.1016/j.trc.2011.02.004.

Kass, G. V. (1980). An exploratory technique for investigating large quantities of categorical data. *Applied Statistics, 29*, 119–127. doi:10.2307/2986296.

Kassin, S. (2003). *Psychology* (4th ed.). New York: Prentice Hall..

Kelly, L., Rowe, A., & Wild, P. (2009). Analyzing the impacts of plug-in electric vehicles on distribution networks in British Columbia. In *Proceedings of the Electrical Power & Energy Conference (EPEC)*. IEEE.

Kempton, W. (2004). *Vehicle to grid power implementation: From stabilizing the grid to supporting large-scale new renewable energy*. University of Delaware..

Kempton, W., & Tomić, J. (2005). Vehicle-to-grid power fundamentals: calculating capacity and net revenue. *Journal of Power Sources, 144*(1), 268–279. doi:10.1016/j.jpowsour.2004.12.025.

Keskinen, E. (1996). Why do young drivers have more accidents? *Junge Fahrer und Fahrerinnen, 52*, 42–53.

Keskinen, E., Hatakka, M., Laapotti, S., Katila, A., & Peräaho, M. (2004). Driver behaviour as a hierarchical system. In *Traffic Transport Psychology: Theory and Application* (pp. 9–23). London: Elsevier..

Khan, M. A., Al Kathairi, A. S., & Garib, A. M. (2004). *A GIS based traffic accident data collection, referencing and analysis framework for Abu Dhabi*. Paper Presented in CODATU XI: World Congress: Towards More Attractive Urban Transportation. Bucarest, Romania.

Kidd, E. A., & Laughery, K. R. (1964). *A computer model of driving behavior: The highway intersection situation* (Report no. VJ-1843-V-1) Buffalo, NY: Cornell Aeronautical Laboratories.

Kim, T. J. (2012). *Application of activity-based transport simulation model to the gangnam-gu area*. (Unpublished Master thesis). University of Seoul, Seoul, Korea.

Kim, C. S., Cheon, S. H., & Hwang, S. Y. (2012). *A decade of change in Korean travel patterns and policy implications*. Seoul, Korea: The Korea Transport Institute..

Kirby, B. (2004). *Frequency regulation basics and trends*. Oak Ridge National Laboratory..

Kitamura, R., Kikuchi, A., & Pendyala, R. M. (2008). *Integrated, dynamic activity-network simulator: Current state and future directions of PCATS-DEBNetS*. Paper presented at the 2nd TRB Conference on Innovations in Travel Modeling. Portland, OR.

Kitamura, R. (1988). An evaluation of activity-based travel analysis. *Transportation, 15*, 9–34. doi:10.1007/BF00167973.

Kitamura, R., Chen, C., Pendyala, R. M., & Narayanan, R. (2000). Micro-simulation of daily activity-travel patterns for travel demand forecasting. *Transportation, 27*, 25–51. doi:10.1023/A:1005259324588.

Kitamura, R., Kikuchi, A., Fujii, S., & Yamamoto, T. (2005). An overview of PCATS/DEBNetS micro-simulation system: Its development, extension, and application to demand forecasting. In R. Kitamura, & M. Kuwahara (Eds.), *Simulation Approaches in Transportation Analysis: Recent Advances and Challenges* (pp. 371–399). New York: Springer. doi:10.1007/0-387-24109-4_14.

Knapen, L., Muhammad, U., Bellemans, T., Janssens, D., & Wets, G. (2012). Framework to evaluate rescheduling due to unexpected events in an activity-based model. In *Proceedings of TRB 2013 Annual Meeting*. Washington, DC: TRB.

Knapen, L., Yasar, A., Cho, S., Keren, D., Dbai, A. A., Bellemans, T., et al. (2013). Exploiting graph-theoretic tools for matching in carpooling applications. *Journal of Ambient Intelligence and Humanized Computing.*

Knapen, L., Keren, D., Yasar, A., Cho, S., Bellemans, T., & Janssens, D. et al. (2012). *Analysis of the co-routing problem in agent-based carpooling simulation.* Niagara Falls, NY: Procedia Computer Science. doi:10.1016/j.procs.2012.06.106.

Knapen, L., Keren, D., Yasar, A., Cho, S., Bellemans, T., & Janssens, D. et al. (2013). *Estimating scalability issues while finding an optimal assignment for carpooling.* Halifax, Canada: Procedia Computer Science. doi:10.1016/j.procs.2013.06.051.

Knapen, L., Kochan, B., Bellemans, T., Janssens, D., & Wets, G. (2012). Activity-based modeling to predict spatial and temporal power demand of electric vehicles in Flanders, Belgium. *Transportation Research Record: Journal of the Transportation Research Board, 2287,* 146–154. doi:10.3141/2287-18.

Knappen, L., Kochan, B., Bellemans, T., Janssens, D., & Wets, G. (2011). *Activity based models for countrywide electric vehicle power demand calculation.* Hasselt, Belgium: University of Hasselt. doi:10.1109/SGMS.2011.6089019.

Knudsen, D. C., & Fotheringham. (1986). Matrix comparison, goodness-of-fit, and spatial interaction modeling. *International Regional Science Review, 10*(2), 127–147. doi:10.1177/016001768601000203.

Kochan, B., Bellemans, T., Cools, M., Janssens, D., & Wets, G. (2011). *An estimation of total vehicle travel reduction in the case of telecommuting: Detailed analyses using an activity-based modeling approach.* Paper presented at the European Transportation Conference. Glasgow, UK.

Kochan, B. (2012). *Application of an activity-based transportation model for Flanders: Activity-based models and transportation demand management policies. LAP LAMBERT.* Academic Publishing..

Kochan, B. (2012). *Implementation, validation and application of an activity-based transportation model for Flanders.* Hasselt, Belgium: University of Hasselt..

Kochan, B., Bellemans, T., Janssens, D., & Wets, G. (2008). Assessing the impact of fuel cost on traffic demand in Flanders using activity-based models. In *Proceedings of Travel Demand Management.* Vienna, Austria: Travel Demand Management..

Kochan, B., Bellemans, T., Janssens, D., & Wets, G. (2013). Validation of an activity-based traffic demand model for flanders implemented in the feathers simulation platform. In *Computational Intelligence for Traffic and Mobility.* Atlantic Press. doi:10.2991/978-94-91216-80-0_6.

Kockelman, K. M., & Kalmanje, S. (2005). Credit-based congestion pricing: A policy proposal and the public's response. *Transportation Research Part A, Policy and Practice, 39*(7-9), 671–690. doi:10.1016/j.tra.2005.02.014.

Koenig, B. E., Henderson, D. K., & Mokhtarian, P. L. (1996). The travel and emissions impacts of telecommuting for the state of California telecommuting pilot project. *Transportation Research Part C, Emerging Technologies, 4*(1), 13–32. doi:10.1016/0968-090X(95)00020-J.

Kohavi, R., & Provost, F. (1998). *Glossary of terms: Machine learning.* Boston: Kluwer Academic Publishers..

Kohonen, T. (2001). *Self-organizing maps.* Berlin: Springer. doi:10.1007/978-3-642-56927-2.

Kok, K., Scheepers, M., & Kamphuis, R. (2009). Intelligence in electricity networks for embedding renewables and distributed generation. In *Intelligent Infrastructures.* Dordrecht, The Netherlands: Springer. doi:10.1007/978-90-481-3598-1_8.

Korea Development Institute. (2008). *A study on general guidelines for pre-feasibility study* (5th ed.). Seoul: Author..

Körner, C. (2012). *Modeling visit potential of geographic locations based on mobility data.* (PhD Thesis). University of Bonn, Bonn, Germany. Retrieved from http://hss.ulb.uni-bonn.de/2012/2811/2811.htm

Körner, C., May, M., & Wrobel, S. (2012). Spatiotemporal modeling and analysis – Introduction and overview. *Künstliche Intelligenz, 26*(3), 215–221. doi:10.1007/s13218-012-0215-2.

Kothari, A. (2004). *Genghis - A multiagent carpooling system.* (B.Sc Thesis). University of Bath, Bath, UK.

Krajzewicz, D., & Wagner, P. (2002). ACME (a common mental environment)-driver a cognitive car driver model. In *Proceedings of the 16th European Simulation Multiconference on Modelling and Simulation* (pp. 689-693). SCS Europe.

Krajzewicz, D. (2010). Traffic simulation with SUMO – Simulation of urban mobility. In *Proceedings of Barceló* (pp. 269–294). Barceló. doi:10.1007/978-1-4419-6142-6_7.

Krajzewicz, D., Bonert, M., & Wagner, P. (2006). The open source traffic simulation package SUMO. In *Proceedings of RoboCup 2006 Infrastructure Simulation Competition*. Bremen, Germany: RoboCup..

Kramer, B., Chakraborty, S., & Kroposki, B. (2008). A review of plug-in vehicles and vehicle-to-grid capability. In *Proceedings of Industrial Electronics* (pp. 2278–2283). IEEE. doi:10.1109/IECON.2008.4758312.

Krumm, J., & Horvitz, E. (2006). Predestination: inferring destinations from partial trajectories. In Proceedings of UbiComp'06, (pp. 243–260). UbiComp..

Kullback, S., & Leibler, R. A. (1951). On information and sufficiency. *Annals of Mathematical Statistics, 22*(1), 79–86. doi:10.1214/aoms/1177729694.

Kumar, R., Ali, M. S., & Ahmed, A. (2010). An appraisal of signal free corridor in Karachi via empirical study of road accidents and pedestrian movement concerning road crossing. In *Proceedings of the 3rd International Conference on Infrastructural Engineering in Developing Countries* (pp. 379-388). NED University of Engineering and Technology.

Kurban, H., Gallagher, R., Kurban, G. A., & Persky, J. (2011). A beginner's guide to creating small-area cross-tabulations. *Cityscape (Washington, D.C.), 13*(3), 225–235.

Kusumastuti, D., Hannes, E., Janssens, D., Wets, G., & Dellaert, B. G. C. (2010). Scrutinizing individuals' leisure-shopping travel decisions to appraise activity-based models of travel demand. *Transportation, 37*, 647–661. doi:10.1007/s11116-010-9272-2.

Kutner, M. H., Nachtsheim, C. J., & Neter, J. (2004). *Applied Linear regression models* (4th ed.). New York: McGraw-Hill..

Kyte, M., Khatib, Z., Shannon, P., & Kitchener, F. (2001). The effect of weather on free-flow speed. Transportation Research Board, 1776, 60–68..

Lämmel, G., Grether, D., & Nagel, K. (2010). The representation and implementation of time-dependent inundation in large-scale microscopic evacuation simulations. *Transportation Research Part C, Emerging Technologies, 18*(1), 84–98. doi:10.1016/j.trc.2009.04.020.

Lawe, S., Lobb, J., Sadek, A. W., Huang, S., & Xie, C. (2009). TRANSIMS implementation in Chittenden County, Vermont. *Transportation Research Board Record, 2132*, 113–121. doi:10.3141/2132-13.

Lee, D., Yang, X., & Chandrasekar, P. (2001). Parameter calibration for PARAMICS using genetic algorithm. In *Proceedings of the 80th Annual Transportation Research Board Meeting*. Transportation Research Board.

Lee, D.-H. Sun, & Erath. (2012). *Study of bus service reliability in Singapore using fare card data*. Paper presented at the 12th Asia Pacific ITS Forum & Exhibition. Kuala Lumpur, Malaysia.

Lee, W. D., Kim, C. S., Choi, K. C., Choi, J. M., Joh, C. H., Rasouli, S., & Timmermans, H. J. P. (2012). *Analyzing changes in activity-travel behavior in time and space using household travel surveys in Seoul metropolitan area over 10 years*. Paper presented at the Workshop on Transportgraphy: Advances in Spatial-Temporal Transport Analysis. Hong Kong, China.

Lee, D., Shiah, S., Lee, C., & Wang, Y. (2007). State-of-charge estimation for electric scooters by using learning mechanisms. *IEEE Transactions on Vehicular Technology, 56*(2), 544–556. doi:10.1109/TVT.2007.891433.

Lee, J., & Wong, D. W. S. (2001). *Statistical analysis with ArcView GIS*. New York: John Wiley & Sons, Inc.

Leemput, N., Van Roy, J., Geth, F., Tant, P., Claessens, B., & Driesen, J. (2011). *Comparative analysis of coordination strategies for electric vehicles*. Paper presented at the 2nd IEEE PES International Conference and Exhibition on Innovative Smart Grid Technologies Europe. Manchester, UK.

Lee, W. D., Cho, S. J., Bellemans, T., Janssens, D., Wets, G., Choi, K. C., & Joh, C. H. (2012). Seoul activity-based model: An application of feathers solutions to Seoul metropolitan area. *Procedia Computer Science, 10*, 840–845. doi:10.1016/j.procs.2012.06.109.

Lei, P.-R., Shen, T.-J., Peng, W.-C., & Su, I.-J. (2011). Exploring spatial-temporal trajectory model for location prediction. Mobile Data Management, (1), 58-67.

Letendre, S., Denholm, P., & Lilienthal, P. (2006). Plug-in hybrid and all-electric vehicles: New load, or new resource? *Public Utilities Fortnightly, 144*(12), 28.

Levine, N., Kim, K. E., & Nitz, L. H. (1995). Spatial analysis of Honolulu motor vehicle crashes: II: Zonal generators. *Accident; Analysis and Prevention, 27*(5), 675–685. doi:10.1016/0001-4575(95)00018-U PMID:8579698.

Li, H., Tang, C., Qiao, S., Wang, Y., Yang, N., & Li, C. (2010). Hotspot district trajectory prediction. In Proceedings of WAIM '10, (pp. 74-84). WAIM.

Li, S., Kolmanovsky, I. V., & Ulsoy, A. G. (2011). Battery swapping modularity design for plug-in HEVs using the augmented lagrangian decomposition method. In *Proceedings of American Control Conference (ACC)* (pp. 953-958). ACC.

Li, X., Lopes, L. A., & Williamson, S. S. (2009). On the suitability of plug-in hybrid electric vehicle (PHEV) charging infrastructures based on wind and solar energy. In *Proceedings of the Power & Energy Society General Meeting*, (pp. 1--8). IEEE.

Li, C. T. (2012). Synergistic control of plug-in vehicle charging and wind power scheduling. *IEEE Transactions on Power Systems*. doi:10.1109/TPWRS.2012.2211900.

Liebig, T., Körner, C., & May, M. (2009). Fast visual trajectory analysis using spatial Bayesian networks. In *Proceedings of the 2009 IEEE International Conference on Data Mining Workshops (ICDMW'09)*, (pp. 668-673). IEEE.

Li, G., & Zhang, X. (2012). Modeling of PHEV charging demand in probabilisic power flow calculations. *IEEE Transactions On Smart Grid, 3*(1), 492–499. doi:10.1109/TSG.2011.2172643.

Lim, Y. T., Kang, M. G., & Lee, C. H. (2008). Impacts of number of O/D zone and network aggregation level in transportation demand forecast. *Journal of Korean Society of Transportation, 26*(2), 147–156.

Lin, D.-Y., Eluru, N., Waller, S. T., & Bhat, C. R. (2008). Integration of activity-based modeling and dynamic traffic assignment. *Transportation Research Record: Journal of the Transportation Research Board, 2076*, 52–61. doi:10.3141/2076-06.

Litman, T. (2006). *Mobility management traffic safety impacts*. Paper presented at the Transportation Research Board (TRB) 85th Annual Meeting. Washington, DC.

Litman, T. (2010). *Changing vehicle travel price sensitivities: The rebounding rebound effect*. Victoria Transport Policy Institute. Retrieved from http://www.vtpi.org

Litman, T., & Fitzroy, S. (2012). *Safe travels: Evaluating mobility management traffic safety impacts*. Victoria Transport Policy Institute. Retrieved from http://www.vtpi.org

Litman, T. (2003). The online TDM encyclopedia: Mobility management information gateway. *Transport Policy, 10*(3), 245–249. doi:10.1016/S0967-070X(03)00025-8.

Liu, K., Deng, K., Ding, Z., Zhou, X., & Li, M. (2011). Pattern-based moving object tracking. In Proceedings of TDMA '11, (pp. 5-14). TDMA.

Lopes, J. P., Soares, F. J., Almeida, P., & da Silva, M. M. (2009). Smart charging strategies for electric vehicles: Enhancing grid performance and maximizing the use of variable renewable energy sources. In *Proceedings of International Battery, Hybrid and Fuel Cell Electric Vehicle Symposium and Exhibition* (pp. 1--11). IEEE.

Lopes, J. A. P., Soares, F. J., & Almeida, P. M. R. (2011). Integration of electric vehicles in the electric power system. *Proceedings of the IEEE, 99*(1), 168–183. doi:10.1109/JPROC.2010.2066250.

Lord, D., & Mannering, F. (2010). The statistical analysis of crash-frequency data: A review and assessment of methodological alternatives. *Transportation Research Part A, Policy and Practice, 44*(5), 291–305. doi:10.1016/j.tra.2010.02.001.

Los Alamos National Lab (LANL). (2004). *TRANSIMS: Transportation analysis simulation system: Version 3.0 (LA-UR-00-1724)*. Los Alamos, NM: TRANSIMS..

Lovegrove, G. R. (2005). *Community-based, macro-level collision prediction models*. (Doctoral thesis). University of British Columbia, Vancouver, Canada.

Lovegrove, G. R., & Litman, T. (2008). *Using macro-level collision prediction models to evaluate the road safety effects of mobility management strategies: New empirical tools to promote sustainable development*. Paper presented at the Transportation Research Board (TRB) 87th Annual Meeting. Washington, DC.

Lovegrove, G. R., & Sayed, T. (2006). Macro-level collision prediction models for evaluating neighbourhood traffic safety. *Canadian Journal of Civil Engineering, 33*(5), 609–621. doi:10.1139/l06-013.

Lovegrove, G., & Sayed, T. (2007). Macrolevel collision prediction models to enhance traditional reactive road safety improvement programs. *Transportation Research Record: Journal of the Transportation Research Board, 2019*(1), 65–73. doi:10.3141/2019-09.

Lu, Q. (2011). On pre-processing for least-cost carpooling routing in a transportation network. In *Proceedings of IARIA* (pp. 62 - 68). IARIA.

Lu, E. H.-C., Tseng, V. S., & Yu, P. S. (2011). Mining cluster-based temporal mobile sequential patterns in location-based service environments. *IEEE Transactions on Knowledge and Data Engineering, 23*(6), 914–927. doi:10.1109/TKDE.2010.155.

Luetzenberger, M., Masuch, N., Hirsch, B., Ahrndt, S., & Albayrak, S. (2011). Strategic behaviour in dynamic cities. In D. Weed (Ed.), *Proceedings of the 43rd Summer Computer Simulation Conference*, (pp. 148–155). IEEE.

Lunz, B., Yan, Z., Gerschler, J. B., & Sauer, D. U. (2012). Influence of plug-in hybrid electric vehicle charging strategies on charging and battery degradation costs. *Energy Policy, 46*, 511–519. doi:10.1016/j.enpol.2012.04.017.

Lützenberger, M., Ahrndt, S., Hirsch, B., Masuch, N., Heßler, A., & Albayrak, S. (2012). Reconsider your strategy – An agent-based model of compensatory driver behaviour. In *Proceedings of the 15th Intelligent Transportation Conference (ITSC 2012)*. Anchorage, AK: IEEE.

Lützenberger, M., Masuch, N., Hirsch, B., Ahrndt, S., Heßler, A., & Albayrak, S. (2011). The BDI driver in a service city. In *Proceedings of the 10th International Conference on Autonomous Agents and Multiagent Systems (AAMAS'11)*. Taipei, Taiwan: IFAAMAS.

Lyon, T. P., Michelin, M., Jongejan, A., & Leahy, T. (2012). Is smart charging policy for electric vehicles worthwhile? *Energy Policy, 41*, 259–268. doi:10.1016/j.enpol.2011.10.045.

MacKay, D. (2008). Sustainable energy-without the hot air. Cambridge, UK: Cambridge.

Madireddy, M., Medeiros, D. J., & Kumara, S. (2011). An agent-based model for evacuation traffic management. In *Proceedings of the 2011 Winter Simulation Conference*. Winter Simulation.

Maia, R., Silva, M., Araújo, R., & Nunes, U. (2011). *Electric vehicle simulator for energy consumption studies in electric mobility systems*. Paper presented at the IEEE Forum on Integrated and Sustainable Transportation Systems. New York, NY.

Manzini, R., & Pareschi, A. (2012). A decision-support system for the car pooling problem. *Journal of Transportation Technologies, (2)*, 85–101.

Mathoy, A. (2008). *Definition and implementation of a global EV charging infrastructure (Final Report)*. Gams, Switzerland: Brusa Elektronik..

MATSim-T. (2013). *Multi agent transportation simulation toolkit*. Retrieved March 26, 2013, from http://www.matsim.org

May, M., Hecker, D., Körner, C., Scheider, S., & Schulz, D. (2008a). A vector-geometry based spatial kNN-algorithm for traffic frequency predictions. In *Proceedings of the 2008 IEEE International Conference on Data Mining Workshops (ICDMW '08)*, (pp. 442-447). IEEE.

May, M., Scheider, S., Rösler, R., Schulz, D., & Hecker, D. (2008b). Pedestrian flow prediction in extensive road networks using biased observational data. In *Proceedings of the 16th ACM SIGSPATIAL International Conference on Advances in Geographic Information Systems (ACM GIS '08)*, (pp. 1-4). ACM.

McKnight, A. J., & Adams, B. B. (1970a). Driver education task analysis: Volume I: Task descriptions. Humand Resources Research Organization..

McKnight, A. J., & Adams, B. B. (1970b). Driver education task analysis: Volume II: Task analysis methods. Humand Resources Research Organization.

McKnight, A. J., & Hundt, A. (1971). Driver education task analysis: Volume III: Instructional objectives. Human Resources Research Organization.

McNally, M. G. (2000). The four step model. In *Handbook of Transport Modeling* (pp. 35–52). London: Elsevier Science Ltd.

McNally, M. G. (2007). The four step model. In *Handbook of Transport Modelling*. London: Elsevier Science..

McRuer, D. T., Allen, R. W., Weir, D. H., & Klein, R. H. (1997). New results in driver steering control models. *Human Factors, 19*(4), 381–397.

McRuer, D. T., & Weir, D. H. (1969). Theory of manual vehicular control. *Ergonomics, 12*(5), 599–633. doi:10.1080/00140136908931082 PMID:5823971.

Meister, K., Balmer, M., Ciari, F., Horni, A., Rieser, M., Waraich, R., & Axhausen, K. (2010). *Large-scale agent-based travel demand optimization applied to Switzerland, including mode choice.* Paper presented at the 12th World Conference on Transportation Research. Lisbon, Portugal.

Melhuish, T., Blake, M., & Day, S. (2002). An evaluation of synthetic household populations for census collection districts created using optimisation techniques. *Australasian Journal of Regional Studies, 8*(3), 269–387.

Meloni, I., Guala, L., & Loddo, A. (2004). Time allocation to discretionary in-home, out-of-home activities and to trips. *Transportation, 31*(1), 69–96. doi:10.1023/B:PORT.0000007228.44861.ae.

Menczer, W. (2007). Guaranteed ride home programs. *Journal of Public Transportation, 10*(4), 131–150.

Metro Carpooling Made Easy . (2013). Retrieved from http://metro.kingcounty.gov/tops/van-car/carpool.html

Metropolitan Transport Association. (2007). *Seoul metropolitan area household travel survey (2006)*. Seoul: Author..

Metropolitan Transport Association. (2012). *National household travel survey (2010)*. Seoul: Author..

Mets, K., D'hulst, R., & Develder, C. (2012). Comparison of intelligent charging algorithms for electric vehicles to reduce peak load and demand variability in a distribution grid. *Journal of Communications and Networks, 114*(6), 672–681. doi:10.1109/JCN.2012.00033.

Miaou, S.-P., Song, J. J., & Mallick, B. K. (2003). Roadway Traffic Crash Mapping: A Space-Time Modeling Approach. *Journal of Transportation and Statistics, 6*(1), 33–57.

Michaeli, I., Reenock, C., & Kapoor, D. (2011). *Electric vehicles: Perspectives on a growing investment theme.* Retrieved from http://www.ceres.org/resources/reports/electric-vehicles-report

Michon, J. A. (1976). The mutual impacts of transportation and human behaviour. In *Transportation planning for a better environment* (pp. 221–236). Plenum Press. doi:10.1007/978-1-4615-8861-0_18.

Michon, J. A. (1985). A critical view of driver behavior models: What do we know, what should we do? In *Human Behavior and Traffic Safety* (pp. 487–525). Plemun Press. doi:10.1007/978-1-4613-2173-6_19.

Michon, J. A. (1989). Explanatory pitfalls and rule-based driver models. *Accident; Analysis and Prevention, 21*(4), 341–353. doi:10.1016/0001-4575(89)90025-0 PMID:2669785.

Milton, J. C., Shankar, V. N., & Mannering, F. L. (2008). Highway accident severities and the mixed logit model: An exploratory empirical analysis. *Accident; Analysis and Prevention, 40*(1), 260–266. doi:10.1016/j.aap.2007.06.006 PMID:18215557.

Mitsubishi i-MiEV . (2008). Retrieved March 14, 2013, from http://www.mitsubishi-motors.com/special/ev/

Mobiel Vlaanderen: Onderzoek Verplaatsingsgedrag Vlaanderen . (2013). Retrieved March 14, 2013, from http://www.mobielvlaanderen.be/ovg/

Mohan, D., & Tiwari, G. (2005). Road safety in low income countries: Issues and concern regarding knowledge transfer from high income countries. In G. Tiwari, D. Mohan, & N. Muhlard (Eds.), *The way Forward- Transportation Planning and Road Safety* (pp. 122–135). MacMillian India Press..

Mokhtarian, P. L., & Varma, K. V. (1998). The trade-off between trips and distance traveled in analyzing the emissions impacts of center-based telecommuting. *Transportation Research Part D, Transport and Environment, 3*(6), 419–428. doi:10.1016/S1361-9209(98)00018-2.

Monreale, A., Pinelli, F., Trasarti, R., & Giannotti, F. (2009). WhereNext: A location predictor on trajectory pattern mining. In Proceedings of KDD '09 (pp. 637-646). KDD.

Morzy, M. (2006). Prediction of moving object location based on frequent trajectories. In Proceedings of ISCIS '06 (pp. 583-592). ISCIS.

Morzy, M. (2007). Mining frequent trajectories of moving objects for location prediction. In Proceedings of MLDM '07 (pp. 667-680). MLDM.

Mullen, S. K. (2009). *Plug-in hybrid electric vehciles as a source of distributed frequency regulation.* (Dissertation). University of Minnesota, Minneapolis, MN.

Muller, K., & Axhausen. (2011). *Population synthesis for microsimulation: State of the art.* Paper presented at the 90th Annual Meeting of the Transportation Research Board. Washington, DC.

Murray, G., Chase, M., Kim, E., & McBrayer, M. (2012). *Ridesharing as a complement to transit - A synthesis of transit practice.* Washington, DC: Transportation Research Board..

Näätänen, R., & Summala, H. (1974). A model for the role of motivational factors in driver's decision-making. *Accident; Analysis and Prevention, 6,* 243–261. doi:10.1016/0001-4575(74)90003-7.

Näätänen, R., & Summala, H. (1976). *Road-user behavior and traffic accidents.* North-Holland Publishing Company..

Naderan, A., & Shahi, J. (2010). Aggregate crash prediction models: Introducing crash generation concept. *Accident; Analysis and Prevention, 42*(1), 339–346. doi:10.1016/j.aap.2009.08.020 PMID:19887176.

Nanni, T. Rossetti, & Pedreschi. (2012). Efficient distributed computation of human mobility aggregates through user mobility profiles. In Proceedings of UrbComp12. UrbComp..

Nanni, M., Kuijpers, B., Korner, C., May, M., & Pedreschi, D. (2008). Spatiotemporal data mining. In F. Giannotti, & D. Pedreschi (Eds.), *Mobility, data mining, and privacy: Geographic knowledge discovery.* Berlin: Springer-Verlag. doi:10.1007/978-3-540-75177-9_11.

Nassauer, S. (2009). Zipcar plans partnership with zimride. *Wall Street Journal.* Retrieved from http://online.wsj.com/article/0,SB123915473346099771,00.html

Neisser, U. (1976). *Cognition and reality - Principles and implications of cognitive psychology.* W. H. Freeman and Company..

Nijland, L., Arentze, T., Borgers, A., & Timmermans, H. J. (2009). Individuals' activity-travel rescheduling behaviour: experiment and model-base d analysis. *Environment & Planning A, 41,* 1511–1522. doi:10.1068/a4134.

Nijland, L., Arentze, T., & Timmermans, H. (2008). Multi-day activity scheduling reactions to planned activities and future events in a dynamic agent-based model of activity-travel behaviour. In *Design & decision support systems in architecture and urban planning.* Eindhoven, The Netherlands: University of Technology..

Nilles, J. M. (1996). What does telework really do to us? *World Transport Policy and Practice, 2*(1-2), 15–23.

Nishino, M., Nakamura, Y., Yagi, T., Muto, S., & Abe, M. (2010). A location predictor based on dependencies between multiple lifelog data. In Proceedings of GIS-LBSN, (pp. 11-17). GIS-LBSN.

Nissan Leaf . (2013). Retrieved March 14, 2013, from http://www.nissanusa.com/electric-cars/leaf/

Noembrini, F. (2009). *Modeling and analysis of the Swiss energy system dynamics with emphasis on the interconnection between transportation and energy conversion.* (Doctoral dissertation). ETH Zurich, Zurich, Switzerland.

Noh, S. H., & Joh, C. H. (2011). Change in travel behavior of the elderly: An analysis of household travel survey data sets in Seoul metropolitan area. *Journal of the Korean Geographical Society, 46*(6), 781–796.

Noland, R. B., & Oh, L. (2004). The effect of infrastructure and demographic change on traffic-related fatalities and crashes: A case study of Illinois county-level data. *Accident; Analysis and Prevention, 36*(4), 525–532. doi:10.1016/S0001-4575(03)00058-7 PMID:15094404.

Noland, R. B., & Quddus, M. A. (2004). A spatially disaggregate analysis of road casualties in England. *Accident; Analysis and Prevention, 36*(6), 973–984. doi:10.1016/j.aap.2003.11.001 PMID:15350875.

Noland, R. B., & Quddus, M. A. (2005). Congestion and safety: A spatial analysis of London. *Transportation Research Part A, Policy and Practice, 39*(7-9), 737–754. doi:10.1016/j.tra.2005.02.022.

Nurminen, J., Pakarinen, K., & Hartikainen, J. (2011). *Carpool application quick guide*. Nokia. Retrieved from https://projects.developer.nokia.com/carpoolwindows-phone

Octotelematics. (n.d.). Retrieved from http://www.octotelematics.it/

OECD. (2012). *OECD fact book 2011-2012: Economic, environmental and social statistics*. Paris: OECD Publishing..

Olszewski, P., & Xie, L. (2005). Modelling the effects of road pricing on traffic in Singapore. *Transportation Research Part A, Policy and Practice*, 39(7-9), 755–772. doi:10.1016/j.tra.2005.02.015.

Ozbay, K., & Bartin, B. (2003). Incident management simulation. *Simulation*, 79(2), 69–82. doi:10.1177/0037549703253494.

Ozbay, K., & Kachroo, P. (1999). *Incident management in intelligent transportation systems*. Artech House Intelligent Transportation Systems Library..

Pang, C. (2010). *PHEVs as dynamically configurable dispersed energy storage for V2B uses in the smart grid*. Paper presented at the 7th Mediterranean Conference and Exhibition on Power Generation, Transmission, Distribution and Energy Conversion (MedPower 2010). New York, NY.

Pang, C. (2012). *BEVs/PHEVs as dispersed energy storage for V2B uses in the smart grid*. IEEE Transactions on Smart Grid. doi:10.1109/TSG.2011.2172228.

Panou, M., Bekiaris, E., & Papakostopoulos, V. (2007). Modelling driver behaviour in European Union and international projects. In *Proceedings of Cacciabue* (pp. 3–25). Cacciabue. doi:10.1007/978-1-84628-618-6_1.

Papadopoulos, P. Skarvelis-Kazakos, Grau, Awad, Cipcigan, & Jenkins. (2010). *Impact of residential charging of electric vehicles on distribution networks, a probabilistic approach*. Paper presented at the 45th International Universities Power Engineering Conference (UPEC). New York, NY.

Pappalardo, L., Rinzivillo, S., Qu, Z., Pedreschi, D., & Giannotti, F. (2013). Understanding the patterns of car travels. *The European Physical Journal. Special Topics*, 215, 61–73. doi:10.1140/epjst/e2013-01715-5.

Park, J. Y., Lee, J. S., Kim, Y. H., & Yu, J. B. (2012). *Forecasting individual travel behavior based on activity-based approach*. Seoul: The Korea Transport Institute..

Parks, K., Denholm, P., & Markel, A. J. (2007). *Costs and emissions associated with plug-in hybrid electric vehicle charging in the Xcel energy Colorado service territory*. Golden, CO: National Renewable Energy Laboratory. doi:10.2172/903293.

Peden, M., Scurfield, R., Sleet, D., Mohan, D., Hyder, A. A., Jarawan, E., & Mathers, C. D. (2004). *World report on road traffic injury prevention*. Geneva: World Health Organization..

Peeta, S., Ramos, J. L., & Pasupathy, R. (2000). Content of variable message signs and on-line driver behavior. *Transportation Research Record: Journal of the Transportation Research Board*, 1725(1), 102–108. doi:10.3141/1725-14.

Pel, A. J., Bliemer, M. C. J., & Hoogendoorn, S. P. (2012). A review on travel behaviour modelling in dynamic traffic simulation models for evacuations. *Transportation*, 39(1), 97–123. doi:10.1007/s11116-011-9320-6.

Pendyala, R. M. (2005). Modeling pricing in the planning process. In *Proceedings of the Expert Forum on Road Pricing and Travel Demand Modeling*. Washington, DC: Office of the Secretary of Transportation, US Department of Transportation.

Pendyala, R. M., Kitamura, R., Kikuchi, A., Yamamoto, T., & Fujii, S. (2005). FAMOS: Florida activity mobility simulator. In *Proceedings of the 84th Annual Meeting of the Transportation Research Board*. Washington, DC: Transportation Research Board.

Pendyala, R. M., Chiu, Y.-C., Hickman, M., & Waddell, P. (2009). *SimTRAVEL: A simulator of transport, routes, activities, vehicles, emissions, and land*. Washington, DC: Federal Highway Administration, Exploratory Advanced Research Program..

Pendyala, R. M., Kitamura, R., Kikuchi, A., Yamamoto, T., & Fujii, S. (2005). Florida activity mobility simulator: Overview and preliminary validation results. *Transportation Research Record: Journal of the Transportation Research Board*, 1921(1), 123–130. doi:10.3141/1921-14.

Pendyala, R. M., Konduri, K. C., Chiu, Y.-C., Hickman, M., Noh, H., & Waddell, P. et al. (2012). Integrated land use – Transport model system with dynamic time-dependent activity-travel microsimulation. *Transportation Research Record. Journal of the Transportation Research Board, 2303*, 19–27. doi:10.3141/2303-03.

Perchonok, K. (1972). *Accident cause analysis - Final report*. National Technical Information Service..

Perez, R., Ineichen, P., Seals, R., Michalsky, J., & Stewart, R. (1990). Modeling daylight availability and irradiance components from direct and global irradiance. *Solar Energy, 44*(5), 271–289. doi:10.1016/0038-092X(90)90055-H.

Peters, B., & Nilsson, L. (2007). Modelling the driver in control. In *Proceedings of Cacciabue* (pp. 85–104). Cacciabue..

Phithakkitnukoon, S. Horamont, Lorenzo, G. D., Shibasaki, R., & Ratti, C. (2010). Activity-aware map: Identifying human daily activity pattern using mobile phone data. In *Proceedings of HBU2010*, (pp. 14-25). HBU.

Pieltain, L., Gomez, T., Cossent, R., Mateo, C., & Frías, P. (2011). Assessment of the impact of PHEV on distribution networks. *IEEE Transactions on Power Systems, 26*(1), 206–213. doi:10.1109/TPWRS.2010.2049133.

Pillai, J. R. (2012). *Electric vehicles to support large wind power penetration in future Danish power systems*. Paper presented at the IEEE Vehicle Power and Propulsion Conference (VPPC). New York, NY.

Pirdavani, A., Brijs, T., Bellemans, T., Kochan, B., & Wets, G. (2012). Developing zonal crash prediction models with a focus on application of different exposure measures. *Transportation Research Record: Journal of the Transportation Research Board*.

Pirdavani, A., Brijs, T., Bellemans, T., Kochan, B., & Wets, G. (2013). Evaluating the road safety effects of a fuel cost increase measure by means of zonal crash prediction modeling. *Accident; Analysis and Prevention, 50*, 186–195. doi:10.1016/j.aap.2012.04.008 PMID:23200453.

Pitfield, D. E. (1978). Sub-optimality in freight distribution. *Transportation Research, 12*(6), 403–409. doi:10.1016/0041-1647(78)90028-X.

Polak, J., & Meland, S. (1994). An assessment of the effects of the Trondheim toll ring on travel behaviour and the environment. In *Proceedings of First World Congress on Applications of Transport Telematics and Intelligent Vehicle Highway Systems*. Paris, France: IEEE.

Pritchard, D. R., & Miller. (2009). *Advances in agent population synthesis and application in an integrated land use and transportation model*. Paper presented at the 88th Annual Meeting of the Transportation Research Board. Washington, DC.

PTV-AG. (2004). Vissim microscopic traffic and transit simulation user manual - V.3.70. Author..

Puget Sound Regional Council. (2008). *Traffic choices study – Summary report*. Seattle, WA: Puget Sound Regional Council..

Qian, K., Zhou, Allan, & Yuan. (2011). Modeling of load demand due to EV battery charging in distribution systems. *IEEE Transactions on Power Systems, 26*(2), 802–809. doi:10.1109/TPWRS.2010.2057456.

Quadstone, L. T. D. (2004). *Quadstone paramics v5. 0 modeller user guide*. Scotland, UK: Author..

Quddus, M. A. (2008). Modelling area-wide count outcomes with spatial correlation and heterogeneity: An analysis of London crash data. *Accident; Analysis and Prevention, 40*(4), 1486–1497. doi:10.1016/j.aap.2008.03.009 PMID:18606282.

Quenault, S. W. (1967). *Driver behaviour - Safe and unsafe drivers*. Road Research Laborator..

Quenault, S., Pryer, P., & Golby, C. (1968). *Age group and accident rate - Driving behaviour and attitudes*. Road Research Laboratory..

Rakha, H., Van Aerde, M., Bloomberg, L., & Huang, X. (1998). Construction and calibration of a large-scale microsimulation model of the Salt Lake area. *Transportation Research Record, 1664*, 93–102. doi:10.3141/1644-10.

Rakha, H., Zohdy, I., Park, S., & Krechmer, D. (2010). *Microscopic analysis of traffic flow in inclement weather – Part 2 (FHWA– JPO–11–020)*. Academic Press..

Ran, B., Barrett, B., & Johnson, E. (2004). *Evaluation of variable message signs in Wisconsin: Driver survey*. Academic Press..

Ranney, T. A. (1994). Model of driving behavior: A review of their evolution. *Accident; Analysis and Prevention, 26*(6), 733–750. doi:10.1016/0001-4575(94)90051-5 PMID:7857489.

Rasmussen, J. (1986). *Information processing and human-machine interaction: An approach to cognitive engineering.* London: Elsevier Science Ltd.

Rebours, Y. G., Kirschen, D. S., Trotignon, M., & Rossignol, S. (2007). A survey of frequency and voltage control ancillary services - Part 1: Technical features. *IEEE Transactions on Power Systems, 22*(1), 350–357. doi:10.1109/TPWRS.2006.888963.

REE. (2010). *Informe del sistema eléctrico 2010.* Retrieved from http://www.ree.es/sistema_electrico/informeSEE-2010.asp

Rei, R., Soares, F. J., Almeida, P. M. R., & Lopes, J. A. P. (2010). *Grid interactive charging control for plug-in electric vehicles.* Paper presented at the 13th International IEEE Conference on Intelligent Transportation Systems. Funchal, Portugal.

Renault Fluence ZE . (2011). Retrieved March 26, 2013, from http://www.media-renault.eu/fluence-ze/

Ricaud, C., & Vollet, P. (2010). *Connection system on the recharging spot: A key element for electric vehicles.* Retrieved March 14, 2013, from http://www.evplugalliance.org/en/doc/

Rindt, C., & McNally, M. (2002). *An agent-based activity microsimulation kernel using a negotiation metaphor* (Tech. Rep. No. UCI-ITS-AS-WP-02-7). Irvine, CA: Department of Civil & Environmental Engineering and Institute of Transportation Studies, University of California.

Robinson, D. (2011). *Computer modelling for sustainable urban design: Physical principles, methods and applications.* London: Routledge..

Ronald, N. (2012). *Modelling the effects of social networks on activity and travel behaviour.* (PhD thesis). TUE, Eindhoven, The Netherlands.

Ronald, N., Arentze, T., & Timmermans, H. J. (2012). Modeling social interactions between individuals for joint activity scheduling. *Transportation Research Part B: Methodological, 46*(2), 276–290. doi:10.1016/j.trb.2011.10.003.

Roorda, M., & Andre, B. (2007). Stated adaptation survey of activity rescheduling empirical and preliminary model results. *Transportation Research Record, 2021,* 45–54. doi:10.3141/2021-06.

Rossi, T. F. (2010). *Partnership to develop an integrated, advanced travel demand model and a fine-grained, time-sensitive network in the Sacramento region.* Paper presented at the 3rd TRB Conference on Innovations in Travel Modeling. Tempe, AZ.

Ruelens, F., Leterme, W., Vandael, S., Claessens, B. J., & Belmans, R. (2013). *Day-ahead and real-time planning method of a flexibility aggregator.* IEEE Transactions on Smart Grids..

Ruelens, F., Vandael, S., Leterme, W., Claessens, B. J., Hommelberg, M., Holvoet, T., & Belmans, R. (2012). Demand side management of electric vehicles with uncertainty on arrival and departure times.[rd *IEEE PES Innovative Smart Grid Technologies Europe][IGST Europe][.* IEEE.]. *Proceedings of the, 2012,* 3.

Ryan, J., Maoh, & Kanaroglou. (2009). Population synthesis: Comparing the major techniques using a small, complete population of firms. *Geographical Analysis, 41*(2), 181–203. doi:10.1111/j.1538-4632.2009.00750.x.

Saad, L. (2008). Majority now cutting back elsewhere to afford gas: Appeal of fuel-efficient cars is surging among Americans. *USA Today/Gallup Poll.* Retrieved July 29, 2012, from http://www.gallup.com/poll/107203/Majority-Now-Cutting-Back-Elsewhere-to-Afford-Gas.aspx

Sadek, A. W., Zhao, Y., Huang, S., Fuglewicz, D., Hulme, K., & Qiao, C. (2011). Advanced transportation simulation modeling for transportation system evaluation and management during emergencies. *Journal of Homeland Security on Catastrophes and Complex Systems: Transportation.*

Safarianova, S., Noembrini, F., Boulouchos, K., & Dietrich, P. (2011). *Techno-economic analysis of low GHG emission passenger cars, TOSCA project.* Zurich, Switzerland: ETH Zurich..

Sagl, G., Loidl, M., & Beinat, E. (2012). A visual analytics approach for extracting spatio-temporal urban mobility information from mobile network traffic. *ISPRS International Journal of Geo-Information,* 256-271.

Salvucci, D. D., Boer, E. R., & Liu, A. (2001). Toward an integrated model of driver behavior in a cognitive architecture. *Transportation Research Record*, *1779*, 9–16. doi:10.3141/1779-02.

Saqib, M., Sheeraz, K., & Farooqui, R. (2010). Development of guidelines for road safety audit in Pakistan: Case studies. In *Proceedings of the 3rd International Conference on Infrastructural Engineering in Developing Countries* (pp. 237-288). NED University of Engineering and Technology.

Scellato, S., Musolesi, M., Mascolo, C., Latora, V., & Campbell, A. T. (2011). Nextplace: A spatio-temporal prediction framework for pervasive systems. In Proceedings of Pervasive 2011, (pp. 152-169). Pervasive..

Scheiner, J. (2010). Social inequalities in travel behaviour: Trip distances in the context of residential self-selection and lifestyles. *Journal of Transport Geography*, *18*(6), 679–690. doi:10.1016/j.jtrangeo.2009.09.002.

Schieffer, S. (2010). *To charge or not to charge? Decentralized charging decisions for the smart grid.* (Semester's thesis). ETH Zurich, Zurich, Switzerland.

Schieffer, S. (2011). *Decentralized charging decisions for the smart grid.* (Master's thesis). ETH Zurich, Zurich, Switzerland.

Schmietendorf, G. (2011). *Verkehrsdatenerfassung mit bluetooth-detektion: Möglichkeiten und grenzen.* (Diploma Thesis). TU Dresden, Dresden, Germany. Retrieved from http://elib.dlr.de/72017/1/Diplomarbeit_final_fin_ende.pdf

Schreinemacher, J., Körner, C., Hecker, D., & Bareth, G. (2012). Analyzing temporal usage patterns of street segments based on GPS data – A case study in Switzerland. In *Proceedings of the 15th AGILE International Conference on Geographic Information Science (AGILE'12)*. AGILE.

Schulz, D., Bothe, S., & Körner, C. (2012). Human mobility from GSM data - A valid alternative to GPS? In *Proceedings of the Mobile Data Challenge Workshop*. ACM.

Schüssler, N., & Axhausen. (2011). *Combining GPS travel diaries with psychometric scales.* Paper presented at the 9th International Conference on Survey Methods in Transport. Termas de Puyehue.

Schwanen, T., Dijst, M. J., & Dieleman, F. M. (2005). The relationship between land use and travel patterns: Variations by household type. In K. Williams (Ed.), *Spatial Planning, Urban Form and Sustainable Transport*. Aldershot, UK: Ashgate..

Seo, S. U., Jung, J. H., & Kim, S. K. (2006). Analysis of the elderly travel characteristics and travel behavior with daily activity schedules: The case of Seoul, Korea. *Journal of Korean Society of Transportation*, *24*(5), 89–108.

Shao, S. Pipattanasomporn, & Rahman. (2009). *Challenges of PHEV penetration to the residential distribution network*. Paper presented at the IEEE Power & Energy Society General Meeting. New York, NY.

Sharfman, I., Schuster, A., & Keren, D. (2007). A geometric approach to monitoring threshold functions over distributed data streams. *ACM Transactions on Database Systems*, *32*(4). doi:10.1145/1292609.1292613.

Shaw, L., & Sichel, H. S. (1971). *Accident proneness - Research in the occurrence, causation, and prevention of road accidents*. New York: Pergamon Press..

Shewmake, S. (2010). *Can carpooling clean the air? The economics of HOV lanes, hybrid cars and the clean air act.* (Doctor of philosophy dissertation). University of California, Davis, CA.

Siddiqui, C., Abdel-Aty, M., & Choi, K. (2012). Macroscopic spatial analysis of pedestrian and bicycle crashes. *Accident; Analysis and Prevention*, *45*, 382–391. doi:10.1016/j.aap.2011.08.003 PMID:22269522.

Smart Electric Drive. (2013). Retrieved March 14, 2013, from http://www.smart-electric-drive.com/

Smith, D. P., & Hutchinson, B. G. (1981). Goodness-of-fit statistics for trip distribution models. *Transportation Research*, *15*(4), 295–303. doi:10.1016/0191-2607(81)90011-X.

Smith, M. C., Sadek, A. W., & Huang, S. (2008). Large-scale microscopic simulation: Toward an increased resolution of transportation models. *Journal of Transportation Engineering*, *134*(7), 273–281. doi:10.1061/(ASCE)0733-947X(2008)134:7(273).

Soares, F. J., Peças, J. A., Rocha, P. M., & Moreira, C. L. (2011). *A stochastic model to simulate electric vehicles motion and quantify the energy required from the grid.* Paper presented at the 17th Power System Computation Conference. New York, NY.

Song, S. (2011). *Research on coordinated dispatch of PEV charging and wind power in regional grid.* Paper presented at the 4th International Conference on Electric Utility Deregulation and Restructuring and Power Technologies (DRPT). New York, NY.

Song, C., Koren, T., Wang, P., & Baràbsi, A.-L. (2010). Modelling the scaling properties of human mobility. *Nature Physics, 7,* 713.

Stern, A., Shah, V., Goodwin, L., & Pisano, P. (2003). *Analysis of weather impacts flow in metropolitan Washington D.C.* Washington, DC: Academic Press..

Sterzin, E. D. (2004). *Modeling influencing factors in a microscopic traffic simulator.* Cambridge, MA: MIT..

Sudhir, M., & Sameera, K. (2006). Bangalore: Silicon city or black city? *ArriveSafe Organizations.* Retrieved April 1, 2013, from http://www.arrivesafe.org/pdfs/Bangalore-Silicon_Capital_or_Black_City.pdf

Suh, N., Cho, D., & Rim, C. (2011). Design of on-line electric vehicle (OLEV). In *Global Product Development* (pp. 3–8). Berlin: Springer. doi:10.1007/978-3-642-15973-2_1.

Summala, H. (1996). Accident risk and driver behaviour. *Safety Science, 22*(1-3), 103–117. doi:10.1016/0925-7535(96)00009-4.

Summala, H. (1997). Hierarchical model of behavioural adaptation and traffic accidents. In *Traffic Transport Psychology: Theory and Application* (pp. 41–52). New York: Pergamon..

Sykes, P. (2010). Traffic simulation with paramics. In *Proceedings of Barceló* (pp. 131–172). Barceló..

Tan, P. N., Steinbach, M., & Kumar, V. (2005). *Introduction to data mining.* Reading: Addison Wesley..

Tant, J., Geth, F., Six, D., Tant, P., & Driesen, J. (2013). Multiobjective battery storage to improve PV integration in residential distribution grids. *IEEE Transactions on Sustainable Energy, 4*(1), 182–191. doi:10.1109/TSTE.2012.2211387.

Tarko, A., Inerowicz, M., Ramos, J., & Li, W. (2008). Tool with road-level crash prediction for transportation safety planning. *Transportation Research Record: Journal of the Transportation Research Board, 2083*(1), 16–25. doi:10.3141/2083-03.

Tesla Model S. (2013). Retrieved March 14, 2013, from http://www.teslamotors.com/models

THELMA. (2013). *Technology-centered electric mobility assessment.* Retrieved March 29, 2013, from http://www.thelma-emobility.net

Tian, L., Qi, K., & Jing, A. (2013). Sitting and sizing of aggregator controlled park for plug-in hybrid electric vehicle based on particle swarm optimization. *Neural Computing & Applications, 22*(2), 249–257. doi:10.1007/s00521-011-0687-2.

Timmermans, H. J. P. (2003). *The saga of integrated land use-transport modeling: How many more dreams before we wake up?* Paper presented at the 10th International Conference on Travel Behaviour Research, International Association for Travel Behaviour Research (IATBR). Lucerne, Switzerland.

Timmermans, H. J. P., Arentze, T. A., & Joh, C.-H. (2002). Analysing space-time behavior: New approaches to old problems. *Progress in Human Geography, 26*(2), 175–190. doi:10.1191/0309132502ph363ra.

Tisue, S., & Wilensky, U. (2004). Netlogo: A simple environment for modeling complexity. In *Proceedings of International Conference on Complex Systems* (pp. 16-21). ICCS.

Toroczkai, Z., & Eubank, S. (2006). Agent-based modeling as a decision-making tool. In *Proceedings of Frontiers of Engineering: Reports on Leading-Edge Engineering from the 2005 Symposium.* Washington, DC: The National Academies Press.

Tourism. (n.d.). *Wikipedia.* Retrieved from http://en.wikipedia.org/wiki/Tourism

Toyota Prius Plug-in Hybrid. (2013). Retrieved March 14, 2013, from http://www.toyota.com/prius-plug-in

Toyota RAV4 EV. (2013). Retrieved March 14, 2013, from http://www.toyota.com/rav4ev

Tran, L.-H., Catasta, M., McDowell, L. K., & Aberer, K. (2012). Next place prediction using mobile data. In *Proceedings of Nokia Mobile Data Challenge*. Nokia..

Tran-Quoc, T., Braun, M., Marti, J., Kieny, C., Hadjsaid, N., & Bacha, S. (2007). *Using control capabilities of DER to participate in distribution system operation*. Paper presented at 2007 IEEE Power Tech. Lausanne, Switzerland.

Transportation Research Board. (2000). *Highway capacity manual*. Washington, DC: National Research Council..

Trasarti, R., Pinelli, F., Nanni, M., & Giannotti, F. (2011). Mining mobility user profiles for car pooling. In *Proceedings of the 17th ACM SIGKDD International Conference on Knowledge Discovery and Data Mining*, (pp. 1190-1198). ACM.

Tuffner, F., & Kintner-Meyer, M. (2011). *Using electric vehicles to mitigate imbalance requirements associated with an increased penetration of wind generation*. Paper presented at the IEEE Power and Energy Society General Meeting. New York, NY.

Tulpule, P., Marano, V., & Rizzoni, G. (2009). Effects of different PHEV control strategies on vehicle performance. In *Proceedings of American Control Conference*, (pp. 3950-3955). ACC.

Tulving, E. (1972). Episodic and semantic memory. In Organization of Memory, (pp. 381-403). Academic Press, Inc..

Tzirakis, E., Pitsas, K., Zannikos, F., & Stournas, S. (2006). Vehicle emissions and driving cycles: Comparison of the Athens driving cycle (ADC) with ECE-15 and European driving cycle (EDC). *Global NEST Journal, 8*, 282–290.

Ungemah, D., Goodin, G., Dusza, C., & Burris, M. (2007). Examining incentives and preferential treatment of carpools on managed lane faci lities. *Journal of Public Transportation, 10*(4), 151–170.

Vaa, T. (2001). Cognition and emotion in driver behaviour models: Some critical viewpoints. In *Proceedings of the 14th ICTCT Workshop*, (pp. 48-59). ICTCT.

van der Molen, H. H., & Bötticher, A. M. T. (1988). A hierarchical risk model for traffic participants. *Ergonomics, 31*(4), 537–555. doi:10.1080/00140138808966698.

van der Molen, H. H., Rothengatter, J., & Vinjé, M. (1981). Blueprint of an analysis of the pedestrian's task-i: Method of analysis. *Accident; Analysis and Prevention, 13*(3), 175–191. doi:10.1016/0001-4575(81)90004-X.

Van Roy, J., & Vogt, K. (2010). *Analyse van verschillende batterijcapactiteiten voor plug-in hybride elektrische voertuigen*. (Unpublished master's thesis). KU Leuven, Leuven, Belgium.

Van Roy, J., Leemput, N., De Breucker, S., Geth, F., Tant, P., & Driesen, J. (2011). *An availability analysis and energy consumption model for a flemish fleet of electric vehicles*. Paper presented at the 2011 European Electric Vehicle Congress. Brussels, Belgium.

Vandael, S., Boucké, N., Holvoet, T., & Deconinck, G. (2010). Decentralized demand side management of plug-in hybrid vehicles in a smart grid. In *Proceedings of the First International Workshop on Agent Technologies for Energy Systems (ATES 2010)*, (pp. 67-74). ATES.

Vandael, S., Boucké, N., Holvoet, T., De Craemer, K., & Deconinck, G. (2011). Decentralized coordination of plug-in hybrid vehicles for imbalance reduction in a smart grid. In *Proceedings of 10th Int. Conf. On Autonomous Agents and Multiagent Systems – Innovative Applications Track (AAMAS 2011)*. AAMAS.

Vandael, S., Claessens, B., Hommelberg, M., Holvoet, T., & Deconinck, G. (2013). A scalable three-step approach for demand side management of plug-in hybrid vehicles. *IEEE Transactions on Smart Grids, 4*(2), 720–728. doi:10.1109/TSG.2012.2213847.

VandenBos, G., Knapp, S., & Doe, J. (2001). Role of reference elements in the selection of resources by psychology undergraduates. *Journal of Bibliographic Research, 5*, 117–123.

Varrentrapp, K., Maniezzo, V., & St¨utzle, T. (2002). *The long term car pooling problem on the soundness of the problem formulation an d proof of NP-completeness* (Technical Report No. AIDA-02-03). Darmstadt, Germany: Fachgebiet Intellektik, Fachbereich Informatik, TU Darmstadt.

Veldhuisen, K. J., Timmermans, H. J. P., & Kapoen, L. L. (2000b). Microsimulation model of activiy patterns and traffic flows: Specification, validation tests, and Monte Carlo error. *Journal of the Transportation Research Board, 1706*, 126–135. doi:10.3141/1706-15.

Veldhuisen, K., Timmermans, H. J. P., & Kapoen, L. L. (2000a). Ramblas: A regional planning model based on the micro-simulation of daily activity travel patterns. *Environment & Planning A, 32,* 427–443. doi:10.1068/a325.

Vlaamse-Overheid, & Traject-NV. (2007). *Onderzoek naar hinderpalen en voorwaarden voor het succesvol promoten van carpooling* (Tech. Rep.). Vlaamse Overheid. Retrieved from http://www.mobielvlaanderen.be/studies/carpoolen02.php?a=18

Voas, D., & Williamson, P. (2000). An evaluation of the combinatorial optimisation approach to the creation of synthetic microdata. *International Journal of Population Geography, 6*(5), 349–366. doi:10.1002/1099-1220(200009/10)6:5<349::AID-IJPG196>3.0.CO;2-5.

Voas, D., & Williamson, P. (2001). Evaluating goodness-of-fit measures for synthetic microdata. *Geographical and Environmental Modelling, 5*(2), 177–200. doi:10.1080/13615930120086078.

Volvo V60 Plug-in Hybrid . (2013). Retrieved March 14, 2013, from http://www.volvocars.com/intl/campaigns/v60-plugin-hybrid/Pages/v60-plug-in-hybrid.aspx

Vovsha, P., & Bradley, M. (2006). Advanced activity-based models in context of planning decisions. *Transportation Research Record: Journal of the Transportation Research Board, 1981,* 34–41. doi:10.3141/1981-07.

Vovsha, P., Petersen, E., & Donnelly, R. (2002). Microsimulation in travel demand modeling: Lessons learned from the New York best practice model. *Journal of the Transportation Research Board, 1805,* 68–77. doi:10.3141/1805-09.

VREG. (2012). *Flemish regulator of the electricity and gas market.* Retrieved from http://www.vreg.be/verbruiksprofielen-0

VREG. (2013). *Verbruiksprofielen.* Retrieved March 14, 2013, from http://www.vreg.be/verbruiksprofielen-0

VTPI. (2012). *Online TDM encyclopedia.* Victoria Transport Policy Institute. Retrieved from http://www.vtpi.org/tdm/index.php

Vu, S. T., & Vandebona, U. (2007). *Telecommuting and its impacts on vehicle-km travelled.* Paper presented at the International Congress on Modelling and Simulation, University of Canterbury, Christchurch, New Zealand.

Wang, C., Quddus, M. A., & Ison, S. G. (2009). Impact of traffic congestion on road accidents: A spatial analysis of the M25 motorway in England. *Accident; Analysis and Prevention, 41*(4), 798–808. doi:10.1016/j.aap.2009.04.002 PMID:19540969.

Wang, F.-Y. (2010). Parallel control and management for intelligent transportation systems: Concepts, Architectures, and applications. *IEEE Transactions on Intelligent Transportation Systems, 11*(3), 630–638. doi:10.1109/TITS.2010.2060218.

Wang, X., & Abdel-Aty, M. (2006). Temporal and spatial analyses of rear-end crashes at signalized intersections. *Accident; Analysis and Prevention, 38*(6), 1137–1150. doi:10.1016/j.aap.2006.04.022 PMID:16777040.

Waraich, R. A., Charypar, D., Balmer, M., & Axhausen, K. W. (2009). *Performance improvements for large scale traffic simulation in MATSim.* Paper presented at the 9th Swiss Transport Research Conference. New York, NY.

Waraich, R. A., Dobler, C., Weis, C., & Axhausen, K. W. (2013). *Optimizing parking prices using an agent based approach.* Paper presented at the 92nd Annual Meeting of Transportation Research Board. Washington, DC.

Waraich, R. A., Galus, M., Dobler, C., Balmer, M., Andersson, G., & Axhausen, K. W. (2009). *Plug-in hybrid electric vehicles and smart grid: Investigations based on a micro-simulation.* Paper presented at the 12th International Conference on Travel Behaviour Research (IATBR). Jaipur, India.

Waraich, R. A., & Axhausen, K. (2012). Agent-based parking choice model. *Transportation Research Record, 2319,* 39–46. doi:10.3141/2319-05.

Waraich, R. A., Galus, M., Dobler, C., Balmer, M., Andersson, G., & Axhausen, K. W. (2013). Plug-in hybrid electric vehicles and smart grid: Investigations based on a micro-simulation. *Transportation Research Part C, Emerging Technologies, 28,* 74–86. doi:10.1016/j.trc.2012.10.011.

Weir, D. H., & McRuer, D. T. (1968). A theory for driver steering control of motor vehicles. *Highway Research Record, 247,* 7–39.

Weis, C. Vrtic, Widmer, & Axhausen. (2012). *Influence of parking on location and mode choice: A stated choice survey*. Paper presented at the 91st Annual Meeting of the Transportation Research Board. Washington, DC.

Weller, H. (2010). Smart battery management systems. In *Proceedings of the Joint EC /EPoSS / ERTRAC Expert Workshop 2010*. Retreived on March 5, 2013, from http://www.green-cars-initiative.eu/workshops/joint-ec-epossertrac-expert-workshop-2010-on-batteries

Wheeler, D., & Tiefelsdorf, M. (2005). Multicollinearity and correlation among local regression coefficients in geographically weighted regression. *Journal of Geographical Systems, 7*(2), 161–187. doi:10.1007/s10109-005-0155-6.

White House. (2009). *Fact sheet: US-China electric vehicles initiative*. Washington, DC: Author..

Wier, M., Weintraub, J., Humphreys, E. H., Seto, E., & Bhatia, R. (2009). An area-level model of vehicle-pedestrian injury collisions with implications for land use and transportation planning. *Accident; Analysis and Prevention, 41*(1), 137–145. doi:10.1016/j.aap.2008.10.001 PMID:19114148.

Wilde, G. J. (1978). Theorie der risikokompensation der unfallverursachung und praktische folgerungen für die unfall verhütung. *Hefte zur Unfallheilkunde, 130*, 134–156. PMID:659134.

Wilde, G. J. (1982). The theory of risk homeostasis: Implications for safety and health. *Risk Analysis, 2*(4), 209–225. doi:10.1111/j.1539-6924.1982.tb01384.x.

Wilde, G. J., & Murdoch, P. A. (1982). Incentive systems for accident-free and violation-free driving in the general population. *Ergonomics, 25*(10), 879–890. doi:10.1080/00140138208925048 PMID:7173151.

Williamson, P., Birkin, M., & Rees, P. H. (1998). The estimation of population microdata by using data from small area statistics and samples of anonymised records. *Environment & Planning A, 30*(5), 785–816. doi:10.1068/a300785 PMID:12293871.

Wilson, C. (1998). Analysis of travel behoviour using sequence alignment methods. In *Proceedings of the 7th Annual Meeting of the Transportation Research Board*. Washington, DC: Transportation Research Board.

Wilson, S. R. (1976). Statistical notes on the evaluation of calibrated gravity models. *Transportation Research, 0*(5), 343–345. doi:10.1016/0041-1647(76)90114-3.

Wooldridge, M., & Jennings, N. R. (1995). Intelligent agents: Theory and practice. *The Knowledge Engineering Review, 10*(2), 115–152. doi:10.1017/S0269888900008122.

Wu, H. H., Gilchrist, A., Sealy, K., Israelsen, P., & Muhs, J. (2011). A review on inductive charging for electric vehicles. In Proceedings of Electric Machines & Drives Conference (IEMDC), (pp. 143-147). IEEE..

Wynne, J. (2009). *Impact of plug-in hybrid electric vehicles on California's electricity grid.* (Unpublished doctoral dissertation). Duke University, Durham, NC.

Xiao, X., Zheng, Y., Luo, Q., & Xie, X. (2010). Finding similar users using category-based location history. In *Proceedings of the 18th SIGSPATIAL International Conference on Advances in Geographic Information Systems*. ACM.

Xue, G., Luo, Y., Yu, J., & Li, M. (2012). *A novel vehicular location prediction based on mobility patterns for routing in urban vanet*. EURASIP J. Wireless Comm., & Networking. doi:10.1186/1687-1499-2012-222.

Yavas, G., Katsaros, D., Ulusoy, O., & Manolopoulos, Y. (2005). A data mining approach for location prediction in mobile environments. *DKE, 54*(2), 121–146. doi:10.1016/j.datak.2004.09.004.

Ye, X. Konduri, Pendyala, Sana, & Waddell. (2009). *A methodology to match distributions of both household and person attributes in the generation of synthetic populations*. Paper presented at the 88th Annual Meeting of the Transportation Research Board. Washington, DC.

Ye, X., Pendyala, R. M., & Gottardi, G. (2007). An exploration of the relationship between mode choice and complexity of trip chaining patterns. *Transportation Research Part B: Methodological, 41*(1), 96–113. doi:10.1016/j.trb.2006.03.004.

Ying, J. J.-C., Lee, W.-C., Weng, T.-C., & Tseng, V. S. (2011). Semantic trajectory mining for location prediction. In Proceedings of GIS '11, (pp. 34–43). GIS.

Yuan, Y., & Raubal. (2012). Extracting dynamic urban mobility patterns from mobile phone data. In *Proceedings of GIScience*, (pp. 354-367). GIScience.

Yunus, K., Zelaya, H., & Reza, M. (2011). Distribution grid impact of plug-in electric vehicles charging at fast charging stations using stochastic charging model. In *Proceedings of the 2011-14th European Conference on Power Electronics and Applications* (EPE 2011). EPE.

Zhang, B., & Ukkusuri, S. V. (2009). Agent-based modeling for household level hurricane evacuation. In *Proceedings of the 2009 Winter Simulation Conference* (pp. 2778–2784). Winter Simulation.

Zhang, K., Mahmassani, H. S., & Vovsha, P. (2011). *Integrated nested logit mode choice and dynamic network micro-assignment model platform to support congestion and pricing studies, the New York metropolitan case*. Paper presented at the 90th Annual Meeting of the Transportation Research Board. Washington, DC.

Zhao, L. Prousch, Hübner, & Moser. (2010). *Simulation methods for assessing electric vehicle impact on distribution grids*. Paper presented at the IEEE PES Transmission and Distribution Conference and Exposition. IEEE.

Zhao, N., Huang, W., Song, G., & Xie, K. (2011). Discrete trajectory prediction on mobile data. APWeb, 77-88.

Zhao, Y., Sadek, A. W., & Fuglewicz, D. P. (2012). Modeling inclement weather impact on freeway traffic speed at the macroscopic and microscopic levels. *Journal of the Transportation Research Board Record, 2272*.

Zhu, Y., Sun, Y., & Wang, Y. (2012). Predicting semantic place and next place via mobile data. In *Proceedings of Nokia Mobile Data Challenge*. Nokia..

About the Contributors

Davy Janssens graduated in 2001 as Commercial Engineer in Management Informatics at Limburg University. After his graduation, he worked as PhD candidate and teaching assistant at Hasselt University within the faculty of Applied Economic Sciences. In 2005, he got his PhD at Hasselt University, where he is now working as a professor. He is teaching different courses in the domain of transportation sciences. At the level of scientific research, he is a member of the Transportation Research Institute (IMOB) at Hasselt University, where he is programme leader in the domain of travel behaviour research. His area of interest is also situated within the application domain of advanced quantitative modelling (e.g. data mining), such as Bayesian networks and research about Reinforcement Learning and in activity-based transportation modelling.

Ansar-Ul-Haque Yasar was born on November 18, 1983, in Rawalpindi, Pakistan. He finished his Bachelors of Computer Software Engineering degree from Foundation University Islamabad in 2005. Afterwards, he joined Linkoping University Sweden and finished his Masters in Computer Science and Engineering degree (specializing in Communication and Interactivity) in 2007. In November 2007, Ansar joined the DistriNet research group at the Department of Computer Science of the Katholieke Universiteit Leuven and started his PhD research on context-based communication in large-scale vehicular networks under the supervision of Prof. Dr. ir. Yolande Berbers. During the course of his PhD studies Ansar was involved in the Context-Aware Local Service Fabrics in Large Scale Ubicomp Environments (CoLaSUE) project funded by the Research Foundation Flanders (FWO). Since October 2011, he works as a postdoc research and a part-time professor at the Transportation Research Institute (IMOB), Hasselt University, Belgium. At IMOB, he is working on the European FP7 project DATA SIM. His research interests include ubiquitous computing, context-aware communication, VANETs, intelligent transport systems, and mobility management.

Luk Knapen graduated in 1974 as a civil engineer in Construction Engineering and finished the Applied Mathematics Engineering program in 1979 both at the Katholieke Universiteit Leuven (K.U. Leuven). He worked in software industry developing distributed real-time monitoring systems and engineering applications in the fields of construction engineering and transportation. Currently, he is a Ph.D. student at IMOB (Hasselt University, Belgium). His current research focuses on algorithms to handle schedule adaptation and cooperation in activity based models.

* * *

Mir Shabbar Ali has around 20 years of research experience in the field of Transportation Engineering. He is chairing Department of Urban and Infrastructure Engineering at NED University of Engineering and Technology. He is author of more than 25 refereed research publications, and also reviewer of reputed transport Conferences and Journals. He is recipient of research grant of around 20 Million PKR for five research projects from national and international donor agencies. He is being serving in capacity of technical advisor for national transport related forums, and also part of numerous committee on Road Safety and Transportation.

Muhammad Adnan has obtained his PhD in the field of Transport Modelling from Institute for Transport Studies, Leeds, UK. He is currently serving as Associate Professor in the Department of Urban and Infrastructure Engineering, NED University of Engineering and Technology, the same institute from which he obtained his graduation in Civil Engineering in year 2002. He is author of 15 refereed research publications that were published in International conferences and reputed Journals. His research interests include Transport Modelling, Road Accident Data Analysis and Traffic Flow Models.

Kay W. Axhausen was born in Heidelberg, Germany. He received the M.Sc. degree in civil and environmental engineering from the University of Wisconsin-Madison in 1984 and the Ph.D. degree from the University of Karlsruhe, Germany, in 1988. In 1989, he joined the University of Oxford, U.K., as Senior Research Officer and in 1991 he was appointed Lecturer and later Senior Lecturer at the Imperial College London, U.K. He worked as a full Professor at the University of Leopold-Franzens, Innsbruck, from 1995 to 1999. Since 1999, he is full Professor at the Institute for Transport Planning and Systems at ETH Zurich, Switzerland, where he heads the Transport Planning group. His current work focuses on the agent-based micro-simulation toolkit MATSim (see www.matsim.org). He was the chair of the International Association of Travel Behavior Research (IATBR) and is an editor of Transportation and DISp, both ISI indexed journals.

Qiong Bao received in 2008 her first master degree of engineering in control theory and control engineering from East China University of Science and Technology, and received her second master in transportation sciences from Hasselt University in 2010. She is now a PhD student at the Transportation Research Institute (IMOB) of Hasselt University in Belgium. Her research is situated in the area of activity-based transportation modelling.

Tom Bellemans is a Lecturer at the department Transportation Sciences at Hasselt University, Belgium and is also a member of the Transportation Research Institute (IMOB). Tom Bellemans received the degree of electrotechnical engineering in control theory from the Katholieke Universiteit Leuven, Belgium in July 1998. He received a Ph.D. in applied sciences from the Katholieke Universiteit Leuven, Belgium in May 2003 for his work on advanced traffic control on motorways. Since November 2004, Tom Bellemans is affiliated with the Transportation Research Institute, Hasselt University. The main topics of his research include activity-based transportation modeling, traffic simulation, and traffic control.

Tom Brijs graduated in 1997 from the Limburg University Centre (now: Hasselt University) as Engineer in Business Informatics. From 1997 until 2002, he was active at the LUC as a Ph.D. student. He gained his Ph.D. title in 2002. Since then, he has been working for Hasselt University's Transportation Research Institute as a postdoctoral researcher and lecturer. Tom Brijs is author and co-author of various scientific publications, among others in the domain of advanced techniques for the detection and indication of spatial concentrations of crashes. From 1999 until 2002, he held a National Fund for Scientific Research scholarship for advanced research into model-based techniques for the detection and analysis of hot spots in traffic.

Yi-Chang Chiu is an Associate Professor in the Department of Civil Engineering and Engineering Mechanics, and Director of the DynusT Laboratory, at the University of Arizona in Tucson. Dr. Chiu teaches and conducts research in transportation network modeling and has been at the forefront of developing dynamic traffic assignment methods, algorithms, and software systems. He is the team lead for the development of DynusT, a dynamic traffic assignment software that is used widely for network simulation. He has undertaken a number of sponsored research projects and published extensively in refereed journals such as Transportation Research Record and Transportation Research. He is a member of the Transportation Research Board Committee on Transportation Network Modeling and led the effort to put together the committee's primer on dynamic traffic assignment. He has his PhD from the University of Texas at Austin.

Paolo Cintia was born in Marsciano (PG), 4th November 1983, He is a Ph.d Student in Computer Science at the graduate studies school "G. Galilei" of Pisa. In 2006, he got the bachelor degree in Computer Science at the University of Perugia, with thesis on "Parallels and Distributed Algorithms for Resolution of Propagation Equations." Then He continued his study in Pisa, getting the master degree in Computer Science in 2009, with thesis on "Map Matching of GSM Tracks with Data Mining Technique." Currently, his main research interests involve mobility data mining, with focus on the arising challenges from the availability of the so-called Big Data.

Nicola Corona is graduated in Computer Science at University of Pisa in February 2013. His thesis is about an innovative method for Short-term Location Prediction through Users' profiling. It allows to predict a vehicle's moving using Mobility Data Mining techniques. He achieved the Bachelor degree Cum Laude in Computer Science at University of Cagliari. The thesis was about Query by Sketch on Image Retrieval that, starting from a sketch drawing's borders, allows to retrieve similar images contained in a database. He is interested in Data Mining technologies applied to extract people's regularities and exploit them to improve or explain their activities. He believes in job automation and adoption of any technology that allows improving users' life or routines.

Lieve Creemers obtained her degree of bachelor in Transportation Sciences at Hasselt University. In 2010, she obtained her master degree in Transportation Sciences – Mobility Management. Since 2010, she is employed at the Transportation Research Institute (IMOB) at Hasselt University as a Ph.D. student. She is enrolled in the research group Travel Behavior. Her research task relates primarily to travel demand modeling.

Fjo De Ridder studied Chemistry at the VUB ('99) and made a PhD in system identification under the supervision of Rik Pintelon and Johan Schoukens at ELEC-VUB ('04). His PhD focused on signal processing and statistical model selection. During post-doc interests moved to experimental design, model optimization and forecasting. Nowadays he works on modeling, control and data-analysis applied in the field of energy technology at EnergyVille/VITO. Research focuses on distributed and stochastic control, prediction models and energy market strategies.

Johan Driesen received the M.Sc. and Ph.D. degrees in Electrical Engineering from the KU Leuven, Belgium, in 1996 and 2000, respectively. Currently, he is a Professor with the KU Leuven and teaches power electronics and electric drives. In 2000, he was with the Imperial College of Science, Technology and Medicine, London, U.K. In 2002, he was with the University of California, Berkeley. Currently, he conducts research on distributed generation, power electronics, and its applications.

Jesús Fraile-Ardanuy received his Telecommunication Engineer degree (B.E. and M.S.) from the Polytechnic University of Madrid (UPM), Spain, in 1996. He developed his final project with an Erasmus Grant in University College of London (UCL), England, from 1995 until 1996, and he received the Ph.D. in 2003 in UPM, Spain. He was an Assistant Professor (1997-2003) and Professor (2003-2010) in the Civil Engineering School in the UPM where he was also Studies Chief Assistant from 2009 to 2010. Since 2010, he is a Professor in the Telecommunications Engineering School in UPM where he is the assistant director of the Special Technologies Applied to Telecommunications (TEAT) Department and he is leading the Electric and Energy Area. His research interests focus on modeling and control of renewable energies (hydro power plants and wind farms) using advanced control systems, fault diagnosis, and advanced charging management of plug in and electric vehicles. He is co-author of more than 9 books and 45 papers in international congresses and JCR publications.

Barbara Furletti was born in 1976 in Livorno (Italy). She graduated in 2003 in Computer Science at the University on Pisa. From 2003 to 2010, she collaborated with the Computer Science Department in Pisa working on several National and European projects in the data mining and Ontologies fields. In 2006, she started the Ph.D in Computer Science and Engineering at IMT, Institutions, Markets, Technologies of Lucca (Italy), where she received her Ph.D in December 2009 discussing the thesis "Ontology-Driven Knowledge Discovery." From 2011, she is a Research fellow at ISTI Institute of CNR, Italy. Her current research interests are about urban mobility, spatio-temporal data mining and semantic enrichment of trajectories. She is involved in several National and European Projects about data mining, Tourism flows and mobility.

Lorenzo Gabrielli was born in 1984 in Italy. He graduated in Business Informatics in 2010 at the University of Pisa. He discussed his thesis on Mobility Data Analysis: "A Case Study of the Milan area." Currently he is a Research fellow at ISTI-CNR as member of Knowledge Discovery and Delivery Laboratory. His interests regard mobility data mining with heterogeneous data as detecting urban mobility patterns and anomalies, study individual and collective mobility behavior, semantic enrichment of movements, study of the capability of public transport to attract private vehicular trips.

Matthias D. Galus was born in Swientochlowitz, Poland. He holds Dipl.-Ing. degree in electrical engineering and a Dipl.-Ing. degree in industrial engineering from the RWTH Aachen, Germany, and a PhD from ETH Zurich. He spent research visits at the Pennsylvania State College (PSU), at the Massachusetts Institute of Technology (MIT), and at INESC Porto, Portugal. Currently, he is with the Swiss

Federal Office of Energy (SFOE) where he is in charge for the Smart Grid Roadmapping process for Switzerland, which will coordinate and guide the smart grid developments. He is also leading the activities for defining the minimum requirements for smart meters the terms for their roll out. He has a strong background in modeling, optimization in power systems with a focus on the efficient integration of PEV into power systems as well as other Smart Grid technologies, such as storage, distributed generation, smart metering or virtual power plants. Dr. Galus is a Member of the IEEE (S'07, M'13) and the VDE (German society of electrical engineers).

Brian Gardner is a Team Leader in the Office of Planning of the Federal Highway Administration at the US Department of Transportation. Mr. Gardner's team is responsible for policy, technical assistance, and research related to travel forecasting and analysis. Prior to becoming Team Leader, Brian Gardner served as the program manager in charge of managing a large transport modeling and simulation research program. Mr. Gardner has managed numerous projects and has led major initiatives aimed at deploying advanced travel modeling methods and simulation tools in practice. His team is responsible for the Travel Model Improvement Program (TMIP), which has been engaged in significant capacity building activities through technology transfer, training, and dissemination of best practice. He has made numerous presentations at conferences and workshops and serves as a member of the Transportation Research Board Committee on Transportation Demand Forecasting. Mr. Gardner has his Master's degree from North Carolina State University.

Gil Georges received the M.S. degree in mechanical engineering from ETH Zurich, Switzerland, in 2010. Currently, he is working toward the Ph.D. degree in mechanical engineering with the Aerothermochemistry and Combustion Systems Laboratory at the Institute for Energy Technology, ETH Zurich. His research focus is on the assessment of alternative drive train technology for individual mobility systems. Of particular interest are the factors influencing the end energy demand of electrical propulsion systems. This includes demand-side aspects, in particular the influence of driving patterns and vehicle usage patterns, but also technological aspects such as power train design and component sizing, traction and vehicle dynamics as well as non-propulsive loads - namely heating and air-conditioning.

Frederik Geth received the M.Sc. degree in electrical engineering from the KU Leuven, Belgium, in 2009. Currently, he is working as a research assistant with the division ESAT-Electa towards a Ph.D. at the KU Leuven. He is funded by the PhD School of EIT-KIC InnoEnergy. His research interests include optimal storage integration in distribution grids, batteries for (hybrid) electrical vehicles and controlling the impact of the charging currents of (hybrid) electrical vehicles on the grid.

Fosca Giannotti is a director of research at the Information Science and Technology Institute of the National Research Council, ISTI-CNR, Pisa, Italy. Her current research interests include spatio-temporal data mining, privacy preserving data mining, social network analysis, data mining query languages. She has been the coordinator of various European research projects, including the FP6-IST project GeoPKDD. She is a member of steering committee of the FP7 European Coordination Action MODAP: Mobility, Data Mining, and Privacy. She is the author of more than one hundred publications and served in the scientific committee of the main conferences in the area of Databases and Data Mining. She chaired

ECML/PKDD 2004, the European Conf. on Machine Learning and Knowledge Discovery in Data Bases, and ICDM 2008, the IEEE Int. Conf. on Data Mining. Fosca Giannotti leads the Pisa KDD Lab – Knowledge Discovery and Data Mining Laboratory2 – a joint research initiative of the University of Pisa and ISTI-CNR.

Roberto Alvaro Hermana (1988) received his Dipl.-Eng. degree in Electrical Engineering from the UPM in 2011. In 2011 he joined the DEE from the UPM, researching in transient stability related to wind farms and wave farms. In 2013 he joined the TEAT Department from the UPM, where he is presently working at V2G and V2B and preparing his PhD.

Mark Hickman is the ASTRA Chair and Professor of Transport Engineering in the School of Civil Engineering at the University of Queensland (UQ). He is also the Director of the Centre for Transport Strategy at UQ. Prof. Hickman has taught in the areas of public transport planning and operations, travel demand modelling, traffic engineering, transport economics, and civil engineering systems analysis. Prof. Hickman's areas of research interest and expertise are broadly in the areas of transport systems analysis, with a particular focus on public transport and traffic sensing. Dr. Hickman has published extensively on these topics in journals such as Transportation Research Record, Transportation Research, and Transportation Science. Dr. Hickman earned his PhD from the Massachusetts Institute of Technology. Prior to joining the University of Queensland, he held academic positions at the University of Arizona, Texas A&M University, and the University of California at Berkeley.

Chang-Hyeon Joh is Associate Professor at the Department Geography, Kyung Hee University, Republic of Korea. He received his Ph.D. in Urban Planning from the Eindhoven University of Technology, The Netherlands in 2004. His current research interst is activity analysis and passive data collection for modling travel behavior.

Bruno Kochan currently holds a position as post-doc at Transportation Research Institute (IMOB). He graduated as a master in electromechanical engineering from the Vrije Universiteit Brussel in 2003 and now holds a PhD in Transportation Sciences from the Hasselt University since March 2012. His main topics of interests are implementing and applying activity-based transport models for Flanders and other regions, prediction of future transportation behaviour, and policy evaluation.

Karthik Konduri is an Assistant Professor in the Department of Civil and Environmental Engineering at the University of Connecticut in Storrs. He specializes in the development of behaviorally rigorous activity-travel microsimulation model systems of demand and supply. He has worked extensively with travel survey data sets and specializes in the application of advanced statistical and econometric methods for modeling and understanding traveler behavior and values. He is a member of the Transportation Research Board Committee on Traveler Behavior and Values. His publications have appeared in Transportation Research Record, Transportation Letters, and Accident Analysis and Prevention. Dr. Konduri has his PhD from Arizona State University.

Christine Kopp is research scientist at the Fraunhofer Institute for Intelligent Analysis and Information Systems (IAIS). She studied Business Informatics at the University of Leipzig and Jönköping International Business School, Sweden. She received her Ph.D. degree in Computer Science from the University of Bonn in 2011. Her interest lies in the analysis of spatiotemporal data and mobility mining.

Won Do Lee obtained his degree of bachelor in Geography at Kyung Hee University. In 2011, he received his master degree in GIS and Cartography. Since 2011, he has studied at the iRoute (Urban-Transportation Laboratory) at Kyung Hee University as a Ph.D. student. His research interests are to estimate both individual travel behavior and urban spatial structure using GIS and quantitative methodology.

Niels Leemput received the M.Sc. degree in Electrical Engineering, with specialization in energy, from the KU Leuven, Belgium, in 2010. Currently, he is working as a research assistant with the division ESAT-Electa towards a Ph.D. at the KU Leuven. He is funded by IWT-Vlaanderen. His research interests include the grid integration of charging infrastructure for electric vehicles and power electronics for grid coupling of electrical vehicles.

Marco Lützenberger received his diploma in computer science in 2009 from the Technische Universität Berlin and is currently working on his doctoral thesis in the field of multi-agent based traffic simulations at the DAI-Lab, Berlin. In addition to his works on multi-agent based traffic simulation, Marco Lützenberger has developed applications that optimise industrial processes with respect to energy costs, has implemented applications that control and optimise charging processes of electric vehicles with respect to their CO_2 efficiency and is a member of the group that is developing the multi-agent framework JIAC. Marco Lützenberger has joined many organising- and programme committees and has presented his publications at all major agent-conferences.

Sergio Martinez (Spain, 1969) is Associate Professor of Electrical Engineering at Universidad Politecnica de Madrid (UPM), Spain, since 2003. He holds a M.Sc. in Industrial Engineering (UPM, 1993) and a Ph.D. in Electrical Engineering (UPM, 2001). His current research interests include electrical generation form renewable energy and the analysis of its impact on the electric power system.

Michael May is heading the Knowledge Discovery department at the Fraunhofer Institute for Intelligent Analysis and Information Systems (IAIS) since 1999. His main research interest is in Spatial Data Mining. He studied Philosophy and Computer Science at the University of Hamburg and obtained his Ph. D. 1997 at the DFG doctoral program in Cognitive Science.

Anna Monreale is a post-doc at the Computer Science Department of the University of Pisa and a member of the Knowledge Discovery and Data Mining Laboratory (KDD-Lab), a joint research group with the Information Science and Technology Institute of the National Research Council in Pisa. She has been a visiting student at Department of Computer Science of the Stevens Institute of Technology (Hoboken, New Jersey, USA) (2010). Her research is in mobility data, privacy and anonymity of complex forms of data including sequences, trajectories of moving objects and complex networks, and in privacy-preserving outsourcing of analytical and mining tasks.

Mirco Nanni holds a Laurea degree and a PhD in Computer Science, both from the University of Pisa. He has been a visiting reasearcher at College Park - University of Maryland (1999), SENSEable City Lab @ MIT in Boston, MA (2008), Transportation Research Institute (IMOB) of Hasselt University in Belgium (2010), and Applied Movement Behaviour Research Group at UNB in Canada (2012). Since 2006, he is a researcher at KDD Lab, ISTI-CNR. His current main research interest is data mining and knowledge discovery, especially clustering and sequential patterns on temporal and spatio-temporal data, and mobility data analysis in general. He regularly serves as PC and/or referee for various international conferences and journals on data mining, databases, logic programming and artificial intelligence. He served for several years as teacher and/or collaborator in courses on data mining and databases for graduate and undergraduate students.

Hyunsoo Noh is a PhD student and Graduate Research Assistant in the Department of Civil Engineering and Engineering Mechanics at the University of Arizona. He is also a core member of the DynusT Laboratory and has devoted the past few years to integrating activity-based travel demand models with dynamic traffic assignment models. He has worked on a number of projects involving the application of dynamic traffic assignment software systems and has published several papers in refereed journals. Recently he has worked on the development of transit and intermodal assignment algorithms. Prior to joining the University of Arizona, he served as a Graduate Research Assistant at Seoul National University where he earned his Master's degree in transportation planning.

Luca Pappalardo is a PhD student at the University of Pisa and a research associate at the Knowledge Discovery and Data Mining Lab (KDDLab) at the Information Science and Technology Institute (ISTI) of the National Research Council (CNR) at Pisa, Italy. He received his Master Degree in Computer Science from University of Pisa. His main research interests are focused on the study of human behavior, in particular on human mobility patterns and social networks.

Ram M. Pendyala is a Professor of Transportation Systems in the School of Sustainable Engineering and the Built Environment at Arizona State University. His expertise lies in the study of human activity-travel behavior and the development of microsimulation-based activity-travel demand model systems. Dr. Pendyala has published more than 100 peer-reviewed journal articles and book chapters. He has served on the editorial boards of a number of journals including *Transportation, Transport Reviews, Journal of Choice Modeling*, and *Transportation Letters*. He is the chair of the Travel Analysis Methods Section of the Transportation Research Board and the immediate past chair of its Committee on Traveler Behavior and Values. He is also the immediate past chair of the International Association for Travel Behaviour Research (IATBR). Dr. Pendyala has his PhD from the University of California at Davis.

Jairo Gonzalez Perdomo (1983) received his Electrical Engineering degree from the Universidad de Las Palmas de Gran Canaria (ULPGC), Canarias, Spain, in 2009. After working as Electrical Commissioning Engineer in 2009-2010 in the field of CCGTs, he joined the TEAT Department from the Universidad Politecnica de Madrid (UPM), Madrid, Spain, in January 2012, where he is presently working at projects related to Electric Vehicles.

Ali Pirdavani was born on November 11, 1980, in Tehran, Iran. He received his Bachelor degree in Civil Engineering in 2004 and Master degree in Road and Transportation Engineering in 2007. After his graduation, he served as a traffic safety advisor in Tehran municipality for 2 years. Afterwards, he joined Hasselt University, Belgium to pursue his PhD. He obtained his PhD in 2012 and since then, he works at the Transportation Research Institute (IMOB) of Hasselt University as a postdoctoral researcher. He has published his research in several international peer-reviewed journals such as *Accident Analysis and Prevention, Transport Reviews, Environment International, Injury Prevention, Transportation Research Records*, and *Advances in Transportation Studies*.

Dionisio Ramirez (Spain, 1966) is Associate Professor of Electrical Engineering at Universidad Politecnica de Madrid (UPM), Spain, since 2012. He holds a M.Sc. in Industrial Engineering (UPM, 1999) and a Ph.D. in Electrical Engineering (UPM, 2003). His current research interests include electrical generation from renewable resources and power electronics.

Salvatore Rinzivillo is a researcher at the Knowledge Discovery and Data Mining Lab (KDDLab) at the Information Science and Technology Institute (ISTI) of the National Research Council (CNR) at Pisa, Italy. He received his Master Degree in Computer Science from University of Catania. He holds a PhD in Computer Science from University of Pisa. His main research interests are focused on Data Mining and Machine Learning in particular for spatial, spatio-temporal, and mobility data. He has published several papers in international peer-reviewed conferences and journals (IVS, ACM GIS, JIGIS).

Chiara Renso holds a PhD and M.Sc. degree in Computer Science from University of Pisa (1992, 1997). She is permanent researcher at ISTI Institute of CNR, Italy. Her research interests are related to spatio-temporal data mining, reasoning, data mining query languages, semantic data mining, trajectory data mining. She has been involved in several EU projects about mobility data mining. She is scientific coordinator of an FP7 Marie-Curie project on semantic trajectories knowledge discovery called SEEK (www.seek-project.eu) and a bilateral CNR-CNPQ Italy-Brazil project on mobility data mining. She is author of more than 70 peer-reviewed publications. She is co-editor of one special issue for *Journal on Knowledge and Information System* (KAIS) on Context aware data mining and for *International Journal of Knowledge and Systems Science* (IJKSS) on Modeling Tools for Extracting Useful Knowledge and Decision Making. She has been co-chair of three editions of the Workshop on Semantic Aspects of Data Mining in conjunction with IEEE ICDM conference. She is co-editor of the book *Mobility Data: Modeling, Management, and Understanding* published by Cambridge Press.

Adel W. Sadek is a Professor in the Department of Civil, Structural and Environmental Engineering at the University at Buffalo (UB). He also serves as the Director of UB's Transportation Systems Engineering Lab and Chair of UB2020's Strategic Strength in Extreme Events. Before joining UB in 2008 to lead the development of the department's interdisciplinary program in transportation systems engineering, Dr. Sadek was an Associate Professor in the School of Engineering at the University of Vermont (UVM), and held a secondary appointment in the Department of Computer Science. He also served as co-Director of UVM's Complex Systems Center. Dr. Sadek is the recipient of the 1998 Milton Pikarsky Award for the best dissertation in the field of Transportation Science and Technology, awarded by the Council of University Transportation Centers, a National Science Foundation (NSF) CAREER award, and a 2011 IBM Smarter Planet Faculty Innovation Award.

Daniel Schulz works as a project manager at the Knowledge Discovery department of Fraunhofer IAIS since 2006. He studied Geography, Geology and Soil Science at the University of Cologne, Bonn and Gothenburg. His current research interests focus on mobile analytics, spatial business intelligence, and traffic simulation.

Filippo Simini is a lecturer in the Department of Engineering Mathematics at the University of Bristol. Previously he has been a postdoctoral associate at the Center for Complex Network Research at Northeastern University in Boston, and at the Department of Physics at Budapest University of Technology and Economics. He received his PhD in Physics from the University of Padova.

Roberto Trasarti was born in 1979 in Italy. He graduated in Computer Science in 2006, at the University of Pisa. He discussed his thesis on ConQueSt: a Constraint-Based Query System aimed at supporting frequent patterns discovery. He started the Ph.D. in Computer Science at the School for Graduate Studies "Galileo Galilei" (University of Pisa). In June 2010, he received his Ph.D. presenting the thesis titled "Mastering the Spatio-Temporal Knowledge Discovery Process."Currently, he is a researcher at ISTI-CNR as member of Knowledge Discovery and Delivery Laboratory. His interests regard data mining, mobility data analysis, artificial intelligence, and automatic reasoning.

Juan Van Roy received the M.Sc. degree in Electrical Engineering, with specialization in energy, from the KU Leuven, Belgium, in 2010. Currently, he is working as a research assistant with the division ESAT-Electa towards a Ph.D. at the KU Leuven. He is funded through doctoral scholarship of the Flemish Institute for Technological Research (VITO) and the PhD School of EIT-KIC InnoEnergy. His research interests include integrating and controlling the charging of (hybrid) electric vehicles and their interaction with thermal energy flows in buildings.

Paul Waddell is Professor and Chair of City and Regional Planning at the University of California at Berkeley. Dr. Waddell teaches and conducts research on modeling and planning in the domains of land use, housing, economic geography, transportation, and the environment. He has led the development of the UrbanSim model of urban development and the Open Platform for Urban Simulation, now used by Metropolitan Planning Organizations and other local and regional agencies around the world. Professor Waddell has published extensively in the urban analysis and planning domains and serves on the editorial boards of a number of journals including *Transportation Research Part A, Transportation*, and *Journal of Transport and Land Use*. Dr. Waddell has his PhD in Political Economy from the University of Texas at Dallas.

Liming Wang is an Assistant Professor in the Toulan School of Urban Studies and Planning at Portland State University. Dr. Wang's research takes a data-driven approach to address challenging issues in planning, in particular those intersecting land use and transportation. Relying on data analysis, simulation, and visualization techniques, his research aims to inform policy makers and the public of the effects of infrastructure and policy choices on community outcomes such as accessibility, environment, and equity. He has been a leading developer of UrbanSim, an open source land use and transportation modeling system widely used by planning professionals and researchers, and was involved in its application in a dozen cities around the world. Before joining Portland State University, Dr. Wang was a post-doctoral researcher at the University of California, Berkeley. He has his PhD from the University of Washington, Seattle.

Rashid A. Waraich studied computer science at ETH Zurich, Switzerland, with an exchange year at KTH Stockholm. He wrote his master's thesis in the area of distributed systems and information security, during his final masters semester at University of California, Berkeley. He received the M.Sc. degree in computer science from ETH Zurich in 2007. In 2008, he joined the Institute for Transport Planning and Systems at ETH Zurich, where he is working towards the Ph.D. degree. The main topic of his dissertation is related to microscopic electric vehicle demand modelling. Based on an agent-based traffic simulation, he has developed an open source framework for electric vehicle modelling, which has been utilized in several projects. His research interests also include large-scale parallel micro-simulations and transportation economics.

Geert Wets received a degree as commercial engineer in business informatics from the Catholic University of Leuven in 1991 and a PhD from Eindhoven University of Technology in 1998. Currently, he is a full professor at the faculty of Applied Economics, department Transportation Sciences at Hasselt University where he is director of the Transportation Research Institute (IMOB). His current research entails transportation modelling, traffic safety modelling, and data mining.

Daehyun You is a PhD student and Graduate Research Associate in the School of Sustainable Engineering and the Built Environment at Arizona State University. He specializes in the development of algorithms and computational procedures for efficient implementation of activity-based travel micro-simulation model systems. He is an expert in the application of agent-based model systems to the study of transport policy impacts and has performed a number of studies examining various facets of traveler behavior and activity patterns under a wide variety of scenarios. He has worked on a number of projects for agencies such as Federal Highway Administration of the US Department of Transportation, Maricopa Association of Governments, and Southern California Association of Governments.

Yunjie Zhao received the B.S. degree in mechanical engineering from Fudan University, Shanghai, China, in 2009, and the M.S. degree in civil engineering from University at Buffalo (UB), The State University of New York, Buffalo, in 2012. He is currently a Graduate Research Assistant with the Department of Civil, Structural, and Environmental Engineering at UB. His current research interests include connected vehicles applications (e.g. eco-signal, green routing), emission modeling, intelligent transportation systems, and traffic simulation.

Index

T

U

V